NEURO

A Contemporary Approach to Mental Health

Ronald Milestone, M.D.

NEUROMIND
A Contemporary Approach to Mental Health
All Rights Reserved.
Copyright © 2022 Ronald Milestone, M.D.
v3.0

The opinions expressed in this manuscript are solely the opinions of the author and do not represent the opinions or thoughts of the publisher. The author has represented and warranted full ownership and/or legal right to publish all the materials in this book.

This book may not be reproduced, transmitted, or stored in whole or in part by any means, including graphic, electronic, or mechanical without the express written consent of the publisher except in the case of brief quotations embodied in critical articles and reviews.

Outskirts Press, Inc.
http://www.outskirtspress.com

ISBN: 978-1-9772-5729-1

Cover Photo © 2022 www.gettyimages.com. All rights reserved - used with permission.

Outskirts Press and the "OP" logo are trademarks belonging to Outskirts Press, Inc.

PRINTED IN THE UNITED STATES OF AMERICA

Preface

This book began as talks for Psychiatric residents and other trainees at the Inner Harbour treatment center between 1992 and 2000. The plan to compile them into a book of "clinical challenges" has evolved into a different approach to clinical practice. The neurologist Oliver Sachs wrote several popular books telling "stories" of persons with brain problems. *Neuromind* tells a different "story" about brain pathways that carry messages back and forth, interacting with each other. When a pathway's messages are garbled symptoms are the result. This "story" emphasizes the adaptive role of the pathways working together. For decades, the pathways were hypothetical, but in the last twenty years, brain research has discovered new information about them, and *Neuromind* integrates these findings with clinical experience. It is written for mental health providers, to inform a range of professionals in "psychiatry", "psychology", "social work", "mental health services", and others.

My greatest debt has been to the patients whose life struggles have revised my approach throughout my career. In my formal education, Professor Rose Olver at Amherst College was an early influence. Alan Epstein, George Gerstein, and other faculty at the U of Pennsylvania Department of Psychology and Biology, were mentors. I learned about clinical challenges at University of Pennsylvania school of Medicine, University of Michigan Department of Medicine, and the Department of Psychiatry at Yale University. I discussed earlier versions of the manuscript with Stanley Possick, MD, Douglas Kramer, MD, Robert Winston, MD, James Thompson, M.A., and Dale Johnston Ph.D., but take responsibility for the all the ideas and statements. I am grateful to my wife who has been a supportive listener, and never complained about the time taken by the writing.

The book is dedicated to my wife's uncle, Manuel Pearson, MD, now gone from us, who practiced psychiatry in Philadelphia, taught at the University of Pennsylvania, and supported my entry into the field.

Table of Contents

Chapter One: The brain and mental health. 1
    Appendix: Limitations of Current Brain Research 15
Chapter Two: The social brain 24
Chapter Three: The motivation system 58
    Appendix: Suicide and Depression 80
Chapter Four: Memory and significance 89
Chapter Five: Attention organizes mental activity 114
Chapter Six: Choice in behavior and thought 137
Chapter Seven: Learning attachment 174
Chapter Eight: Learning fear and anxiety 203
Chapter Nine: Addiction and motivation 231
Chapter Ten: Assessment 263
Chapter Eleven: Biological interventions 298
    Appendix: Other Biophysical Interventions 333
Chapter Twelve: Information interventions 337

CHAPTER ONE:
The brain and mental health.

Neuromind is about mental health, the ability to adapt to the social environment. Mental health is not the absence of symptoms of disease but an interactive process with the community. The members create the community, which modifies the members. The brain enables this by **processing information** over neural pathways.

There are many problems adapting:

CLINICAL EXAMPLE *(1) A dazed homeless person yells at cars on the street. He seems "crazy", psychotic, and inappropriate to others passing by. Is his brain impaired? Does he have a supportive family? Can he stabilize in a residence?*

CLINICAL EXAMPLE *An anxious housewife has panic attacks that prevent her from going anywhere. She takes tranquilizers to do everyday activities but worries about the side effects and getting addicted. Does she have a trauma that left her anxious?*

CLINICAL EXAMPLE *A teenager uses drugs and believes he cannot cope without them. He was an honor student but is failing, and fighting with his parents to get money for drugs. Why is he vulnerable? How can his parents help?*

The problems are different but the common thread is the inability to deal with others. *Neuromind* explores the neural pathways guiding interaction with the social environment, and how the social system organizes them, a view presented by Siegel in several books. (2) Adapting is not a reflex response, but also involves agency, intentionally choosing appropriate actions.

The brain is a biological system using biological processes to represent and process information. Just as DNA molecules "encode" (represent) genetic information, neural pathways "encode" (represent) information for adaptation. Shannon and Weaver defined "information" as a group of messages with probabilities of transmission between sender and receiver sites. (3) Biosemiotics is the study of how information is represented and transformed in biological systems. (6) In the brain, messages are sent from sensory receptors along neural pathways from region to region. Pinker proposed that the brain could be understood "in patterns of data and in relations of logic that are independent of the physical medium that carries them." This concept is the "computational theory of mind". (4) Pinker omitted specific biological pathways, while current neuroscience texts emphasize the biological components, ignoring the representation of information. (5) Kendler reviewed the disciplines of mental health for articles published in the APA Psychiatric journal over a decade, and found biological, psychological and environmental studies, but none about information systems (and he did not notice the omission). (6) An approach is needed that combines them. Lerner presents an overview of the communication in the brain over synapses across regions, using neural pathways. (7) Electronic computers perform similar information functions, and comparisons of brain and computer have been discussed since the Hixon Symposium of 1949 (the following SIDEBAR reviews some aspects (8)). The brain/computer comparison is useful for understanding how symbolic information is organized differently in computer and biological systems. This clarifies certain issues, but the differences limit the comparison (see below).

The synapse is the local brain region where information processing, computation, occurs at millions of locations throughout the brain. Neural signals arrive on axons from other neurons, and interact along dendrite surfaces. In an example from cortex, axons from different cells converge on the dendrites, combining to determine ("compute") a response in the target neuron: axon firing, or no axon firing, or a stream of pulses. Abbott et al describe multiple

SIDEBAR The relationship between brain and computer. Computational devices and calculators originated in the 19th century. Soon after electronic computers were developed, the Hixon symposium (1949) convened a group of scientists and engineers to explore parallels in the computer and central nervous system.(8) Attendee Norbert Wiener coined the term "Cybernetics". (9) The question: "Is the brain a computer?" reverses the historical relationship because computers were developed to perform brain-like operations to relieve humans of repetitive cognitive tasks. Human brains and computers share the ability to modify "symbolic messages". Searle and Dennett reject the comparison because computers do not have subjective awareness of their actions. Edelman rejects the comparison, preferring one based on biological statistics (discussed in chapter five). Biological and silicon systems both modify information, in different ways, so the debate is mostly about definitions. (10) Information science is a discipline in engineering with specialization in hardware, software, and systems analysis. Information processing principles can be studied independently of the physical system in which they operate, and sometimes are applied to brain operations.

Are brains and computers equivalent? Alan Turing, a mathematician and early computer scientist defined the "Turing machine", a logical model of electronic computers, a "tape" that runs past a "head" which can perform specific operations. (11) He (and others) proved that this simple definition of computing is *mathematically equivalent* to the operations of all binary electronic computers, and predicts operations that are not computable (in finite steps) by computers. Some authors, e.g. MacLaren in ***Humanizing Psychiatry***, think the brain-bio computer is also a "Turing machine", and that electronic computers and brain computation are equivalent. But the brain uses analog "fuzzy logic" at synapses and no proof exists that "Turing machines" using "fuzzy logic" are logically equivalent to binary ones, or to the brain. (12) Other features of brain operation also question the equivalence. Turing proposed "the Turing test" for determining when a computer could **emulate** a human successfully: A "judge" submits questions, answered by separate inputs from human and computer. When the judge cannot decide which is which at better than chance, the emulation is successful.

operations that may occur at these sites. (13) The FIG 1-1. Depicts interactions in a unit of cerebral cortex. This unit is proposed as the basic logic unit of cerebral cortex layers.

Isolated synapses do not clarify brain operations. D.O. Hebb's theory of cell assembly pathways links synapses together into networks. **Hebb's principle states "neurons that fire together wire together"** to create cell assembly pathways ("a diffuse structure

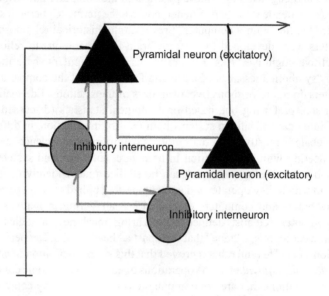

Fig. 1.1 Simplified network diagram of synaptic unit of cerebral cortex, the basic "logic unit"(with added paths). This network is repeated vertically to form one of six layers in a column unit, that repeats throughout cortex.

comprising cells in the cortex and diencephalon, capable of acting briefly as a closed system, delivering facilitation to other such systems" (14)). **Neurons operate in pathways, and a specific neuron may participate in multiple pathways, transmitting different "messages" in each network.** Cell assembly "messages" are organized around specific activities. Hebb's principle extends understanding brain processes beyond the local synapse, which is the limit of most current research.

The pathways of **Neuromind** *perform the adaptive behaviors, but no current technique is capable of measuring the pathway signals over any distance.* Each axon uses membrane electrical charges to transmit the signals, but the message is the aggregate of multiple signals along axon bundles (which may be pulse coded, when the frequency of pulses carries the signal (27)). The inability to record and observe messages over pathways leaves only indirect

SIDEBAR The brain and computer have different organization:

1) Digital vs. analog. Electronic computers are binary digital devices with all or none values (0,1) in circuits. The brain is a mixed analog and binary system. Analog electrical charges build up along synaptic dendrites to produce all or none depolarization with binary axon firing (or a pulse train of repeated firings). This analog/binary combination is called "fuzzy logic", a probability response. (12)

2) Local vs. distributed processing. Electronic computers perform computations at specific "central processing units" (ALU) (a computer may have more than one). Each ALU processes data in a specified sequence. (15) In the brain, computation occurs at numerous synaptic regions simultaneously, in parallel. Information is differentiated by anatomical location. Different "cell assembly pathways" generate separate information messages at the same time.

3) Local vs. distributed storage. Electronic computers store information in separate memory chip units or external storage. Storage in the brain occurs at the same synaptic membranes as computation, so "memory" is distributed to multiple locations, conferring redundancy. The "message content" depends on the pathway in which the information is stored. Kandel proposed a set of principles emphasizing how local synapses are modified by activity using messenger RNA protein production. (16) This applies to storing all synaptic information, but is not specific for what is stored, which is defined by the "cell assembly pathways".

4) Syntax and semantics. In the silicon computer, the data to be "computed" is stored separately from the instructions for the computing (syntactic and semantic content are separate). The stored instructions guide operations to process the data, and are not changed in the computation. In the brain these two streams are combined: the "message" may modify the pathway links while computing the message. In the computer, a different data set can be entered into the same program. In the brain, new data alters the processing. (17)

5) The data flow rate of electronic computers is determined by the processing speed of the ALU unit and other physical factors. This has been dramatically increased (Moore's Law) by design of components. (18) The brain component speeds are much slower, and cannot be rapidly redesigned; so speed is improved by parallel processing, and pre-computed patterns.

6) Operating system. Electronic computers manage the complex tasks of memory, display and other input-output functions by "operating system" programs (19), stored in the computer and computed by the (ALU). (The design of computer systems with the ability to execute computer operations and perform data processing was proposed by von Neumann in the 1950s, and incorporated into all modern systems.) Parallel "cell assemblies" in the brain require a mechanism to switch from one pathway to another. The switching process, related to attention, is discussed in chapter five.

methods of observation (details of these limitations are discussed in the Appendix to this chapter). Until more precise measures are possible, a verbal description of neural pathways as "information pipelines", like the fiber optic transmission in modern digital communication systems, provides an approximation. Computers can model the information process of local brain networks using data from neurophysiological studies; examples are the local "cell assembly" activity in the visual system, (20), action selection in basal ganglia (21), and attention (22). Model "perceptrons" simulate pattern recognition (23). But aggregating local models to produce a "bottom up" brain simulation has not been accomplished. Instead, a total network approach or *connectome map* attempts to model the brain pathways between brain regions, requiring "big data" calculations on supercomputers.

SIDEBAR The connectome project attempts to build a complete map of connections of the human brain, an analogy to the "genome project". The neural connections in primate and human brains have been mapped in low detail. In contrast to the genome, the *connectome* is organized partly through genetic programming and partly by experiential events that are constantly changing. Synapses are dynamic regions that re-organize over the lifetime of the individual. The same dendritic field participates in many different "cell assembly" pathways receiving different information from each pathway, so *connectome* pathways are not unique. The neuron firing pattern may carry different messages over the same pathways. For all these reasons, the *connectome* provides information about basic links, but dynamic models are needed to map pathway activity, as illustrated in the recently published study of cortex. (25) The scale of the data makes the *connectome project* a multicenter effort. (An application is available on the desktop computer to allow scientists to explore current models.)(24) The grandiose claim of creating a "whole brain emulation" to upload and simulate the information activity of a person's brain on a super computer (and provide "personal immortality" for that person's "brain activity") is science fiction. It ignores the dynamic changes of the living brain, treating brain activity at one moment as static and eternal, and is an example of the failure to understand the differences in brain and computer operations. (26)

Pathways for specific functions are described in this and following chapters. Each contributes to adaptation, and disturbances in one or more pathways produce symptoms. The normal pathway function must be understood to understand the dysfunctions. Some neuro-anatomy is necessary to define each pathway, not complicated details, but enough to anchor the discussion, including simple diagrams. (Resources for more detail about each region are at: (28)) The three major groups of pathways are: A) the input/output component including the sensory systems, the spinal cord, and autonomic network that modifies body response. These functions are involved in mental health indirectly, the damage to them is often local, and they are studied and treated by Neurologists. B) The subcortical nuclei include thalamus, basal ganglia, midbrain extensions of the tegmental, and regions of the brain stem. These core integrative regions are essential to all brain activities, and are involved in mental health, and discussed in later chapters. C) The surrounding layer, the cerebral cortex (and cerebellar cortex) encloses the other regions and is connected with them.

The cerebral cortex is a highly folded multi layer sheet of cells covering deeper regions. The cortex has dramatically enlarged in the course of primate/human evolution, and is the last brain region to fully mature during human development. These evolutionary changes are associated with new capacities not seen in other animals, and associated vulnerabilities when the complex networks do not develop or are damaged. The networks perform the integrating functions that "make us human". (29) Different regions of cortex will be discussed in several chapters. This outer brain layer is vulnerable to injury, and easier to access for research. (29)

The cortical sheet can be differentiated into four quadrants using two anatomical landmarks, the *longitudinal fissure* and *central sulcus*, with different tasks in each region. The longitudinal fissure divides the cortical sheet into right and left sides (usually called "dominant" and "nondominant" in association with handedness) that use different modes of processing. Regions in front of the central sulcus are involved with selecting and activating actions; the regions posterior organize sensory reception and analysis. The posterior cortex receives sensory input from vision, hearing, and somatic receptors, (and indirectly from olfactory receptors and taste receptors), analyzes this information, interacts with thalamus and other subcortical nuclei, and transfers the analyzed data to frontal brain regions. The temporal lobes extend bilaterally from the posterior region as extensions and have both sensory and storage functions. This chapter focuses on the posterior pathways of cerebral cortex. Chapter two reviews brain pathways for social interaction.

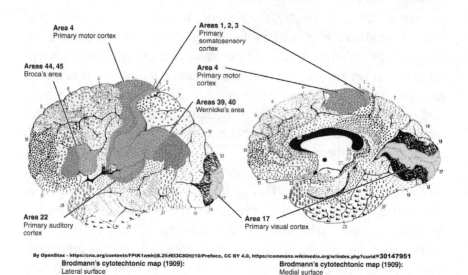

Brodmann's cytotechtonic map (1909): Lateral surface

Brodmann's cytotechtonic map (1909): Medial surface

The cortex is divided into sub regions, termed Brodmann's regions, after the anatomist who first described and numbered them, by detailed microscopic studies of neuroanatomical degeneration, and functional connection. (Fig. 1-2.) (29) These are used in imaging research to specify the regions. Glasser et al, have published a more complex mapping combining neuroanatomy, function, and connectivity. (37) As with other *connectome* studies, there are questions about the study which used a small number of adults and no children, the stability of these measures over time, and the "standard conditions" of the measurements. (See Appendix discussion) The folded surface is the result of fitting a large planar sheet of cell columns into a barely accommodating space in the skull. If taken out of the skull, and metaphorically unfolded, the cortex can be visualized as a curved layer of multiple subunits. (The mathematics of calculating this mapping is complicated. (30)) To understand pathways, it helps to open up or "unfold" the compressed human brain to clarify its components. (See FIG 1-3.). In the diagram, one side of the cortex is spread out as a flat sheet of cells. (The cerebellum is omitted for simplification but is closely linked to cortex.) The cortex and subcortical nuclei have bidirectional pathways, transferring information between subcortical regions and cortex.

> **SIDEBAR Cortical columns.** Microscopically, the sheet is a series of roughly 100 vertically oriented multi-cell cylindrical columns containing interactive neurons with 6 or 7 layers, first described by Mountcastle. Column cell interaction is described in the earlier diagram (FIG 1-1.) Each column of cells contains six layers of double units of Fig. 1.1. These interact with nearby columns on the cortical sheet, and with more distant regions via input and outflow axons. This creates both "local" and "distal" pathways of interaction. The neurophysiology of the cell column connections has been studied and the local regions modeled to predict the local interactions (rules are listed in footnote (31)). The more distal interactions require an increase in axon ("white matter") pathways. (The cortical/cerebellar ratio remains relatively stable over evolution in primates and cerebellar operations expand processing in cortex. (32)

The corpus callosum is a large axon path between the R and L cortex that maintains interaction between the sides. The Nobel prize-winning studies of Sperry, Gazzaniga, and others, on patients who have surgical bisection of the callosum for control of seizures provides information on the different modes of each side. (33) The Right (nondominant in R handed people) cortex uses simultaneous relationship patterns ("gestalt" processing) to organize data.

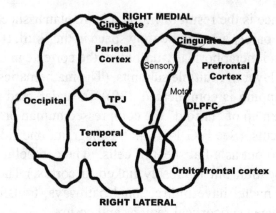

Fig. 1.3. Cortical regions drawn in unfolded form. (Based on calculations of Hurdal (30).

Facial recognition, musical melody, spatial orientation and similar tasks are processed on this side. Jung characterized this as the "intuitive" cortex. (36) The "dominant" Left cortex (in a R handed person) uses sequential processing of spoken language and other sequential tasks. Language capacity involves three separate skills: vocalization-speech, auditory verbal recognition, and reading, the last to develop. Development of vocalization and verbal recognition are closely linked to core evolutionary capacities for sound production and auditory pattern recognition. (34) The capacity for language acquisition may have genetic elements, but children learn the language of each culture by social interaction, the "original word game", described by Roger Brown, the social transaction between child and social environment for learning language. (35) Local injury to the speech region gives rise to different aphasias (Broca, Wernicke) often the result of stroke/vascular occlusion. Developmental abnormalities are also important, and speech therapists address a range of these disturbances in children (a list at (35)). Reading is last to develop and more difficult in some languages than others. Children who have major difficulties learning to read require special attention, and the clinician may not immediately consider this. Written language has major social, cultural, and personal significance, the basis for historical records, legal documents, and recording commercial transactions, all the fundamental elements of modern society.

CLINICAL EXAMPLE A 15 year old young man was hospitalized for recurring truant behavior, fighting with peers, social isolation and depression. He was born prematurely, without resuscitation, to a single mother with limited social support. He had no siblings, and problems in school from first grade with difficulty relating with peers. By middle school he dressed in counter-culture style, and favored "heavy metal" music, which expressed his anger and depression. He could recite lyrics from memory but used no written references. Teachers reported that he was unwilling to participate in class, never read assignments and was failing. When a teacher asked him to read a simple text, after some hesitation he admitted that he was unable to read. He began a remedial reading program, and in 6 weeks could read simple words. He became excited about this, and his mood changed. He actively practiced reading skills and even volunteered to read a selection he had carefully practiced to the class. His anger and mood improved and he returned home with special reading interventions in school. COMMENT Children unable to read are excluded from many aspects of education and life activities, creating major problems in self-esteem. The embarrassment invariably leads to hiding the difficulty, making remediation more difficult. If there is no major impairment of capacity, when the ability is acquired there is with a strong sense of empowerment.

The posterior cortex receives visual and auditory signals via thalamic relays, and has been studied extensively in Psychology. The signals are deconstructed, and no "image map" of visual space is stored there, instead features are abstracted for analysis. (38) The "Pattern Recognition Theory of Mind" transforms sensory data is by into "thoughts". Bruner, an early pioneer in cognitive Psychology, proposed that all cognitive experience is categorization taking sensory perceptions to more abstract properties in a pathway sequence that "abstracts" (extracts) sensory data into perceptual and cognitive units. (38) This conserves time in sequential perception (e.g., speech) and space in visual perception. The simplest coding processes are wired genetically as basic operators in the sensory field, and additional perceptual coding is learned from experience. Meaning is abstracted from sensory data, stored in pathways, and compared with new experiences. Rewards organize the process, identifying signals for social attachment or other needs. (39) This process has been modeled in computer "pattern recognition" for recognition of words, speech, and faces.

The development of cognitive ability occurs in a defined sequence, first studied by Jean Piaget in children using a unique interviewing procedure, which has been replicated by academic research. (40) The three stages of perceptual organization are: a) Sensory motor organization in the first year of life. External sensory information is linked to motor responses. This includes development of basic motor coordination, visual following, first proto-words and early social patterns. b) Symbolic operational organization begins later in childhood, giving the child a simple vocabulary, and organizing sensory experiences into pattern categories. These categories are not fully abstract but linked to specific real objects of immediate experience. Important at this stage is development of *object constancy*, the persistence of sensory objects even when they go out of the sensory field for short (and eventually longer) time intervals. The child is also able to create fantasy from memory based on stored sensory information. c) The Abstract-representation develops in the teen-young adult years, when categories of experience are detached from immediate sensory events, and actions can be linked to abstract categories, not just sensory data. (The development of social interaction is described in chapter two.) Research has modified the specific ages and precision of Piaget's categories, but there is general agreement on the progression of stages, which are similar across cultures, and may be delayed or prevented by injury or cognitive impairment ("retardation").

The skills are genetically programmed and modified by experiential learning. Recent reviews, using fMRI and other imaging techniques, find that both progressive myelination of pathways across cortex, and a decrease in gray matter volume indicating synaptic thinning (not cell loss) are involved in cognitive development. Experience enhances active pathways and deletes less relevant ones, modifying networks. Meyer and Lee propose, *"the process of pruning is largely experience driven. As with synapse production, the timing of synapse pruning is dependent on the area of the brain in which it occurs"* (41) Myelination permits more rapid transfer of information, allowing more distal interactions. Local connections, early in development, extend to more distal regions as myelination proceeds. Anatomical maps provide a general picture of the genetically programmed connections, but micro-connectivity depends on experience, and is modified throughout life.

The cerebral cortex illustrates several features of information processing: a) Many similar neuron groups process signals simultaneously in parallel. b) Local regions are differentiated by input/output pathways. c) Local interaction and sequential hierarchies analyze features of the signal. (Several computational models of cortical column processing have been created and tested. (42)), d) Maturation adds distal interaction and more complex pathways. e) Initial organization is polygenic, and additional programming occurs by experience throughout life.

CLINICAL SYMPTOMS

The external layer of cerebral cortex is exposed to trauma, vulnerable to stroke, tumor, and other injury. Malfunctions of processing may produce local or general clinical symptoms. The historic controversy between Halstead, who developed the Halstead-Reitan test for local regions, and Lashley, the neuropsychologist, who defined an "equipotential" role for total damage, characterizes the differences. (43) Local processes produce local changes, and *symptoms* related to the region affected. (42) Clinical studies using X-ray, CAT scan, MRI, and EEG localize functions and abnormalities to detect local changes. Non-local problems, like encephalitis, alter multiple brain regions with *symptoms* of multiple region dysfunctions. (44) (45) *Delirium* and *dementia* are examples of diffuse cortical problems. (46) In mental health, changes of pathways do not involve the entire brain, but present complex symptoms.

CLINICAL EXAMPLE The Young Man Who Lost His Mind. *A twenty-two year old male was evaluated for loss of motivation, confusion, and passivity. He spent time surfing, had successfully completed HS and was enrolled in community college, but now rarely attended because he could not concentrate. Treatment for depression by another provider with SSRI made him worse. There was no history of drug use or family history of mood disorder. The onset of the changes came approximately one month after a surfing accident in which he was trapped underwater for several minutes and required resuscitation. He recovered consciousness and mental functions within hours, was hospitalized for several days and discharged home. In the next few months, he had progressive loss of mental capacity and emotional confusion. He began using cannabis in low doses and was not sure if it helped. He had symptoms of occasionally "freezing up" in which he would be confused but did not lose consciousness or postural control. He was placed on a low dose anti-seizure medication and reported some improvement in symptoms, slight benefit in concentration, but little change in motivation.* ***COMMENT*** *The cognitive impairment and confusion were not responsive to SSRI medication, which suggested that mild diffuse cortical injury was sustained in the hypoxic episode. Diffuse injury to cortical function, even when relatively mild, can result in significant changes of function and not be visible on x-ray or MRI. Young adults often have accidents with brain consequences, so the history is essential for etiology and treatment.*

The **etiology** *is the process that alters the brain pathway and produce the symptoms; it is the "cause" of the changes.* (Research that finds changes in brain pathways, and claims that the changes are the "cause" of the symptoms, does not understand that pathway changes and symptoms are the same process. See discussion in the Appendix.) Important etiologic factors include genetics, other biological disturbances, programming (learning) experiences, and the impact of the current social environment. A normally functioning pathway has standardized operation, the basis for comparison that is often omitted in documentation. (An example is E.R. John's QEEG system. (46)) Treatment may shift brain processing back to adaptive patterns, or develop new adaptive patterns. Disturbances may have different durations: a) Early onset and lifelong problems are seen early in development, i.e. several genetic syndromes of cognitive disability. (47) (There are multiple genetic loci for cognitive disability.) b) Sudden and transient disturbance seen in trauma or intoxication showing delirium. (46) c) Sudden onset and residual, or chronic symptoms of trauma, birth hypoxia, and long term infection create specific areas of impaired cognitive function, which may persist. d) Gradual and progressive impairment is seen in the many dementia syndromes, with a variety of neural mechanisms, genetic and other, etiologies. (Scales for evaluating the level of impairment are listed in references. (48))

Howard Gardner's ***Frames of Mind***, expands consideration to other capacities beyond basic cognitive skills, but has not yet been integrated into mental health. (48) The effects can be local or change pathways that range across regions, or impact the entire brain. Several pathway descriptions have been proposed by Williams et al, and by Buckholz and Meyer-Lindenberg. A description of functions is presented in the Research Domain Criteria (RDoC) of Insel et al at NIMH. None of these correlate neural pathways with current diagnoses, as noted by Gillihan and Parens. (49)

There is no mind/body confusion in information processing. Computers receive input in symbolic form and use it to perform tasks that modify the physical world. This is not considered a philosophical mystery. No one asks: "How can text input to a computer operate automobiles, robot production facilities, etc.?" Information systems can transform the physical world; there is no "software/hardware problem", no "mind/body" problem. Information is configured in material components. Brain pathways use biological processes that produce physical outputs: movements, changes in sound waves, secretion of chemicals, etc. The brain information system converts "information", symbolic messages into material effects.

APPENDIX: LIMITATIONS OF CURRENT BRAIN RESEARCH

Neuromind explores how the brain interacts with society to create individual behavior. Each chapter presents a hypothetical pathway with complex synaptic links, and messages sent over multiple units of the pathway. Currently, there is no way to observe, measure, or decode these messages into biophysical measurements. This section discusses technical limitations in measurement and interpretation of current techniques. Later chapters cite research using these methods, so understanding these limitations is essential, and will not be repeated, so other chapters will refer back to this appendix.

What is a science of the brain? (The analogy to computers is helpful here.) There is no single "science of computers". Computers have basic circuits, which are programmed, and connected into networks, and each stage is studied using different techniques. The relationships of the levels are worked out in practical situations. A similar situation exists in brain information systems. The biological components can be studied in the biological sciences. The way they are organized, and the messages they produce are organized as information must be studied using different methods, similar to programming. The connection between separate persons (and computers), the transfer of messages, is studied using social science techniques. There is no single science of mental health, and efforts to reduce or explain it to one component will never be successful. The last two decades have emphasized study of biological components. Detailed pharmacology of the synapse led to new drug development, discussed in chapter eleven. Gene research expanded hopes that the organization of (abnormal) pathways would result from genetic programming, which is not the result, as described in chapter ten. Hebb's basic principle links pathways of neurons to form networks that store and represent information. This hypothesis fits the observable pathways studied by anatomy, but no current technique is able to visualize the specific activity of a pathway performing a specific information task. (The closest so far has been an ingenious experiment by Ross Adey, many years ago.)

The last decade has seen an explosion of studies of the brain using imaging techniques. The use of imaging techniques in Psychiatry and mental health overlaps Neurology and the findings have progressed from localizing functions in specific regions to observing the interaction of regions.

Techniques of anatomical localization include:

1) **XRAY.** Beginning in the 1980s, XRAY and later *computerized axial tomography* (CAT SCAN (uses a computer to manipulate both the x-ray source and the collecting device to create computed two dimensional "slices" through brain or other tissue)) procedures were looking for anatomical abnormalities to explain mental health symptoms. (50) The techniques can visualize tumors, some trauma, and are useful in Neurology and Neurosurgery for preliminary evaluation. In Psychiatry, when large anatomical abnormalities contribute to the symptoms, due to tumors or atrophy, similar findings are observed. But variations in specific regions that explain various symptoms are rarely conclusive. Results have not been consistent or replicated, and no meta-analysis has identified a brain region specific for a psychiatric disorder on the basis of anatomical measures, increased or reduced. (51) This contrasts, for example, with Huntingdon's Disease, a genetic disorder with local brain atrophy visible in basal ganglia. (52) This may be partly an issue

of normalizing anatomical measurements, but it suggests that mental health syndromes do not have gross anatomical features.

2) **Magnetic resonance imagery (MRI), developed in the 1970s, uses a magnetic field to interact with body tissue, and generate and measure RF signals originating from the tissue.** X-rays are not transmitted through tissue, so there is less danger from repeated studies. The signal can be can be detected/scanned by tomography, which provides more precise information about local anatomy, and is used frequently in Neurology to localize anatomical changes in tissue (and in other specialties in other parts of the body). The signal is influenced by the geometry of the region, motion of the subject, and other variables that produce signal noise, and interpretation requires computation to compensate for the different factors. MRI scanners are expensive devices, and marketing and demand for these in hospitals and offices has dramatically increased their use. MRI is a more precise, anatomical method but studies in Psychiatry and mental health have not seen a dramatic discovery of new information. (53) The essential problem in X-ray and MRI technology is the inability to measure brain activity.

Two techniques have been developed to explore regional function and activity.

3) **SPECT (PET) scanning uses radioactive labeled oxygen as a signal source.** The individual is injected with radioactive oxygen and then measured under active and inactive conditions, and again after the tracer "washes out" after the oxygen is metabolized. This technique allows visualization of localized brain cell activity as it consumes oxygen, the energy source for all neural activity. Because of radioactive decay and oxygen metabolism, studies must be carefully timed, depend on reliable administration and blood flow, and safe management of radioactive material. All these factors introduce variability into the data, the need for a constant source of radioactive material, and special handling in the lab, which combine to make it inconvenient, and so it has never become a major research technique. Amen uses this clinically to define brain injuries more subtle than observed by other imaging methods but the results are not standardized (see following) and his interpretations are challenged. (54) A more convenient method is needed for studying brain activity.

4) **The technique that fills this gap is BOLD ("blood oxygen level dependent MRI" often called fMRI).** In 1990, Ogawa and colleagues utilized changes in the oxygen content of hemoglobin (the blood carrying protein in red blood cells) to generate MRI signals. The entire brain uses oxygen as an energy source, so by itself this method does not improve localization. But if one region is "activated" by a specific task to use more oxygen than other regions, fMRI becomes a measure of the difference in activity. (55) Studies confirm that this method can produce differential results, and it has become the major technique in mental health research for over a decade.

In contrast to basic MRI, fMRI is a **comparison measurement** that introduces measurement and interpretation problems. The statistical variability of fMRI scanning is multiplied because fMRI requires (multiple) comparison scans at different time intervals. (And differences between subjects.) The sources of noise/variability include:

a) Basic MRI requires standardizing the signal capture with brain tissue regions, including various corrections for anatomy, overlying tissue, and environmental factors.
b) Scanner drift, head movement, and physiological noise from other body tissues may change on repeat measurement.
c) Environmental factors which may change at different times the fMRI is obtained.
d) Comparison of active and inactive states requires timing the activation of brain regions to the timing of fMRI measurements, when increased blood flow is expected in a certain tissue.
e) Comparing abnormal function to "normal" requires standardization of signals across groups. When two groups are compared with "before and after" treatment effects, both group standards and timing noise is multiplied, with at least four measures. "Normalization" must be done in advance, and compared for the study groups. Often not done.
f) The geometry of blood flow of different brain regions which is related to the location of blood vessels to neural tissue, limits observation. Blood flow to brain regions is not equally distributed: some regions like cortex have large well separated vessels, while some deep brain regions have small closely overlapping ones. *The closer, more overlapped the vessels, the more difficult it will be to separate values under different conditions, and the more likely they will be lost in background noise.* This is observed by the failure to identify subcortical neural regions in most studies. (These regions can be visualized in high resolution MRI, but not the differences in BOLD.) This does not mean they are not active, or that they are not active in different ways. The data simply do not tell what is happening.
g) Some regions may be actively involved in pathways in all states and not differentiated yet still involved and active.
h) If more than one region shows changes at the same time how to interpret the relationship? The fact that they are statistically correlated signals does not assure they are directly connected, nor activated by the same signals, and the activation of one region may reflect active *inhibition* of another.
j) When multiple regions are observed, the values may be measured against selected regions or "nodes", which are defined statistically, or by prior anatomical location, or some other method. How nodes are selected may change the results.
k) The time scale of shift in oxygen flow for different regions may alter the timing of the activation.

A technical review of the issues in design and measurement in these studies can be found at (56) and recent editorial comments and review discussed by Kalin. (55)

The oxygen utilization techniques in (SPECT) and (BOLD) (fMRI), measure differences in brain activity in different regions. Early studies focused on specific regions of increased activity, generating a list of "centers" associated with externally defined tasks, which is not consistent with networked pathways. Recent studies compute "network correlations" across multiple regions, comparing which regions are simultaneously more active or inactive. *(57)* The authors propose that the correlations identify "networks", which sound like Hebb's "cell assembly pathways", **but they are not recordings of pathways**. The relationship of these signal correlations to "cell assembly pathways" is speculative. Attempts to associate these "network interactions" with diagnoses have been unsuccessful. The result of more than a decade of studies and meta-reviews is confusion. fMRI studies are unable to track changes in cortical/subcortical pathways. The sources of noise (listed above) raise questions about the reliability of the data which is confirmed by failures of replication. Researchers have replicated several "network" correlations of cortical regions, *default mode network, salience network, and attention network.*(49) Differences in the active/inactive dimension do not indicate if neural activity is stimulated or inhibited. To understand the activity involved in the "network correlation", experiments must be designed using brain tasks performed in fMRI, to identify specific pathway activity. Some researchers have been creative in designing such tasks, and interpretation of tasks is sometimes "abstracted" from the actual tasks. These studies are found in cognitive neuroscience research, not in clinical situations. Defining the appropriate "nodes" to correlate is difficult. (57) "Node" in this context, does not mean anatomical region, though it may be associated with one after the analysis. (58) (59) BOLD is the primary method for observing brain activity in awake human subjects, despite many difficulties in measurement and interpretation. There is a need for standardization and coordination across the research community. (60) There is no reason to think that single pulses are the only important signal, the same pathway may carry different messages and information depending on the signaling, and the time course for signal transmission is much faster than any fMRI measurement. (27)

5) **Another MRI technology, diffusion-tensor MRI, measures the water space around axons and their changes using MRI fields** *(comparing brain spaces with models of tubes in water).* This is an anatomical measure, not a functional one, and the transmission of impulses over the axons is not observed. This has proven useful for neurological injuries or diseases of white matter. Some findings have been reported in Psychiatric patients, but since no literature on white matter changes in in psychiatric disorders exists, interpreting the results awaits further analysis. The supposed localizations are not typical disorders, and the technique may give new insights or be artifacts. (61)

6) **Brain pathways carry electrical depolarization over axons.** Magnetic field techniques (MRI) look at relatively large brain fields over time intervals of seconds to minutes, while brain activity occurs in microscopic zones over microseconds. The surface of the skull has a low voltage, variable frequency, electrical energy waveform that can be recorded by surface electrodes, the "EEG". This occurs in real time, not the time scale for averaging fMRI oxygen consumption measurements. The spontaneous electrical activity measured in EEG is created by the electrical activity of the brain, but problems of interpretation limit its usefulness: 1) The surface EEG is a complex AC waveform combining multiple sources in the underlying brain regions. The sources closest to the skull contribute the most voltage and the power decreases with distance so that subcortical regions make little contribution, and the waveform is an average of many electrical events. 2) A technique is needed to organize the information of this complex waveform, and identify significant features. A Neurologist is trained to identify specific visual patterns, reading 10-30 min sheets of EEG data, with no statistical standardization and undocumented reliability. "Sharp waves" indicate potential synchronization may be associated with seizures; "slow waves" suggest areas of underlying damage; the EEG has been used to track the variation in different stages of sleep.

QEEG. Small time units of the EEG signal can be digitized and a "Fourier transform function" used to separate the signal into frequency ranges, which can be correlated to different states of brain activity. (62) This analysis of power of each frequency range is not possible by visual inspection, and the digitized QEEG (quantitative EEG) can only be measured practically for short time intervals (due to the enormous number of data points collected in 24 lead standard placement, a data load even for modern computers.) This technique was originally developed with visual display called BEAM, but was not standardized so abnormalities were not predictive of clinical states, similar to the current dilemma in fMRI. John and associates carried out the heroic study of 4000 (presumed) normal subjects to accumulate standard scores for the frequency spectrum at each electrode location (this database is propriety and available as part of the cost of QEEG evaluations by various providers). (64)

When a patient record is compared against the standardized values, it is possible to make a statement of abnormal values with statistical precision, but these abnormalities are not associated with diagnostic or symptom categories. This requires developing "discriminant" scores of patient groups with similar symptoms compared to controls. This has been done for one small study differentiating depressed from ADHD teenagers, of questionable use. (63) *Studies like those of fMRI comparing changes in local regions under different brain tasks have not been carried out for this technology but could be a useful method. QEEG measures are real time measures of brain activity and have not been correlated to pathway activity.*

LORETA is a method for combining digitized EEG with tomographic re-computation that attempts to localize the sources of EEG. (65) So far this has been utilized for localizing sources of epilepsy, but might prove useful in localizing activity in mental health. There are also efforts to combine EEG and fMRI techniques. Proponents who champion the idea suggest that the result will generate greater ability to localize brain interactions, but both techniques have high noise to signal ratios, and the sources of the noise are entirely different and not easily standardized. Neither technique localizes networks so the hypothesis that combining them would do so is not intuitive. (The hope that "big data" number crunching might find relationships not immediately evident in simpler analysis is aspirational.) Another localizing technique combines magneto electrical activation with EEG, with unknown value to date. (The reader is encouraged to consult the technical sources to form a personal conclusion.) (66)

7) *Evoked potential.* Electrical activity in localized sensory cortex can also be recorded in synchrony with sense organ stimulation, visual and auditory. Such "evoked potentials" have complex waveforms with experimental analysis of hypothetical components. These have been correlated with diagnostic conditions related to sensory input in neurology but not to mental health symptoms. They might prove useful for analyzing aspects of attention but have only been used in relation to schizophrenia so far. (67) *The concept of "evoked potential" using an external event to correlate to neural electrical activity might be generalized to other information beside simple sensory signals, but this has never been tried.*

The problems in measurement and interpretation of current biophysical techniques for evaluating brain function indicates their limitations. Each of these technical problems can be addressed by studies that focus on specific adaptive functions, by animal studies that correlate regions not easily observed by human methods, and by using other biological markers to clarify the information. (68) A major problem in current research has been the attempt to associate biophysical findings with clinical diagnoses despite the known problems of the diagnostic system. Emit has summarized similar observations in an editorial. He, among others, has also proposed abandoning the current diagnoses, and aggregating the findings using "big data" analysis. (68) It is doubtful that "big data" by itself solves anything (in computer language: "garbage in, garbage out"). Before comparing "patients" and "non-patients", it is necessary to define normal pathway functions. fMRI is a "noisy" procedure, requiring statistical standardization that no one seems willing to perform, which contributes to the many inconclusive meta-analyses of fMRI studies. When these relationships are better defined, prediction of brain function will still be difficult. The component operations of a computer system can be designed and produced, but in operation, the input and other factors determine its performance.

This summary of methods of brain imaging indicates:

A) Current measures of synaptic activity, and neural firing in animal models are useful.

B) No current technique measures pathway activity or is directly correlated with this activity.
C) fMRI (BOLD) is producing some useful information but needs standardization. Despite brain changes in development, standardizations of pathways for development have not been done.
D) Current techniques have major statistical noise, not easily resolved, which reduces the accuracy and sensitivity of testing. (Increasing the n of subjects in studies does not lower the variability between subjects.)
E) Social systems data is rarely studied in conjunction with pathways. These are needed to extend the understanding of the process to the social system.
F) Studies comparing the difference between diagnoses of "normal" and "abnormal" add additional noise to the data because the current diagnostic system is insensitive to variables in neural processes.
G) Standardizing "normal brain functions", and then sorting patient groups by categories of dysfunction may give better results. A few researchers have begun to explore this approach. (68)

Different brain regions and functions are described in chapters of *Neuromind,* but the concept of isolated "modules" is rejected. The brain consists of pathways joining multiple regions. Environment-organism interactions program these pathways. Destruction or disconnection of brain regions interferes with processing.

Along with technical issues, brain characteristics put limitations on research: a) Neural signals are probabilities that vary over time so only an average summary of messages is possible. (It is this probabilistic averaging quality that suggests "quantum properties" to scientists coming from a background in physics.) b) The scientific understanding of the *processes* that generate brain activity cannot predict the *content*, which is dependent on the statistical variation of individual experience. Brain operations are both logical processes and information content, and the processes can be understood using the language of cognitive neuroscience, but the content is always changing. The *content problem* includes different modes of representation in the brain: linguistic and "non-linguistic" or symbolic. The scientific theory of the brain is a representation of brain operations in linguistic mode that may not be able to describe some non-linguistic modes. Other "languages of experience" including literature, painting, dance, etc. use features of neural activity not easily represented in neuroscience formulations. Neuroscience can produce a scientific model of pathways with more detail and accuracy over time, but the output at a certain moment also depends on the stream of input data, the content. c) The relationship between external observation of brain activity and internal processes must be understood. The output on the computer screen (or other output) is produced by the operations of the computer. Changes of output depend on changes of input including the human operator, the programming, hardware changes, and operations that change output. The output observed includes these multiple elements. This is not the usual sense of "causation" in physical sciences. It is the same for the brain. *Pathway operations and their interactions "produce" the observed output.* Etiologies that alter the pathway patterns change the observed output, which are different observations of the same process. (In philosophy, this is called "psychophysical parallelism"; the operations of an information system and its outputs are the same process.) In reporting research, the author may describe differences in fMRI data (of pathways) as the "cause" of observed symptoms. This is incorrect, the **etiologies** cause both the changes in pathways and what is observed.

The technical limitations in mental health research create difficulties applying research to clinical practice. Uniqueness of the individual is a statistical property: The average shows statistical similarity, but does not discriminate details. Unique values give low statistical similarity but good discrimination. "I am very different from you or anyone else, and it is very difficult to predict my response." Determining a useful level of generality for mental health research and clinical applications is a balance between average prediction and individual specificity, the problem of standardizing "evidenced based treatments" against specific individual patterns. The *Neuromind* solution is to *standardize adaptive patterns*, and *specify unique abnormal variations*. Philosophers who state that human consciousness is a unique individual property are correct: each person's conscious experience depends on many experiential and genetic features, which makes predicting the content of consciousness from moment to moment impossible. However, the processes that generate this changing conscious experience are similar across humans and can be described (discussed in chapter five). *There can be a model of the neural process of subjective experience, but not a model for the current subjective experience of each person.* It is too rare a statistical event. Subjective report and scientific observation are two different representations of the world and overlap, but do not map onto each other with precision. Scientific description averages across a population of observations (of many individuals), providing useful information for a variety of tasks, including mental health tasks, but is limited for describing the individual. This problem occurs repeatedly in mental health research, complicating the use of subjective report as data about brain activities. Scales and other techniques "normalize" the subjective report, but do not capture the individual variation needed for differentiating individuals. Human observers are often capable of identifying important elements in interaction with other humans that are not captured in statistical measures. There is a "sweet spot" for each process that maximizes the effectiveness of generalization, and preserves uniqueness. Theories of mental health (and mental illness) do not include all the unique features of each individual. This does not diminish the value of group studies for treatment options. The interaction of the conscious experience of provider and client, "agency" both in the patient and the provider, are most effective. Replacing this interaction by computations always converges toward average results.

CHAPTER TWO:
The social brain

CLINICAL EXAMPLE A confused elderly man was brought to a board-and-care home for evaluation. He was seated in a chair in the lobby and left alone. He asked staff passing by to notify someone of his arrival. An hour passed without any contact. He became impatient and called out for attention and was told that someone would be with him shortly. After two hours, he began to take off his clothes, and had begun removing his pants when several staff responded. He was taken to an examining room and allowed to put his clothes back on. After some discussion, it was decided that he was not suitable for this placement and transportation was called to return him to the previous one. COMMENT Sometimes abnormal communication is the most effective.

Social adaptation is the most important of the brain's many capacities. Humans group together for hunting, agriculture, defending territory, protection against other species, breeding, and raising the next generation. The group replaces musculoskeletal speed, toxins, claws, and other individual survival mechanisms. Primary attachment to a caregiver is necessary for the neonate's survival. (Societies practice infanticide by leaving newborns unattended, subject to starvation and predators, even in contemporary society.) Messages between the brain and the social system are the reciprocal interactions that program the brain to learn physical skills, cognitive skills including language, and social skills to become a functioning member of the community. If a group member experiences problems satisfying personal needs in social interactions, problems often occur. The human cortex is similar to other mammalian species that live in social groups, including chimpanzees and dolphins, (1) and the British anthropologist Dunham proposed the "social brain hypothesis" (SBH) as an explanation: the evolution of brain function in primates (including humans) is selected for adaptation in social groups. (2)

SIDEBAR The social brain hypothesis. As evidence for the SBH, Dunham observed correlations between the neocortex/medulla ratio (a measurement of relative cortex size) with the size of foraging groups: the larger the foraging group, the larger the cortex relative to the core brain across primate species. (He has gone on to find other suggestive evidence.) The idea appeals to The Group for the Advancement of Psychiatry who advocate it as a basis for clinical psychiatry (2002):"…the brain is a body organ that mediates social interactions while also serving as the repository of those interactions." (3) The GAP authors (Bakker, Gardner et al) embrace this evolutionary hypothesis, rejecting the "bio-psycho-social model". (5) By emphasizing evolutionary principles, Psychiatry is linked more directly to the biological sciences, and brain functions are linked to adaptive social behavior, bridging the divide between social and biological approaches, described by the anthropologist Luhrmann in "Of Two Minds: The Growing Disorder in American Psychiatry": "Young psychiatrists are supposed to learn to be equally good at both talk therapy and drug therapy, psychotherapy and biomedical psychiatry,…Yet they are taught different tools, based on different models, and used for different purposes." (4) The appeal of integrating biological and social levels is strong, but evolutionary selection leaves no place for cultural factors. These issues are discussed in a SIDEBAR at the end of the chapter.

Social adaptation raises several questions (whether or not it drives evolutionary selection):

What specific regions of the brain are involved in social interaction?

How is adaptation related to mental health?

Can adaptation be measured in order to differentiate health from illness?

How are pathways are organized by social experience?

The answers are the link between brain and community.

Many brain regions contribute to social interaction, certain regions are crucial for social messages. Four reviews of the "social brain" (between 2007-9) offer different perspectives, including Frith (6) and Van Overwalle (7) who organize their data of the "social brain" using abstract concepts of "mentalizing" and "prediction of intention of others". Their subjects are isolated in fMRI performing mental tasks hypothetically related to social interaction. Adolphs (8) adds evaluation of social stimuli. Hari and Kujala (9) focus on interaction with others, gathering social information from studies of joint measurement of interacting subjects, and also the development of social perception. Soto-Icaza, et al, present a detailed overview of development of social skills from a neural perspective (10). The following summary uses these reviews and related studies, to identify stages of social development:

Perception of social stimuli. With developing sensory capacity, the child differentiates "social stimuli", facial patterns, auditory intonations, physical actions, and touch, (and probably also release of pheromones not yet understood in children), from inanimate objects. Eye gaze is an important indicator of social response (and evidence for impairment), involving pathways of visual perception. (10) Facial expression and eye gaze are major channels of communication between mother and child, using non-dominant hemisphere and amygdala for facial signals. (11) The face stimulus must be interpreted as a special stimulus, (12) based on research by Ekman and Friesen of emotion in older children and adults. (13) There are rare cases of "facial blindness" that involve abnormalities of the fusiform gyrus. (14) Olfactory stimuli are likely important but less understood in humans. (15) Sensory significance pathways create an internal representation of "other" (see chapter four and seven). The social rewards of the maternal-child interaction motivate learning and create primary attachment. (See chapter seven.)

Interpretation of Social stimuli. "Social" data must be interpreted by combining sensory stimuli with social/reward information in parietal and temporal cortex. Ramachandran studied persons with "capgras syndrome", emotional/sensory disconnection, who recognize "stimulus familiarity" of another person, but do not connect the emotional data. "it may look like the person you know, but it doesn't "feel like" that person, so identification is rejected." A person is only "recognized" when the sensory and emotional links are jointly activated. (16) (This also occurs in the Kluver-Bucy syndrome (see chapter four). (17)) The role of amygdala in studies of facial recognition emphasizes negative emotions and aversive threat because positive emotional assessment is not linked there. (6) The regions for facial recognition may be genetically programmed, but connecting facial patterns with specific caregivers requires social experience. (18) A particular region of hippocampus, dentate gyrus/CA3, is associated with the memory for social information. (19) There is less data on the emotional content of auditory stimuli, though one study explores this in the blind. (20) There is research on the role of music and its interaction with brain and amygdala. (21) The loss of social recognition in dementia combines losing both stimulus and emotional connections. (Much of the data and impetus for current research on the "social brain" is from studies of autism, discussed in a later section.)

Mirror neurons *discriminate self/other to organize responses.* After receiving and interpreting social signals, the child responds. The simplest response is repeating the message sent by the other, mimicking. Certain "dual response neurons", first discovered in nonhuman primates and later in humans, show activity when behavioral patterns generated by the person, are similar to visually observed behavior performed by another: "Mirror neurons in the motor and associative cortex of humans and monkeys discharge not only when specific actions are executed, but also when these same actions are observed in other animals or humans..." (9) Hari and Kuhala review data that mirror neurons are the mechanism for imitation/mimicry, reproducing behavior observed in others. (22) Brain imaging techniques locate these cells in two main areas, the temporal-parietal junction (TPJ) where visual and somato-sensory signals interact, and the medial prefrontal cortex of reward pathways. (9) The "mimicry pathway" combines visual and somatosensory data (self-motor actions) with reward signals that confirm "matching", by social rewards. The research combines microelectrode recordings in awake monkeys and fMRI of human subjects. The cells organize movement on the basis of visual feedback in a developmental sequence starting from simple motor patterns (eye gaze is an early response), to more coordinated actions, (e.g. bipedal locomotion of adult movement), eventually imitating complex social responses. (22) (23) *"Mirror neurons"* are located close to the speech region of Broca's area, the likely basis for speech acquisition by mimicry, in the sensory-motor phase of cognitive development. (24) Other mirror functions are being explored. (25) There is agreement that cells respond to linking visually observed and self generated action, and that the cells are located in specific brain regions, but various interpretations are given to their functions from simple mimicry, to "anticipation of actions of another", and "the ability to differentiate self and other"("theory of mind").

SIDEBAR The Mirror Neuron Puzzle How mirror neuron responses are produced is not explained by the studies that show convergence on different sensory paths, intersecting at TPJ, of motor behavior and observed behavior. The response is not genetically organized because a range of different motor behaviors can be linked. "Similarity" must be programmed by outcome (=reward?) when similarity conditions are met, as in practicing mimicking trials until the behavior is "just right". The TPJ junction cells provide the comparison signal data, and the OFC region gives the confirming reward signal that links them. Several authors have proposed explanations for the separate development of parts of the mirroring system. (32)(33)

Awareness of "self" uses sensory feedback of somesthetic, muscle, and connective tissue signals, and also emotional responses. (23) (Separate representation of separate self/other occurs in the transition from a symbiotic early child/caregiver bond to independent separation in child development, discussed in chapter seven.) Adolphs speculates that motor feedback is crucial to "self awareness", not sensory data, and motor interaction with others is more important than sensory data about self. *(8)(25)* Damasio identifies *insula* as the major region for self-data, based on symptoms of neurological patients with damage to this region and fMRI studies. He includes both storage of self-experience, and the subjective sense of self. The *insula* is a distinct cortical region hidden inside the Sylvian fissure, less than 2% of the total cortical surface area and densely connected to other regions (sensory thalamic nuclei, association cortex, the amygdala, and other limbic nuclei) over complex pathways. Both sensory and motor data are linked over pathways to *insula*. Large "Von Economo neurons" in the region have complex dendritic trees for multiple integrative functions. (26) (27) *Insula* is involved in many different pathway activities: general sensory reception, smell, response to pain and modulation of pain response. Damasio views the insular cortex as a "detector node" converging sensory information from key body inputs, to represent "self", and has incorporated this into a theory of "self consciousness". (28) (29) Insula is distant from TPJ, so mirror neuron data must use long axon pathways to connect. Gogolla reviews much of the information processed in *insula*, including "self memories" (experiences), and "actions" expressing "self intention". (29) The overlapping pathways store information defining "self" as learned experience. (30) Menon and Uddin have proposed a model for the interaction of insula and cingulate cortex, linking "self" pathways to the motivation system and pre-frontal choice system (see chapter six.). (31)

Hari and Kujala review studies on dynamic interaction between child and caregiver creating a mix of sensory, motor and reward information. (9) A complex multistage attachment and separation process occurs in mammalian development, studied in detail in humans, (reviewed in chapter seven). Neural data related to the process, reviewed by Long et al, are preliminary. (31) A detailed review of social development by Izcata-Soto, describes the changes of the sensory information of early childhood, stored later as abstract "intentions" and "traits". (10) The sensory/perceptual elements become "person-objects" which acquire "meaning", i.e. reward links, and other associations. (35) *No one neuron, pathway, or region stores the representation of person or thing. Sensory and motor information are linked with rewards and other data, to form the representations, which are stored along multiple pathways.* These intersect and interact with other representation pathways. The relationship between attachment/separation and self/other determination is an example of this complicated process, requiring further study. (34)

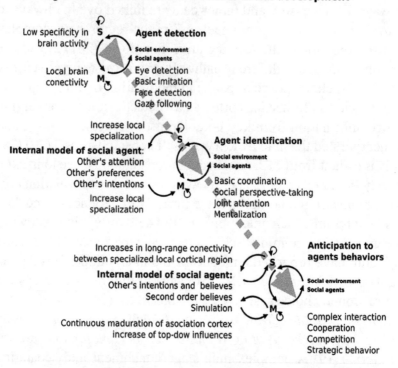

A general framework for a model of social development

Copyright © 2015 Soto-Icaza, Aboitiz and Billeke.
This is an open-access article distributed under the terms of the
Creative Commons Attribution License (CC BY)

Higher order social cognition. The ability to generalize from specific social interactions to more general patterns depends on abstraction, a cognitive development in adolescence. The mirror neuron-mimicry process changes from simple to complex motor mimicry, to emotional expression, and then to complex verbal and cognitive behavior. Adult research on the "social brain" emphasizes these capacities in studies of fMRI on isolated subjects performing verbal tasks assessing hypothetical "other". Ventromedial prefrontal cortex (mPFC) figures prominently in these "social" assessments. (See chapter six) (35) Social stimuli activate this region in studies of "perception of others" with several features reported: i) both positive and negative evaluations of self and other, ii) monitoring behavior inhibits irrelevant cues, (6) iii) activity over time suggests long term storage of social information, which includes enduring traits of others and the self, including interpersonal norms and "scripts" (see chapter six). (36) (37) Van Overwalle thinks "mirror neurons" provide an "inference of other's intentions", an abstract function. Keysers and Perrett question these interpretations. *(23)* Abstract functions are inferred from fMRI studies in adults requesting complex cognitive activity. Patients with right-sided damage (non-dominant hemisphere) have more problems interpreting social signals. Storing interpersonal information over pathways of mPFC is affected by damage at earlier life stages, with more impairment with earlier damage. (37) Problems of adaptation may result in confusing the source of emotion in self *or* other. (38) Neurosurgical (frontal lobotomy) or traumatic injury (Gage case) disconnect the mPFC pathways producing syndromes of reduced social capacity, impaired motivation, and poor self-management. (39)(40)(41) Hickock's 2009 critique rejects formulations that mirror neurons provide "action understanding", as unproven by the studies, and difficult to formulate as neural activity. (42) Functions attributed to **mirror neurons** involve the pathways in which they are embedded. Newer "hyperscanning interaction" techniques use real time EEG correlation to measure subjects interacting live (in real time), which may provide additional information. (43) Neurofeedback driven reward offers the possibility of manipulating this variable to study its impact. (44) (45)

Adolphs and Kennedy emphasize that the "social brain" is not a region but a network integrated with other neural pathways. (8) There is no one region of the "social brain" but multiple pathways integrating social functions. Many studies of the social functions were stimulated by the "epidemic" increase, beginning in the 1960s, of autism spectrum, a disorder of impaired social interaction. (Discussed in later section.) (Documentation of the increase can be found at (46)(47).)

> **SIDEBAR Group Process.** Other evidence for the neural pathways of the social brain comes from the research on group process. Active research on the formation and development of work groups began during WWII and continued into the 1960s. Studies by social scientists, "T-group" programs, the Tavistock clinic, and U of Michigan center all document that individuals experience social messages, in small groups as they are forming in a process that proceeds in definable phases. The process is often outside of the participants' awareness, but can be brought into awareness by an experienced observer who gives feedback to the group. Groups can be created to study this group forming process and its relationship to historical and anthropological evidence, as described by Slater in **Microcosm**. **(47)** The universality of this process is one more indication of the neural basis of human group participation, regulated by the pathways of the "social brain" and programmed by life experiences.

Emotions are messages for group communication. Emotion in mental illness focuses on dysphoric subjective states, ignoring the full range of emotional events and their role in communication. Moors reviewed the psychology of emotion, defining an "emotional episode" as: (a) a cognitive or assessment component; (stimulus evaluation or appraisal), (b) a feeling component, the emotional experience; (c) a motivational component, the action tendencies or states of action readiness (e.g., to flee or fight); (d) a somatic component, consisting of central and peripheral physiological responses; (e) a motor component, consisting of expressive behavior (e.g., facial and vocal expression). Researchers question which components are essential, and emphasize particular components and sequences. (48) Ekman and Friesen have done extensive studies of facial expression of social/emotional signals which has several properties:

aa) humans can discriminate several basic expressions, bb) facial patterns are consistently identified with the basic emotions, cc) the facial pattern/emotion association has cross cultural validity, and dd) a person can produce the emotional facial patterns on demand. Facial motor recognition and production are important components of social communication in primates and humans. (49) For Ekman, recognition is the key to understanding emotional communication, an automatic appraisal mechanism which detects the facial emotions: fear, anger, joy, sadness, disgust, and surprise (universal features based on the recognition of facial expressions). Anthropologists raise questions of the specificity of facial patterns, but the major ones listed above have 70% validation across cultures. Facial motor patterning has a "wired in" component that conveys a "behavioral message" about the subjective state of the individual. (50) Studies by Parkinson and his colleagues observe emotion in social settings of interpersonal interaction as communications between individuals, not just the individual response to a stimulus. (51) Emotion messages lead people to engage in social encounters or withdraw. Rom Harré emphasizes language, social practices, and other elements of culture in the social role of emotion. (52) Most humans possess an assessment-expressive communication system, involving body and facial configurations, along with verbal communication, to convey information about internal emotional states to others (and may also be used to convey false information). Some individuals can "read" somatic aspects of emotion, like pupillary response, better than others. Others emphasize different aspects of the process: James-Lange and Damasio emphasize the somatic response. (54) For Damasio, mental activity triggers the bodily response that then triggers a cognitive recognition, a part reversal of James-Lange. (1994, p. 145). (55) Johnson's review of emotion focuses on three features: evolutionary, social, and internal. *"Evolutionary theories attempt to provide a historical analysis of the emotions, usually with a special interest in explaining why humans today have the emotions that they do. Social theories explain emotions as the products of cultures and societies. And internal approaches attempt to provide a description of the emotion process itself.*" (53) "Evolutionary" and "social" contrast the genetically prewired and socially learned components. Johnson also differentiates **emotion** and **mood**: An *emotion* is related to a specific stimulus context and changes in response to new stimulus. *Mood* is a persisting state not related to a specific stimulus context, and often appears independent of context. This distinction is useful for clinical applications, because normal emotional experience is transient, while abnormal states are persistent, with pathways "stuck" in maladaptive patterns.

Moors reviews the areas of agreement: All the theories agree on the majority of components including a) initial stimulus, b) appraisal of the stimulus, c) internal emotional response, d) with or without bodily response, e) motivational significance, and f) output of emotional expressive behavior. Several theories assume that emotion-antecedent processing is cognitive, that it can be automatic, and multiple mechanisms and representations are involved. The theories have evolved from step-wise processes toward more automatic, parallel, multistage processes with subjective and behavioral components used in social exchange. *Questions remain*: what stimuli elicit emotion and how it is related to intensity? What neurophysiological mechanisms process elicitation and output? Is elicitation more conscious or subconscious? (48)

The sequence described by Moors identifies the four elements important for social communication: (i) acquisition and appraisal of data/"message" produces (ii) an internal change, the motivational impact of message on the receiver, which influences (iii) the response, producing (iv) a new "message" to the group. Adolphs summarizes the same brain areas for social functions. (14) The pathways involved are the same "perception of others", "theory of mind", and other operations of the social brain, here described in terms relating to "emotion". The neural pathway for emotion first described in the historic paper by Papez, described the "emotional brain" as a memory reward system (described in chapter four). (61) This temporal-hippocampal "limbic circuit" stores reward and motivation experiences of all modalities especially emotion-social interaction.

The amygdala uses a different circuit for danger information, including facial expression, (discussed in chapter eight). Learning social patterns of emotional expression involves the mimicry of mirror neurons discussed earlier in this chapter. The insula & cingulate coordinate the "self" experience of emotion states. The organization and expression of emotional responses are coordinated in the action-selection pathways of chapter six. Kassam et al used fMRI to localize regions of social brain cortex for emotional patterns. (60)

Communication of emotion is a component of social adaptation that utilizes the same social brain pathways. The survival value of emotional communication is an alternate formulation of the social brain hypothesis. The strongest argument for genetic programming of "emotion" is the similarity across cultures and species of patterns of facial and other motor expression. (60) This was clear to Darwin, and to any contemporary pet owner. Mammals have the capacity to coordinate emotion states and needs, communicating them to others of their own and other species (esp. humans!). The genetic patterns are modified by social norms for expression of emotional communication by social pressure. Human interaction can be habitual-automatic, but awareness provides opportunities for change. (57) Subjective awareness of emotional state of self and other provides the opportunity for choice. (58) Emotional signals can be intentionally modified, to some extent ("agency"), providing some control of emotional expression and social interaction, but some emotional responses are difficult to revise, creating "stuck" patterns. The ability to "act" in life, theater or film, shows the ability to produce emotional behavior not determined by an internal motivational state. The emotional component of the tic behaviors in Tourette's syndrome is another example of disconnection of emotional expression and internal states. (See chapter six.) (62) Emotional communication between humans creates group stability, cohesion, and coordination of actions, also found in other primate societies and non-primate groups like dolphins. Emotional communication coordinates social activity within the group and signals others outside the primary group. (59)

Social Adaptation Defines The Boundary Of "Mental Illness". Mental health is the adaptation to social systems, so "mental illnesses" are problems of adapting. "Labeling Theory" defines mental illnesses as statements of impaired social adaptation, "deviance". In the 1960s, T. Szasz and R.D. Laing proposed that "mental disorders" are socially deviant behaviors, not illnesses in the medical sense. (63)(64)(65) The Rosenhan study tested this issue (see chapter ten). Society determines the boundary of acceptable behavior, and *mental illness,* crime, and other "deviant" behaviors are violations of social boundaries. The societal definition of "deviant behavior" is not the same as "symptoms". Individuals may experience symptoms without seeking care or demonstrating behavior sufficiently impaired to require intervention and be labeled "mentally ill". Individuals may show impaired adaptation and be labeled "mentally ill" while denying symptoms. There is no absolute mental health, adaptation is always relative to the community of the individual, and someone poorly adapted to one culture, may fit very well in another. Maladaptive behavior can be produced by many etiologies, "Labeling Theory" emphasized only social/developmental etiologies, ignoring the others, and opposing purely biological psychiatry. (66) The waning interest in social psychiatry ignores its contributions including the "stigma" associated with mental illness, described by Goffman (67). Differentiating criminal and mental health problems did not occur until the 19th century with the emphasis on "compassionate care", and the return of incarceration of mentally ill in the last twenty years suggests that the differentiation is breaking down again. In consultation-liaison psychiatry, in the general hospital, a patient who refuses to conform to the treatment expectations of the "patient role", refusing treatment or failing to cooperate in prescribed treatment may generate a mental health intervention for deviating from the "patient role".

Autism spectrum disorder(ASD) is an example of impaired social adaptation. (68) In the most severe form, the person is unable to experience himself or others as social beings engaged in interpersonal events (lacking "theory of mind"). (69) A less severe presentation allows the individual to develop some social competence, learn language, and live independently. Beginning in early childhood with failure of eye gaze, face recognition, and other responses to maternal interaction, the child demonstrates impaired social engagement and response to social rewards. This can be shown in comparison EEG measures, and early deficits in facial tracking, which support the importance of the face in bonding. (70) These children do not lack the sensory motor capacities, and respond to punishment modalities, including painful self-stimulation, but lack social rewards including attachment bonding. Object reward and punishment are used to shape behavior. In less extreme examples, some capacity for social reward develops. This may deprive the parent(s) of the gratifying aspects of parenting, while leaving the tasks of structure and management of behavior. (71) Autism patients develop idiosyncratic self-reward systems, the repetitive non-social rewards of "asperger's phenomenon". Working with or living with such a person is a profound lesson in the importance of social reward for participating in a community.

CRITERIA FOR DIAGNOSIS OF AUTISM

Persistent deficits in social communication and social interaction across multiple contexts:

Deficits in social-emotional reciprocity, ranging from abnormal social approach to failure to initiate or respond to social interactions.

Deficits in nonverbal communicative behaviors used for social interaction from abnormalities in eye contact and body language to a total lack of facial expressions and nonverbal communication.

Deficits in developing, maintaining, and understand relationships, ranging, from difficulties adjusting behavior to suit various social contexts to absence of interest in peers.

Severity is based on social communication impairments and restricted, repetitive patterns of behavior.

> Restricted, repetitive patterns of behavior, interests, or activities, at least two of the following, currently or by history: Stereotyped or repetitive motor movements, Insistence on sameness, inflexible adherence to routines, or ritualized patterns of verbal or nonverbal behavior.
>
> Highly restricted, fixated interests that are abnormal in intensity or focus.
>
> Hyper- or hypo reactivity to sensory input or unusual interest in sensory aspects of the environment.
>
> Symptoms must be present in the early developmental period (but may not become fully manifest until social demands exceed limited capacities, or may be masked by learned strategies in later life).
>
> Symptoms cause clinically significant impairment in social, occupational, or other important areas of current functioning.
>
> These disturbances are not better explained by intellectual disability (intellectual developmental disorder) or other global developmental delay.

After a brief period of attributing the syndrome to "cold unresponsive mothers", a genetic etiology was proposed from familial patterns, males are more often affected, and a specific "fragile X" variant is found. Several genetic markers are associated with a small percentage of cases, and a large number of markers associate with autism at low probability. (72) Neural pathway studies show problems involving the mirror neuron system, but also changes in habituation and generalization suggest an impact on the attention system. Different social brain pathways are altered in different presentations, showing variations of the syndrome. Abnormalities in response to face patterns are a consistent feature, with reduced connectivity between the fusiform face area (FFA) and amygdala and prefrontal regions, especially in severe ASD. A review of learning deficits indicates problems of generalization and goal focused learning, but not reward. (74) Much emphasis has been placed on abnormalities of eye gaze, and a scale observing social patterns has been developed. (75) (76)

Genetic variables change too slowly to explain the recent dramatic increased incidence, so some environmental factor must also be contributing to the increase. Some studies point to risks of medication, environmental toxins, and ultrasound as possible factors. (73) Early intervention with specific training can improve the individual's adaptation, and the level of social impairment may change across development. **Autism** provides a dramatic example of the importance of effective social interaction for achieving life goals. Other pathway disturbance syndromes, discussed in later chapters, may also impair social adaptation. *A separate assessment of social adaptation is needed, independent of symptoms, to track effects of treatment, and the contributions of multiple pathways.* Symptoms are an indirect and inconsistent measure of social adaptation, not a reliable basis for determining course of recovery. (A tentative scale is provided in appendix to chapter 10, with reference to other scales.) (77) (78)

How does the social environment influence the brain? Life experiences modify "social brain" pathways: i) the events of the developmental sequence in the family and transition to society, ii) traumatic life events, iii) socio-economic factors in individuals and groups, and iv) cultural differences (which are discussed in chapter ten). The current diagnostic system (DSM V) omits social factors, locating the problem entirely in the individual, ignoring the interaction between the person and the social system. The developmental sequence can be organized by a "life cycle history" of the effects of developmental transitions: a) adaptation to family, b) transition from family to local community, and c) transition to engaging with the general society. Events at each stage modify pathways, which is difficult to document because of the cost and complexity of longitudinal studies, with large populations and multiple events that are beyond the resources of private organizations. Governments seem uninterested in evaluating the "human resources" of their citizens, and so private foundations may be the best resources for identifying the long-term effects. The life cycle approach is useful for gathering and organizing information, and allows the provider to anticipate significant events that are missing, as well as those present. (106)

The life cycle indicates positive responses to challenging events that document **resilience**, the ability of individuals with social and economic challenges to achieve successful life adaptation. Persons who grow up in negative social circumstances to become highly, sometimes exceptionally, effective adults have learned how to facilitate the developmental process. Without documenting adjustment to challenging environments, it is impossible to study. The following overview uses the life cycle approach to describe a few of many possible examples:

The family (or other primary caregivers) experience is the first stage in the social life cycle. The evolutionary role of the family is supporting the survival of offspring, and preparing them for adult roles in the community. Family function begins with reproduction/fertilization, protection of the fetus in utero, and continues with birth and support of the neonate. In utero children and neonates are highly vulnerable, documented in several recent references. (79) An important bonding process, "attachment", occurs at this stage involving a special learning process (discussed in chapter seven). *The family is a dynamic interactive group performing functions or tasks.* The assessment of the individual/child is closely linked with the family system. The Beavers-Timberlawn method of family assessment separates family "competence" and "family style", using the clinicians' observations of the family. Leadership, enmeshment/autonomy, intergenerational boundaries, communication of task, communication of emotion, decision making, and material support, maintaining the physical needs of the family, scale competence. Style is rated as "centripetal, centrifugal, or mixed". Real families have complex patterns, and vary widely in "culture", so evaluation is individualized. (80) Chess and Thomas identified birth features which persist to young adult life (one of the few longitudinal studies) which are not genetic, nor learned, (perhaps the result of in utero effects). Birth order is another significant variable. (81) Polygenic multi-site loci present a complex picture of genetic influences on social interaction, consistent with the multiple brain regions of the *social brain*. Separating genetic and social influences in family interaction is an intellectual fantasy with little clinical relevance. The two interact in complex patterns. (82) The family supports the child's development for autonomy, and early departure through placement, voluntary or involuntary, or excessive dependence, interfering with autonomy, may result in problems.

The balance between the severity of problems posed by the child(ren) and the limitations of the parental unit determine the capacity of the family to care for them. The concept of the identified patient illustrates this. The small child is critically dependent on the parents' support for survival. So dysfunction of the presenting "patient", the child, may reflect problems in the parents, a dynamic interaction validated when changes in the family improve or resolve the child's symptoms. (85) Family intervention of placement out of the family also addresses this, but is costly and does not address the problems of remaining family members. Minuchin's group at Philadelphia Child Guidance Clinic pioneered work with families with limited resources, using a method of reorganizing the family with all family members participating. (84) Reports of "feral" children who grow up with little or no human contact also show the impact of the social environment: case reports provide a basis for assessing the role of social conditioning. (Are some of these feral children on the autism spectrum?) (87)(88)

The symptoms presented by children are variations of disturbed social behavior, poor emotional control, and developmental delays or regression to earlier behaviors. (A discussion of behavior symptoms in childhood is presented in chapter six.) The evaluation must include a mixture of biological and social issues: 1) is there intrinsic neural pathway dysfunction? 2) What is the impact of the family system? 3) Can the child engage the family network to satisfy the needs? 4) Do certain developmental experiences negative or positive impact the child? 5) Is the child able to separate from family to attend school, etc.? 6) Is the family able to provide emotional support? Assessment of the child without including the social context misses many factors.

SIDEBAR. The American family has changed dramatically in the last 75 years. The literature on families and family therapy in the 1950s and 60s considered the two parent lifelong marriage with multiple children the norm, and other family systems variants or dysfunctional, even though many families at the time did not fit the pattern. The lifelong two parent family is not statistically representative of current American families. Beginning in the 1960s attitudes about joint parenting, the gender of parents, and assumptions about values for raising children have changed. By 2000 more than 50% of American children were born into single parent households across all socio-economic groups, including mothers who decided to raise children without another involved parent. (86) Homosexual couples now marry and adopt (or bear) and raise children as a family in many states. These changes impact clinicians working with families, and how they understand an effective family. Changes do not invariably result in family dysfunction, but require new approaches to parenting that may not always be appreciated by the participants.

CLINICAL EXAMPLE Twins. The birth of twins is a normal event, 32 per 1000 births in recent years in the US. And every instance challenges the family unit. Two totally dependent infants require constant attention, and feeding, comforting, and etc. Some families may solve this challenge with additional help from other family members or childcare workers. If both parents are not actively involved, the attending parent will have most of her (or his) time consumed in the task. If it is the mother, she will be recovering from childbirth or surgery or both, and also experiencing the hormonal post pregnancy changes. Unless extra childcare is available this will be an intensely stressful time for the separate family unit. Only one study discussing this has been found in recent literature! (89)

*CLINICAL EXAMPLE **A family with two pre-teen daughters**. The "identified patient" was the younger daughter reported seeing monsters coming into her room at night. The therapist noted that each parent sat together with a child, apart from each other. In an attempt to "reorganize the family", he suggested that the parents sit together, re-arranging the seating. The family complied, and almost immediately, the mother began to blush, became anxious and left the session. None of the remaining family members could explain this, and the session ended. The father called next week to cancel the next session and report that the mother left the family to live with a female companion. After several months, the mother and "identified patient" returned. The "identified patient" was no longer seeing things or having trouble sleeping, but was in trouble at school and admitted to using cannabis and trying other drugs. COMMENT The family is a delicate system, and abrupt interventions may seriously destabilize the process. The false "closeness" reported in the first session, evaporated leaving an emotionally empty space, so the daughters had to seek support elsewhere.*

Loss of a family member is especially difficult in childhood. Nagera reviewed the impact of early loss of a parent. (90) It removes an available parent, and creates issues if a new parent enters the family system. The death of a sibling is also difficult. The parents' grief may interfere with helping the child grieve at a less cognitive level. If the loss is not accepted, the remaining children are "asked" to fulfill expectations of the deceased child. "Replacement" children, who are sometimes born *after* the death, become "doppelgangers" for the lost child, carrying their own life tasks along with those of the deceased. (91) Incomplete grieving may leave "ghosts" in the family.

CLINICAL EXAMPLE Failure to accept a child's problems. *A mid adolescent male had mild autism, but expressive language, and was mainstreamed in the classroom. He had recurring fights with his mother, who never felt that he bonded with her. Father was mediating between mother and son, and became increasingly frustrated by the angry exchanges. The family decided it was best to place the child in a residential placement. COMMENT Although the autism syndrome was moderate, a parent's inability to accept the problems of bonding obscured that the child was only able to bond with mother in anger. This is also an example of inability to grieve for the loss of the "ideal child. At birth, every child born is a "fantasy child" in each parent's mind, and each imagines who the child will become. The child will never completely fulfill either parent's expectations, so they must grieve for the part of the unrealized "fantasy child". Under ordinary circumstances this process occurs gradually in the child's development, with "desirable" features celebrated by the parent, and "failures" accepted. When a parent does not accept the child's actual characteristics, negative feedback about the inability to live the ideal impacts the child's self esteem.*

Family violence has many forms. Domestic violence is a failure of the parental unit. (93) The emotional needs of family relationships are powerful and members depend on each other for emotional gratification and support. When expectations are not met, intense anger may lead to violent behavior, and physical assault of one parent on the other. The parental unit fails to establish a safe interpersonal group which impacts the child in many ways: a) it teaches the use of violence as a coping strategy; b) it creates fear in young children resulting in PTSD; c) it degrades the child's respect for both parents; and d) it encourages inappropriate faux-parental behaviors in older children to protect the abused parent. Multiple factors contribute to domestic violence, a difficult problem to modify. Legal interventions do not provide an effective barrier, and domestic violence calls are highly dangerous situations for police intervention. Child abuse is also family violence. The spectrum of child abuse ranges from violent acts leading to dissociation and PTSD, or seductive interactions that bind the child in a dysfunctional relationship that prevents autonomy. This may occur as physical abuse, sexual abuse, and/or protracted emotional abuse to one or more children. The perpetrator may be a parent, stepparent, or related family member. It may be associated with domestic violence. The dysfunction includes: a) A breakdown in the intergenerational incest boundary. b) Inappropriate competition between one parent and a child for emotional gratification by the other parent. c) The perpetrator makes the abuse the responsibility of the child, distorting the child's sense of agency and complicating later recovery. (94) **Every clinician is required by state law to report suspected abuse, so state agents can perform an evaluation.** This may, at times, complicate intervention by introducing an outside agent in the situation, and the ability to frame this in a manner that does not disrupt treatment can be challenging. State agencies are not always effective in creating protective boundaries, and the clinician must remain vigilant to possibility that the victim is still vulnerable. (95) Complicating issues include the situation in which a teen is involved in sexual behavior with another teen, younger than the age of consent, and instances of false accusation. The task of determining the true situation can be very difficult, especially in older teens, or when it occurs in the context of divorce proceedings.

An addicted parent (/parents) does not make parenting the primary motivation. The child who seeks emotional support while the parent is intoxicated, or when the parent is experiencing withdrawal, will face rejection and/or abuse. Addictions often lower moral boundaries allowing intergenerational abuse, both violent and sexual. The addicted parent is unable to perform the parental role, producing premature

CLINICAL EXAMPLE Continuing abuse in a young adult. *A 19-year-old female was seen for evaluation of mood swings. She was taking high dose steroids and other medications to control symptoms of lupus. This had onset several years before, and in evaluation she reported that the onset was during a period when mother left the family for a short time, and during that absence, father began a sexual relationship with her, which did not end when the mother returned. A series of interventions led to the end of the abuse, and the father's departure from the family. There was gradual reduction in symptoms of lupus. The father never admitted to the abuse but the patient's mood improved.* **COMMENT** *This situation was complicated by the patient's adult status, her reluctance to confront the father, and the stress related autoimmune disorder.*

efforts at self-parenting and ineffective autonomy in the child, with anxiety about the self-parenting. "When I can open the refrigerator door to get something to eat" is the symbolic indicator of self-parenting, but the "child" does not trust the self-parenting and focuses on "fixing" the addicted parent. (96) Winnicott (see chapter seven), describes how the child "internalizes" emotional soothing from interaction with parental figures, so instances in which the parental interaction is inconsistent result in alternative outcomes. The child may develop practical skills in feeding, clothing, and even helping manage a dysfunctional adult ("put mommy to bed when she is sick"). But cannot "internalize" managing dependency needs, which are not being addressed by the parental figure. The result may be a "pseudo adult", a person with a high level of practical function, who is unable to self-sooth, and suppresses emotional needs. The history will reveal a life long pattern of driving achievement, and hidden, immature emotional demands, with periodic depressive episodes. Epidemiology research identifies early trauma experiences that contribute to success or failure in adult life. (97) But more subtle and complex effects are missed, and the impact on adult mental health is retrospective and misses resilient responses. Studies do not clarify which children are able to survive early trauma successfully, while others do not. *(98)*

The transition from family to community adds additional problems. The family (or alternative placement) has responsibility for coordinating the child's entry into the social community, which differs in tribal and contemporary settings. Tribal, and small rural communities in more developed societies, are able to maintain small group face-to-face interaction between family and community. In large cities, the transition from face to face contact in small groups to more anonymous multi-family groups is influenced by the family's relationship to the community, their ethnic group, social class, cultural values, and other labels. The experience of going off to school with students from unfamiliar families creates challenges for both student and family. In modern society, cognitive skills, reading, writing, arithmetic, self-management, staying seated for periods of time, and behavior control are essential. (The first problems typically encountered are problems of motor control and are discussed in chapter six, as "ADHD".) The age for transition to school should reflect the child's neural maturation, which occurs across a range of ages. The same age for starting school puts slower developing children at a disadvantage; girls are typically started sooner than boys because of earlier maturation.

Difficulty in giving up emotional support of the family, labeled "school refusal" (formerly "school phobia" or "anxiety"), involves many factors that interfere with the child's separation from family. The diagnostic challenge is determining when the problem is anxiety in the parent and when it is the child's anxiety about school or peers. Some providers recommend treatment with anxiety medications, ignoring the role of the family and social system. Individualized assessment is needed for the relationship of the child to both social systems. (98) Many other small group activities, including scouting, sports teams, and hobbies involve other children and families, and introduce the child to the wider social system that requires developing group skills. Bullying is a serious consequence of poor social skills, when peers are hostile and rejecting of the student. (99) This has become a greater problem with peer communication over social media for older children, which can lead to suicidal behavior, or gun violence toward peers and teachers. (100) The demands for academic performance increase by middle school, where difficulties in speaking, reading, writing, mathematics and other cognitive performance become more obvious. Specialists, identified by schools, address the child's cognitive problems (and minimize the cost of alternative education to the school system). The decision about where the child should be schooled should address multiple adaptive challenges. The choices of (i) home schooling, (ii) specialized public school, (iii) general public school or "mainstreaming", (iv) private (parental payment) and (v) special needs school involve both costs, adaptive capacity of the child, and flexibility of the school system. Placement of children with *autism spectrum symptoms* is an example. Weighing the benefit and challenges of peer exposure depends on the severity of the disability, the ability to provide special support, and the value of a more "normal" developmental experience to prepare for later life. The society makes the institution of education responsive to the needs of the society, but no studies confirm that this occurs. Assessing the transition from family centered to school centered childhood reveals individual vulnerabilities and continuing effects of family issues. The issues of other families and their children now also impact and modify the child and family, complicating the assessment. Labeling all of these events as individual pathology fails to assess the impact of the social environment of contemporary children and teens.

The transition from local community to adult role in society. Adolescence, not recognized until the early 20th century, involves multiple changes of physical, cognitive, sexual development, and social engagement (see sidebar in chapter six). The changes may result in identity confusion. (101) Adolescents are neither "big children" nor "small emotional adults" but a complex transitional stage. Significant changes in the understanding of gender identity and the acceptance of alternative identities are a feature of the 21st century and add to the challenge of defining identity. (See chapter six.) Increased peer interaction may provide emotional support outside the family or rejection. If the teen has difficulties individuating, it predicts future problems in adjustment. If the teen is very separated from family, it creates more vulnerability to peer pressure and external demands.

> **CLINICAL EXAMPLE The absent teen.** *Parents were seen for evaluation of their teenage son who was reported to be depressed, and addicted to cannabis, but the son did not arrive at the session. The parents described his lack of cooperation, problems in school, and drug use, but without the "identified patient" nothing could be achieved. The son was contacted and agreed to one session without his parents. In the session, he revealed that his mother was dying of a progressive chronic disease, but she refused to talk to him about it. He and his father were constantly fighting about trivial arguments and the father was abusive. The son admitted his life was falling apart, but had a small support group of friends and could not stand to be around his parents, and refused to have joint family sessions. Another session was held with the parents, and the mother admitted her illness, and justified suppressing the information because "it was not relevant" to the problem. Couples sessions allowed the mother to grieve for the life she was slowly losing, with support from her husband who stopped focusing his anger on the son. Over several months, they reported that the son had "gotten back on track", was doing better in school, and spending some time at home. In an individual session, the son discussed his fear and sadness about what was happening to his mother, and how he would deal with her death, but still needed separation from his parents. COMMENT In family sessions, the "absent member" is the one who holds the key to the problem. The family could not deal with a major crisis together, so it had to be managed in separate generations.*

Teens test their emotional and social identities in peer groups to get alternative emotional support, but also from family when needed. If the teenager has significant limitations in adaptive function, keeping the child close to the family delays developing necessary adult coping skills. All three levels of individual, family and social interaction are influencing the teen, and providers without this perspective often have problems with adolescent interventions. Problems of adaptation may be dramatic. Emergence of "first episode psychosis" may occur at this developmental stage, especially with a separation from family. Depression and suicidal behaviors are also common. (103) Hypomania or mania may be obscured by the emotional intensity of teens, who mask emotions using alcohol and other drugs. Teens, confronted with challenges and overwhelmed, retreat to denial, childhood coping methods, substance abuse, or despair, all very confusing to the family. The dramatic alternation of autonomy and dependent regression is difficult to follow. Under the best circumstances, the family will "be available" to support the adolescent's need for support while "backing off" to allow the teen to develop support from the peer group, which can be dangerous when the peer group is negative, a gang, or alcohol and drug focused. (104)

CLINICAL EXAMPLE The silent sailor. A 19-year-old male was hospitalized with severe anxiety while in basic training in another state from his family, from whom he had never been separated before. The patient, a small thin, anxious WM was totally mute. He was visually responsive, and able to speak, but refused to engage verbally. Medications had no benefit on either anxiety or his mutism. The family visited him from their home in another state, and participated in a family session which revealed that a half-sib, several years older than patient, had lived with the family for three years, but left at the mother's request. He appeared to have no contact with the family, but the father revealed in the session that he was still in touch with the son, who lived in a nearby city, and was doing OK. Both mother and patient showed surprise, and the patient began asking the father about him, the first words he had spoken publicly since coming on the unit. This clarified that the other son was not abandoned, and that the parents were not angry or upset about the patient's inability to complete training and he would not be abandoned. He was enormously relieved and went out of session to spend time with the parents. Over the next several weeks, his anxiety diminished, he spoke openly on unit and in sessions, and expressed a strong desire to be discharged and return to family as soon as possible, which was arranged. COMMENT The misperception of a sibling's banishment from the family, convinced the patient he too was banished. One session resolved this confusion and he returned to the support of family. He had difficulty individuating which was addressed in later outpatient sessions with the family.

The transition to adult life begins sometime in adolescence, extends into the 20s when first mental health contact sometimes occurs. The assessment of social adaptation includes consistent social engagement, ability to form intimate personal relationships, productive work, and the ability to enjoy life. The role of the family is internalized and the influence of peers becomes more important.

Certain rituals like graduation from high school sometimes mark the transition, which also occurs in different form in "primitive" cultures. Eric Erikson recognized these life stages, and Levinson describes them in detail (his work popularized by Sheehy). (105) The hypnotherapist Milton Erikson used the "family life cycle" and the challenges individuals master at each stage. Access to work is a constantly changing factor with mental health significance rarely considered by providers, (except when it impacts payment). Certain jobs increase the personal stress of working at them, including firemen, policeman, air traffic controllers, prison personnel, etc. When employees suffer stress, but do not seek mental health services for fear of losing employment other problems occur. Airline pilots are the most frightening, as in the pilot who crashed a plane full of passengers. (111) For much of human history (and prehistory?) the cycle of reproduction and entry of offspring into society was also the end of the parental generation. Life expectancy to age 50 or so, ensured only a brief period after child emancipation to demise of the parents, who also died sooner in childbirth and disease. This has changed in the last half of the 20th century, and old age, the last stage of the adult "development", is experienced more often, including a group of adults with an additional 10 to 25 years of activity after age 60, though these "survivors" vary widely in health and mental capacity. Society has done little to organize a coherent response for using their skills productively, and managing the increased burden of their illnesses. How to include the "elders" in society is a total mystery both economically and socially.

Social and economic factors impact mental health through work, the lack of work, and the environment of economically challenged individuals, especially limited access to healthcare. Economic deprivation is associated with social dysfunction, though the causal relationships are debated, according to the preconceptions of the authors. (108) Hollingshead and Redlich, in *Social Class And Mental Illness,* presented a correlation between schizophrenia and lower social class, interpreted as the disorder reducing economic potential in society, the consequence of disability, or growing up in a lower economic class makes experience factors that cause the disorder more frequent. Mental disability limits one's economic and social position, so both factors are possible.

The Social Psychiatry initiative of the 1960s raised many issues about social variables in mental health with almost no impact. The major initiative of the 1960s, was ending long-term institutionalization of patients, without providing functional alternatives, which has contributed to the expansion of homelessness, and problems of poorly stabilized patients. Social Psychiatry also tried to identify what other factors were important. Exposure to toxic substances in the environment of newborn and young children is documented for lead poisoning in poor children, they have less prenatal care, and more birth related trauma. Poorer children have a higher exposure to drug abuse, though this is more balanced since the recent opiate epidemic. (109) Contemporary epidemiologic studies confirm the impact of these and other factors. (110) Books like **The Culture Of Poverty** propose that economic deprivation creates a different set of life expectations. Vance's **Hillbilly Elegy** described his family dysfunction and was met with empathy by reviewers. The TV series "Breaking Bad" idealized the epidemic of meth abuse in rural white farm communities. These examples try to "normalize" the social inequities. Children are impacted whenever parents are unable to perform their role. It is necessary to address these factors to avoid losing these children. More money is spent every year in the US on marketing toys and trinkets to children, often with dysfunctional messages about adult behavior, than spent providing healthcare services to them, a social and political decision that values children as consumers. This issue cannot be addressed by individual providers, or even the professional organizations of providers, but must be a political priority for the society. How to make protecting children, and their mental health needs a priority of the society is anybody's guess.

Sociological studies show the impact of social isolation on health, positive and negative, depending on engagement or isolation. (112) Opportunities for casual social interaction are different in large cities, small towns, and low-density rural areas. Churches, informal sports teams, and other interest groups are created to offset the isolation of people and families living alone. A trend toward more isolated life-style was already apparent when the Covid-19 epidemic imposed quarantine isolation to the world's population, and numerous studies suggest its impact. (113) Social interaction, including living with a stable partner is predictive of better long-term health, mental and physical. (114) The Weissman group has focused on the role of interpersonal factors contributing to mood disorder symptoms, especially in women, and the relationship between addictive behaviors and social support systems is underestimated. Interpersonal challenges can emerge from too strong interpersonal dependence in relationships. (114)

> *CLINICAL EXAMPLE Individuation and Support. A female health professional entered psychotherapy to deal with her "controlling mother". The patient and mother lived in different cities, but were in daily contact, and the patient sent part of her earnings to "support" her mother and resented doing so. The patient had not been in a serious relationship with another because she did not think her mother would approve. After several months in therapy, she went to visit her mother and returned reporting the following story: She was shopping alone downtown in the mother's city and realized she did not have any cash. She went to the bank that her mother used and asked to withdraw money from "her mother's account". The teller went to speak to a manager, and returned to inform the patient that it was a joint account with her name also, and she was free to withdraw whatever she wanted. The patient had a sudden realization that her mother was not "controlling" her earnings, and she was free to use them as she wished, which immediately changed her view of the relationship.*

War, and the aftermath of disintegrating social systems have demolished the orderly "life cycle" in many regions of the world. Providers are asked to evaluate residual family members whose lives have been altered by loss of parents, kidnapped children, victims dealing with torture, and instability of social systems. (115) (116) For those who are able to begin a new family, current economic, social, and emotional problems may create more difficulties. (R.J. Lifton has made a personal specialty of interventions with these individuals, discussed in chapter twelve. (117)) Individuals who are captives, or who join cults, either as teens or young adults, or who are raised in them as children, have problems of identity called "Stockholm syndrome". (118) The dramatic result of mass suicides in Jonestown, and conforming behavior in other cults gives ample evidence of the impact of social systems on individual behavior in groups. Cannon explored the phenomenon of "taboo death", the death of individuals who violate major social boundaries. (118) This is the most extreme example of the impact of aversive social events on the individual. The social system literally has control of life and death over the individual mediated through cultural norms and brain controls, and social systems can apply this power. A less dramatic example is shunning or banishment in religious groups.

SIDEBAR Stockholm syndrome: The individual is placed in an inflexible social environment under mental and emotional stress and must adapt to the environmental demands to survive. In some instances the person will take on the values and behaviors adaptive to that situation. When released back to a different social environment, significant problems may occur readjusting to the society, which may question the moral basis of the adaptation. This is typical with prisoners of war, like the brainwashing of prisoners of North Korea, where adaptation is considered a treasonable offense, or surviving in a concentration camp. Children and young women who are kidnapped and held captive for years must adapt to that life. The Patty Hearst kidnapping is a famous example because of crimes she committed while a captive and later trial. When released survivors face major adaptive challenges. Highly abusive family systems sometimes approach this level of control and isolation from the values of the rest of the society. Small cult-like groups pressure members to deviate from the extended society, as in the "Manson family". All military training involves altering the behavior of trainees to accept aggression, including killing others, as an acceptable value, which complicates return to civilian life. Changes in behavior of prisoners of war revealed the power of coercive persuasion during the Korean War. The ability to use a coercive environment to change attitudes and behavior is exploited in many situations. (118)

> **CLINICAL EXAMPLE** *The residue of growing up.* A woman was raised in a religiously isolated group in the west, with a father who dominated the wives and children. The woman was resentful but conforming, and "escaped" from the family and its social group at maturity. She developed a successful career, but had difficulty committing to relationships and became depressed about her life. She had recurring problems with male partners who were either controlling, in her perception, causing her to reject them, or passive and emotionally unappealing. Medications were ineffective. COMMENT The individual may reject the cultural patterns of the community and seek a new pattern, but the person has not grown up interpreting the social cues of other groups or relationships, and must learn them or be frustrated.

Cross Cultural Considerations. Tart coined the phrase *"consensus consciousness"* to characterize the general system of beliefs that each society teaches its members and to which they must adhere in order to remain members. (119) A uniform consensus still exists in some areas of the world, but in Europe and the United States this is not so. Two centuries of immigrants in the US, many in the last 30 years, has created a highly diverse, multicultural society. In many areas of the country, providers are involved in delivering services to persons with different cultural backgrounds. The "social norms" of mental health are not universal, and differ in different cultures:

i) The cultural understanding of mental illness varies. The American conception of "mental illness", part of the healthcare system of illnesses, is not valid in some cultures. (120) Other cultural systems have other differences from the Western medical model regarding mental illness. A provider of mental health services must be familiar with the understanding of the individual's culture (and subculture) in order to get effective collaboration in treatment.
ii) Patterns of abnormal behavior, "symptoms", reflect cultural values. The abnormal behavior in different cultures includes "running AMOK", "Windigo psychosis", etc., which reflect deviation from particular social norms. (121)
iii) Cultures use different treatment methods. Entering the mental health treatment system has expectations of the treatment

process, the patient role, the consequences of mental disability, etc. The changing mores of successive generations of immigrant families illustrates how this impacts on the family's ability to raise children integrated in the larger society. This complicates the expectations of treatment between the parental generation and the child or teenager. (122) (123) (See chapter ten)

Socio-economic status, social controls, and multi-cultural societies influence neural pathways in complex ways. Studies in social research confirm different effects, but not which brain pathways, or methods to use for modification and stabilization. No one has formulated a model for the effects of social variables on neural pathways and adaptive functioning. Individual examples have been cited here, and many more are available. Integrating social etiology in mental health is a multidisciplinary opportunity. Genes and experience combine to organize pathways, coding symbolic information in synaptic membranes to store experience.

SIDEBAR Return to the SBH. *The Social Brain Hypothesis, described at the beginning of the chapter, seeks ways to demonstrate that pathways are selected for social adaptation. There are several unresolved questions: SBH states that evolution selects brain characteristics that favor social adaptation. Conceptualizing Psychiatry using the Social Brain Hypothesis is not easily applied to clinical settings: A) Evolutionary studies require a multi-generational time scale (or controlled mating!), while most clinical research rarely extends for one or at most two generations. (Evolutionary changes by selective breeding are not easily accomplished in human populations!) B) Human selection by reproduction is not well documented. Do decisions about reproduction include assessment of social participation, along with other characteristics? There is little research on human reproductive choices. The relationship of reproductive success to adaptive success, or reproductive limitations of mental illness have rarely been studied. "Sex appeal" might be an important factor in social selection, but "group appeal"? Studying measures of reproductive choice for social adaptation might be useful if it could be measured. A study in the 1980s looked at features in reproduction of seriously mentally ill patients. (124) C) "Evolution in groups". The basis of evolutionary theory is selection of the individual's genetic contribution. Models that calculate group survival effects have been calculated, and modern evolutionary theory defines a process of group influence on selection.*

(125) Geneticists have struggled to define statistical models of evolution for noncompetitive interaction, supporting the survival of others, i.e. "altruism". This phenomenon occurs across the range of species from insects to primates, and is characteristic of group participation. Harmen discusses these in The Price Of Altruism. (126). Luo provides a meta-review of brain regions involved in all types of altruistic, prosocial behavior which localizes mostly to pre-frontal areas of motor choice. D) What role does social experience or cultural norms play in the selection process? Social experience can only influence reproductive selection of genes. Learned behaviors do not become part of the genome and cannot be genetically passed on. Classical evolutionary theory (including the SBH) rejects non-genetic factors, the basis for the GAP rejection of non-biological factors. (Lamarckianism is the (discredited) belief in inheritance of acquired traits.) The ability to acquire social skills may have a genetic basis, but the content is learned in the social/cultural environment and cannot be transmitted genetically. (Sapolsky chapter 10 "The Evolution of Behavior" in Behave. (127)) This is illustrated by language skill, which enhances adaptation, probably by genetic selection. (128) The ability to learn language may be genetic, but each person must learn his/her specific language(s) through social experience, that is not passed on genetically! E) Combining genetic and cultural information is presented in "dual inheritance theory". Donald T. Campbell published the first theoretical work that adapted principles of evolutionary theory to culture. Richard Dawkins's The Selfish Gene introduced ideas of cultural evolution to a popular audience. Geneticists Feldman and Luca Cavalli-Sforza published the first dynamic models of gene–culture co-evolution. In their theory, a parallel system of "culture" maintained by the group preserves important survival information. The term "meme" serves as a "gene" analog, though less precisely defined. This extends biological evolutionary theory to acquired knowledge. (129) Genetic selection occurs by reproductive advantage but how the elements of "cultural selection" are chosen is not defined in Dual Inheritance Theory. (130)

For social scientists and mental health clinicians who wish to combine genetic effects with social processes, the SBH is too limited, because transmission of social and cultural information are important to survival. Experience is transmitted from one generation to the next through the intergenerational processes that "preserve wisdom": elders teaching skills to youth, ancestor honor or worship, oral sagas memorized and retold, the stored documentation of values in traditional religious texts, the vast compilation of libraries, and modern digital data storage. Dual Inheritance Theory (DIT) combines biological and social transmission to include them. Genes and experience combine to organize pathways, coding symbolic information in synaptic membranes to store experience. The society must choose what cultural information to transmit to the next generation.

CHAPTER THREE:
The motivation system

A pathway receives information about internal body states to balance the data received from the social environment. The combined data from the body and external sensors is transmitted to frontal brain pathways to make choices of response, and also sent to cingulate and insula over a separate pathway for subjective experience.

The pathway that links body and brain begins in the ventral pons, and continues along the underside of the brain to pre-frontal cortex. Depending on the location and species it is called midbrain "tegmentum", "midbrain motivation system", or "hypothalamus", and in *Neuromind* is "the motivation pathway". The pathway goes through several nuclei (neuron groups) with varying functions. The body sends messages: "I am hungry, seek signals for food." or "I am in pain, seek safety, or attack!" (in neural code, not words) to receptor neurons in the pathway. Motivation uses information about body states to select adaptive behavior, indicating how body states produce changes in behavior. It can be defined operationally by inputs that reward or "reinforce" behavior: Behavior followed by a "positive reinforcer" is likely to be repeated, by a negative reinforcer, suppressed. (1) This can be studied using electrical stimuli to the motivation system in animals, intracranial self-stimulation (ICSS). In Olds and Milner's classic study, a rat presses a bar, closing a circuit that sends an electrical pulse through an implanted electrode to a brain site. (2) Stimulation at certain sites leads to recurrent bar pressing, "positive reinforcement", while other sites turn off stimulation, "negative reinforcement". Valenstein identified areas in hypothalamus and other limbic regions that facilitate or inhibit behavior, a "go/no-go system". (3) The effect is not easily replicated in humans, who have more cortical regulation of behavior, but do report the stimulation sensations as "pleasurable". (4) ICSS demonstrates motivation by repeating behaviors with positive rewards. The animal/subject wants more of this input (vice versa for negative reinforcement). (5) This operational definition of reward is also a method for probing the animal brain for location of reward sites, but is not the natural reward signal, and ICSS does not produce "satiety" signals that turn off behavior like natural rewards. An increase in blood glucose signal after ingesting is rewarding to a point and then inhibits behavior. (6) The motivation pathway is an information "cable" gathering data from the body and from other brain regions, and transferring this information to the decision making pre-frontal brain for choosing behavior. *(9) (10)*

The neurotransmitters of this pathway are biogenic amines, more densely distributed in this region than other parts of the brain. Although dopamine synapses are prominent in reward areas, GABA neurons are also in the reward area of nucleus accumbens in the mesolimbic reward pathway, a region of convergence of positive reward pathways. (7) (8) Neurotransmitters code motivation, but not specific motivations. (11) The amine system has been the pharmaceutical industry's major focus of drug development for the past 50 years. The activating or "go" effects of noradrenaline and dopamine, contrast to the mixed reward-satiety-inhibitory effects of serotonin. GABA transmission is also inhibitory. (11) Additional peptide transmitters code specific motivations, e.g. orexin for eating and arousal. (12) (Sternson has developed sophisticated techniques for activating and identifying these circuits in mice, using special genetic strains, and photo activation of brain regions. (13)) Outflow from the amygdala also goes through the motivation pathways providing "fight/flight" signals from the external environment, and internal pain signals. The amygdala receives direct input from the olfactory system, and other sensory inputs (reviewed in detail in chapter eight).

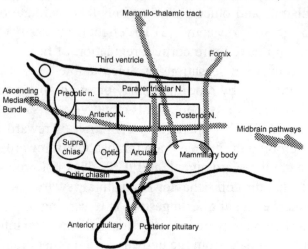

Fig 3.1 Diagrammatic view of hypothalamic nuclei and related pathways.

The hypothalamic nuclei have multiple functions, and are linked by connecting pathways both forward (anterior) to pre-frontal cortex, and descending to brain stem. There is anterior-posterior balance with the more anterior regions activating approach response, and posterior, especially amygdala, sending messages of inhibition, avoidance, (or attack). There is also a lateral balance on each side, with more lateral regions activating (documented especially in control of eating), and medial (periventricular) nuclei more inhibiting. Linking pathways between the medial and lateral pathways are observed in neurophysiological studies with inhibitory connections, but are not visualized in human fMRI studies because of their location and blood supply anatomy in the region (see appendix chapter one). (14) These produce mutual inhibitory interaction in animal research. (15) A multi-paper research summary indicates the other interactions of this region. (16) The inhibitory pathways provide a "governing mechanism" for balancing variations in the system; an increase of one side of the system is balanced by inhibition from the other. If the mechanisms are ineffective, or overpowered by other factors, clinical syndromes of motivation imbalance may result in intense bidirectional swings, or hyper- or hypo activation.

The information pathways in the motivation system are the

body's homeostatic controls for a) feeding (gluco-receptors and other signals), b) thirst (osmolality receptors), c) temperature, d) sleep and wakefulness, e) maternal & social bonding (see chapter seven), f) regulation of hormonal pathways to the pituitary, including cortisol for stress response, thyroid for energy metabolism, and sexual hormones with related responsive body tissues for sexual behavior, and g)immune system regulation (psycho-neuro immunology). (17) Major damage to the region results in coma, as seen in post-viral encephalitis. (18) The extensive role of the hypothalamus in mental health, described briefly here, deserves a comprehensive review. The motivation system transducers transform somatic signals into brain activity, directing responses, and producing subjective experience, an interaction between brain and body called "psychosomatic medicine". (The term emphasizes the "mind-body" separation, and should be replaced by one that emphasizes data interaction, e.g. neuro-somatic information transfer.)(19)

The regulation of each function is a complex interaction of multiple signals. Eating behavior has been studied in detail in humans with many metabolic control elements: a) blood glucose levels, and hormones, including adipokines from fat tissue, activate brain pathway receptors, b) the brain melanocortin system, which links sleep and energy metabolism/eating using orexin, c) and other transmitter and hormone factors. Lateral hypothalamic areas activate eating behavior, and destruction of these pathways leads to starvation and death in animal studies. The ventromedial area generates satiety signals to inhibit eating behaviors, so destruction of these sites results in dramatic overeating to obesity. Evidence of genetic programming of the "set point" for homeostatic regulation is found in some families with obesity. (20) In humans control of eating combines metabolic set point variables, with local stomach sensations, the immediate feedback of eating behavior, and interpersonal controls from the history of dependence on others for early feeding. And social-body image factors also influence behavior. Eating has become a focus for mental health because disturbances in eating cannot be accounted for by changes of metabolic control factors in many patients with serious health consequences of their disturbances.

From early development, internal homeostatic controls and external factors influence the balance. The earliest eating disturbance, "Failure to thrive" after birth, may be caused by body organ system malfunction, or failure of the maternal-child bond. (20) Social control of human eating can produce eating problems in adolescence related to patterns of family interaction, explored by Minuchin in family therapy. (20) Social interaction also creates a "body image" for the individual who seeks social acceptance. How these biological and social factors interact to influence eating behavior is different in different situations. Diagnostic groups may not have individuals with the same dysfunctional patterns. Studies targeting specific brain regions, or chemical regulators, do not evaluate the range of variables, and often get inconclusive results. Anorexia Nervosa (AN), a difficult to treat, potentially lethal eating problem, does not have a specific genetic basis despite exhaustive GWAS studies. A more recent review identifies locations for specific cases but not a local genetic etiology. (21) fMRI response of anorexia nervosa patients finds statistical changes in medial cingulate cortex, related to motivation system pathways. (22) It appears doubtful that all patients with AN have the same abnormal pathway. A study of adolescent eating disorders showed differences in regional brain response with different diagnoses, consistent with different mechanisms and etiologies. *Eating disorders are problems in management of motivated self-directed behavior with complex controls that combine metabolic regulatory and social factors that are poorly documented.*

Many factors may produce "excess weight" (by statistical definition). Diagnoses are based on how the weight is acquired: "binge eating disorder" and "bulimia" are defined episodes of excessive consumption, with the occurrence of "compensatory behaviors" to offset the impact of excess consumption. The role of "nervous eating", episodes of eating which have a role in affect regulation, are reported by patients with anxiety, but this is not a diagnosis, and has never been explicitly researched. (23) Managing obesity (and body image) may use treatments like surgical stomach banding to prevent absorption, or diets that throw the body into "starvation" metabolism. Bariatric surgery works against the "set point", but psychological complications activate new or recurring symptoms. (24) A study evaluating subitramine found significant weight loss in the experimental group, but a 38% drop out rate, which was not explained, but may reflect loss of emotional control. (25) Eating disorders may be associated with mood disturbance, or may mimic addiction and be associated with addictive families. (Metabolic changes are a prominent effect of newer "second generation" antipsychotic medications, and data on the regulation of eating is relevant to understanding these effects. (See chapter eleven)(27)) Rao et al have proposed a common factor for certain adolescent syndromes related to anxiety. (26). *Searches for universal genetic mechanisms, or common regulatory hormones have not produced definitive results; control of eating depends on the interaction between somatic variables, social variables influencing consumption, and body image- "self" variables – interaction of separate neural pathways.* A multi-level approach to the interaction of information from different sources is needed to clarify the control issues in each person in order to design effective interventions. The complexity is frustrating, but typical of the motivation system that integrates social and metabolic data. Sleep will be discussed in chapter five. Maternal bonding will be discussed in chapter seven. The diagnostic system should be revised to include the category "motivation system dysfunction" with variable clinical patterns and etiologic factors. (See chapter ten)

*CLINICAL EXAMPLE **Dramatic weight gain**. A woman in her 30s was evaluated for weight gain. She weighed less than 120 pounds (at 5' 7") 6 months prior to evaluation, but gained almost 200 pounds in the next 3 months despite efforts at diet and exercise. Six months prior to evaluation, she suffered an episode of encephalitis and was comatose for 3 weeks. Her weight went down to 85 pounds during this period. After regaining consciousness, she rapidly began gaining weight until she reached 285 at which she plateaued. Efforts at a variety of medications, diet and exercise interventions had not been successful in reducing weight by more than 15 pounds, which she rapidly regained. COMMENT The clinical picture suggests the woman had significant ventromedial hypothalamic damage during her encephalitis. Multiple syndromes were observed after the great flu epidemic of 1918 which was also marked by the development of post encephalitic Parkinson's disease due to damage of the substantia nigra. (29)*

The motivation system includes receptors, & effectors for endocrine regulation that control pituitary release of cortisol, growth hormone, sex hormones, and thyroid hormone. Feedback loops between hypothalamic receptors and end organs modulate the body systems associated with stress adaptation, energy metabolism, physical development, and sexual differentiation. Receptors, located in several hypothalamic nuclei, receive hormone feedback from the body, and generate releasing hormones to stimulate pituitary release of hormones, both directly and through a blood portal system. (30) An oscillating timing center coordinates 24hour cycles with melatonin from pineal. (See chapter five) (31) Problems in endocrine system disorders may have overlapping mental health symptoms. Thyroid hormone regulates a wide range of body energy functions, serves as a transmitter-like substance in certain brain regions, hypothyroid patients present a cognitively impaired depression syndrome, and high thyroid levels may present as mania. Manipulating hormone levels intentionally to modify psychiatric symptoms has been attempted, most often using thyroid hormone supplements to modify depression symptoms. (32) (See chapter eleven) Certain antipsychotic medications have a releasing effect on the prolactin system. (33) The interaction of endocrine and psychological functions allows for more complex adaptive regulation, and also problems resulting from the interactions.

CLINICAL EXAMPLE Endocrine Psychosis. *A woman in her 50s was referred by a mental health professional for worsening symptoms. On evaluation she was confused, disoriented, and depressed. This had been developing over several months. She was in ongoing treatment for lymphoma. She was admitted to hospital with diagnosis of delirium and a consult requested from Neurology and her chemotherapist. The neurologist performed a spinal examination looking for tumor cells that were not found. Her laboratory screen came back with a very low thyroid hormone level. COMMENT Low thyroid can produce severe symptoms. This problem was corrected over several months with careful thyroid replacement by her endocrinologist.*

The neuroendocrine regulation of sex hormones at different life stages influences behavior in several ways. Development of adult reproductive capacity and physical development for reproduction depends on hormonal release during puberty. In both sexes, the changes of puberty are hormonal and associated with changes of body size and shape, sexual motivation, and fertility. Adapting to changing body configuration and regulating its impulses is a major task of adolescence. The peak of sex hormone activity in the early 20s for men is often a time of disruption of function in schizophrenics, though the causal relationship is unclear. Onset of anorexia in females and some males is seen at puberty. Variations in sexual hormone levels are sometimes correlated with depression and anxiety. (34) Sexual hormone effects on *female mental health* include the mood variations during menstrual cycles, pregnancy, and at menopause, all of which are associated with clinical syndromes. Anxiety is also sometimes a menstrual cycle symptom. (35) Premenstrual dysphoric disorder is an example of different brain response in different women, as documented in the study by Baller et al. (39) Hormone factors affect sexual response, as do anti-depressants. (36) (37) Interpreting the boundary between normal and disturbed function is controversial: if normal variation is stigmatized, or the severity of symptoms is ignored. (38)

Pregnancy and post-partum (delivery)(PPD) are associated with dramatic changes in women. Pregnancy represents three changes for the pregnant mother, (and sometimes the father): 1) hormonal changes in the woman's body along with other physical changes may be experienced as positive or aversive; 2) the mother recognizes a change in her independent status sometime in the course of the pregnancy with the responsibility for care of another human being (which may be shared by the father); and 3) the mother experiences changes in her personal social system, becoming isolated by the limitations of activity, which may include temporary separation from work or career. The challenges of the pregnancy may be congruent to the woman's goals and expectations or significantly incongruent, or both. If serious mental health symptoms emerge (or continue from the pre-partum state) the mother and provider must decide on the relative contribution of these factors, and implement a treatment strategy that considers the risks to both mother and fetus. The strongest PPD biological risk predictors are hypothalamic-pituitary-adrenal dysregulation, inflammatory processes, and genetic vulnerabilities. The strongest psychosocial factor predictors are severe life events, chronic stress, relationship quality, and lack of support from partner or mother. (42) Dramatic hormonal shifts at delivery, and the ensuing first few weeks post partum, along with major sleep deprivation, and psychological challenges of caring for the newborn are challenges. Some women experience post partum depression or psychotic symptoms which result from the interaction between hormone changes and life space issues. Reviews of the syndrome emphasize presumptive hypothalamic-pituitary factors, or changes in monoamine oxidase, and the literature on social factors is separated from the biological, making an integrated approach difficult. (40) Using psychopharmacology during pregnancy or post partum risks negative impact on the developing fetus or newborn, while not using it risks negative impact on the mother. (A dilemma explored in chapter eleven.) (41)

CLINICAL EXAMPLE Post Partum (I) A 19 year old married woman in first pregnancy became agitated, anxious and distressed about her husband's infidelity. This was their first marriage, and her first pregnancy, without complications, until delivery. She became anxious and withdrawn after delivery, had difficulty caring for the newborn, and became increasingly depressed and suicidal. She had no prior mental health history, but a family history of anxiety disorder. Initial treatment with SSRI anti-depressants and anti-psychotics did not alter the symptoms that continued for months. Because of the mixed depression and anxiety features, the woman was tried on an MAOI, and responded over several weeks with improved mood and function. She was able to recover, return to care of the child, and later, and return to work. The marriage was dissolved. COMMENT Post partum psychosis responsive to MAOI has limited documentation, despite recent evidence of increased binding of dopamine (Sacher et al) (40). Dramatic changes in MAO at delivery have been reported.

***CLINICAL EXAMPLE* Post Partum (II)** *A married woman in her 20s became depressed after the birth of her second child. There was no similar episode after the first pregnancy, but a family history of mood disorder. The newborn was healthy, the mother came home in two days, and there were no complications of the delivery. Before the delivery, the patient had been working full time in a high stress career, and on leave for only two weeks prior to the delivery. She was due to return to work from maternity leave two weeks after delivery. The demands of two children, sleeplessness, and post delivery recovery were draining her energy. She was receiving help from her husband, who also worked full time, but there was no additional childcare. The patient was started on low dose of an antidepressant, and given a medical letter to remain off work at the end of her maternity leave. She improved both in energy and mood over two months, and returned to work in the 3rd month. On return to work, her mood and functioning were stable; she discontinued the medication, and arranged childcare for both children. COMMENT the problem of balancing work demands and the biological and psychological demands of childbirth can be difficult in a woman who has strong motivation for both. The physical recovery from the birthing, the hormone shifts, the childcare demands, and a desire to bond to this child all contributed to her conflicts, and it is impossible to separate the separate contribution of each one. Her employer had difficulty finding temporary coverage for her three-month leave. The needs of business and individual were in conflict, and were mediated by a statement of medical leave, with positive outcome for both. Maternity leave should be standard in all work settings, and individualized to the specific circumstances. The idea that a woman seeks "excess" time off from work with a newborn to "relax" is ludicrous.*

Gender Identity has both hormonal and social learning components, and this complex topic is discussed in chapter six.

Sex hormone levels decrease in midlife and create a menopause syndrome in some women, and men. The changing hormonal cycle at menopause may change the motivation states, worsening or improving prior dys-regulation, or produce new problems. The prevalence of depression syndromes in menopausal women has been statistically documented by several sources, and both social and hormonal factors are likely etiologies. (44) Hormone replacement is often effective in altering the symptoms, but carries other risks. The effect of diminished testosterone in males has been studied, though less often, and a depressive syndrome associated with decreased testosterone levels in middle age has also been reported. The desire to preserve hormone levels and behavior capacity of earlier ages is typical for men, who seek a variety of hormonal adjustments to accomplish this, whose safety is controversial. (45)

The regulation of ACTH secretion via the hypothalamic-hypophyseal pituitary pathway stimulates adrenocortical function and cortisol level, varies with time of day, season, and stress level. Cortisol is essential for adjusting body systems to activity level. The control of cortisol secretion has a normal diurnal variation, and is released in response to "stress demands" both physical, and emotional. Linking motivation system activity with pituitary cortisol secretion coordinates the internal response with external demands. Selye carried out the early studies on what he called the "General Adaptation Syndrome" identifying the hormone response to stress, and subsequent research has confirmed the multiple systems impacted and psychological effects. (46) Persistent arousal creates hyper-arousal clinical syndromes in some individuals with job stress like air traffic controllers, and high dose steroid administration (which may produce a manic psychosis). (47) The syndrome of PTSD, (discussed in detail in chapter eight) is associated with chronic changes in cortisol secretion. The "Dexamethasone suppression test" is a test of pituitary adrenal function. The patient is given Dexamethasone to suppress adrenal response but severely depressed patients sometimes "escape" from that suppression more quickly than normals. *(49)*

Response to life experiences is stored in the brain with both immediate and delayed body reactions, often grouped under the term "chronic stress reaction". (These are discussed in more detail in chapter eight.) Holmes and Rahe studied stress events in Navy personnel and found that a high level of life stress events in the previous year is a valid predictor of medical illness in the following year. Mental health episodes are also observed. (50) The hypothalamic-hypophyseal axis plays a crucial role in the survival of the species by bringing the endocrine system under the regulation of the brain so that external environmental inputs, learned behavior patterns, and other neural demands influence the system.

The immune system and brain interact in the motivation system. The AIDS epidemic of the 1980-90s provided insights into the relationship of the brain and the immune system. Mental symptoms were generated by direct attack on brain regions by the virus (encephalitis), secondary inflammation of immune response cells damaging cells infected by viruses, and immune damage of altered immune cells. Syndromes of depressed mood, confusion, and problems with attention and focus were observed. This resulted in a new understanding of brain/immune system interaction. The immune system combines cellular elements and blood circulating proteins to detect and neutralize foreign cells, viruses and proteins that might be harmful to the organism. (51) Many newly discovered proteins and blood particles provide immune system responses with targeted functions. Immune cells cannot pass the blood brain barrier (unless it is damaged), and microglia are the immune cells that perform cellular immunity functions in the brain. The study of *psycho-neuro-immunology* identifies brain regions that interact with the immune system showing evidence that brain states can enhance or impair immune response. (51) This is demonstrated by conditioned responses of the immune system. (52) Cytokine immune mediators produce mental health effects in some depression syndromes, pediatric inflammatory syndromes including PANDAS, and in stress syndromes. (53) Anti-viral medications sometimes have brain side effects, as seen in treatment of AIDS. (54), Different brain/immune interactions are seen: **Type I:** Somatic illness causes neural pathway damage and brain illness. This may be infectious, like viral encephalitis, meningitis, etc. **Type II:** An illness in the body produces immune system responses that damage neural pathways. A common example is the syndrome associated with fever in viral and bacterial illnesses, which changes the thermoregulation set point. NMDA antibody disorder, CNS symptoms of lupus, and multiple sclerosis are other examples. It is sometimes difficult to determine whether the primary problem is a direct infection or a secondary immune response, as in PANDAS. A vivid description of the experience of an inflammatory encephalitis producing psychosis can be found in **Brain on Fire** describing the effect of inflammatory change in the recently recognized NMDA antibody disorder. (55) **Type III:** An autoimmune disease in the body with chronic disability creates symptoms of depression related to the pain and other responses of chronic illness. This is seen in arthritis, certain cancers, producing depressed mood, which can modify the immunological system, making it more vulnerable. **TYPE IV:** Changes in the brain modify the immune system. The immune system has complex interactions with the hypothalamic region of the brain. Frichione has written a general review of this topic. (56) Stress states may make a person more vulnerable to medical illness or cancer. The following example illustrates an environmental factor.

CLINICAL EXAMPLE **Couple with rare immune disorder**. *A middle-aged woman was evaluated for depression in referral from her rheumatologist. She was being treated for a rare immune disorder. She responded to SSRI medication and asked if her husband could also take the medication since he was also depressed. The same Rheumatologist was also treating him for a different rare immune disorder. The coincidence of two persons, in the same household, both of whom have a rare immune disorder is unlikely. The patient was asked to investigate her environment for potential toxic chemicals. She returned to report that their well water supply was in groundwater that had been shared by a now closed tannery. The patient was advised to begin using only bottled water for a month. Both she and her husband had significant improvement in their immune symptoms and remission of the depression. COMMENT The immune system brain interaction goes both ways. Her brain was affected by the immune dysfunction, and the chronic illness. The depression syndrome responded to medication and improved completely when the environmental stress was removed.*

To understand a neuro-immune process one must know which way(s) the information flows; how each system affects the other. Medical disorders including Crohn's disease, lupus erythematosis, rheumatoid arthritis, and fibromyalgia syndrome are produced by immune system changes that also impact the neural pathways creating mood changes in these disorders. Brain/immune system interactions are in early stages of research and the direction of flow of information and effects is likely to be bi-directional.

Another recent area of effects is the relationship between GI tract flora and brain function. Information may travel across two pathways, the neural connections between gut and brain, mostly via the vagal nerve and parasympathetic nervous system, and the humoral pathway of molecules released from gut into bloodstream that travel to the brain. (A third pathway is the internal migration of parasites to brain.) (57) Vagal nerve stimulation has been explored as a potential intervention for various mental health conditions, including depression, with mixed results. (58) There is clearly an impact on brain activity but how to achieve benefits is not clear. The role of humoral substances and direct chemical transmission is just beginning research. Gastro-intestinal illness has strong subjective components and GI reactivity has been demonstrated as a response to situational stress and personality types, in a review of irritable bowel syndrome. (59) The connecting pathways are important for clinical symptoms but how to control the symptoms depends on understanding the flow of information that is bidirectional.

Other body systems also have important interactions with brain documented by recent studies in the relationship of psychology to cardiac disease, lung and other organs. *Type A personality style* is associated with increased cardiovascular risk.

*CLINICAL EXAMPLE **Man with heart disease**. A middle-aged male was being treated in psychotherapy for anxiety and agitation. He was upset about his teenaged daughter's lack of respect for him, and her promiscuous behavior. The therapist inquired whether the patient had sexual feelings about the daughter and the patient became severely agitated, reported heart pain, and was taken to the emergency room where an acute myocardial infarction was diagnosed. COMMENT Working with a patient with strong emotional reactions, the person's overall health status must also be considered. Exploration of major emotional triggers must be done cautiously when the patient has the potential for major illness. In this situation, the patient had previous episodes of angina for which he had not sought treatment.*

Clinical patterns of the motivation system. In additional to their specific regulatory functions, motivation pathways integrate messages into a general level of activation sent to the pre-frontal region to influence behavior. An increase in activity may be adaptive for situations of high demand, environmental crises, war, etc. Reduced activity is associated with repair, recovery states, avoiding danger, and may be an environmental adaptation to ice age climate using hibernation. The sleep-waking cycle is a variation of arousal, and becomes maladaptive if the level does not match the situation. Major Depressive Disorder (MDD) with deactivation of behavior, and Mania/Bipolar Disorder with hyperactivity are the two prominent syndromes with neuro-vegetative symptoms of motivation system activity that is not coordinated with external situations. (Current diagnosis emphasizes the subjective mood, not the motivation symptoms, and among current rating scales, the Beck Depression scale includes fewer neuro-vegetative items than the HAMD. (60)) The following categories use current data on brain pathways and etiologic factors to differentiate syndromes of activation and mood.

Motivation system patterns:

1a) Tegmental system mood swings of hyper and hypo-activation. Swings between extreme activation and inhibition ("bipolar syndrome") may be due to ineffective lateral inhibition. (The hypothetical mechanism for pathway problems is the evidence of lateral/medial inhibition in animal studies, which is not visualized in fMRI. See earlier discussion in this chapter.) Psychosis symptoms may be produced over a different pathway. (See chapter five) Etiologies include traumatic injury, endocrine state, and other influences on motivation pathways. The genetic factor has been researched for decades, but no common genetic factor is found for any of the syndromes. Fears reports a 25% overlap of multiple genes associated with "bipolar patients" (which may also be psychosis genes). Evidence for SNP locus is found in a few specific families and may regulate overall activity level. (61) Endocrine state variations play a role in the Stanley foundation data, women who are more depressed or "rapid cycling bipolar" also experience post partum triggering. McIntyre has reviewed the multiple metabolic abnormalities seen in association with bipolar symptoms including obesity, metabolic syndrome, dyslipidemia independent of medication, obstructive sleep apnea, and hypothetical mediators include insulin/IGF, glucagon like peptides, ghrelin, leptin. *These observations document the overlap with the regulatory functions of the motivation system that are modified in bipolar states.* (63) Studies comparing these changes during abnormal states and in recovery would clarify the persistence of changes. Medications for depression may shift some patients to mania, especially when medication for control of mania is discontinued (64) Abnormalities in the non-dominant frontal prefrontal cortex are associated with manic episodes, and dramatic mood swings. (Waltz, 62) supporting fMRI data on the role of the prefrontal region for regulating the system.

*CLINICAL EXAMPLE **Woman with bipolar symptoms***. *A 20-year-old married woman was evaluated for a post partum psychotic episode. She had post partum depression, but when treated with antidepressants she switched into mania and was eventually treated with lithium to stabilize. She and her second child had bonded and she was stable but confused about what had happened, and whether it could happen again. There was no previous history of emotional problems, including any after her first delivery. But she had a hemangioma (blood vessel abnormality) removed from her R eye as a child, which appeared to heal without problems. CAT scan that revealed a vague R frontal vascular abnormality. She wished to go off medications due to side effects of lithium, and lowering the dose resulted in some return of symptoms. Eventually a compromise was achieved using a low dose of medication that was adjusted each time she felt the sense of increasing agitation and inability to sleep. COMMENT Reports of R frontal abnormalities associated with disturbances of mood regulation suggest this contributed to triggering her symptoms. (62)*

1b) Tegmental pathway activation without associated shift to de-activation and depressed mood is also seen. Mania includes prominent neuro-vegetative symptoms and is only diagnosed when extreme enough to produce psychosis. How this pathway syndrome differs in controls from the bi-directional variation is unclear. Chemical triggers of stimulant, cocaine and amphetamine, abuse are triggers that suggest external factors. Post developed a "kindling" theory based on them. (65)

SIDEBAR Kindling Post proposed a hippocampal/amygdala source driving the tegmental pathways into mania. Cocaine, amphetamines, and other stimulants are known to create manic- activation in users. Based on the effects of cocaine and other stimulants in producing manic psychosis, and data from EEG studies, hippocampus/amygdala abnormalities were the source of the "kindling". This may also be observed after head injury, chemical toxicity, or post-encephalitic infection. Post's theory of bipolar/mania by "kindling" is similar to subclinical seizure activity giving rise to potential syndromes discussed in chapter 4, and may account for some mixed "schizo-affective" syndromes. (66) QEEG and other scan evidence sometimes shows regions of injury or abnormal activity. "Kindling" is an alternate etiology for driving the tegmental out of balance. It may be an important factor in behavioral instability in children and teens with a history of head injury or encephalitis. (67)

CLINICAL EXAMPLE Mania in a young woman. An 18-year-old woman was evaluated for sudden onset of manic symptoms of agitation, confusion, and expansive behaviors. There was no prior history of mental health problems, and no family history of mental illness, but she had recently moved away from her family and home to start a new career. On physical evaluation she had tachycardia and a mass in her neck, but no exophthalmos. She was evaluated for hyperthyroidism, confirmed by laboratory data, and treated with radioactive iodine. She did well on replacement thyroid, and had a successful career, marriage, and personal life, with occasional return of hypo-manic symptoms, while maintaining replacement thyroid. She used a mood stabilizer, to avoiding lithium complications with thyroid function. COMMENT The discovery of thyroid etiology was a surprise. The occasional return of hypomania suggests a pathway alteration was created by the hyperthyroidism episode.

1c) Tegmental pathway with neuro-vegetative symptoms (without hyper-activation) means that pathways are deactivated.

Poor response to reward is predicted. Subjective mood symptoms result from network pathways to cingulate/insula. The depressive symptoms are generally severe, have functional impairment, are anhedonic, dysphoric and may have suicidal ideation. Etiologic factors for this pattern include the etiologies of the tegmental system: medical illnesses, drug side effects, nutritional deficiencies, infections, and toxic chemicals that have tegmental sites of brain action.

Tegmental depression without mood swings is often diagnosed as MDD with prominent neuro-vegetative signs. Poor response to SSRI treatment, and switch to mania indicates a different pathway is involved. (Historically, these patients responded to mixed transmitter anti-depressants. Medication treatment is discussed in detail in chapter eleven.) The difficulty in visualizing the tegmental pathways by fMRI has contributed to emphasizing the mood symptoms produced by pathways to cingulate and insula, while ignoring the tegmentum.

2) Amygdala pathway syndrome is a response to aversive life events. Amygdala output goes through motivation system pathways, and also has direct autonomic nervous system output (see chapter eight for more details). (68) Anxiety is the subjective experience often associated with amygdala messages, along with behavior inhibition. Loss, trauma, stress, and "learned helplessness" are all associated with amygdala symptoms, life events that produce depressed mood. Amygdala pathways usually produce a mixed anxiety and depression, and more autonomic signs along with tegmental neuro-vegetative symptoms.

Depression of loss, described by Bowlby (and others), is a withdrawn (sometimes agitated) state with depressed mood seen in children, and some adults who experience a major attachment separation or loss. The motivation system is involved in the process of attachment (see chapter seven). Freud described intense grief, "melancholia", and a recent study confirms that grieving subjects are more focused on grief related subjects, consistent with the attachment literature. They also show increased correlation of pre-frontal and amygdala regions. (69) A mixed aggression/depression seen in the male attachment syndrome of abusers may be another example (see chapter eight). (The specific syndrome panic anxiety with separation anxiety and depression is described in chapter seven.)

Depression of chronic stress. Individuals in stressful situations have elevated cortisol, depressed mood, and may have neuro-vegetative symptoms. If the person is aware of the situation, but chooses not to change, or is unable to change for various reasons, tegmental abnormalities are more likely. This pattern is discussed in chapter eight.

Trauma with PTSD may be associated with subjective depressed mood. The tegmental changes often include increased cortisol secretion, and an associated hyper-arousal, a mixed picture. The depressed mood and inhibition of behavior in the early stage may be controlled for months or years by coping methods and then re-emerge with a triggering life situation. PTSD is discussed in detail in chapter eight. (70)

3) The cingulate cortex pathway involving the Default Mode Network (DMN) has a relationship to mood states. Cingulate & insula activation are essential for the subjective experience of mood states, so messages from the motivation system to these regions generate the subjective moods. (Subjective experience is discussed in detail in chapter five) The cingulate-insula connects with prefrontal cortex over the hypothetical salience network to influence behavior (see chapter six). Do cingulate cortex and insula produce depressed mood that does not originate in motivation system pathways? Mayberg's group studied depressed patients using SPECT scanning and reported a primary cingulate group, but her method did not visualize the motivation system. The cingulate symptoms are sometimes responsive to SSRI treatment, but attempts to alter cingulate activity by implanting electrodes in chronic depressed patients have inconsistent results. (73) The Default Mode Network (DMN) is a statistical correlation of regions (not neural pathways) that includes cingulate cortex. (74)

Studies comparing depressed patients and controls sometimes show *increased correlations in the DMN,* with withdrawal and cognitive impairment in the depressed group. DMN correlations are observed in multiple scanning studies when the person is "turning inward", at wakeful rest, during daydreaming, mind-wandering, when "thinking about others" or self, remembering the past, and "planning for the future", so changes are not specific for depressed

SIDEBAR The default mode network activates "by default" when a person is not involved in a task, and was originally noticed to be deactivated in certain goal-oriented tasks (sometimes referred to as the task-negative network) such as working memory of social interaction. The DMN is negatively correlated with attention networks. The components that are correlated:

Posterior cingulate cortex (PCC) & precuneus: Combines bottom-up (not controlled) attention with information from memory and perception. The ventral (lower) part of PCC activates in all tasks which involve the DMN including those related to the self, related to others, remembering the past, thinking about future, and processing concepts plus spatial navigation. The dorsal (upper) part of PCC involves involuntary awareness and arousal. The precuneus is involved in visual, sensorimotor, and attentional information.

Medial prefrontal cortex (mPFC): Decisions about self processing such as personal information, autobiographical memories, future goals and events, and decision making regarding those personally very close such as family. The ventral (lower) part is involved in positive emotional information and internally valued reward.

Angular gyrus: Connects perception, attention, spatial cognition, and action and helps with parts of recall of episodic memories. DMN develops statistical overlap in its connectivity, with limited evidence of the DMN in the infant brain, but more consistent in children aged 9–12 years, suggesting that the default network if formed in development. This supports its creation by experience, and also possibly through myelination. The DMN is most commonly calculated with resting state data by putting a calculated value in the posterior cingulate cortex and examining which other brain areas correlate with this area. The DMN can also be defined by the areas **deactivated** during external directed tasks as compared to rest. It is the "background state" of brain activity associated with many different events. (Full description is found in (74).)

mood. Chronic pain patients also activate the DMN. GABA is involved in the increased correlation, consistent with its role as an inhibitory transmitter. Hamilton et al identify the DMN data as the source of several depression symptoms, including rumination, the sense of being "stuck". DMN is a correlation, so etiologies that that maintain the correlation define DMN. (76) Meta reviews report variable DMN components in depression, some more closely linked than others, or different for different syndromes. (Mayberg,

73) The depression is less episodic, more chronic, and if responsive to treatment, improves with either SSRI or cognitive behavior therapy for depression. (75) The relationship between depression symptoms related to cingulate/insula/DMN and the motivation pathway is unclear. The cingulate/insula/DMN system may produce mood symptoms and inhibit the motivation pathway to produce secondary neuro-vegetative symptoms. If DMN maintains a deactivated (correlated) state, a sustained effect blocking the motivation system might result. Or, the *motivation pathway* may produce the changes in cingulate- DMN. The pattern of withdrawing to an "internal rest state" is typical of some depression syndromes, while others are agitated. (See discussion of cingulate and insula in chapter six.)

The primary tegmental and amygdala syndromes are associated with anhedonia, but no clear relationship to reward has been documented. Ng's recent meta-analysis of fMRI studies produced the peculiar report of opposing abnormalities in the reward circuit: hypo-responses in the ventral striatum and hyper-responses in the orbitofrontal cortex. (76) The striate has limited visualization, and this probably accounts for the inconsistency (see chapter six). More promising is Admon and Pizzagalli who found impaired response to altered reward in OFC, a more likely measure, still indirect. (76) Naranjo et al attempted to measure the effect of "amphetamine probe" with suggestive results. (76) Gotlib found decreased response in teen females "at risk" by family history. The current data suggest that the dysfunctions of the motivation system that modify the reward response are not the **result** of impaired reward response.

4) Cortical activity and Default Mode Network (DMN) may be affected by etiologies that shift the DMN. The "obsessional anxiety depression" of the elderly is associated with prefrontal OCD features. Aging with reduced sensory input and cerebral cortex atrophy associated with dementia has depressed mood. ECT is often the preferred treatment in this syndrome, a "disruption" of the pathway. The relationship of motivation system orbito-frontal cortex pathways sustains activation, so damage, as in head trauma (i.e. Nicholas

Gage), lobotomy, or dementia cell loss, can decrease motivation and activity. (See chapter six) (77)

Four hypothetical pathways of the motivation system produce activation or de-activation associated with clinical syndromes: 1) tegmental pathways, 2) amygdala tegmental pathways, 3) cingulate cortex/insula and DMN pathways, and 4) a residual but important cortical function. Many clinical situations may involve more than one etiology and pathway, as when two pathways are linked, so combination patterns are observed. This creates overlapping findings in genetic and pathways research.

SIDEBAR Meta studies of connectivity. Meta reviews emphasize the cingulate and DMN patterns because most studies select subjects with mood symptoms and fewer neuro-vegetative ones. The met-analysis of Seminowicz et al, is an heroic effort to define pathways using studies across multiple labs, recalculated using a 7 region model. (It did not include the hypothalamic-tegmental pathway.) Three pathways were defined: A) limbic–cortical connections (latF9-Cg25-OF11-Hc) differentiated drug treatment responders from nonresponders. B) nonresponders showed additional abnormalities in limbic–subcortical pathways (aTh-Cg24-Cg25-OF11-Hc). C) more limited limbic–cortical (Hc-latF9) and cortical–cortical (OF11-mF10) path differences differentiated responders to cognitive behavioral therapy (CBT) from responders to pharmacotherapy. The pharmacotherapy was SSRI. The pathways suggest variations of a cingulate/DMN model. The B) group may reflect more tegmental function. (78)

Drysdale's study attempted to identify MDD pathways. In a large group of patients studied by fMRI connectivity, Resting state fMRI were obtained for patients and controls, and signal variations were separated (differences from controls) and **then the depressed patient findings were categorized by a data analysis AI program**. Regions that had strong correlations were removed from the data, and four biotypes generated from the residual differential data were:

Type 1= hypoconnectivity of frontal/amygdala with increased anxiety, and hypoconnectivity of cingulate-orbito-frontal with anergia

Type 2 = hypoconnectivity of cingulate-orbito-frontal with anergia

Type 3 = hyperconnectivity of thalamic striatal anhedonia and psychomotor retardation

Type 4 = hypoconnectivity of frontal amygdala increased anxiety and hyperconnectivity of thalamic striate anhedonia with psychomotor retardation. They showed Hypoconnectivity frontal-amygdala Types 1 and 4 > increased anxiety. Hyperconnectivity thalamic-striatal Types 3 and 4 > anhedonia and psychomotor rtd. Hypoconnectivity cingulate-orbito-frontal Types 1 and 2 > anergia and fatigue.

These differences in symptoms were not associated with different levels of depression by HAMD scale scoring, and had some correlation for response to rTMS (but not to medication).

The attempt to use purely statistical correlations created only noisy patterns. The types show no obvious relationship to clinical categories or local brain regions, and slight differential response to treatment. The results of the statistical sort were partially replicated on a new data set. These (odd) findings may reflect: 1) the decision to omit data common to all patterns, leaving data of symptoms common to all groups. (79) Several other attempts are listed in the references, which also have not been replicated. (80)

At one time, a serotonin depletion theory of depression and related suicidal thoughts was proposed, but a recent meta-review found no consistent support for this unitary hypothesis. (81) Many reviewers now question treating "depression" (MDD) as one disorder, a convenience for pharmaceutical research, and have begun to identify separate syndromes. In an epidemiology study, the anxious/distressed specifier characterized 74.6% of major depressive disorder cases, and the mixed-features specifier characterized 15.5%; both of these surprisingly large groups might show differential treatment response. Comparing syndromes with and without major neuro-vegetative signs (tegmental vs. cingulate/insula) may provide another method for differentiating patterns. GI related syndromes; response to dermatology medications, and presence of significant (amygdala) anxiety might also define etiology. (81)

APPENDIX: SUICIDE AND DEPRESSION

Suicidal behavior is a potentially lethal mental health problem, which can be viewed from three perspectives: The **social perspective** decides whether suicide is morally acceptable, and seeks suicidal prevention if preservation of life is a social value. Durkheim's **social perspective** review, at the turn of the 19th century, asked whether changes in society increased suicidal rates. He attributed changes to anomie, the failure of group support for the individual. Both Freud and Darwin struggled with explanations for a behavior that is clearly counter to evolution. (82) The **personal view** is the individual decision to continue to live, or die. These two intersect with the **clinical perspective** of assessing the client's risk to prevent suicide. The three perspectives are not always in alignment, complicating the task.

Is suicidal behavior always a symptom of mental illness? This is a cultural issue. The Judeo-Christian tradition emphasizes the preservation of life and makes suicide morally unacceptable. The sanctity of life is the basis for cultural and legal restrictions against suicide, but heroic altruistic suicide is honored, the death of soldiers on a mission sacrificing themselves for the needs of the nation. (83) In historic Japanese culture, *seppuku*, suicide after personal disgrace, was an honorable outcome. Altruistic suicide is morally acceptable in some cultures, an exception to the evolutionary goal of advancing one's own genome in reproduction. In recent years, the view that an individual may choose death without demonstrating mental illness is trending. There is acceptance of voluntary euthanasia/suicide as an outcome for incurable chronic disease, especially cancer. (84) More complicated is the decision in the Netherlands, and certain other European countries, to accept voluntary euthanasia/suicide by persons with "incurable" depression: Having an incurable mental illness does not make the decision to end one's life a symptom of "mental illness"! This puts the mental health provider in a conundrum by authorizing suicide under certain circumstances with the aid of a physician, but also placing a person in protective custody when he is a "danger to self". Which legal standard applies to which situation is not always clear. These differences in legal status require a careful assessment and documentation of the situation. (85)

The epidemiology of suicide and suicidal attempts poses problems for evaluating completed suicide, compared with the incidence of non-lethal suicide attempts. Increase in the frequency of attempts in the 20th century does not reflect completed suicides. (86) Oquendo has presented an overview of these issues. (87) Suicidal thoughts, attempts, and completed suicide are not the same events as indicated by sex rate differences. Females have a much higher rate of attempts with lower lethality than males. There are also differences in national rates, which suggest the role of social or environmental factors. The low frequency of completed suicide to attempted suicide makes determining effective interventions difficult. The completed suicide rate in the US is about 11/100,000, and this increases in some populations like the elderly, to 14/100,000 (including those not in treatment). The ratio of attempts to completed suicide is reported at 25/1, but probably is much higher as many attempts do not get recorded. People considering suicide often seek help: 64% of people who attempt suicide visit a doctor in the month before their attempt, and 38% in the week before. So, for about 2/3rds, some mental health contact occurs for attempted suicides, but not completed suicides, since history for them is incomplete.

A large number of persons in treatment will present suicidal communications or behaviors, most of which are not imminent, or pose long-term risk of death. Persons at high risk must be differentiated from low risk, to measure the outcome of interventions and assess their effectiveness. (88) Intensive study of the dramatic increase in suicide and attempted suicide in the US military illustrates the role of stress experience, in a population with prior screening for mental illness. (89) These difficulties in evaluating statistics impact the choice of interventions and results.

Are all suicidal behaviors the same? Self-destructive acts may have a lethal (completed suicide) or non-lethal outcome (attempted suicide). A completed suicide is always a death, no matter the situation in which it occurs, but whether the person intended the death is not always clear, and some suicides do not appear to have death as the intended outcome. They can be intentionally self destructive, and unintentionally self destructive, (the latter are situations when an individual dies as a result of actions with a lethal lack of judgment, including high risk adventure behavior, poor management of firearms, dangerous driving, improper use of dangerous substances, etc. (It is usually impossible to be certain that no "subconscious" self-destructive intent was involved, but it is not overt.) Among suicidal behaviors with clear intent (by firearms, overdose of medication, or hanging, etc.) the ratio of lethal/non-lethal is still very small, even when the method is lethal. In the group of intentional self-destructive acts, some persons are involved in mental health care (or previously involved), and some are not. Oquendo emphasizes that only general public health measures can impact the latter group, who are inaccessible to clinicians. (87) Mental health contacts allow further analysis, and Oquendo's group differentiate risk factors of *Suicidal Affective Disturbance*, the context of an affective disorder, from *Suicide Crisis Syndrome*, a life crisis situation, by using subjective verbal reports. The two can overlap. (89) Affective disturbance is only one of several risk factors they have identified in recent studies, which include childhood abuse, borderline syndrome, and scales measuring impulsivity, aggression, and pessimism. These create a broader categorization:

A) REACTIVE sudden and intense suicidal thoughts proximal to some major life event, as in a major loss and/or failure of personal self-esteem
B) INTERMITTENT RECURRING intermittent suicidal thoughts which may be associated with suicidal actions, sometimes triggered by external events, and associated with depression syndromes
C) CHRONIC PERSISTING THOUGHTS AND OBSESSIONS persistent suicidal thoughts associated with one preoccupation about lethal suicidal actions over more than 3 months, sometimes associated with anhedonia, hopelessness, obsessional preoccupations about dying, and recurring treatment failures (related to depression?)
D) NON LETHAL SELF-INJURY COPING STYLE recurring self-injury behavior, verbalized as non-lethal and used as emotional coping, especially in teenage girls, and not intended to be lethal. (90) This behavior has the goal

of emotional control, and might protect against lethal suicidal behavior, or evolve into it.

This grouping, similar to Oquendo's, separates "reactive" from the other forms, but D) is not included in her categorization, though a frequent observation in clinical practice (esp. with borderline syndrome, see chapter seven).

The Oquendo group reports an extended ***prospective study*** of persons identified with initial suicidal thoughts or behavior, which confirmed the depression/reactive difference, with a high percentage of persons reactive to life events. Depression episodes had a higher predictive percentage of completed suicide, and the two were independent. Imaging studies trying to localize and confirm 5-HT effects were variable, as were the role of salivary cortisol measures. These both seem more reflective of long-term risk factors, not acute events. The results must be interpreted in the context of a) patients identified at risk, b) low long term risk, the future events were low, and c) a significantly varied group. *No measures gave clear prediction of imminent risk. (89)*

Theories seeking genetic sites for suicide pose an obvious evolutionary puzzle: how does a gene persist which reduces its contribution of the individual to the gene pool? This makes a gene or genes for suicide unlikely, but genes for *adaptive behavior* may have secondary correlations for suicide, secondary effects of lower *protective* value. (91) (92) GWAS studies to find multiple SNP loci correlated with clinical features have not provided clear results for suicidal acts. Wilbur et al tried to narrow the findings by associating loci with bipolar patients who did/did not attempt suicide. They found only one SNP 2p25 with a site also identified with bipolar suicide. (93) Efforts to identify brain pathways highly correlated to suicidal behavior are also inconclusive. This reflects the current limitations in technology (see chapter one) but studies emphasize the cingulate/insula system, which is consistent with emphasizing "self" representation in risk. (94) Sullivan et al show serotonin abnormalities, in two locations that do not separate attempters from non-attempters but differentiate lethality in attempters (in Raphe but not prefrontal regions.) The role of increased von Economo neurons in a recent study suggests the insula role. (95) The amygdala is also identified in one study. The previous list of different patterns of suicidal behavior supports the lack of consistent findings in neurophysiologic and genetic studies. Suicidal behavior is not one entity and will not be understood by narrow classification. The following CLINICAL EXAMPLE illustrates this problem. This event does not fit categorization in any current method:

CLINICAL EXAMPLE Suicide By Cop with Survival. *A preteen male, not involved in any mental health treatment, was unhappy with his life and intended to commit suicide. He took a toy gun, called the police to a location near his home, and pretended to threaten them when they arrived. He was shot several times but* *survived, and decided on interview that it had been a bad idea. Despite his lethal intent he survived. There was no family history of prior suicidal behavior, but significant social and economic dislocation. COMMENT This situation illustrates the difficulty in sorting out suicidal behavior at the statistical level.*

SIDEBAR The Puzzle Of Toxoplasma Gondii. Individuals infected with the Toxoplasma gondii parasite are at significant risk for later suicide attempts. A cohort study of 84 adults from Sweden showed those infected with T gondii were 7 times more likely to participate in nonfatal, self-directed violence compared with their counterparts. The host immune response in *T. gondii* infection produces pro-inflammatory cytokines such as IL-6 and TNF, and it activates T cells, which secrete IFN-γ, blocking *T. gondii* growth by inducing the activation of an enzyme, indoleamine 2,3-dioxygenase (IDO), which causes tryptophan depletion and ultimately results in a decrease in serotonin production in the brain. Resultant tryptophan depletion leads to a decrease in serotonin production in the brain, which may contribute to depression. Expectant mothers who were infected with T gondii at time of delivery were 53% more likely to self-injure than their uninfected counterparts. The same researchers found a link between T gondii and development of schizophrenia in women who had recently given birth. The parasite influences some pathway component that increases self-injury behavior, but is not limited to that effect and also produces other diagnostic findings. (96)

The goal of most suicidal studies is prevention. This is consistent with cultural values that view suicide as an immoral, illegal, or deviant act, though as noted above the perception is changing. Preventing completed suicides outside of the mental health setting requires that energy, money and emphasis be concentrated in public health efforts, and does not answer the question "is the number of completed suicides lower in clinical settings because of effective interventions?" That currently has no clear answer. (88) Current clinical perspectives on treatment strategies for suicidal ideation are based on differentiating risk assessment, and implementing effective interventions. Prediction of lethal outcome is difficult to study.

The only intervention for persons at imminent risk of self-destructive behavior is protective isolation. This medico-legal intervention is not imposed without serious concern, and indications. What factors differentiate high risk patients and justify this intervention? Assessment of imminent risk includes statistical facts, determination of severity of depression symptoms, existing protective social environment, and, rarely, explores subjective variables that are likely to be most important predictors. Statistical correlations of completed suicide to attempts have low predictive value. Glenn and Nock have reviewed the identified factors in risk, with special attention to the issue of *imminent risk.* (97) Lifetime and 12 month risk factors include socio-demographics, stressful life events, family history, and past suicidal behaviors, which conform to the diathesis/risk model of Oquendo, but *have little value for assessing immediate danger.*

What Factors Predict Transition from Suicidal Thoughts to Attempts Over Hours, or Days?

What are the Important Objective Markers of Short-Term Risk? These have no current answers. The current state of the art in acute suicide risk assessment is asking: *Do you have a plan or intent to kill yourself?* Do you have a strong urge to kill yourself right now? The clinician can use scales, the most recent a detailed assessment of immediate risk, the "Chronological Assessment of Suicide Events" with validity for future attempts but not completions. (98) A relatively simple formula for risk is the combination 1) The patient has strong anhedonic, anergic feelings, with inability to perform daily activities due to the severity of the depressed state, and 2) strong self hatred, rejection, and issues of abandonment or social isolation. Medication may be useful for the first, but not the second. (99) Sometimes a suicide attempt resolves the obsession, as in the following:

CLINICAL EXAMPLE The suicide that walked away. *A married father in his 30s was depressed for several months after he lost his job, and began ruminating about suicide. He was not in mental health treatment, formed a plan, and shot himself aiming for the temple, but missed, with minor damage to the scalp. He was rescued by passers-by, hospitalized, and recovered. He was treated with medication, and started a new job with no residual depression, and no suicidal thoughts. COMMENT Suicidal obsessions may be recurring, or may resolve with changes in the situation. Survival from a lethal attempt may provide a disruption of the previous patterns, and return the person to adaptive goals.*

Initiating procedures for safety, which requires infringing on the personal freedom and self-control of the individual, is a further injury to an already damaged self-system, but prevents the immediate danger. A controlled study allowing a "control group" of patients with imminent risk is unlikely to be approved by any review committee. The result is studies predicting future attempts not lethal results. Different state jurisdictions have different procedures and requirements illustrating the lack of understanding of safety interventions in prevention. Financial considerations often limit the duration of confinement to one or two days, limiting what can be accomplished. If the risk is not "imminent", the provider has the opportunity to help the patient/client develop a life-affirming outlook. As with other areas in mental health, medication and psychotherapy are alternative strategies (see chapters eleven and twelve). Medications to treat depressed mood are inconsistently effective, take weeks to evaluate, and have the occasional risk of augmenting suicidal thoughts. (Chapter eleven). (100) Many patients, already on a medication, will be offered a change, based on the apparent ineffectiveness of the current choice. Referral from non-medical therapists to Psychiatrists for inauguration of medication may occur with onset of suicidal thoughts. Depression is one of several risk factors for suicidal behavior, but the initiation of medication for depression, if appropriate, should not wait until suicidal thoughts develop, nor be expected to rapidly reverse them. Evidence for the effectiveness of medication in reversing suicidal thoughts is weak, because these patients are excluded from most drug studies, providing no evidential basis. Recently ketamine infusion has been promoted as an option, much like ECT in treatment of depression, and a study shows some reversal of suicidal thoughts. (101) (See chapter eleven)

The role of psychotherapy is unclear. Whether CBT treatment is effective in preventing completed suicide is difficult to assess due to the low rate of occurrence. CBT has been shown to improve depression and reduce suicidal thoughts. (102) Addressing specific issues in self-injury may be more important than general techniques. For the patient who has suicidal thoughts or performs self destructive acts, the treatment task is addressing issues that influence negative self experience that motivate destroying the "self". (This is an information processing, subjective task, described in chapter twelve.) Etiologic factors include childhood trauma, and associated shame, anhedonia, problems in social interactions, and loss of attachment support. Hopelessness is often seen in youth and chronic medical illnesses. Childhood abuse and trauma are identified as consistent precursors to suicidal behaviors, but not clearly correlated with lethality. Some behaviors can be interpreted as injuring oneself to avoid being abused by the other. A pattern of causing physical pain to substitute emotional pain also uses the mechanism of self-trauma to prevent external trauma, but does not clarify whether this pattern has a higher or lower likelihood of completed suicide. Sexual abuse is also strongly associated with a history of suicide attempts in women, and both factors are associated with borderline personality. (See chapter seven) (103)

Common to all suicidal behavior is the self-destructive act, strong hostility toward the (internal representation of) self, which has not been studied as a key feature because the subjective component is difficult to integrate into biological formulations. DeLeon et al have explored their changing perspective on suicide from a highly biological model based on serotonin levels to what they call "mental pain". Based on problems differentiating attempters from completed suicides, and using Odds Ratio instead of traditional statistical models, they now favor approaches based on a more subjective evaluation of the person's "mental pain" and related subjective symptoms. This is consistent with the importance of insula in the "subjective pathway" of aversive data. (104) (It illustrates the challenge of using individualized assessment data, as described in the appendix to chapter one.) The recent development "The Interpersonal Theory of Suicide" emphasizes subjective "belongingness" and "burdensomeness" as key interpersonal factors, along with the capacity to suicide. This approach is most applicable to planned suicidal thoughts, less to impulsive reactive ones. It is the more deliberate planned suicidal patients who are often seen in therapy and accessible to changes in thinking. (105) According to the theory, the most dangerous form of suicidal desire is caused by the simultaneous presence of two interpersonal constructs—thwarted belongingness and perceived burdensomeness—and the capability to engage in suicidal behavior is different and separate from the desire to engage in suicidal behavior. Suicidal desire with lowered fear of death is the condition for suicidal desire to transform into suicidal intent. This approach does not address all the issues of suicidal events, as noted in an extensive critique, (105) but it provides a conceptual model for designing interventions, not provided by more statistical or biochemical theories.

In the clinical setting, the client's wish to live is essential to prevent completed suicide. In an outpatient setting, only the patient can prevent him or herself from performing a suicide. The provider can offer an interpersonal connection that encourages the client to take steps of self protection. A clear indication of a problem in the relationship is the provider belief that he can protect the client from suicide. Efforts to assess this by asking "what percent of you wishes to die?" are probably less accurate than the provider's assessment of the client's intentions. If the client intentionally withholds the information of a determination to die, the provider has no capacity to prevent the death. In any situation where suicide is a possibility, this simple fact must be explained clearly to the client in language easily understood. It represents the basic interpersonal reality of using another to help protect yourself, the fundamental reality of suicide prevention in the treatment setting. The therapist can **align** with the patient who wants to live. The therapist can **protect** the part that wants to die, by an intervention that interrupts the treatment.

Much of the pressure for the evaluation of suicidal behavior comes not from the patient's state of mind or brain, but the clinician's counter-transference. The death of a patient by suicide is emotionally difficult for the clinician, and a potential malpractice, which every clinician wishes to avoid. Most suicidal statements and behavior in the clinic do not predict completed suicide, but this is ignored in favor of the conservative position that any risk of suicide must be prevented, which may lead to ineffective responses:

1) Shift responsibility: have the client evaluated by some other clinician. Refer the client to an ER or "suicidal evaluation team" set up by the mental health system for this purpose. Whenever possible include others in the responsibility for the decision, so that IF completed suicide occurs someone else will have made the final decision.
2) Make a non-suicide contract: the client and clinician make an agreement that the client will not kill him/herself, as the basis for treatment to continue. This strategy is based on the doubtful assumption that the client is *both* mentally unstable enough to be seriously considering suicide, and also *rational enough*

to contract not to do so, an inherently self-contradictory position.
3) Terminate the treatment in some unspecified manner: the clinician will either directly or covertly indicate an unwillingness to work with the patient who is struggling with suicide and recommend transfer to another clinician, or less professionally, create circumstances which result in the termination of treatment.

Clinicians generally 1) document that they have fulfilled the legal obligation to consider the risk, and made a good faith effort to protect the patient, 2) intensify the treatment for depression, as this is generally considered part of suicide prevention, and 3) assess the immediate social and personal context of the individual patient and institute controls for the patient's safety. (The major impact of confinement is the change from home environment to hospital environment, which patients usually describe as unpleasant, disruptive, and they are highly motivated to revise their suicidal reporting.)

Suicidal behavior is a complicated phenomenon and deserves a multi-dimensional approach. Whether suicidal behavior should always be considered a mental illness in need of prevention is a social decision that must be answered politically, not by the clinician. This is currently shifting with confusing impact on providers. Suicidal behaviors are not one phenomenon, not one genetic vulnerability, and not one specific neural system. Parsing the behavior into subtypes gives a clearer understanding of the problem statistically, clinically, and therapeutically. For example, differentiating persons with persistent obsessional suicidal thoughts from those with sudden impulsive suicidal acts is important, but the relation of these patterns to completed suicide is not understood. Suicidal behavior is sometimes associated with depressive syndromes, and mechanisms explaining this association have been presented, but it is not likely that one genetic or developmental process accounts for most of the variance, and many clinical states have suicidal behavior as a risk factor. The current emphasis on the relationship with depression overshadows the key issues in regulation of self-destructive impulses.

Suicidal behavior is associated with major psychiatric diagnoses and not a consistent feature of any diagnosis, which suggests that self directed destructive thoughts and impulses need separate consideration, and perhaps separate diagnostic formulation and suicidal behavior should be considered a motivation symptom.

Treatment intervention depends on assessing imminent risk, and providing treatment modalities relevant to the etiologic factors, which may be multiple. The assessment of imminent risk is not possible by current statistical measures or instruments and may not ever be assessed in this way. The client is the absolute expert on the severity of imminent risk and only a close collaborative relationship with the client can be effective in prevention. A client whose wish to die exceeds the wish to live presents a difficult problem in clinical collaboration.

CHAPTER FOUR:
Memory and significance

*The brain stores information at every modifiable synapse. Different types of storage have different functions. The memory process linking external stimuli with motivation system rewards gives **significance** to the stimuli. The pathway may be disturbed by intermittent events, or persisting abnormalities.*

Research differentiates several types of memory: (1)

Explicit or declarative memory is conscious, can be intentionally recalled

Implicit memory of experience, is not available to immediate recall

Semantic memory is verbal, or conceptual information, including language

Episodic memory of events is stored sensory experiences

Spatial memory is the location of specific elements in the surrounding world

Sensory memory provides spatial-temporal continuity, constancy, and the persistence of the sensory world that develops in childhood.

Missing from the list are the memories necessary for adapting to social situations and survival, adaptive memory. The other types all contribute to this group. The term **significance** describes information significant for adaptation. (2) Memories reported in clinical interviews are generally episodic, semantic, and usually (but not always) explicit: "things that happened to me, that I remember, and can talk about". Clinical problems with memory include the inability to store or retrieve information, and problems of significance, the assessment of the adaptive importance. Research evidence documents the hippocampus as the region for pathways storing adaptive **significance** memory. An anatomical review by Papez named this circuit the "emotional brain", later amended by McLean to the "limbic system", to indicate the circular route of the pathways, on side view of the split brain. (3) The spatial arrangement in the brain is illustrated in Fig 4-1. The connections in 4-2.

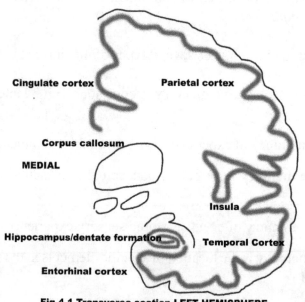

Fig 4.1 Transverse section LEFT HEMISPHERE

The pathways link sensory data analyzed by the cortex to reward outcomes in the motivation system, storing the *reward significance of the sensory signals*. Kluver and Bucy removed the temporal lobes bilaterally in a classic study in monkeys, and postoperatively the

Memory and significance

confused adult monkeys demonstrated a pattern of dis-inhibition: inappropriate oral contact of inedible objects, and sexual behavior toward inappropriate objects. The monkeys lost the ability to recognize the *significance* of environmental objects with bilateral loss of the regions damaged, which included most of the hippocampus. (4) This syndrome has been observed transiently in humans in subclinical temporal-ictal states. (5) (6) Children learn the *significance* of objects by exploring the environment, monitored by their anxious parents. The child touches or ingests objects, receives positive/negative reward experiences and repeats/avoids the actions, building a "significance model" of the environment (which may be modified by parents in dangerous situations!).

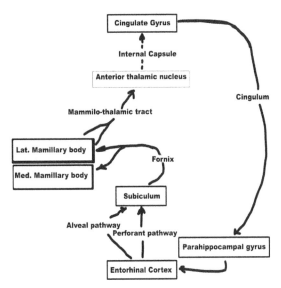

Fig 4.2 The Papez's pathway clockwise
(from multiple sources)

FIG 4-2. shows the connection diagram of the papez- hippocampal memory circuit. The sequence can be described as: sensory information goes to cingulate cortex, and via cingulum to entorhinal cortex, to hippocampal formation (subiculum), via fornix to mammillary bodies, via mammillothalamic tract to anterior thalamic nucleus, and cingulate cortex . The case of H.M. also demonstrates the function of the temporal-hippocampal region. In this patient, the temporal-hippocampal pathways were damaged bilaterally, on one side by seizures, and, on the other side, by surgical resection that (mistakenly) removed the remaining functional tissue. (7) H.M. lost the ability to form new memories of experience and emotional response. (4) He did not lose all previous memory patterns, because he did not have complete ablation of both sides. Learning motor patterns was still possible, because this capacity is stored in basal ganglia (see chapter six.) Damage to the pathway through the hippocampus to mammillary bodies is seen in Korsakoff's syndrome, a complication of alcoholism due to the destruction of the mammillary bodies, and CM of thalamus. (8) Penfield's neurosurgery on awake, locally anaesthetized patients, stimulated the temporal lobe surface of the hippocampal region, which sometimes resulted in patients reporting earlier life experiences, interpreted as evoking "memories" from the surface of the temporal lobe. (9) These and other studies using specific memory tasks and fMRI in normal and brain injured patients associate different memory functions with brain regions, as summarized by Eichenbaum. (10)

The "nodes" are regions of pathways where data converges. For example, sensory memory requires the intact sensory source pathways for recall. Memory "athletes" can enhance memory by mapping it onto spatial images, showing that overlap and "crosstalk" between the modes occurs. (11) Memory recall and fantasy creation utilize the same data, often intermixed by the individual. Persons with mental dysfunction may present emotionally intense "stories" about the world created from emotional states, memory storage, external sensory data, or a mixture of both, producing the symptom of "impaired reality testing". This process contributes to the experience of hallucinations. (58) (The functions of creating fantasy, intentional storytelling, for rehearsal of events or simulation of challenges are reviewed in chapter twelve.) LaBar and Cabeza reviewed the topic

SIDEBAR Rugg et al summarize fMRI studies of hippocampus localizing different features of memory storage:

i) **hippocampus** (medial temporal lobe) Declarative memory: recognition memory, and the entorhinal-CA1 system major region for reward memory, recall of detailed information (but not for "familiarity" (dorsolateral frontal regions are also involved) ii) **peri-rhinal cortex**: The interior surface of temporal lobes, store "context", spatial temporal memory, and familiarity-based recognition (something is "familiar"), parahippocampal cortex also contributes to recollection, retrieval of contextual (especially spatial) information. iii) **dorsal/caudal medial entorhinal cortex (dMEC)** contains a spatial grid a topographically organized map of the spatial environment in grid cells. This brain region transforms sensory input from the environment and stores it as a durable representation in the brain to be used for negotiating paths. iv) **dorsolateral frontal cortex** is needed for retrieval of memories not initial creation. v) **language areas of frontal cortex** are involved in retrieval of semantic/verbal information, which is stored in the dominant side. vi) **primary sensory receiving areas** must be intact for sensory memory, abstract information recall depends on intact association regions. (Sensory memory involves the original sensory pathways.) vii) hippocampus trisynaptic loop (entohinal-dentate-CA3-CA1) stores place recall memory. Viii) The hippocampal CA2 region is essential for social memory. (12) These locations are estimated by studies of localized damage.

of "emotional memory" focusing on negative events and the amygdala. Emotion with subjective awareness must include the cingulate cortex. Memories of intense emotional arousal, as in an accident or assault, are often recalled inaccurately: the individual's belief in a clear "flashbulb" image of the event is not supported by objective data, revealing distorted "reconstruction". This, and other factors biasing recall make witness testimony unreliable, and complicate psychotherapy. (13) *Memory is always a variable reconstruction of experience, challenging to use clinically.*

Memories change or are "lost" in several ways, including neurogenesis-based forgetting, interference-based forgetting, and intrinsic forgetting, the ongoing signals that slowly degrade molecular and cellular memory traces. Intrinsic forgetting may be the basic mode, constantly promoting erasure by everyday experiences that "overwrite" previous episodes with new information, and modify what is stored. Other processes promote memory stability by consolidation.

Pioneering research studies, using Drosophila, have identified a molecular and cellular mechanism for active forgetting. Zhong, a neuroscientist at Tsinghua University in Beijing, and his team have also successfully manipulated forgetting in mice by inhibiting a specific protein called Rac1 in hippocampal neurons that prolongs the retention of memories from less than 72 hours to at least 120 hours in many cases. Increasing the activity of Rac1 reduced the life of memories to less than 24 hours. (14) The blocking of emotionally intense events, associated with PTSD, does not erase in this way, instead active pathways block re-experiencing of troubling memories (discussed in chapter eight). Temporal lobectomy, as in H.M., is not usually the cause of memory loss, but temporal dysfunction may interfere with memory consolidation, documented in patients with temporal seizure disorders, and the effect of ECT seizures that interfere with memory consolidation. (14) Aging is also a factor in decreasing acquisition of new memory, involving both prefrontal and hippocampal changes.

Clinical reports, accumulated since the 1950s, document mental health symptoms associated with seizures. Slater and Beard described a syndrome associated with temporal seizures: "The Schizophreniform Psychoses of Epilepsy". (16) Patients with previous brain injury and symptoms of temporal lobe epilepsy presented subjective experiences and symptoms fitting the (older) diagnostic criteria for schizophrenia, including auditory hallucinations, delusions, and psychotic disorganization. The seizures were often "partial complex" type, including inter-ictal features, disturbances in interpersonal functioning, paranoid trends, and grandiosity. The 69 patients had documented temporal lobe abnormalities on EEG and active seizures at some time. The mental symptoms came 5-15 years *after* onset of seizures in the report. Some had a history of traumatic birth with anoxic complications of delivery. The authors reviewed previous reports in the literature of this phenomenon and concluded that this overlap showed that epilepsy directly caused the schizophrenic symptoms, not a co-incidence of two illnesses. 10 of 14 cases, in a related series, showed evidence of damage to the small

SIDEBAR Seizures are the spread of local brain activity to surrounding areas. (Epilepsy is the disease.) Large voltage low frequency brain waves are observed on EEG recording replacing the usual low voltage, high frequency pattern, indicating excess synchronized firing. A "seizure episode" results when this activity spreads to surrounding regions and produces symptoms, from brief loss of awareness to complete loss of motor control, tonic-clonic limb movements, and unconsciousness. (15) The pattern of seizure activity, and the immediate pre-seizure activity ("aura") give clues to the original location of the seizures. The surgical treatment of patients with intractable seizures, resulted in patient H.M., Sperry and Gazzaniga's studies cutting the corpus callosum and the lateralization of brain function, and Penfield's stimulation of temporal cortex during surgery. "Partial complex seizures", which do not involve complete loss of consciousness, or complete loss of motor control, have varied symptoms including emotional reactions, and emotional experiences. These atypical seizure patterns can sometimes be confirmed by recording EEG activity with concurrent video monitoring in special centers, or using ambulatory recording devices. If the observed behavior or experience is correlated with EEG abnormalities it is a "seizure episode", if not, a "non-seizure event". In patients with epilepsy, some symptoms are observed during epileptic activity (**intra-ictal**), while others occur between seizure episodes (**inter-ictal**). Brain abnormalities that alter brain activity without producing seizures may sometimes be observed as local EEG "spikes"(sharp wave activity) or slowing in the EEG. Abnormalities observed in EEG without associated seizure episodes do not justify the diagnosis of epilepsy but may still give rise to symptoms. (14) Seizures may develop in many regions of the brain, but the hippocampal/temporal region is a frequent site of damage that results in abnormal activity (for reasons of blood flow and other anatomical factors). (15)

interneurons of the dentate nucleus of hippocampus, whose blood supply is highly vulnerable to hypoxia. (17) Falconer concluded that mesial temporal lobe sclerosis, caused by lack of oxygen, was not a result of the epilepsy but the original source of the abnormal activity, possibly at birth. (18) Malamud presented a series of psychiatric patients, not initially diagnosed with tumor or epilepsy, who were later found to have temporal tumors and epileptic events. (19) Wall et al presented a series of patients with panic attacks and epileptic activity from a blood vessel abnormality (AVM). (20) The seizure literature was reviewed by Dietrich Blumer in 1975, describing a Temporal Lobe Syndrome with two patterns: abnormal environmental response like Kluver Bucy oral inappropriateness and other hyperemotional features, or reduced emotional response, lack of reactivity, symptoms of poor emotional regulation, and other features. (21) Waxman and Geschwind wrote about the inter-ictal characteristics of patients with temporal lobe seizures, describing altered sexual behavior, religiosity and compulsive writing. (Associated spikes in temporal areas were observed). They proposed that the spike activity indicated abnormal activity in the region between seizure episodes, though it was not always possible to correlate with symptoms. (22) A review from British Medical Journal identifies other related brain regions likely affected in patients with psychotic episodes and epilepsy. Symptoms are sometimes seen first in childhood or adolescence. Szabo and Magnus did a case review of adolescents admitted to inpatient unit who were all subsequently confirmed to have abnormal EEG but had not had seizure episodes. They demonstrated a wide variety of psychiatric disturbances inter-ictal, including psychotic features. Some of the symptoms were associated seizure episodes, while others were inter-ictal. The phenomenon of "abdominal aura" from outflow pathways, which can activate GI symptoms, poses a diagnostic confusion for the clinician. Patients with this had both diagnostic seizure findings and non-diagnostic abnormal EEG and associated symptoms of hallucination, aggression, dissociation, and cognitive deterioration. (23) Recent studies suggest that consequences of injury in some athletes are more pervasive than previously appreciated, the syndrome of CTE. These studies summarize a large body of evidence that abnormalities of temporal-hippocampal region may produce seizure activity and/or associated mental health symptoms. The importance of this etiology is not emphasized in current clinical practice.

Temporal/hippocampal injury may produce different clinical patterns:

TYPE #1: Symptoms develop after seizures. The classic pattern in the Slater and Beard series, with seizures and then inter-ictal Psychiatric symptoms, sometime (up to 5-15 years) after the seizures are diagnosed. A variety of seizure patterns occur.

***CLINICAL EXAMPLE** A 50 y o veteran was being followed for psychosis.* His birth history was not obtainable, but in his 20s he had onset of partial complex seizures, with indication of fronto-temporal source. Roughly 8 years later, he had the sudden "religious experience" of being told by God to become an opera singer. At the same time, he was agitated and confused and briefly hospitalized and treated with antipsychotic medications in addition to his anti-seizure treatment. He proceeded to study voice for the following 30 years with little aptitude and no history of public performance. He remained staunchly convinced that he was fulfilling "God's order" for his life. He had no further psychotic episodes and his seizures were well controlled.

TYPE #2: Seizures produce symptoms that have mental health features. The patient has seizure episodes often associated with inappropriate affect (panic anxiety), or behavior (see example). They are documented by concurrent EEG and video recording.

***CLINICAL EXAMPLE** Spitting in class.* A 15-year-old high school student began having episodes of spitting in class at other students or teachers who tried to stop him. He was noted to be in a "trance" state and was referred for a Neurology evaluation. Concurrent recordings revealed that he was having active seizure episodes while hyper salivating and spitting out the saliva to avoid choking. He maintained fixed posture and often aimed the spitting, but had no response to visual or auditory stimuli, suggesting partial complex seizures. COMMENT The particular challenge of this example is the mixture of dissociated consciousness and apparent ability to focus the behavior. He responded to medication to control seizure episodes.

TYPE #3: EEG abnormalities without seizures produce symptoms. The patient has evidence of brain abnormality by scan or EEG and shows Psychiatric symptoms but does not have seizure episodes (which may develop later). Lewis reviewed studies of EEG abnormalities in severely violent and uncontrollable criminal offenders many years ago, many were not diagnosed with seizures but had violent explosive episodes. The identification of traumatic brain injury (TBI) by might identify some of these patients. The qEEG study group on TBI formed the following conclusions: Individual qEEG measures provide limited diagnostic utility for TBI. ERP(Event related potentials) offer utility in TBI detection because there is evidence that ERPs can identify abnormalities in cases where qEEGs do not. (27) Amen and his group have reported local abnormalities in SPECT scans interpreted as patterns of damage in temporal and other regions. (26) Because large population studies are not feasible with this expensive test, diagnostic criteria do not exist. (28) (See chapter one appendix for further discussion of techniques)

> **CLINICAL EXAMPLE Teen implanted with creature.** *A teenage male was referred for substance abuse of cannabis. He was grandiose and paranoid about other peers, but had a small group of similarly "outcast" friends. He had mood swings mostly toward mania and difficulty concentrating in school. He had been a nuchal cord birth with significant hypoxia. There was no history of epileptic activity, nor any family history of epilepsy or psychosis. Treatment with antipsychotic medication precipitated a new symptom: he insisted that a large creature was growing inside his abdomen and he could feel it moving around from time to time. (At the time, a popular movie included a scene where a creature was implanted into a character.) After changing to anti-seizure medication, the symptom was controlled. He continued to use cannabis, and complained of poor focus and requested stimulant medication, which was refused. He did not return for follow-up. COMMENT There was a strong history suggesting of a temporal type birth injury. The new atypical symptom might have been abdominal ictal activity activated by the medication, and improved with anti-seizure medication. EEG was never obtained. The breakdown in treatment over request for stimulants is a frequent issue with teens in contemporary treatment. (24)*

TYPE #4: Symptoms with no sign of local brain injury on biophysical tests, and no seizures, but history suggestive of temporal injury. Patients without seizures or EEG abnormalities, with behavioral symptoms, may still have brain injuries. The EEG is an unreliable indicator of underlying abnormalities. Certain patients have atypical mental health symptoms, especially in late childhood and young adulthood, with mixed psychiatric and neurologic symptoms, but no seizures. They do not fit into current diagnostic categories and are labeled as mood disorder, schizoaffective disorder, etc., depending on the presenting symptoms. (28) Traumatic brain injuries are typical, along with a history of unsatisfactory response to traditional treatment, and many prefer benzodiazepines. Currently, the only way to identify this group of patients is by specific details of life history:

History of birth hypoxia. The dentate cells in hippocampus are most sensitive to perinatal oxygen deprivation to the infant. Prematurity, CPD with fetal distress, nuchal cord, and other obstetric complications can produce sufficient hypoxia for this type of injury, and later symptoms, and several studies report effects often missing the role of local damage. (29)

History of brain trauma in either childhood or adolescence. Sports injuries are often clues. Concussion may injure different cortical areas after head trauma. The hippocampal-amygdala region can be injured by brain swelling after head injury resulting with partial tentorial herniation damage. Changes in function are observed after the acute syndrome, in weeks to months. Onset of severe problems may be observed in childhood or not until adolescence in milder injuries. (28)

Symptoms not typical of psychiatric diagnoses. A summary of these symptoms are found in a Neurological screen for possible temporal lobe seizure disorder. (28) Some Psychiatric symptoms are reported as *intermittent and episodic* than seen in major psychiatric disorders.

Four symptoms, not typically seen with psychiatric disorders without temporal injury, are useful for screening neurological dysfunction, especially if the **temporal quad symptoms** improve along with emotional ones on anti-seizure medication trial.

a) Increased frequency of déjà vu, jamais vu, and other disturbances of context interpretation: DÉJÀ VU Déjà vu, jamais vu, and depersonalization are sometimes experienced by adolescent patients, but more frequently with disturbances in this region, along with problems of "memory context". In *déjà vu*, the current space is misperceived as identical to a previous experience. In *jamais vu* a current space is NOT recognized as familiar from previous experience. Depersonalization describes misinterpreting current sensory signals related to self. Sometimes there is a feeling of "religiosity", of "spiritual transcendence" that may be an aspect of the context of life experience. These

symptoms broaden the understanding of the role of **significance.**
b) Olfactory hallucinations or heightened olfactory response, The symptom of intensified smell or olfactory hallucinations, usually of disagreeable odors, indicates the close connection of the olfactory lobes to the temporal hippocampal-perirhinal cortex. This olfactory connection is a separate feature of the temporal system, very evocative of memory, producing incorrect olfactory perceptions.
c) Intermittent brief staring spells which may be unrecognized "absence seizures" sometimes correlate with EEG abnormalities confirming seizures.
d) Problems in memory consolidation. The immediate recall of current data is usually maintained, but there is difficulty in storing new information similar to the experience of H.M. but less severe.

CLINICAL EXAMPLE: TWO BROTHERS *Two brothers were evaluated in their early 20s. Both had a history of abnormal delivery with hypoxia and skull compression. Both appeared to develop normally with minor reading and other cognitive challenges. Neither displayed seizure episodes. Both elected to play football in high school, and both suffered recurring concussions. Over the next year, each began to show severe cognitive impairment, confusion, and hallucinations. The older had more severe symptoms, withdrawal, emotional blunting, and active hallucinations. The younger had milder symptoms with confusion, sudden anger outbursts, and impulsivity. Both had problems maintaining focus of attention. They were initially treated as "psychosis" with increasing doses of antipsychotic agents, and became worse. In re-evaluation by a different Psychiatrist, the diagnosis of brain injury was made, and medications changed to anti-seizure medication that significantly improved the younger brother. The older brother became more manageable. Both were referred for EEG and SPECT scanning, confirming damage to both frontal and temporal regions. COMMENT Milder birth related hypoxia can worsen by later brain trauma in unpredictable ways. CTE is now a recognized syndrome, though not often seen this early. The effect of treatment with high dose antipsychotics is typical, since it interferes with processing and focus, and may lower thresholds for seizure activity. Neither had active seizures at any time, though EEG showed a variety of abnormalities. This situation illustrates the narrow margin between safety and injury in some head trauma situations, especially with an earlier developmental history. A high index of suspicion about preventing further damage is needed to avoid unfortunate outcomes.*

CLINICAL EXAMPLE An irritable woman. *A woman in her 60s was seen for lifelong problems with mood instability and panic episodes. She had been a difficult birth and her mother told her "she almost didn't make it". The episodes had started in childhood, with intermittent spells, and worsened with maturity, were not well controlled with SSRI, or SNRI, but responsive to benzodiazepines. The patient was scrupulous about controlling her use of benzos for fear of addiction. At no time had she been psychotic, or had a seizure episode, or sudden loss of consciousness. She had never been tried on another anti-seizure medication. After starting a gaba-active medication she reported significant and sustained improvement, and discontinued use of benzodiazepines.* **CLINICAL COMMENT** *The author's clinical experience includes many referrals with temporal-hippocampal symptoms not recognized by other clinicians, who respond to appropriate medications. Exploration of etiologic events and symptoms can identify these patients, even in the absence of seizure activity. Exotic syndromes described by Ramachandran and others (capgras, etc.), are also observed, but rare. (29)*

Hippocampal syndromes help clarify the pathways of Schizophrenia. Patients with temporal lobe/hippocampal symptoms are sometimes diagnosed as "schizoaffective disorder", "bipolar disorder", "mood swings", or anxiety disorder, as well as schizophreniform psychosis (i.e. Slater and Beard). The relationship between the temporal lobe syndromes and the "schizophrenia syndrome" has been reviewed, with differences in onset, and persistence of symptoms, but definite overlap. (30) The relationship is complicated by the variations in both syndromes, and in etiologies. (The DSM V requirement for psychosis symptoms in schizophrenia also confuses the relationship (see discussion in chapters five and ten).) Hippocampal syndromes overlap the spectrum of schizophrenia, yet some clinicians still seek "real schizophrenia" of genetic etiology, viewing the others as "variants". Barch defines a range of "schizophrenia spectrum disorders" as the alternative. MacDonald and Schulz list 22 statements with corroborating evidence about "schizophrenia syndrome" (most are **not** DSM criteria), and no patient group presents all the features.

TABLE 4-1. "20 things I know about schizophrenia"
(adapted from MacDonald and Schulz(31))

1. The diagnosis identifies a heterogeneous population.
2. There is a roughly 0.7% prevalence across cultures.
3. The gender ratio is equal male to female.
4. The peak onset is in mid adolescence.
5. The genetic factor shows a 50% concordance in identical twins.
6. Linkage studies show multiple gene effects.
7. Dopamine D2 synaptic blockers improve psychotic symptoms, not the negative.
8. Cognitive deficits are found in other family members, involving hippocampus.
9. There are multiple other risk factors documented in population studies.
10. The time course of response to treatment with current medications is inconsistent.
11. Amphetamine substances may trigger the syndrome in some persons.
12. PCP and NMDA drugs can trigger the syndrome.
13. The longer the duration of unresolved psychosis the poorer the prognosis.
14. Pyramidal cells and hippocampal dentate regions are damaged in post mortem.
15. The Gaba transmitter system is reduced in some studies.
16. Changes in ventricle size are seen in patients with longer course.
17. The hippocampus is smaller in anatomical scan studies.
18. Verbal memory, performance and coding tasks deficits are cognitive symptoms.
19. Social skills therapies are effective in improving social interaction.
20. Cognitive deficits correlate with employment and social adaptation problems.

The list does not require psychosis, and others have called for removing psychosis as necessary for diagnosis, and recognizing a wider spectrum. (31) Based on their summary, the following features describe the **schizophrenia spectrum**:

1) a collection of varied symptoms (31)
2) with multiple etiologies: Genes influence some patients and families. This has been a research obsession for over twenty years, as summarized by several authors. Arnedo et al review multiple GWAS studies showing that groupings of SNP (multiple genes at single nucleotide locations) weakly predict occurrence of the syndrome,

but no single group predicts with high probability, in their words: "a group of heritable disorders caused by a moderate number of separate genotypic networks associated with several distinct clinical syndromes". (32) GWAS studies also show overlap of multiple disorders including schizophrenia syndrome and bipolar disorder, which may reflect psychosis as a separate symptom/syndrome (see chapter five). (33) The genetic studies document that schizophrenia is groups of symptoms, without a common gene or genetic group. Proposals to add genetic analysis to include regions for risk (PRS) yield marginal benefits and fail to improve diagnosis for clinical purposes. Much of the confusion may lie in searching for genes for diagnoses, rather than for adaptation, (discussed in chapter ten).

Other etiologies are associated with the syndrome, and how genetic and non-genetic factors interact is unclear, or even whether different etiologies damage the same or different pathways. Failure to include etiology in diagnosis prevents gathering this data. Reported etiologies include (34): vitamin deficiency (B12 and niacin), brain injury, temporal lobe tumor, maternal starvation during pregnancy, etc., nutrition at age 3, maternal infection during prenatal period, toxoplasma infection in mother, herpes simplex infection, obstetric complications predict abnormalities when there is also developmental delay, a relationship between serious infectious autoimmune disorders (Danish series), autoimmune anti NDMA. The list shows the range but is far from complete. The role of substance use is confusing: Does abuse of certain substances eventually produce psychosis and/or schizophrenia syndrome or does it manifest vulnerability? A study of the Swedish national register suggests that the effect of substances depends on familial vulnerability. A study by Riglin et al indicates the possibilities and difficulties of evaluating effects. They found that children and teens with PRS scores indicative (statistically) of schizophrenia syndrome were reportedly more subject to peer victimization. (34) The observation of psychosis and other brain symptoms in patients with Epstein-Barr infection stimulated a surge of research into immune system components of *inflammation*. Muller describes recent findings that associate nonspecific immune system changes in some patients. Gilmore's editorial is clear: there will be no one etiology, genetic or other, for the range of schizophreniform syndromes; the search for "THE" must evolve into documentation of multiple etiologies, some preventable. (34)

3) with no specific synaptic chemistry. A "disease model" in which dopamine was the key transmitter has been dismissed. (35) D2 blockers reduce symptoms of psychotic arousal, but do not modify the cognitive impairment. GABA factors are identified in post mortem, localized in specific regions, and this neurotransmitter is important in hippocampal function but also widely distributed in brain. Benes and Beretta see GABA neurons as abnormal in amount and therefore decreased inhibition in hippocampus, which they ascribe as a factor. The Frankle et al study: "demonstrates, for the first time, an in vivo impairment in GABA transmission in schizophrenia syndrome, most prominent in antipsychotic-naive individuals."(36) The extensive input to gaba cells and their extensive ramifications make it likely that they play a role in many different syndromes, not specific for one mental disorder. Recent studies seek a role for glutamate due to its broad effects. (37) The desire to find a specific neurotransmitter substance is a holdover from the dopamine era, and the wide distribution of major transmitters makes specificity for schizophrenia doubtful.

4) cognitive deficit is an essential feature. Historically called "dementia praecox" (premature dementia), cognitive impairment has been recognized as a basic symptom of schizophrenia syndrome from its inception. (The emphasis on symptoms of psychosis including hallucinations, delusions, and mental disorganization distracts from the major features.) Defining this "core cognitive deficit" is a confusing trail, starting with attention and reaction time studies (which did not support a primary sensory/attention basis for the problem as reviewed in 1977, Schizophrenic Bulletin (vol 3 #3)). The cognitive deficits include traditional neuropsychology tests, Battery For The Assessment Of Neuropsychological Status, Matrics Consensus Cognitive Battery, and the UCSD Performance Based Skills Assessment. (38) Bosch's review of cognitive deficits identifies four core problems: a) difficulty considering "context" for organizing cognition to integrate information into more complex systematic organization. Context is derived from para-hippocampal memory. b) difficulty in working memory, inability to maintain organization of information in ongoing life activities, DLPFC is the region associated. Other memory is also involved, patients are impaired on their ability to recall, recognize, and learn both visual and verbal materials with greater impairments in verbal memory than in other modalities.

Various studies show problems in processing speed, vigilance, working memory, verbal learning and memory, visual learning and memory, reasoning and social cognition. (The role of psychosis creating attention problems is separate and not been clarified.) c) symptoms of social withdrawal, lack of spontaneous affect. No specific region has been identified for these symptoms, but the link between hippocampal memory and regions that activate emotion are likely to be important. d) Psychotic symptoms of hallucinations, delusions, which are associated with problems in context memory storage and working memory, and which are driven by psychotic arousal (see chapter five). It is unclear if these symptoms and reality distortion persist without psychotic arousal. Halder and Mahato describe cognitive deficits consistently observed: (39) Problems in reading, auditory sensory detection, and motion sensing difficulties are also reported. (40) (These core schizophrenic symptoms are also sometimes seen in other temporal network syndromes.) There is early indication of impairment in some patients before psychosis symptoms. In one study, New Zealand youth had cognitive deficits and developmental delays before emerging with schizophrenic diagnosis, but not children who later became depressed. Keefe's review identifies the longitudinal course, which supports the cognitive impairment as the basic element in the syndrome, with other symptoms consequences. (41) Leeson et al differentiated "first episode psychosis" which does not a progress to schizophreniform spectrum, from patients that do, by presence of cognitive abnormalities. The best correlation was "negative symptoms" of social impairment, the result of cognitive disturbances. (42) A scale for documenting the "negative symptoms" has been standardized, and correlates to long-term outcome. (The historical "first rank symptoms" have *not* been validated statistically.) (43) Understanding the spectrum of cognitive impairments and their relationship to etiology is an unfinished research task. The cognitive deficits have not been associated into specific neural processes. Factors considered in original studies are sometimes lost in meta-analyses.

SIDEBAR Cognitive Symptoms Summary. The following disturbances are selected from reviews and other data as the most frequent, but are not seen in every patient: a) memory difficulties: especially linking external sensory and internal reward data (significance) to social interaction, b) attention problems: the "binding problem" (see chapter five) of how attention follows a specific target, c) self identity, the representation of self and other (also referred to as "Theory of Mind"), differentiation of self and other in social interaction, learned during development, d) failure to mature from sensory to abstract cognitive function. Most IQ testing depends in part on achieving a level of abstract intelligence typical for age, which is different from "pure cognitive disability" (mental retardation), e) experiencing emotion. The anhedonic quality reported by some patients in recall despite normal emotion/pleasure experience, suggests that memory storage of emotional memory is impaired, f) poor executive decisions. The data regarding executive control points to the difficulty using working memory to select and prioritize activities, including formulating goals, planning and organizing goal-directed behavior effectively, and monitoring self-correction of behavior, g) problems in interpretation of semantic component of language. The classic verbal distortion seen in severe schizophrenia syndrome reflects confusion of semantic properties of language and difficulties in verbal memory.

Some reviews propose unifying hypotheses to account for the symptoms: Lesh et al propose a deficit of "cognitive control" with localization in prefrontal and dorsolateral prefrontal cortex failures of "top down" control. (44) (45) Some scan studies to show deficits in this region, and the region has important linking functions between the prefrontal system and the hippocampal system. Frith explains the disturbances of consciousness in schizophreniform patients as difficulty in monitoring abstract (especially mental) events, describing the experience as separate and alien. (46) Regulating response to stimuli has two modes, proactive and reactive control, and schizophrenia syndrome patients are unable to anticipate and guide proactively. This is also a frontal control ability (discussed in chapter six). (46) Brune uses the **theory of mind** conceptualization for cognitive deficits in schizophrenia syndrome. There is evidence that this is impaired in schizophrenia syndrome, though not as severely as in autism. (See chapter two) (47)

The core deficit is a cognitive/memory task, with problems in memory system pathways: (48) The ability to assign significance to sensory information, and store this for future use in attention and behavior selection is impaired. Most of the other deficits described can be linked to this core impairment, and the testing procedures used to assess the deficits. This directs to studies of pathways in the next section.

CLINICAL EXAMPLE The man who wouldn't give up. *A 20-year-old Hispanic male had recurrent hospitalizations with psychotic symptoms, that resolved taking antipsychotic medication, and resumed on discontinuation. Confusion and disorganization suggested adding a GABA agonist, which proved useful in maintaining his mental stability for months without hospitalization. He began a simple job, and a relationship with a young woman, but after a few months, she moved back to Mexico. For several weeks he was extremely distressed about her departure. He decided that he would visit her in Mexico to continue the relationship. This was discouraged and he was lost to follow-up. Months later he returned and reported that he had traveled to Mexico and visited her, but she was not interested, so he became angry and hostile and was hospitalized briefly in Mexico and returned to the US. COMMENT This person demonstrates the potential value of GABA agonists and the executive decision problems seen in patients with relatively good adaptation. He was unable to make effective social decisions even when he was not psychotic, and might have benefited from therapy. Instead he obtained a lesson from experience.*

5) the brain pathway(s) involved is(are) debated. The temporal/hippocampal and DLPFC frontal brain regions combine in a pathway often associated with schizophrenic abnormalities, so involvement of both regions is indicated. Excluding symptoms of psychosis, which involves DLPFC by a different pathway, the emphasis shifts to the hippocampal region.

Cutting the DLPFC/hippocampal pathway connection that transfers data from hippocampus to prefrontal regions blocks one of two major links between subcortical memory and action. Deciding which pathway tracts are essential has been difficult. The obvious pathway is the Papez-McLean circuit: thalamus to cingulate cortex and then to DLPFC, while the entorhinal connection to DLPFC

SIDEBAR Role of hippocampus: Tammiga frames the cognitive impairment as dysfunction of hippocampal memory: *"Declarative memory is one of the most consistently impaired functions in schizophrenia. Abnormal performance on memory tasks that depend on conjunctive representations has been repeatedly reported" (51)* Several lines of evidence show schizophrenia syndrome patients have variations in hippocampal activity, and hippocampal abnormalities. Based on this research, she proposed a specific anatomical disturbance: *"significant, but localized, reduction in glutamatergic transmission within the dentate gyrus and in its efferent pathways,..."* are crucial. Rasetti proposed altered hippocampal-parahippocampal function during encoding as the phenotype for increased genetic risk for schizophrenia. Measuring hippocampal-parahippocampal function represents a potentially useful approach, but is difficult to visualize. A study of stimulus encoding by hippocampus using fMRI successfully screened both schizophrenic patients and siblings against normal controls. (51)

SIDEBAR Dorsolateral Prefrontal Cortex (DLPFC) focuses attention and coordinates working memory (part of the prefrontal region, see chapter five), and may contribute to schizophrenic syndromes by psychosis symptoms or direct effects on memory pathways. It is readily visualized in fMRI making it easier to document. DLPFC pathways link temporal/hippocampal areas with executive prefrontal regions. (51) Task related changes have been observed in fMRI of schizophrenic patients in DLPFC and thalamic nuclei interactions. (52)

Barch and Ceaser (54) review research focused on the DLPC. They emphasize the problems representing goal information in working memory to guide behavior, a DLPFC function (see chapter five). A meta-analysis by Minzenberg reported similar differences between schizophrenics and normal patients with reduced activity in DLPFC and connected regions. Cohen's theory proposes that DLPC is involved in processing "context", which also involves parahippocampal cortex. DLPFC is involved in attention focusing, and is consistently dysfunctional in psychotic disorganization of any origin (see discussion in chapter five). Schizophrenia syndrome patients are unable to anticipate and guide their responses by anticipation (proactive) in studies regulating response to stimuli. The interaction of DLPFC and hippocampus described by Lisman and Grace involves *"a hippocampal ventral tegmental loop, triggered by novel stimuli, activates the hippocampus to initiate memory storage and the attention system to focus or "attend"* (see refs for detail). Data from animal microelectrode and other sources reconfirms the "orienting reflex" model linking DLPFC with "working memory" and hippocampal areas for long term information storage. Other pathways link multiple sensory sources with reward history (the multi-region pathways of "significance") in hippocampus. (56)

cortex is more direct and also a route through basal ganglia. *The different pathways may be affected in different ways, resulting in variations of the syndrome.* (53)

Leivada et al. review evidence that the syndrome of "congenital cortical blindness" protects against developing schizophrenic syndrome. (57) The difference in organization of sensory input to memory storage appears responsible for this protective effect. The phenomenon suggests that schizophrenia syndromes result from difficulties managing the interaction of information across adjoining dentate pathways.

> **SIDEBAR Studies showing changes in connectivity in patients with hallucinations illustrate the role of local interaction.** Hare et al combined two resting-state functional magnetic resonance imaging (fMRI) analysis methods – amplitudes of low-frequency fluctuations (ALFF) and functional network connectivity (FNC) – to explore the hypotheses that (1) abnormal FNC between salience and sensory (visual/auditory) networks underlies hallucinations in schizophrenia, and (2) disrupted hippocampal oscillations (as measured by hippocampal ALFF) beget changes in FNC linked to hallucinations. Increased auditory connections were observed, and ALFF also showed a difference between normal and patient FNC in resting state. These findings provide *indirect* support favoring the second hypothesis. (58) This is a different approach to examining cross sensory response. Disturbances of hippocampal connection to DLPFC, hippocampal thalamic cortical oscillation changes, and abnormal frontal activation are all consistent with a primary hippocampal DLPFC pathway disturbance with secondary manifestations.

Each of the primary senses is linked to the other modes in association cortex, and the results sent to entorhinal cortex and dentate/hippocampus. The hippocampus pathway integrates these multiple sensory pathways. Separate memory systems are organized in hippocampal regions (see earlier SIDEBAR.) Spatial, emotional, and verbal memory must have some crosslinking of storage. For example, "Memory palace" techniques for enhanced memory use spatial memory to store symbolic/verbal data. (58) GABA inhibitory interneurons are essential to maintain the separation of memory types, but some crosstalk across modalities is needed to link different information. This provides a theory of the disturbance: **The schizophrenic syndromes are problems managing the "crosstalk of information" in neural pathways through hippocampus/dentate and its pathway connections with DLPFC. When "crosstalk" is too strong, confused messaging occurs; when "crosstalk" is too restricted difficulty in integrating sensory/reward occurs.** Different etiologies may modify different components. There are several new studies in animal models mapping the interaction across this region. (58) The cognitive impairments described in the syndrome all involve effective use of memory, working memory, and links to executive functions. The hippocampal-DLPFC is the essential pathway linking memory/reward and PF/BG choice, and produces the range of cognitive disturbances. All could be the result of confusing memory messages of different modalities affecting decision making and behavioral choice. (see chapter six)

6) *the core deficit is not the psychosis but may produce psychosis.* The DSM V requires an episode of psychotic disorganization for the diagnosis, but the cognitive deficit is the core disturbance, and psychotic disorganization, a secondary manifestation, the result of maladaptive social behavior and poor decisions. This is the view of Tammiga, and Kahn and Keefe, who see the emphasis on psychosis syndromes interfering with a broader understanding of the cognitive disturbance. Persons with core cognitive deficits, who do not become psychotic, but still have impaired social skills are found in clinical settings (family members with similar cognitive problems are identified in genetic studies). Severity of cognitive impairment is rarely measured in them because a psychotic episode is necessary for diagnosis. (50) The core cognitive deficits generate the clinical presentation, and may produce psychotic disorganization. (45)

7) *evidence for progressive deterioration is inconsistent.* Schizophrenia was originally classified as a form of dementia with brain atrophy. The clinical course depends on many variables, and atrophy may be the result of functional impairment, lack of social activity, or other cognitive changes. (60) Patients with more

disorganization are noted to have poorer outcomes, though the severity concept is vague. A predictor of relapse has been developed. (61) Cognitive deficits may emerge concurrently with the onset of psychotic symptoms, or be observed before, with early deficits of executive function, attention and long term memory, social difficulties, stress, and anxiety which lead to psychosis. Differentiating an episode of "first episode psychosis" as "schizophrenia spectrum" vs. some other etiology, uses cognitive impairment identifying the group with brief course and high probability of recovery from others. (The diagnosis Attenuated Psychosis Syndrome was created at least in part to recognize the mis-diagnosis of first episode events for lack of another category. (63)) Some patients have a slowly developing chronic and progressive course, some recover with little residual, and a third group have chronic symptoms. Whether deterioration is a biological feature of a specific subgroup, or the result of treatment failure or social isolation, (or all) is unknown. The effect of medication, especially chronic high doses, failure to improve cognitive symptoms, the impact of disability compensation, and socio-economic-status on level of social adaptation may all influence the course. The impact of hospitalization or institutionalization has decreased over the last two decades with inconsistent benefit. (62) Does treatment interfere with recovery of life function? A retrospective review of patients in Suffolk county NY showed a difference maintaining executive function, and loss of verbal and IQ that reflects intellectual experience. Memory problems were seen across diagnoses. There was a larger GAF decrease in schizophrenic diagnoses compared to others. Is this a "self fulfilling prophecy" or the effect of the core disability? Shanks identified two different courses, one of which was less severe, but he was unable to identify differential factors. (61) Poor outcomes observed may reflect poor access to treatment, poor engagement in ongoing care, poor treatment response, poor adherence, inherent cognitive deficits, substance use disorder, pre-existing developmental disorder, disabling side effects of medication, social factors and poverty. (Wow! A lot of variables to consider in studies.) Medications may have a biphasic impact on

recovery (see chapter eleven). (61) To make a meaningful statement about the optimal course of schizophrenic syndromes it is necessary to
  i) separate other first episode, and variant psychoses without core cognitive abnormalities,
  ii) institute effective treatments promptly, and discontinue unnecessary ones when not needed,
  iii) avoid institutionalization and optimize social setting for functional capacity,
  iv) avoid factors that encourage disability,
  v) create life expectations consistent with cognitive capacities and vi) provide training and therapy for them

No current treatment situation meets these goals, so specifying the "optimal course"(with appropriate treatment) is not possible. The actual course is often one of progressive disability and loss of function, but it is not clear whether this reflects the underlying disorder or failures in performing effective treatment.

Pathways through the temporal lobes provide the link between sensory data and motivational data. Often described in the psychological literature as "memory" or "declarative memory", the region stores spatial, context, verbal and social information. Total damage, as in pt H.M. impairs storage. Partial damage interferes with **significance**, the ability to interpret the adaptive significance of sensory data. The "schizophrenia syndrome" is a multi-etiology, multi symptom syndrome of impaired memory processing, attention, decision-making, social interaction, and other cognitive functions that involves this region. The core cognitive impairment is difficulty organizing sensory/external (especially reward linked) information, in different modes of memory storage. The syndrome has multiple etiologies, no specific gene loci or GWAS combinations, but multiple loci regulate the balance of cognitive operations in ways not currently understood. Not all persons with the cognitive impairment present with psychosis, so the emergence of psychosis is a separate process. The clinical presentation often emerges in adolescence when abstract cognitive ability does not develop, and evidence of cognitive impairment is observed (and may be prior to this age). The term "schizophrenia" should be subsumed under **temporal/hippocampal syndromes** with a list of symptoms related to dysfunction, identified etiologies, and the presenting patterns of the type. Specification of multiple cognitive impairments and other features are the symptom variations of different disturbances. No chemical treatments exist for correction of the cognitive deficit. D2 blockade reduces the arousal and related symptoms of the psychosis without appreciable benefit to the cognitive disturbance. (See chapter eleven) The role of glutamate and GABA synaptic intervention should be considered.

The prevalence of violence and attacks on (groups of) strangers has stimulated questions about violent behavior in mental health patients, specifically schizophrenia syndromes. (63) Little is known about the successful prediction of violent behavior. No evidence links violence to mental health or to one specific diagnosis. Using chemical control based on the fear of potential violence is "preventive detention", counter to effective recovery, which requires legal authorization. So many societal factors contribute to violence that focusing on the contribution of mental health patients is political scapegoating, with little benefit for services, or for protecting the society from violence.

CHAPTER FIVE:
Attention organizes mental activity

The attention pathway coordinates messages from the internal and external world including the immediate response to sensory stimuli and internal signals, the 24hour daily cycle. The focus of attention is influenced by other pathways and coordinated by the prefrontal basal-ganglia pathways (chapter six). Attention augments other pathway activity performing an **operating system** *function and produces the subjective experience of consciousness.*

Pathways located in the brain stem, with origins early in vertebrate evolution, coordinate the internal and external environment, both tonic and phasic aspects. The tonic process coordinates the sleep-waking diurnal (circadian) cycle, and the solar rotation seasonal cycle. Species choose the diurnal or the nocturnal pattern (humans sometimes violate this by doing both, and suffer the consequences). The seasonal cycle is created by the variation of the duration of the daily cycle, a result of the earth's asymmetric solar rotation, which produces seasonal changes in sexual activity, hibernation, and other functions. (1) The phasic process is attention, the immediate response to stimuli. The tonic and phasic components use overlapping pathways, which also regulate sleep cycles (its neural mechanisms, and clinical features including dreaming, are discussed at the end of the chapter). (2)

Responding to external stimuli is called "the orienting reflex", "awareness", or attention. (3) Sensory receptors transmit signals over pathways to receiving areas in the thalamus for most senses (not taste and smell), and pathways from thalamus to sensory reception areas of cortex (visual in the occipital lobe, auditory in the temporal, etc.). The attention pathway focuses on the most important current signal. Descartes' "cogito ergo sum" declared that the experience of attention/awareness was the significant brain activity until the 19th century, when observers "discovered" that other brain activity occurred outside of awareness. The discovery of the unconscious, a major 20th century event, was the "re-discovery" of ongoing brain activity sometimes inaccessible to awareness. (4) (5) (The "Unconscious" (capital) in Psychoanalysis is a different topic.) Attention is studied in human cognitive neuroscience using response tasks to sensory signals, and in animals by recording brain responses to stimuli. Posner and colleagues, working in the visual system, have proposed that attention involves three related processes: alerting, orienting, and executive function. (6) (7)(8) (13)

Alerting is the arousal state, the sensitivity to incoming stimuli that varies with the sleep/wake cycle, as when a loud noise that awakens from sleep changes arousal state. Classic neurophysiological research on the core of the ascending reticular activating system (which begins at the top of spinal cord and terminates in the diffuse nuclei of thalamus, ARAS) shows how it influences the response of cortex. (9) The extension of this pathway in the diffuse thalamic projection system (DTPS) activates the focus of attention- arousal. (10) Alertness is, in effect, the arousal state of this system for receiving external stimuli.

The *orienting response* to a specific stimulus maintains the focus of attention on that stimulus until habituation decreases the response. Two related processes a) response to changes in the stimulus field triggering the orienting reflex, and b) "locking on" for maintaining, are described by Posner et al. (13) Habituation (the decreasing response to sustained stimulus) uses a "stimulus model memory" that fades unless changes occur. (14) (In the visual system, visual cortex, the superior colliculi, frontal eye fields and temporal-parietal

> **SIDEBAR Neurophysiology of the ARAS.** In a series of classic neurophysiology studies in cats, the Italian neurophysiologists Marouzzi and Magoun showed that transections through the midbrain and posterior brain stem determine at which level "disconnection" would prevent the cortical electrical desynchronization response to electrical stimuli. They also examined the effects of injuries on the functioning of unanesthetized animal subjects. Sections through the midbrain that disconnected basic central core pathways resulted in a comatose state in the animal. It is clear that this "reticular arousal system", as they termed it, is essential for activating cortical response to external input and for maintaining cortical arousal activity. These results are confirmed in humans who have brain injuries to these pathways resulting in comatose states despite intact cortex. Anaesthesia, using chemicals to induce coma-like state, has been used for surgery since the late 19th century. A wide range of chemicals, both injected and inhaled, induce this state, but no current theory of how neural changes induce the state, and studies suggest that there is not one mechanism common to all procedures. (11) The *arousal* component of attention is sensitive to day-night and other tonic phase cycles. (12)

association areas combine to visually track the stimulus.) Crick and Koch called this the locking on response (15). Sokolov and Razran called it the orienting reflex, a systemic response to novel stimuli that includes pupil dilation, GSR changes, EEG de-synchronization, evoked potential (EP) response, etc. (16) The EP has been dissected into multiple components, and correlated with other psychophysiological data. (17) (18) A theory that integrates attention and memory to account for stimulus locking on was first proposed by Norman in 1968, and is associated with a hippocampal theta frequency rhythm linking to memory in hippocampus. (19) The attention process uses pathways between thalamus and cortex. Thalamic nuclei (neuron cell groups, right and left) are located on the ARAS and connect with it through DTPS pathways. Specific thalamic nuclei also have reciprocal pathways to sensory reception areas of cortex illustrated in Fig 5-1. The thalamic nuclei generally do not interact with each other, but create projection and relay loops to specific cortical regions. The integration and processing of data is done in cortex, but the recursive loops back to thalamus allow for more complex processing and sustained focus.

Attention organizes mental activity

Fig. 5.1 Thalamic projections to cortex

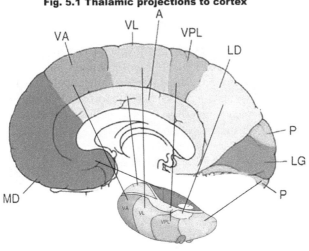

Medial view of cortex with non-anatomical placement of thalamus and it relation to cortical regions.

Control of the focus of attention, the third component, involves the prefrontal cortex executive control network, (of chapter six). The attention pathways can be directed by different inputs:

a) *Sensory/perceptual:* The more intense the sensory stimulus, the more likely to capture attention, especially sudden changes in stimulus values, loud, brief changes, etc. which are the opposite of habituation to a constant stimulus, (which depends on a frontal-parietal cortical pathway). (20)

b) *Other brain regions:* activation signals direct attention to messages of high emotional/ motivational value especially threat. (24) Pain somatic responses received in insula/cingulate cortex can rapidly direct focus of attention. (25) (The role of PTSD in redirecting attention is discussed in chapter eight.)

c) *Scanning the environment for stimuli linked to current needs or dangers.* Internal motivation states may direct the focus of attention seeking social interaction, or other needs. Thirst drives the attention system to seek stimuli indicating water. The fear network, if activated, seeks indications of danger in the

> **SIDEBAR Sensory deprivation** creates habituation of the total sensory field by reducing all sensory changes. Classic experiments, first done by Hebb et al in Montreal, placed subjects in an environment lacking sensory variation, and resulted in confusion, disorganization of mental state, and hallucinations. (21) In the absence of external stimuli and loss of external sensory control, internal stimuli dominate. A dynamic balance between external stimuli and internal control is needed for cognitive stability. Fisk and Maddi call this stimulus variation "novelty", critical to maintaining some level of activation. (22). A "default mode network" DMN of statistically correlated brain regions (see chapter three) are linked when the subject is not attending to external stimuli. Correlations of the DMN components are "decoupled" by the attention process. The relation of novelty to the DMN network has not been studied. The clinical situation of "sundowner syndrome" in the elderly occurs when sensory impaired individuals show cognitive deterioration in reduced sensory environments, and is important in eldercare settings. (23)

surrounding environment (as when walking in a dark place at night).

d) *Salience signaling.* A person who has been attacked at a certain location will have heightened sensory awareness at that location and somatic responses associated with the attack. These signals come from previously stored associations in the hippocampal *"significance"* system of chapter four. The ongoing balance between external stimuli and internal motivation is managed by attention. (26) The *salience network,* couples with data from motivation system to direct specific responses. Menon and Uddin identify the insula in switching, and build a model around "salience", involving frontal systems and motivation. (See chapter six)(27) (28)

e) *Intentional focus of attention*, e.g. "I will look at my computer screen". If focus is accompanied by subjective awareness, conscious intent is involved. All attention experiments use verbal instructions to intentionally direct the subject's focus to specific features. In everyday life, someone may choose to focus attention. Peterson and Posner extend their model, in the 2012 review, to include "self regulation", but do not discuss subjective awareness: "One might think of focal attention as the entry to the conscious state, which may involve widespread connections from the midline cortex and the anterior cingulate cortex (ACC)..." (Peterson, 29) For example, the Stroop procedure (29) requires the individual to focus attention to the color or text of the word by instruction. Choosing to attend to specific signals requires awareness, though the research subject may not always be "conscious" of doing so. Intent influences action when it changes the focus of attention. (29)

A computer simulation of human attention responses validates the Posner model. The model "simulates" human attention, but does not model the neural interactions of specific pathways. Multiple inputs influence the focus of attention, both "bottom up" and "top down" sources of control, described by Posner and Graziano. (34) For example, sensory input influences the focus "from below", and intention directs the attention pathway "from above" by other signals. In addition to responding to external stimuli, **attention performs the "operating system" function of augmenting activity in selected cortical regions (a computer system analogy originally suggested by Crick and Koch). (30) (31) Baars describes this facilitation as the "Global Workspace Model" with a metaphorical "attention spotlight".** (32) This does not explicitly depend on subjective awareness, but both the Crick and Koch, and Baar "workspace" models include "consciousness" as part of the control.

Consciousness, (i.e."awareness","subjective experience"), the meta experience of attention, is controversial. (For a philosophical overview see Blackmore, for a neuroscience review see Gazzaniga. (33)) Orienting ("locking on") to a stimulus is usually associated with subjective awareness, the ability to report the focus verbally, and influence the focusing. (31) Posner identified three meanings that capture the use of "consciousness": (a) the neurology of the state of mind allowing coherent orientation to time and place, (b) the selection of sensory or memory information for awareness, and (c) the voluntary control over overt responses. (34) A broader list of features might include:

C1) *neural pathway activity* consciousness/subjective awareness requires brain activity, and is lost with certain interruptions of cortical activity. (35) (53)

C2) *an information property of the attention network*, produced by the organization of pathways, not isolated elements. (This adds confusion to many discussions of "consciousness" when it is treated as a biological property, instead of an information property.)

C3) a *network property organized by experience* (Edelman and Koch) Links over thalamic pathways have a genetic, evolutionary basis but connections in the individual are built by experience. Edelman calls this "Neural Darwinism", enhancing synaptic interactions to assemble "cell assembly pathways" by external (and internal) activity/rewards. His measure of "dynamic complexity" assesses the organism's (genetic) capacity for consciousness, a graduated capacity that increases to primates. (36) Tononi has extended the concept to Phi, measuring integrated information across all pathways, as yet unproven.(Tononi, 36)

SIDEBAR Specific thalamic pathways produce the relationship of attention and consciousness. The Posner model of attention combines primary sensory pathways with thalamic-cortex recursive loop pathways which "lock on" focus of attention and subjective awareness (also the basis of the Crick and Koch model): "linking together of sensory or other properties of these stimuli in order to achieve awareness recognition of the object." The sensory thalamic nuclei receive external sensory data and project it to specific regions of cortex. (See fig.) *The intralaminar nuclei (DTPS) and Dorsal Median nucleus have diffuse pathway interactions throughout cortex augmenting local activity.* Activation of cortical regions by diffuse thalamic pathways (DTPS) augments attention, supported in animal studies, and "locking on". A dramatic increase in research in the last five years on these thalamic regions confirms these bidirectional recursive interactions. (37) These interactions provide the wider cortical activation needed for awareness.

C4) *adds subjective awareness to attention*. Attending is usually associated with *subjective awareness*. (38) The experience of *consciousness* is the combination of an attention focus combined with activation of DLPFC working memory, linked to that focus.

SIDEBAR Working memory and awareness. Baddeley and Cowan were the first to propose that "working memory" was related to subjective awareness, which is the memory process of "keeping something in mind" for a limited time interval. Baar, Cowan, and others propose that "subjective awareness" requires *activating the "working memory" region of DLPFC along with another focus.* (39) (40) (41) DLPFC has extensive interconnections with other regions supporting this function, and is related to pre-frontal control networks that direct attention. (41) The DLPFC working memory region is connected to Dorsal Median thalamus by recursive feedback loops. (39)(40) Most brain activity is not in awareness at any moment, and Posner, et al; propose that the relationship of attention to conscious awareness depends on the relationship of the DTPS and dorsal median nucleus of thalamus. (41) (34) When the attention process activates a region of cortex along with pathways of DLPFC (working memory), by using thalamic linkage, conscious awareness is experienced. This awareness may involve verbal pathways without overt verbal behavior, or non-verbal activation, i.e. "intuition". (42) The time "decay" of working memory, and frequent change of attention are also typical features of subjective awareness/consciousness. There is no *subjective awareness* of nothing: *working memory (DLPFC)* "points" to the current active focus of attention. (42)(A recent review by Silvanto et al proposes that "consciousness" component is a separate representation in working memory and there might be other "representations" without specifying them.) (43) (41)

C5) the "higher order" recursive, level of attention. Awareness of a specific item, integrates information across multiple brain areas into a "representation". Conscious attention integrates information over the brain-wide "global workspace". The "attention schema theory" posits the specific pathway that produces the "attention schema" which allows the attention process itself to be the focus. (Graziano, 34)

C6) Self consciousness is another feature of human attention. Being aware of self focuses attention on pathways of *self/insular cortex*. Damasio and others identify the insula as the region for the storage of "self experience" and his theory of "consciousness" is based on awareness of insular cortex activity: consciousness is always "**self-consciousness**". (44)

SIDEBAR *Self* is a developmental acquisition, so Damasio's view of "consciousness" is based on emotion, other body states, and behavior, requiring a significant learned component, and differentiation from "other". (44) Varela also has a theory about the internal representation of self-action, "embodiment", as the organizing property of consciousness. He studied mental visualization on motor performance, a common technique in athletic training. (45) Humans are aware of the attention process, which Baddeley calls an "emergent property", (39) and Graziano calls the "*attention schema*". *(34)* Edelman's network property assumes that many mammalian species have attention, with some "awareness", but only smaller groups have the capacity for separate awareness of self, e.g."theory of mind".

C7) Subjective awareness can influence choice of attention and action. The significance of consciousness/subjective awareness is its role in 'top down control'. Subjective awareness can change focus of attention to (intentionally) modify behavior. This is **agency,** choosing behavior for selected goals, not determined by pre-programmed patterns or specific external demands. The capacity for making choices not entirely determined by genetic or social programming is "free will". (47) Libet claimed to show experimentally that awareness associated with decision-making did not influence it, but this was the result of the limited task. From an evolutionary perspective, it is doubtful that this elaborate process developed with no contribution to survival. The information approach suggests that the pathways allow "top down" selection of various behaviors (see chapter six), and produce the *"subjective experience"* that influences choice. Not all choices require conscious attention. (It is always puzzling when biologists decide that something with a long evolutionary history has no importance for survival.)

The evolutionary significance of the attention system is the ability to use the dynamic focus of attention to synchronize internal demands with the external environment. "the ability to voluntarily focus awareness provides an additional adaptive tool for the organism for learning new habits attending to critical aspects of the environment and certain other practical applications."(Crick and Koch) Agency is programmed into pathways by social interaction.

SIDEBAR Debates about consciousness. Debates about consciousness involve both the process of *subjective awareness/consciousness* and its potential for guiding *agency/intentional choice*. i) The "uniqueness of subjective experience", that every person's experience of "red", or "hot" or whatever, is different from everyone else's: qualia. Philosophical riddles like "What is it like to be a bat?" resolve to "What is it like to be anyone but yourself?" Each human experience is unique and no one else has direct access except by external presentation (the "beetle in the box" of Wittgenstein). The unique content of each person's conscious experience is the result of its individual programming by experience. Every person's conscious experience is unique, but the processes producing conscious experience do not depend on the stored experiences. *Qualia describe the content of experience, not the process*. Most computers have different content depending on the user, but very similar information operations. (See discussion in the Appendix chapter one). ii) The concept of "zombie", a fully functioning information system without conscious awareness, is contrasted with humans who have both. A human zombie is conceivable if a critical region of brain does not develop. Inability to maintain "working memory" is a typical problem with aging. In early dementia, the continuity of self is lost, and only prior information available. Does this make some elders and victims of dementia "partial zombies"? (46) The addition of subjective awareness makes human focus different, but might be simulated in AI systems. (See later) Whether consciousness allows the individual to have an active role is the **Libet challenge**: A series of experiments by Benjamin Libet at the University of California claim to refute the control by conscious intent. In his study, individuals in a stimulus choice showed brain signal changes indicating the choice before the individual had conscious awareness of intention to choose. Libet was able to predict subject's choice, use the indicator, before the subject. So he interpreted the subjective sense as an epiphenomenon that does not determine choice. The studies were done on subjects giving rapid motor responses to stimuli, with no time for deliberation. In such situations, the awareness of choice often comes after it is made. Do such tasks generalize to situations in which the subject deliberates among a series of alternatives? Scanning chess board for the appropriate move is more like a social situation that requires choosing an appropriate response to a complex situation. Libet's experiments do not reject the possibility of agency in other situations. (48)

Gazzaniga, in ***Who's in Charge: Free Will and the Science of the Brain,*** sees "choice" as a property emerging from the interaction of brain and social system, a view similar to Siegel's *social neurobiology*, (49) and Bandura's *self efficacy*. (50) The individual chooses among adaptive responses to the environment, conscious of some choices, but not others. *Consciousness* augments the ability to develop new choices. It guides training of skilled performance of athletes, artists, musicians, and martial artists, using consciously designed sequences to learn complex visual-motor patterns (that eventually become "subconscious" and automatic). (51) Subjective attention provides the capacity for sequencing activity according to priorities, and selecting new responses to challenging situations. Choosing to make adaptive choices and modifying them when they are no longer adaptive is the basis of mental health. Symptoms of all mental illnesses involve the failure to adaptively modify feelings or actions. It provides a tool for social remediation using psychotherapy (see chapter twelve).

The attention pathway can be altered or disrupted many ways. Examples of impaired attention including coma, anaesthesia, delirium, dementia and psychosis. The first four are usually associated with biological etiologies altering attention system pathways, and often seen first in medical or ER settings, though Psychiatrists are evaluating dementia more frequently in older patients as the population ages. (53) The key characteristic of mental illness is the patient's loss of *agency*. Pathways that are "stuck" are unable to change the focus of attention as needed. The fundamental task of mental health interventions is enabling the patient/client to become "unstuck" and recover *agency*.

Psychosis is the disturbance of the attention system most often seen by mental health providers. It may have a biological etiology or be produced by other pathway disturbances of the motivation system (mania) and significance/memory system (schizophrenias). The evidence for a separate psychosis syndrome includes: i) psychosis syndrome fMRI connectivity in DLPFC is altered in all psychotic states regardless of etiology. (54) ii) The capacity to shift to psychotic mechanisms is personal, some never have this syndrome while others are more susceptible to psychosis from drug use, or other etiologies. Family members of patients with psychosis syndrome may never become psychotic despite similar features in other brain pathways, the difference being the vulnerability to psychosis. This is an issue in studies of "prodromal" patterns which may not progress to psychosis (55) iii) GWAS studies show overlap between schizophrenia and bipolar groups (and other psychoses when included) suggesting a genetic vulnerability for the psychotic syndrome, not the overlap of the core syndromes. (The alternate interpretation, that the two syndromes are a "continuum" is summarized in the Mueller paper, a conclusion rejected here and by others.) Perkins et al used a PRS method of overlapping these genes to modestly predict future psychotic episodes regardless of other diagnosis. Further studies with other psychoses may help pinpoint the overlapping genetic loci. (56) (Kelleher and Cannon have put an alternative spin on this idea proposing that psychosis should be associated with *every* diagnostic category, which amounts to considering psychosis as a separate feature. (Kelleher, 57)) Psychosis separate from etiology uses the diagnostic category *psychosis, unspecified*. (58) The course of psychosis is variable, and may resolve without long-term disability. A useful account of organic psychosis, the myriad symptoms that result, and the difficult process of "putting yourself back together" (a task for all post psychotic patients) is found in the memoir by Susannah Cahalan. (59)

Psychosis is the clinical manifestation of altered attention pathways. The symptoms include a) heightened sensory arousal response with reduced stimulus barrier, b) increased arousal which does not progress to seizure activity, c) changes in interpretation of perceptual information, including hallucinations, and incorrect cognitive explanations, and d) increased anxiety. The symptom patterns may varying with etiology, but these are the most consistent. Sensory input goes through thalamic relay nuclei to cortical sensory regions, and a component goes through the DTPS and DM driving the thalamic locking on process. The sensory system also uses memory information from hippocampus/DLPFC. Motivation system pathways enter prefrontal regions through OFC regions, (with separate pathways through the thalamus connecting to cingulate cortex, and insula, the "salience network"). These message streams converge on prefrontal regions at DLPFC. Psychosis syndrome can be produced by changes in either pathway. Changes in primary sensory/perceptual pathways create errors in perception, experienced as confusion and anxiety, with maladaptive responses to the outside environment, e.g. when LSD ingestion or other "psychotogenic" substances trigger anxiety ("bad LSD trip"). Excessive motivation system activation is seen in mania, stimulant drugs, sleep deprivation, and other arousal states, producing excess activation over the OFC pathways. The incorrect assessment of sensory data temporal pathway dysfunction (chapter four) produces psychosis with gradual deterioration of adaptation and secondary confusion and anxiety (the schizophrenias). (61) Stahl also recognizes three pathways: the "dopamine pathway" is his version of the motivation system pathway, the "NMDA pathway" is associated with the ARAS and sensory/thalamus, and the third, "serotonin pathway", is based on the effects of LSD. He is less clear about the hippocampal pathway. (62) The DLPFC is the key region of convergence because it links pathway information with the focus of attention. It connects with other pre-frontal regions, with basal ganglia, with distal regions of cortex, and with hippocampus and other temporal lobe pathways, and dorsal median nuclei of thalamus. Sleep disturbances can alter attention pathways, and the psychosis syndrome alters sleep functions, showing the reciprocal relationship of the overlapping pathways. (63) Increased dopamine is likely to be an important factor, but whether this is prodromal or secondary to the anxiety/arousal is unclear. (64)

The psychosis syndrome may develop slowly or rapidly depending on the etiology. Toxic chemicals, and infectious or inflammatory processes produce rapid changes, while impaired response to social situations may develop over months to years. (This footnote summarizes the range of etiologies, associated with varied clinical syndromes of psychosis:(65)) The prodromal interval, described by Bowers in **Retreat From Sanity,** is often seen in the first episode. (66) The new diagnoses, attenuated psychosis syndrome and prodromal psychosis, identify psychosis syndrome as a specific entity, but currently have limited use. (67) The important role of anxiety in the syndrome suggests that amygdala activation must play a role, different from its role in general anxiety, which has not been clearly documented. (62) (68) Psychosis is a syndrome of disorganized information processing, so recovery must re-establish functional processing. Bowers notes that delusions and hallucinations often recur intermittently in some patients, suggesting that an alternate psychosis organization remains after psychotic pathways have been established, to which the individual may "return" in response to stress, as an extreme coping mechanism. Although clinicians often note that patients who have previously been psychotic and become psychotic again report similar hallucinations and delusions, there is little research on the significance of this phenomenon.

Is psychosis ever adaptive? The control system that regulates arousal and attention also risks excessive arousal and disorganization. *"Psychosis is a disturbance of brain information processing with dramatic changes in cortical activity, heightened arousal and disorganization that can disrupt previous habit patterns."* (70) This description suggests a potential evolutionary adaptive function. The English Psychiatrist RD Laing, in his essay "Journey to Metanoia", proposed that the psychotic process is a method for reorganizing brain patterns when the individual's life is no longer adaptive, and put his theory into practice at a treatment center in which residents decompensated and reconstituted new lives without using medication. No outcomes were reported and the center was closed after a few years. A similar program was started by Mosher at NIMH under a special grant, and terminated without conclusive results. (71) Treatment of psychosis without medication was the only option for centuries. The wealthiest were treated in select institutions, and some recovered functional lives. This is similar to using rituals as treatments in other cultures. (72) Leary, and others proposed "LSD as therapy" in the 1960s, claiming temporary mental disorganization could open the self to new avenues of creative and adaptive functioning in a society broken and dysfunctional, but no formal process of re-organization was provided, and the chemicals were outlawed. (73) A return of interest in this method suggests that its previous restrictions were not based on adequate scientific evaluation. (74) (See chapter 11 for more detail). C.G.Jung provides a dramatic report of living through a psychotic state in his memoirs. (75)

> **CLINICAL EXAMPLE Jung's Psychosis.** *C G Jung has written the striking account of a period of psychotic disorganization in his life, during which he was able to maintain some level of function, and from which he recovered, to continue his career. This is one of a few personal accounts reported by a psychiatrist or other mental health professional. Jung was involved in an intimate relationship with a patient, Sabrina Spielrein, and had intense anxiety about the situation, which led to the end of his mentorship with Freud. In his account, Jung describes a series of troubling dreams, that he decided were not related to earlier life experiences (as a Freudian interpretation would have proposed) but to "archetypes" from some deeper unconscious, which Jung presumed was genetic. These created anxiety: "I was frequently so wrought up that I had to do certain yoga exercises in order to hold my emotions in check" p177 "I was afraid of losing command of myself and becoming prey to the fantasies—and as a psychiatrist I realized only too well what that meant....I plunged down into dark depths..."p179 He describes hallucinations which he associates with a "psychopathic woman patient who has a strong transference to me". He mastered these symptoms: "I learned to distinguish between myself and the interruption. When something emotionally vulgar or banal came up, I would say to myself, "It is perfectly true that I have thought and felt this way at some time or other, but I don't have to think that way now."... "The essential thing is to differentiate oneself from these unconscious contents by personifying them, and at the same time to bring them into relationship with consciousness. That is the technique for stripping them of their power."p187 Jung's ability to recount his episode and his management of it is valuable for the insight into the struggles of someone going through such an experience, and the potential for using cognitive techniques in recovery. (75)*

Psychosis is a disturbance in information processing in which the brain "arousal systems" interact, become disorganized, and interfere with adaptation; and may also provide an opportunity for change. Current efforts to define and intervene in "early psychosis" syndromes might enhance adaptive potential if early changes could be reliably identified, and new interventions developed. (76) The accuracy of prediction is better than chance, suggesting that syndrome vulnerability can be determined, but not using any current prodromal research protocol. (78) Psychosis has many etiologies, so it is necessary to understand both the process and the etiology to design an effective intervention. Many "risk predictors" are specific to schizophrenia, and not relevant to other psychoses. (77) Caution is needed to avoid premature use of medications, which have not been shown effective in prodromal states.

The **disconnection syndromes** of neurology include loss of subjective awareness the effects of local pathology, tumors, strokes, etc. interfering with awareness of regions. The example of hemi-spatial neglect, a Neurologic condition that occurs with damage to parts of the non-dominant hemisphere, producing "inattention" to visual, auditory, somatic, or multiple sensory fields in patients has not defined a specific location for the effect. This is a disconnection between the local damage and the attention pathways that produce subjective awareness. (79) The Neurological emphasis on local regions does not consider the pathway, though Geschwind's later work extended the focus beyond local regions, but not to the attention system. (80) The "disconnection syndrome" associated with surgical disconnection of corpus callosum produces the loss of subjective awareness of the other side, but Gazzaniga doesn't relate this to disconnection of thalamic pathways. (81) **Dissociation** is a symptom associated with the attention process, seen in PTSD, borderline syndrome, and dissociative disorders in which access to memory is altered in these syndromes (discussed in chapters seven and eight).

A better understanding of the attention process suggests new treatment options like ***meditation***. A history of meditation in American culture can be found at (82). The techniques of both traditional Eastern and contemporary Western traditions use focusing attention on the sensations of breathing (or other focus). (See chapter twelve)

Meditation, Breathing, And The Diving Reflex. Nixon's review of neural mechanisms emphasizes the thalamic-cortical interactions that are most easily observed in fMRI studies. But all the traditions emphasize focus of attention on the breath as the initial training method, and crucial to the process. The human (mammalian) ability to control breathing voluntarily, while also regulated by PO2

SIDEBAR Can focus of attention help manage and prevent disorganization?
Does practicing focused subjective awareness train the brain to focus more effectively? Eastern cultural traditions suggest that training in meditative states can enhance regulatory control of brain and body functions with observable consequences:
a) Maintaining one's focus of attention enhances with practice.
b) The arousal system can control autonomic and other emotional and motivational arousal states. In Buddhist tradition, training is also associated with improved management of emotional arousal and the power to modulate and reduce these states in meditators after long practice. (82) A most dramatic example of this control was demonstrated during the Vietnamese war, when Vietnamese Buddhist Monks poured gasoline on themselves and self-immolated. The ability to make the decision to suicide is in the realm of ordinary human understanding, but the ability to maintain a focused meditative posture while one is burning up in flames clearly suggests a level of control over motivational variables not available to most persons in ordinary states of mind. These demonstrations greatly impressed Western appreciation of the potential for managing the state of awareness. (83)
c) Wallace et al, using the TM method, studied meditation as a "4th state of consciousness": i) the awake state, ii) the deep sleeping state, iii) the dream {REM} state, and iv) meditation, based on the EEG, and peripheral autonomic variables. Meditation has properties of deep stage 4 sleep but not the EEG findings. (84)
d) Meditation is "agency" in its purest form: learning to manage the focus of attention itself. Nixon, a neurologist and Zen meditator, has carried out an ongoing review of research in the neural pathways of meditative processes in a series of texts. (85) His conceptual model, based on fMRI and anatomical data, emphasizes the role of DTPS and the n. centrum median of thalamus, corresponding to the role emphasized by neuroscientists studying "consciousness". Kabat-Zinn and colleagues have developed an approach to using meditation for therapeutic goals of emotional management and pain amelioration (see chapter twelve). (86)

and PCO2 levels in the blood receptors in pons, indicates a pathway from pre-frontal cortex to respiratory controls that can override the pO2 controls. Whales and dolphins, mammals returned to the sea, have enhanced ability to use this control, but the ability to control breathing under water is possible for all mammals within certain limits. The combination of control of breathing, reduced heart rate and reduced external blood flow are a reaction to immersion, the "diving reflex", adapted by sea-going mammals for diving and hunting underwater, and by humans for recreation and also fishing in some cultures. The technique of focused breath meditation probably accesses the same control pathways of respiration in the "diving reflex". *The diving reflex has been studied in "free divers" but has not been linked with studies on meditative states. Perhaps a profound regulation of body states is possible with training. (87)*

The Western tradition most closely resembling meditation is *hypnosis*. Hypnosis is a two-person experience: a "hypnotist" induces changes in the "hypnotic subject". Initially explored in mental health by Janet (and Freud), it was perceived for many years as a parlor "magic trick", and became a research focus in the 1960s, when studied by Hilgard, and Shor and Orne, and recent research reviewed by Jensen. (89) Spiegel, father and son, have studied and written extensively on clinical use. (88) Milton Erickson, a psychiatrist practicing in the 1970s, became famous for his ability to use hypnotic techniques therapeutically. (Discussion of his methods is in chapter twelve.) The studies support several statements:

a) Individual susceptibility to hypnosis can be measured as a quantifiable variable and has a relatively normal (bell shaped) distribution when measured in a young adult population. b) The techniques used for inducing and measuring this state use suggestions of conflicting sensory focus that reorganize the focus of attention. c) In the "altered attention state" of hypnosis, persons can be motivated to perform a variety of tasks, which do not differ significantly from "simulating subjects". d) Perceptual distortions can be induced in hypnotized subjects that are not replicated by persons "simulating" trance. e) Subjects vary in the intensity of their experience of the "altered attention state" (trance), and those with an intense state can be trained to alter significant bodily responses in ways similar to meditators. Hypnosis is a method for facilitating a person's access to managing attention, mediated by another trained person. In meditation, the person must learn to modify the attention process by continued practice, in hypnosis, "induction" can teach the person to modify attention more quickly.

Biofeedback is another method for managing awareness. (90) The subject is given sensory feedback, auditory or visual or both, about a somatic variable and instructed to use the feedback to regulate the value of the somatic variable. The subject may be given frequency feedback from EEG leads in the scalp, and directed to use the feedback to modify the frequencies generated by the brain. The attention process is linked directly back to brain activity providing the opportunity for potentially interesting interventions.

SLEEP CYCLES ARE THE TONIC REGULATION OF AROUSAL.

The sleep cycle occurs throughout the vertebrate phyla (and may be found in some invertebrates). It has both internal controls, and synchronization to an external light source. The cycle of sleep and activity is the most basic element of adaptation. Sleep symptoms are observed as mental health symptoms, have a separate group of dysfunctions and related symptoms, and are sometimes explored in information based therapies for their content (see chapter twelve). Excellent reviews of the process, and its evolutionary development, describe the following features: (91) A) 90 minute cycles of activation and inactivation of cortex occur during the stages of sleep (and less prominent cycles occur during waking hours), defined by variations in EEG frequency, eye movements, and physiological measurements. B) Four stages of sleep: Stage 1, 2, 3, and REM (rapid eye movement) are defined by EEG frequencies and other indicators. Slower EEG frequencies indicate deeper stages. Stage 1 is the closest to being awake. Stage 3 is the deepest and least responsive. The frequency shows the relative synchronization of groups of neurons firing together, not the absolute level of activity, which is different in different stages. At no time is cortical activity completely inactive. During stages N1 and N2 and, N3, slow-wave sleep (SWS), heart rate, breathing, and blood pressure decrease, muscles relax (slightly), and the restorative functions of sleep occur. C) The sleep cycle has gradual slowing of the cortical EEG frequencies until the person arrives at (SWS) stage 3 sleep, and remains in this state for some time, before rapidly shifting to high frequency cortical EEG activity (REM) state for a period of 3 to 5 minutes of "emergent" sleep. D) During REM there is suppression of muscle activity, increased autonomic signs of arousal, and rapid eye movements, and increased reporting of vivid cognitive dream activity if the person is awakened during this stage. Response to external stimuli is attenuated in REM stage, even though cortical EEG activity appears awake. (Velluti, 92) (REM is also seen in other mammals: cats and dogs in REM are flaccid with paws twitching. Large muscle group inhibition prevents body posture and movement, but fine motor activity persists.) E) Sleep follows a pattern of alternating rapid eye movement (REM), and non-REM (NREM) sleep throughout the night in a cycle that repeats itself roughly 90 minutes. Sleep requirements vary from person to person and throughout the life cycle. During development, children spend more time in the deeper stages of sleep compared with older adults.

F) The two factor model of sleep regulation includes <u>process C</u> (circadian), an endogenous "clock" that drives the rhythm of the sleep-wake cycle, by the "circadian pacemaker" with oscillators in suprachiasmatic nucleus (SCN) and regions linked to energy metabolism (observed in SCN-lesioned arrhythmic animals, as well as in human subjects during internal de-synchronization). Orexin, a neuropeptide is a wakefulness maintaining neurotransmitter, also involved in regulating eating behavior, creating a complex relationship between sleep neuropeptides, and eating patterns, which sometimes vary by gender. And <u>process S</u> "sleep propensity" is related to the recent amount of sleep and wakefulness, a "fatigue factor". The SCN interacts with both processes. Melatonin secreted in response to darkness travels to SCN linking the control to the external light. Melatonin has two effects on the sleep-wake cycle, it entrains and shifts the circadian rhythm (process C) in a "chronobiotic" function, and promotes sleep onset by increasing the homeostatic drive to sleep (process S). These effects appear to be equal. (93)(94)

G) Exogenous melatonin given in the morning delays the phase of circadian rhythm and subsequent evening sleepiness. Melatonin given in the evening can advance both of these phases. Excitatory signals from the SCN and subsequent melatonin suppression are thought to promote wakefulness during the day in response to light and the suppression of melatonin inhibition of the SCN. This inhibition is released in the dark phase and leads to melatonin synthesis/release with consequent sleep promotion. (94) Recordings from the suprachiasmatic nuclei (SCN) suggest that S and C interact continuously. The model supported the development of novel non-pharmacological treatment paradigms in psychiatry, based on manipulating circadian phase, sleep and light exposure.

H) Many exogenous and endogenous factors (called zeitgebers) can shift a circadian rhythm. The sleep-wake cycle becomes entrained to the 24-hour solar day by these factors, and by far the most powerful is ocular light exposure. Performing activities at different day/night periods leads to 24 hr. cycle disturbances, Jet lag, and in the blind Non-24 disorder. (95) (The pharmacokinetics and pharmacodynamics of exogenous melatonin (high first-pass metabolism, short half-life, and weak MT1/MT2 receptor binding) may lead to the inconsistent effects.)

I) Sleep pathway changes are associated with a range of clinical symptoms. Narcolepsy is a disorder of this regulatory system. A common form of Narcolepsy is due to degeneration of orexin cells and reduction in release. (96) Infection that invades the tegmental region and impacts the orexin system more severely can lead to intermittent somnolence, or coma. A variety of genetic and other etiologies give rise to disturbances in the locus coeruleus pontine pathways producing problems with the control of stages and arousal, including sleepwalking, night terrors, sleep paralysis, etc. (97) The sleep controls are embedded in the tegmental motivation pathways, producing associated disturbances including depression with neurovegetative signs, mania, and insomnia of severe anxiety. Problems are experienced when persons disrupt synchronization with time zones, i.e. "jet lag", or shift workers who change day to night shifts, etc. Frequent changes in sleep synchronization create risks for secondary disease manifestations including increased oxidative stress and inflammation, type 2 DM, higher cardiovascular risk and triggering of mood disorders.

CLINICAL EXAMPLE POLICE CHIEF WITH TUMOR. *A police chief in a small rural city in the Midwest was operated on for a pituitary tumor of cortisol releasing hormone cells. The neurosurgeon reviewed his records and discovered three other cases, all his procedures of this type, involved law enforcement personnel.* COMMENT *This is one of several jobs in which frequent uncontrollable changes in the 24-hour cycle occur on a random basis. It suggests that such changes, which are known to produce elevated cortisol levels, can result in chronic changes in secretion and in some instances tumors.*

A rare disorder of disturbance in sleep and sexuality is the **Klein Levin syndrome**, which presents the combination of hypersomnia, hyperphagia, and in some cases hypersexual motivation, when awake. Most are teenage males, and this rare disorder of unknown etiology appears to involve dysregulation of motivation pathways associated with hypothalamic changes of puberty. (98) The etiologies that modify sleep cycle control include both biological and experiential events, producing disturbances in sleep cycle coordination, and motivation. (99)

J) Hibernation is a complex synchronization of these regulatory functions: light cycles, external temperature, sleep cycle length, metabolic activity, and energy metabolism, to produce an adaptive pattern! A human clinical syndrome, seasonal mood disorder **(SAD)**, suggests that a residual of this linkage persists.

Dreams are reports of subjective recall on awakening, and occur most consistently when awakening from REM (but also when awakened from other stages). Cortical operations continue during sleep but "subjective awareness" and associated memory consolidation often do not occur. The cognitive activity of dream experience occurs without significant external sensory input, and is derived from memory traces. REM stages of sleep are a recurring feature of the normal sleep process, but do not determine the cognitive content, and do not always result in awakening and the ability to recall content. (100) The PSA view that these are related to "unfulfilled wishes" is one of many ways of contextualizing dream activity in different cultures. (The use of dream states as part of treatment is discussed in chapter twelve.)

SIDEBAR In "Lucid dreaming" a person is able to experience the subjective awareness of being in a dream state; aware the experience is a dream. This is an infrequent aspect of dreaming for most people, but can be enhanced by training. Some people can be trained to lucid dream more often. This might provide significant opportunity for learning new coping skills. In a unique experiment, La Berge showed that subjects in the lucid dream state could be trained to signal this by controlling eye movements. This demonstrates that 1) intention can direct actions in lucid dreams, and 2) intention can occur in a state it was not presumed to be present, suggesting intention is an independently controllable factor. (101)

The overlap of sleep cycle and attention pathways creates symptoms of interaction between the two systems. Many mental health dysfunctions are associated with changes of regulation of the sleep cycle, a common "neuro-vegetative sign" in mood disorders. The following presentation is one example of *narcolepsy*.

***CLINICAL EXAMPLE Not really ADHD**. A physician in training was evaluated for continuation of medications. The patient was treated by another physician with Adderall and wished to change doctors for reasons of insurance. There was no childhood history of ADHD, no family history, any use, or need, for medication for school in childhood, as she had performed well in academics. Problems in focusing began in late teens and the person began taking Adderall for difficulty concentrating. According to the history this was at the time that a sister died of an infections illness (encephalitis?). Records were not obtainable from the previous physician. The prescription was filled for a limited period, with the intention of reducing the dose over time, and no increase was needed, but any effort at decrease over the next several months resulted in reduced function. COMMENT the patient showed consistency of use, no indications of need for increase or signs of stimulant intoxication. With closer details of history, the problem was not "decreased concentration" but "excessive sleepiness" to the point of falling asleep at work without the medication. This was Narcolepsy, in mild form, responsive to stimulants, which was misdiagnosed as "adult ADHD". There was no indication of obstructive airway problem or nighttime interference with sleep. Narcolepsy has variable etiologies but an infectious encephalitic form is recognized and may have been fatal to sister.*

CHAPTER SIX:
Choice in behavior and thought

The prefrontal pathways, along with the attention pathways, combine data coming from other pathways to select actions. The multiple variations in human behavior are organized and stored in basal ganglia loops, which are activated by the prefrontal system. All the data messages of the first four chapters are coordinated by the attention system and integrated by prefrontal pathways to select behaviors that manifest personality, childhood patterns of behavior, and specific patterns of dysfunction of basal ganglia networks.

Some part of the brain must be "in charge" of what happens and what output the brain produces, the behavior. Executive functions are the interaction of attention and pre-frontal pathways. The attention system (chapter five) directs focus from one region to another, performing the "operating system" functions of a computer. The attention pathways direct the focus of attention to use the pathways in this chapter. The two systems are closely linked, which makes defining the separate functions for each region inaccurate. The executive tasks of the (combined) region are selecting a specific behavior "option", organizing, storing, and activating specific patterns to use for performing the behavior. The final "execution phase" combining pathways of primary and accessory motor cortex, thalamic relays to cerebellum, and spinal motor neurons in a complex motor system is not discussed here, because problems are usually addressed by Neurologists. (1) (2) Specific symptoms of basal ganglia that are important in mental health are described in a later section. The model has both "top down" control for selection of the specific "action", and organization "from below" that creates and stores the behavior options. Malfunction in either system interferes with adaptive behavior. As with other brain regions, the organization is developmental, more complex patterns are learned with experience. (3)

The "pre-frontal cortex" lies anterior to the "motor cortex" (in front of the central sulcus). The sub-regions are named by their spatial location to each other and skull landmarks, and differentiated by anatomical pathways and cellular structure (see Brodmann regions diagram chapter one). (4) It is easier to visualize the spatial relationships by opening the frontal cortex onto a two-dimensional plane showing the regions: Dorsal Lateral Prefrontal Cortex (DLPFC), (Dorso)medial Prefrontal cortex, Anterior (and posterior) Cingulate Cortex (ACC), Orbito-Frontal Cortex (OFC), and Insula. Fig 6-1. The gray area is the pre-frontal "executive" region.

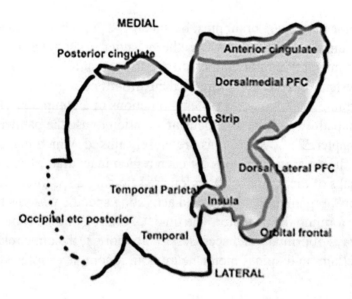

Fig. 6.1. Expanded view of prefrontal cortex showing the relative relationship of diffferent regions. Shaded area in chapter six. (Based on calculations of previous image Fig 1.3)

The organization of behavior is produced by the subcortical nuclei of basal ganglia that have direct connections to the prefrontal region. Axons from the prefrontal regions have connection to basal ganglia regions, and the basal ganglia nuclei interconnect (see below) and send data back to cortex in loops through thalamus. There are the same local/distal interactions between neighboring regions and distal axon pathways from distant regions as other regions of cortex. No simple schematic diagram shows this complex network. DLPFC has input from most other regions of cortex, a "projection map" of the cortex. (5)

The following description of decision-making includes the major pathways, but simplifies the complex process. The functions of each region have been studied using anatomical mapping, human pathology/injury, human fMRI, and inference from animal microelectrode recordings, (see references at (6)).

Step #1) The message about motivation state is sent over pathways through orbitofrontal cortex (OFC): "This is the current motivational state, this is what is needed now", and a related message, based on historical reward data: "This is the history of reward in this environment."

The orbital frontal cortex (OFC) receives sensory input including direct input from olfactory sources (the main target of primary olfactory cortex, and taste receptors), reciprocally connects to insular cortex (*self* data), Para hippocampal regions and the hippocampus, and the amygdala. All sensory modalities are represented in the orbitofrontal cortex particularly somatosensory areas associated with innervation of the hand and trigeminal complex, indicating the importance of face and hand sensation, two regions with strong reward potential, and visual input, i.e. proximal and distal sensory input. These inputs provide data on the available rewards including social rewards. (7) The close proximity of mPFC to OFC probably indicates an overlap of function of the two regions. mPFC may be the location where prefrontal data converge and then are "stored" in hippocampal pathways for future use. Social data, especially negative inhibitory data, seems to transmit via mPFC. (8)

SIDEBAR Gage Injury. Human injury of OFC includes the famous injury of Phineas Gage (9) an engineer with an accidental injury to this region, who did not suffer major impairment, but had more subtle changes that prevented him from continuing his career. In the 1950s, the psycho-surgical process of "frontal lobotomy", developed by Neurologist Muniz, was endorsed by Psychiatry as a "cure" for a variety of mental disturbances. Subsequent observation of results indicated that patients were less violent, but unmotivated, and managed ADL poorly. The result was "loss of personality", reduced motivation, release of impulsive behavior, and insensitivity to others showing problems of social rewards.

The reward value of the current sensory field comes through OFC: "This stimulus gave positive/negative reward in the past". Neural units in OFC respond to a wide range of external reward parameters. The OFC is reciprocally connected to hippocampal memory (significance) pathways, and through the mediodorsal nucleus of the thalamus to nucleus accumbens – the major integration of reinforcement and reward information. Many studies of OFC use fMRI activation in humans performing tasks that involve cognitive estimates of reward. This results in abstract descriptions for OFC like "look up table for rewards" and "maintenance of set". The *Iowa gambling task* shows that damage to OFC interferes with assessing changes in reward. (but see footnote) OFC responds to "reversal learning" changes in reward. (10) Rudbeck and Murray call this "predictive", though it is the accumulated data of past responses. (11) Stalnaker et al reviewed these studies and question more abstract interpretations, emphasizing the primary motivations. (12) OFC provides information about the current motivation state, the historic reward value of stimuli/reinforcers, and current stimulus information about rewards.

Step #2) Data about the current sensory field includes **significance** data. "What is the current stimulus situation of available rewards?"

The Dorsolateral Prefrontal Cortex (DLPFC) receives stimulus information through sensory/association cortex (chapter one), and hippocampal reward pathways (**significance**, chapter four). DLPFC provides working memory information about current options and current brain activity from three subsystems (Baddeley model): the phonological loop (verbal information), the visual-spatial sketchpad (visual environment map), and the "episodic buffer" that integrates short-term with long-term memory. DLPFC converges this data and updates the current task, using relevant information. (13) Subjects with injuries in this region show deficits in *Wisconsin Sorting Task,* the ability to learn sensory reward signals and then alter the response to changing information. (14) This region malfunctions in psychosis, some types of dementia, and after stroke or tumors, creating problems of attention and organization of behavior. (15) The dorsal lateral pre-frontal cortex (DLPFC) converges data from current sensory fields, association cortex, and hippocampal memory sites for interpretation of the sensory data and reward significance. The relationship between working memory and reinforcement is not simple, the reward value of sensory memory must be linked to working memory. *Yoo, et al discuss the issues and possible solutions to this problem that is still unresolved.* (15)

Step #3) The "option command" is computed and sent to basal ganglia to activate of specific behavior: "Execute selected choice!" The pathway interactions produce an "option-command" to choose specific behavior(s) appropriate to the current environment, *a process that has no current computational model.* (16) This is transmitted to basal ganglia over pathways between the prefrontal region and basal ganglia, that are too complex to be separated in fMRI studies, but documented in neuroanatomical studies showing direct inputs into the region. The verbal equivalent might be "execute this option using a previously defined behavior sequence".

Step #4) "Perform the selected behavior." The basal ganglia multi-loop pathways execute the "option-command" on previously organized patterns, activating the selected sequence.

Humans, with bipedal posture and multifunctional upper limbs, have complex behavioral options combining hand movements, multi limb and body movements, facial muscle patterns, and intricate patterns of speech. These are organized (as subroutines) by experiential learning and stored as *basal ganglia pathway sequences*. The basal ganglia are a collection of cell nuclei under the cortex, and closely connected, on each side. (It is difficult to visualize the three dimensional shapes embedded in the surrounding cortex.) Mahlon and colleagues using microelectrodes in awake behaving primates, and human fMRI have studied the anatomy of basal ganglia and their relationships to cortex. (The cell assembly loop activity observed in microelectrode techniques is not visualized in fMRI.)

SIDEBAR The Basal Ganglia Network has several features:
i) Recursive loops link cortex and basal ganglia starting from specific regions of cortex to basal ganglia pathways, then to lateral thalamic nuclei, and back to the original areas of cortex (see diagrams in Fig. 6-3.). Thalamic feedback returns to the original cortical region. The thalamic relay nuclei intersect with vestibular and cerebellar loop pathways providing balance and sensory field information to refine the motor sequences. (17) (18) The cell assembly patterns on basal ganglia loop relationships to cerebral cortex are diagrammed in Fig 6-3.
ii) The loops include nonmotor regions of cortex: The loop pathways activate a broad range of actions: a) general motor patterns start at the supplementary motor area, b) visual attention inputs from frontal eye field controls, c) emotional response input originates from orbital frontal cortex, and other cortical regions provide sources for cognitive activity. iii) The basal ganglia loops are activated by dopamine synapses from substania nigra (SN), pars compacta. SN is the "activator" for movement sequences by dopamine activation, as other tegmental pathways "motivate" prefrontal cortex by dopamine. Loss or damage to cells in substantia nigra results in Parkinson's disease (or syndrome), which begins as problems initiating of motor activity, progresses to motor tremor, interference with postural control, and eventual impairment in overall frontal cortical function including dementia. Without SN dopamine input, the basal ganglia become inactive and freeze movement. iv) The synaptic connections within basal ganglia are both inhibitory and excitatory; some activity is facilitated by inhibition of inhibition, some by direct excitation. (The inhibitory system avoids regenerative positive feedback. The combination may help smooth motor action but also provides opportunities for "locking up" in abnormal states.) v) The organization of this network is accomplished by connectivity (experiential) learning. (Hebbian programming). An engineering analysis of the network is described by Wolf.

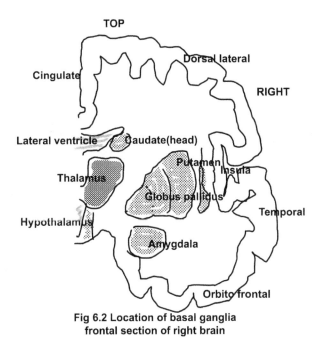

Fig 6.2 Location of basal ganglia
frontal section of right brain

Graybiel's research documents learning behavior patterns stored in pathways of multiple nuclei, which she calls "action repertoires", different options. (19) These are different for each individual and change with new experiences. An example is the ability of humans to revise their locomotor patterns in development from quadrapedal to bipedal, and to adjust to later situations. Houk proposed fixed computational models for these loops (20), but newer studies suggest that experiential connections build complex behaviors that are activated on demand. (21) The loop sequence should not be thought of as a single event, but a series of cycles repeated to produce a complex behavior. *The computational model for this recursive process has not yet been developed, but Michako discusses possibilities.*(21)

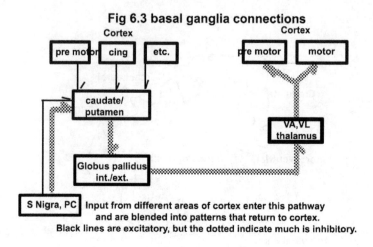

Fig 6.3 basal ganglia connections

Input from different areas of cortex enter this pathway and are blended into patterns that return to cortex.
Black lines are excitatory, but the dotted indicate much is inhibitory.

Step#5) Reward data, the results from actions performed, are sent from reward centers to anterior cingulate cortex (ACC) for evaluation: "This action produced positive reward. Continue action." Or error correction: "This did not produce reward, alter selected pattern." The feedback appears to go through OFC to cingulate through unknown connections.

Anterior Cingulate Cortex (ACC) has multiple sub-regions and three related functions. It receives input from the limbic circuit by way of thalamus. Studies of ACC activation suggest it provides *error detection,* though different procedures give varying results. (22) The response is temporary, related to the specific reward, social or other of current behavior outcomes, and in some studies, associated with inhibition of inappropriate (wrong) responses. Studies of this process involve a special error-related negativity (EN) generated in the ACC with error occurrences. Evidence by fMRI studies indicates the ACC has an evaluative component. This notion of "error detection" is the investigator's perspective. From the organism's perspective, ACC is registering reward outcome to change of behavior selection for improved reward and survival. Lesions also produce an inability to detect errors, severe difficulty with resolving stimulus conflict in the *Stroop task*, and emotional instability.

Giving feedback after responses sometimes confuses the response (adding conflicting social rewards?). (23)

SIDEBAR Other Features of anterior cingulate cortex. The *posterior/ventral system* of ACC is connected with amygdala, nucleus accumbens, hypothalamus, hippocampus, and anterior insula: pathways of the reward system gathering reward and motivation data to influence behavior choice. It forms an alternative papez-like circuit. It may be differentially activated by negative reward information since negative outcomes indicate a need to change behavior, activating a message sent to behavior modules. This reward information is transferred to the prefrontal decision process. ACC receives information from pain systems to activate behavior modules, a negative-reward "warning signal". The ACC registers physical pain in fMRI studies that show an increase in signal intensity, typically in the posterior part of area 24 of the ACC correlated with **pain intensity**.

Critchley reviews the evidence of an autonomic feedback information pathway about body states to ACC. (27) The ACC is the cortical area that has been most frequently linked to the experience of pain, (not the perception of pain). These studies interpret pain as a "negative reward" stimulus. Lesions in this area lead to low drive states for basic needs of food or water and decreased interest in social and vocational activities, sex, apathy (and possibly akinetic mutism), probably correlated to extent of cingulate damage. The ACC may also be involved in monitoring "painful" (aversive?) social situations as well, such as exclusion or rejection: When participants felt socially excluded in an fMRI virtual ball throwing game in which the ball was never thrown to the participant, the ACC showed activation, this activation was correlated with a self-reported measure of social distress. (Rushworth, 24) Lead exposure toxicity shows greater atrophy of ACC. (25) The posterior region of cingulate cortex is highly metabolically active and may be the aversive correlate to the positive reward anterior cingulate, but fMRI and other data do not yet confirm the differentiation. Critchley has reviewed the data on posterior CC autonomic functions that produce autonomic *effector output* for specific negative signals. (28) Leech et al believe the posterior cingulate is a crucial node for the DMN shift away from the external world. This would create a complementary relationship between anterior cingulate related to external reward, and posterior to internal, signals. ACC is associated with subjective experience of "self" emotion, when linked with attention. The ACC area in the brain is associated with *conscious experience* of somatic sensations of emotion, the feedback of body states in subjective experience, which link to *insula* for "self" experience. (29)

Rushworth's Theory. Rushworth proposes an expanded view of anterior cingulate, emphasizing the social rewards not defined in experimental settings. ACC is the reward pathway in social settings in his theory, based on data from human and primate game studies, especially "prisoner's dilemma" games. (24) His theory balances ACC and OFC: ACC is a more general reward evaluation system across different reward inputs, and, according to him, the "error detection" is an interpretation of how certain studies are designed. (26) OFC gathers immediate stimulus reward value, as in the Iowa gambling task. This is part of his theory of the evaluation in "evolutionary forage" the animal must evaluate differences in environmental rewards, including social rewards.

SIDEBAR Insular Cortex. The **insula** region is hidden under overlying cortical tissue, but continuously connected on its margins. Though less than 2% of cortical surface area, it is widely connected to sensory systems and limbic areas. Deen et al define three regions: a) a posterior region, functionally connected with somato-motor cortex, a pathway for self related motor activity, b) dorsal anterior-middle region, connected with dorsal anterior cingulate cortex, has inputs from pain, temperature, gustatory, gut, muscle, and skin receptors via the thalamus, and connects to the anterior insula. The dorsal insula pathways link interoceptive inputs with emotional and cognitive information from motivation system (limbic) pathways and association (sensory) cortex, and c) the ventral anterior region, connects to anterior cingulate cortex. (Deen, 29) This provides the cortical area for somatic- visceral and somato-motor data: the subjective experience of body sensations. (See chapter five) The insula has visceral-motor sympathetic and parasympathetic output through pathways in the lateral hypothalamus, indicating a role for directing autonomic somatic response. The self-referential information is sent to pre-frontal areas for executive decision-making. (29) Understanding insula functions is emerging in recent studies, and the lack of parallel systems in non-human primates and other mammals (without detailed self-systems) makes research more difficult. The relationship to self/other differentiation using mirror pathways is not understood. Self consciousness, discussed by Damasio, emphasizes the subjective state activated by this region and cingulate. The accumulation of experiential events of personal-self experience forms the basis of the "self" identity. This may include the experience of positive reward states and negative states like "hyperkafeteia" described by Koob. (See chapter nine). Current research gives suggestions of these functions but is preliminary.

The combination of cingulate and insular cortices provides a separate pathway between the motivation system and the PF/BG system that does not depend solely on reward outcome of actions. Menon and Uddin define a ***salience network*** that includes cingulate, insula and other prefrontal cortical regions involved in the selection of behavior. The regions do not influence specific behavior choice in fMRI studies, and are difficult to visualize independently so the effects on the pre-frontal system are unclear. (30)

Summarizing this model of executive function:

STEP #1) Motivation data arrives through OFC, both internal body signals and external warning signals, to "prime" the executive system for response.

STEP #2) Information of the current sensory field is presented on pathways to DLPRC from association areas and hippocampal memory data, to generate a current world message: "this is what is available". Input from insula may also suggest patterns of response from previous experiences.

STEP #3) The data combine to generate an option command, a decision to act: based on needs and situation, respond with specific behavior.

STEP #4) The option command activates a specific pattern of response over pathways of the basal ganglia loop system, where response patterns are stored.

The resulting behavior may, or may not lead to the desired reward.

STEP #5) Outcome data from the response (do/do not) result in reward changes in the motivation pathway. This is transmitted to anterior cingulate which evaluates the response, and sends a message back to prefrontal cortex if change is needed.

The network connections of the regions are genetically determined, but specific patterns of interaction are programmed (learned) by social and reward experiences. (21) (30) Established patterns of PF/BG activity, learned by repetitive training, can be performed without starting a new decision making process, using established links. This is done in martial arts, acting, playing piano or musical instrument, tennis and other sports, etc. Learning the sequence is guided by the attention process, to set up training. Dramatic studies of pre-frontal social interaction use "hyperscanning" of two interacting persons either by EEG or fMRI. Montague has been a developer of this technique, which is still dealing with problems interpreting the signals. (31)

Consciousness/subjective awareness may guide choice in "top down control". This is agency, consciously choosing behavior for selected goals, not solely determined by habits or external demands. (32) (Experiments by Libet challenging the role of consciousness in choice are discussed in chapter five.) The purpose of **agency** is choosing new adaptive responses to changing situations, and it is programmed in pathways by social interactions that create the internal representations of social goals, in the "social brain". **Agency** is not involved when the individual is responding to social situations using habitual responses, but it is needed when the individual is challenged with unfamiliar situations. A two person competitive game like chess includes immediate data about the board situation, hypothetical data about the other player, and experiential data from past games. The player must balance all three, so games are useful training for developing decision-making skills. Is **agency** just adaptive learning? Yes, if the learning process has "meta" properties that include representation of, and changes in, the choice system itself. Athletes, artists, musicians, and martial artists learning complex visual-motor patterns use self-awareness to train skilled performance. (36) Chapter twelve discusses the application for changing social behavior pathways. "Free will" does not mean random choices, or choices that are counter to expectations, it means making choices not totally determined by the external environment and past experience, and responsive to changing situations. These choices may not always be adaptive if pathways malfunction. (37) (38) Any information system, which can execute this process, can demonstrate "adaptive behavior". Kurzweil, Manzotti, and Varela all come to a similar conclusion in describing computational systems. (39) The reverse situation, the subjective experience of loss of agency in movement disorder reflects a pathway malfunction (see later paragraphs). (Maurer, 39)

The pre-frontal executive control system is essential for adaptation, so pathway malfunctions produce symptoms. The following examples illustrate selected problems of executive pathways: i) behavioral symptoms of childhood, ii) special syndromes of the basal ganglia, and iii) personality and identity.

Behavior symptoms of childhood are early indications of pathway problems, because mastery over motor functions develops before verbal cognitive skills. The baseline for identifying behavior problems comes first, and emotional, verbal and cognitive symptoms are recognized later. The Prefrontal/Basal Ganglia Pathways (PF/BG) generate motor sequences for bipedal walking by observing other bipedal humans, and for social interaction by observing facial expressions, vocalization, and speech. The social rewards for learning them are immediate (the ability to say "mama" is huge!). The stages are documented in developmental psychology, and assessment determines whether the child falls outside of the normal developmental range for the behavior. (40) (Attachment and autonomy, learned in social development, are discussed in chapter seven.) The syndromes of *Autism spectrum disorder*, *Intellectual Disability*, and *Specific Learning Disorders* (mentioned in chapter one and two) are often differentiated from other childhood problems though they sometimes share social and behavioral difficulties. (40) Other mental health diagnoses of childhood, including anxiety, depression, and mood disorder, present behavioral symptoms before verbal/emotional ones. Trauma and stress (discussed in chapter eight) may also present in childhood. The similarity of behavior symptoms for different childhood disorders makes evaluation difficult. The syndromes can be associated with **Neuromind** pathways, using hypothetical relationships consistent with clinical findings. (*Pathways changes do not "cause" symptoms, but are the correlated brain* *activity associated with them. See Appendix chapter one.*)

Group A) ATTENTION, EXECUTIVE CONTROL, (ADHD). Attention deficit disorder, with or without hyperactivity is the most common diagnosis in the child and adolescent age group with prevalence of up to 10% in some populations. Children with behavior problems were identified in mid 19th century, but only "diagnosed" attention deficit hyperactivity disorder in the mid 20th, and infrequently until 1963, when Connors reported an (unexpected) positive response to stimulants in certain children, and a "syndrome" was declared. (41) The PF/BG control system focuses attention. (Barkley (and others) favor the label of *impaired frontal executive control syndrome*, which is more precise, but not used.) The research for pathways associated with ADHD identifies multiple pathway changes, including the thalamic projections (DTPS), DLPFC attention pathways, and limited data in PF/BG pathways. (45) Patients present problems integrating sensory information, working memory, orientation, and maintaining task focus, and other symptoms of "attention problems", (which are also symptoms of hippocampus! (See chapter four)). A meta-analysis by Curatolo describes hypo function of all the pre-frontal areas in patients with ADHD, with multiple etiologies, and different areas of frontal brain affected, producing multiple syndromes. (46) Other reviews also show the lack of specific findings, or fail to identify specific correlations. (47) Problems of executive function and task integration that involve the DLPFC network, DTPS, and other attention pathways of the executive control system, all contribute to symptoms of ADHD. The response to dopamine and stimulants, suggests an important contribution of basal ganglia circuits. The differentiation of motor/GP and cognitive/caudate features in ADHD may reflect the different role of these BG units. (Teicher, 48) Studies have been unable to separate the role of basal ganglia due to the technical limitations of fMRI. (Studies that identify PF/BG regions focus on anatomical volume not function, because fMRI has problems visualizing separate components of BG.) A review by Makris, Biederman, et al summarizes various studies and presents models of potential pathways, and recognizes the multi-pathway features of this dysfunction. (49) *If there are unique features of PF/BG abnormalities in ADHD, they have not been identified.*

Improving behavior with stimulants encouraged the belief in a unique (genetic) syndrome. Instead, multiple variations are found, as in Ball's study describing different ADHD groups associated with 1) head size, low SES, math & reading performance, 2) delayed development, 3) hyperactivity, less family history, low SES, and 4) poor cognition and irritability independent of ADHD sx. Children differ on primary motor, primary cognitive, or a combination of symptoms. (Ball, 41) Stevens concluded: *"ADHD is a collection of discrete disorders for which a comparable behavioral endpoint arises through different neurobiological pathways. The findings raise caution about applying common cause, single-deficit conceptual models to individual ADHD patients and should prompt researchers to consider biologically-defined, multifactorial etiological models"* (Stevens, 41) Meta-reviews of ADHD genetics show the paradox of 74% concordance in twin studies, but less than 30% convergence of specific loci in GWAS searches. Thapar notes strong genetic overlap between ADHD and autism spectrum disorder (ASD) and intellectual disability, suggesting a nonspecific factor. ADHD also shows substantial genetic correlation with a much broader group of neuropsychiatric disorders as well as with non-psychiatric conditions (e.g., lung cancer). The evidence of multiple etiologies, including head injury, fetal alcohol exposure, birth hypoxia, childhood infections, neonatal jaundice, and a range of developmental behavioral disturbances associated with "soft neurological signs" (disturbances of handedness, etc.) are evidence that many factors that produce the symptoms. (42) Humans have delayed myelination of cortical tracts compared with other primate species, an extended period of local network, delaying frontal control. The rate of myelination has been correlated with symptoms, and likely contributes to frontal function in the course of development. (43) Whether degree of myelination is a factor has not yet been fully resolved. Multiple factors with polygenic loading make it difficult to specify a major etiology. Given the findings of multiple features in the syndrome, the expectation of a common genetic factor is misguided. Extensive research on the genetics does not support a single genetic abnormality, but evidence of multiple clinical patterns, with multiple etiologies, over several different pathways.

The complex pathway variations are only part of the diagnostic assessment. Social adaptation plays a significant role in ADHD diagnosis that is usually ignored. Entry into school places new demands on the child's executive control, and scales and observation systems are available to document the child's inability to perform at "expected age level". (See refs 44) These introduce variability into the definition of the syndrome (and do not separate different pre-frontal functions). Stimulant trials with positive response are often taken as indication of a correct diagnosis, though not an official criterion. Social expectations define the degree of executive control expected, validated by scales that "standardize" social assessment. Three aspects interact: a) the more severe the pathways disturbance, the sooner the assessment. b) Expectations for peer group social environment (like preschool), or children living in confining living spaces, are higher than on children living in open areas permitting free activity, and are likely to be diagnosed later, or not at all. c) Adult expectations, especially parents, are a major factor. (50) If cognitive problems (not behavior) are the major feature, the diagnosis may not be made until the challenges of middle school or high school, when the academic expectations of parents and teachers are not met, creating a strong pressure to diagnose and treat. When there are low academic expectations for the child, the diagnosis and treatment may never be made! These factors are ignored, rarely reported in studies, are difficult to validate, and yet obvious to the practical clinician.

Stimulants, dopamine, norepinephrine and stimulant agonists enhance PF/BG function to a point, and activate the OFC pathways, but excess dopamine stimulation causes pathway disturbances. If the stimulant effect is more on motivation pathways than PF/BG, risk of addictive use is higher. Detailed studies of the reward aspects of dopamine and other stimulants do not provide a clear model of its multiple effects. (51) Assertions that ADHD (attention/executive difficulties) resolves by age 18 have been discredited by population studies, but may be valid for a subgroup with developmental issues. Given the different etiologies and pathways, some changes may be associated with myelination/maturation, while others are intrinsic brain injuries, confounded by failure to document etiology. Frontal brain injury patients will not "outgrow" the damage but may adapt, or if symptoms persist impairing adult function, they may benefit from continued treatment. There are also studies suggesting *onset* of ADHD problems in adults. These may reflect injury or other factors not identified without considering etiology.

CLINICAL EXAMPLE Adult ADHD *A married woman in her late 30's was evaluated requesting renewal of her stimulant medication. Her previous psychiatrist had prescribed it for over five years to help her focus. She gave no history of early problems in behavior or focusing in childhood, but developed viral meningitis in early teens and had problems in school, and "confusion" after her recovery. This was not evaluated or treated until approximately 5 years before the evaluation, when a previous psychiatrist began prescribing stimulants. She had one child, who did not have symptoms, and she worked part time in retail. She was having marital problems and felt, for most of the marriage that her husband had dominated her, but she did not consider this until she started medication. The medication was adjusted; she started a new business of her own, and got more frustrated in the marriage, eventually separated and divorced. She continued to manage her life and family successfully. COMMENT there are multiple etiologies for ADHD syndromes, and not all start early in childhood. Failing to recognize this resulted in lost years of the woman's life, but eventually the ability to function more effectively, evidenced by changes in adapting, improved her life.*

Multiple etiologies alter PF/BG pathways producing executive problems managing motor and cognitive responses. Evidence indicates that ADHD, "frontal executive control syndrome", is not one specific disorder, and decades of research reveal no unique genetic or pathway disturbance. Regulation of executive function is polygenic, less focus may benefit farmers and other active occupations balancing negative features, to be selected. The mechanism of action of stimulants improving focus is based on enhancement of adrenergic or dopaminergic activity, based on in vitro studies. (51) *The extensive use of this diagnosis in childhood, along with the pervasive use of medication, needs a better understanding of etiologies and treatment options.*

Group B: MANAGING EMOTION AND MOTIVATIONAL STATE. (*impulse-control disorder, intermittent explosive disorder.*) All childhood behavioral syndromes are associated with problems in emotional control and symptoms of anger, impulse control and problems of social interaction. (52) Motivation and emotional information enters prefrontal regions over pathways of OFC and mPFC from hippocampus and tegmentum. The messages may include a) Increased activation of the motivation system, due to genetics, damage to motivation pathways, excessive (amygdala) anxiety, changes related to attachment, etc. The role of genetic/biologic and experiential factors may differ in each situation. Or b) Prefrontal inability to regulate the incoming data which overlaps Group A and may reflects pre-frontal injury. Viding and McCrory review challenges in this assessment: genetic risk is likely to be polygenic and statistically weak, neuro-imaging studies do not link hypothalamic changes to mOFC changes, (due to technical limitations! see Appendix chapter one), and the role of social environment is disregarded. Different mechanisms may produce similar behavior symptoms ("equifinality") and the same disturbance may produce different behavior outcomes ("multifinality"). (53) Metareviews of neuro-imaging studies find both dorsal cortex and ventral cortex abnormalities, not clearly associated with syndromes. (54)

The diagnosis of childhood bipolar disorder was proposed by Akiskal et al, based on the adolescent emotional and behavior problems of offspring of bipolar adult patients in his clinics. This group might have genetic vulnerability for the syndrome and present earlier in life as behavior problems. Biederman and associates at Harvard found "comorbid" overlap in symptoms for ADHD and bipolar disorder, with some children benefitting from bipolar rather than stimulant medications. (55) The Disruptive Mood Dysregulation Disorder diagnosis was created to address GROUP B symptoms without making a commitment to the adult bipolar diagnosis. It has limited research for differentiation or treatment, and does not correlate with development of mood disorders in adults. (55) Techniques to identify intense emotional activity in motivation pathways are not currently possible, leaving the assessment to clinical skills. *Whether the symptoms in children evolve into adult mania or bipolar disorder is unknown, there are no longitudinal studies.*

The diagnosis of Explosive Disorder (IED) is also confusing. Although reports describe a high prevalence of such behaviors in children, they do not persist, or predispose to future problems. The reported high prevalence and the lack of research activity suggest it is a transient developmental stage for most children. The diagnosis "intermittent explosive disorder" remains a residual category for diagnosing aggression, and no differentiation is made between patients with ineffective socialization and those with primary neural deficits. Neuroimaging supports abnormalities in several subcortical regions in a few studied cases. (56) *Disturbances of Group B), the motivation pathways, are easily confused with problems in executive control, and consistent methods of differentiating them have not been developed.*

CLINICAL EXAMPLE. The Explosive Teen. *A teenage girl had recurring episodes of explosive anger in home, school, and with friends. She was socially connected to peers, and the episodes had started about a year before admission to a locked adolescent facility. The episodes continued were not controlled by dopamine blocker, and staff were becoming frustrated. A trial of valium provided almost immediate termination of the episodes, suggesting that some subclinical seizure activity was involved. More specific testing could not be obtained, but on low dose valium, and then a replacement antiseizure medication she rapidly stabilized and had no further episodes. She met behavior criteria for discharge and return to outpatient in the referring state was arranged. However, one of her previous outbursts occurred in front of a juvenile court judge, who refused to authorize her release, the court sent her to a different locked facility. COMMENT This illustrates both being aware of a potential etiology leading to effective treatment, and also how prior behavior and "conduct disorder" diagnosis can negatively bias the course of a person's life.*

Group C) OPPOSITIONAL DEFIANT DISORDER (ODD). The diagnoses "Oppositional Defiant Disorder" and "Conduct Disorder" differ from other groups by criteria for behavior as socially unacceptable, (labeling theory). Conduct disorder describes behavior that violates social prohibitions, especially without expected emotional distress. ODD is based on symptoms of negative interaction with (parental) authority, which may include emotional outbursts. The child is brought to treatment by the parent or family, who decide that the defiance is inappropriate, so the evaluation must take into account the child's socialization and family dynamics. Children demonstrate individuation in the developmental period between 2 and at 4, which can involve opposition to parental authority; so the diagnosis ODD must be differentiated from normal patterns. It is generally diagnosed later in childhood, or if extremely persistent. Persistence may be "perseveration", mistaken as opposition. OCD features may be associated and the two are often confused. Overlap with perseveration in disorders like Tourette's locates the behavior to frontal pathways, though a recent review did not mention this possibility. (57) *If ODD is an "excessive need to demonstrate autonomy" with issues in development of the "self" system, this has not stimulated any research.*

Conduct disorder is diagnosed by behavior that violates social norms, so the child must have awareness of social norms to perform behavior that "intentionally" violates them. This is Kohlberg's "Preconventional" stage during much of early childhood, so deciding when the behavior is severe enough, and later enough in development to diagnose, becomes an issue. (The historical "triad" of cruelty to animals, fire-setting, and persistent bedwetting, proposed by Guze to indicate some "basic problem", is not confirmed statistically with this syndrome, but persists as a "professional legend".) The current basis of diagnosis is lack of remorse or guilt about the behavior, lack of empathy, unconcern about consequences of unsatisfactory academic, professional, or other achievement, and "shallow or deficient affect". (58) These descriptive features imply capacities which emerge later in development, and are often diagnosed in the juvenile justice setting, raising questions of when this is a "mental disorder" or social deviance. Nothing about the socialization of the individual is included in the defining features, but it may play a role. Similar behavior patterns are reported in a type of attachment disorder, and in patterns of inappropriate socialization (external type of Rotter). The diagnosis is often made retrospectively after legal problems occur. Youth diagnosed with "conduct disorder" may go on to criminal behavior or "antisocial personality disorder", but also to other psychiatric diagnoses, or some other abnormality, misunderstood in childhood. Identifying which children who have "limited pro-social emotion", "callous unemotional" traits, and will develop into antisocial personality as adults, is less important than identifying the children who will not and can benefit from treatment. (Issues of the amygdala that may influence this process are discussed in chapter eight.)

Group D) Compulsive repetition. Perseveration, repetitive behavior, or automatically repeating another's observed behavior is a symptom of frontal brain injury in Neurology. This is observed in behavioral syndromes, motor tic disorder, repetitive motor patterns, and obsessive–compulsive disorder with repetitive thoughts. (59) Parents often report an angry defiant response occurs when attempting to redirect the child from ongoing activity, regardless of whether it is appropriate or inappropriate. In this situation, the key element is not the opposition, misinterpreted by parent or other adult as "not doing what I tell him (or her) to do", but the child's difficulty changing actions. Perseveration has been explored in Autism spectrum, and is seen in other childhood problem behaviors. Many children go through a developmental phase of obsessional patterns for coping with anxiety, but only a few persist with OCD. Genes, frontal brain injury, response to excessive anxiety, or other etiologies play a role. A symptom scale describes typical symptom patterns in older children and adults. (Goodman, 60) A pre-frontal OFC-ACC- caudate pathway is documented in several studies of the syndrome reviewed by Maia et al. (Maia, 59)

There is an inherent duality in PF/BG function, not yet simulated in model systems. Impaired focus of attention-executive operations, *contrasted with* over-focusing, perseveration, and tics are complementary patterns of the same pathways. Dopamine and agonists drive this "duality" toward focus (and perseveration, when excessive). In children (and adults) with deficits, stimulants can improve focusing until perseveration and irritability occur. Tics are sometimes revealed by stimulants, (though loss of appetite, weight loss, and interference with sleep usually occur first). Treating OCD or other perseverative PF/BG response using serotonin reuptake modifiers reduces perseveration and also focus and executive control. The goal is a balance. If brain injury is a factor, both problems may occur together. (60) Multiple etiologies produce specific changes in PF/BG. Birth is a complex and potentially dangerous time of life for the brain, which may create disturbances in pre-frontal motor control in syndromes of "cerebral palsy", or PF/BG management of behavior. Head trauma also produces disturbances. Streptococcal infection, and more recently other infections can cause basal ganglia syndromes, e.g. Syndenham's Chorea and PANDAS (Pediatric Autoimmine Neurologic Disorder Associated Streptococcus), with symptoms of chorea, tics, perseveration, and OCD. It is unclear whether this damage is by the infectious agent, or a secondary autoimmune reaction, and typically occurs weeks after the infection. (61) The following case indicates how this can be confused with other mental health syndromes:

Group E) Inappropriate response to reward. Anterior Cingulate Cortex is essential in validating behavior choice and positive experience of the result. Issues in in the development of sense of self and behavior may occur if this reward data is not experienced. This problem may be an associated with other childhood disturbances, but becomes catastrophic in autism spectrum, discussed in chapter two. The connections to anterior cingulate cortex and insular cortex store sequences linked to "self identification". The importance of the "self-other" distinction for salience, goals, and behavior choice were explored earlier in this chapter. This problem may be hidden

CLINICAL EXAMPLE The Girl Who Lost Her Spark. *A teenage girl was admitted to a Psychiatric hospital for a third time after two previous short hospitalizations did not clear her of patterns of anxiety, social isolation, and "semi-catatonic" slowing of behavior. She had developed a series of repetitive patterns of behavior and complained of obsessional thoughts. This was diagnosed a schizophrenic syndrome of sudden onset but efforts to treat with anti-psychotic medications worsened the symptoms. The parents brought in photo albums documenting that one year before, the patient had been a happy cheerful teen cheerleader with no history of intervening trauma or abuse. There was no family history of major mental disorder. She was taken off medications, with mild improvement, but no return to normal activity. She was transferred to an academic center where the Psychiatrist planned to administer ECT (diagnosing this as "mild catatonia"). In the pre ECT procedure, a Neurologist observed that the patient's spasms and tics disappeared with the IV preoperative valium and (correctly) diagnosed a basal ganglia disorder. ECT was canceled and she was maintained on benzodiazepines and improved significantly. The Neurologist obtained the history that four weeks before onset of the syndrome, the patient had experienced an infectious illness with fever and respiratory symptoms. She was diagnosed as possible PANDAS with a Parkinson-like presentation. COMMENT Failure to identify etiology in an unusual presentation delayed effective treatment. (61)*

in symptoms of depression, body dysmorphic disorder, or other motivation syndromes. The development of self/other is related to attachment and may also be part of this syndrome. Recent data on the role of both of these cortical regions warrants a wider research agenda. (62)

Childhood problems regulating behavior involve different pathways, or combinations, with difficulty specifying syndromes. Multiple etiologies may alter different systems, complicating assessment. The following questions help guide the clinician: "Is there a problem focusing on specific task, or motor behavior that interferes with decision making? This suggests DLPFC attention network pathway, and control of basal/ganglia networks, with unfocused pattern. "Is there a problem in emotional control?" This suggests problems in OFC, or mPFC pathways, increased motivation system messages, or regulatory failure of emotional messages in prefrontal regions. "Is there a problem with appropriate assessment of social behavior and response?" This suggests a problem in amygdala response to social context, a result of genetic, attachment or social factors, or mild autism spectrum syndrome. "Is there perseveration, obsessional thoughts, or recurring behaviors?" This suggests malfunction in the pre-frontal system/ basal ganglia pathways with perseverative pattern. "Is there a problem integrating reward including social reward?" This suggests problems of the ACC, INSULA, and motivation centers.

Abnormal attachment or childhood abuse with PTSD generate separate findings. Multiple pathway disturbances are identified, describing the combination of features in each child's presentation.

Disturbances of basal ganglia pathways produce distinct clinical syndromes in children and adults, including iatrogenic etiologies. *OCD and repetitive motor actions (tics)* are the compulsive repetition of behaviors or thoughts occur in both children and adults. An activated motor or cognitive PF/BG pathway produces intermittent spontaneous motor or cognitive behavior. (Other compulsive behaviors, alternatives of OCD, e.g. trichotillomania, and (according to some) hoarding behavior, may also be produced.) Differentiating OCD as a symptom of anxiety or a basal ganglia dysfunction *or both* is confusing. PF/BG can produce OCD symptoms, and the same pathways are involved in coping skills for anxiety (see chapter eight) as described by Huey et al. (64) *Tics (and tic disorders)* are brief repetitive units of behavior, emitted in (semi) periodic fashion, experienced subjectively out of the person's control, that may produce social problems. They are examples of behavior without agency! The most dramatic, *Tourette's,* has sudden verbal and emotional outbursts similar to intermittent explosive disorder behaviors but without evidence of intent. Tourette's combination of verbal and emotional elements validates DeLong's model that all cortical regions, including verbal and emotional, are involved in the basal ganglia- thalamic loops. (65) PF/BG pathways with lower threshold for activation are more likely to be activated and produce spontaneous motor/other system response. The pathways of Tourette's and

OCD overlap in PF/BG pathways, with common genetic markers. Treatment with stimulants may result in onset or worsening of tics. (65) Dopamine blocker treatment causing a generalized increase in threshold to block dopamine transmission reduces tic frequency in Tourette's, but may release tics in tardive dyskinesia.

Tardive dyskinesia. Patients treated with dopamine blocker medications sometimes develop tic-like motor movements, which may persist even after discontinuation of medication. All strong dopamine-blocking agents can produce this iatrogenic tic disorder, though the "first generation" strong D2 blockers are more often involved. (66) The tics, often oro-facial or finger movements are intensified by emotion as in other tic disorders, and a source of embarrassment. The tics of tardive dyskinesia sometimes emerge when the dopamine blocker is reduced. The condition has been described and the role of D2 blockade understood since the 1960s, but studies linking it to basal ganglia network changes have been limited by the difficulty visualizing basal ganglia by fMRI and other considerations. Motor thresholds are involved, and whether the threshold for particular regions is critical is unclear. The statement that the symptoms are an indication of individual genetic vulnerability has never been documented, but provides a basis for avoiding liability. Recent developments in medication treatments for TD are described in chapter eleven. (Tiwari, 66)

Parkinson's syndrome. This is a progressive neurological condition from damage to substantia nigra (SN-PC) in the basal ganglia with depletion of dopamine and accumulation of "Lewy bodies" in the cells of SN. (67) The first and most comprehensive symptom is difficulty initiating movement, akinesia. Associated with this are release symptoms: tremors, postural instability with characteristic postural changes, and later, cognitive symptoms of dementia. A similar syndrome is produced iatrogenically when dopamine transmission is blocked by medication which results in deterioration of behavior control. The first antipsychotics, particularly at higher doses, produced unresponsive affect and various extrapyramidal symptoms (EPS). (67) Newer medications that also facilitate serotonin transmission or dopamine partial agonism, cause less basal ganglia disruption. (See chapter eleven) In the tradeoff of managing psychotic arousal these side effects are tolerated, but patients often choose to discontinue the medication after the resolution of psychosis, giving rise to debates about "compliance". (The management is discussed in detail in chapter eleven.) The Parkinson syndrome shows the effect of global interference with PF/ BG activation.

Dystonic reaction is an iatrogenic symptom of the basal ganglia, when a patient, taking a D2 blocker, reports sudden onset of muscle spasm in some local region often of head and neck. The effect is rapid, terrifying, and bizarre. This may occur soon after starting a medication, with dose increase, or after extended use. Administration of a benzodiazepine, IM Benadryl or Cogentin will usually result in rapid resolution of the symptom (though it may recur if other changes are not made to the regimen). The balance of facilitation and inhibition of motor activity the region has been disrupted by dopamine inhibition, and put the muscles into spasm. (68)

Neuroleptic malignant syndrome is a potentially life-threatening side effect of medications that block D2, a diffuse pattern of activation & inhibition in flexor/extensor muscle groups creating rigid muscle tremors. The excessive motor activity at the micro level causes rabdomyolosis (muscle breakdown) and hyperthermia, possible seizures, muscle damage, and even death. Rapid treatment with a GABA inhibitor, diazepam or lorazepam, releases the spasm. The mechanism of D2 trigger of this syndrome is not clear, but high doses of medication along with environmental factors like heat and dehydration are contributing factors. (69) This failure of balancing opposing motor system muscle groups might be a "total body dystonia".

Catatonia is another problem of integration of motor excitation/inhibition. Catatonia has a long history in the psychiatric literature of patients who show dyskinesia or akinesia with "waxy flexibility" (the ability of an evaluator to place the limbs in any posture, that is maintained for considerable time). Fricchione has studied catatonia describing features of akinesia and loss of motor postural control, similar to NMS and advanced Parkinson's Disease. (70) The diagnosis of catatonia is reported in bipolar disorder, schizophrenia, and other medical conditions, and not always related to use of D2 blocker. The symptoms are dysregulation of PF/BG motor control. (71) The use of inhibitory agents especially diazepam (or the disruption by ECT) are utilized to end the state, which sometimes terminates spontaneously. In contrast to NMS, catatonia does not usually lead to muscle damage. (60)

*CLINICAL EXAMPLE **Walk-In Catatonia*** *A 30 year old man was seen in the ER for anxiety and confusion and admitted to a short term mental health unit. Within several hours of admission, he layed down in bed and did not move or get up for 72 hours. He did not appear to be asleep, and demonstrated some limb positioning effects, especially when being moved to avoid pressure sores. Laboratory panels were entirely normal and there was no outward sign of trauma or head trauma. At the end of three days, he "woke up", reporting that he was confused about where he was and what happened. When the circumstances were explained, he reported that he had had a similar incident about a year before. He had been working as an engineer in an aerospace company, and was not married, nor from the local region. Toxicology screens showed no blood alcohol or other drug level. He was treated with no medications. He could give no explanation for these episodes and denied any family history. Possible treatment options were discussed but he refused any further treatment and discharged. Approximately 6 months later, the same man returned to the same hospital and had a similar episode lasting about 48 hours, treated by another physician. He refused follow-up treatment, and was not seen again in the area. COMMENT The patient's presentation was suggestive of an acute episode of catatonia, with no clear precipitating factor. Case reports of intermittent catatonia tend to focus on prefrontal system epilepsy, which is consistent to abnormal activation of basal ganglia networks, but this was not observed or reported by this man. (70)*

These PF/BG pathway disturbances are clinical boundary conditions of prefrontal executive control. Tics, choreiform movements, tardive dyskinesia, and Tourette's are **release phenomena** of pathways spontaneously activated, unrelated to the ongoing motor activity. Parkinson's, dystonic reaction, NMS, and catatonia are syndromes of inhibition that interfere with motor activity. (Carroll proposed a "universal field hypothesis" of catatonia and NMS in

2000 based on similar synaptic activity. (72)) In contrast to these neuro-pathway syndromes are patients who report loss of control (agency) of movement without evidence of impairment. These "functional movement disorders" were some of Freud's original patients, now mostly seen by Neurologists. Hallett et al report findings of regional changes in these patients on fMRI, consistent with insula self-system variations. (73) These potential problems in the PF/BG system impact clinical situations by their interference with adaptive functioning. Some are dramatic and intermittent and more obvious, while others are more pervasive and subtle.

Personality (plural) are patterns created and stored in PF/BG pathways. *Personality* is the expectation that people interact socially with consistent behavior: "I have a consistent pattern of behavior which does not change dramatically, and "you" also have a consistent way of behaving towards me." This is accurate but also highly misleading!

PERSONAL EXAMPLE a personal "memory experiment" demonstrates personality in-stability. Attending your 20th high school reunion, you may notice that everyone's interactions revert to the high school patterns with other students they knew at the time. This has, on occasion, resulted in resumption of old high school romances and even marriages. But most attendees sense that the behavior is different from and inconsistent with their current adult behavior and emotions. An adult may have the same experience playing a children's game with a child, which elicits childhood behavior, while observing it from an adult perspective. The examples demonstrate that personality patterns change over time and context, and old patterns persist in storage to be elicited in suitable situations. Earlier modes of interaction are replaced by new patterns appropriate to current life, and are not erased.

How stable is "personality"? If behavior is adaptive to new situations, new patterns must be learned, including all the developmental changes of growing up. Yet personality "types", stable "traits", have been a research interest of psychology since the 1920s. This suggests that a person stays "stuck" in a stable "personality type". There is little formal research on this assumption of persistence.

SIDEBAR ADOLESCENT DEVELOPMENT Adolescence is the life stage with the most dramatic changes in social interaction. This developmental stage includes five transitions that impact social adaptation: The **physiologic** changes of adolescence combine rapid somatic growth with the changes of puberty associated with a general increase in emotional intensity. The timing of pubertal changes, which may be as early as age 11 or as late as age 16-17, are relative to the peer group and also impact emotional development. Societal valuation of specific physical features, and expectations about sexual identity are contributions to personal identity. The **cognitive** changes associated with myelination of cortical tracts enables abstract thinking. The ability to abstract properties from the sensory elements of perception, and disconnect from immediate life situations, enables increased frontal control of behavior. Under ideal circumstances the hormonal and cognitive changes balance each other. But the changes can occur early or late in the age range and are not synchronized with each other, producing different patterns of self-control in different children. (Sexual changes occur ahead of cognitive ones, often in females, while the reverse is often true in males. This gives rise to the teen slang of "sluts" and "geeks".) **Personal gender identity** is different from physical puberty and builds on childhood experiences of sexual identification, normal and abusive childhood sexuality, and other pre-adolescent issues. It occurs in two stages. In the initial stage, the person develops a strong identification with a person of the same perceived gender orientation, which is sometimes obsessional, emotionally charged, idealizing and may become sexual. This identification enhances gender identity in teenagers by modeling. After the experience is sufficiently integrated, a second stage of sexual experimentation ("dating") begins, which provides opportunities for exploration of differences in gender stereotyping and the ability to understand and develop an intimate interpersonal relationship. In the traditional developmental process, this leads to mate selection. In the current society, a much wider range of gender choices has emerged and the blurring of the first and second stages is common. **Social development** is the transition from dependence on family for emotional and physical support of childhood to using the peer group in adolescence. Changes in the contemporary American family have exaggerated and modified this trend. The existence of gang activity is an extreme alternative peer group, as are other emotionally charged peer relationships for some adolescents. Adolescents may have difficulty separating from the family and ambivalent autonomy. **Social identity**, a concern of later adolescence from 18 to 35, is the task of becoming a productive member of society.

(74) "Personality tests" repeated on the same persons over time intervals often have different results, and when they are stable reflect abnormal characteristics (see following). Erickson offered an early formulation of the interaction patterns associated with PSA developmental stages, relating problems to the social "tasks" at each stage. Levinson et al, popularized by Sheehy, extended his formulation through adult life stages. (74) Dramatic developmental changes occur in adolescence that modify behavior and personality.

The "stability" of personality is both everyday consistency and persisting "abnormal" patterns that do not adjust to new situations. (Though, even clinical "personality disorders" have evidence of change over time (75)). People interact differently in everyday situations, as when the supervisor comes around, and co-workers change their demeanor. Patterns of social interaction ("personality") change with development, experience, and social situations, maintaining some consistency. Rigid unchanging patterns or highly dramatic changes indicate problems. Patterns of social interaction are organized and stored in the brain as behavior choices. Earlier DSMs defined "personality disorders" on a separate axis, but there cannot be two brains, one for "personality", and another for "other mental illness". The same brain pathways are involved in all mental health. Dramatic changes of function are labeled "mental disorders", and more chronic persisting problems in adaptation are called "Personality Disorders" because they are more consistent, and not as disruptive as "Mental Disorders". Personality is a set of adaptive capacities, stored as cognitive, emotional, and motor behavior patterns in PF/BG loops, programmed by social experience. The procedural learning of BG loops is created and stored differently from the significance learning of the hippocampal circuits, and is not lost in bilateral hippocampal damage. (19)

Posture is the coordination of behavior oriented to gravity. Motor sequences must be integrated with vestibular input, and external sensory signals, and change depending on the walking surface, angle of body, etc. Basal ganglia pathways coordinate complex behavior sequences with vestibular and cerebellar pathways to manage posture.

Posture changes across the lifetime from quadruped to biped movement (and then to bipedal plus cane). Certain human "play" activities are based on the challenge of maintaining biped stance under gravitational challenges. Adult "posture" is stable and consistent, but humans adapt to different gravitational environments, e.g. developing "sea legs" while at sea for an extended period, and noticed on return to land. Astronauts have dramatic problems recovering from zero gravity. (76)

SIDEBAR Kohler Goggle experiment. *A German Psychologist had subjects wear goggles with prisms that inverted the visual field vertically: up was down. Adjustment took several days but all the subjects were able to accommodate. Weeks later, when the goggles were removed another period of adjustment occurred. Even in adults, the visual-motor-vestibular pathways can be reprogrammed.* (77)

Personality is the analog of posture for social interaction. Behavior patterns of personality are organized by expectations of the social environment, an analogy to gravity. These behaviors include gestures, "tone of voice", speech, large motor activity as in bowing, and, more often, small motor, and vocal behaviors. The responses to social situations are learned (programmed) by social experiences, stored in basal ganglia loops in patterns of response, and assembled into complex sequences, what Graybiel calls the "behavior repertoire". (19) (78) Social interactions are consistent, yet re-programable (as in military training to overcome the social inhibitions of aggression). Do early experiences of the family leave lasting behavior patterns ("transference")? The PSA concept of "transference" states that patterns of social interaction are learned in the family. (79) Freud's early emphasis on "traumatic experiences" that caused "fixations" was later expanded to general experiences of childhood. Effects of trauma are more easily documented and appear more persistent (see chapter eight). Is the relationship between childhood and adult behavior modified by intervening events? Reviews of the genetics of *personality* show patterns of polygenic involvement, and inability to differentiate gene effects from other sources of dysfunction, (the PF/BG system was not recognized in the research, so "genetics of personality" does not address PF/BG variables). (81)

Interaction between posture and personality occurs when emotional patterns influence body posture. This can be transient in situations of fear or frustration (visible in the posture of athletes during moments of competition), and also may create persisting effects on posture. Emotional reactions stored as chronic muscle tension in postural muscles were described by Wilhelm Reich in **Character Analysis** as "body armor", and addressed in treatment by his student Lowen in **Betrayal Of The Body**. (See chapter twelve). (80) Like posture, the actions of personality, are often performed unconsciously, but are accessible to conscious attention. Surfing, snowboarding, skiing, rollerblading and other balance sports require conscious awareness during training, and are performed spontaneously, or in competitive situations with intense focus. Social and cultural variables establish the boundaries of acceptable social interaction. Social choices are often performed unconsciously in everyday encounters, but consciously in social situations of different cultures when one is unfamiliar with expectations for behavior. Language, the most social behavior, requires little attention to speak in the native tongue, but may demand great concentration when learning a new language, or overcoming a disability. Social pressure can dramatically modify personality patterns. A person imprisoned or abducted can be forced into morally unacceptable behavior in "Stockholm Syndrome" when victims of wartime "brainwashing" modify behavior to adapt to incarceration. Whether a "breakdown", a "failure of personal integrity", or the intentional result of the training, patterns change, and may later revert to earlier ones, or persist. There is some research on the aftermath of torture and interrogation, the extremes of social indoctrination. (82) Accounts of "feral" children also give information about the impact of the lack of social programming. (83) The patterns of personality configuration are stored in the PF/BG pathways, but the cingulate and insular cortex provide self-referential experience, past and current, for the *sense of self.*

Personality patterns are experienced consistently across time, but multiple patterns are stored, and can be expressed when triggered by circumstances. *The relationship between the PF/BG patterns and the self/identity patterns of Insula is unknown, a topic for research.* Personality patterns are compartmentalized, separated into life epochs, relatively accessible for most people, but not always in certain syndromes.

What is the best method of observing and categorizing patterns of personality? The most direct evidence of personality is observing the person in various social situations. This is the method of anthropology but is impractical in mental health, and replaced by interviews in a research or clinical setting, which do not give the data of interacting with a spouse, child, or another person in the everyday social environment. The observer bias must be "standardized" to minimize errors (H. S. Sullivan and anthropologists call this "participant observation"). The Personality Disorder categories of DSM IV documented the most obvious maladaptive patterns observed. The desire to standardize the process lead to structured procedures and scales. A series of questions by the interviewer, or printed questionnaire, is designed to differentiate personality "types", by statistically scoring the answers against the responses of "personality types" separately defined by clinical interview or some other method. (84) These rating scales, verbal choice tests, are based on self-report, and most, like the MMPI, on responses of patients with "diagnosed" mental illnesses. All current scales in clinical use are designed to document abnormal aspects of personality. (85) An alternative approach would define the dimensions of adaptive social interaction, and design scales for them. The Five Factor Method (FFM) was developed by statistically aggregating many other scales, "factor analyzing" consistent features, and selecting the items associated with them. The resulting components range between positive and negative values, not just abnormal categories. Weston and Schedler developed another multi-factor approach. (86) (See footnotes for details) Whether personality patterns are a continuously varying range or specific abnormal patterns is debated, but the FFM has not been accepted clinically because of the focus on abnormality.

Coping mechanisms are pathway patterns that manage fear, anxiety, or other emotions and behavior. They are called "defense mechanisms" in PSA, and codified by Freud's daughter in *The Ego And The Mechanisms Of Defense*. Bellak developed a scale of defense mechanisms, based on structured interviews, and was able to differentiate severe ("schizophrenic") from less severe ("neurotic") patients statistically. The procedure is cumbersome, and the terminology difficult to translate from its PSA heritage. (87) Vaillant observed patterns of coping in men followed across adulthood, and found poorer adjustment for those with less "effective" types. (88) The concept of "coping" focuses on positive adaptive capacities rather than maladaptive patterns when studied under the term **resilience**, and a literature on the topic has developed mostly outside of the domain of mental health providers. (89) Some method for organizing and cataloging the pattern of social interaction and emotional regulation is an essential part of the assessment of the individual's adaptation.

Self is an important component of social interaction. The differentiation of self/other is a basic skill (discussed in chapter two and seven). The pathways of "self" use data from multiple sources including body sensations, experience of behavior, outcomes of social interactions, and memories of prior experiences. Damasio defines the "self" as the learned data that creates "self awareness". Hood calls this the "illusion of self" because so much of it is acquired in, and depends on, social interaction. (90) The "self" is best understood as the node of pathways that combine personal experiences, differentiated from experiences of "other". The pathways have some genetic organization, but self is created in a process of accumulating experience. The individual's subjective sense (consciousness of self) is produced by the interactions of these pathways with the attention system, and allows the individual to select choices that reflect "self" goals, or reject them. An example **is gender identity**, an aspect of self currently undergoing transformation.

Gender identity illustrates aspects of personality and self. Gender includes the experience of body, social perceptions, and performance of specific social behavior. Genetic programming, in-utero hormonal exposure, anatomy, social conditioning, pubertal hormones, and cultural messages all influence gender. (91) These factors are organized in *the Olson-Kennedy gender-identity abacus*, "calculating the relative gender of each person". (92) *Each feature can have a male or female value or be bimodal.* Altering one's anatomy does not resolve the issue of social acceptance; the experience of growing up in a "mixed gender role" does not simply dissipate. The variables identify a range of gender-identity alternatives. (93) Sexual identity in the 21st century is not determined by biological/anatomical characteristics. It is unclear how the influences work, what changes they effect, and whether significant gender differences in the brain are the result. The issue of gender shows that multiple pathways interact to produce aspects of self. Understanding the options are important for helping the person define their personal identity. *From Olson-Kennedy "gender-identity abacus", the relative of each person:* (92):

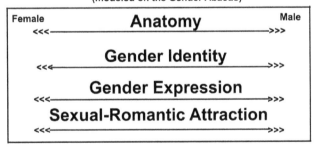

Figure 6.4 Assessing gender as a mixture of multiple characteristics. (modeled on the Gender Abacus)

*ANTHROPOLOGY EXAMPLE **Gender in New Guinea**. An anthropology report described adolescent behavior in a remote region of New Guinea. Male children and teens performed fellatio on adult males, believing that this increased their "maleness". The community had no adult male homosexuality, which confirmed the cultural belief, and disputes the view of the 1950s that male-to-male sexual behavior in adolescence contributes to the development of adult homosexuality. The key difference is* **culture.** *How the culture configures the relationship between behavior and later identity must be an important part of the determination.* (93)

Personality disorders are persisting pathway patterns that interfere with adaptation. They do not involve a separate part of the brain, or require a separate category. Severe impairment of interpersonal adaptation is seen in *autism syndrome* (see chapter two), though it is not usually considered a personality disorder. (94) Personality diagnoses are disturbances of major pathways with varied severity and persistence. Obsessive Compulsive (Personality) Disorder describes symptoms of the PF/BG system, discussed in this chapter, which vary in severity, persistence, and etiology. Schizotypal Personality Disorder describes symptoms of the schizophrenia spectrum without psychosis, which is not needed if schizophrenic symptoms are separated from psychosis. (See chapter four) Similar reformulations are possible for many other syndromes. Borderline Personality Disorder has increasing evidence supporting abnormalities in attachment. (See chapter seven). (94)

Dissociative disorders and Dissociative Identity Disorder are patterns of the control mechanisms associated with trauma, (discussed with PTSD in chapter eight). Dissociative Identity Disorder ("Multiple Personality Disorder" (MPD)) is the most controversial because it directly challenges the notion of consistent personality: "One self or many?" Clinicians, who have not had experience with this syndrome, view the diagnosis as clinical fantasy, although it has sufficient support to acquire a DSM diagnosis. (95) After seeing a person enact this diagnosis, its significance becomes clear. MPD, PTSD, and borderline syndrome all depend on understanding dissociation as a coping skill. (This is discussed in detail in chapter eight.) MPD is associated with early childhood abuse-trauma, and dissociative defenses that are used for coping. The diagnosis, like PTSD, often does not present to the clinician for decades, during which dysfunctional coping methods impair adaptation. The clinical significance of both MPD and borderline syndrome is that patterns of social interaction from different life stages can coexist in the brain, and can be elicited by different circumstances. These shifts in behavior are more dramatic but not different in kind from the shifts experienced by everyone. The confusion that surrounds them, and differentiates them, is the person's denial of awareness of the shifts. In borderline personality, the emotional state and coping methods shift dramatically, the person is aware of this, but claims no control, no *agency*. In MPD, the shifts occur and the person denies both control and awareness of the shifts, of at least some of the "alter" states. When personality is understood as patterns of social interaction, dramatic variations that use alternative, sometimes mal-adaptive, coping patterns are recognized. There is only one *person/body*, and working with multiple personality disorder may result in awareness of different patterns of personality enacted by the individual, (and which may eventually come to co-consciousness). There is no magic or mystery in MPD, just the effects of dissociative control of awareness/attention, and switching among previously stored coping patterns.

CLINICAL EXAMPLE Another Eve. *A married mother in her 30s was severely depressed with recurring suicidal thoughts, who had taken several overdoses. She felt unable to care for her two children, though her husband remained very supportive. Months went by with no response to therapy or medication, when one day the patient entered the session with a dramatically different tone of voice and movement. She appeared to be a young child, perhaps 7 or 8, in mannerisms, voice, and movement. She introduced herself by a child's name and remarked that she had been observing the sessions for sometime and wanted to attend one. The dramatic difference in behavior and mannerisms was associated with an entirely different affect. The person in the room was cheerful and happy, and aware that this differed from her "other self". A multi year course ensued in which the person was able to modify and organize her sense of self more effectively. COMMENT A provider who has not experienced this "multiplicity" will be unable to appreciate the extent to which enacting another "self" is different from "pretending" to be someone else. The change in affect is often dramatic, as in borderline syndrome, and conscious awareness of different components of self is variable. In this instance, the child-self had more overall awareness than the adult-self. The child-self appeared to have been "protected" from a long history of childhood abuse, which was part of the adult-self awareness.*

CHAPTER SEVEN:
Learning attachment

Each pathway performs functions essential for mental health. Genes, other biological events, development, and life experience organize each pathway. The programming of attachment is done by interactions of the brain and social environment. A similar process is involved in sexual behavior, but is not understood as well.

Attachment is an example of pathway organization by gene-environment interaction. It depends on the genetic capacity for attachment, and requires environmental stimuli to form the bond between newborn and parent. This mammalian (and avian) survival strategy produces a small number of protected live births instead of the profusion of reptile eggs released to the environment, and vulnerable to predators. Birds are the intermediate stage, with a few protected eggs. The helpless human newborn requires a nurturing parent to feed and protect it. The bond between parent and offspring, called "imprinting" in birds by Lorenz and Tinbergen, occurs when hatched chicks link with their first visual stimulus, usually the mother bird. Other stimuli can trigger attachment, ensuring attachment to some supportive figure in the absence of the mother bird. A similar phenomenon has been observed in puppies and other mammals. (1)

HISTORICAL PERSPECTIVE Several classic studies have contributed to the understanding of attachment. *McLean reviewed the comparative neuroanatomy of reptile and mammalian brain structure, describing the "triune brain", three "evolutionary stages" in brain organization, with reptilian, mammalian and primate characteristics. Reptilian species have instinctual (genetically* *programmed) behavioral options with limited capacity for modification, and reproduce through environmental dispersion. The paleo-mammalian "Limbic cortex" develops on this core, with three characteristics that differentiate early mammals from reptiles: 1) generating and responding to the infant cry, 2) nesting behavior, and 3) the ability to "play" or organize behavior to non-instinctual cues. All three have reproductive significance, and the third is the basis for attachment. MacLean's "triune brain" model emphasizes maternal functions of the mammalian brain. (2)*

Harry Harlow, a primate researcher at Wisconsin in the 50s to 60s, demonstrated the importance of maternal infant bonding in primates by taking infant chimpanzees away from mothers at birth, and placing them with two different inanimate "surrogate mothers". (Two wire mesh cylinders mounted on bases, one with a bottle for feeding, the other wrapped in a towel.) The chimps, who used the other only for feeding, preferred the "surrogate mother" with cloth surround. The chimp sought the cloth mother when exposed to a fear stimulus, emphasizing the role of touch in primate attachment. Monkeys separated from their mothers in Harlow's original studies remained permanently disabled in social relationships indicating that the attachment relationship in primates is the foundation for other relationships. (3) A similar phenomenon had already been demonstrated in human infants by Spitz. (4) Infants with "failure to thrive" in prison nurseries recovered growth when caregivers gave them contact beyond feeding, while infants who were only touched while feeding did worse. Directing all the caregivers to pick up infants on a regular schedule corrected the developmental delays. Physical contact is also an essential element in the nurturing process of human infants.

The **attachment process** in humans does not occur in the one trial "imprinting" of birds. **John Bowlby,** a behavioral biologist (ethologist) studied human maternal-child attachment. "The Nature of The Child's Tie to His Mother" was published in a psychoanalytic journal in 1957, and merged the British psychoanalytic exploration of early maternal-child relationships with ethology. (5) Bowlby emphasized the importance of the child's seeking both physical contact and oral feeding, and described the transactional events occurring between mother and infant, initiated by both. His work stimulated the fusion of biological and psychological understanding of attachment, and his students Ainsworth and Main are major contributors to the study of patterns of attachment.

Oxytocin is a neurotransmitter that facilitates mammalian bonding. Studies by Insel and colleagues working at the Yerkes Primate Center in small mammals (voles) showed oxytocin and vasopressin peptides play a role in supporting pair bonding and attachment in certain species that show permanent pair boding. He reviewed this model of "attachment" and the role of these hormones in the maternal-infant bond in mammals. (8)

The studies reveal several principles:
1) Attachment is a learning/programming process in which genetically defined pathways are organized by environmental experience. There is only nature + nurture.
2) Somatic touch is as important as feeding for attachment in humans and other primates.
3) Humans emerge less genetically hardwired, requiring longer "programming time" for attachment. The human neonate is less pre-programmed for selfcare, for coordinated locomotion, for organized perception, and for communicating needs in recognized patterns. (6)
4) The neonate-maternal bond includes crying, mutual gazing, and the mother's smile response, holding ("contact comfort") and feeding. These elicit strong mutual responses in infant and caregiver, described by Bowlby and others. (7) The details of these first years of development are reviewed in many surveys documenting the stages of acquisition of perceptual organization and basic motor control of the infant. (6)
5) Oxytocin is a transmitter that facilitates attachment, along with other neurotransmitter effects on body regulation and behavior. (8)
6) The dopamine reward system may also be involved in maternal behavior. (9) Breast feeding activates oxytocin and is shown to reduce maternal neglect and enhance other aspects of maternal interaction. (10). Prolactin which stimulates the growth of milk producing glands and ducts at the late stages of pregnancy and post partum, may have a (as yet undocumented) role in attachment. The regions of hypothalamus involved in hormone release are easily identified and neuropeptide transmission and other reward pathways overlap. Insel has proposed that genetic coding of neuropeptide variants will explain variations in human affiliation. The hormones do not produce attachment without physical interaction, but facilitate bonding when it does. An extensive literature demonstrates serious adaptive consequences when the attachment process fails. (10)

Stranger anxiety is the evidence for internal representation. Humans do not "imprint" in one stimulus event. Human attachment to a specific caregiver is demonstrated by the stranger anxiety phenomenon, a developmental event observed throughout the world in children with a consistent caregiver over the first 9-12 months: In the first 8 months of life (approximately) the child will accept care and holding from many individuals, without strong preference for a "primary caregiver". Between 9 and 12 months, the child will have an emotional "protest response" if the primary caregiver is not available which includes crying and searching for the caregiver, and has been termed "separation anxiety" or "stranger anxiety" (it occurs in situations when the child is separated from the primary caregiver and put in the care of a "stranger", and is also seen in testing situations that involve separation from caregiver and challenge by another). This is observed even if the substitute caregiver is a family member who previously provided care, e.g. the father or grandmother. After a period of adaptation, the child once again accepts care from others. (11) In this sequence, the child differentiates a particular caregiver from others, creating an internal representation of sensory data of the primary care giver. This representation has **significance** associated with nurturing reward. The child preferentially responds to the "unique caregiver" for an interval, and then generalizes caregiving to others again. (The importance of the emotional reaction has been challenged. (12)) **Stranger anxiety** is the evidence of specific attachment, of the child's internal representation for nurturing with the sensory pattern of a specific caregiver. Fraiberg summarized the development of the representation, noting that this emotional constancy occurs after perceptual constancy (the awareness of permanence of entities when they are out of the direct sensory field of the child). (13) She studied the object constancy and representation of blind children and showed that they too develop stranger anxiety and form representations and primary attachments, with a slight delay, without the sensory input of visual stimuli, making the tactile element very important, as with other primates. (The role of smell and pheromones has not been studied but is also likely to be important. (14)) Human Primary Attachment depends on multiple sensory/reward experiences in the first year. The internal representation of "mother" is a multisensory pattern of the primary caregiver linked to the infant's reward experiences of nurturing activities. "Mother" is not stored at one location; the experiences of nurturing link sensory, reward-motivation system, and hippocampal reward significance storing mother-child attachment information. (15) The information in these pathways creates the representation of a specific caregiver who provides satiation from hunger and calming touch. (The self/other differentiation in *insula/cingulate* is also involved later.) There is some data observing pathway activity in mothers, but not in infants due to limitations of fMRI management. (15) The protest response is likely to originate in amygdala recognition of an aberrant state (see chapter eight) and related to other amygdala reactions to loss of nurturing support. (Redlich,15) A child who has acquired this response to a caregiver will calm from crying on being picked up, before any feeding, diaper change, or other corrective action is taken.

The child and mother are combined in the experience of "mother". Bowlby described this as a bilateral interactive experience of brain pathways in mother and child both responding to the interaction. Psychoanalysis calls this the "primary mother-child symbiosis", which is not a metaphor but a description of the child's representation of the primary caregiver in the pathways. The extended duration of bonding in humans reflects the maturation of perceptual pathways, reward systems, and physical capacity. It favors survival by allowing attachment to a wider range of possible caregivers, when the primary caregiver is unavailable, so attachment can develop on a substitute. The role of the mirror neuron system is important in primary attachment, but has not been clarified. Laurita et al present a theoretical review of the interactions based on current studies. (Laurita, 15) A complex multivariable study by Lenzi et al explores the variations in attachment in adults, and illustrates the difficulties in neural studies that address multiple variables. (Lenzi, 15) Praszkier proposes a relationship between empathy and mirror neurons that involves attachment. (Praszkier, 15) The study of mirror neurons and attachment in different research domains has delayed finding bridging variables to integrate them. Primary attachment synthesizes multiple reward interactions into a representation of "general social reward", that influences relationships throughout life. The multisensory nature of the representation has implications for emotional memory in clinical situations. The profound dependence of the human neonate, and the extended duration of the attachment make this an intense motivation, with strong ***significance***.

Primary attachment is followed by separation-individuation. Children grow heavy, the need to be picked up for soothing becomes physically demanding, and there may be a new infant to nurture, so the child must find comfort without the direct contact of the primary (or even secondary) caregivers. The internal representation of "mother" is transferred to something other than the person for comfort, a process first described in detail by the British psychoanalyst-pediatrician Winnicott. (Though it has been observed and appreciated by parents over time immemorial.) Tactile physical objects, blankets, teddy bears, pillows, etc. (in accord with the Harlow data) become nurturing surrogates when the mother is not available. These transitional objects define the transitional period, when alternative objects satisfy the child, and the child begins individuation. "Transitional object" gives psychological meaning to the importance of "cuddly" objects in development, and observes the relationship between interactive human nurturing, self-stimulation, and external objects. (16) A study by Fortuna suggests that both situational and genetic factors contribute to attachment to transitional objects. (Fortuna, 15) The establishment of transitional objects occurs after primary attachment, and is probably an indicator of successful primary caregiver attachment, though there is no validating research confirming this. (PSA describes the child "hallucinating" the mother implying transfer of memory of maternal nurturing to the object. (17)) An alternate situation, when nurturing emphasizes feeding rather than tactile contact, may teach some children coping patterns using eating, and create problems with tactile nurturing. Do some eating disorders reflect disturbances in touch attachment? This deserves further study. (Ward, 16)

Winnicott's concept of a holding environment, created by the mother, provides not constant nurturing but good enough mothering, sufficient to provide an experience of nurturing, while leaving space for separation. The separation-individuation stage has more research than primary attachment, which reflects the difficulty doing research with neonates, but also the interest in "separation anxiety" in later life. After creating an internal representation of the caregiver, and transferring its emotional power to external objects, the child is less dependent on the caregiver. Individuation has been studied in two different research paradigms. Bowlby's students, Main and Ainsworth (and others), explored the quality of attachment in young children using the "strange situation": placing a child in an unfamiliar situation with the mother and studying the way the child and the mother responded to the situation. They identified 4 patterns: A) secure response, B) avoidant response, C) ambivalent response and D) disorganized response, patterns similar to Bowlby's descriptions of the child's reactions to maternal separation in earlier studies. (18) Adult patterns of relationship were studied by questionnaire to develop a corresponding description of adult relationships: A) secure, B) autonomous, C) dismissing, D) pre-occupied and E) unresolved-disorganized. Longitudinal evaluation across time does not give replication of the childhood categories in adults. (Bartholomew, 19) It is unclear whether children with a particular response pattern maintain this pattern as adults. Johannes studied adult couples and parents as dyads, and showed more consistency of parents, than young adults, but some in both. (Johannes et al,19) The transfer of the childhood pattern of attachment to adult life is unresolved, and it is possible that other life situations modify these patterns. (20)

Mahler used an observational mother/child situation similar to the "strange situation" but interpreted it as patterns of separation-individuation (perhaps reflecting cultural differences). Mahler's children were 18 months to 3 years of age, a range thought to give increased autonomy from the primary caregiver by locomotion. She categorized a three stage process: i) symbiosis, begins soon after birth and represents the changing proprioceptive patterns in response to mother, and development of "object constancy", then ii) separation/ rapproachment, at 16-18 months, locomotor capacity permits some autonomy from mother, but the child shows fear with rapid returns, "rapprochement", and then iii) individuation, including sub-stages, with infrequent rapprochement by 24 mos. This includes a period of "peek-a-boo", hiding games, and other forms of rapprochement, followed by more consistent autonomy. Mahler proposed that some children might be developmentally fixated at a stage of the process and unable to complete the sequence to explain adult dysfunctions. (21) Where the English group saw patterns of interaction emphasizing attachment, the American presented a developmental sequence with stages leading to individuation. Both paradigms assume the quality of the attachment created in the maternal/infant situation is revealed in the older child or adult.

After thirty years, Fonagy, a psychiatrist working with both the US psychoanalytic community at Menninger's Clinic and the Tavistock Clinic in London, integrated the two approaches correlating findings from Mahler's "separation/individuation" with Ainsworth and Main's "disturbed attachment". (22) His synthesis observed i) the role of mutual cueing between mother and child at the two year old transition point, ii) the "ambivalent response" is noted in both, iii) "rapprochement" is key to autonomy in Mahler and a pattern type in Ainsworth, iv) Fairburn's formulation of "obsessive attachment" is related to trauma in Main, but not clearly identified in the Mahler paradigm though it is suggested by children who do not progress through the stages. v) Both link personality development to early life experiences. vi) Both emphasize the pattern of maternal response (more than the child's). vii) Both emphasize the internal representation in the child for later relationships, including the experiences of security and vulnerability to trauma. viii) The persistence of patterns forms the basis for adult relationships. He proposed that the symptoms of borderline personality disorder are attachment problems. His more recent review incorporates new research and expands his theory to combine genetic vulnerabilities with the effects of early trauma. These principles relate developmental experience to adult interactions, but are not based on longitudinal studies. His comparison of the two approaches does not have an overlapping data set. The child's experience is open to interpretation: a 2 year old, struggling with autonomy, may be a problem in interpersonal relations, or the ambivalence of separation/individuation. (23) A contemporary ethologist sees similar phenomena in comparative studies of animal and human family systems. (24) Siegel, a pediatrician/psychiatrist developed a similar approach emphasizing the role of interpersonal interaction, including the attachment process, in brain and social functioning, along with an overview of the different areas of brain and social function. (25) A key assumption of his approach, the longitudinal relationship between the childhood events and adult responses, and the stability of internalized attachment patterns also needs documentation. (26) Later experiences may influence the process, modifying the initial programming. Fonagy linked the attachment literature and PSA in two paradigms; Siegel linked the attachment literature to cognitive neuroscience. (Fricchione, puts a similar emphasis on attachment as primary in healing and healthcare. (27))

The attachment literature has several unresolved issues: *The neural pathways involved lack confirming studies. Measures of neural activity during attachment in infancy are difficult to perform, measurement of changes in separation individuation are transient and unstable. Does attachment change throughout life or become fixed at a certain point in development? Extending "Adult Attachment Modes" to parenting offspring, mirroring the relationship of one's own parenting, is unresolved. Attachment in old age includes both the ability to remain attached, as partners and friends are lost, and the role of previous attachment experiences in facing death. Are attachment patterns discrete categories or a continuum? Can one person have multiple attachment patterns at the same time to different others? Are patterns of attachment programmed to situations? Are attachment patterns culture specific?* (28)

CLINICAL EXAMPLE Daycare and the kibbutz. *Kibbutzim, communal farms in the 40s and 50s in Israel, used a communal process for childcare. Children were cared for in groups and school but returned home to parents at night. As young adults, these children had a stronger peer group attachment than transgenerational attachment to older authority figures. The Main-Ainsworth school examined contemporary daycare in the United States, and found that children who go to daycare for a portion of everyday and then come home to be with their mothers go through separation anxiety. When the time they have with the mother is adequate, it will provide the primary caregiver experience. Data on situations where the mothering isn't adequate and the child doesn't develop strong primary attachment are not clear. (29) Similar issues arise in any situation where the child is raised partly in a group setting and includes the myriad variations of daycare now common in Western societies where both parents are working. (30)*

How does the attachment process create patterns for social interaction in later life? PSA uses the terms "internal object" or "internal representation",for what Bowlby calls the "internal working model". The internal representation of caregiver is distributed across synapses of various pathways crossing multiple brain regions; there is no "attachment center" or localized "mother". *Self/other differentiation is created during the separation-individuation sequence and probably stored in cingulate cortex, insula, and mirror neuron locations, though research on this has not been done.* Internal representations of patterns of social behavior involve multiple sensory-reward experiences, the basis for patterns of social behavior (see chapter six, personality). During adolescence, transition from family attachment to peer group tests the process with a new separation challenge. This is accentuated in boarding schools, especially the English system, where clinical symptoms and maladaptive patterns are sometimes reported. (31) The contemporary development of audio-visual media and social media complicates the nature of "transitional objects". The practice of placing children in front of television for emotional control suggests other changes in the nature of the **transitional object,** with very limited current research on the consequences. Very young children watching and hearing images designed to be comforting on video screens create an alternative basis for *non-tactile transitional objects* (but note the fuzziness of the puppets in Sesame

Street). How do these experiences alter the sensory programming nurturing of modern children? (32) The availability of social media interactions may alter social patterns, and reduce the isolation from peers, or exaggerate it. *Research is needed to understand the emerging emphasis on visual attachment, replacing tactile (touch) attachment, the normal mode of primates.*

The clinical consequences of attachment problems can be obvious or subtle. The social brain includes pathways involved in attachment. (See chapter two) **Autism spectrum syndrome** includes the lack of response to social rewards, and difficulty in attachment. Persons with severe problems have an inability to attach, while milder syndromes have complex attachment issues. The impairment in contact/touch in these children, along with excessive self-stimulation, are consistent with the problems using the touch sensory channel for attachment. *The brain regions impaired in this syndrome overlap regions essential for attachment, but the relationships lack documentation.* Attachment is fundamental to all relationships, so isolating its role in clinical situations is difficult. What is the role of attachment in anxiety or depression? Few mental health diagnoses specify attachment symptoms. Is the individual's capacity for attachment impaired? Are symptoms associated with separation? The following are some clinical examples:

Failure to thrive. The neonate's inability to take nourishment and grow can be fatal. The inability to engage in the feeding process and absorb nutrients may be due to malfunction of heart, lungs, digestive track or other organs. "Non-organic failure to thrive" is diagnosed when growth is impaired, not by somatic organ problems but failure of attachment bonding to mother. The historical data of Spitz are an example (see sidebar above). Factors in child-mother bonding have been studied to improve bonding with the caregiver, to mitigate long term effects in growth and development. This is the most basic form of the infant's dependence on the caregiver for survival, showing the importance of bonding in human relationships. (33)

Attachment Issues In Childhood. The departure or death of a parent(s), especially the primary caregiver, has been studied using naturalistic experiences of separation. Bowlby studied children who were temporarily separated from parents, and developed an anxious, depressed, withdrawn state, usually temporary, but for some with lifelong impact. The age of occurrence may be a factor in developing long-term effects, with studies reporting higher impact at certain ages, but not always the same age range. (34) Perhaps there are "critical periods" in the human attachment process when the loss has more impact. A prospective study in 2007 found psychological effects, but did not reference attachment as a primary variable. (Marks, 34) Nagera reviewed earlier literature relating child losses to later depression, with adult symptoms a mixture of anxiety and depression. (Nagera, 34) Early adolescence is another vulnerable period, due to the concurrent separation individuation issues expected at this stage. (Rice, 34) There is a presumption that problems in grieving in children reflect both the loss and other associated issues, associating loss and anorexia is an example (Delvecchio, 34) *Understanding the role of loss and attachment in childhood can only be studied if the event is documented in later evaluations.*

Disruption of the caregiver-child connection due to problems in the family unit, domestic violence, child abuse, or issues external to the family is difficult to assess. Incarceration of the caregiver with placement of the child outside the family in an institutional setting, orphanage or foster family, may threaten the process of primary attachment and its organizing effect on the brain, or provide a more stable experience. The changes may be temporary or permanent, and may depend on when they occur, during or after "stranger anxiety" and "separation individuation". (35) If an alternative primary caregiver is available, the attachment process can continue with the alternative. In some cultures, a designated caregiver, a nanny, is assigned this task, to complete the attachment process. If there are multiple caregivers and no primary, the child receives adequate nurturing, and group identification of nurturing occurs, as in children raised on Kibbutz, or in communes or cults. (28) (36) If no replacement occurs, and the child does not form representation of a primary caregiver, symptoms of Reactive Attachment Disorder may result. (36) If the replacement is abusive this may create an alternative attachment bonding and result in abnormal adult social functioning. (37) Zeanah et al review practical issues in the evaluation of attachment: questions of parental maltreatment or foster care maltreatment, post-institutional and inter-country placement, divorce and child custody, and families with inter-parental violence issues. (38)

School Refusal (historically, School Phobia) is one indication of attachment issues. Johnson's classic review identifies different factors: an acute anxiety in the child, which may be caused by organic disease, or by some emotional conflict, precipitated by arrival of a new sibling, promotion in school, etc. Equally important is anxiety in the mother, due to threat such as economic deprivation, marital unhappiness, illness, etc. If there is an unresolved dependency relationship between the child and mother, problems may occur. The role of issues at school or home is a diagnostic challenge. (38)

Reactive Attachment Disorder. Some children in orphanages, or in situations without consistent primary caregiver may not develop a primary attachment, and present symptoms of Reactive Attachment Disorder, with two subtypes: emotionally withdrawn inhibited, and social disinhibited. Zeanah and Gleason describe the two patterns, with young children under the age of 5, especially in orphanages, described as *withdrawn and non-interactive*, with poor social communication. Emotional dyscontrol, regressive behavior, and developmental delays are also sometimes observed. (39) Other developmental factors including cognitive disability, and mild autism may confuse the data. The *disinhibited pattern symptoms* overlap with antisocial personality features, and teenagers with this life history and adults with severe attachment may later be diagnosed with Antisocial Personality Disorder. The two patterns may be alternative coping strategies for absent parenting: 1) failure to seek interaction due to the experience of no previous reward, or 2) excessive attempts to manipulate others for reward. Clinical assessment of the child-caregiver bond depends on intuitive observations, and shows poor reliability. (39) Cassidy, Jones, and Shaver review areas in need of clarification. (40) Early foster placement benefited inhibited pattern children more than the socially disinhibited form in one study. The life histories of Ted Bundy and some other serial killers appear to have life circumstances consistent with the Reactive Attachment Disorder diagnosis, giving this concept a high forensic profile, but the documentation is retrospective and biased by defense attorneys seeking exculpatory explanations. Bierer et al, report that certain childhood experiences lead to later adult personality disorders, suicidal behaviors, and poor social adjustment. (37) This is also the retrospective assessment of maladapted persons, subject to the distortions of recall. The lack of consistent social rewards, and socialization by a hostile externalizing parent could explain the pattern in reinforcement terms, according to Rotter. (38)

CLINICAL EXAMPLE Socialization Problem. A female teenager of was evaluated for social problems. She was adopted through international channels as a child, at 4 years old, and lived in an orphanage prior to this. No information on biological mother or father was available to the adopting family. As a teen, she was oppositional to parents, rejecting of parental authority with hostile outbursts, using cannabis, and not sexually active. The parents, a religious Christian family adopted the child both for personal reasons and "religious commitment". The teen was stocky, not "feminine" by Western standards, and casually groomed. She formed intense temporary bonds with other females, at school and on the treatment unit, but not with parents or other adults. The parents reported her inability to make physical contact from her earliest time in the family. COMMENT The teen illustrates the complex and confusing issues in the RAD diagnosis. She manifests both inhibition and hostility toward the adoptive family, and excessive attempts at "attachment" to peers, perhaps mirroring earlier orphanage attachments. Gender identity issues may also be involved. Other than parental conflicts, the patient did not show symptoms of a psychiatric diagnosis, or respond to any intervention. She discharged unchanged.

Many contemporary international situations create issues of attachment. Parental deprivation, associated with social calamities, has produced studies of children in orphanages of Eastern Europe, displaced children in African civil wars, children raised in cults, and children participating in migrations. (42) American families, who adopt orphans from other nations, may find they do not bond to the adoptive family. Whether this is due to RAD, or confounded by lack of prenatal care, fetal alcohol, birth injury history, early childhood abuse and neglect, unrealistic expectations of the adoptive family, or other factors is unknown. Evaluating if foster care or group home experiences create primary attachment problems or reactive attachment disorder is controversial; studies are influenced by the politics of placing children out of the family. *A broad review of the literature is needed.* The child's response to traumatic abuse is poorly understood, and some children demonstrate withdrawal, isolation and depression, others bond strongly to the abuser, and others take on the abusive role and traumatize children later in development. These variations reflect different modes of responding to the interaction of abuse and attachment and the critical variables have not been clarified, though the concept of "trauma bonding" is described. (43)

CLINICAL EXAMPLE The Girl Who Abused Others. *A young adult woman, adopted as a young teen from an orphanage, had poor emotional control, and did not bond to her adoptive mother. She reported that she had been abused, physically and sexually in the orphanage, and (eventually) acknowledged aiding staff in abusing other residents. She ran away from her adopted mother to live on the street, and bonded with another homeless female for support, but also triggered the other female's problem behavior.* COMMENT *Individuals with attachment problems with antisocial features have difficulty sustaining intimate relationships, interfering with adult relationships. The patient sought treatment services as a victim, concealing her role in abusing others and the guilt involved, which slowly emerged. When abuse victims are also abusers, modeling "identification with the aggressor", healing the trauma is more difficult. (44)*

Controversy over the treatment of RAD adds to the confusion. Children with the *social disinhibited* pattern often do not enter treatment until they have legal problems as pre-adolescents and are diagnosed with behavior problems, especially "conduct disorder". Withdrawn inhibited children present earlier and are usually diagnosed and treated as depression. The inability to bond to a therapist may lead to residential referral, creating another separation from the adopting family. Treatment that attempts to build the child's attachment using various paradigms to encourage (or "force") interaction are sometimes physically coercive, have been criticized as abusive, and are sometimes helpful. (45) No data predict which children will respond to particular interventions. The importance of touch in primary attachment suggests that touching could be helpful, but is difficult to include in traditional psychotherapy, which views it as a boundary violation. For children capable of connecting to animals, "pet therapy" can build a transition to human attachment by first bonding with a therapy animal, but some children abuse animals and must be closely watched. Whether connection with the animal transfers attachment to the family caregiver is unpredictable. The difficulty in resolving attachment in older children and teens lends credence to a "critical period for attachment" in humans, and makes rebuilding the missing connection more difficult as the child gets older, or whether it is even possible. (46) The most recent recommendations of Mayo Clinic confirm no agreement on the treatment of this problem, especially when issues emerge in late childhood and early adolescence. (47)

Attachment problems in childhood may be obscured by family compensation until adolescence. "Home schooling" can delay the challenges of individuation from the family, and provide more time for maturation, but deprives the child of experiences with peers. The separation/individuation process in adolescence may reveal problems with family or extra-family life stresses. Rice correlated studies on adolescent interpersonal relationships with the attachment literature and found different levels of attachment in teens. (48) Schafer emphasized the importance of a stable sense of self in adolescent separation-individuation. Problems in individuation include the dilemma of ambivalence, rejecting parental influence but fearing parental rejection. Autonomy can open up feelings of loneliness and emptiness. (49) In the adolescent, social experiences are more urgent and intense, and rejection more devastating. It is a time of developing coping skills and/or suicidal feelings of hopelessness. (50) The core issue for attachment theory, both the psychoanalytic reports of adult clinical situations and child development studies, remains: *does the pattern of interpersonal communication and behavior learned and stored as representations in the mind/brain become the ongoing framework for social engagement, or is it revised throughout life?* These questions are not answered by measuring fMRI or other brain responses, because no brain measures have been correlated with degree of attachment.

Borderline syndrome and attachment. For most adolescents emotional instability will be temporary when new relationships stabilize. If symptoms persist into adulthood, the individual may be diagnosed *Borderline Personality Disorder*. The person has episodes of anxiety, sudden loss of emotional control, and poor coping skills. Social skills seem effective, but are unstable showing dramatically intense emotions after (seemingly) mild provocations. Sudden dramatic shifts to immature personality configurations with poor emotional regulation are common. The loss of emotional regulation is often associated with suicidal behavior, or non-suicidal self-injury used as a coping skill. (*These shifts may involve changes in configuration of cingulate/insula and PF/BG system described in chapter six.*) Dissociation may be important in creating the dramatic changes, (see chapter eight). The prominent role of suicidal self-injury is also seen in PTSD and dissociative states. The emphasis on using suicidal self injury as a "coping skill" can be understood as: an escape from intolerable emotional experience, a coping device that substitutes physical for emotional pain, self injury for guilt related to the experiences, or interpersonal efforts to intensify the treatment engagement with therapist. Several of these factors may be involved in the same person at the same or different times. (See Appendix to chapter 3).(56)

The syndrome has been extensively researched with conflicting viewpoints that mimic the patients' internal conflicts. Gunderson has written an historical "ontogeny" review of the "development" of the diagnosis. (51) The diagnosis transitioned from a PSA term for a specific group of patients to a DSM diagnosis with emphasis on sudden changes in emotional state in the late 70s. The patients respond poorly to medications, (to the point of doubting the diagnosis: "Is the patient borderline if he or she responds to medication?")

Difficulty regulating emotions and behavioral loss of control are the basic symptoms, with sudden dramatic failure of coping skills in social situations (in someone who appeared to have effective coping). Dramatic emotional response occurs to perceived loss of attachment of support persons. Genetic etiology varies from a high of 69%, to as low as 37% in different studies, indicating a different balance of genetic and developmental factors in different persons. There is significant incidence of childhood PTSD. There is no relationship to bipolar disorder and no response to bipolar medications. *Gunderson concluded that BPD is a "brain disorder with good prognosis" challenging previous theories of developmental etiology and poor prognosis. (51)* Several theories (etiologies) for the development of the *borderline syndrome* have been proposed: Fonagy is a strong proponent of the disturbed attachment in early development view. Vulnerability for attachment may be the result of no consistent nurturing object, failure of calming to the nurturing object, or failure to internalize a representation of the caregiver. (51) Individuals with borderline diagnosis often have early life history of traumatic events that contribute to difficulties in attachment, i.e. PTSD/childhood trauma. Patients with/without PTSD history report different symptoms. A genetic (presumed) impairment of affect regulation varies from a high of 69% to a low as 37% in different studies, with no specific defined loci. (In more recent papers, Fonagy includes a genetic vulnerability as well as traumatic events. (53)) The meta-review summary of Amad notes the confusion between 40% heritability in families and a lack of overlapping gene loci in population studies, and posits "a paradigm shift, in which "plasticity genes" (rather than "vulnerability" genes) would be involved." (Amad, 54) The opiate theory, based on the effect of opiates calming emotional reactivity, proposes a deficit, genetic or other, in endorphin response. (New and Stanley, 54) (Prossin, 54) Insel suggested the neuropeptide theory of changes in oxytocin because oxytocin is important in human bonding. One study demonstrates a positive interaction effect on patients after nasal administration of the hormone. (Bertsch, 54) *Competing theories of borderline syndrome mediated through brain pathways that produce the syndrome, are potentially interrelated, but never researched together, and are all still opportunities for new research.*

Pathways associated with insecure attachment may be involved in borderline syndrome. (Ruocco, 55) Several small studies used PET scanning show increased activity in amygdala, and in cingulate-insula. The results are often lateralized to the non-dominant cortex. When amygdala is visualized it is active, but not always the same region in different studies (which may be a technical problem). The role of amygdala is consistent with its role anxiety, described in the next chapter. The current imaging research on borderline patients does not indicate increased activity in cingulate cortex, insula, and amygdala produced by triggering stimuli. *There is no indication of how triggers alter pathways, and if there is loss of frontal control.*

Therapy using Linehan's and Fonagy's methods emphasizes subjective experience of the interpersonal space, with limited use of short-term hospitalizations. (52) Patients who have not learned to attach may learn this skill using "reprogramming", per Gunderson's comment: *"In modern psychiatry, borderline personality disorder has become the major container for sustaining the relevance of the mind, an arena that has been endangered by our growing biological knowledge".* (51) *Borderline syndrome deficits in coping skills may benefit from a treatment strategy that teaches missing skills.* (59)

Intimate partner violence often arises in a context of fear of separation, or loss of attachment. The borderline syndrome of anger/suicide is more common in females, is the male equivalent anger and partner violence? Is stalking or inter-partner violence the male alternative to borderline symptoms seen in females? McClellan and Killeen proposed that male partner violence is related to insecure attachment. (57) Velotti et al reviewed the data supporting this hypothesis correlated with attachment patterns. Sansone and Sansone found a relationship to borderline/attachment issues, and Patton et al examined the relationship in stalking. Why this connection took so long to reach the literature is puzzling. (58) The references, found in criminal justice literature, question whether defining a "mental illness" is used to avoid legal consequences. Corvo et al proposed specific "evidence based practices" for treatment that prevent avoiding accountability. (Corvo, 58) Other studies support the connection of attachment with violence and suggest an alternative association with amygdala response (see chapter eight).

The relationship of attachment issues to other mental health conditions has not been studied systematically. *Hoarding* may be a coping mechanism of problems of secure attachment, childhood use of "transitional objects" for comforting that becomes extreme in adults. Almost everyone has a collection of favorite "something or others", a childhood teddy bear, jewelry, or other emotionally comforting object. News stories about people whose houses are filled with accumulated things extend this to the extreme. If one's residence becomes uninhabitable, the process becomes a syndrome. Two theories of hoarding have been proposed: an example of the attachment phenomenon of *"transitional objects"* taken to the extreme, related to unstable primary attachment, or *obsessional repetition*, a defense using repetition of buying or collecting to ease anxiety. *Are these two different explanations or variations of the same brain activity, phrased in different terms?* Mathes et al present a review paper showing correlations between severity of hoarding and attachment measures in the same subjects. (61) (63) Persons who hoard animals, who constantly "rescue" animals from street or shelters, and keep "herds" of dogs, cats, etc. seem to be *hoarding living transitional objects*! A recent review did not identify specific diagnostic features in a group of identified American and Canadian animal hoarders, but noted addiction and OCD explanations, not attachment issues. Animal hoarders rarely seek treatment, until neighbors and county health departments become involved when health concerns are violated. (62) *The boundary between separation anxiety, attachment to transitional objects, and OCD symptoms offers opportunities for research and clarification.*

Attachment may also play a role in other clinical situations. Hellmuth Kaiser, one of Freud's students, claimed all psychopathology was driven by the desire to recapture the early attachment of childhood. This did not fit with the PSA view and was generally disregarded (and even now seems an overgeneralization), but leaves open the question of which symptoms are driven by attachment, and how to link these with the attachment process. The schizophrenias have problems in social interaction, and separation issues are often seen in these patients that might be problems in attachment. Attachment loss may trigger manic or depressive episodes in bipolar patients.

CLINICAL EXAMPLE A Woman Becomes Manic On Anniversary Of Mother's Death. Every year a single woman in her 20's would have a manic episode at the anniversary week of her mother's death, often on the day. She did not live at home at the time of the mother's death and was impaired by addiction at the time. After the death, she became sober, acquired a career and had a productive life, but at the time of the anniversary she would get agitated, go back to using drugs, and require hospitalization for days to weeks. This had occurred two previous years, when first seen in treatment after the third episode. The sequence was explained to her (for the first time!) and she was able to use the information to use medications to interrupt the cycles. COMMENT Anniversary reactions are more frequent triggers for problems than often appreciated, especially associated with grieving. Attachment issues played a role in the relationship between patient and her mother, and persisted after mother's death. It was possible to work on the grief when the pressure to shift to mania was controlled. (64)

Every interpersonal exchange involves attachment, especially sustained psychotherapy. Attachment is activated when a patient is admitted to an inpatient treatment setting and the confusion and resulting dependency may exaggerate the search for support, even when not reciprocated. A classic paper describes this with inpatient treatment of children, who were perceived by the staff as "victims" of defective parenting that the treatment would correct. This view is often incorrect since the child presents both personal issues and parental conflict. (65) A related problem is the VIP patient (or one who wishes to be) seeking special connection to the therapist or staff. Attachment is inherent in all treatment relationships. Cassidy et al presented a comprehensive overview of attachment in 2013. (40) From its historical origins to the contemporary approach to mental health problems, the topic has remained "slightly outside" the mainstream of research, creating its own path. The emphasis in mental health of the medical model leaves little room for attachment. *Interpersonal approaches that focus on positive attachment are disappearing with the loss of trust in social relationships, just as the American family as an environment for safety, security, and support is disappearing.*

Sexuality is the other motivation for attraction that is important for the species. The sexual act is evolutionary because it mixes the human genome. It provides no survival benefit for the individual, only for the species genome, and requires a physical interaction to achieve its (reproductive) goal. Sexual behavior promotes one's genome to the next generation in preference to the genome of others Many regulatory processes influence this behavior, with or without intention. At the individual level, hormones, and distal and local sensory stimulation coordinate the "behavioral exchange of genes" (i.e. sex). The seasons, display behaviors, and other instinctual factors also influence human and animal sexual activity. The study of sex has diminished over the past 50 years in mental health, leaving many unanswered questions. What motivates the person to engage in sexual behavior? How is a suitable partner chosen? What is the relationship between sexual behavior and attachment?

Sexuality can be studied at the individual, group, and societal level, and each provides different information. Because of the personal/private nature of sexual acts, direct observation is limited. Kinsey and coworkers performed an extensive self report survey of sexual behavior in the American adult population in the 1950s, an impressive sociological feat, which was read with great interest, but treated more as a source of personal comparison than for understanding norms of sexual activity. It did not address the role of mental illness in sexual behavior. (73) Defining statistical "norms" of sexual behavior was biased by respondent selection and disclosure, and not accurate data on actual behavior at the time, and less so now. The contemporary changes in gender identity, acceptance of different relationship patterns, and changes in reproductive choices all make defining the "normative" behavior difficult, and blur even statistical patterns. Even assessing appropriate childhood sexual boundaries is controversial. (73) Contemporary critics object to studies revealing gender differences in current research claiming the gender bias of the researchers, which makes research even more difficult. (73)

Demography studies factors that influence the rate of reproduction in human populations. Multiple factors change rates across societies including public health, economics, and social structures. Demographers associate varying rates of reproduction with these variables. Many developed societies are currently experiencing reductions in reproductive rate, the result of the aging of the population, and other factors. But sub-groups within these societies preserve higher rates, a clue to changes in the society. (74)

Psychiatric research into the genetics of mental disorders does not include gene effects on reproductive rates of persons with mental disorders. (Mental health geneticists do not seem to understand how gene transmission occurs.) One recent study by Mullins et al addresses the issue. (75) They wondered why, if "heritable psychiatric disorders reduce reproductive fitness", they don't get eliminated in human breeding. (A similar argument might be made for all genetic influence on disease.) They obtained genomic data from 150000 Icelanders not diagnosed with Psychiatric diseases and evaluated the reproductive rates of the individuals grouped by known CNV and PRS (polygenic risk)scores. They found reduced reproduction only for sites associated with autism and schizophrenia syndrome, not others. This may be interpreted as difficulty identifying risk in the absence of the clinical syndrome, but *a different interpretation (suggested throughout **Neuromind**) is that these are not sites for mental illness, but sites for adaptive effects which are not understood because genome research in mental health is correlated to diagnoses not adaptive mental functions.*

What motivates an individual to engage in sexual behavior? The endocrine effect in puberty is documented. The correlation of hormone level and "drive"(= motivation?) for sexual behavior is documented at times of increasing hormone levels in teens, (and also a weaker period in mid childhood), and by the effect of castration or hormone block in reducing sexual drive in male sexual predators. Smell, touch, and visual stimuli are all effective for arousal of sexual response as "documented" by the use of sexual imagery for advertising and other promotions. Human sexual response depends on hormone levels, the sexual "drive", social conditioning, and the response to sexual arousal by stimulation, "sexual appetite". Studies have explored the differences in stimulus arousal response of men and women. The neural basis of sexual response is inferred from studies with brain damage and seizure activity. fMRI response to arousing images are observed in OFC, and subjective awareness in cingulate and insula. (68) Problems in female sexual response led Masters and Johnson to study the physiological features of sexual arousal and orgasm in females, and in males, based on their background in gynecology. The studies addressed both normal individual sexual response and problems. The visual documentation provided a basis for understanding the physiological sexual response, but the goal of facilitating female sexual response ran counter to social values, and was viewed as "objectification of sexual behavior removing the emotional component". Their work succeeded in opening public discussion of the topic, but was strongly criticized as unscientific and closed down. (69)

Fisher, an anthropologist, identified three component factors in sexual relationships: attachment, lust, and attraction, and related each component to a different neuro-transmitter. "Lust" depends upon the sexual hormones, testosterone and estrogen, and is part of the process of sexual maturation. "Attachment" is the process discussed so far in this chapter, and (according to Insel and Young) depends on oxytocin and vasopressin. "Attraction" is used to describe the state of enhanced motivation usually called "falling in love", a strong motivation directed toward a specific love object who is perceived as "rewarding", involving the reward transmitters, norepinephrine and dopamine. This account is too simplified, but provides some differentiation. (70)

In addition to biological controls, social factors also play a role in sexual behavior at the group level. Until the mid 20th century, sexual behavior was also reproductive behavior. The introduction of reliable contraception has separated the two decisions for a significant proportion of the population in developed countries. They can be separated in non-reproductive acts, motivated by sexual pleasure (or other), and reproductive behaviors for producing offspring, (there is a third category when the intention is not conscious, but the actions support reproduction). Socially constructed, anthropological-social rules of allowable sexual acts, influence human decisions about sexual (and reproductive) behavior. They usually involve some restriction against adult/child sexual behavior, and between genetically related individuals (incest). Societies differ in these rules, expressed in cultural norms and prohibitions.

What motivates an individual to engage in sexual behavior with a specific person? Just as *attachment* is programmed by interpersonal experiences in development, there is evidence suggesting that this occurs with sexual attraction. Observations of children document sexual play, and verbal expressions of attraction toward others in ways that imply "marriage" or other sexual connotation. Freud was sharply criticized for his observations, but contemporary data validate this information. (71) Freud's PSA theory proposes that behavior is motivated by conscious (and unconscious) desires to satisfy "needs", the "pleasure principle", which is based on sexual motivation ("libido"). Current reading of Freud, reframes "pleasure" as both sexual and non-sexual gratification, but his writing emphasized sexuality. The "complexes" are explicitly sexual, and cases often involved sexual events or traumas. (78) Significant attention is given in PSA treatments to patterns of sexual attraction presumed to develop in childhood that interfere with adult relationships. This focus is not associated with consideration of the genetic factors in mate selection. Other methods of interpersonal therapy, especially the EST paradigms, do not emphasize sexual factors unless the therapy is explicitly focused on sexual problems. (72) The developmental issues in patterns of sexual attraction do not seem to have stimulated the research focus seen in attachment. *For example, male and female children have different dynamics in the relationship between maternal attachment and sexual attraction, which have not been studied.* (This may be the result of contemporary cultural opposition to identifying factors in sexual differentiation. This rejection of differences in male/female identity and brain function is part of the "equality of genders" view that rejects differences in brain and behavior as not significant for social behavior. The view has academic support that discourages (or attacks!) studies and investigators who claim to show differences.)

Though contemporary American society appears more open about sexuality, interest in sexual behavior in mental health has diminished. Advertising and media openly portray provocative sexual images and behavior, while the society pretends to be outraged by the sexual behavior of leaders and politicians. The sexual side effects of medications are more important than what might be interfering with sexuality in relationships. How individuals choose sexual partners for reproduction has not received study, especially regarding mental health strengths and vulnerabilities. (79) As in other areas of contemporary life, the digital/internet world has expanded the access to sexual encounters using online dating sites, with (often inaccurate) information about both parties. The links produce encounters, which may lead to ongoing relationships, and eventually reproduction, broadening the available pool of genetic choices, for better or worse.

None of these methods of studying sexual behavior (individual, group, or demographic) address the selection of an "evolutionarily suitable" partner. The individual rarely thinks of sexual choice as, "I will select that female/male for positive phenotype/genome characteristics." (Women seeking donor insemination do request detailed information about the donor's genetic strengths and vulnerabilities.) In all cultures, individuals select reproductive partners motivated by a range of conscious and unconscious assessments, yet identifying the important determinants in mate attraction is not often shared in verbal reports. A recent study exploring these questions, by Robinson et al in Australia, showed common genetic traits in married partners, assuming that these characteristics were consciously (or unconsciously) selected. (76) No studies selecting partners by features of mental health have been reported (apparently individuals do not select partners for positive mental health characteristics).

> **SIDEBAR Huntington's disease.** Huntingdon's disease, illustrates this issue: the disease often does not manifest until after age 30, reproductive age or after, so the individual must decide whether to reproduce, and risk passing on an autosomal dominant gene. Dominant genes that produce major adaptive problems before reproductive age are rare because they interfere with passing themselves on to the next generation. Just as genetic research has shifted to the study of large populations, the understanding of the factors influencing the differential rate of reproduction are more easily understood at the population level. (77)

The role of attachment and sexuality in relationships is variable. The Greeks had 7 different words for love relationships (with no evidence that it clarified their relationships): Storge = empathy, parental love, Philios =deep friendship, Ludic = playful love, dancing, flirting, Eros = physical romantic love, sexual passion, Agape = unconditional, God love, universal love, Pragma = enduring love, mature realistic love of enduring relationships, Philautia = love of self, narcissitic, self-focused. (80) Current scholars are unclear about the relationship between these terms and the motivations of attachment and sexuality. The examples suggest that each has an "appropriate object" on which to attach, and that some emphasize primary attachment, others, sexuality, and a few involve both.

Studies on the relationship between attachment needs and sexual behavior examine whether sexual motivation or attachment drives the relationship. (81) Problems of attachment that create tension in relationships are not resolved by sexual satisfaction, but generalization is difficult, and the possibilities include: a) Both motivate the relationship, women with stable attachment to parental figure had more "stable" sexual involvement in marriage. (82) b) Problems of attachment are "compensated" by sexuality, anxious attachment and avoidant styles motivate sexual compulsivity. c) Attachment and sexuality oppose each other. (72) Attachment may be related to problems in intimacy, especially patterns of avoidant attachment. (83) d) Fear of loss of attachment(separation) may lead to abuse (if sexuality does not compensate). The term "separation assault" has been used to describe this situation, a major public health issue. (84) Birnbaum summarized her research on the types of interaction. (79) Couples therapy often involves imbalances between the two motivations, especially fear of abandonment. Problems of Intimate Partner Violence may be related to attachment. (85) The connection between abuser and victim in which the victim continues to participate has been called "trauma bonding". *Documentation of the relationship between attachment and sexual motivation requires further research.*

Fetishism is the parallel of hoarding in sexuality, experiencing sexual arousal from objects associated with a sexual partner (or intended partner), or used to generate sexual experiences. Sexualizing objects is similar to transitional object behavior of attachment transferred to sexual motivation. Several PSA, including Greenacre have remarked on this, and formulated theories based on experiences with adult patients in PSA. Her observations confirm that patients experience the process as fantasy and gratification. (86) She attempts to reconstruct transitional object responses in childhood from adult statements in therapy sessions, but (given the discussion of memory in chapter 4) it is usually impossible to verify the accuracy of the historical narrative.

Sexual arousal from audio-visual stimuli is a feature of *pornography* (regardless of the "appropriateness" or "artfulness" of content). Touch has a complex role in communication, and touch information is necessary for mammalian/primate attachment in the Harlow studies and in "fuzzy transitional objects". (87) Human sexual arousal can be activated by audio-visual stimuli without somatosensory stimulation, though the stimuli vary for individuals. This may be used for arousal in preparation for the couple's sexual behavior, for autoerotic sexuality, or for the pleasure of experiencing arousal stimulation. This appetitive stimulus has the ability to activate pleasure responses, and research on persons with habitual use of audio-visual sexual arousal suggests that this can produce an addictive pattern. (The relationship between "sexual addiction" and compulsive sexual behavior is discussed in chapter nine.) *The growing role of audio-visual and digital media is expanding the importance of these channels while reducing the role of touch, with unknown long-term results. How this relates to the neural processes of sexual behavior and mate selection are also unknown.* (There are a lot more people caring for pets!) Touch sensory channels carry messages for both attachment and sexual arousal, with potential for overlap of messages and confusion that must be differentiated by developmental experience. The current concerns about child sexual abuse and the warnings to children about touch by others may create confusion by labeling all touch as sexual. (An example is a family practice article that emphasizes abuse issues. (88)) A comprehensive view by Cascio et al, does not differentiate them. Spitoni et al studied the effects on touch perception of persons with attachment issues, and a few references exist on research about touch in sexuality. The lack of studies probably indicates the lack of support for sexual research as seen in the Masters/Johnson outcome. (89) Several studies confirm a negative impact of psoriasis on touch and intimacy, along with a recent surge in new medications for its treatment. (90) *Touch communication of emotion depends on visual and auditory signals to link the two participants in the interaction, and there is little research to understand how they interact in specific individuals.*

CLINICAL EXAMPLE The Couple With Too Much Sex. *A mid 30s woman sought treatment for the problem that her husband of several years wanted to have sexual intercourse too often. Inquiry revealed that the couple had a positive relationship, with good social interaction, and a stable economic base. The husband requested intercourse up to several times per day, and had been doing so for several years. A couples session was scheduled to evaluate the situation, and the husband reported that he requested intercourse in order to have an opportunity to hold, and be held by, his wife. He reported a developmental history that men in his family only had contact with women when having sex. This was discussed and a suggestion offered that they try physical contact without sex to explore whether it was suitable. Returning a month later, they reported the problem resolved, and did not return. Is this an example of confusing attachment and sexuality?*

CHAPTER EIGHT:
Learning fear and anxiety

Walking down a dark street at night in an unfamiliar city, you feel your senses heightened, become aware of strange noises, and notice your heart is beating faster. You are getting organized for a possible threat by evolutionary pathways of the amygdala, that warn of danger.

Adaptation has two aspects, seeking rewards and avoiding dangers. The child must learn to avoid dangers, and the first aversive infant experiences are body sensations: cold-wet, hunger contractions, and pain receptors in skin and connective tissue. Crying brings a caregiver response. Increased motor control, crawling, then walking, enables exploration of the surrounding world with more encounters of dangers. "Visual cliff", large moving objects, and loud noises are pre-programmed sensory warnings. (1) The child must also learn to avoid aversive smells and tastes, toxic ingestions, pain from bumps, sharp objects, and other dangers. In modern urban childrearing, caregiver warnings may protect the child from some experiences, so social messages (partially) replace direct danger experiences. But danger and anxiety must be avoided, and since all children experience anxiety, they must learn coping methods from adults and other children.

The amygdala is the "center" that coordinates the response to danger. The nuclei are located under the cortex near the temporal lobe-hippocampal region on both sides of the brain, with pathways to other regions. "Hardwired pathways" give immediate "reflex responses" to pain and some other dangers, and conditioned responses are formed to complex sensory input associated with danger. LeDoux (2) discovered that the lateral nuclei link specific stimuli and aversive responses forming aversive conditioned stimuli, and the medial nuclei produce the output of somatic responses and activate behavior. LeDoux and Pine present a "dual" system in humans, both a direct amygdala response to danger stimuli, and associated cortical pathways for subjective experience of anxiety. The amygdala receives input from all four senses of sensory-association areas of cortex. The interactions of amygdala with other pathways have been termed the extended amygdala, and the amygdala-stria terminalis loop for danger signals and negative internal states parallels the hippocampal-fornix loop associated with positive reward signals. Stimuli are linked (conditioned) to warn of "anticipated" danger, including social stimuli, and the internal negative somatic states of addiction (see chapter nine). Social interactions can generate aversive stimulation, e.g. punishments (spanking, yelling, or threats, etc.), and the potential loss of attachment from caregivers (*separation anxiety*). Parents using aversive stimuli are the same caregivers involved in attachment. Aversive social interaction becomes "dominance" behavior controlling the "subordinates" in groups, as observed in primate social cultures with dominance hierarchies, including humans. (4) Fear conditioning, stress reactions, and attention bias are all linked to amygdala pathways. Anxiety signals can be generalized to similar signals in new situations, or refined in repeated experiences, or extinguished if danger does not recur. The danger signals of modern life use hippocampal memory pathways connected to amygdala to create warning signals about hot plates, traffic signals, warning signs, and other secondary danger signals. (This is different from primary attachment which integrates multiple sensory components into a complex representation (see chapter seven).) If the intensity of the anxiety response is excessive, or the ability to avoid the anxiety is blocked, the experience is stored by a modified process that creates Posttraumatic Stress Disorder (PTSD).

SIDEBAR The concept of **extended amygdala** describes amygdala connections with other regions. The dorsomedial nuclei are smaller, evolutionarily older, and primarily connected to olfactory input (bad smells!). The ventrolateral group are evolutionarily newer, and linked reciprocally with the limbic/hypothalamic motivation system. Conditioning links with aversive stimuli are created in the lateral amygdala nuclei, and involve sensory-memory processed by hippocampus. The amygdala has extensive overlap with hippocampal neurons linking (memory) sensory data for assessing danger risk current stimuli (the significance of chapter four). The centromedial group joins the other two regions and provides output to brainstem connections, and to hypothalamus to generate autonomic responses. The primary output, stria terminalis (and "bed nuclei") goes to ventromedial hypothalamus, an inhibitory ("no go") region, then to thalamus and back to amygdala, a control loop. The ventral amydalofugal pathway also goes to hypothalamus, septum, and to dorsal thalamus (centrum median) and then to cingulate cortex (for subjective awareness). The outflow pathways combine i) autonomic nervous system response, ii) hypothalamic signals to pre-frontal brain PF/BG, and iii) to the cingulate/insula cortex for subjective experience. (3) **Amygdala pathways** shown in Fig 8.1 show the parallel pathways of amygdala (via stria terminalis) and hippocampus (via fornix) to hypothalamic nuclei. The pathways continue to thalamic and cingulate cortex and prefrontal cortex. The ventral amygdala has an alternative pathway directly to hypothalamus and to autonomic nervous system. Amygdala and hippocampus also connect directly.

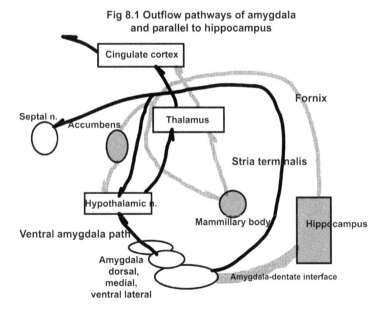

Fig 8.1 Outflow pathways of amygdala and parallel to hippocampus

Though the amygdala nuclei are visualized in recent fMRI studies, the internal subregions are not visualized separately, and nearby anatomical structures reduce accuracy, so most of these functions have only been documented in animal studies. (5) The response of amygdala pathways can be characterized by five parameters associated (hypothetically) with clinical symptoms:

1) the **sensitivity** of amygdala response to input,
2) the **intensity of the somatic response,** from mild subjective anxiety to "panic anxiety"
3) the **ease of creating conditioned aversive pathways**,
4) the external **control** of amygdala response
5) the response to **"intense stimuli"**

The parameters summarize amygdala functions, and may reflect the DSM V categories of anxiety syndromes. No current studies validate this hypothetical association. Table 8.1 compares the DSM V Anxiety diagnoses sorted by amygdala response. (The categories "other specified" and "other unspecified" are ignored, only necessary for completeness and billing.) (6) The DSM calls the anxiety symptoms "disorders". Discussion of the pathways will be organized around these "properties". Despite the name, agoraphobia, this is not typically associated with phobias, and often is a vestibular response sensitivity.

Each of these potential syndromes is described:

Table 8.1 of DSM V ANXIETY DISORDERS (RECLASSIFIED)
1) *Sensitivity of amygdala response to aversive input.*
F41.1   Generalized anxiety disorder
2) *Intensity of the somatic anxiety response.*
F41.0   Panic disorder [episodic paroxysmal anxiety]
3) *The ease of creating conditioned anxiety pathways.*
F40.2   Specific phobias (long list!)
F40.1   Social phobias
4) *Regulatory control by frontal-cortical pathways.*
F42   Obsessive-compulsive disorder
F44.4   Conversion disorder (various types)
F45   Somatoform disorders Briquet's disorder
F45.2   Hypochondriacal disorders
F45.22 Body dysmorphic disorder
5) *The intensity of stimulus*
F43   Reaction to severe stress, and adjustment disorders
F43.0   Acute stress reaction Acute crisis reaction
F43.2   Adjustment disorders Culture shock Grief reaction
F43.1   Post-traumatic stress disorder (PTSD)
F44.0   Dissociative amnesia
F44.81 Dissociative identity disorder Multiple personality disorder
F40.0   Agoraphobia Despite the name this is not typically associated with other phobias, and likely reflects a vestibular-neural sensitivity.

Sensitivity Of Amygdala Response. The sensitivity of amygdala to activation by fear/anxiety stimuli is not measurable by current techniques. ("Emotion Appraisal Theories" (see chapter two) suggest that this is an individual characteristic depending on evaluative factors.) It is not measured by the intensity of the somatic response, a separate variable produced by a different region of amygdala, because sensitive individuals may show a strong somatic response to mild threat. The lateral nuclei are responsible for "appraisal of danger" in animal studies, and this sensitivity might be measured in that region. It is a lifetime characteristic, first noted in childhood. (6) Generalized Anxiety Disorder is the current diagnosis best describing someone with high sensitivity to anxiety signals, the diagnosis based on the range of different anxiety stimuli and pervasiveness of symptoms. The sensitivity does not usually produce "panic attacks" (somatic responses). Without a measure of intrinsic sensitivity, the genetics cannot be assessed specifically, but polygenic sites are reported for anxiety. Amygdala sensitivity may be a continuous variable, with syndromes at both extremes, or separate subgroups with high or low reactivity, and genetic studies miss this distribution issue. Etkin at al report variable connectivity in studies separating lateral and baso-medial regions in fMRI. (Etkin, 6) Social Anxiety and Agoraphobia have anxiety symptoms when leaving one's "comfort zone", also a feature of generalized anxiety. The breadth of anxiety responses might be a useful measure of this variable but is not usually documented.

SIDEBAR Social anxiety is an intense expression of "shyness", a lifelong individual characteristic. As a separate diagnostic category it has more than 66% overlap with other diagnoses, starting as "Social Phobia" in DSM II. The change to a separate form of anxiety, in DSM IV, as "Social anxiety disorder", was in response to the development of criterion scales, and the publicized episodes of famous personalities, rather than new evidence. Persons with this syndrome may have fear of being in social situations, being judged by others, performing socially, or other concerns about interpersonal behavior and its consequences. (7)

Intensity Of Somatic Response. The intensity of the subjective experience of anxiety ranges from mild discomfort to intense somatic autonomic symptoms experienced as "panic attacks" (Panic Anxiety Disorder). The symptoms include rapid heart rate, rapid shallow breathing, and other reactions to danger that activate the body for survival, which occur when the person is not facing a survival threat. (The differential diagnosis often overlaps with certain cardiac syndromes, and patients often get to mental health by way of cardiology.) The central nuclei outflow pathway activates these somatic symptoms. Many people with anxiety do not experience "panic attacks", which indicates a separate vulnerability not simply associated with "sensitivity". The intense subjective experience of the somatic response is not correlated with the seriousness of the threat, and episodes often end by reassurance, or "rebreathing", not resolution of a serious personal threat, but a somatic reaction. Panic episodes can be recurring, triggered by various situations, and may result in a generalized agoraphobia (typified in the O'Neill play "The Iceman Cometh"). Not all agoraphobia patients have panic, but many panic patients limit their excursions, not always to the point of agoraphobia. A syndrome of panic associated with fear of separation from attachment figures suggests a relationship between Panic Anxiety Disorder, and Separation Anxiety Disorder, and requires further study. (See CLINICAL EXAMPLE) The vulnerability to panic may have a genetic component. (8)

CLINICAL EXAMPLE: A panic-separation anxiety syndrome. *Kline and Kline described a syndrome in children with panic episodes associated with symptoms of parental separation. Patients of varying age may present the following symptoms: (1) panic anxiety episodes, (2) may be associated with episodes of depression, (3) a multigenerational family history of anxiety/panic often with matrilineal pattern, (3) life long intermittent sleep problems, (4) low normal blood pressure, sometimes symptoms of postural hypotension, (5) onset, especially in females, at a time of hormonal shifts of puberty, pregnancy, or menopause, and (6) childhood history of difficulty with separation from parents on entry to school, or major separation anxiety at some other stage. The patients, often female, have perfectionist coping style, and are very sensitive to separation including strong attachment to their children, which creates intergenerational problems of individuation. All six* *features are found in some patients, and a cluster of 4 or 5 warrants a clinical trial of specific treatment. Other authors have identified other panic disorder clusters, one around respiratory features and another vestibular (see above) unrelated to the syndrome described. The importance of separation anxiety is noted in the Klein series (and the author's) that does not produce a borderline syndrome. The multi-symptom subgroup is effectively treated using an MAOI, (for example Nardil 15mg bid to qid). This treatment does not alter the general level of anxiety, but within two weeks of treatment, patients report the anxiety no longer escalates into panic episodes, allowing major life changes. The treatment must be viewed as a clinical trial, as not all patients respond. If the patient responds, hypertensive crises on MAOI rarely occur, and patients typically violate the diet and even medication restrictions, without consequences, which suggests a bio-amine vulnerability. The literature on use of MAOI has sporadic reports of special benefit in certain patient groups, (e.g. Quitkin in 1990) without specifying the particular features described here. (8) This syndrome is one of several panic disorders that appear to have evidence for genetic vulnerability. It is likely that the transition from anxiety to panic is a genetically controlled amygdala response.*

CLINICAL EXAMPLE: VESTIBULAR ANXIETY. *A subgroup of patients who report panic symptoms, especially associated with driving in a car, running, etc. have vestibular abnormalities like Meniere's disease. (A review of this group of disorders and its relation to anxiety symptoms is available from NETCE.) A childhood history of multiple ear infections is a helpful clue that the problem may be vestibular. An example is a twenty two year old female who was seen in referral for onset of panic episodes after a respiratory infection. The panic came on suddenly while she was driving in a familiar location. These recurred while driving over several weeks, and a therapist referred her for further evaluation and medications. No other changes in her social environment were noted, and treatment with local vasodilators and decongestants were effective in resolving the symptoms. She was advised that recurrence with future infections could be managed with similar treatment. A similarly dramatic syndrome is seen in middle aged or older persons with "benign positional vertigo" which is often of sudden onset and stimulates panic anxiety. In this situation, resolution is accomplished using certain positioning maneuvers. (8)*

Ease Of Creating Conditioning Aversive Pathways. Fear and anxiety can be triggered by immediate pain stimuli, but, in the complex modern world, most anxiety is the result of programmed signals of potential threat. Some individuals acquire an anxiety reaction after one or a few exposures. This could be amygdala sensitivity (#1), or a separate feature, "ease of conditioning". Anxiety to a specific stimulus or situation is a phobia and patients manifesting phobias often have many different triggers for anxiety with no common thread but the anxiety, Phobic Disorder. LeDoux's studies show that lesions to the lateral nuclei prevent conditioning, and input from hippocampus is part of the conditioning pathway. The number of conditioning anxiety trials needed may indicate the ease with which "aversive conditioning" occurs in vulnerable individuals. (9) Easily ending the anxiety response to a specific phobia by extinction methods also suggests the role of conditioning/extinction. Studies exploring the cortical correlations of extinction are useful for monitoring the changes. (9) A list of "Phobias" is available in DSM and other sites. Some of these seem associated with childhood experience, and some are responses to stimuli that provoke anxiety in most human subjects. (10) Ease of conditioning may be a separate characteristic, different from amygdala sensitivity.

> **CLINICAL EXAMPLE Adult Anxiety to Childhood Event.** *A middle-aged man, born and raised in England, was evaluated for recurring episodes of depression and anxiety. Anxiety episodes occurred intermittently and seemed not to depend on time, location, or access to his primary partner. He would call the therapist in great distress, and the timing of the calls seemed random. During one episode the therapist noticed a thunderstorm outside. The patient confirmed hearing the thunder, and remarked that he got very nervous around the sound. He recalled that as a small child he was taken to bomb shelters away from his mother during bombing raids in London, and had terrible anxiety during these separations. The thunder reminded him of sounds of bombing. He would never know if his mother would be alive and return for him. After discussion and a series of cathartic reminiscences, he was markedly improved.* **COMMENT** *This example illustrates both the anxiety related to separation issues of childhood, and being conditioned to a specific stimulus. The patient was not consciously aware of the triggering stimulus, probably because it occurred in an earlier sensory-motor stage.*

Regulatory Control Of Anxiety. The experience and expression of anxiety are modulated by "coping skills", "defenses", etc. Prefrontal cortical pathways (discussed in chapter six) channel and manage arousal activity from the amygdala-anxiety pathways to PF/BG, (but not autonomic pathway activity which goes directly to the autonomic system). A study of the impact of anxiety on attention tasks shows anxiety interferes with task performance, illustrating effects on pre-frontal pathways. (11) PF/BG controls interact with anxiety messages in mPFC, and also at cingulate-insula. Certain DSM V diagnoses are examples of these coping responses, and not the anxiety state per se. *Whether the syndromes identify specific anxiety patterns or responses to #1 or #2 is unknown and requires further study.*

Obsessive-compulsive disorder, (and related symptoms of picking disorder, trichotillomania, and hoarding) are repetitive patterns of the PF/BG system, presenting as symptoms, often activated by anxiety. They vary from mild obsessive-compulsive behavior seen in daily life, to persistent recurring patterns of obsessional thought and compulsive behavior, which must be performed to avert intense anxiety, and disrupt the patient's life. Anxiety increases if the rituals are not performed, suggesting that they help "manage" anxiety by directing anxiety activation along specific pre-frontal pathways. (12) Brain studies suggest increased activation of OFC, expected in any emotional activation. The YBOCDS self report scale gives a symptom criteria checklist; more symptoms define a more severe diagnosis. (12) A developmental period of obsessive rituals is a normal stage in child development, suggesting the source for later development of the symptoms, and posing the unanswered question: *Are OCD symptoms a genetic or injury based pattern of PF/BG perseveration (see chapter six), or does intensity of anxiety activate specific defenses in certain individuals?* (13). (14) No research indicates whether these mechanisms are more prominent in anxiety related to separation, or all anxiety.

Regression is the use of less mature behavior or coping skills to deal with challenges, seen across the life cycle. In children, stress, the birth of a sibling, or a sudden change in family situation increasing anxiety produces symptoms of "regression" to a younger developmental coping pattern. Thumb sucking, pacifier use or other "soothing" oral behavior (eventually smoking or vaping!) are examples. In PSA, "regression" is potentially adaptive in some situations ("regression in service of the ego"). (15) The boundary between effective coping to manage anxiety, and dysfunctional patterns of OCD, hoarding, and regression, is a boundary of mental illness. Some coping strategies have separate "personality diagnoses" which use the same brain pathways (see discussion of chapter six):

Somatoform Disorder. The person has somatic symptoms with no biological cause by medical testing. The production of somatic responses by amygdala outflow provides a direct pathway for their production. The patient may focus on the somatic features, ignoring the subjective anxiety, experiencing anxiety as physical complaints. In *Conversion Disorder*, symptoms are reported that cannot be validated with other tests, and often relate to local areas of emotional focus. (Nothing is "converted" and the term is historical.) Many of Freud's early patients presented these symptoms. Currently they are often seen by Neurologists, who report subtle differences in fMRI. (Hallett, 16) Medical providers often search for medical illnesses until the failure to find a treatable condition is accepted, and the patient is referred to mental health. (16) *Factitious Disorder* (and Factitious disorder presented by another) are situations in which the patient (or the presenting person (usually parent of a child)) is aware that no medical illness is occurring, and presents symptoms, and often false evidence to suggest an illness is present. Because of the "intentional" aspect of these disorders, they may be dismissed as "manipulating" instead of exploring the emotional need to have medical attention. A rare but dramatic variation is presenting another, usually a child, with an alleged illness (Munchausen by proxy).

*CLINICAL EXAMPLE **The problem is not "factitious"**. A 22-year-old woman was seen in Consultation Liaison at a general hospital for concerns about continuing symptoms. She had just undergone one of many gynecological procedures for dyspareunia that interfered with sustaining intimate relationships with men. She did not have confidence that the current procedure would make any difference and was hostile about being discharged. The referral was from her gynecologist, who had decided that the patient would not benefit from further surgery, because she had a "factitious disorder". In a bedside evaluation, the patient gave a history of growing up in a family with stepfather, emancipating to college, and was currently employed. She had several short frustrating* *relationships with men, marked by sexual problems. She denied either depression or anxiety symptoms, and did not understand why referral to mental health was done. But after building rapport, the patient acknowledged being sexually abused by her stepfather for several years, and that her departure from her family was to escape from this experience. She had not reported this, even to her mother, but described vaginismus on intercourse as a regular event. There was a strong emotional catharsis at the disclosure and patient was referred for psychotherapy. She eventually experienced a positive outcome. COMMENT Her symptoms were somatized, and though the patient was aware of the origin, she did not make the emotional connection, and was unable to disclose it for some time, in order to get help. This illustrates the challenge of formulating the source of symptoms, an area with risk for malpractice and inappropriate care.*

CLINICAL EXAMPLE Nursing Home Patient With Anxiety. *Anxiety is also the response to serious medical problems which that must be considered. A 70 year old woman was evaluated in hospital consultation for anxiety symptoms. She had recently been hospitalized, from a nursing home for a urinary tract infection and was improving, and planned for discharge that day. She suddenly became anxious and a mental health consultation was requested. The woman was sitting up in bed, dramatically anxious, complaining of chest pain localized to the R upper chest and with rapid shallow breathing and a pulse of over 120 BPM. She appeared to be in respiratory distress, denied any problems at nursing home or with family, and said that she was fearful because she was "sick". The consultant agreed, and advised the referring physician to get a chest x-ray which showed infiltrate, and on subsequent scan, a pulmonary embolus, fortunately not fatal. COMMENT The possibility of medical factors triggering an anxiety response, especially in an ill or elderly patient, must always be considered. Defining a physical problem as an emotional one can have serious health consequences, especially if treatment of the physical problem is ignored. Persons with anxiety also get serious, mortal illnesses.*

CLINICAL EXAMPLE Body Dysmorphic Disorder(BDD). *In BDD, a person with an obsessional preoccupation with imagined or slight defects in appearance is considered an obsessive compulsive disorder, based on similarities to obsessive-compulsive symptoms. It is associated with impairment in psychosocial functioning, poor quality of life, higher suicide rates, and high rates of elective, but unsatisfying cosmetic surgery. The opposite of focusing on somatic symptoms to ignore emotion, in BDD intensive preoccupation about somatic features is linked to intense negative affect, depression or anxiety. Negative self-image is associated with specific bodily features, depressed mood, obsessional thoughts, and impaired function. If weight is an issue, eating disturbances may be observed. Categorizing this syndrome illustrates the issue of multiple pathway interaction.*

> *The "self system" of somato-sensory data produces strongly negative signals. Frontal obsessional pathways are involved, as well as intense motivation system (amygdala?) activity. (63) (17)*

Effective coping techniques reduce anxiety and allow adaptive functioning. The Middle Eastern tradition of "worry beads", like Rosary beads, is a coping skill. Self administered psychoactive chemicals, manufactured or naturally available, are used for control of anxiety throughout the world, e.g. alcohol; and the boundary between effective and maladaptive coping is often blurred using them. How coping skills modify amygdala pathways is not understood, though inhibitory GABA interneurons play an important role in reducing amygdala activity, and decreasing cingulate-insula activation. Pharmaceutical treatment of anxiety can alter pathway outflow through the motivation pathway to PF/BG by altering amine transmission, or use direct GABA drugs on amygdala. Most GABA agents have potential for addiction, complicating their chronic use. Theories of addiction recognize the amygdala as a crucial element in maintaining addiction, which creates problems trying to differentiate coping skills from addictive behaviors. (18) (Chapter nine examines the addiction process that does not **initially** depend on, or be related to anxiety.)

Stimulus intensity is the most difficult anxiety parameter to characterize. Can the intensity of the anxiety stimulus be defined independently of the individual's response? Why does one person develop anxiety symptoms when exposed to a stress, when another does not? What is the relation of amygdala sensitivity (#1) to the stimulus intensity? It cannot be measured by the somatic response, which does not correlate. Stressful events may be: Recurring moderate to severe stress producing a mixed neuro-humoral syndrome, first studied in detail by Hans Selye, the *General Adaptation Syndrome (GAS).* (This is not included in the DSM and is usually diagnosed as Adjustment Disorder.*)* The experience alters HPA axis regulation of cortisol (see chapter three), as studied in air traffic controllers, and may lead to other symptoms. (20) GAS is initially an adaptive response, but a gradual deterioration in social and physical capacity with depressed mood occurs when it endures for too long, "burn out syndrome". A similar phenomenon studied by Seligman in dogs prevented from escaping aversive situations is termed "Learned Helplessness". (21) These changes are often the "background" of other life situations and not recognized in evaluations. An approach developed by Holmes and Rahe, assessed the long-term result of stress experiences. A severity rating scale of stressful life situations measured stressful events, showing an increase in mental and physical illness in the year after significant stress events proportional to the scale measure of stress experienced by the individual. There is no ideal "stress free life", some psychologists see a "zone" balancing boredom and stress as the desired goal. (19) Individual differences in tolerance for external demands are likely to be a factor, but research is needed defining them.

CLINICAL EXAMPLE Work stress. *A man in his 50s was evaluated for continuing use of stimulants. He had taken them for several years, prescribed his family doctor who did not wish to continue them. He had no childhood history of ADHD or treatment with stimulants, and had completed high school, and two years of college before beginning to work. He had not used stimulants until his forties, working at a job that required constant focus for 8 hours per day, with intermittent rest intervals. In recent years, the job required alternating day and night shifts of two weeks each. This was creating more and more problems focusing and staying awake and he had increased the use of stimulants in response. He reported that the work prevented him from any real social life; he lived alone and was getting increasingly moody and depressed. The man was afraid to ask for a change in schedule fearing he would lose the job. At evaluation, he was put on a four-week disability leave and his use of stimulants tapered off without incident. The problems posed by the job were not under his control, and he was encouraged to seek a different, less stressful, position at the company, and accept a reduction in pay. Placing him on disability helped encourage HR to arrange the changes. COMMENT The use of stimulants to manage job stress has a long history in over the road truckers, military situations, and related work. The stress of Air Traffic Controllers has been given special attention due to the potential risks involved. (19)*

Post Traumatic Stress Disorder (PTSD). The syndrome of response to a strong anxiety/fear stimulus is literally: "symptoms that occur sometime after a significant stress". One or more stressor events in the past, brief or sustained, produce persisting abnormalities in attention, memory, and the cortisol system, that continue after the stress stimulus ends. PTSD and GAS differ in time course, and the way the experience is stored. In GAS, the symptoms are ongoing and additive, and the subject is aware of the life situation. In PTSD, the event(s) are in the past, and awareness of the sensory/emotional event(s) are partially or totally blocked, dissociated, and unavailable to full recall. (22) Any incident which produces intense emotional arousal, especially fear, may block emotional response, be felt as "numbness", or "not feeling anything", as in the first stage of grief. Short-term memory and consolidation are not impaired (unless there is concurrent brain trauma) but consolidation is modified. Blocking in PTSD is an active process that alters the attention process. PTSD patients perform poorly on a variety of neuropsychology tasks that involve attention and memory, documenting the change in attention. Event-related potentials and functional neuroimaging also indicate abnormal stimulus processing, and the persisting state of hyper-arousal. The symptoms of anxiety indicate the *defenses fail* in breakthrough moments, with partial recall of the event.

The diagnostic features of PTSD also describe the symptoms:

A) intrusion Symptoms (one required) *The traumatic event is persistently re-experienced: Unwanted upsetting memories, Nightmares, Flashbacks, Emotional distress after exposure to traumatic reminders, Physical reactivity after exposure to traumatic reminders*

B) avoidance (one required) avoidance of trauma-related stimuli after the trauma: *avoiding Trauma-related thoughts or feelings, Trauma-related external reminders*

C) negative alterations in cognitions and mood (two required) *Negative thoughts or feelings that began or worsened after the trauma: Inability to recall key features of the trauma, Overly negative thoughts and assumptions about* *oneself or the world, Exaggerated blame of self or others for causing the trauma, Negative affect, Decreased interest in activities, Feeling isolated,*

D) alterations in arousal and reactivity: *trauma-related arousal and reactivity that began or worsened after the trauma: Irritability or aggression, Hyper vigilance, Heightened startle reaction, Difficulty concentrating, Difficulty sleeping*

Dissociative features: *an individual experiences:* **Depersonalization.** *Experience of being an outside observer of or detached from oneself (e.g., feeling as if "this is not happening to me" or one were in a dream).* **Derealization.** *Experience of unreality, distance, or distortion (e.g., "things are not real").*

Delayed Specification. *Full diagnostic criteria are not met until at least six months after the trauma(s), although onset of symptoms may occur immediately.*

((AND ALSO: Symptoms last for more than 1 month. Symptoms create distress or functional impairment (e.g., social, occupational). Symptoms are not due to medication, substance use, or other illness.)) All these symptoms indicate changes in sensory/information processing. An exclusion for substance use is needed because the frequent association of heavy substance use in adults experiencing the syndrome, makes it difficult differentiate the loss of memory from intoxication from that of dissociation. (Differentiating persons with current PTSD from previous symptoms after resolution is not indicated in the criteria.) (22)

The key question of PTSD is: what makes an experience "traumatic"? What determines that a stimulus situation is severe enough to activate the PTSD process? The official diagnosis includes criteria related to the incident: Exposure to actual or threatened death, serious injury, or sexual violence in one (or more) of the following: 1) directly experiencing the traumatic event(s). 2) Witnessing, in person, the event(s) as it occurred to others. 3) Learning that the traumatic event(s) occurred to a close family member or close friend. In cases of actual or threatened death of a family member or friend, the event(s) must have been violent or accidental. 4) Experiencing repeated or extreme exposure to aversive details of the traumatic event(s) (e.g., first responders collecting human remains; police officers repeatedly exposed to details of child abuse). (The criteria do not apply to exposure through electronic media, television, movies, or pictures, unless this exposure is work related.) The assumption that PTSD is created by "objective parameters" of stimulus severity (direct physical threat, "life threatening") ignores individual differences in response and makes the definition too narrow. *Stimulus intensity is dependent on the individual appraisal:* ***A TRAUMA is an experience of anxiety/fear that exceeds the individual's tolerance for emotional arousal.*** This is intentionally circular; ***a TRAUMA is an event that causes PTSD in some person***. Much of the literature on this subject and the demand for precise definitions comes from military and civilian situations where disability compensation is involved. North et al have reviewed the complex issues in this determination. (23) Secondary gain and other motivations in patients, and objectives of the evaluator, confuse measuring the response with other considerations. Identifying symptoms of persisting stress and altered arousal is the clinical task, assessing other motivations is a separate additional task. Specifying details of the circumstances are useful but cannot be used to make a complete determination without omitting many persons with PTSD. The dramatic increase in suicides in the military in recent years documents the inability to resolve this syndrome both in active duty, and with veterans. (24). (The interval between the stress event and the development of PTSD did not have a diagnosis, preventing access to treatment, which has been addressed by the diagnosis Acute Stress Disorder. This provides a basis for initiating treatment after an event in an effort to prevent PTSD from developing which remains only an aspiration in current treatment. (25)) The coping technique in PTSD alters recall to prevent recurring emotional overload. Activation of glucocorticoid and autonomic arousal systems, and heightened arousal show that stress continues. The blocking is variable and depends on the age of the individual and other factors, and the protection against the intense emotional recall is inconsistent, so a person with PTSD may go through daily life without major anxiety when the blocking is effective, and not seek treatment until the blocking mechanism breaks down. The person may use substances for control of anxiety, or other coping skills to help manage breakdown episodes. The triggering may occur when the person is exposed to trigger stimuli, or in nightmares, or from other breakthroughs. Emotions often reemerge when experiences are explored in therapy. The **dissociation process** in PTSD regulates attention pathways. (26) Until recently, the study of amygdala interaction with dissociation or other regulatory neural processes was not possible. A group recently reported on a technique of sequential fMRI observations over short intervals while giving the person sensory input that would be likely to trigger PTSD or other anxiety response. (26) This is the first step toward a temporal live measure of pathway responses, but the technique is statistically complex, has not been replicated, and awaits further validation.

Warning response signals alert the individual to take evasive action, but if blocked by dissociation, warnings are unavailable or activated at inappropriate times. So PTSD patients demonstrate maladaptive responses: lack of warning in situations of triggering, and missing danger signals, as when women, molested in childhood, are vulnerable to rape later in life. (29) The *dissociative disorders* are recognized diagnostically and provide symptoms for the diagnosis though many providers do not recognize them clinically. (30) The extent of dissociation varies from one person to another, and the younger the age of the person at PTSD, and the more "overwhelming quality" of the situation, the more likely that dissociation will be used. (It is not usually seen in schizophrenias because these patients have problems regulating memory pathways).

PTSD is seen in civilian and military settings, including: childhood abuse, assault, rape or other traumatic child or adult experiences, battle trauma, and dramatic, lethal, natural and man made disasters. Childhood abuse, both physical and sexual, frequently produces the symptoms, because dissociation is the initial mode of coping for intense anxiety in children. Children use dissociation because their survival depends on parents or caregivers, and so they are unable to escape abusive situations. Dissociation can block the experience for years, so the individual enters adult life with limited understanding of certain reactions, and may even continue to engage

SIDEBAR Dissociation pathways and hypnosis. Understanding dissociation has been aided by research in hypnosis. Hypnotic trance is an observable, repeatable *dissociation* phenomenon studied in people without PTSD (often college students). Subjects experiencing "trance" and are measured for "susceptibility" on a scale developed by Hilgard. Herbert Spiegel, researcher, teacher, and practicing clinician has provided an approach for use in clinical settings. (27) Neural pathway changes have been documented in this process, though not clearly correlated to PTSD. The link between amygdala and "subjective cortex" (cingulate, insula) is altered. Current fMRI research is unable to visualize the thalamic recursive process or its modifications that are probably involved. Etkins, in meta-review, concluded that PTSD included a mechanism for the emotional regulation symptoms in PTSD that extend beyond an exaggerated fear response. (Etkin, 28) He did not formulate what it was, or introduce the dissociation concept.

The pathways that control attention are discussed in chapter five. Access to stored information allows recall, re-experiencing of memory(s), and gradual emotional resolution. Clinical techniques, e.g. EMDR (a treatment which manipulates the attention process), and hypnosis, are used to gain access to the traumatic memories. (See chapter twelve). The associated symptoms of depersonalization and derealization, indicate that the *signification* system is modified in this process. The association of working memory and long term memory is needed to maintain focus of attention. In PTSD the intense arousal of amygdala pathways blocks this link on a consistent basis using dissociation. Controlling "choice of attention" depends on the pre-frontal choice network. (See chapter six) So warning signals must be perceived, be recognized as PTSD (=overwhelming) and a signal sent through pre-frontal controls to block attention to these signals or memories. *The precise pathways have not been documented.* When they occur early in childhood, they are often replaced by more complex coping methods later, because they are dangerous to use, inherently mal-adaptive.

with the abuser, experiencing trauma again and again, often complicated later by addiction, or other dysfunctional coping skills. (31) (32)

Adult exposure to trauma in civilian life includes auto accidents, assault, observing or being threatened by gun violence, vehicular homicide, gang violence, etc. PTSD is often ignored, leaving the survivors with stress responses, without recognition or support for the symptoms. Failure to inquire about traumatic events ignores this etiology.

CLINICAL EXAMPLE (Repeated from chapter six.) Another Eve. *A married mother in her 30s was severely depressed with recurring suicidal thoughts and had taken several overdoses. She felt unable to care for her two children and husband, who remained very supportive. Months went by with no response to therapy or medication, when one day the patient entered the session with a dramatically different tone of voice and movement. She appeared to be a young child, perhaps 7 or 8, in mannerisms, voice, and movement. She introduced herself by a child's name and remarked that she had been observing the sessions for sometime and wanted to attend one. The dramatic difference in behavior and mannerisms were associated with different emotion. The person in the room was cheerful and happy, and aware that this was different from her "other self". A multi year course ensued in which the person was able to modify and organize the sense of self more effectively. COMMENT A provider who has not experienced this "multiplicity" will be unable to appreciate the extent to which enacting another "self" is different from "pretending" to be someone else. The change in affect is often dramatic, as in borderline syndrome, and conscious awareness of different components of self is variable. In this instance, the child-self had more overall awareness than the adult-self. The child-self appeared to have been "protected" from a long history of childhood abuse, which was part of the awareness of the adult-self, and the source of the severe depression and low self-esteem.*

CLINICAL EXAMPLE Adult Auto Crash Survivor. *A 25-year-old female journalist was hit by another vehicle while driving through an intersection. She had no major physical injuries, some whiplash soft tissue injuries, and a brief moment of unconsciousness. In the immediate recovery period, she had increased anxiety, dreams of the incident, and headaches for several weeks. Over the next year, she persistently avoids driving through the same intersection, unaware of her change in routes until it is pointed out. She noted anxiety when back at the spot and over several months was able to drive in that location with "exposure" that extinguished her anxiety. COMMENT such typical adult PTSD incidents are common and often only mildly disrupt the person's life space. Physical assault, especially rape is much more disruptive and benefits from a focused psychotherapy intervention.*

Trauma may occur in conjunction with natural disasters, and the Psychoanalyst R J Lifton has written a series of studies on the adult experiences of mass traumatic events and prisoner trauma, emphasizing the sense of "discontinuity" of life that results. This corresponds to the discontinuity in the dissociative process of memories, although most of his situations involve selective dissociation, with recall of events, but blocking of emotion. Many of the same information processing and storage issues seen in childhood trauma are observed in adult treatment of survivors. Stevens et al have a detailed study of neural subtypes. (33)

Military PTSD includes soldiers in battle, and recent military engagements have extended the zone of attack to civilian areas, and "rear echelon" personnel providing support services. Every military encounter in recorded history has resulted in psychological impairment of some participants and not others. Research designed to determine why some are more vulnerable to PTSD than others, done primarily post exposure with patients at VA hospitals, have not identified which parameters are important in determining PTSD vulnerability. (34) Identifying predictors in advance could avoid placing vulnerable persons in battlefield or other high stress situations. The amygdala panic response is not the critical factor in PTSD; some disturbance in integrated attention is key. The extended service of soldiers in Iraq and Afghanistan, with high rates of suicide, has prompted the Army and Veterans Administration to review interventions for these veterans. Complicating this is the high percentage of close range explosive injuries with brain trauma in many patients. The relationship of brain trauma and impaired response to sensory overload makes diagnosis and treatment more complicated. When redeployments are at the discretion of commanders, with two or three deployments over a two-year period not unusual, the likelihood of redeployment prevents reversal of "battle conditioning", and the subsequent deployment does not ensure return to the previous unit support system. All these factors likely contribute to intensifying PTSD problems. (34) The result may be a persisting reorganization of personality for combat, as in the following report.

*JOURNAL REPORT **Addictive combat attachment**. This journal report describes the desire to return in various ways, verbal and in role game playing to combat situations. The case series describes several features: Veterans had a strong ambivalence about re-experiencing combat-like situations. "Glorifying" combat experiences from memories, and imagining new combat scenarios was observed,* *which supported group bonding. Men sought activities with high arousal including video games, war movies, etc. and were generally unaware of these preferences, and were surprised by their attraction to combat related actions and thoughts. The physiologic highs were followed by depressive lows. Veterans eventually noted the patterns but felt helpless to stop them. COMMENT Military training is social conditioning to prepare soldiers to suspend control over violence, bond to a support group, and tolerate an environment of high danger. The training creates problems for reintegration into civilian life. The authors of the case report expressed surprise, ignoring the explicit features of training, as illustrated by the situations, including the need to find a support group with similar experience and training. The real surprise is that the society does not provide a relearning path to "untrain" soldiers for return to non-battle situations. Instead this is done inconsistently on an individual basis, and often leaves the veteran unable to make the adjustment. (35)*

The development of human civilization is motivated by the need to control anxiety about potential dangers. The caves, walls, wisdom about safety, and protective devices are adaptive efforts to reduce exposure to potential dangers. In the process societies have created new dangers in lethal weapons, "ordinary household devices", automobiles and other vehicles. Social hierarchies and the legal structure of societies are created to provide a clear definition of dominance and avoid recurring hostile interactions, but also encourage challenging the hierarchy with violence. Some societies manage social violence by lowering the population density, but this is not possible in urban settings. Defense of territory against strangers is an instinctual process adapted from earlier evolutionary stages to (modern) human societies. Danger, and the associated fear and anxiety are an intrinsic component of living and cannot be eliminated. The experience of anxiety is inherently protective and adaptive. The alternative is difficult to imagine, but an analogue is life without awareness of pain, a rare congenital condition, which is extremely dangerous because the individual cannot take precautionary measures to avoid self-injury. (36) The inability to access memories of danger in PTSD events poses a similar risk. *The more general question, what life might be like with reduced sensitivity to anxiety, is discussed in the next section.*

The response to danger is termed "flight or fight", and the previous sections describe the fear/anxiety, "flight" aspect. The danger signals of amygdala pathways also activate aggressive behavior, the "fight" component. Humans express anger/aggression in many ways, and the boundary between normal and abnormal expression has cultural variations. Several statements are possible in Blair's overview from animal research, though the topic is not so clear as fear/anxiety: a) anger/aggression is an observed response to threat throughout mammalian species, b) there are sequences favoring fear/anxiety response, withdrawal escape, and activating aggressive response, coordinated by the proximity and intensity of threat, c) amygdala activation occurs in both fear and aggression in animal and human studies (38), d) prefrontal regulatory systems sometimes provide inhibition of amygdala aggression, e) planned or premeditated aggression does not follow the same pattern as reactive aggression. (37)

Expression of anger and aggression is modified during development to conform to the expectations of the person's social system. Coordinated patterns of anger-assertive behavior are learned, like other emotional behaviors, from observing parents' or other caregiver's responses, modeled at the child's level of cognitive-motor development. The expression of anger progresses from a) diffuse behavior, the earliest expressions of anger-assertion are non-specific responses and crying. to b) focused less destructive motor and emotional expression, seen in the autonomic arousal and behavioral response of two year old "temper tantrums", poorly coordinated motor and emotional behavior expressing internal demands, to c) use of expletive verbal behavior, and d) to verbal behavior instrumental in achieving social goals. Many adults do not complete this sequence. Participation in sports is a social technique used for shaping anger into focused aggressive behavior. The society may also use military training, aggressive interpersonal games (martial arts), and hunting to develop focused aggressive behavior. (39) *No current research is designed to understand this developmental range; instead it focuses on individuals with problems in anger control, as if they constitute a specific (diagnostic) group, which is unlikely.*

Understanding anger and aggression means understanding what stimulus situations elicit the response and what brain pathways carry out the behaviors. Efforts to understand human differences in anger/aggression focus on differences in amygdala and pre-frontal controls. *The study of aggression is at a preliminary stage compared to the study of fear/anxiety, which is puzzling given the extent to which the human society has experienced lethal aggression in various forms over the last millennium!* Little is know about the controls that determine which pattern the amygdala produces, or even at what level the determination occurs. Recent reviews suggest the amygdala/hypothalamic pathways combine to produce an aggressive message sent to the pre-frontal basal ganglia system. Siever's review of etiology and epidemiology identifies "bottom up drive" data from genetics of amygdala and loss of "top down control" from cognitive impairment, sensory deficits, developmental trauma, etc., but no statistical data are presented to measure the contribution of each factor, or the distribution of differences in individuals. (37)

Amygdala "sensitivity" for anger-aggression may be different from the sensitivity for anxiety or part of the same response. A person may have high anxiety reactivity, and low threat/aggression response, or other variations. A high response to threat/aggression, with low fear response, may produce more aggressive responses, if frontal controls are not effective. A Swedish study on "normal adults" found that a "smaller amygdala", measured by MRI volume, was correlated to more aggression, even within the normal range of aggressive episodes. They proposed that lower anxiety, associated with smaller amygdala, is associated with more aggression, because amygdala anxiety helped control aggression. This model has been popularized but not replicated, and other variations are also seen. (41) Fowles created a mixed model of arousal separating two components. The BAS (assertion) is more associated to aggression or assertion, the BIS (inhibition) is associated with anxiety, and the two converge on a general arousal system (motivation pathway to PR/BG via orbito frontal cortex?) to initiate behavior. His differentiation is based on the assumption that heart rate does not associate with other anxiety measures and can be used to differentiate them. (Fowles, 41) The two patterns can take several forms: *Aggression and anxiety responses are linked and have similar sensitivity.* a)The person's response is balanced, so fear of consequences and aggression balance each other.) *Aggression and anxiety have separate sensitivities*, b) with anxiety high, and aggression low, the person is more vulnerable to fear, c) anxiety response is low, aggression is high, producing a person with high tendency to aggression and little anxiety. These variations have not been validated in studies of separate groups.

How amygdala pathways are triggered to initiate violence in different situations is unclear. The aggressive response to threat may involve: the sensitivity of amygdala to aversive input: anger arousal activated by threat, the intensity of the immediate somatic response may be a trigger for aggressive response, (James Lange theory of emotion), or the ease of creating conditioned pathways, associating threat to anger in defined experiences, as in domestic violence. Or all may be involved. Military training is an example of exposing young persons to "hypothetically danger arousing situations" (fear) and training them to perform focused aggressive behavior in place of fear. All aggressive sports require the participants to experience threat, or aggression, and respond with aggression. Does regulatory control of prefrontal pathways involve similar mechanisms for fear and aggression? Most of the studies focus on the role of PF/BG inhibiting aggressive responses, not how they focus to express aggression or use more appropriate patterns. Does amygdala respond to "severe threat": Is there a sense of dire threat the equivalent of an overwhelming PTSD stimulus that directly triggers reactive aggression?

A low fear arousal level, and less anxiety response to danger situations produces a person comfortable in life situations that provoke anxiety in average responders. The person reacts to life situations with less hesitation, and has less concern for consequences. The amygdala reaction does not activate somatic responses of anxiety, so the person shows little emotional reaction, often called "callous and unemotional", because of the lack of somatic reaction. Such persons are identified by reduced polygraphic response in testing, and diagnosed as Anti-social Personality if they arrive in the legal system. In Fowles model, this would be the type c) with low anxiety and high aggression-arousal. (42) There is no current method of measuring this parameter of amygdala responsiveness directly, but data showing the reduced autonomic arousal in persons with antisocial features supports this distinction. An alternate explanation of Anti-social Personality emphasizes impulsivity, the failure of prefrontal controls. *Whether this is an aspect of amygdala pathways or pre-frontal pathways PF/BG("impulsivity") or their interaction, is unknown.* None of the papers include the developmental process, even though applying treatments to children is proposed. *Little is understood about the difference in information signaling in amygdala pathways that leads to fear responses or aggression responses, and how they are regulated in pre-frontal pathways.*

Anti-social Personality has been studied in detail because of its legal significance. Much of the research is based on inconsistent patient group selection, not specific to aggression or reduced anxiety. Blair identifies problems of the interaction of amygdala and orbito-frontal cortex. Raine and Yang map a circuit of amygdala and cingulate-insula cortex as the "moral reasoning" region impaired in these patients but other brain regions and role of injury factors was not considered in the study. (Raine, 43) Koenigs et al review the inconsistencies in a meta-analysis. (Koenigs, 43) A high comorbidity with chemical addiction is noted, though is difficult to interpret. Comorbidity of aggression and anxiety disorders varies, some report this is rare as expected in amygdala low response, and some report high co-morbidity, which suggests an attachment basis for APD. An oversimplification attributes all the variance of anxiety response to genetic variations in amygdala sensitivity, but it may be a component, as reported in several studies. (43) The accumulation of current studies tend to affirm that the amygdala response is lower for individuals, including children, with higher level of aggression, suggesting reduced inhibition by anxiety. The relationship of this variable to pre-frontal controls is not consistently evaluated, so both may be involved. The emphasis on low amygdala response in antisocial personality focuses on the maladaptive features. Persons capable of enduring dangerous situations with low anxiety have opportunities to use this ability without illegal activity. They are suited to careers with high levels of danger and risk, i.e. airplane pilots, soldiers, arctic explorers, etc., facilitated by ignoring danger. The emphasis on the negative clinical aspect is typical of research driven by the clinical perspective.

The DSM V has few diagnoses for aggression, and the clinical assessment of "dangerousness", an important concern of the individual risk for mass violence, uses scales with poor validation. Relating aggressive behavior to diagnostic categories misses several features: What is the role of social control, is this an attempt to manipulate with threat? Is the individual responding to external reality or focusing on internal emotional threats (Is this psychosis)? Do cognitive or developmental limitations reduce the range of potential anger responses making physical responses more likely (due to cognitive impairment or dementia)? Is the current state of agitation immediate and temporary, or are there extended periods of hostility, and previous situations with hostile events? Is this a consistent adaptive pattern? What social factors in the individual's life play an important role? For adolescents, problems of social integration, and frustration about negative peer interaction may lead either to suicide or "school shooting" as hostile alternatives. Gang association often requires hostile behavior to bond or continue bonding to the group. In young adults, failure to satisfactorily integrate into the surrounding society is seen in job site violence, and "terrorist" violence of persons with alternative cultural backgrounds, or persons who feel that the "others" are taking over. Mothers or fathers, who kill their children, or entire family, are indications of failure of social engagement. "Suicide by cop" illustrates the complex interplay between the two modes of hostile expression: suicide and aggression. All of these situations present aggressive episodes with specific personal triggers, but do not identify the critical features that lead to the actions. The socialization of the individual plays an important role in willingness to use physical aggression. Temporary impairment of pre-frontal inhibition, as in alcohol intoxication can play a role. *How each of these situations produces aggressive behavior, deviating from norms, in one person and not another is not understood by any current diagnosis.* Violence may occur, as in suicide, without any mental health contact. Some violent persons perform lethal acts for no particular purpose other than the enjoyment of the experience, but it would be a serious error to presume this underlies all violence. None of these factors is specific to a particular diagnosis, and the urge to diagnose public situations "from afar" creates a false impression of expertise in mental health providers where none exists.

There is no evidence that one common identifiable feature unites individuals with poorly controlled aggressive behavior, or that they have excessive aggressive motivation compared with the general population. The hypothesis that "serial killers" and other aggressive behaviors reflect prior child abuse does not follow the PTSD pattern of failure of access to information. They are more likely to be examples of "modeling" aggressive behavior, as in the "school shooters" who wear clothing similar to the character in the Matrix film series. (40) The importance of the developmental sequence in learning to express aggression is so obvious that failure to gather this data in studies of persons with anger control problems is a major research omission. Poorly controlled aggression often places the individual in the legal system, and once there, is rarely evaluated for mental health concerns. The public's fascination with planned aggressive behavior, "serial rapist-killers", "mass shootings", etc. focuses interest on a minority of aggressive behavior, emphasized by a media motivated to capture viewers. Mass shooting attacks on fellow workers, in educational settings, and toward groups of strangers (based on group identification) are declared mental health problems before any study of the contributing factors. These episodes are not representative of most aggression, focus research on patterns of aggression with small statistical risk to the society, and divert resources from more comprehensive studies. *The wish to find a simple identifier that differentiates and isolates such persons, in order to protect the community, ignores the likely possibility that aggressors have different motivating factors and problems of control.* The pressure on mental health providers to identify persons at risk for violence toward others is not consistent with the multiple issues provoking violence in the society, and the complex individual data for risk, make one or a small number of critical factors is unlikely. Many factors may combine in each situation to increase the risk, and if the variables are identified in a person, in advance, intervention enters the legal realm of preventive detention, the restraint or treatment of individuals before any justifying event has occurred. (The story "Minority Report" by Dick is a famous warning about this situation.(44))

CHAPTER NINE:
Addiction and motivation

Addiction is a paradox. The person seeks the addiction with single-minded focus, yet seems unable to attend to other life needs. He may be charming, and appear engaged in the social scene, but closer attention shows that everything he does is organized around pursuing the addiction. Addiction is the hijacking of the motivation system by non-survival based motivation. The vulnerability of individuals to addictive hijacking depends on many variables, some of which are controlled by the society. Treatment of addiction using addiction is a paradox.

Historically, addiction was considered a problem of chemical use, and the current diagnostic criteria of DSM V apply mainly to drug addiction, though gambling has been added. (1) The criteria are the same for each addiction, with specific symptoms for withdrawal or intoxication of a specific drug. Withdrawal symptoms are the basis of the DSM definitions, hypothetical changes in brain regions where the substances are active. (In opiates and sedatives, the withdrawal symptoms are the opposite of the synaptic effects of the drugs.) An old NIDA monograph outlines this theory (1) and a review by Nestler describes the synaptic studies related to stimulant addiction. (2) This chemical tolerance/withdrawal model does not account for many features of addiction. Cannabis may produce addictive craving in some persons, without the "withdrawal syndrome" changes of synaptic receptors. The opiate withdrawal model of addiction does not account for initiation of use, especially opiates that produce negative initial effects. The model does not explain differences in vulnerability, or differences in development of addiction in different situations. The chemical model does not address other behaviors that interfere with life activities, including gambling, sexual compulsions, and dysfunctional eating. The concept of addiction needs a new approach. The American Society of Addiction Medicine proposed: *Addiction is a treatable, chronic medical disease involving complex interactions among brain circuits, genetics, the environment, and an individual's life experiences.* People with addiction use substances or engage in behaviors that become compulsive and often continue despite harmful consequences. *(3)* This definition adds etiologic factors, cognitive symptoms, and does not mention tolerance/withdrawal. But it does not capture what "addiction" *IS*, the paradox it presents, something else is needed.

Behavior that is reinforced promotes survival by satisfying basic needs. When humans do things that "feel good" (Freud's "pleasure principle"), that are "positive reinforcers" (Skinner) they are also fulfilling basic needs. But ICSS in rats (chapter three) does not enhance survival, no nutrition is acquired in self-stimulation, so it is possible to motivate rats to bar press for ICSS to death by starvation. (4) ICSS is both the prototype of motivation and a prototype for addiction. Addicts ignore necessary tasks to obtain the addiction. **Addiction is hijacking of the motivation system by a non-survival motivation.** The motivation system is "reprogrammed" to prioritize maladaptive goals and the behaviors of the addiction, which have a higher priority in motivation than other goals. Volkow and Boyle observe addiction causes: *"disruptions of an individual's ability to prioritize behaviors that result in long-term benefit over those that provide short-term rewards...even when associated with catastrophic consequences."* (Volkow, 5)

In the Wise and Koob approach to addiction: (6) (7) The addictive motivation is learned by initial reward of the chemical (or other experience), then, a secondary learned motivation, "the craving", augments and substitutes for the primary; the combination is the **hijacking**. In the dopamine dependent binge-intoxication stage, the "reward" effects of the addiction activate the reward centers in nucleus accumbens, reinforcing addictive behavior. This fits best with stimulant and cocaine addiction, but any reward with strong accumbens response can initiate the process. Most drugs of abuse cause a release of dopamine in the nucleus accumbens, though the intensity, in animal studies, is not correlated with addictiveness. (6) Chemicals may desensitize the reward system response, accounting for increasing drug use. The "Gateway Hypothesis" summarizes evidence that initial drug use facilitates later addiction as a model of how one drug "primes" the use of another. It is better evidence for learning to use chemicals to alter brain states. (8) The reward process indicates how use is initiated, but does not explain how the addictive reward overtakes other motivations, the hijacking. In the withdrawal-negative affect stage, the negative effects of withdrawal become motivating, craving the pleasurable experience creates a "need state". Wise and Koob call this negative emotional state *hyperkatefeia* (an amygdala response described in chapter eight). The extended amygdala pathways produce a negative affect, "craving" message motivation. (9) In the third, preoccupation-anticipation stage, these messages create the motivation that pre-empts (*hijacks*) other motivation: The individual is motivated by both the initial reward, and by a learned anticipation to seek addiction to avoid withdrawal/craving symptoms. Studies confirm changes in the PF/BG system as this region is "taken over", and new behavior habits are formed to pursue the addiction. In gambling, or sexual behavior, the motivation becomes the "craving for another episode". The anxiety-like subjective state generates a need for addictive experience, only partially satiated by fantasies like subjective "glorifying" of previous addiction experiences. The authors focus on chemical addiction, but the theory is applicable to all hijacking. Understanding addiction has evolved from local effects on accumbens, to a multi-pathway learning model of changes in motivation. (Piazza and Deroche-Gamonet present a model of stages of an addiction that also reflects this process. (10))

Does the addicted person "choose" to perform the addictive behavior? The motivation definition clarifies this confusion about "intentional choice": Yes, seeking the addiction is conscious and guided by intent. No, because addictive motivation has taken priority over other motivations, resulting in loss of the ability to make **adaptive choices**. Addiction can only occur if the person introduces the substance into his system, or performs the addictive behavior to produce **the loss of control of motivation**. (Nancy Reagan's "Just say no" is a typical confusion.) Symptom lists try to define when the person changes from being able to choose not to perform addictive behavior to hijacked motivation that controls the choice. In some chemical addictions, a physiological explanation for this loss of control is based on changes that result in "withdrawal symptoms", in other chemicals, or nonchemical addiction, similar cravings are created by changes of motivation that prioritize the for the addiction. ***Hijacking means the motivation for the addictive behavior dominates other motivations.*** Factors favoring hijacking include ones that apply to everyone, specific individual vulnerabilities, and general social factors that influence the process. The use of chemical substances for management of emotion and social behavior is not new, unique to American society, or inherently dangerous. Whenever this method is used, the negative messages of the amygdala are activated, either as the stimulus to be moderated, or as a reaction when the chemical or other addictive moderation is not available. The influence of multiple factors, genetic, personal, social, and political-economic combine to influence the use of chemical coping, and development of addiction. These include:

Enhanced Reward Learning. (DeltaFosB) Human motivation depends on generalizing rewards to abstract stimuli, "secondary reinforcement". Modern society depends on the capacity to abstract reward signals. Oddly marked pieces of paper (paper money) or entries in a digital bank statement provide goods and services needed for survival. Secondary rewards activate behavior after being linked to primary rewards, and substitute for primary rewards, becoming motivations. They extinguish if the reward system no longer responds. (11) Vulnerability to hijacking may involve differences in the ease of conditioning *secondary rewards*. The DeltaFosB gene protein is a critical element in learning secondary reinforcement, and enhances learning in regions involved in addiction. (2) Studies confirm that secondary reward stimuli activate the same reward system as primary rewards. DeltaFosB is activated in reward centers by addictive drugs. But the DeltaFosB factor is not specific and enhances all reward learning. (12) *It magnifies sensitivity to reward cues in the environment which is potentially adaptive, but may make the person more vulnerable to non-survival based rewards, which needs further research.*

Reward Effects. The reward effect of the chemical (or other experience) is the individual response to the chemical/drug/experience, including genetic vulnerability in some addictions. A family history of chemical addiction in previous generations, may "skip" a generation who are "strongly abstinent" in recognition of addiction problems of parents, and re-emerge in their children. If the individual avoids exposure to the addiction it cannot be learned, but the genetic vulnerability will persist. Studies of genetic vulnerabilities have not produced a clear picture. Shukit, et al showed that young men with genetic loading for alcoholism by family history have an immediately stronger reaction to alcohol on first drink. This supports the AA belief that members have a specific "sensitivity" to alcohol making it more "reinforcing". (13) Alcohol is part of the normal diet in most European cultures, with a long history of preservation of calories by fermentation of grains and fruits for energy. So the genetics of alcohol use must balance attraction and the dangers of excessive use and may differ from other addictions. Candidate factors like dopamine sensitivity are not specific for addiction, but apply to all reward. Certain populations have evidence for a genetic contribution to vulnerability, e.g. Native Americans, but not how the vulnerability operates. (14) Estimates that multiple genes account for 50% of the vulnerabilities in heavy drinking, do not give specific loci, or mechanisms for the hijacking. The subgroup of the population that experiences alcohol as "spiritual", the "society of dionysis", may have this factor. (14)) A GWAS study showed overlap of alcohol vulnerability with 17 other mental health conditions, questioning its specificity. AA and NA groups differ in focus at meetings: does this reflect differences in genetic vulnerabilities? (15) Other factors studied in the genetics of addiction include endorphin variations, GABA system abnormalities, etc. The emphasis on finding a genetic explanation does not impact treatment, since it does not discourage addicts from reproducing!

Individual vulnerabilities were documented in the soldiers experiencing heroin use while in Vietnam which did not trigger a nationwide heroin abuse epidemic, but a subgroup who did become addicted, and Stanton reviews the differences. Patients given opiates after surgery or in anesthesia have similar variations. (16). Differential amygdala response may also be a factor in individuals. This is a key element of the multi-component theory of addiction, but measuring the amygdala response is not currently possible. *Research quantifying amygdala sensitivity is needed. (17)*

Addictions lack an intrinsic satiety signal. In survival-based motivations, feedback from the reward of the behavior creates somatic messages that "turn off" the motivation signal activating the behavior. Drinking water quenches thirst by altering receptors in hypothalamus. The effects of addictive chemical use dissipate, and the body returns to the pre-use state without a sustained interval of satiety. For non-chemical addictions there is no explicit satiety response, so, in gambling, the appetitive reward is immediately reversed by negative outcomes. The peri-ventricular (medial) component of motivation pathways is involved in satiety behavior, so addictive hijacking bypasses this system in ways that survival motivations do not. This has not been studied in humans due to technical problems of fMRI (see chapter one appendix). A few studies have been done related to food "addiction", a meta review of available studies at (17)

Addiction changes PF/BG pathways associated with the developing addictive habit. These changes may be useful for charting the course of recovery, but current data are too variable for clinical use. Studies on the differences in prefrontal regions suggest "impulsivity" is sometimes associated with difficulty in stopping use. This seems too simple a formulation, and not consistent with the Kolb model of focused re-programming. (17) Volkow found specific differences in transmitter response. (Volkow, 18) Variations in cocaine and alcohol addiction indicate problems in control of choice. (18) Personality characteristics that interfere with social interaction and social reward reduce the power of social reward relative to addictive reward. These may be the result of genetic factors or early life experiences. Childhood and adult trauma events are strongly associated with vulnerability to addiction. Different types of alcoholism have different patterns of onset and response to treatment: Type A have a generally milder history and course, while Type B have earlier onset, more traumatic events history, and poorer course. (Babor, 18) Shukit also validated this difference. (18) The differences in pathways have not been studied.

The developmental stage contributes to vulnerability. Adolescent vulnerability includes physical changes, transition from family-based emotional support to peer group-based support, and changes in self-awareness and sense of personal identity. The brain is developing defensive strategy/coping mechanisms to be used later, and integrating the experiences of childhood. Substance use during this stage can be disastrous by interfering with the development of the pre-frontal system to regulate choice of action (see chapter six). When addiction captures the motivation system it also hijacks "identity" to make drugs or other addictive goals the focus. This distorts identity until the hijacking can be controlled, and may persist. In 12 step programs, comments begin " I am so and so, I am an "addicted person (alcoholic)", acknowledging that the addiction has taken over identity. All societies recognize the need to manage the experiences of children and adolescents, based on the incomplete development of prefrontal control systems. Heavy drug or other addictive behavior in teens before the development of internal coping skills, usually blocks further development of adult coping. (19) Kendler et al reported on young adult patterns of alcohol addiction. The young adult subtype accounts for about 32% of U.S. alcoholics, the largest group. They rarely seek help for alcohol dependence, became alcoholics by age 20, on average, and tend to binge drink. The young antisocial subtype comprises 21% of U.S. alcoholics, are 26 years old on average, and more than half have antisocial personality disorder. They tend to start drinking at 15 and became alcoholics by 18, earlier than other subtypes. The two types do not overlap. (Other types in the study: The functional subtype accounts for about 19% of U.S. alcoholics. They are middle-aged, working adults who have stable (sometimes) relationships, more education, and higher incomes than other alcoholics, and drink every other day. The intermediate familial subtype makes up nearly 19% of U.S. alcoholics, and nearly half have close relatives who are alcoholics. The chronic severe subtype, the rarest subtype, accounts for about 9% of U.S. alcoholics, mainly includes men, has the highest divorce rate, and frequently includes users of illicit drugs. (20) The total 100% appears to include both males and females, but does not separate issues of abuse/trauma, or the overall rate of recovery with age. The data shows different life patterns associated with excessive alcohol use.)

Three social variables are important factors in addiction: i) access to other rewards, ii) social support, and iii) availability. If the individual's other available rewards are limited, the motivation system becomes more vulnerable to hijacking, whether chemical, sexual, etc. The opium addiction of the collapsing empire in China in the late 19th century, encouraged and facilitated by European traders was an example. The prevalence of addiction, especially stimulants and opiates, in "inner city" US, throughout the mid 20th century, was and is associated with the lack of opportunities. Declining economic and social opportunity spread to rural communities in the 1990s and early 21st century, facilitating methamphetamine and opiate addiction. Covington et al document that adolescent drug use is now prevalent in both minority and majority teen culture. (21) The recent lowering opportunity for "middle class youth" in suburban and urban America in the early 21st century, has fueled a dramatic increase in opiate use, supported by opiate manufacturers, including an "epidemic" of opiate overdose deaths of middle class children, unprecedented in its extent and distribution. (This has raised concerns not expressed when other ethic groups experienced similar consequences.) (22) Persons facing difficulties accessing life rewards are more vulnerable to addictive hijacking. Not everyone in a vulnerable community chooses an addictive escape; the impact of limited social opportunity can only be appreciated at the population level.

Social reinforcement and support counters motivation for addiction. The family and social matrix are important, because addictions replace social rewards with addictive ones. Early attachment or abuse problems may interfere with the person's ability to experience positive attachment to others, interfering with social reward, and increasing vulnerability. A specific transcription factor has been identified with both stress and vulnerability to addiction. (24) The role of the family can be crucial in adolescent addiction. Adolescents are intrinsically dependent on their family (or other) support system. The addictive process disrupts this dependency. The family is confronted with the reality that the child is functioning in immature, helpless ways, which encourages excessive family intervention, while the addiction encourages the family to withdraw. There may be current substance abuse in the parental generation, acknowledged or unacknowledged, an added factor in adolescent substance abuse. The pervasive use of alcohol in the American West during westward expansion reflected the lack of social rewards from family, and social system, which were replaced by the saloon. The Temperance Movement of the 1920s grew out of this Western culture. Addiction interferes with social relationships, which compete with the addiction to motivate behavior. Intimate relationships fail, leaving the addictive motivation unopposed. The loss of social interaction and support in modern societies contributes to an overall increase in addictive behavior, replacing social support. (***Bowling Alone*** describes these trends but not the trend to increasing alcohol consumption alone.) The experience in Japan illustrates the series of changes in relation to chemical coping that are the result of social transformations. (24) The "Rat Park" experiment suggests this is also a factor in animal vulnerability to addictive substances. (23)

Politics can influence addiction by creating solutions or, more often, promoting it. Laws against addictive use resulted in massive incarceration of addicts in the Nixon-Reagan era, by making the problem the addicted person, "blaming the victim". It did not reduce addiction or its financial benefits, because drugs were clandestinely distributed in prisons. The cost to society of incarceration exploded, and created new, for profit, corporate organizations to manage the prisons, and created more socially isolated persons on discharge to return to addiction. The "war on drugs" and other policies that address controlling addiction by legal consequences to addicts always fail, costing the society more in expenses and lost lives than they gain in recovered lives. They ignore the "loss of control", *hijacking,* aspect of addiction. Using legal consequences to increase the negative motivation against addiction by is not supported by any data. The threat of legal consequences may be a weak inhibitor of initiating the process, but is ineffective once the *hijacking* occurs. Hart, an addiction specialist has published advocacy against legal penalties for even "hard drugs" emphasizing social factors in the effects of drug use. Andreas' book ***Killer High*** describes the way that drugs get enabled as part of war efforts. (25)

The strongest social contribution to vulnerability is the availability of addictive substances or situations. "If there is no substance "X", the addicted person can not get addicted." If an addiction is not available, it cannot hijack the system. This is the justification for the long history of attempts to restrict the availability of addictive chemicals. The logic of controlling availability seems clear, but the ability to limit access turns out to be difficult or impossible to achieve. Various "social experiments" like the 18th Amendment for Prohibition of Alcohol in US failed to impact addiction, only encouraging intensive efforts to bypass legal controls. The commercial relationship between the US, Mexico, and South America demonstrates that "off shoring" production also applies to illegal substances produced for consumption in the United States! Restriction is generally ineffective, but increasing supply has become epidemic.

Between 2000 and 2010, the US experienced a dramatic increase in the production and distribution of highly addictive opioids that was not prevented by either the FDA or the DEA. These were generally prescribed by physicians, in amounts and dosages inconsistent with any known treatment regimen, but promoted by pharmaceutical companies with claims of no addiction risk. A dramatic increase in opiate addiction and OD deaths in young persons is the result. A surge in illegal opiate distribution is occurring as the legal source is cut off. (In many ways, this parallels the situation in 19th century China, but the source of addiction is internal.) The recurring inability to manage opiate addiction is a significant aspect of mental health in the United States. Cannabis use and addiction is a developing concern. This natural substance went from a designated component of the U.S.P. natural formulary to a Class I restricted substance of abuse in 1973, a political reaction to the social rebellion of the 1960s. No evidence existed then or now to make the substance more addictive and dangerous than morphine (Class II). (Class II drugs are manufactured by pharmaceutical companies.) Social pressure has gradually altered the legal restrictions on cannabis with new research on possible medical uses, as well as recreational use. There is evidence that cannabis use can evolve into addiction in vulnerable persons, and also trigger severe symptoms, so a regulated approach is warranted, which is not occurring. Cannabis, a natural product, cannot be patented; so intensive pharmacognosy research is attempting to synthesize mentally active substances that can be patented. Cannabis related products are being tested for use in MAT, and so becoming part of the drug-addiction cycle. (52)

Addiction makes money! From an economic-business perspective addiction is the ideal product: it creates a continuing demand, which is not sensitive to supply, and therefore allows for dramatic price increases, or virtually unlimited distribution. An important feature in efforts to contain addiction is the profit it generates. (26) There are a few research studies on corporations profiting directly from addictive behavior, and many studies on the effects of "poverty" or personal variables in producing addiction. How much of the economy depends on addictive behavior is unknown, it is built-into other activities. The relationship between capitalism and addiction assures that business and political leaders continue to support the economics of compulsive use. The world opiate market share is estimated at $4.4 billion, and this does not include illegal sales! The recent campaign for "preventing chronic pain" was created to expand opiate prescribing for minor injuries. Pharmaceutical manufacturers expanded production and distribution of opiates, encouraged physician prescribing, and passed responsibility for the excessive use onto the prescribers. The FDA and DEA both failed to prevent this expansion. Aggressive marketing to teens engaged them in long term use. The ambivalent position of verbally discouraging access, while providing easy access commercially, and marketing products with special appeal to children and teens illustrates the society's role in promoting addiction. The expanded marketing of opiates is the latest example in the succession of alcohol products, nicotine/tobacco products, and cannabis. Providing access to addiction, whether chemicals, gambling, or other experiences generates large financial returns. Legal addiction, e.g. alcohol in the U.S., does not reduce the distribution or control the number of alcoholics, but channels the economic benefit to corporations. Gambling access, both casino and internet variations, state run lotteries, and betting on sporting events are all expanding commercial efforts to exploit this addiction, while warning gamblers to "not exceed their limit". The mental health community also benefits from addiction. The medically based treatment of addiction, MAT, for chemical addiction, continues the use of addictive chemical treatments. The estimated market share is $2.5 billion, of which 80% is currently suboxone. Total addiction treatment of $16.5 billion in 2018 does not fully incorporate the recent epidemic. Treatment of addiction is a major facet of healthcare, mostly supported by governmental agencies, i.e. taxes. (28) Corporations can be held liable for the consequences of addiction, as in the case of tobacco companies, but whether this reduces addiction to tobacco products is unclear. Vaping has become the alternative nicotine addiction. Holding corporations responsible for the distribution of addictive substances is analogous to holding addicts responsible for their decision to use, or identifying poverty as a significant factor in producing addiction. All three factors are relevant and interact, and require social and political processes that foster an integrated solution. The most powerful social variable promoting addiction is the ability to profit at the expense of addicts and society. A society that encourages addiction is saying that exploiting addiction for economic gain is appropriate. This is a moral issue. (27) The current situation in the US of virtually unregulated availability of many addictive substances is expanding the percent of the population addicted and is unsustainable.

Addiction results in the loss of *agency*. Telling an addicted person to "just say no" to addiction ignores the changes in motivation. The paradox of addiction is the high motivation for the addiction while losing control of motivation for other goals. Multiple individual, and social factors influence the prevalence of addiction in a society. No current approach addresses interaction of these factors. (The emphasis on genetic variables is particularly odd, since they are the least accessible to change, and center the problem only in the addicted person, and there is no record of addicts refusing to reproduce to control this risk.) *The essential key to understanding and managing addiction is dealing with the factors that increase the likelihood of **hijacking***. There is not one overall **hijacking** factor. The combined role of the positive and aversive pathways, the accumbens positive reward, and the extended amygdala negative state, are important to understand the process. *The **hijacking**, results when both pathways join for specific motivation. The motivation pathways are involved, but "hyperkatefeia" ("craving") is a subjective experience, suggesting that cingulate or insular cortex is where the two motivation systems are joined to influence BG/PF behavior choice and hijack behavior, research is needed to understand how they are linked.*

Mental health treatment is discussed in chapters eleven and twelve, but the treatment of addiction is included here because treatment is closely linked to understanding the process of addiction.

Managing the access to addiction, and teaching the dangers of addiction seem useful steps but are ignored by a society already heavily addicted. Individual or group treatment processes that attempt to "reprogram" individual addicts are sometimes successful, but are hampered by the reality that the recovering person returns to a society saturated with addiction, which he or she must manage somehow. The treatment of addiction has four stages:

I) Evaluation: validation that an addiction is occurring, that the motivation pathways have been hijacked.
II) Participation: creating a relationship between the addicted person and treatment program with a commitment to resolve the addiction.
III) Intervention: carrying out agreed upon steps aimed at resolving the addiction.
IV) Re-Evaluation: assessment of the changes in the state of the addicted person.

Two strategies have evolved for working with addiction, which make different assumptions about the process, so a decision must be made to use one of them: Medication based treatments (MAT), often termed "harm reduction", withdraw the person from dangerous addictive substances to stabilize on an alternative chemical regimen. **Psychosocial recovery** programs require abstinence from all addiction to resolve the hijacking of the motivation system and redirect the person to recovery of appropriate life goals. Motivation is different in each approach, but essential to both. The individual must choose 1) to participate in actions that modify addiction, or 2) choose to be abstinent, **either /or**. The treatment of addiction follows a definite sequence, and may begin before the addicted person acknowledges need for treatment.

I) Evaluation. The evaluation of a person for addiction means documenting that the motivation system is controlled by an addiction. How much is the person using? Can the person stop using consistently? Is the person hiding or lying about use? Most important

> **SIDEBAR DETOX.** There may be a need for an interim detoxification stage to moderate chemical withdrawal in either approach. Opiate withdrawal syndrome is associated with multiple very unpleasant symptoms, and depending on the current daily dose, the addicted person may be very insistent on a gradual withdrawal that spares experiencing them. Sedative-alcohol withdrawal, including benzodiazepines, is associated with a range of neural hyperactivity symptoms and can lead to "delirium tremens", seizures, and possibly death. Safe withdrawal in this addiction is mandatory. The duration of the chemical detoxification can take days to weeks, often done in hospital for safety, and usually overlaps with the beginning of one of the two treatment interventions. (35)

of all these criteria is the failure of adaptation: Are there indications of failing make adaptive life choices influenced by the addiction? These may be work consequences, relationship consequences, negative events (assault, rape, DUI, etc.) while intoxicated, and legal consequences (fighting while intoxicated, inappropriate public behavior). (29) Programs ask the person to make a list of life problems that have resulted during addictive behavior to increase awareness of the adaptive failure and overcome the element of denial. (30) A major difficulty in assessing adolescent addiction is the limited extent of life activities that may have been affected, though school failure, and problems in relationships are useful.

Denial is a fundamental feature of the mental state of the addicted person, which is often misunderstood. The motivation system is **hijacked** making addiction the life goal, therefore negative events occurring during addiction are perceived as "obstacles" to addiction, not indications of addiction. Inability to see the impact of addiction, the *denial*, must be taken into account in the assessment. Un-ambivalent denial is evidence that the addiction is in control of motivation. So problems at work, with family, or the legal system may need to be provided by others. Discomfort about consequences of addictive behavior may suggest ambivalence in the hijacking and be utilized in treatment. Recognizing addiction in the "functional alcoholic" who continues to work despite heavy use, and denies the impact of use is typical. If a person with addiction seeks treatment because he or she has become aware of the losses that result from addictive choices (called "hitting bottom" in recovery programs) it may help him or her recognize the hijacking.

Pretreatment occurs when the treatment process begins before the individual acknowledges the need for treatment especially if life events trigger entering treatment from legal or other consequences. This is typically the situation with teens referred for drug use by parents. The interviewer uses whatever information is available to explore the addiction, while avoiding direct contradiction of the denial, because if the person is motivated by the addiction, *hijacked*, addictive behaviors are "normalized". Problems that interfere with addictive behavior are ignored in order to pursue the addiction. Direct confrontation at this stage fails to recognize the cognitive changes. The technique of *motivational interviewing* has been used in the pretreatment setting, because it avoids direct confrontation while exploring the intensity of use with the client and exploring alternatives. (31) If the person with addiction continues to make non-survival based choices they will suffer more consequences. This is sometimes helpful in confronting denial, but may intensify it. The "inventory" of negative consequences that is a part of most modern addictive treatment assessment addresses the denial by documenting the "loss of control". The clinician must make an estimate of the extent of use, and often a recovering person will have a more realistic appreciation of the extent of denial than someone unfamiliar with the process. A variety of scales and self-report instruments have been created to obtain information about the addictive behavior. (30) The clinician will often encounter street names for drugs unfamiliar to the non-addiction community, which creates a sense of exclusivity, so addicts often use street names to confuse the extent of use. Data on the amount and types of chemicals used gives apparent numerical precision, but is usually unreliable, because of the addict's inability to recognize the extent of use, and the need to hide it. The amount of chemical use is mainly important to stabilize withdrawal symptoms. (Explaining the dangers of incomplete stabilization of withdrawal can motivate inexperienced persons in recovery, while those with prior attempts at withdrawal know the symptoms all too well, and will amplify reported use to acquire higher withdrawal dosage and moderate the withdrawal experience. There is no evidence that severe withdrawal experiences are aversive motivation to prevent relapse.)

CLINICAL EXAMPLE Problem Drinking Or Addiction? *Stanton Peele, a Brooklyn psychologist who has studied substance use for decades is a longtime critic of the A.A. model. He reports that a majority of college binge drinkers do not go on to become alcohol dependent, and while binge drinking and other drug use are risky, multiple studies show that most people "mature out" of recklessness when they begin to have increased responsibilities. The National Epidemiologic Survey on Alcohol and Related Conditions, or Nesarc, found that 75 percent of those who are heavy drinkers eventually regain control without rehab or A.A., Dr. Peele said. The survey, which was conducted in the early 2000s and was designed to be representative of the larger United States population, was aimed at helping researchers understand high-risk drinking patterns, design better-targeted treatment programs and monitor recovery. It found that over half of those who recover managed to cut back instead of abstaining. (32)*

Traditional approaches emphasize loss of control in assessing addiction because the *hijacking* controls motivation producing a loss of *agency*. The paradox of *agency* in addiction is the addicted person's fixed intention to choose addictive behaviors. The *loss of agency*, the inability to make adaptive life choices, is not "all or none", so determining when life goals are compromised can be challenging. If a person manages use of drugs, sex, or other behavior without disruption of other life goals diagnosis of addiction is not supported; the motivational system has not (yet) been hijacked, so there is nothing to treat. Interventions, often in teens, to "prevent" drug use from "progressing to addiction" are based on a "gateway concept" that has little validation and requires a different treatment approach. An addicted person cannot make changes in their motivation system without some external process to facilitate the change. Once the paradox of agency is understood, the treatment approach must include features that operate outside the person's control.

> **SIDEBAR The relationship of addiction and spirituality.** *Treatment in the recovery community method includes the issue of spiritual focus. Jung embraced this in a letter to Bill W ("You see alcohol in Latin is "spiritus" and you use the same word for the highest religious experience as well as for the most depraving poison. The helpful formula therefore is: spiritus contra spiritum.").* **(33)** *Addiction* **hijacks** *the person's motivation away from other life goals; so* ***every effective "recovery" includes a return to making meaningful life choices.*** *How each individual determines this life path varies from person to person; the process of finding it is the "spiritual journey" in recovery and may involve personal commitment, use of a "higher power", or specific religion. If motivation is ignored in addiction, it cannot address this process. The interaction of genetic and experiential programming influences development of addiction. Spirituality is the process of combining genetic and learned experience to maximize life opportunities. The motivation for one's life, one's Tao, is hijacked by addiction, so the goal is to recover one's life path.* **(34)**

FORMULATION If there is sufficient data to document that addiction is occurring, the provider prepares a formulation that describes the hijacking and provides a pathway for the individual to recover a non-hijacked life. If the information is incomplete or not definitive, the outcome of the evaluation may be "provisional" to be continued at a future time in order to observe the impact of the initial contact. The formulation is shared with the individual, and the phrasing and presentation depends on whether the individual has engaged treatment voluntarily, or has entered into treatment by legal or other pressure. The formulation provides the person with an external, objective documentation of impairment, challenging the denial.

PARTICIPATION If the addicted individual agrees to participate (or is required to participate), a plan of treatment that addresses the addiction is created. The agreement to "participate" does not imply that the individual is no longer hijacked by the addiction, and is making this choice with **agency**, only that both the client and provider agree that hijacking is occurring and a plan of action will be designed to reverse it. This is a behavioral contract between provider and client to engage in the plan. The specific plan depends on the treatment approach, with behaviors performed by the **hijacked** person, actions performed by the caregiver-support system, and others by the provider. These are observable, defined actions that permit assessment of performance. Some way to measure continuing addiction (i.e. "relapse") is necessary. This involves abstinence from the addictive behaviors, and urine or other measurements performed to test for relapse of chemicals. Measuring treatment as reduction in "relapse events" or intervals between "relapses" is common in recovery programs, but not favored in medically based programs, which claim to target "complete abstinence" (while continuing to prescribe addictive substances). The person's participation may be entirely voluntary, or be a condition of work, court ordered after legal consequences of addictive behaviors, or required by other life situations. So reporting requirements to outside agents may be incorporated in the plan, including release of confidentiality. Other details like location of treatment, requirement for incarceration or residential placement may be included. Addiction is behavior, so active participation in non-addictive behavior can be effective even when external factors coerce the participation. In treatment programs, this is termed "fake it 'til you make it". **The addicted person must actively participate in the process, treatment is what the addicted person does, not what the provider does.** When addictive motivations no longer entirely control behavior, some progress has been made. False starts are common, with addicted persons verbalizing complete change without difficulty, while continuing addictive behaviors in secret. The resolution of the hijacking requires time, and depends on the individual and the life situation. Without a commitment to participate, interventions cannot begin, and if the agreement to participate is coerced by external requirements, the participation must be more carefully monitored. Agreement to participate by the addicted person does not mean the person is expected to suddenly "just say no" to the addiction, yet this is often assumed in treatment programs. Given the control of motivation by the addiction, both provider and addicted person understand that continued motivation for addiction remains, and the plan addresses steps for a path to recovery.

CLINICAL EXAMPLE ***The successful addicted person who died.*** *A mid 20s heroin addicted person was treated in hospital for endocarditis, a bacterial infection resulting from using infected needles. He was working in industrial production, had a wife with one child, and a girlfriend who was a regular relationship and also visited to him in hospital. The treating physician emphasized the seriousness of the infection and danger to his heart. The man had been using heroin for three years, never entered a treatment program, and was able to afford his addiction by work and a series of "side hustles". He was discharged with the cardiac infection cleared, and a regimen of narcotic withdrawal that allowed him to be drug free. After discharge he returned to his addictive life, and believed that the treatment meant he could overcome any danger. He believed and verbalized that he was a "successful addicted person". Roughly six months later, he was seen again in hospital for recurring endocardial infection that now involved the valves and impaired cardiac function and put him in heart failure. He died in surgery attempting to replace the damaged valves.*

TREATMENT INTERVENTIONS

Medication Assisted Recovery Model. This method provides an alternate substance for controlled addiction to avoid the social and legal consequences of illegal use. Providers using this approach call the method "Medication Assisted Treatment" which identifies it as a "medical" treatment model. When previous medications were used, the term "harm reduction" was often used, which has broader implications for the social impact of addiction, but also does not imply "treatment". Variations of this model began with heroin as a treatment for morphine addiction in Civil War Veterans. (36) Treatment with substitute drugs was thought to treat the addiction until heroin was recognized as also addictive, so the "treatment" was redefined as transfer to a "safer" option. The basis for all pharmacological intervention is blocking craving. If the person is not craving, he is not motivated for addictive behavior. (This is the 2nd phase of the Koop model of addiction, *the aversive withdrawal phase.*) Without exception, drugs that block craving use the same synaptic pathways as the addictive drugs, by the same pharmacology, and can also be used for detoxification/withdrawal. Methadone, a more recently synthesized opiate, replaced heroin treatment, to prevent withdrawal symptoms, and has little euphoria even at high doses, while blocking the "high" of street drugs. The methadone strategy of the 1980-90s was restricted to specialized clinics. England provided government directed *heroin maintenance*, though it has recently been discontinued. (37) Buprenorphine was introduced in the US in 2002 as an alternative detoxification and maintenance drug to methadone, better tolerated by patients. This was combined with naloxone, as suboxone, both opiate and antagonist (to counter euphoric effects and block response of illicit use of other drugs). Despite its opiate structure, addictive potential and other risks, the FDA scheduled buprenorphine and suboxone as schedule III, not IV, which allows it to be administered in office based practice by physicians specially licensed, a significant change from methadone, which was only approved for use in specialty clinics. (38) Why the government changed this policy, and whether there is less problem of diversion and illicit use with these drugs is unclear. The marketing of treatment focuses on private practice and is less accessible to uninsured addicts. As in other examples of legal regulation of addictive substances, the economics may drive the decision more than pharmacology. The marketing of the term Medication Based Treatment (MAT) coincided with use of naloxone. The effects of this treatment include bypassing the craving and withdrawal symptoms, reducing the motivation to seek other addictive substances. Whether it reduces criminal activities that support addictions and the negative impact on the surrounding society ("harm reduction") have not been documented. It provides an ongoing treatment regimen to prevent "relapse" to more dangerous drugs. Success of MAT depends on the ability to engage the addicted person in new life activities (as in all recovery). Office clinicians do not typically have the resources, nor are compensated to provide rehabilitative interventions, so the outcome depends on the hijacked individual's ability to create a new life plan, while continuing to use addictive substances. If this is accomplished, the treatment can change motivation, but most studies are too short term to document this goal, and only document continuation (vs. dropout) in the program. (38) At least one study showed methadone superior in patient maintenance. (39) The motivation for eventually weaning the patient off all medication is unclear, because financial incentives favor maintenance.

A similar strategy for sedative and alcohol addiction, which has the risk of a lethal withdrawal syndrome, uses benzodiazepines for safe withdrawal (detox) from addiction to avoid seizures or "delirium tremens", and sometimes as chronic "maintenance treatment", though this maintenance on benzodiazepines is not advocated by any official program, but is reported in one case series. (39) After the acute withdrawal from alcohol, some patients describe up to 90 days of recurring confusion and other symptoms termed *Post Acute Withdrawal Syndrome*. (40) No definite physiological data is been correlated with this syndrome, that is presumed to reflect instability of transmitter pathways, and may occur with other sedative withdrawal.

A survey of medical and psychiatric practitioners in every region of the country, would find some patients maintained on moderate doses of benzodiazepines, prescribed for "co-morbidity" of anxiety disorder, PTSD, etc. This is equivalent of opioid Medication Assisted Treatment, but not an acknowledged or advocated by research for sedative/alcohol addiction.

Recovery Of Motivation Model. (The DETOX listed above may also be needed prior to beginning this method.) The *psychosocial recovery* model is based on *abstinence from all addiction*. Non-medical "recovery programs" often staffed by previous addicts, are the alternative to continuing addiction under medical supervision. The programs promote "abstinence" from all addictions, and potentially addictive drugs (except caffeine!), and substitute a program of "steps" intended to guide the addicted person back to non-addiction motivation. Psychosocial interventions are utilized to support return to adaptive motivations. For most hijacked persons, this transformation is difficult, requires months or years, intensive support of the recovery community, and is often associated with relapse and return of addictive behavior. A few individuals report the change occurs suddenly and spontaneously, often in conjunction with a religious or

> **SIDEBAR Other medication options.** The one with longest history is disulfuram (Antabuse), a chemical that blocks the liver metabolism of alcohol to formaldhyde resulting in a toxic and extremely unpleasant temporary state when alcohol is consumed, not usually fatal. This has been used to augment abstinence in alcohol recovery, giving the individual additional motivation to avoid drinking. The medication must be taken daily; its effects wear off over approximately one week. So the individual must be responsible for self-medication, (unless the administration is supervised in a treatment program).
>
> Acamprosate is used in alcohol recovery treatment, but the mechanism of action has never been documented, perhaps because it is thought to work at GABA sites, which might make it a substitute addiction, *and require distribution as a controlled DEA substance*, (which it is not). It has a number of side effects, and has not been proven to enhance recovery when used alone. (54) A number of other GABA agonists or "positive allosteric modulators" have been utilized with varying results. The most studied is topirimate. (See (54) for others)
>
> Treatment of *stimulant addiction* often requires initial antipsychotic medication when the patient presents with a paranoid psychosis. The depressed mood state that invariably occurs with stimulant withdrawal uses "activating anti-depressants" which are only rarely effective at maintenance treatment. The inability to meet the need for "pleasure reward" may result in a depressed dysphoric state that triggers return to use. Bupropion is an antidepressant often used in the aftermath of stimulant addiction to offset the depressive mood that remains. Mirtazapine has also occasionally been used in this way. The use of methylphenidate which is a controlled non-amphetamine stimulant, and atomoxetine another antidepressant used off label as alternative treatments for stimulant abuse are not supported by controlled studies but observed clinically. (49) *The willingness to utilize undocumented treatments reflects both the lack of more effective alternatives and the reluctance to carry out large population studies of recovery for proof of efficacy.*
>
> Several newer proposals include ketamine, LSD, and psilocybin. These disrupt neural pathways and suggest a strategy that disrupts the drug related hijacking to re-establish other reward patterns. Successful use of any of these currently undocumented strategies must also include extensive *relearning of positive life rewards* lost to addiction. (51) This method might be a valid Recovery approach.

spiritual reawakening outside of any established treatment program, or in a church or religious community. The "spiritus contra spiritum" that Jung described. (32) Most programs use some modification of the "12 steps" originally developed by the AA community:

THE TWELVE STEPS

STEP 1) ADMITTED TO BEING POWERLESS OVER MY ADDICTION. (LOSS OF CONTROL) This is the initial step, the individual must acknowledge that hijacking has occurred.

STEP 2) CAME TO BELIEVE THAT A POWER GREATER THAN MYSELF COULD RESTORE ME TO SANITY. "I turn my life over to a higher power, to restore me to sanity." This may be translated as: "I have lost my meaning for life, am controlled by my addiction, and so I must have outside help to recover my life." The "insanity" of addiction is the hijacking by maladaptive motivation to do destructive actions.

STEP 3) MADE A DECISION TO TURN MY WILL AND LIFE OVER TO THE CARE OF GOD AS I UNDERSTAND HIM. Some outside control of my decisions is necessary.

STEP 4) MADE A SEARCHING AND FEARLESS MORAL INVENTORY OF MYSELF. Identify factors that contribute to my vulnerability.

STEP 5) ADMITTED TO GOD, TO MYSELF, AND TO ANOTHER HUMAN BEING THE EXACT NATURE OF MY WRONGS. Publicly admit the vulnerabilities, a confession.

STEP 6) WERE ENTIRELY READY TO HAVE GOD REMOVE ALL THESE DEFECTS OF CHARACTER. Get help dealing with the problems.

STEP 7) HUMBLY ASKED HIM TO REMOVE OUR SHORTCOMINGS. Accept the changes with help.

STEP 8) MADE A LIST OF ALL PERSONS I HARMED, AND BECAME WILLING TO MAKE AMENDS TO THEM ALL. Recognize the social impact of the addiction.

STEP 9) MADE DIRECT AMENDS TO SUCH PEOPLE WHEREVER POSSIBLE, EXCEPT WHEN TO DO SO WOULD INJURE THEM OR OTHERS. Try to repair social connections.

STEP 10) CONTINUE TO TAKE PERSONAL INVENTORY AND WHEN I AM WRONG PROMPTLY ADMIT IT.

STEP 11) SOUGHT THROUGH PRAYER AND MEDITATION TO IMPROVE MY CONSCIOUS CONTACT WITH GOD, AS I UNDERSTAND HIM.

STEP 12) HAVING HAD A SPIRITUAL AWAKENING AS THE RESULT OF THESE STEPS, I TRY TO CARRY THIS MESSAGE TO OTHER ADDICTS, AND TO PRACTICE THESE PRINCIPLES IN ALL MY AFFAIRS.

These "steps" define a psychological strategy to progress from "hijacking" to "recovery":

STEPS 1-3 define the loss of control and need for outside direction. Recovery programs offer strong social community engagement, emphasis on physical activities, and mental distraction to substitute for the euphoric pleasure of drug use. Managing craving is addressed by a series of recommendations including isolation from prior friends and users, and a "sponsor" available to respond. Regular participation in meetings and frequent interpersonal contact is an important component. An organized process of review occurs with a counselor or sponsor.

STEPS 4-7 address personal characteristics that provide vulnerability to **hijacking.** This sequence can be interpreted as personal characteristics associated with addiction; often the basis for poor choices, so recognizing these and changing patterns is revising motivation. It can also be interpreted as damage caused by the addiction on personal development. "Relapse prevention" skills are taught. The defects are not guaranteed to disappear, only that they are "asked to be removed". An organized review using a structured interview encourages the recovering person to become self aware of problems contributing to addictive behavior. This is often stressful, posing risk of relapse.

STEPS 8-9 address the breakdown in social support and efforts to rebuild it. The task here is to identify persons injured and then seek their acknowledgement of an apology. This is an active process.

STEPS 10-12 repeat the previous process throughout the rest of life.

Recovery is an ongoing day-by-day process.

Redirection of someone's motivation is a major undertaking, and there is no controlled evidence that a specific sequence of phrases or steps is effective, the processes outlined in the "12 steps" was derived from practical experience.

When contracting with the addicted person for participation in a plan, one of the two methods must be specified. A few programs have attempted to create overlapping plans using both approaches but these are suspect due to the contradictory assumptions.

The plans must include a number of other features: A plan for interruption of addictive behaviors either by isolating the person, supervision, or urine testing or other methods. The interruption of addictive behaviors may have special challenges if chemical addiction is involved, and require a plan of detox and stabilization to have the person return to a drug free state. Treatment of symptoms that reflect the longer-term residual effects of chemical toxicity. Medical and neurological complications, especially with long-term alcohol use, may require medical intervention. Data supporting these steps is missing especially when programs are already prescribing an addictive substance. Interventions for sexual and food addiction behavior invade personal space and is difficult to monitor. (43) A plan for improving access to other personal rewards. This may include attendance in programs or meetings, emphasis on physical activity, prior rewarding activities, or other behavior. Etc. Having the person engage socially in the community and rebuild damaged social skills and exchange is essential. In recovery programs, this is done by encouraging or requiring attendance at 12 Step meetings. These have risks of exposure to relapsing members and social pressures but provide a community in which all the members share a common problem. Some programs provide explicit attention to problems of the disrupted family, while others avoid this early in recovery as an unnecessary stress. A plan for addressing associated factors facilitating addictive behaviors may require eliminating associates, new social settings, residential placement, or incarceration, and include dealing with abuse, PTSD, or other vulnerability factors.

Personality features are an important vulnerability in acquiring addiction, outlined in the "4th step" of recovery. The combination of self-centered with immature defenses describes an immature narcissistic person called "the King Baby profile". Research to determine whether these are consequences of addiction or antecedents or some combination has not been done. A classic series by Vaillant studied men with poorer coping skill patterns in a longitudinal study, and substance abuse, especially alcoholism, emerged over time and therefore not a consequence. (42) It seems likely that persons with certain features are more vulnerable to developing hijacking.

RE-EVALUATION. A recurring assessment in either method determines whether the member is participating, and if the plan is effective, or if modifications are needed. Not getting full participation indicates problems. These must be addressed and examined, as they reflect the motivation of the addiction. The primary outcome of recovering the life space from non-addictive behavior may be temporary and not reflect a change in the hijacking of motivation. Regular monitoring of the tasks, including signatures from meetings and other documentation, help to maintain consistency. In abstinence programs, chemical relapse can be measured and documented. In MAT, chemical relapse is less likely, and discontinuation is an indication of program failure. Effective programs recognize that relapse or drop out will occur, and seek ways to anticipate this and develop interventions to return the person to recovery. Addiction is an acquired disturbance in motivation that cannot be reversed quickly by any current treatment method. The likelihood of return to the addictive motivation, "relapse" is high. The tracking and management of these episodes identifies factors that contribute to "relapse", and removing or altering them may change the future course of the treatment. Several organized approaches and workbooks outline various ***relapse prevention strategies***. (44)

DUAL DIAGNOSIS. The role of alternate treatment. Addictive behavior may occur in association with other symptoms: Anxiety symptoms often emerge during withdrawal from sedative medications. *Bipolar mania* is often associated with alcohol addiction. Patients with a childhood or adult history of head injury may have attention problems, soft neurological signs, and difficulties in emotional control, and concentration, and seek addictive substances. The association with anxiety disorders, PTSD, depression, and addiction is documented. (45) The relationship of co-occurrence of addictive behavior and sociopathic or anti-social traits may be a disregard for personal controls, lack of social support, or some more direct link. (44) Identifying one of these problems adds consideration for additional medication in the recovery plan. This is justified by the "self medication" hypothesis (SMH) described by Khantzian, who proposed that the choice of addiction related to a specific mental health deficit and would be resolved by appropriate treatment. Lembke did a meta-analysis of papers in 2012, which concluded a lack of evidence for this proposal. Awad concluded that self-medication was a factor in their study of addicted schizophrenic patients. (45) Koob et al have recently reformulated the theory of the addictive process in "coping response" terms, that Hyperkatifeia (derived from the Greek katifeia for dejection or negative emotional state) is a basis for vulnerability, including when created by other syndromes, which indirectly supports the SMH. (Koob, 10) Medical provider programs are more favorable to the SMH, while abstinence programs tend to discount the need for other medications. The **disease concept** of addiction means makes the **hijacking** is a unique treatment issue, not a symptom of other problems.

> **CLINICAL EXAMPLE Dual Diagnosis.** *A young adult male was evaluated for use of cannabis, alcohol, sedatives, benzodiazepines, nitrous oxide, etc. beginning in high school. He began having anxiety as a child and developed prominent obsessions, and the anxiety symptoms continued. There was no family history of anxiety or addiction, but he was a difficult c-section birth with hypoxia. He failed several drug treatment programs, and was currently unemployed living with parents. A trial of gabapentin proved effective in improving his anxiety and gradually reducing his obsessions. He was prescribed Accutane by a dermatologist, and began becoming depressed after a month, which was not helped by antidepressants and was discontinued. He continued to have focusing issues, and these improved using welbutrin. COMMENT Young adults often begin using "street pharmacy" to address mental health symptoms, and experience brain changes that are viewed as helpful until addiction ensues. Both cannabis and GABA agents have stabilizing properties, and are typical choices. After stabilizing on a regimen, the young man needed to re-evaluate his life choices and begin finding a life interrupted as a teen. This pattern is more common in teens and young adults than appreciated.*

The emphasis on opiate and sedative addiction ignores the importance of cocaine, and methamphetamine/stimulant addiction, especially in rural areas, for over 20 years. (21) This addiction does not readily respond to either treatment modality and has not stimulated a pharmaceutical MAT (other than continuing use of stimulants at lower doses). As a result, there is less focus on this addiction though its consequences are as severe.

Nicotine addiction is a special example, an exception of much current theory. Nicotine is a natural transmitter for nicotinic receptors, which does not strongly stimulate accumbens dopamine, but has a prominent effect on arousal and awareness. It should be a minor addictive substance, yet it creates a powerful habit for smoking, which does not usually interfere with other life activities, often enhancing them. Cigarette smoking causes systemic damage to lungs and other organs from continuous use, including lung cancer, but these come from other components of burning tobacco. It is an especially difficult addiction to quit, and often involves substitute nicotine gum or other MAT. There does not seem to be evidence of addictive use by Native-Americans despite history of use long before Europeans refined the leaf. Evidence for genetic vulnerability suggests that only certain groups are highly vulnerable. The potential benefits of nicotine for focus and other effects have some documentation. (51) Taken together these facts illustrate the confusion in its restrictions. And the significance of a dangerous highly addictive substance, that is also facilitative to other activities.

Choosing between MAT and "drug free" Recovery is difficult. Without studies that provide head-to-head comparison of outcome, especially the long term benefit of social adaptation, choosing the one with the best outcome is difficult. Several issues guide the decision:

Non-chemical addictions, gambling, compulsive sexual behaviors, etc. have no **MAT**, and can only choose **Recovery**. Whether gambling, shopping, video games, pornography or sexuality can become addictive is rejected by some, though they fit into the concept of "hijacking", show other characteristics of chemical addictions, are seen in families with other addictive patterns, and a few studies show similar brain patterns. (46) The addiction is a learned motivation, so any strong reward might "hijack" the motivation system under suitable circumstances. The only DSM recognized non-chemical addiction is **gambling**. Persons who gamble to the point of financial consequences and breakdown in personal life are labeled as "compulsive gamblers" or "gambling addicts". But like other hijacked persons, they are good at hiding the behaviors as part of the normalization of their motivational system, the denial. The

---

SIDEBAR The "hijacking" of motivation by sexual drive is controversial. Control of sexual behavior is related to changing hormone levels, the natural regulator of sexual motivation. What pattern, and how much sexual behavior should be considered deviating from norms? Defining "normal" participation in sexual behavior is not clear, the boundaries are changing, and some variations in sexual behavior are no longer considered abnormal or have diagnoses. How does society, i.e. the practitioner (and DSM), decide when the behavior crosses a boundary? Compulsive use of pornography? Frequent desire to engage in sexual intercourse or other sexual behavior ("don Juanism")? Are these "obsessional behaviors", "addictive behaviors", or just differences in sexual motivation? Defining them as "compulsive behavior" rather than "addiction" does not offer any clarification. Compulsive use of pornography, paraphilias between consenting adults, and repeated compulsive sexual behaviors are examples of the current challenge in defining the boundary between acceptable sexual activity and need for treatment. The boundary for sexual behavior reaches clinical concern if this behavior displaces motivation from other life objectives. **The relevant concern for hijacking is the extent to which the person's life is substantially interfered with by the motivation, including disregard of legal boundaries.**

Children must be protected from sexual exploitation, child pornography, or be forced to engage in sexual behavior with another older child or adult. But when two underage teenagers have consensual sex, who is the offender? These are not artificial questions since every mental health provider has mandatory reporting requirements to legal authorities if he/she suspects that an underage person has been involved sexually. The sexual use of adult women by coercion, drug or alcohol sedation, or overt force is illegal, yet occurs frequently enough to have generated a #METOO movement of victims. Does the partner to these events have a hijacked motivation system or is this just an "excuse" to participate in unrequested behavior? The confusion is both about **hijacking** but also personal responsibility. In sexual behavior, addictive or not, the consequences often involve another person. If an addicted person does not have **agency,** can he/she be held responsible for actions, or be "not guilty by reason of insanity"? This is an issue in legal responsibility. (49) *There are many unanswered questions regarding the boundaries of sexual behavior.*

SIDEBAR The relationship of eating disorders and addiction is not clear. Eating is a survival-based motivation (discussed in chapter three), regulated by a complicated combination of physiologic and social factors. Some individuals report modifying (amygdala outflow of) anxiety by altering eating. Has the motivation for eating has been "taken over" (**hijacked?**) by other demands? Not all changes in eating behavior are driven by emotional regulation. And some people with problems regulating caloric intake do not have problems in other life adjustments. Difficulties in control of eating do not always translate into a disturbance of other motivations, as seen in addictions. The hypothalamic-tegmental motivation system is involved, but documenting **hijacking** is not always clear. *The relationship of eating and addiction remains unresolved, and treatment for eating disorders requires different management.* (50)

activation of acumens, and variations in prefrontal activity have also been documented. The demonstration that this is a hijacked behavior comes from the destruction in life space function as with all addictive behaviors. (46) The boundary of abstinence for gambling addiction seems simply to not participate in any gambling activity, but all sorts of minor personal gambling activities can be defined for someone strongly motivated. Gambling represents a huge financial industry with strong political influence. The access to gambling addiction in the US has expanded dramatically in the last 25 years. A person, who once had to journey to Las Vegas, or offshore, can now ride to a casino, within a 50-mile radius of most major cities and rural areas, with devices that strongly stimulate the nucleus acumens!

Non-medical providers favor the repair of motivation "recovery" approach. If the *hijacking* of the person is crucial, reversing the "learned addiction motivation" can allow the person to live drug free. The lack of direct interventions for the lost euphoria and increased craving makes relapse more likely, so the recovery method has frequent relapses and dropouts with consequences. Programs accept "relapse as a part of recovery", and count "days sober", not "days to relapse". The AA motto is not "sobriety forever", but "one day at a time" and illustrates the "here and now" perspective of managing on a daily basis. Cochrane Library, an independent research group, reviewed four decades of global alcohol treatment studies and concluded, "No experimental studies unequivocally demonstrated the effectiveness of AA or TSF approaches for reducing alcohol dependence or problems." Despite that research, A.A.'s 12-step model is the dominant approach in America. (47)

Medication Assisted Treatment uses prescription drugs and is the basis of Psychiatric opiate addiction treatment. The measure of effectiveness depends on whether the goal is the society's or the individual's. The treatment requires Psychiatric/medical care and is not always funded by public agencies. The access to an addictive substance relieves the problem of access, but continues the dependence.

Documenting long-term stability in either method is rare. (48)

After 100 years, the choice has not been resolved because of the social and economic issues, and the many individuals who use both methods at different times, confounding which one is effective. Neither approach has collected extended data to see which method provides a) more days free of addiction, and b) more success in returning to an effective life. Different individuals may respond better to one approach or another, and self-referral may indicate this, now that an outpatient individualized MAT is available. A recent study suggests that abstinence in alcohol is not necessary to get reduction in use, and moderated consumption is possible. (48) The idea of using neural pathway measurements to predict recovery seems unlikely to be useful because the goal of recovery is recovery so pathway changes must be correlated with that. (48)

Addiction is the *hijacking* of the motivation system, a learning process, which depends on reward signals of chemical consumption, or other behavior rewards. This unifies several patterns of dysfunctional motivation into one model, and proposes principles of treatment. In *hijacking*, the control of motivation for behavior that satisfies the addiction becomes primary, ***prioritized over other survival motivations***. Basic principles for a treatment model are: 1) Control of addictive access. 2) Alteration of the motivation system priorities, and link to behavior. 3) Repair of impact of previous addictive behavior. Two strategies have been developed: **MAT** using addictive substances to control craving, and substance free ***"recovery"***.

CHAPTER TEN:
Assessment

*Current procedures must be modified to apply **Neuromind** to clinical practice. This chapter and the next two explore some of these changes, using examples from current practice. These chapters do not state "how to intervene". The task of improving mental health services requires the coordination of all the teachers, providers, and organizations involved in mental health. These suggestions are directed to them.*

Every effective mental health intervention begins with an assessment of the problems interfering with a satisfying, socially adapted life. In medical practice, this is called "making a diagnosis" and "formulating a treatment plan". Neurology, the other field of medicine concerned with the brain, follows the medical model, and emphasizes bio-physical tests. Psychiatry and the other mental health services cannot follow this approach. There are significant differences between mental health and medical disorders, and assessment must address the difference. Assessment is a strategic interaction between the clinician who represents the healthcare system and the patient-consumer being evaluated, voluntarily or involuntarily. The clinician must decipher the patient-customer's strategic goal in the assessment. Goffman calls this the "frame analysis" of the "strategic interaction". (1) Lazare's "customer approach to patienthood" describes several possible services the patient may be requesting, which must be identified for the outcome to be ineffective. (2) If the clinician categorizes patients with a standardized system for recording observations, in an effort to make assessment "scientific" and "objective", the assessment is abstracted from the actual events and misses important information. "Acting like a mental patient", the failure to conform to social norms of behavior, is the sine qua non for access to mental health services. Every "diagnostic event" must identify these behaviors, the social and economic consequences for both patient and provider/healthcare system, and what the patient is seeking to accomplish. (3)

SIDEBAR A short history of mental health diagnosis. The history of mental health care began in the late 18th and early 19th century. This was custodial (prison-asylum) care of socially dysfunctional individuals, attended by *"Alienist"* clinicians with limited options for intervention of patients with severe social impairment. (4) A frequent cause of mental illness in late 19th to early 20th century was "general paresis of the insane", tertiary syphilis, called the "great imitator" because it produced varied symptoms depending on the region of the brain damaged by the infectious parasites, (and later documented by post mortem). (5) Effective treatment with PCN in the 20th century lowered the rate of CNS infections, an example of successful treatment of a biologic etiology, now often overlooked. (6) It was assumed those infectious agents or other biological factors, especially inheritance, caused mental disorders, but were difficult to assess by the autopsies and anatomical evaluations of the period. Kraepelin proposed a diagnostic system *differentiated by observed symptoms of behavior in the 1890s.* (7) In the late 19th and early 20th century, Freud and others began treating out patients with milder symptoms and labeled problems as "neuroses" or "traumas". (8) DSM I (1952) the first comprehensive diagnostic formulation in American Psychiatry, included diagnoses for severe hospitalized patients, and others for less severe outpatients. It differentiated biologic and non-biologic causes. DSM II (1968) was more explicit in defining severe mental disorders and less severe neuroses. Inconsistent use of the categories was common and reliability from one evaluator to another poor. In 1972, the Rosenhan study, "On being sane in insane places", shocked Psychiatry. (9) Actors were paid to arrive at psychiatric hospitals and report that they were hearing voices and the result documented. The actors were usually admitted to the hospital with the diagnosis of a psychotic disorder, usually schizophrenia. *The fact that they were feigning the disturbance was not recognized.* The results, published in Science, the most prestigious research journal in the U. S., reported that Psychiatrists couldn't tell the difference between real patients and actors. (Rosenhan intended this paper to support "labeling theory": that societal deviance is an arbitrary decision of a selected elite who decide which persons are deviant and label them with scientific sounding names.) The study raised questions about valid indicators of mental disorder and naïve assumptions of the clinicians. At the same time, research studies for new medication treatments were hampered by inconsistencies in patient diagnosis, another indication of the weakness of DSM II. To solve these problems, a major revision of the diagnostic system, DSM III, was created based on diagnostic criteria by Guze, Feighner and others (released in 1980).

APA president Carol Bernstein MD, summarized her view of the history (in 2011), and the problems that remain (10): *"...creating a system of explicit, operationalized diagnostic criteria, DSM-III addressed the pressing problem of inter-rater reliability in psychiatric diagnosis. It became necessary in the 1970s to facilitate diagnostic agreement among clinicians, scientists, and regulatory authorities given the need to match patients with newly emerging pharmacologic treatments and the associated need to conduct replicable clinical trials so that additional treatments could be approved."* She noted that DSM III did not identify "etiologically determined diagnoses" because the field was not that advanced, and lacked more "objectively" ascertainable abnormalities of anatomy, physiology, or biochemistry. The "Research Diagnostic Criteria" excluded etiology claiming insufficient knowledge to make accurate determinations. (11) The data was gathered from the *present interview*, including historical data, often structured versions like the Wing PSE to provide more "objective" data (all clinicians would ask the same questions). (12) If different observers ask the same questions, and get similar answers from patients, inter-rater reliability improves. (This does not solve the Rosenhan problem; DSM III criteria give a detailed blueprint for how to "feign" mental illness more precisely if desired!) DSM III did not produce the intended result that each clinical syndrome described in the Feighner criteria would ultimately be differentiated from the others. Clinical use resulted in multiple "comorbidities", overlap of multiple diagnoses. (Are "co-morbidities" the occurrence of two different co-occurring diseases, or the result of the same symptom criteria in multiple categories? (13)) Patients with the same diagnosis did not have the same response to treatment, and studies failed to identify specific genes associated with the syndromes. DSM III did not provide clear differentiation of syndromes, and subsequent modifications, DSM-IV, and -IVR did not produce better differentiation.

Bernstein described the new alternative, DSM V: *"The idea is to assemble existing disorders into larger clusters suggested by the scientific evidence and then to encourage researchers, granting agencies, and journal editors to facilitate research within and across clusters..."* The thirteen years between DSM-IVR and DSM V did not result in a reorganization of the diagnostic system. DSMV abandoned the "multi-axial structure" of previous DSMs, acknowledging that different "axes" did not clarify the components. The use of rating scales for diagnosis increased, despite their limitations. (13) The new structure was not implemented in the revision, but suggested in the organization of the manual. (Insel et al, at NIMH, developed new symptom categories, NIMH RDoC, intended to link to biological factors but these were not included in the DSM V. (14) (15)) Attempts to "biologize" Psychiatry using genetics, neural markers, and imaging techniques have all led to the same situation: The data are statistically noisy, complex, and do not converge on current Psychiatric diagnoses, or discrete syndromes. Kendler, an experienced researcher and thoughtful explorer of the dilemmas of contemporary Psychiatry worried that using biological tests to clarify the nosology would get evaluations stuck in "box canyon" results, categories without connection to other issues in diagnosis. (15)

This short review of DSM diagnosis identifies problems that have persisted through its evolution. A detailed critique of DSM as an effective tool for organizing treatment can be found elsewhere. (16) A different approach is needed, and previous chapters suggest the following principles:

Neurophysiological pathways process information for adaptation, and produce maladaptive responses (symptoms) when altered or damaged. (Pathway malfunctions do not **cause** the symptoms, but are **correlations** to them.) The same pathways are involved in many syndromes, through pathway interactions.

Etiology is a separate component of assessment. Etiology identifies the processes that modify pathways. The balance of genetic and development/experience is important, but other factors including social variables and somatic illnesses also impact pathways.

Severity is defined by impairment of social adaptation, the boundary of health and illness, which determines diagnosing a "mental illness", not symptoms. The DSM has always included **symptom severity** as a criterion for diagnosis, but not functional severity (which was included in now discarded Axis V). Assessment of social adaptation is obtained from the life history of accomplishments (or their absence), and immediate problems of current adaptation. In psychosis and addiction the clinician must deal with the denial of severity, using alternative sources of information. Some individuals with significant symptoms are able to function adaptively, an indication of **resilience**.

Assessment is an interpersonal process with bilateral intentions that must be documented. Both parties influence the outcome of assessment. The claim that the evaluator has no other motivation but "scientific objectivity" is inaccurate, unscientific and not objective! The impression that the patient is solely motivated to receive "treatment" often misses the point. How the social context of the assessment influences the result can only be accounted for by its documentation.

Symptoms are the expression of neurophysiological pathways. Pathways, described in chapters 1 to 9, perform functions producing adaptive behavior, and present symptoms when they are altered. They are organized ("programmed") to coordinate internal states with the external environment. There is no current method for directly observing pathway activity in behaving humans; current studies of functional connectivity and other research must be combined to approximate pathway functions. (*See the appendix to chapter one for a more detailed discussion of this distinction and the limitations of current methods.*) Each pathway has connectivity to other pathways for coordinated interactions. Pathway disturbances manifest specific symptoms alone, by interactions with other pathways, or often both. They are changed by *etiologies that* improve or impair pathway activity. Current diagnoses are not closely related to pathways because the diagnoses are not defined functionally. (Gillihan and Parens, 16) Several other proposals describe pathways as the basis for symptoms. (17) Buckholz et al define brain functions which specify networks: attention and control, affect arousal and regulation, amygdala, reward and motivation, default mode and social cognition, similar to the pathways described in ***Neuromind***. (18) The following pathway descriptions combine these, and other models, and the pathway descriptions of chapters one to nine:

Sensory input- and perceptual categorization (Chapter 1): The posterior cerebral cortex receives sensory data through pathways passing through thalamus and analyzes perception by "pattern recognition", the basis for perceptual categorization and cognition. Special syndromes of child development can be identified that impact education, and interventions to modify them. Generalized disturbances include delirium (acute), cognitive disability (life long), and dementia (chronic) *with various etiologies.*

The Social Brain. (Chapter 2): Specific pathways combine sensory and motivation information for social adaptation. The pathways link hippocampal memory, posterior cortex, insula, attention, and pre-frontal action selection regions to organize social behavior. Self /other is differentiated using **mirror neuron** networks. Symptoms can be dramatic as in the disorder **autism**, or subtle, and incorporated into other diagnoses without differentiation. Attachment, object constancy, and related symptoms are important aspects of social function and internal representation. (Chapter 7.) Linking caregiver and child creates both child and adult patterns of social interaction. A combination of genetic programming and sensory cues are necessary for the process.

Motivation system (Chapter 3): The tegmental-hypothalamic pathways are the interface between brain and body, including input of peripheral pain. Data about the "state of the organism" and "rewards" are received and linked with other pathways for action (frontal action selection), and subjective experience (cingulate cortex and insula). The pathways regulate motivation which may result in problems of sexual motivation, eating, sleeping patterns, thirst, attachment, etc. The pathways transfer data between brain and body for pituitary hormone release and feedback regulating thyroid, adrenal (cortisol secretion), sex hormones, oxytocin, etc. Interaction with the immune system produces symptoms in viral and other infections. Opioid receptors that regulate affective experience and pain are located in this area. General activation or deactivation produce subjective symptoms of depression and mania and associated neurovegetative symptoms.

The signification-memory system (Chapter 4): The hippocampal-septal-hypothalamic loop (the Papez circuit of "limbic system" neuroanatomy) links cortical sensory analysis with reward centers over hippocampal loops storing information about rewards, the **significance** of sensory data. The interaction of hippocampus with DLPFC is necessary to provide this data for "attention" and disturbances in hippocampal DLPFC pathways interfere with integration of information. Symptoms include a range of memory disturbances, problems of evaluation and interpretation of rewards, and variations of the "schizophrenic syndrome".

Anxiety And Response To Danger (Chapter 8): Nuclei in the amygdala receive sensory information directly from somatic and olfactory warnings of danger, and a separate system of "conditioned aversive signals" of potential danger. A loop similar to the Papez circuit connects the nuclei with a wide range of other pathways. Pathways go through the motivation system to influence pre-frontal controls, to the cingulate-insula to register subjective warning, and directly to the autonomic system to prepare arousal for response. Various anxiety syndromes are presented in chapter eight.

Dysfunctional Motivation (Chapter 9): The response to rewards includes learned sensory signals for reward, and direct reward events. Acquired motivations can displace basic rewards, hijack the motivation system, and direct behavior to maladaptive choices. This is *addiction,* any motivation that overpowers survival motivations. In addiction, the loss of agency describes how the hijacking of motivation for dysfunctional goals directs the person to perform "intentional" maladaptive acts.

Executive functions include two closely linked pathways:
Organization and control of attention. (Chapter 5): A central core pathway links the external environment with cortical response. This system manages the sleep/wake cycle, seasonal variations in motivation, and the immediate attention response to environmental stimuli (which has evolved the subjective experience of "consciousness"). Control of focus of attention has multiple sources focusing

other pathway activity to current demands (shifting the "spotlight", the "operating system" hypothesis). Symptoms in the attention system, either directly or due to disturbances in other systems are a heightened state of arousal that may present as **psychosis**, loss of controlled focus, confusion, and impaired adaptation. Problems in the regulation of sleep/waking also originate in this system producing a range of symptoms distinct from mental health but overlapping in specific situations.

The action selection system (Chapter 6): The frontal/prefrontal cortex receives information from motivation pathways, significance-memory pathways, social/self pathways and attention pathways and integrates the messages into decisions for action. (The system is also essential for focusing attention of chapter five.) The basal ganglia region stores patterns for behavior output, including emotional responses, cognitive functions, speech, posture, etc. Symptoms from this region include: problems in choice of behavior, and characteristic pathway malfunctions of basal ganglia. The patterns of social interaction, *personality*, are stored in this network, and disturbances can produce transient or persisting changes in social interaction.

An assessment specifies both pathway disturbances in the clinical presentation, and pathways that are functioning adaptively. A "pathway vector" (used as a metaphor) summarizes the changes in multiple pathways. Pathways interact to create symptoms, which are not "co-morbidity" or "multiple diseases" but interactions of pathways that produce clinical events. Some patterns will have a specific etiology disturbing a specific pathway, as in a localized brain tumor, but more often the etiology will modify multiple pathways. Each pathway performs **specific adaptive functions** (not clinical syndromes). The basis for evaluation is **normal pathway functions**, and how they are altered. *The failure to establish normal standards for "controls" makes this difficult.*

Pathways have both tonic and phasic changes. Consistent pathway function is the baseline, and persistent maladaptive function is usually diagnosed as "personality disorder", while a sudden dramatic worsening in adaptive function is generally diagnosed as "major mental disorder", e.g. psychosis. There is only one brain, and one a system of pathways producing behavior, both chronic and transient. Assessment must specify the transitions between levels of function: chronic persistent, sudden deteriorating, sudden recovering, and recurring, etc. Effective treatment facilitates transition to stable adaptive patterns. In the next two chapters, a variety of treatments are described which attempt to return maladaptive patterns to more adaptive ones; there has been little focus on maintaining stable adaptive patterns. Because there is no current biophysical way to measure pathway activity the behavioral manifestations of pathway activity are the current evidence. (Biological measures many eventually be associated with the behavioral performance, but have little current documented validity.) The clinical presentations of pathways, described in earlier chapters, are not unique, and frequently overlap when multiple pathways are involved. The importance of clinical observation does not change in **Neuromind**, but the observations are linked to specific functions, not "diseases". Separate mental health symptoms are unusual, and represent local etiologies. The brain does not operate this way in general; multiple pathways (the pathway vector) are usually involved with combined symptoms. *Seeking one unique pathway per diagnosis is a carryover from medical diagnostic thinking, which does not represent the complex interaction of brain networks.* This is similar to the view recently discussed by Kendler in an editorial. (19)

An etiology is an event or process that alters pathway activity. Etiology is usually defined as producing symptoms, but all life events create pathway changes, and some may also improve adaptation. Etiology plays a role in treatment planning, prevention, and social issues in mental health and research, differentiating patient groups with unique features. (20) Documenting etiology uses the tripartite biological-psycho-social model, a well known, though denigrated concept. (21) Pathways are altered by i) biologic disturbances, ii) learning maladaptive patterns, or iii) the direct impact of the social environment. The list of potential etiologies is too long to include in a chapter or a book and essential learning for the development of an effective clinician. The pathway changes are not specific for different etiologies.

Biological variables modify pathway functions by directly altering biological properties. Some effects are localized to specific pathways while others have a regional or total brain effect. These include genetics, other biological effects, infections, neoplasms, and physical trauma.

Is mental illness genetic? This depends on the meaning of "genetic". Research seeking specific genes for "mental illnesses", with Huntington's disease as the model has been generally unproductive. (22) (In Neurology such loci are also rare.) Research in twin and other family studies show "concordance", in *identical twins* studies of schizophrenia of 50%-70%, (a pure gene effect would be 95-100%) so other factors play a role. Lieff summarized reasons for difficulty identifying genetic factors: a) the biological variables associated with psychiatric diagnoses are unknown, b) many diagnoses may have multiple etiologies some of which are not genetic, how much the phenotype depends on genes or experience differs by conditions and patients. c) Allele sites ("copy number variants" CNV) that code for a specific syndrome are rare. Several recent reviews confirm his summary. (23) The failure to find specific genes for syndromes led to the GWAS approach: study of large populations looking for multiple genes associated with diagnoses, with confusing results: a) Rare CNV and rare specific alleles contribute a very tiny component of risk for mental health disturbances. b) The major effect is polygenic: *"The evidence is strong that many genes are involved in the etiology of AD, ALC, ASD, BIP, NIC. Projections for ASD and SCZ suggest that variation at hundreds of different genes will ultimately be shown to be involved."* (Sullivan, 23) In a more recent review *"few individuals with a psychiatric disorder have a single, deterministic genetic cause; rather, developing a psychiatric disorder is influenced by hundreds of different genetic variants, consistent with a polygenic model."* This recent review in Science concludes that gene loci impact multiple brain sites, and multiple gene sites modify different pathways, a complex overlay of effects. (23) These findings echo the historical perspective on mental health genetics described by Kendler in his review, describing the effect as a "predisposition", a probabilistic variable in familial transmission, with similar features in other family members— all observed in current results. (23) *After 50+years genetic research in mental health, genetic data are not coded in DSM, and were not included in the "medical" Axis III.* (24)

These results can be interpreted two ways. Continuing the search for genetic factors for mental diagnosis may lead to statistical polygenic measures for each diagnosis. This has little clinical value, but documents the complex genetic influences on brain activity. The alternative, evolutionary approach is *gene selection for adaptation*, with maladaptive genes culled by natural selection. *There are no genes for Psychiatric diagnoses because evolution does not select for DSM diagnostic categories.* Certain CNV and rare variants persist in populations until culled, or because of associated adaptive value. Much human DNA has regulatory influences on other parts of the genome; polygenic regulation balances different sites to adjust adaptive function. **This suggests that genetic research focusing on adaptive traits will be more productive and reflects gene functions. Genes play a polygenic role in the etiology of mental health *capacities*, not diagnoses.** (25) Genes associate with the adaptive functions of pathways, but pathway organization is polygenic and experiential, so simple correlations are unlikely. The clinical importanceof polygenic information would be more useful if the known sites were linked to adaptive abilities. Polygenic effects on adaptive traits provide the clinical perspective, *"play the hand you are dealt"*: that each person has strengths and weaknesses in his or her genome, which create adaptive advantages and limitations. The genetic overlap between bipolar disorder and schizophrenia populations (discussed in chapter five) illustrates the nonspecific relationship of genes to diagnostic categories. Calling them "cause of diseases" confuses their adaptive role. Calculating polygenic "risk scores" for individual genomes is not a useful indicator of diagnoses but eventually be recalibrated to measure the strength of specific adaptive functions.

Other biological processes also alter pathways. Pregnancy and delivery includes maternal factors of fetal distress, abnormal placenta, twins, maternal illness during gestation, cerebral palsy and related mesial temporal sclerosis and hippocampal syndromes. These are examples of pre-natal (in utero), and early post-natal effects. Chess and Thomas found puzzling effects at birth that continue at least to adulthood, that are not genetic. (26) Infectious disease plays an important role in mental health, from the era of syphilis to the AIDS epidemic with mental symptoms an important feature. (27) Viral and bacterial infections sometimes produce brain dysfunction, often with coma, usually diagnosed by other clinicians. Sydenham's Chorea, and related PANDAS, are examples of inflammatory reactions of systemic illnesses. (See chapter six). NMDA receptor inflammation with psychosis is a rare syndrome with active research interest because of its clear pattern, frequent recovery, and published description. (28) Primary and secondary *brain tumors* are occasionally first identified at mental health evaluations when the localization involves pathways with major mental health symptoms. Vascular occlusion or stroke may result in mental health problems even after initial recovery. Numerous references are available in the Neurology literature regarding typical symptoms. (29) Abnormalities in hormone regulation and release are an important factor in mental health, and may result from abnormal hypothalamic regulation or secondary to other illness. Biologic etiology is identified by the mental health clinician when the early symptoms are behavioral, and by others, when not.

Traumatic Brain Injury frequently produces mental health consequences. Childhood may include falls and head injuries, sometimes inflicted by abusive adults, affecting multiple pathways. From mid childhood to late adolescence, sports injuries, assaults, and recreation related activities may produce, often ignored, brain damage. Adults have auto trauma, assault, and sports activities, including

CLINICAL EXAMPLE A Lady With Hypothyroidism. *A patient was referred for evaluation by a psychotherapist when she became increasingly confused during therapy for depression. On evaluation she was disoriented, confused, and was accompanied by a peer friend. There was a history of blood system cancer currently in treatment. The patient was hospitalized with the assumption that the cancer had infiltrated the brain, but evaluation by a Neurologist showed no indication. Laboratory findings indicated severe hypothyroidism. COMMENT Low thyroid is known to impair brain function with symptoms of depression. The obvious biological disturbance may not be the important one. She was treated with thyroid hormone and depression and other symptoms improved.*

professional sports. The recent "discovery" of Chronic Traumatic Encephalopathy identifies mental symptoms and cognitive dysfunction from head trauma of contact sports; a syndrome of "punch drunk" boxers was long ignored. A significant number of young persons with mild symptoms are diagnosed as various psychiatric disorders without considering the etiology, and the failure to consider head trauma, means not avoiding further head trauma, essential to prevention of further deterioration. (30) Treatment includes avoiding overmedicating the emotional reactions, which make the situation worse. (31) The combination of PTSD and TBI has become a major assessment and treatment problem with military deployments in Syria and Afghanistan where the enemy used IEDs producing this combination (see chapter eight). (32) These non-genetic biological factors play a role in etiology, modifying pathways.

CLINICAL EXAMPLE (repeated from chapter 4). TWO BROTHERS With Birth And Football Injuries. *Two brothers were born with some fetal distress, both elected to participate in high school football. In the first year of participation, both had recurring concussions with unconsciousness and later confusion. They continued participating until more serious symptoms developed and they were evaluated. They have persistent cognitive impairments COMMENT This illustrates the narrow margin between safety and injury in some head trauma situations, especially with a developmental history. A high index of suspicion about preventing further damage is needed to avoid unfortunate outcomes.*

The interaction of genes and experience requires a more nuanced understanding of etiology. Kendler has reviewed this concept showing its origins long before it was formally presented in the 1950s. He and Gardner present a study to quantify the contribution of genetic and stress factors in producing depression, with variable impact from the stress factor. The role of the 5-HTTLPR gene locus and stress has gone through major claims and non-replications, suggesting that a meaningful relationship requires large population studies, and probably is not related to a specific diagnosis. The "statistical noise" of genes, diagnoses, and severity of trauma, makes finding associations difficult, even with large populations. Several other reviews of this interaction find similar results. (33) An Australian study looked at genetic and "personal factors" in "psychotic like experiences" using cannabis and found the "experiential" to have more impact than the genetic. (34) Both traumatic events and subjective responses combine in altering pathways.

CLINICAL EXAMPLE Man with a motorcycle accident. *An otherwise active and healthy young man suffered a serious motorcycle accident with significant head injury, while wearing a helmet. Leg and back injuries healed in several months, but he had ongoing episodes of confusion, inability to stay focused, and problems in balance. He was frustrated and depressed about the situation, and refused to accept this disability, seeking evaluation and treatment by a long series of "experts". After more than a year, he accepted that he would have some chronic disability. His mood improved, though his cognitive impairment did not.* **COMMENT** *Difficulty grieving for a loss of function or physical capacity is difficult, especially someone with an active lifestyle. The depressed mood had less to do with the brain injury, and more with the unresolved grief, which improved with acceptance.*

The "Psycho" in Bio-Psycho-Social refers to the role of life experience in structuring pathways, (as revised to bio-*experiential*-social). The relative helplessness of the human neonate, compared with other mammalian species, makes experiential programming important in brain organization. PSA proposes that children modify their "instinctual" behaviors to fit the demands of the social environment (usually family) during development. The formulation appears obvious to everyone who has parented, but documenting the impact on adult pathways has been difficult. The PSA "trauma theory" specifies events at specific developmental stages that produce **fixation** in maladaptive patterns. How "traumatic" does the event have to be? The effects of childhood abuse and trauma are documented retrospectively and there are few longitudinal studies. Strongly negative life experiences are associated with a variety of mental health syndromes including depression, anxiety, and PTSD. (See chapters seven and eight) (35) Developmental problems alone do not produce mental health issues later in life, **resilience** must also be considered, with the potential to revise problems in later experiences. The *anniversary reaction* is a particularly clear example of how experiences produce symptoms. (36)

CLINICAL EXAMPLE The Medication stopped working. A man in his thirties was treated with medication for depression. He responded well and on follow-up visits he reported that his mood had returned "almost to normal". At 8 months he reported that, in the last week or so he was getting depressed again, that the medication had "stopped working". An inquiry into any recent events or problems in his life was negative. Asking about the calendar season revealed that about a week before was the anniversary of sister's death (which had triggered the onset of his initial symptoms). He had not remembered this, and was visibly sad at mentioning it. After several minutes this improved and he stated that he was feeling better. No change in medication was made, and he was seen in a month and reported that the depression symptoms were improved, and he was feeling better again. "The medications are working!" COMMENT Though medications sometimes stop being effective, it is worth inquiring about other factors that may impact the person's response that can avoid incorrect assumptions. The "anniversary reaction" is a classic example of a conditioned emotional response, associated with a calendar event.

Chronic life stress may affect somatic or psychological adjustment, including chronic medical diseases, and intermittent medical (e.g. pain) symptoms. The interface between the brain and body brain states may intensify physical disorders, e.g. the effect of stress on heart disease, especially with "Type A" personality. The Holmes-Rahe data are evidence of this effect. (37) The clinician does not observe the client's social situation. Is the spouse emotionally abusive or being blamed for symptoms, and mis-perceived? Is a boss harassing the patient or being blamed by a disturbed employee? The interaction of biological and experiential factors challenges the clinician to be attentive to both. Assessing experiential (learned) events is not solved by scripted symptom questionnaires which omit this information. (38)

The Social in Bio-Psycho-Social is the impact of the immediate social environment. The social environment includes persons who have influenced the individual in the immediate past, making it is difficult at times to separate the immediate social impact from learned experiences until after the person departs from a stressful environment. The social environment can impact in several ways. In personal development, life events alter pathways, including early abuse and trauma, problems in adolescent social transition, adult life challenges, and challenges of aging and illness. The dynamics of family interaction have special importance in developing neural patterns as discussed in more detail in chapter two. (40) Poor children in the 19th century in Europe and US were required to participate in work at a full time adult level, and missed much of what is considered necessary in modern views of childhood. Non-ordinary life crises include kidnapping, torture, civilian war experiences, and environmental disasters that result in migration and loss of home and family. These are disturbingly common world events, with major impact on human mental function that is rarely studied in aggregate. The work of Lifton (41) and others (42) illustrate the power of these events, as discussed in chapter eight.

Socio-economic inequality looks at the differences in life options for need satisfaction in different social-economic classes. Pathways are organized to satisfy needs in the current social environment. Low educational achievement, unemployment and job insecurity, poverty and income deficit, adverse physical environment, pollution, housing and food insecurity, and limited access to health services all influence the ability to satisfy internal needs. Every society has social inequality, and some authoritarian control; so different groups may experience problems in varying degree. Hollingshead and Redlich associated the risk of developing the diagnosis of schizophrenia with reduced socio-economic status. (43) Their correlation did not specify which is etiology or result, only the correlation. Even in the peak of 1960s social Psychiatry, social etiologies were never included in the DSM. The economic factor of inequality and the multiple material factors of air and water pollution, etc., overlap biological effects and opportunity in combinations producing the impact. Different clinicians will have dramatically different experiences of this, because care of affluent patients does not present these factors, while clinicians working with economically challenged individuals often observe their effects.

CLINICAL EXAMPLE Lead Poisoning. *The toxic effects of lead on the developing brain have been studied for decades, originally the result of poor children chewing on wood with lead based paint. In recent years, the battery plant near Los Angeles was polluting the surrounding environment of homes with lead from battery production. The children in the area had dangerous lead blood levels. Even more dramatic was the change in the water supply of the city of Flint Michigan, a mostly working class city, with a dramatic increase in the lead concentration of the entire water supply(and blood stream) of its inhabitants. It was necessary to provide supplemental drinking water for the entire city. Studies show that lead poisoning affects both cortical cognitive development and cingulate cortex in particular. COMMENT These are examples of an array of toxic factors that produce both physical and mental impairment. The clinician must be attentive to this possibility in any situation.*

Including etiology in assessment is essential to understand the problems and intervene effectively. Most mental health situations involve the interaction of multiple etiologies not a specific "cause" for which is the "most important". Some etiologies may be speculative, or ignored. How can this be documented? The clinician must list "possible" etiologies, and assign a hypothetical weight to each, estimating their importance for generating the current problems in adaptive functioning. Different providers may make this estimate differently, but the aggregate data over time will converge toward an accurate formulation.

CLINICAL EXAMPLE: Estimating etiology.

A) A 25 year old woman with no prior mental health history, and no developmental problems, develops psychosis/delirium with ANTI NDMA inflammatory disease =100% biological

B) A healthy female college student with no prior history of mental health problems is assaulted and raped in her dorm and after recovering experiences sudden overwhelming anxiety. =100% experiential

C) A 20-year-old male, with chaotic family including substance abusing parent and brother, and history of "difficult birth", has difficulty establishing himself in school or work, and begins having delusions of religious nature. = 30% genetic, 30% other biological, 20% experiential (school challenges), 20% social (family problems)

This is simplified but illustrates a workable system. Most syndromes are nuanced, so the judgment depends on the information available and the skill of the clinician. A rating sheet listing major factors in etiology in each category would be a convenient scoring sheet. (See APPENDIX) The clinician makes "educated guesses" of the probabilities identifying bias in the field and to guide future training. The documentation provides data for development of more accurate assessment of different factors, and how etiologies interact. The process improves the clinical assessment by asking the clinician to consider all the variables in the situation. The fantasy of a single etiology for a specific disorder should be replaced.

The severity of impaired adaptation defines the boundary of mental health. Mental health is adaptation, and its "diseases" are failures of adaptation that occur when pathways get "stuck" in altered brain patterns. (Pathways do not "cause" symptoms but are correlated with them.) Mental health problems may be behavior problems in social situations, dramatic behaviors designed to escape from social norms, or emotional experiences (anxiety) that create problems of adaptation. Goffman, described a "heightened demand for normalcy" which tightens the boundaries of acceptable behavior in *STIGMA: The Experience Of Mental Illness In The US*. (44) His writing was an important source for "labeling theory" proponents, who reject all diagnostic labels as arbitrary labels for deviance from the social environment. The English Psychiatrist RD Laing saw all adaptation as the compromise between individual needs and social demands, with some choosing less effective strategies. In Laing's view, socialization always creates dysfunction, and "psychological health" depends on an acceptable adaptation. The "social construction of mental illness" means that symptoms are defined by the society, but also treatment modes. An example of this is the change from "homosexuality" as a treatable disorder to no diagnosis at all; a behavior is no longer classified as a "mental illness". (45) The social system's definition of mental health is influenced by the culture's conception of mental illness. Mental health problems are problems of social adaptation, not just arbitrary decisions of the elite, but the result of many etiologies—- genetic, medical, experiential, and social—- that impact adaptation. "Labeling theory" emphasizes social variables and ignores others.

Persons who are functional do not seek services and are not diagnosed until social disruption occurs. Addiction does not lead to assessment until the consequences of the addiction disrupt the person's life (even then may be denied by the addict). Entering treatment means someone, the patient or another, determines that the person is sufficiently adaptively impaired. Symptom severity is an unreliable measure of adaptation, as determining when normal mourning becomes pathological grief. Cultural factors play a role in defining the boundary, and individuals vary in their ability to maintain function and tolerate subjective dysphoria, so *resilience* is also important. Persons seeking mental health services, world wide, are deemed by others around them to be deviant from the group norms of their community, so adaptation criteria allow better international comparison. (46)

The method of coping is also important. "Coping skills" are pathway operations for adaptation. Immature coping patterns show less adaptive flexibility. Using substances for coping is vulnerable to addiction, other health consequences, and may be unavailable. (A similar consideration involves psychopharmacology treatment as an adjunct for adaptation.) Vaillant's study observed that some coping patterns are associated with better long-term outcome, and therefore relevant to understanding the adaptive process. This is similar to Kernberg's concept "levels of personality", which characterizes high/low personality types. (48) Are persons with mental health issues only quantitatively different from other family members in adaptation? What shifts the patient from "just another family member" to clinical presentation? This involves assessment of *resilience,* when one person with a traumatic childhood goes on to become successful while another becomes disabled. **Resilience** involves actions that help adapt to challenging or stressful environments; adaptive capacity is the combination of these cognitive operations, patterns of "adaptive style". (49) They are stored in the PF/BG pathways (reviewed in chapter six) and the *social brain* pathways (in chapter two). The differential factors are not understood and research into clarifying the role of genetic, developmental and learning effects in resilience is needed. Assessment must include an effective measure of the current level of adaptive function, recent changes if any, and the long-term level of effectiveness. These are never consistently documented in DSM. *The measure of adaptive function should improve with effective treatment, an essential element in evaluation.* (50)

The clinician observes the "present state" of the patient at the time of evaluation (in the "mental status"), along with some understanding of the historical pattern of the person's life. The historical unfolding of the life space begins with the early genetically programmed patterns, the developmental experiences of the brain in childhood, and continuing influences, injuries, illnesses, etc. that affect pathways later in life. Evaluating adaptation at the assessment, and over the previous 7-14 days, also includes a general evaluation of life adaptation. This data is best organized in a longitudinal life space review, identifying significant potential events, and adaptation at different stages, and symptom patterns of previous assessments. The ease with which a person reveals these details on the first interview varies, but many facts can be obtained by simple inquiry. (It may be difficult to obtain valid information from older patients with

Assessment

memory impairment, and data from family or others may be unreliable as well, but if an attempt at "life space" inquiry does not take place no data will be obtained!) (The history recounted as a series of DSM diagnoses, it is less likely to be useful and more likely to reflect the bias of previous clinicians.) An easy to use assessment scale that includes the important areas of human adaptation at different life stages and present function does not exist! Several self-report scales have been developed that are biased by the subject's perception. A scale of major life accomplishments could provide better validation. The measure must differ across development stages for measuring childhood adaptation. The following headings at appropriate developmental levels are useful: **LIVE** What is the current level of activity and arousal? Is the person able to self-care? **LOVE** Can the person use interpersonal interaction to get needs met? Does he or she have age appropriate romantic, intimate, and dependent relationships? **WORK** Doe the person have productive life activities? Or school or other training? **PLAY** Does the person have adequate activities to enjoy life?

Evaluating adaptation compares social function in different patients. Some symptom patterns produce more adaptation problems than others, e.g. *autism*. Measuring adaptation is essential for evaluating treatment interventions, linking assessment to treatment outcome. Treatment interventions that improve social adaptation are effective; those that do not, are not. Most current evaluations of treatment depend on symptom improvement, not adaptive improvement, and some side effects impair social adaptation. The scales developed for symptoms do not include social functioning. (47) If a person is deemed "chronically mentally ill" with a lifelong disability not modifiable beyond certain dysfunction, it creates a need for disability support. The adaptive level of the individual at pre-adult or "pre-morbid" (before first treatment episode) level of function is sometimes useful in setting the potential level of capacity.

Mental health assessment is an interpersonal event within the larger society. Each individual is embedded in the social matrix of the society. The larger society impacts the interaction in the assessment interview. The mental health system is responsible to the society for three fundamental tasks: 1) maintaining the functioning of members of the community, 2) protecting the community from potentially dangerous (or annoying) behavior, and 3) managing the organization and the cost of delivering mental health services. Each of these tasks comes into play in the assessment process. Both participants have intentions that reflect the larger society:

Financial Resources and Payment. The cost to society of a mentally impaired person combines (A) the loss of productivity + (B) cost of providing mental health services + (C) additional cost of housing/services when the person cannot manage for himself = TOTAL COST. *Each person who is returned to a productive life reduces the expense to the society.* The cost can be subsidized by *everyone paying into a common fund,* the "mental health fund (a single payor!)", or by having *functioning individuals* pay a direct fee to have their services paid as needed, and a fee to cover the other non-functioning persons, i.e. by taxes. This arrangement complicates payment and provides marginal benefit for those paying for separate coverage. (This is not the issue of "parity" for equal coverage of medical and mental health services, but is related.) The society wishes to spend the least amount possible to maximize the return of impaired members to some level of function, but the current methods of funding do not accomplish this.

The society regulates the economic access to the healthcare system including mental health services. The four questions are: What services should be provided? Who is entitled to receive them? Who is responsible for paying for them? Where and how should they be delivered? All these depend on the socio-economic status of the individual and family. Currently three levels are operating in the US: totally private self-pay care, insurance based care, and publicly funded care. In totally private care of high net worth individuals, all services utilize special facilities, and selected providers, who contract on a direct payment basis. Institutional care is delivered in private facilities that may also deliver some insurance care. In publicly funded care, all services are provided in mental health clinics, or publicly funded hospitals, and the amount and quality of services is determined by how much state and federal programs are willing to invest in care. Limited resources are triaged, and admission for social welfare needs is balanced against mental health disability. If payment is based on *number of services* delivered, diagnosis of chronic mental illness is more likely, and patients are deemed "seriously mentally ill", which rewards continuing illness, not recovering health. Insurance funded care is a mixed version of the others: more options for care are available, but criteria and qualification for services are limited. Insurance carriers and state mandated payment systems require patients to meet specified criteria to receive services. Payers seek to reduce costs while providers are motivated to provide services that increase personal compensation. This sets up a tension between payers and providers that can distort assessment and alter diagnoses. The patients and assessment process are caught in the middle. The number of patients using each group varies over time, and the society is challenged to allocate economic resources to deliver the services. *Both the provider and the patient will be aware of the funding available for potential services 90% of the time, and these options will create a "fence" around the scope of the assessment and treatment options.* (51)

The alternative, sending the mentally disabled to institutionalization had poor results and high expense in the past, and sending the mentally disabled to "internment camps" with minimal cost to the society is not morally acceptable, but with increased incarceration it is becoming the de facto situation.

Personal and professional responsibility: Maintaining the function of members of the community is rarely measured as an outcome by any medical specialty. The capacity to "return to work" is a significant outcome for any intervention, yet in previous chapters there is a consistent failure to record functional outcome. The assumption is that persons with "serious mental illness" are chronically disabled, while those with milder problems require few services.

Clinical experience does not support this dramatic difference, but becomes a "self fulfilling prophecy" when patients are classified this way. The *sick role* carries with it relief from social responsibility for performing certain societal tasks. This is most clear in the area of work disability and certification for missing work. The payment systems for disability try to limit this compensation by requiring documentation. Factors lumped in traditional diagnosis as "secondary gain", and benefits derived from taking the "sick role" are not assessed and documented in the DSM, (or other medical diagnostic system), yet most practicing physicians in every specialty are aware of them every day. The opposite situation is also encountered: qualifying applicants for work activities, military duty, or dangerous activities, like piloting aircraft, driving large vehicles or operating dangerous machinery. Certifying or denying the "sick role" is a basic boundary task of the clinician's assessment.

Is the professional performing his/her role according to the terms specified by the society? This is the legal issue of **malpractice.** The society specifies, usually through separate organizations, the roles and responsibilities of professional providers, including training, licensing, etc. Providers are expected to maintain standards of care when providing services to patients, and can be held responsible for failing to follow these standards. An obvious example is sexual behavior with a patient, with or without consent. Appropriate administration of treatment, e.g. medication, is also a standard of care. Advising a person regarding administration of a medication, or prescribing a regulated medication creates a legal responsibility for the provider. FDA and DEA regulatory laws define the boundary for prescribing. Failure to observe this boundary can result in tort liability for malpractice, or termination of professional license to practice, and criminal charges. Malpractice involves the duty to perform specific services safely, and dereliction of that duty may occur if the provider performs outside of the limits of acceptable practice. Several situations arise in prescribing. i) Involuntary administration of medication, injectable, under the direction of another. ii) Consent for services and informed consent are important: What to disclose, off label use, competency to consent, and full documentation of consent. Some typical issues are off label use, poly-pharmacy, risk of tardive dyskinesia, lack of medical exam, failure of notification of rare side effects, and negative effects of use while driving, using machinery, etc. iii) The continued use of medications also poses the risk of long term side effects, especially the metabolic issues. The recommendations of pharmaceutical companies promote pharmacology to providers and transfer most liability for prescribing and usage to them. The individual may face financial consequences as a result of tort actions, and also may experience loss of license, on a permanent or temporary basis. If mental health or addiction issues occur in the provider, the professional must be evaluated to determine if he/she can continue working, and the board notified if he/she is no longer safe to practice. It may require another determination to return after suitable treatment. The society withdraws its authorization for the provider to continue in that role. (52) *The patient and provider have symmetrical roles: both patient and provider are assessed by the society for performance of the expected social role assigned to each.*

Defining the boundary of the legal and mental health systems. The mental health system addresses social deviance, a legal problem with responsibility for one's actions until it becomes a mental health issue and responsibility is reconsidered. The boundary of law and mental health addresses two issues: Does the person have responsibility for the acts performed? Is the person competent to evaluate this? Is the person a danger to self or others that justifies loss of liberty? When someone performs an illegal behavior, in most jurisdictions, there is an option to claim that the behavior was the result of mental illness, over which they had no control, **no agency,** while performing it. The legal community often objects when illegal behavior becomes a diagnosis, and mental disorder becomes a mitigating or exculpatory factor in criminal proceedings. Determining the boundary of personal responsibility is a complex issue, handled differently in different states of the US, and relates to the issues of intention and *agency* discussed in chapter five. (53) How this relates to the determination of legal responsibility is a decision of the legal system, and often is associated with longer, less well-defined incarceration.

The other connection between mental health and the legal system is the assessment of dangerousness. The idea that mentally ill persons are dangerous, and that the society must be protected from them is not based on the frequency of their violent acts, or on the relationship to various illnesses. Media accounts of the sudden unpredictable violence of a few individuals reinforce a deep fear about the person "next door" whom we don't know. (Most murders are by someone familiar to the victim, and mass shootings of strangers are the exception.) Mental health clinicians have little influence over the factors beside mental capacity contributing to violence in the society. Persons contemplating violence to self or other are not statistically likely to see a mental health provider, and if they do, the provider is not likely to have the skills to evaluate the likelihood that the person will *imminently perform a violent act*.

The criteria for evaluation "danger to self or others", usually allows placing an individual in 48-72 hour involuntary evaluation, depriving the individual of legal rights and liberty. The assessment of both suicidal risk and interpersonal violence are inaccurate, but has several important implications for the patient and the evaluator: The determination asserts that the person may not be trusted as a functioning individual in the society, and must be isolated and monitored to evaluate this, an extreme level of social labeling which requires isolation and control. The person is no longer afforded the rights and opportunities of an adult member of the society. This loss of rights may extend beyond the period of isolation or incarceration and interfere with later life activities. (As in not receiving security clearance for a job.) If a person is deprived of autonomy on an invalid basis, the evaluator may be vulnerable to legal action for infringement of rights. If the danger is not contained and the patient kills himself or others, the evaluator may incur a liability for failure to protect the society. Professional responsibility demands the clinician take personal and professional responsibility for accurate assessment in order to avoid a dangerous outcome. The ***Tarasoff decision*** makes it clear that the evaluator faces a dilemma of a significant risk with either error. (54) The situation illustrates that the motivations of both persons in the assessment process play a significant role in the outcome of at least some assessments (which resembles a "prisoner's dilemma" configuration). Placement in a secure facility involves the location of care, the availability of space and services, and priority of placement; these factors are often not in the control of the provider, but determined by the social system. If the provider assesses a need for placement, but no space is available what is the society's responsibility? (55)

Institutional issues bias both the evaluator and patient. When the assessment occurs in an institutional setting, school, college, military, or corporate EAP, the clinician has a responsibility to the institution paying for the assessment as well as the client seeking help or evaluation. It helps to make this explicit at the outset of the assessment; at the very least it should be clearly stated in the report of the evaluation, and whether the assessment fits the institution's expectations. The person being evaluated will often have an institutional agenda, which may be counter to institutional policy, and should be documented. The evaluator who is performing an evaluation with institutional bias may, or may not, benefit the person evaluated. The evaluator should not be confused about objectivity in this situation. (56)

All the data collected in the "diagnostic event" are behaviors. Behavior observed directly ("mental status") is an important source of data, independent of its verbal content. Verbal reports about internal subjective states, verbal social interaction, and reports of consuming addictive substances or other activities are behavior. Verbal self-report of subjective experience and verbal report of symptoms are "objective" in the same way: they are observable verbal behavior. *Verbal report of symptoms may describe experiences of mental states but are not objective data about an internal state,* **this is the "Rosenhan Fallacy".** Verbal report of a symptom is not the experience of the symptom. This error occurs both intentionally by patients seeking to present symptoms, and inadvertently when evaluators ask for symptoms and assume that the patient's agreement corresponds to the subjective experience. *Determining if verbal behavior provides "accurate" information about the patient's internal state depends on careful assessment of the associated meaning and context of the verbal report, the patient's openness to share, and the skill of the interviewer.* An unfocused interview can obtain valuable information when interpreted by a trained listener or be wildly off target. The balance between structured and unstructured techniques for gathering verbal data is important but rarely discussed. "Participant observation", combining interaction and observation occurs when the observer interacts with the subject, while distorting the exchange as little as possible, and observing the interaction objectively. The symptoms of Freud's patients did not correspond to his understanding of the nervous system, which led to the idea that they were communicating something other than Neurologic symptoms. He had to "listen beyond the verbal content to understand the symptoms", as described in Reik's **Listening With The 3rd Ear**. (57) The challenge of training others to perform this process accurately has never been solved, and is ignored by many mental health professionals, who seek structured verbal interviews and scales thinking that the consistency corresponds to internal accuracy with the patient. *The relationship between verbally reported symptoms, subjective emotional experiences, and related brain pathways needs clarification, which is not solved simply by structuring the interview into a limited set of responses.*

Cross-cultural issues must be considered. If the assessment occurs in a setting with a shared cultural tradition, the assumptions and values of both assessor and patient will overlap and difficulties of understanding are less obvious. The United States has always included immigration of new cultural groups, and is trending toward a more diverse, less homogenous culture in many regions. Cultural differences between assessor and client impact several areas of the evaluation. Cultural issues were also discussed in chapter two.

The most basic cultural issue is language. If the assessor and patient do not speak the same language, an interpreter is needed who will affect the evaluation. When the interpreter is a mental health professional introduced to relate the symptoms across languages, the interpreter's mental health concepts will influence the translation. If the interpreter is a bilingual family member, the bias in the family will influence the translation by the relationship to the patient.

Differences in cultural interpretation of symptoms will influence the assessment. Different cultures have different models of disease. A recent book about a Hmong child with epilepsy is a good example of this. (58) Mental health theories of spirit possession present an alternative model of disease that must be transformed into Western concepts for understanding between patient and clinician.

CLINICAL EXAMPLE The woman who saw her dead partner. A Hispanic woman in her early 20s with one child was evaluated for recent recurring visions of the dead father of her child. He had been murdered several months before in a gang shooting. She was profoundly depressed, with multiple symptoms, but was caring for the child and personally maintaining herself. She was not suicidal. Walking down the streets where they lived, she would suddenly be convinced that he was there walking, only to disappear or turn into someone else. A previous clinician had decided that she was "psychotic" and wanted an evaluation to place the child in foster care. The patient expressed a strong loving feeling for the child and did not seek any more help than what was already provided by her mother, who was helping her. The patient refused medication because she was still nursing and "did not want to hurt the baby". Her mother knew of her visions and considered them part of grieving for the lost father. COMMENT This severe grief reaction would definitely be considered abnormal in American psychiatric assessment. The lack of complete functional impairment, and the availability of alternative caretakers reduced the danger to the child. These symptoms are considered serious in Hispanic culture, but not indicative of danger or loss of control.

Crossing generations presents another complication. 2nd generation children of immigrant families often display behaviors unacceptable to the first generation, considered deviant by their parents, but fit appropriately in the new culture in which they are adapting. In addition to different conceptual models of mental illness, cultures differ on the evidence for appropriate behavior, the "labeling theory" of how each society defines the boundary of "deviance".

> **CLINICAL EXAMPLE Family Issue Misdirected.** *A female college student, in a family that had emigrated from another country, reported that her college professor was abusing her. She became anxious and paranoid about him, and refused to return to college despite excellent grades. The college investigated and could not confirm any contact between student and faculty member, who taught in a lecture class of 400. After multiple sessions, she revealed that her father was being abusive to her mother. This was at first strongly denied by both parents, but the father's brother came to a session and confirmed the situation. After a family session in which another family member confirmed the abuse, she reported in later sessions that the abuse had stopped, and she returned to college without further problems. COMMENT The woman's conflict over revealing or keeping a family secret while allowing her mother to be abused was expressed by displacing the problem onto someone else. Her status as the second generation created an especially strong conflict between the family's values and her view as a young American woman.*

Certain "core syndromes" are expressed culturally in different ways, for example syndromes of psychosis, though each involves violating norms of the culture:

"Running AMOK" (sudden violence) in a culture that values deference and self-control.

"Windigo monster" (excessive eating) in a culture that requires strong discipline over food to avoid starvation. (59) "*Nymphomania*" is considered a mental illness of women in European culture, but not similar male behavior, associated with the character Don Juan. Women are presumed to value chastity, while men to value sexual prowess and conquest, a further validation of the concept of "labeling" deviance from the values of the society. Individuals who perform symptoms that violate social norms are labeled mentally ill. We are all similarly human, with similar brain pathways, and life experiences, but these are interpreted differently by cultural memes. Finding a common language to communicate can be challenging in the mental health setting with a goal of patient centered care. (60)

The assessment is influenced by many factors that include the financial and social context of the assessment, the issues of personal and professional responsibility, the legal boundaries of danger, criminal responsibility, and professional responsibility, institutional bias, data interpretation, and cross cultural awareness. The clinician will be aware of some, and the interviewee others. These considerations should be documented by the evaluator.

For the interviewee: What are the person's financial limitations in care? Does the person seek relief of symptoms? Is the patient seeking to be removed from current situation?

Is the patient seeking disability or other compensation? Is the patient attempting to avoid legal consequences?

For the clinician: Where is the evaluation occurring? What institutional boundaries influence the evaluator? Does the patient seem threatening or dangerous? Does the evaluator feel a risk of personal liability? Is the patient understand-able; is there a cultural barrier? Does the situation provide sufficient resources to address the patient's problem?

(An interviewer will not be in touch with all the bias he brings to the interview, or always discover the patient's intentions, but comments may clarify the later review.) This approach to assessment is a good fit for "patient centered care". Defining the motivations and context of the interview provide important information about the objectives of treatment for each participant. Clarifying the intentions of the client seeking evaluation can help the provider focus on what is important to the client. This may or may not have anything to do with traditional ideas of treatment. Engaging the client as an active participant in all modalities improves the likelihood of a positive result. There is no way to force the patient to be honest about his intentions, nor the provider about his. As a ***legal document,*** the comments support the treatment process and be appropriate for later review. (60) Sharing this information with the client may improve the treatment alliance.

What Makes An Assessment Correct? What makes a diagnosis "correct"? The criteria of "reliability" and "validity" are often used: Reliability means that different evaluators will produce the same assessment of patients, that the approach yields consistent observations. A method with only one diagnosis yields perfect reliability every time but is not useful. One diagnosis for Major Depressive Disorder improves reliability but creates problems in treatment. (See chapter eleven) Reliability is often misinterpreted to mean that every clinician obtains the same evaluation of the patients, that beginning students, or computer evaluations, will get the same results as experienced observers. This can only happen if the format of observation is so rigid that experience provides no additional benefit. This sounds absurd, but financial pressures on delivery of care require patients use computerized self-assessment to lower cost. The emphasis on reliability has become so rigid its value is lost. (61) Validity measures whether patients, grouped by categories, have similar responses to external conditions. Validity defines categories that are useful for treatment decisions, management of care, and prediction of course. Current DSM diagnoses have poor validity. Treatment response to medication or psychotherapy is poorly correlated with diagnosis. Genetic and network assessments do not correlate with diagnoses. Outcome correlates with diagnosis only for symptoms over limited intervals. *The most important measure of validity is the effectiveness of treatment.* The treatment of psychosis appears to be successful because almost every patient with psychosis has some resolution, usually rapidly, but is not always associated with return to social function, because some core symptoms do not respond. (Explored in chapter eleven.) The validity of the DSM is poor, but the problem is hidden behind statements like "treatment resistant depression" and "chronic mental illness", which make treatment failure a characteristic of the patient not the diagnostic category or the treatment. Kendall and Gebrinsky, *Distinguishing Between Validity and Utility of Diagnoses*, challenge the idea of discrete disease entities assumed in the development of the Feighner criteria (and DSM III). (62) Fusar-Poli reviews the current issues in prognosis, that are not encouraging. (62)

The IT industry is a strong advocate for using AI as the solution to problems in evaluation. An example is using large data sets to improve retinal examination. (Mandl, 62). There are several reasons to doubt this will improve mental health assessment. The experience with EHR shows that the IT industry is profit-centered, and will not prioritize patient and clinician needs in design of systems. There is no direct relationship between improved assessment and profits. (63) "Big data" analysis depends on the quality of the input data. Increasing the amount of data and associated noise will not improve the result ("garbage in, garbage out"). How the data is gathered impacts the value. Much current mental health data derived from scales does not capture important variables. AI methods are based on learning processes that converge toward meaningful categories, as in accurate facial recognition. What are the "meaningful categories" of AI analysis in mental health? They are not DSM diagnoses. So "big data" learning processes do not provide a solution without first clarifying the goals of AI analysis. This understanding of AI is not appreciated either by clinicians or most tech developers. *Another challenge of mental health data is privacy, ensuring that the information is not used to compromise the individual. This issue is not unique to mental health, or general health data, but a core issue in the use of personal data in all information systems.*

Will the approach described here improve assessment? The value of the process can only be assessed by implementation. Clinical trials can answer the following questions: Does identifying pathways guide more effective treatment decisions? Does specifying etiology differentiate treatment interventions and lead to preventive interventions? Is the boundary between well/ill clear and the transitions observable? Can the parameters influencing the interview be documented and inform the limitations of the assessment?

The system proposed has not been implemented; to do so would require significant changes in clinical practice. (The appendix includes some forms and suggestions) These must be learned, with some increase in complexity, but no more than iterations of DSM.

A MODEL FOR DOCUMENTING ASSESSMENT

Pathways produce symptom patterns
    Sensory input- and perceptual categorization NL ABN MAJ
    The social brain and self-system NL ABN MAJ
    Motivation system NL ABN MAJ
    The signification/memory system NL ABN MAJ
    Anxiety/aggression response to danger NL ABN MAJ
    Internal-external integration and attention NL ABN MAJ
    The action selection system NL ABN MAJ

COMMENT:
(add description of major symptom patterns for each abnormal finding)

Etiology (specify where possible)
GENETIC %FACTOR
OTHER BIOLOGICAL %FACTOR
LEARNING/EXPERIENTIAL %FACTOR
IMMEDIATE SOCIAL %FACTOR
COMMENT: (Available documentation and identification of etiologies:)

CRITICAL LIFE STAGE EVENTS

ADAPTATION
ADAPTIVE SUCCESS current
LIVE
LOVE
WORK
PLAY

ADAPTIVE SUCCESS immediately prior (1 to 3 mo)
LIVE
LOVE
WORK
PLAY

ADAPTIVE SUCCESS highest level last five years (or lifetime)
LIVE
LOVE
WORK
PLAY

MAJOR COPING METHODS
INTERVIEW CONTEXT
ESTIMATED INTENT OF CLIENT/PATIENT
CIRCUMSTANCES OF CLINICIAN

CHAPTER ELEVEN:
Biological interventions

The brain is a biological tissue so biophysical interventions can alter its pathways. Psychopharmacology became the dominant treatment in Psychiatry in the 1970s, promoted by practitioners and pharmaceutical companies who claimed they were correcting a "chemical imbalance" in the brain ("no twisted thought without a twisted molecule"). There is (and was) no evidence for the phrase, which has been abandoned, (some deny it was ever made). (1)

Psychopharmacology is the most widely used biological intervention in mental health. (Discussion of other biological interventions is presented in the chapter Appendix.) The research literature of psychopharmacology is vast, repetitive, and contradictory. Several multi-volume summaries quickly became out of date with new developments. This information cannot be summarized in one short chapter, but certain basic principles apply to the use of most medications, which are presented with specific examples, and summarized by four questions:

Does the medication work? (How does it work? What if it doesn't work?)

How to balance the "intended effects" with "undesired effects"?

How to decide when to discontinue the medication?

How to use medications in special high-risk circumstances (childhood and pregnancy)?

HISTORICAL NOTE *Traditional cultures used natural substances to alter brain activity. Biological treatments began in the 20th century by inducing fever (malaria) (1917) as treatment for syphilis, and causing seizures using metrazol (1934), and electric shock (1937) as treatments. Surgical lobotomy was endorsed for treatment in the 1940s, but was discontinued after a brief surge in use. Barbiturates, other sedatives, and amphetamines (a popular medication, not for children) were prescribed starting in the 1930's. (2) The use of medications was sporadic and not focused on mental health treatment.*

Chlorpromazine (CPZ) treatment (1954, in the US) began a new era of biochemical treatment of hospitalized mental patients, ending custodial care for some, and enabling discharge to the community. The medications before 1960 were discovered serendipitously, and then variations of the CPZ molecule by organic chemists were developed for treatment of psychosis and depression. All had problem side effects with frequent discontinuations. New medications seeking fewer side effects were developed. Clozapine was the first "second generation antipsychotic" in 1974 (in US), and a new selective serotonin reuptake inhibitor (SSRI) antidepressant, fluoxetine, released in 1984. Fluoxetine improved depressed mood in some with fewer side effects and became a sales "blockbuster", and the economic potential for psychopharmacology expanded dramatically. Seeking a substitute for the hypnotic-sedatives chlordiazepoxide (1958) and chloral hydrate, led to development of diazepam (1963), a "breakthrough" for managing anxiety, which was the highest selling medication in the world between 1968 and 1982. Other pharmaceutical companies synthesized "me too" drugs, similar molecules with similar (or better) effects modeled on successful ones. For three decades, psychopharmacology drug development was the major focus of Psychiatry, and funded training. The search for new medications continues, but the opportunities in mental health have diminished.

PHARMACEUTICAL COMPANIES. *It is impossible to discuss psychopharmacology without addressing the role of pharmaceutical companies. Critics often misinterpret this role, despite certain facts that are not in dispute: (3)*

Pharmaceutical companies are for-profit businesses developing and selling products that can be marketed to benefit their executives, employees and investors. Their products must treat illnesses to be marketable, but they are not in the business of caring for patients. (The two goals overlap but are distinct.)

Pharmaceutical companies perform research to develop products for profit. This research is sometimes made public, especially in studies done to secure FDA approval, and some studies are published in peer-reviewed journals, while others may never be published. The companies maintain confidentiality about the development of their products, and details of research procedures, in order to secure patent protection. The companies have no obligation to reveal the research for any reason but securing approval for sale, or promoting use, so publication is limited, and negative results are suppressed, which has been documented. (4) The FDA requires public disclosure of potential side effects in new products, but reporting and documentation of side effects after approval and marketing are less consistent.

The pharmaceutical industry encourages the use of medications by supporting research and training in academic training centers; and psychiatry training programs have relied heavily on pharmaceutical funding until very recently. How this funding influenced treatment decisions is debatable. Sponsorship of studies must be documented in papers published in major journals. Most colloquia and symposia, including the American Psychiatric Association meetings, require presenters to disclose their source of funding, and some presentations are separated as "industry funded programs" to indicate the funding source of the presentations.

Pharmaceutical company marketing includes recommendations for use of each company's products. The information is limited to what published studies document, and biased to favor the company's products over others. Providers must consider this data objectively to maintain an independent perspective on use of medications.

These are reasonable practices for producing and marketing products for profit.

The economic value of psychopharmacology has diminished since 2010. Medications with similar effects are mutually competitive, not uniquely beneficial. Health insurers are reluctant to pay the increased cost of new medications, preferring older out of patent and less costly ones. This discourages the funding of new research and reduces the financial support of Psychiatric training, research, and advertising in publications. How this will impact mental health treatment remains to be seen.

Strong support for use of psychopharmacology in American Psychiatry is based on the evidence of its effectiveness. This evidence comes primarily from studies used to establish efficacy for FDA approval. The psychopharmacology literature is a mixture of company financed studies and papers by researchers not compensated by pharmaceutical companies (often in Europe or Canada) which show effectiveness for specific psychopharmacologic agents compared to placebo. There are few studies comparing effectiveness of one agent to another in the same study, or differential effectiveness of medications for specific patient-symptom groups. Evidence supports the use of each agent without specifying which symptom-groups are most likely (or less likely) to benefit or how each drug compares with others in the same study. (5) ***Meta-analyses*** attempt to compensate for this lack of data by combining results from different studies, but the selection of patients, recording of effects, and analysis of data are not the same including differences in assessment. Statistical techniques in meta-analyses attempt to compare the data from different studies on a hypothetical basis. (6) (7) *For the practicing clinician, meta-analyses are often the only guide for comparing treatments.* Different meta-analyses do not always produce the same conclusions. Treatment study design also influences the evidence: Results presented as averages for the active and placebo groups do not indicate the percentage of active patients who were poor or non-responders. A small number of strong positive responders in the active group may account for the benefit. The criteria for patient selection may not reflect community patient populations. Comparing the rate of relapse (return of symptoms) in patients taken off medications does not support maintaining *all patients* on medication, some go off without relapsing and do not need continuation. Flow charts or "algorithms" for sequential use of various agents indicate the high rate of failure in antidepressant treatment, and are based on personal opinion, not research. (The Star*D study on treatment of depression by NIMH (reviewed later) did not favor any algorithm.) Clinical use of medications may be *off label*, used in clinical situations not included in the original FDA studies, and not documented in publications (for liability concerns), so the effects are difficult to summarize. The limitations in evidence of effectiveness of medications are discussed in later paragraphs.

How do the medications work? Psychopharmacology medications modify synaptic transmission (*with a few exceptions*). (8) Medications, characterized by chemical structure and pharmacologic effects, have receptor sites that interact with sites in the brain. The pharmacological reactions between the chemical site and receptor site can be studied experimentally in isolated brain tissue, and a single molecule often includes more than one site, interacting with multiple sites in different brain (and body) regions. The brain has a small group of major neurotransmitters and a large group of others including more than 50 peptides with transmitter properties (and new ones discovered every day). Three neuro-transmitters: glutamate, acetylcholine, and gama-amino butyric acid (GABA) (are estimated to) account for over 75% of all brain neurotransmission. Glutamate and acetylcholine are the major activation transmitters, so methods that alter these transmitters risk hyperactivity and seizures, e.g. organophosphate insecticides, and nerve gas poisons. (8) Glutamate, the most prevalent transmitter, is excitatory at well over 90% of the synapses in the human brain, and release of pre-synaptic glutamate activates several post-synaptic receptors including the NMDA receptor. Glutamate produces synaptic transmission for learning/memory in hippocampus and neocortex by *long-term potentiation,* the process of plasticity. (9) Because of its wide effects, it is difficult to devise an agent for this system with limited effects. (Recent interest in ketamine as an antidepressant illustrates this problem (see later section).) GABA transmission is inhibitory throughout the brain, and agents that enhance GABA transmission pose the danger of excessive inactivation and coma. Acetylcholine is also widely distributed, the transmitter at the neuromuscular junction connecting motor nerves to muscles, and also in regions of the brain, over nicotinic and muscarinic receptors. Nicotine has been in human use for centuries, and the current focus on its "addictive" properties distracts from use in some cultures to improve cognitive function.

The other major neurotransmitter group are the monoamines, amino acids with amine side chains: adrenaline, nor-adrenaline, dopamine, and serotonin. These play an important role in brain neurotransmission of the *motivation system* (chapter three), are less widely distributed in other regions of brain, and are less likely to cause excess activation. The *motivation system* is richly supplied with biogenic monoamine synapses, and the combination of pathways and synaptic receptors creates a regulator, *activator-inhibitor function,* for brain activity. Medications currently used in psychopharmacology act mostly on the biogenic amine receptor systems, directly or indirectly. A graphical method of presenting receptors has been developed by Saklad. (10)

SIDEBAR Several factors influence receptor effects: Receptor sites are distributed in multiple brain areas even within a single region, giving different effects on activation at different sites and different drug levels. The bonding between drug and receptor site is a chemical reaction, characterised by the Michaelis-Menten equation (relating the amounts of substrates and product in this case binding to the receptor) with a rate constant, Ki, an indicator of the relative strength of binding of different medications: high values indicate weak binding, and vice versa. (11) The Ki is measured on receptors extracted from the brain and thus is not specific to synaptic locations. Chemicals may act on different components of a receptor site to moderate effects on the receptor. Single drug molecules may interact with more than one receptor type. This may produce desirable or undesirable consequences as when "second generation antipsychotics" produce metabolic changes. (See later discussion)

How the synaptic effects of medications modify the *information function* in pathways is not understood. Most medications work on monoamine pathways, or GABA synapses, which are located in many pathways, producing multiple effects. Recent research on changes in fMRI patterns of networks using patients on medications, provides rudimentary data, but does not lead to FDA approval, and does not validate effectiveness, so they are not done routinely (see appendix to chapter one). Because "diseases" are defined as symptoms, the effectiveness of medications is measured by symptom improvement. The documentation of "efficacy", that the medication "works", are studies that compare changes of symptoms measured by standardized scales, compared with placebo. These are not correlated with improved function.

What if the medication doesn't work? The individual's response to the medication involves many factors including distribution and metabolism of the agent, genetic variability, and local brain response. Some of these can be estimated in advance but others are discovered only by clinical experience. Genetic variability may create a response to a specific medication, and there is limited evidence for genetic variation in metabolism of certain agents. (12) Pharmaceutical companies have pulled away from exploring genetic factors, unsure if genes will identify a company's products as less effective. The genetic variability of individual response to specific medications has little documentation. Earlier chapters summarize the disappointing results trying to define genetic markers for mental diseases. Polygenic influences are most often observed, and the interactions with medications are not studied. Candidate gene loci do not account for most depression syndromes, or predict medication response. (21). The genetic variations in metabolism of certain medications, especially by liver enzymes has been studied in detail, but the results have very little benefit for most clinical situations.

Psychopharmacological agents are always given in, and impacted by the social context. Evidence for effects of the social environment comes from anthropology where native cultures have used psychopharmacology in healing rituals for eons and social context and ritual are essential features, not incorporated into Western practice. In drug development every effort is made to minimize the role of these social factors, described as *placebo response*, to isolate the chemical response. In clinical practice, the placebo effect should be enhanced as part of effective treatment. Research on the placebo response, how it depends on variables in the prescriber, and the social dynamic of the setting, might guide providers to enhance the response and expand the pharmacological benefit. But it is unlikely to be medication specific and therefore of little marketing value. (*13*) This is *patient centered* rather than illness/diagnosis focused, and supported by Enid and Michael Balint, among others, who recognize the patient as an independent person with his/her own expectations and decisions, which may enhance the response. (13) The reality is that the provider does not control the use of medication, but facilitates access for the patient, if it is appropriate, and the patient chooses to use it.

Ineffective response is frequently observed in antidepressant treatment. Antidepressants have varied chemical structures and pharmacologic effects for treating symptoms of the motivation system (see chapter three). The motivation pathways regulate changes in sleep, sexuality, and eating, i.e. the "neuro-vegetative signs". The subjective experience of depression/mania involves motivation system pathways to cingulate and insula. Current antidepressant medications evolved, from MAOIs, and tricyclic antidepressants (TCA), which had troublesome side effects, to the current selective serotonin reuptake inhibitors (SSRI) (which prevent reuptake of a proportion of the released serotonin on the presynaptic side). There is no explanation of why serotonin is more important, or how the changes modify pathways, though several theories have been proposed. (14) The Mayberg fMRI studies make it doubtful that only one system is involved in depression symptoms for all patients and the SSRI effect is observed for the group that involves cingulate pathways. (See chapter three) Some newer anti-depressants (SNRI) alter both serotonin and norepinephrine (and dopamine) release, and their effects on patient symptoms may be different for specific symptoms but have not been studied selectively. (15) (16)

SSRIs are not effective for many patients with depression, and even have problems demonstrating efficacy, and in the results of the STAR*D trials. (17) The popularity of these medications, described by Kramer, suggests the effect on mood is a general "feel good" effect, not specific to depression, for persons with mild symptoms. They are not effective for severe depression syndromes. (18) Explaining the problem as "surprisingly high rate of placebo responders in research studies" is misleading; it can be restated "spontaneous improvement is as effective as the medication" which makes clear that the medication has limited effect. (19) Major Depressive Disorder is not a uniform syndrome. Depressed patients have different symptoms and features. In STAR*D out of 1,030 separate symptom profiles, 864 profiles (83.9%) were endorsed by five or fewer subjects, and 501 profiles (48.6%) were endorsed by only one individual. The most common symptom profile exhibited a frequency of only 1.8%, yet research on treatment of depression by specific symptoms is not done. (20) Different patterns of depression involve different pathways (see chapter three): Depressed mood without Neuro-vegetative signs, Recurring depressed mood with Neuro-vegetative signs, Recurring depressed mood with positive Neuro-vegetative signs and history for BPD, Depressed mood with separation and loss, with or without panic, Depressed mood with anxiety. They do not respond the same way to medications. (22) Psychopharmacological agents are always given in, and impacted by the social context of administration. All these factors contribute to (in)effectiveness. Predictors of poor outcome in one study were the timespan between first and last depressive episode, age at first antidepressant treatment, response to first antidepressant treatment, severity, suicidality, melancholia, number of lifetime depressive episodes, patients' admittance type, education, occupation, and comorbid diabetes, panic, and thyroid disorder. The combination predicted poor response 75% of the time, but did not identify an adequate treatment for any patients! The results can be summarized as "patients with poor response to depression treatment, continue to have poor response", which defines a group of patients with **chronic persistent depression**, i.e. *non-responders* for unknown reasons. Measures like cortical connectivity and EEG patterns are not predictive. (23) Treatment of "psychotic depression" with high symptom severity is challenging, and a meta-review suggests the combination of anti-psychotic and anti-depressant medication. (24) Because Major Depressive Disorder is treated as one disease, studies on groups with different symptoms are not usually performed to compare effects of different medications on symptoms. (25)

What strategies can be used for non-responders? Clinical studies in the 1990s did not seek relationships between specific symptoms and medication response. Instead, NIMH performed the **STAR*D study** to evaluate intervention strategies for depressed patients (completed in 2006, with data analysis to 2008). Summaries can be found on the NIMH site, and in reviews. (26) The treatment for non-response in the STAR*D study was: A) increase dosage, B) switch to a different agent, and/or C) combine the antidepressant medication with a second medication or treatment.

***CLINICAL EXAMPLE The Star*D Study.** The study design had no placebo groups, only active treatments. Patients and clinicians had joint involvement in choosing the steps for second treatment when the initial treatment with SSRI was unsuccessful, i.e. it was not "blinded". This made statistical analysis difficult, but supposedly mimicked the "typical clinical procedure". There were four steps: 1) The first treatment step (citralopram) had 33% effectiveness. This supported the need for an alternative strategy for the remaining patients. 2) The second step involved an add-on (Level 2) a) CBT + citralopram b) citralopram + buspar, or c) bupropion or venlafaxine or sertraline. The add on of second agents or combined agents was not based on symptoms. (CBT, though identified as effective in independent studies, did not improve remission rates). Results of Second step were 55% effectiveness. Level 3) Switching to a new agent gave variable improvement: a) mirtazapine +12%, nortryp +8% or lithium or T3 small %) total 45% remission. Level 4) Other interventions tranylcypramine, or (mirtazapin + venlafaxine xr) for previous nonresponders generated little additional improvement. Multiple treatment steps were associated with decreased response and higher relapse rates. Level 3-4 patients showed higher improvement and higher relapse effect on discontinuation.*

The overall total treatment response rate of STAR*D, including relapse, was 47%; *almost half the patients had no benefit at the end of the 6 months study!* A third of patients who entered the study never responded at all during the 6-month course despite receiving multiple treatments. **STAR*D confirmed the problem of poor treatment response in patients with depression, without indicating a solution.** The selection of subsequent treatment options did not consistently improve outcome. Neither augmenting dose nor switching, without differentiating symptom patterns, was endorsed: *neither option was superior.* Add on treatments did not show benefit either. ***STAR*D received extensive criticism about the procedures, patient selection, etc., but it documented the core dilemma of antidepressant treatment.*** The weak results of STAR*D challenge a unified concept of depression, different symptom patterns of depression must be considered in treatment selection.

The clinical approach to non-responders did not change after STAR*D. Increasing dosage, changing to a different SSRI or SNRI, and augmentation with other medications are still typical responses in treatment. Research for special groups for bipolar depression, confirmed that bipolar patients with depression required a different approach. (27) Neuro-vegetative symptoms, and the relationship between severe depression and attachment/loss, have not yet been used to differentiate groups. Research on adding on other treatment agents is a "shotgun effort" looking for alternatives for non-responders based various theories of non-responding, but ***not differences in patient symptoms***. These include combining multiple drugs from start of treatment, CBT, l-methylfolate, stimulants, vit D, body therapies and exercise; references to multiple strategies are listed at (28). Pharmaceutical research has developed new medications with multiple receptor sites without identifying symptom targets for their use. *After multiple treatment failures, the patient may enter the group of **chronic refractory (persistent) depression***. Providers sometimes turn to electroconvulsive therapy (ECT). (The procedure of ECT is discussed with other biological interventions at the end of the chapter.) The following example illustrates a situation of "non-response" in which failure to identify a critical factor was associated with ineffective treatment.

Chronic, refractory depression has replaced the term "treatment resistant depression" for the patients with do not respond to current medications. (29) ("Treatment resistant depression" is inappropriate: depression is not animate and it cannot "resist" anything. The patient is not resisting. The reality is that "a depressed patient is given ineffective treatment".)

CLINICAL EXAMPLE A Woman Who Got ECT. *A married woman in her 40s was evaluated by a Psychiatric resident for medication follow-up, after being treated with ECT. She did not respond to antidepressant medication at a university treatment program that resulted in the ECT course. In the follow-up evaluation, she reported being depressed because her husband was "cheating on me", and gave evidence of lipstick stains on collar, mysterious phone callers who hung up when she answered, etc. According to the patient, the university psychiatrist dismissed this as paranoia, which explained why the medication did not work. There were no children. The resident asked why, if she was so upset, she had not left her husband. She replied that she had nowhere to go, but on reflection, she realized that a sister lived in the next town. She was given a prescription for an antidepressant and scheduled for next visit, but did not return. About 6 weeks later, the resident received an outside call for an appointment. When asked how the caller selected him, the man answered that the resident had treated the man's wife. Inquiring about her, the caller answered that she was doing fine, had left him, and was living with her sister, and was not depressed anymore, but now he, the husband, had become depressed and was seeking treatment. COMMENT: The interpersonal dynamics of a relationship can be the source of depressed mood not responsive to usual interventions, which requires a different approach. Would the woman have improved without ECT or medication if the social situation were addressed from the start?*

SIDEBAR Two definitions have emerged for the Non-Responder: The European definition is an insufficient response after full dose, and full course, of two types of medications. The Harvard/MGH definition is an "insufficient effect after full dose, max dose, or effective blood concentration, for at least 6 weeks on two types of medications". The definitions emphasize two medication trials because of the frequency of non-response from one, and the occasional positive response from a different agent. Note that this defines a treatment course of at least, 12 weeks, which is within the range of spontaneous remission of symptoms in some patients. (30) The definitions appear rigorous, but since "effective blood concentration" is not established, they are not.

A new chemical intervention, ketamine, has been promoted (also not specific to etiology or symptoms). Ketamine is an example of the search for a "universal solution" to non-responders without identifying characteristics, with an unusual history of development.

SIDEBAR The "Miraculous Ketamine Cure" For Refractory Depression.
Ketamine is used in anaesthesia, and was reported to give transient improvement in persons with "chronic refractory depression" after use. Trials using IV ketamine on a group of depressed patients produced transient improvement after emerging from the confused semi-anaesthetized state, but benefit was transient (days). Ketamine is a NMDA glutamate agonist, with no clear pathway action. (Suggestions that it influences mu opiate activity are reported.) Given the broad effects of glutamate, a wide range of effects is possible. The observed effect is similar to ECT (see appendix): patients have mental disorganization that may disrupt the pathway patterns producing symptoms, and then return. This has been tested in a recent study that claimed better results for ketamine vs. ECT. (30) Multiple weekly IV administrations are impractical (and not consistent with previous FDA approval for use of ketamine as an anaesthetic). The transient benefit of IV administrations required a more continuous method of administration for sustained benefit. So a pharmaceutical company developed an intranasal spray that would allow self-administration on an ongoing basis, and it was authorized within months of development, on a special use basis, with limited control over availability, shifting the liability for administration to the prescriber. (31)

Ketamine development illustrates several trends. Use for "chronic refractory depression" is not based on diagnostic, pathway, or any other understanding. Does Ketamine treat or merely "disrupt" abnormal pathways? If it disrupts, some additional intervention is required to stabilize after the short-term use. This is a similar issue to ECT, and has not been considered. (The relationship of biological and information treatment is discussed in chapter twelve.) Ketamine is also a "party "drug ("Vitamin K") used for altering mental states, and addictive for some. No evaluation of long term addictive risk for nasal administration was possible in the short time it has been available. Given the national disaster created by the oxycontin, and now fentanyl, it seems incredible that another potentially addictive substance would be authorized without careful study. *Anyone currently using ketamine intranasal long term is participating in the assessment of its addictive risk.* (32) (33)

Ketamine had previous FDA approval for another use, so it was possible to use IV ketamine "off label" without further FDA review for a new indication, an opportunity for entrepreneurial drug development without extensive research expense, which fails to provide data on the long term use of a drug previously used briefly. The cognitive disorganization associated with each treatment has the potential for long-term cognitive impairment, which has not been evaluated because the development did not follow any protocol of risk assessment. A "review" by senior members in the field weighed in on this issue giving ambivalent support for use, which did not include any new research, an unusual statement of advocacy for a "new" medication. (32)

The "ketamine story" illustrates the pressure to find new solutions to treatment problems without understanding the failure of previous approaches. The long term benefit and risk of ketamine remain hazy, but it is a clear example of how development of treatment has changed, with disregard for the risk of addiction, a factor in many mental health treatments. The current evidence indicates that psychopharmacology of antidepressant medications, when administered to persons with depressed mood without differentiating symptom groups is ineffective at least 30% and perhaps as much as 50% of the time. And the long list of attempted solutions does not result in significant improvement. The need for research that identifies differential response of symptom subgroups is not supported by the pharmaceutical industry, which would not get any marketing benefit, so other research support must be found.

Understanding what the medication treats is essential for assessing effectiveness. Knowing what pathway is altered, and the result of the changes explains the effect(s). This applies to "antipsychotic medications" which are very effective for treatment of *psychosis syndrome* (see chapter five). Reduction in arousal, and major symptoms (of the BPRS scale) are typically achieved within days using current anti-psychotic medications. They are effective for most etiologies of *psychosis* including the schizophrenia syndromes (see chapter four), but there is no evidence that they alter the core cognitive disturbances in the schizophrenias. (34) *For patients with schizophrenia syndromes, control of the psychosis syndrome without improvement of the underlying disorder is partial treatment.* The basis of treatment of psychosis is the ability to block dopamine D2 transmission, also perhaps nor-epinephrine. Treatment of the cognitive symptoms of the schizophrenias has recent evidence favoring GABA for synaptic transmission in hippocampal regions. (See chapter four). The effectiveness of two medications, olanzapine, and clozaril, may reflect this treatment in selected patients. (Leucht, 34)

CLOZAPINE   CARBAMAZEPINE   BENZODIAZEPINE

SIDEBAR The Mystery Of Clozapine. Clozapine (Clozaril) is an example of serendipity in drug development. Though developed in 1958 (for unknown use), it was not marketed in US until 1990 as a treatment for "schizophrenia", the "initial SGA". (See later discussion) It is a weak blocker of dopamine D2, a dibenzodiazepine chemically unique from other FGA molecules, and distantly related to carbamazepine, an anti-seizure medication with similar bone marrow toxicity, very distantly to the benzodiazepines (see diagram). (35) Its side effects include weight gain, siallorrhea, cardiotoxicity, seizure problems, and agranulocytosis (bone marrow toxicity), which became apparent in clinical use, requiring regular WBC monitoring for liability protection. These three uncommon but dangerous side effects limited use of clozapine for 20 years. The Novartis patent expired in 1998 and generic manufacture was transferred to Mylan (supported by Novartis), who instituted a new monitoring system and new marketing. Advocacy for its use spread through academic psychiatry, with reports that difficult to treat patients, referred to academic centers, responded to clozapine. This was not based on controlled studies but case reports and series. The reports claimed the drug was effective in schizophrenic patients not responsive to other medications, including other SGAs. (35) It was used despite the bone marrow toxicity, and other serious side effects. Reports of improvement in social isolation and other symptoms suggested the ability to "cure schizophrenia"! A toxic medication, previously rarely used, had suddenly been re-discovered to be highly effective without controlled research.

The chemical structure suggests clozapine may have GABA agonist properties (only recently been confirmed in *published* studies) and the clozapine effect may be GABA activity in combination with weak D2 blockade. (36) A subgroup of "schizophrenic syndrome" patients with temporal lobe injury, or hyper-excitable brain tissue might improve with GABA agonists like carbamazepine and clozapine. (And respond poorly to high dose D2 blockers that lower the seizure threshold.) The role of GABA in the schizophrenias is discussed in chapter four. The effectiveness of clozapine and olanzapine was noted in a Finnish study, and in the Catie study as a phase 2 finding. Clozapine and olanzapine have similar chemical structure (along with major weight gain). No effort has been made to

Biological interventions

identify the special characteristics of "non-responding" patients, another example of the failure to explore specific symptoms in medication response. The hypothesis that both clozapine and olanzapine have significant GABA activity along with D2 effects may explain their special effectiveness in selected patients, (and metabolic side effects), also reported by Shrestha et al. (Shrestha,36)

OLANZAPINE   BASIC BENZODIAZEPINE

CLINICAL EXAMPLE *The author explored this concept clinically by transferring patients referred, who are taking clozapine, to a combination of low dose SGA medication, and GABA agonist. In every instance, the patient remained stable, psychosis did not return, and bone marrow risks were eliminated. (This is not a controlled study but encourages doing one.) (36)(37)*

When evaluating medication treatment, effectiveness is related to what pathways the medication is treating. D2(anti-psychosis) blocking agents are effective for psychosis but not other symptoms and failure to recognize this interferes with effective use, and research on the differences.

Primary and Secondary Effects. The receptor sites on a medication activate different receptors in brain and body. After oral administration, the clinical effect is the combination of the effects at all sites. The *primary site* is the effect used for marketing the agent (and getting FDA approval), and other sites are labeled *side effects,* which differ only by the intended use, and may have stronger affinity (Ki) for the medication. Side effects are sometimes useful clinically and the distinction between primary site and side effects is a marketing consideration, unless the *side effects* on brain or body are **dangerous**. (Highly toxic side effects especially on organs outside the brain, usually prevent FDA approval, but sometimes result in a Black Box Warning, as in the danger of antipsychotics in dementia.) (38) *The effect of each medication is the aggregate impact at clinical dosage of the multiple sites activated or inhibited by the drug.* The other, non-primary effects are used in marketing, to favor one product over others, though studies by the company producing the medication do not include head to head comparisons on the same patient group to validate differences in side effects. To organize this data, a table of primary and secondary effects of medications is useful, but limited because most tables are based on both *in vitro*, and meta-analysis clinical information. When the effects and side effects are recognized as common features it is possible to design utilization optimizing the combination of effects for each patient. An example is this table 11.1 of receptors of antipsychotic medications (from Siafis et al, 37): A clinician considering the use of an antipsychotic is presented with this range of synaptic effects with varying pathway interactions. The table is created from a meta-analysis of different studies not direct comparison of patients on different medications. There is no indication of GABA activity, only recently reported. The table shows the limited comparative data for decision making involving multiple factors. The Risk column comes mostly from studies designed for marketing.

Side effects play an important role in the choice of anti-psychotic medications. Medications developed before clozapine (released in US 1990), designated first generation antipsychotic (FGA), have significant motor system side effects. Clozapine and subsequent medications, are designated second generation (SGA) though the clinical differentiation is not sharp. Blocking dopamine is effective treatment for psychosis, but the effects in basal ganglia (see chapter six) interfere with activity, emotion pathways, and cause motor system disturbances. The most serious motor system symptom, *tardive dyskinesia*, produces **permanent** motor tics. (39) SGA agents were

Biological interventions

Table 11.1: range of receptor activity in selected antipsychotic medication collected from multiple studies. No GABA receptor listed.

	D$_1$	D$_2$	D$_3$	D$_4$	H$_1$	H$_2$	H$_3$	5-HT$_{1A}$	5-HT$_{1B}$	5-HT$_{2A}$	5-HT$_{2B}$	5-HT$_{2C}$	5-HT$_6$	5-HT$_7$	M$_1$	M$_3$	α$_1$	α$_{2A}$	α$_{2B}$	α$_{2C}$	Transporter	Weight Gain	Glucose Abn	Lipid Abn
Olanzapine	++	++	++	++	+++	++	+		+	+++	++	++	++	++	+++	++	+++	++	++	++		++++	++	++
Zotepine	++	+++	+	+++	+++	+		+	++	+++	+++	+++	+++	++		+	+++	+	++	++	SERT, NET	+++/++++	(LD)	(LD)
Cloxapine	+	+	++	+	+++	+		+	+	++		++	++	++	+++	++	+++	+	++	++		+++/++++	++	++
Chlorpromazine	++	+++	+++	+++	+++	+		+	++	+++	+++	++	+	+++	++	+	+++	+	+	++		+++/++++	+/++	+/++
Sertindole		+++	+++	+++	+			++	++	++++		+++	+	++			+++	+	+	+		+++/++++	+/++	+/++
Iloperidone	+	+++	+++	++	+		+	++	++	+++	++	++	+	+++			+++	++	++	+		+++/++++	+/++	+/++
Risperidone	+	+++	+++	+++	+++	+		+	++	+++		++	++	+++			+++	++	++	++		+++	+/++	+/++
(Nor)quetiapine	+	+	+		++	++		+++	++	++		+	+	++	+	+	+++	++	+	++	NET	+++	+/++	+/++
Paliperidone	+	+++	+++	+++	++	++	+		++	+++		++	+	+++			++	++	+++	+++		++	+	+
Asenapine	+++	++++	++++	+++	+++	+++	++	++++	++	++++	++++	++++	+++	++++			+++	+++	++++	+++		++	+	++(LD)
Amisulpride		+++	+++								++							++	++			++	+	+
Aripiprazole		+++	+++	+	++			++++	++	+++	+++	+	+	++			+++	++	++	++	SERT	+(LD)	+(LD)	+(LD)
Brexpiprazole	+	+++	+++	++	++			+++	++	+++	+++	+	++	+++			+++	++	++	+++	SERT, NET	+(LD)	+(LD)	+(LD)
Cariprazine		+++	++++	+++	++			++	+	++	+++	+	++	++			+	+	+			+(LD)	+(LD)	+(LD)
Haloperidol	+	+++	+++	+++		+		+		+++							++	++	++	+		+	+	+
Lurasidone	+	+++	++	++			+	+++		+++				++++			++	+	+	+++		+	+	+
Ziprasidone	++	+++	+++	++	++	+		+++	+++	+++	++	+++	++	++++			+++	+	++	+++	SERT, NET	+	+	+

SOURCE Siafis, S., Tzachanis, D., Samara, M., & Papazisis, G. (2018).
Antipsychotic Drugs: From Receptor-binding Profiles to Metabolic Side Effects.
Current neuropharmacology, 16(8), 1210–1223. https://doi.org/10.2174/1570159X15666170630163616 (Creative Commons Authorization)

GRAY INDICATES ANTAGONIST, STIPPLING AGONIST, + = intensity.

designed with serotonin release sites to reduce this danger, but clinical experience shows only modest reductions in motor side effects, and a lower risk (not zero) of tardive dyskinesia. (40) The combination of serotonin activation and dopamine blockade increased **metabolic effects**: weight gain, increased cholesterol, and risk for DM. The variations in available medications have marginal differential benefit. Strong marketing of the newer agents emphasized the reduced risk of *tardive dyskinesia,* but the relative benefit of FGA and SGA medications is unclear with no head to head comparative studies performed by pharmaceutical companies or academic centers. (41) (41) *Side effects* are also synaptic effects and may be undesirable in one situation but useful in another. Enhanced sedation with quetiapine has milder motor system side effects, useful for promoting sleep in agitated patients. *Balancing desirable and undesirable effects is a challenge using these medications.* It is likely that these effects are the combination of adrenergic and serotonergic alterations in the motivation system, but studies confirming this have never been published. Such studies would clearly link responsibility for metabolic effects to the medications.

NIMH initiated the CATIE study to clarify the relative benefit/ risk of first or second-generation antipsychotics, whether EPS/ parkinsonism/TD or metabolic dysfunction was more important in selection. The multiple available medications, and individual variations led to an unusual research design, comparing several SGA agents with perphenazine, the most frequently used FGA at the time. This was not blinded and the targets were a) *tolerating the medication* (non-discontinuation) and b) *efficacy at FDA dose.* (42)

CLINICAL DATA The CATIE results showed: *a) PERPHENAZINE had the same discontinuation picture as the SGAs, its side effects did not result in more discontinuations, had the most EPS motor side effects, and the lowest cost. b) OLANZAPINE had the lowest discontinuation of all, was best tolerated, had best symptom resolution, but* **worst metabolic picture** *of both weight gain and increasing lipids. c) RISPERDONE had discontinuation in some patients for* **lack of symptom benefits** *(ineffective dosage), high prolactin level* **led to breast enlargement and discontinuation**, *and had significant EPS. d) QUETIAPINE* seemed best on **low EPS** *(it had been created for that), but high metabolic problems with weight gain and lipid elevations,and also QTC prolongation heart risk, with the **highest discontinuation.** e) ZIPRASIDONE had the **best metabolic** spectrum, had **good efficacy,** and second best tolerance by discontinuation. (43)*

The results failed to support a clear value for using SGA agents, or justification for the increased expense. None of the agents proved definitively superior to the others, even FGA perphenazine had relative advantages. The design has been criticized for not providing "blind" alternatives, but mimics clinical practice. The clinical reality is that individual patients respond differently to medications and experience different levels of side effects. Meta-analyses attempt to bridge the information gap of side effects by comparing different patient groups, and reflecting the biases of the original studies. A meta-analysis (in the Cochrane review database) of the few head to head studies (Leucht et al, in 2009) favored olanzapine and clozapine in separate arms, but only effectiveness on symptoms were evaluated, side effects and discontinuation were not considered! By ignoring the major problem side effects of clozapine, the review biased the conclusion. (44) The CATIE study was partly replicated in a similar study in adolescents. The outcome of CATIE sends a message that drug side effects play an important role in selection and use, and no medication has unique superiority. CATIE did not address the variability seen in individual response, so *predicting the individual response in advance of clinical use is not possible.* **The need to individualize care by using the patient's response to the medication does not benefit from "evidence based" statistical data.**

The options for managing "problem side effects" of anti-psychotic medications are:

A) Change to another medication with less of the problem effect. This can be done gradually without precipitating a return of psychosis.(45) (Papers reporting the danger are usually by authors funded by companies, and there is an obvious benefit to discouraging changes.)

B) Add an additional medication to counter the problem effect. The use of statin cholesterol medications, and metformin for managing glucose intolerance are examples, each of which produces other problems and risks. For basal ganglia side effects, atropinic agents (benztropine, etc.) have been used, but are not effective for TD. Medications developed for TD include valbenazine, documented to improve some instances, and now aggressively marketed for that use. Only long-term clinical experience will clarify valbenazine's benefit, optimal dosing, and risk. TD remains a risk for using D2 blocking agents. (46)

C) Poly-pharmacy: combine agents with different side effects at lower doses to combine efficacy with less problems from other side effects, minimizing the undesirable effect of eachmedication, while providing enough D2 for the antipsychotic effect. *Poly-pharmacy* poses the problems of allergic reactions to either medication, and multiple side effects, sometimes a benefit for reducing the intensity of undesired effects. (47) One study reports up to 50% use of poly-pharmacy in some settings. A large number of studies suggest this strategy, both independent studies which often support the practice, and studies by authors, company sponsored, who invariably warn against the practice. (48) The financial motivation for pharmaceutical companies against poly-pharmacy is obvious: it undermines the claim that each company's medication is sufficient for treatment.

D) Develop multi-receptor medications. New medications with multiple receptor sites have been developed to address side effects and also treat a wider range of symptoms with one (patented!) medication. This strategy creates several problems: site effects cannot be adjusted because they are on the same molecule, which was observed combining 5HT and D2 sites on the SGA molecule with undesirable metabolic effects of different intensities. The benefit of each site cannot be separately adjusted by changing the dose of the whole medication. Differences in individual response to each receptor site cannot be managed independently. *All these problems are avoided by using poly-pharmacy.* (49) For pharmaceutical companies, these multi-receptor site medications provide a new opportunity for patents, and are examples of the marketing fantasy of one "universal medication" to treat all mental health symptoms. (They are currently advertised in this way.)

This discussion of primary and secondary effects in anti-psychotic medications is an issue for all the medication types. A similar analysis can be done for evaluating the primary and other effects of 5-HT receptor actions of SSRI medications. (39) These have less marketing impact because of the efficacy problem in SSRIs, but may lead to discontinuations. The side effects of stimulants do have important clinical impact because their major use is in children. GABA synapses are so generalized that large doses of agents are not feasible, and the difference of primary and other effects is difficult to differentiate. Many drug interactions, and problem effects are only discovered after clinical experience. These are summarized in various locations, and become part of the medication's warning section documentation.

The use of every medication includes the decision to discontinue at a suitable time or continue use indefinitely. Medications may treat illnesses of short duration, or life long conditions. The inability to secrete insulin requires lifelong substitution. Bacterial infections are often reversed by a one to two week course of antibiotic, after which the medication is discontinued. The decision in mental health also depends on the basis of the pathway changes, and their course: is this a life long "chronic mental disorder", an intermittent episodic change, or a brief transient event? Pathway changes that are not reversible may benefit from ongoing treatment to prevent future problems. In some instances, recurrences may be prevented, but documentation of this benefit is poor. *Given the many side effects of medications, the shortest course is preferred.*

Psychosis syndrome, defined in chapter five, is a malfunction of the attention, activation, and choice pathways. The medications used to treat *psychosis syndrome*, from any cause, block D2 (dopamine) and are usually effective. Several questions guide the decision to discontinue. *Are the target symptoms resolved?* The target of antipsychotic medication is *psychosis syndrome*, so when the psychosis resolves, the medication can be discontinued. A short course reduces the risk of major side effects, and allows the mental status to clear from the medication effects. Patients often request this discontinuation when they are feeling clearer. In current treatment, an in-patient provider stabilizes the patient, who is transferred to a different practitioner for follow-up. The interruption makes medication adjustment more complicated. Medications usually reduce psychosis and allow the patient to return to a nonpsychotic state, a major advance in the field, but they do not treat all conditions that produce the psychosis, so some other intervention is needed or psychosis will return.

Is there another reason to continue the medication? The evidence that D2 blockers do not benefit the negative, withdrawal, or cognitive symptoms of schizophrenia syndromes, the core elements of the disorder (see chapter four) means this is not a reason to continue, especially if there is another medication or treatment to use (the use of clozapine, and olanzapine are discussed above). (50) Other etiologies of psychosis syndrome have other treatment options, for example, lithium and some anti-seizure medications show effectiveness in stabilizing bipolar syndrome, and preventing its recurrence after psychosis resolves. (50) Organic etiologies resolve by treatment of the biological disturbance. Understanding the etiology of the psychosis syndrome is essential in determining the treatment of the cause(s) of disturbance, and decisions about continuation. This is especially important in treatment of first episode psychosis, when a young person with onset of psychosis syndrome improves with medication. Ending the psychosis with dopamine blockers without treating the associated etiology may lead to return of psychosis. *Research studies that demonstrate continuing medication "prevents return of psychosis syndrome" also document the failure to offer any alternative treatment by omission.* In a frequently quoted paper, Wyatt reviewed a series of older studies of schizophrenia syndrome patients, including first episodes, which suggested that early use of medications led to more rapid improvement, and that discontinuations interfered with full recovery of function. He noted "little consensus among the authors" and his conclusions were based on his "reanalysis of the data". This led to the conclusion that early and continuous treatment of "schizophrenia" was beneficial. The meta-analysis included non-schizophrenic patients, and was unclear if "schizophrenia" and other psychoses were treated. (50)

> **SIDEBAR Psychosis syndrome and medication compliance.** *Psychosis is an aversive human experience that the individual is motivated to avoid. Medication non-compliance is an ongoing problem not because the person wishes to return to psychosis, but because, at typical doses of anti-psychotic medication, the person is dysphoric. The response to patient "non-compliance" is developing products for IM depot administration, at first for a month, but now approaching 6 mos per dose. (55) The IM route of administration overcomes efforts to discontinue medication; the depot delivery reduces the cost of management of long-term patients, but ignores the potential for chronic disability. Research studies confirm that IM depot medications prevent re-hospitalization, and psychosis syndrome, but do not document effective return of social function. (55) For pharmaceutical companies, altering the mode of delivery creates new patentable products using old molecules at reduced development cost. Some patients benefit from the control of psychosis syndrome and are also able to manage their own functional recovery.*

More recent studies have raised questions about long term treatment. Harrow et al identify the heterogeneity of long-term outcomes. (52) In a small prospective study participants with schizophrenia not on antipsychotics after the first 2 years had better outcomes than participants prescribed antipsychotics. The adjusted odds ratio of not on antipsychotic medication was 5.989 (95% CI 3.588–9.993) for recovery and 0.134 (95% CI 0.070–0.259) for re-hospitalization. That is, regardless of diagnosis, *after the second year, the absence of antipsychotics predicted a higher probability of recovery and lower probability of re-hospitalization at subsequent follow-ups.* Goff et al found that early treatment is beneficial, but long-term use less clear, and a need to identify which patients were at risk for relapse. A small study of first episode psychosis patients revealed that some were successful in discontinuation while others did better with continued use, and that collaborative involvement early in the process was helpful, but the study did not differentiate etiology or type of psychosis. (51) *The failure to differentiate schizophrenia syndrome from other "first episode psychoses" is another example of the failure to differentiate clinical syndromes.* Antipsychotic medications do not correct other etiologies that disrupt the pathways that produce the psychosis syndrome. Because the anti-psychotic medication does not treat the (other) etiology, if it is not treated some other way, then large continuing doses are needed to block the return of psychosis. (52) Whitaker has written an extensive critique of the dangers. (53) The multiple side effects produced by these medications (see earlier paragraphs and chapter six) involving PF/BG, interferes with learning changes in the PF/BG pathway which affects the ability to learn corrective socially adaptive patterns. (54) Careful discontinuation of dosage does not happen because no other treatments are instituted to facilitate learning new patterns. There is a need to identify which patients are most likely to benefit, and who might need some other treatment intervention. *This is another example of the failure to individualize treatment and evaluate outcome of social function.* "Evidence based treatments" which depend on statistical results are useful for indicating general patterns of treatment response, but ineffective in identifying differential individual response unless the data is examined in more detail. The trend to find evidence that supports continuation of medication is understandable in studies funded by pharmaceutical companies, but few alternative studies are available. *There is no pharmaceutical industry benefit for funding research on other treatments that stabilize syndromes without medication. This research must be funded some other way, and comparison studies with medication ignore the negative medication effects, focusing only on return of psychosis.*

After 5 decades of psychopharmacology, only 20% of patients on chronic anti-psychotic medication function independently. (53) Does this indicate that medications have long-term benefit? The focus on suppressing psychosis, positive symptoms, while ignoring other functions leaves cognitive and social impairment, and contributes to the syndrome "chronically mentally ill". Continuing a treatment for a problem without addressing the factors that create the

*CLINICAL EXAMPLE **Learning to manage mania**. A woman in her twenties was evaluated for recurring episodes of mania. She also had substance abuse problems. The manic episodes were predictable as she went into mania every year at the anniversary of her mother's death, and had become manic for the first time at the funeral. The woman was not manic at the time of evaluation, and was using cannabis. She contracted to discontinue cannabis and begin a low dose of an anti-manic medication, but refused to take a larger dose saying she didn't want to be "foggy". She agreed to increase the dose before becoming manic again, because previous episodes had cost her jobs, and created legal problems. She called within three months, around the anniversary time, stating that she could feel the symptoms starting with trouble sleeping and agitation. She increased her medication to slightly above the usual therapeutic dose and was seen the next week. She reported the symptoms were still there but mild, and she was starting to sleep more regularly. The dose was increased and she was seen the following week and was now back to her "normal" mood state. She was very pleased to discover she could control her manic episodes with adjustment of medication, and did not add an addictive substance. She maintained her function through the year, and was able to anticipate and adjust dosage with visits to prevent the next episode. COMMENT The anniversary of a death is an example of a trigger for recurring psychosis. In some persons with manic vulnerability, continued use of a high dose of medication is not acceptable because of the depressed mood. In this instance, an acceptable dose could be adjusted in time to abort a full manic episode because the patient and provider worked out an alliance to avoid the dangers of future episodes. (repeated example from chapter seven.)*

problem is not effective treatment. *Effective treatment re-establishes the patient's sense of agency over symptoms and restores social adaptation.* In children, teenagers, the elderly, and cognitively impaired, the same principles apply and must be adjusted to the developmental capacities of the individual. Similar issues arise in the discontinuation of antidepressant SSRI, and other medications. Persons with persisting depressed mood, with or without neuro-vegetative signs, pose a treatment challenge. (56) Continuing use of antidepressants does not appear to be helpful. It is difficult to understand the continuous use of SSRI medications when their effectiveness is low, and ineffective in severe depression, while milder depression is often self-limiting. Studies on "relapse" after discontinuation in a select patient group, fail to separate out the percentage that do not relapse and could be discontinued. *Discontinuation should always be based on resolution of target symptoms, treatment of underlying etiology, and effective return of functional capacity.*

Problem "side effects" become more complicated in special populations: pregnant women and children. Medication impacts the developing body and nervous system with unknown effects that may become life-long disabilities (or benefits!). Longitudinal multi-year monitoring is necessary to document the effects, which is expensive and rarely done. Evidence that some drugs produce immediate risk of fetal malformation (the historical example of thalidomide) has been challenged, but specific abnormalities are documented by independent studies, e.g. heart vessel abnormalities from some SSRIs. (57) Are these abnormalities more frequent than expected statistically? In some instances, yes, in others, less clear. Paroxetine for example is associated with a significant increase in cardiac defects by Berard et al, who was also consultant on a lawsuit. Einarson et al. collected the outcome of 1,174 infants from eight services and found no increase in cardiac problems; they concluded that studies that show an increase are minor, transient defects that resolve spontaneously; several of the authors were funded by pharmaceutical companies. Malm et al. used national population-based registries in Finland to compare the offspring of women who were and were not prescribed antidepressants during pregnancy and determined that use of paroxetine was associated with a small absolute increase in right ventricular outflow track defects; they had no competing financial interests. (57) *Are some studies compromised by financial bias in a subject with significant risk for patients? A clinician cannot spend time sorting through the disclosure statements of multiple studies, yet they may impact the findings.*

The FDA has rated psycho-pharmaceuticals by A/B/C/D risk classification. These are NOT based entirely on clinical outcomes but also use teratogenicity data from animal studies. According to this classification, certain medications have lower risk than others, and would be preferred:

Category A *Adequate and well-controlled studies have failed to demonstrate a risk to the fetus in the first trimester of pregnancy (and there is no evidence of risk in later trimesters).*

Category B *Animal reproduction studies have failed to demonstrate a risk to the fetus and there are no adequate and well-controlled studies in pregnant women.*

Category C *Animal reproduction studies have shown an adverse effect on the fetus and there are no adequate and well-controlled studies in humans, but potential benefits may warrant use of the drug in pregnant women despite potential risks.*

Category D *There is positive evidence of human fetal risk based on adverse reaction data from investigational or marketing experience or studies in humans, but potential benefits may warrant use of the drug in pregnant women despite potential risks.*

Category X *Studies in animals or humans have demonstrated fetal abnormalities and/or there is positive evidence of human fetal risk based on adverse reaction data from investigational or marketing experience, and the risks involved in use of the drug in pregnant women clearly outweigh potential benefits.*

The contentious debates in publications (a sample are included in the references) are not helpful. (58) The wish for a "correct answer" to this issue is a fantasy. Medications have different effects on different individuals, including the developing fetus. Many effects on neural development and behavior, positive or negative, are graduated, manifesting in subtle ways over the lifetime of the person, and may be more powerful at specific stages in development. The task of monitoring and documenting these different possibilities would only be possible with a complete birth registry and "big data" computational support. (59) The lack of long term monitoring of the health of individuals in the United States, and the cost of long term data management, (and the privacy issues), make it impossible to gather the long term data needed to answer these questions with precision (Scandinavian countries are more effective.) *The government could make this a cost of business for pharmaceutical companies wishing to use medications on pregnant women and children, but so far no effort has been made, and the companies have not taken on the responsibility as an industry.*

The clinician, considering medication for a pregnant woman should follow a conservative course:

1) *Don't use psycho-pharmacology medications during pregnancy if possible.*
2) *If mental health symptoms interfere with management of pregnancy and self care,* **avoid agents with documented teratogenic effects**, *even when sponsored studies say this is only "statistical", use medications with low risk,*
3) *Inform the pregnant mother of the known risk level when seeking consent*
4) *Start medication as late as possible into the pregnancy at lowest dose, and discontinue with improvement if possible, especially a few weeks before delivery*
5) *Restart after delivery if symptoms return, unless nursing is involved.*

In post-partum, the child is no longer directly exposed to the mother's medication (unless nursing at the breast), but treatment is urgent when the mother is unable to care for the newborn. The role of dramatic hormonal changes in producing or facilitating post partum disturbance has been documented. And a new medication appears to address some of these directly. Discussion of medications for post-partum syndromes is referred to the references where several syndromes are observed and treated. (60) As in other interventions, understanding pathway syndromes guides treatment, there is no single "post partum" illness. (See chapter three)

Using medications in children has several issues. Some conditions, like *autism syndrome*, have no proven benefit from medications. The decision to initiate medications for problems in *behavior control* seen in early childhood (chapter six) depends on the family's tolerance of the behavior. The syndromes of executive control treated with stimulants may improve focus of attention for school cognitive performance, and better social integration. *Is the medication effective?* Studies that show improved ratings of behavior control, and cognitive performance are available, but the effects are not equal across children, some do worse. (61) ADHD was originally considered a specific disorder, but newer studies suggest that multiple etiologies disrupt the pathway, and the diagnosis covers a range of frontal-prefrontal pathway changes than interfere with motor and cognitive focus. (See chapter six) (61) *How to balance effects and other effects?* Stimulants suppress appetite and have been used in adults as weight loss medications, a problem when used in children with effects on development. The dosage and type of stimulant is different for different patients, and comparative studies determining the factors have not been done. (62) So the practitioner is required to select among agents based on the child's response and personal preferences. Pharmaceutical companies focus on changes in mode of delivery because short acting medications do not cover the time interval needed for afternoon school function.

When to discontinue stimulants in children? Historically, workers, and the military, use stimulants to maintain attention, in adults, used stimulants and long haul truckers still sometimes use them. (63) The degree of focus needed for specific life tasks varies and adult work responsibilities vary in their demand for focus. It is likely that some adults diagnosed and treated with stimulants for "ADHD" use them to enhance performance of tasks demanding intense focus. Do stimulants treat a pathway dysfunction or augment a natural capacity: is the medication being used to correct a deficit or enhance performance? This is not an FDA approved use for a controlled substance, but probably occurs more frequently than realized. Others use stimulants to improve deficits in PF/BG pathways that are childhood residuals.

Deciding if stimulant medications are overprescribed children, and what long-term effects, positive and negative, they have, requires more study. Is the decision for discontinuation of stimulant medication related to the maturation of pathways? Assuming that all children or teens "grow out" of the syndrome of ADHD is not confirmed by some longitudinal studies. (64) Some children have etiologies that are not reversible, not delayed development. Since etiology is not differentiated in studies, these differences cannot be targeted in treatment. Narcolepsy is not reversible, so discontinuation is inadvisable. A concern that using a potentially addictive substance, a stimulant, makes the child more vulnerable to addiction is not documented, but might be an issue for vulnerable individuals. (64) The long term impact on the developing nervous system requires long term studies that have not been carried out. Does correcting a pathway dysfunction, temporary or ongoing, enable the child to stabilize the pathway and eventually allow discontinuation? Does using medication to stabilize a pathway interfere with long term self correction of the pathway? Does using medication that improves social function benefit independently? Limited short-term studies cannot differentiate these outcomes.

Do SSRI antidepressants increase suicidal thoughts and behaviors in children and teens? This is another example of an important unresolved issue. Unsponsored studies from England reporting this, were countered by a series of studies, performed by sponsored investigators who concluded that there was no "statistical difference" in the incidence of these behaviors or thoughts between treated and untreated depressed teens in various studies, reviewed retrospectively. This allows deniability of responsibility for effects of medication, but it seems odd that no one commented that this also shows *the failure to reduce the suicidal manifestations of treatment in this group.* An effective treatment for depression in children would reasonably be expected to reduce these symptoms. This is another example of the controversy that emerges in the treatment of vulnerable populations and the failure to obtain clear evidence for a resolution using conflicting "evidence based" studies with varying interpretation. Black box warnings were eventually added to these medications for children and teens.

Pharmacological interventions are not information specific. Chemical agents modify synaptic transmission in pathways transmitting information and the changes may be beneficial or detrimental alterations. If the medication reduces anxiety signals, it may do so for all anxiety, both emotional and real life dangers; and the reduction of fear in dangerous situations may be undesirable. SSRIs are sometimes effective in modifying mood, regardless of etiology; but using medication for mood changes in grieving has been challenged. Medications may enhance social adaptation by reducing symptoms at lower doses, as in the social effects of alcohol, and impair social adaptation at higher doses by reducing emotional sensitivity. Finding this inflection when prescribing must involve the patient. If the dose is optimized, the patient experiences the medication as an ally for improving life. Biological and information interventions (chapter twelve) can interact to alter the same pathways. *After pathway symptoms improve, the person must still solve the problems of life. Pharmacologic interventions are not "curative" without interventions that produce corrective life adjustments.* The current separation in providers and methods disconnects the discussion into different chapters of interventions, a reality that limits effective use. The client may make the adjustments without counseling or fail to do so. "Experts" have different opinions about the interactions: An expert in psychopharmacology describes psychotherapy as an "alternative drug" intervention, ignoring the difference in information content. (65) The "mind/body split" persists for someone who suggest that the two methods are separate, unrelated, and act in different ways. (66) An *information pathway* model of how the different methods overlap includes ways to balance their effects for optimal use. (Some comments on their interactions will be presented in chapter 12.)

Government agencies regulate psychopharmacology. Regulations differ from country to country based on social and political issues not closely related to pharmacology. The guidelines are misleading, but must be followed for legal reasons, and address three aspects:

a) clinical benefit: In the United States, a company must prove medication "efficacy", a significant benefit improving some disorder, to be marketed. Because of the added expense of proving efficacy for different uses, studies are often not repeated, and a proportion of current usage is *"off label"*, i.e. not for the use originally approved. (67)

b) safety: A company must prove safety to FDA standards showing low toxicity and "tolerable" side effects observed during clinical trials. These are reported in clinical trials, but other problem effects often emerge in later use with a longer course of treatment. The side effect risk differs for different drug classes, and risk of addiction is an important consideration. There is growing FDA tolerance for releasing medications with increased risk for unknown reasons.

c) The designation and control of distribution of chemicals considered a risk for addiction. This depends on historical, social, and legal traditions that ignore psychopharmacology, and do not reflect potential addictive dangers. Alcohol, an extremely dangerous psycho-chemical, with known addiction, side effects, and toxicity to major organs, is readily available in US without prescription (at food stores in some states), while gabapentin, a low toxicity neuroactive drug with no known addictive potential is available by prescription only. Thomas Szasz wrote **Ceremonial Chemistry** (1970) giving examples of this inconsistency and criticizing the regulatory process. (68)

The safe use of psychopharmacology can be viewed as a three legged stool: 1) the pharmaceutical manufacturers do studies of the efficacy and safety, 2) the government regulatory agency evaluates reports and guides or restricts use, and 3) providers administer according to these guidelines and inform users of dangers. When all three "legs" perform their functions effectively, the public is protected, and has effective treatments available. If any of the "legs" fails, the public is put at risk. This has become a problem for more than a decade. The continuing production and distribution of excessive amounts of addictive substances is epidemic today in the US. This is not a hypothetical issue but a description of the opiate crisis of the last twenty years, which is not over. (70)

> **SIDEBAR An example of regulatory confusion is cannabinols.** Herbal products incorporating cannabis or related substances were part of the National Formulary and marginally regulated until the Marijuana Tax act of 1937 that taxed and monitored the product's sale. The Controlled Substances Act of 1970 placed it in Schedule I, the most restrictive category, making it illegal to use or experiment with for any purpose. The decision to limit the research and development of cannabinols was a conservative political reaction to the turmoil of the 1960s and bears no relation to pharmaceutical reality. Schedule I prohibited research in the US on these chemicals, so developing potential uses and safety was delayed for several decades. Several points are clear: 1) There are brain receptors specific to cannabinol-like substances which have a range of potentially useful clinical properties. 2) Evidence that some of the medications impact the motivation system is also clear, but how to use these actions effectively is not clear. 3) There is some risk of addiction and/or psychosis syndrome, but the widespread use makes it unclear if this statistical or specific to certain individuals. Psychiatry appears to be divided in exploring or rejecting legalization of cannabis. An industry has developed to produce and market the natural substance. The pharmaceutical industry is currently attempting to develop synthetic alternatives that can be patented. The failure of the scientific community to accurately address the issues in the face of political pressure is an example of the complex social context of mental health practice. The most recent and extensive example has been the expansion of cannabis use among patients in states where it is legalized. (71)
>
> **Nicotine** is an especially interesting example because there is evidence that it improves cognitive function and might be useful in treatment, but it is very addictive, not patentable, but economically valuable to tobacco companies, so currently it is not under FDA regulation. (It is taxed under the supervision of the ATF administration.) (69)

The naming of psychotropic drugs is confusing. It has been guided by marketing and patent regulation, and should be revised. When the synthesis of a new *chemical structure* is confirmed by spectroscopy, a *chemical name* is created that is unique to the chemical structure and part of the patent application. If the chemical proves to have marketing potential, a second name is given which is easier to remember and can be *trademarked* for protection. The *clinical application* creates a third name/description, "antidepressant", "antipsychotic", etc. related to FDA efficacy and use. The nomenclature/classification of psychopharmacologic agents should reflect all these basic properties, a view also advocated by European union providers. (72) A proposed system is shown in the following table using the chemical **diazepam**. The proposed system clarifies confusion over drugs like atomoxetine, labeled for depression in Europe, for ADHD in the US, and chemically, an SNRI, and all valid. The proportion of drug usage that falls in the category "off label", which can be used, but not promoted without incurring penalties, should be included in naming *if documented*. Pharmaceutical marketing that promotes only the trademark has resisted changes of nomenclature. The following is a slight variation on the European proposal but has the same objective of improving categorization of medications. (73)

REVISED PSYCHOPHARMACOLOGY NOMENCLATURE:

<u>**A (chemical) chemical family:**</u> The chemical structure links to the primary chemistry generating the product. The family includes similar agents. **(Example, diazepam: benzodiazepines)**.

<u>**B (pharmacological receptor effects):**</u> The main action at synaptic receptor sites, and the primary information pathway affected. This category is complicated because drug development combines different receptor properties within one molecule. The pharmacological properties overlap, and the primary receptor target may be arbitrary. **(Example: GABA agonist)**

<u>**C (demonstrated clinical effects, treatment and side effects)**</u>
Clinically demonstrated effects indicate the therapeutic goals, FDA **approved,** and **documented off-label effects. (Example: antiseizure, antianxiety, OffLabel: alcohol detox.)** Side effects: (including toxic or dangerous side effects are a subcategory): sedation, respiratory depression.

<u>**D (social-political) agency certified uses and restrictions, regulatory controls, schedules etc:**</u> The FDA status along (and other national regulatory agencies), must be recognized for clinical purposes. what restrictions on use are in place (Example: **FDA Class IV.**)

APPENDIX: OTHER BIOPHYSICAL INTERVENTIONS

The other biophysical interventions used in Psychiatry are surgery, convulsive treatment, trans cranial magnetic/electric stimulation, and direct brain or vagal stimulation. Most, like psychopharmacology, were discovered serendipitously, and none has a theoretical basis. They are generally used for patients who do not respond to psychopharmacology. The following comments suggest the current role they play as minor interventions. *These methods should all be considered experimental treatments with limited evidence of effectiveness, though this is not always how they are promoted.*

Convulsive Interventions were the first to be developed and utilized in the 1930s. Sakel used newly discovered insulin injections to lower blood sugar and induce coma in patients. von Meduna explored a similar technique using metrazole injections, which produced seizures, because, according to his "theory", his hospitalized patients with seizures did not have psychotic episodes. (A finding at odds with the later studies of Slater and Beard, see chapter 4.) The technique was refined by Cerletti in 1937 using electrical stimulation across the scalp to induce seizures, the only convulsive intervention still in use. Although the procedures are carefully designed and electronic devices administer the treatment, there is nothing inherently "scientific" about the process, including the limited documentation of optimal administration parameters. The review by Kellner et al summarizes that the treatment requires full seizures, bilateral placement of electrodes, and repeated episodes over a short interval of days, typically three times per week for several weeks, and memory consolidation is impaired for some time after the course of interventions. Without these effects the treatments are not effective. (74) Four theories are proposed: monoamine neurotransmitters are altered, that neuroendocrine stress causes the effects, that ECT causes "protective" changes against convulsions, and a neurotropic theory that nerve growth is enhanced. Despite over 80 years in use, no evidence for these mechanisms is conclusive. A range of studies have shown a variety of transmitter and MRI activity changes after ECT, which are correlations of the effect, consistent with disrupting pathways, and understood in the same sense that changes in brain after psychotherapy or psychopharmacology document the effects, not causal. Practitioners take great pride in ECT as a "biological treatment", but the most likely explanation is ECT acts like the RESET on the brain computer, disrupting pathway activity, with loss of *significance* memory, and interference with a broad range of pathways, including ones associated with the clinical dysfunction, i.e. *its effect is information based. Studies consistently show that some measurable cognitive disruption must occur for change.* (75) The disruptive effects of ECT provide no guarantee of a return to a more desirable pattern of brain function, but the patient may "reset" to a previous desirable mode. (76) A major effort over the years to identify the ideal parameters of treatment to minimize the negative and maximize the desirable effects has limited agreement. Evaluation of effectiveness of ECT as a treatment is complicated because it is employed when other methods are ineffective, so comparison evaluation is not typical. "Heroic care" means there is no other option. Many uncontrolled case series report positive results, but few are blinded controlled studies. Less severe patients respond better but are not the usual ones selected for treatment. (76) Redlich et al used an AI method of identifying MRI abnormalities in "subgenual cingulate cortex" a relatively large area, to identify patients most likely to respond, which has not been replicated. (77) ECT is not performed by most providers, which creates a group of "ECT specialists" who promote its value. Recent FDA and British regulatory agencies have narrowed the use, and regulated the equipment. (79) Nothing is known about the long-term cognitive impact of repeated treatments. The interaction of ECT with other treatment modalities is affected by the interference in memory consolidation in the immediate phase that means that psychosocial interventions cannot be used immediately. *To include ECT in the range of treatment options, studies identifying the preferred characteristics for patient selection, treatment course, dosing, electrode placement and pulse characteristics should be documented. At present, there is no database for these parameters.*

Trans cranial Magnetic Stimulation (TMS) ECT is not localizable to one region, because the seizures must affect the total brain. The alternative, altering specific regions by local intervention lead to the development of TMS. Instead of an electrical current applied across the skull surface, a magnetic field pulse is applied locally, which creates a *local electric current*. This prevents spread of the applied current and avoids seizures (though they occur occasionally). The *rheobase level* (the current needed to induce neural axon depolarization) can be evaluated and pulses created at twice this level to *produce local axon discharge*. The more localized less traumatic effect is offset by less clear results. A variety of systems have been developed for the technique, and localization and pulse parameters of the method are still in development. The original technique only affects surface transmission; the ability to induce deep brain effects requires a special H coil system. FDA approval exists for treatment of depression in the surface device, and for the H coil device. (80) A short paper by Hallett gives a feeling for the potential for local control, though not for mental health symptoms. He reviewed localizing response to motor cortex, showing the control possible using the surface TMS device. (81) Reports of effective treatment for depression and OCD have weak documentation, and duration of effects is limited. The cortical regions most identified in emotion: cingulate, insula, and OFC, are not readily accessible by surface TMS stimulation. DLPFC is accessible and effects on working memory have been documented. But this region is not primary for affect. The development of the H coil makes deeper areas accessible, but with less localization and control, and an increase in seizures. (82) It would make sense to have academic centers carry out detailed studies to assess effective procedures, instead of studies by equipment manufacturers' seeking rapid support for the method. A study at Stanford attempts to refine the parameters. (83) The presumption that

TMS can provide a more localized effect is offset by the problem of not reaching deeper brain regions. Evaluation of parameters is also incomplete. The area of cortex stimulated may be important for the local effects. Future studies will determine whether the procedure extends beyond the exploratory stage. (83)

Electrode Implantation. To access deeper brain regions, with accurate localization, it is necessary to implant electrodes, guided by a stereotaxic frame, for direct stimulation of a local region. This technique has been used for a decade as an intervention for controlling some symptoms of Parkinson's disease. The experience in PD suggests that these procedures do not significantly alter the disease course but improve function and reduce medication use. If psychiatric conditions involve abnormal activity in pathways there should be a similar method for modifying the pathway activity. (84) Mayberg and others have explored the electrode technique with direct stimulation to the brain regions they identified in depressed patients. This approach maximizes every aspect of the physical intervention: it is local, non convulsive (usually) and depolarizing, producing a response intended to enhance the relevant cell assembly pathways. A case example and discussion is provided at (86) Report of a 20 patient series in 3-6 yr. follow-up showed generally improved symptoms and life function over the time course. The subcollosal cingulate gyrus white matter bundle was the location of the implants. 4.7v 124Hz stimulus delivered. Despite the positive summary, 2 suicides, several re-hospitalizations, and ongoing use of medication were reported. These results do not indicate a sudden dramatic improvement but rather some modest amelioration of a chronic condition. For the NAc target, it has been shown that continuous stimulation was more effective than intermittent stimulation, but does not resolve the condition. Several other labs have reported using the techniques, sometimes varying the location of electrode. The results are also modestly positive but not dramatic. One key issue in implanted stimulation is the relationship to pathway function. Generally only one electrode can be implanted, and sites helpful in PD have been identified. For depression and other mental health pathways, finding the most effective node is challenging, and current pathway modeling is of limited value for this task. (85) This technique is in the early stages of development, and the parameters and location for best effects remain for future research. And this is an "heroic" intervention. There is no obvious corporate source for funding such procedures, and so it will depend on NIMH or other government sources for future development.

An approach to stimulating the vagus nerve external to its entry to the skull has been tried by several research groups. The multiple functions of vagus, and its connection to primary motivation system sites, made it a likely choice for intervention. The initial trials did not show significant changes in non-responding depression, but FDA approval was awarded as an adjunct treatment. A meta-review of 255 nonrandomized cases also failed to show a significant effect. Vagus stimulation does not appear to be a significant treatment for non-responding depression, but might be more valuable in dealing with somatic symptom illnesses, which has not been evaluated. (86)

Psychosurgery. Using surgery to intervene in brain and mental health issues has an unsuccessful history. In the 1950s-60s surgery to interrupt seizure spread led to the discovery of the functions of corpus callosum (described in chapter one). The unfortunate accident of Nicholas **Gage** in the late 19th century encouraged Moniz to develop the procedure of lobotomy, in 1948, awarded the Nobel Prize in 1949. This procedure transects axon pathways between sub cortex and the orbital region (parts of the OFC). After a surge of interest and use in the 1950s, poor results, persistent failure of social adaptation requiring institutional care, and the irreversibility, all led to abandonment of the procedure. More precise techniques might be possible with gamma knife radiation methods, but the interpenetration of brain tissue and overlap of critical regions makes precision difficult for surgical methods. Reports of surgery on *amygdala for aggression in children* and teens seem premature given the potential for development in children and the limited understanding. It also seems to ignore data on amygdala hippocampal damage and risk of Kluver Bucy syndrome (chapter four). Lobotomy has not been performed in US since 1967.

Temporal lobe surgery for seizure disorders continues to be a neuro-surgical procedure with 6300 cases from 2000-2013. These patients often have emotionally related symptoms and the review does not clarify the extent to which these are improved. Neurosurgery is not currently a significant element in mental health treatment in the US. (87) There are no current reports of controlled studies or managed case series in which a psychosurgery intervention reliably improves mental functioning. It is likely that some procedures are being done around the country, but the failure to report the results speaks to the failure to accomplish a consistent positive outcome.

A science fiction view of brain stimulation envisions an array of stimulating electrodes sending a complex signal into the brain, something like the MATRIX movies. There are promoters of this technology: "A true fluid neural integration is going to happen," Leuthardt says. "It's just a matter of when. If it's 10 or 100 years in the grand scheme of things, it's a material development in the course of human history." (88) There are currently devices for simpler motor device integration to allow the individual to interface motor direction with a prosthesis limb, and computer linked speech has been developed. (89) In March 2017, Elon Musk, a founder of Tesla and SpaceX, launched Neuralink, a venture aiming to create devices that facilitate mind-machine melds. Facebook's Mark Zuckerberg has expressed similar dreams, and in the spring of 2017 his company revealed that it has 60 engineers working on building interfaces that would let you type using just your mind. Bryan Johnson, the founder of the online payment system Braintree, is using his fortune to fund Kernel, a company that aims to develop neuroprosthetics he hopes will eventually boost intelligence, memory, etc. The ability to create information transmission interface with pathways is currently limited to peripheral motor functions, but as the understanding of pathway transmission expands, other options are possible.

CHAPTER TWELVE:
Information interventions

All life experiences, daily activities, and dramatic events reprogram brain pathways. When the brain is being modified for physical performance, it is called "training". ("She is in training for the Olympics.") When the brain is being modified for cognitive development, it is called "learning". ("He is learning algebra this year.") When the brain is being modified for emotional and social development, it is called "psychotherapy". ("She is learning to manage her depression".) Psychotherapy is learning to modify pathways to improve social adaptation using information.

Healers, "wise men", curanderas, and shamans have counseled others for eons, but current techniques evolved from a method developed by Freud and his followers. Freud was a physician, treating patients with physical complaints, who developed a method of inquiry, psychoanalysis that was helpful in resolving puzzling symptoms. (PSA is used throughout the chapter and book as an acronym for **ps**ycho**a**nalysis.) Other practitioners produced many variations of his method, which raised two questions: Are there basic features for the process to be effective? Is there a "universal psychotherapy" which applies to all dysfunctions or are specific procedures needed for each disturbance?

For decades after psychotherapy became popular, researchers tried to answer the two questions, seeking the "essential components", the factors that would validate all methods, and be the basis for teaching the skill. Rosenzweig's factors (1936) were a)

SIDEBAR Freud and Psychotherapy. Sigmund Freud, a Neurologist-Psychiatrist, treated patients with atypical neurological (and other) symptoms, by listening and talking to them. The detailed history of his methods is covered in several sources (1). "Talk therapy" did not fit the physiological model of disease in the medical community at the time, which was seeking biological causes in postmortem specimens, and his work was criticized. A small community of European providers utilized his method, and refugee physicians fleeing Nazi Germany emigrated to US (Freud to England) expanding its use. Treatment of war trauma in WW2 supported the technique, and by the mid 20th century, it was the favored method of Psychiatric treatment in the US. Psychiatrists were trained to use it, and PSA, the method, had cultural recognition. Variations, developed by other practitioners, expanded the field and created controversies. Jung emphasized cultural imagery and a collective (genetic?) unconscious. The "object relations" school at Tavistock Clinic, London, emphasized early child development, and corresponding interpersonal issues in adult life. Early theories did not include the "self" as separate from "ego", and Erikson added this. Lacan promoted a verbally focused process, suis generis, combining PSA, Marxist, and other cultural memes. By 1975, a diminishing number of providers across the country (and world) utilized PSA, modifying or replacing it by other methods. The two factors most important in the decline in the U.S. were the increased use of psychopharmacology, and health insurers unwilling to cover the extended costs, claiming no evidence of effectiveness. Few current psychiatric residency programs make psychotherapy a required skill, and few current residents enter PSA training.

PSA has been changing in recent years. Since the 1990s, a "relational turn" has shifted from one person psychology based on drives, to interaction between persons and the needs for attachment, and emotional regulation. (see chapter seven) New conceptions of the "self" as a complex experience are recognized as part of development. Data on *mirror neurons"* has influenced the concept of empathy. And the modern authors are attempting to integrate the earlier concepts with corresponding neurophysiologic components. A review of these changes can be found in Schalkwijk's paper on "conscience". (1)

personality of the therapist, b) formal consistency of the ideology and c) creating an alternative formulation of the events of patient's life. Franks' "4 factors" were (a) an emotionally charged, confiding relationship with a helping person (b) a healing setting (c) a rationale, conceptual scheme, or myth that provides a plausible explanation for the patient's symptoms, and prescribes a ritual or procedure for resolving them, and (d) a ritual or procedure that requires the active participation of both patient and therapist and that is believed by both to be the means of restoring the patient's health. Strupp and colleagues did research on the interpersonal features. He was trained in PSA and especially interested in the client-therapist relationship, described by Carl Rogers and developed a process scale similar to Rogers', measuring the "congruence" between therapist and client. Research on "basic factors" was difficult to perform, the results of studies were frequently inconclusive, and eventually the task of identifying common factors was replaced by development of "evidence supported treatments"(EST). (2)

EST research validates a specific technique for clients with specific symptoms. The patients are selected by symptoms, and the technique is performed by trained providers. The studies of effectiveness of EST methods meet insurance company requirements of efficacy, and providers obtain reimbursement. Beck's cognitive therapy for depression, Rational Emotive Therapy, and Dialectical Behavior Therapy are examples. Each requires training and certification of the clinician to be a valid provider of the technique. *The EST strategy provides a path to documentation of efficacy at the expense of identifying essential elements.* Studies do not compare EST methods, and the specification does not identify essential factors, only the procedure. Several reviewers have discussed these limitations. Wampold has reviewed the early efforts to define basic factors and its replacement by EST. Castelnuovo contrasts the current approaches to understanding the common elements and methods. He proposes an alternative strategy to be discussed later in the chapter. There are reasonable doubts that EST provides a broad standard of effectiveness, as reviewed by Weston. (3) The EST approach creates a basis for exclusive training, because insurers require "certification" of EST providers for payment. NIMH has shown no interest in financing research in this area, and there is no obvious alternative source to finance comparison studies. A list of EST is at (4) The "common factors" approach aims to modify a general adaptive skills; the EST approach uses psychotherapy to change specific symptoms. The decline in training and use of psychotherapy by psychiatrists parallels the increased use of EST by non-Psychiatric providers. The difference in providers has increased the controversy over the methods without addressing the key issues. (3) Social interaction is a complex system of self/other pathways, and Weston, et al. question whether treating specific symptoms can be done independent of this context. (Weston, 3) *In the absence of comparative studies, the question cannot be answered.*

This chapter identifies some features common to all procedures, suggesting a basis for comparison of the two approaches. The key factors are unknown, but these variables may be involved. The terms "psychotherapy" and "re-programming" are both used to describe interventions using information presented over sensory channels to modify pathways. With a few exceptions, bio-physical procedures are not involved. "Psychotherapy" is used when more traditional methods are discussed, and "re-programming" to emphasize the general nature of the process. The following are the basic features of reprogramming procedures:

A) the quality of the interpersonal interaction
B) What information is transferred over which sensory modalities
C) Whether the recipient actively or passively involved, or some combination
D) Whether special procedures are used in reprogramming
E) How the brain is reorganized by the process
F) How effectiveness is measured

These features *could* generate useful comparison studies including comparison of effectiveness.

The Characteristics Of The Interpersonal Interaction. Reprogramming is an interpersonal process with varying levels of intensity:

Level 0: The individual uses resources (information) developed by others with *no direct personal interaction*. This method gets little attention from mental health professionals, and little research.

It includes tapes, apps, internet sites (not live), and other prepared materials. These are sometimes incorporated with other levels as an addition. There are sites for self hypnosis on the web! (5) There are few studies of their effectiveness. (6) Persons who self correct using personal experiences ("the encounter with a stranger that changed my life"), do not receive mental health services, so their outcomes are not documented.)(A list of resources for *self correction* is included in this ref: 7)

Levels, 1,2, and 3 have direct interaction with a provider (this may occur in real time (live) over an internet audio-visual channel). Greenson and Wexler describe three features that characterize the levels: (8)

The therapeutic alliance ("professional relationship") includes all the (role) expectations for the interaction as a professional (not personal) relationship. This includes scheduling, payment, general behaviors expected of both parties in the sessions, and consequences if the expectations are not met, i.e. the **structure** of the relationship (e.g. charge for canceling in less than 24 hours). The "therapeutic alliance" is a contract, sometimes adjusted in the real interaction in response to a situation. How goals are defined depends on both parties, and also on external factors, like insurance coverage.

The transference relationship (a PSA term) is the pattern of learned behavior and expectations about interpersonal relationships acquired in childhood and other life situations, and enacted by the client in interactions with the therapist (and with others). Learned behavior patterns are "transferred" from earlier life situations to current ones. Although the term originated in PSA it is a universal aspect of social learning: everyone's social interaction is learned from prior experiences. These patterns are also present in the re-programmer-psychotherapist, where they are called *counter-transference* though their origin is the same, and may also create problems. (Szasz identified these as the same learned behavior as the client's and the difference in terminology as a linguistic convention of PSA. (9)) How the therapist "manages" his or her patterns of *counter-transference* is important. (10) The stronger the emotional intensity of interaction, the more likely emotional transferences will occur, which may be outside of immediate awareness in the patient/client, and also the therapist.

All the features of the interaction, which do not fall under the previous categories, comprise *the real relationship*. This includes the appearance of both parties, the decoration and setting of the office, the tone of voice of the therapist, etc. Neither therapist nor patient can eliminate these aspects, but they may be adjusted (as when the therapist sits behind the patient out of view).

The therapeutic alliance and intensity of the transference vary in different treatment methods. The real relationship varies only with the participants and the physical arrangements. Three different levels of interaction are described, but the actual process is a continuum of varying levels of mutuality and decreasing control by the re-programmer.

Level One: The re-programmer's role is limited to advisory recommendations and structured interventions, and the emotional contact between the parties is minimized. The *therapeutic alliance* is a highly structured, defined role for both parties, limiting *transference*. The client performs actions directed by the re-programmer. Methods might include informing the patient of how to use birth control, suggesting coping techniques for anxiety control, etc. The process is structured.

> **CLINICAL EXAMPLE** *The therapist is a trainer modifying the patient's behavior using a direct reward/punishment process.* Applied Behavior Therapy for children with serious behavior problems including autism uses behavior reinforcement methods. The therapist gives rewards directly to the child, or may instruct a parent on how to do so.(11)

The issue of Level One is **control**. Is reprogramming "brainwashing" where one person control's another person's thoughts and emotions? Trust, reliability, and consistency are emphasized in Rogers' ***Characteristics Of A Healing Relationship,*** using the concept "unconditional positive regard", a *non-judgmental* stance. (12) When this is the intent, the control is centered on the client's needs.

CLINICAL EXAMPLE Therapist as detective. *A woman in her 30s was being treated for depression and other symptoms related to severe abuse as a child. She would occasionally visit her mother who was still alive, but failing, and had never confronted her mother about her abuse. On one visit the patient injured her leg and was seen by the local elderly doctor. She noticed that the doctor had the same strawberry blond hair that she, and no one else in her family, had. The therapist commented that maybe she got her hair color from the doctor. The patient eventually confronted her mother, confirmed the affair that her mother had never admitted, but her father knew anyway, who was severely abusive to the patient. The information helped her understand that she was not responsible for the abuse.*

Level Two: The individual interacts freely with a psychotherapist who responds with controlled participation. This is the level of interaction in PSA and most psychotherapy. *Theory of mind* assumes that both therapist and patient are actively aware of each other's participation, and the intended outcome. The client enacts the **transference** of previously learned patterns of emotion and behavior, while the therapist/re-programmer *manages* the reciprocal ***counter-transference***, to maintain a "neutral" environment. Newton has written a detailed social-psychological role description in neutral interaction terms, not dependent on PSA language. (13) The client develops expectations, a "fantasy relationship", while the therapist responds only *enough* to be involved. Ideally, the therapist does not express emotional reactions to the patient, a capacity developed through training, but many have written about the real, sometimes intense, emotions that occur, requiring discipline to manage. (14) When preparing to make important life changes, it helps to have an "imaginary world" in which to "play", to "try things out", a safe place to make mistakes without major consequences. (15) The relationship is asymmetric, with limits on the re-programmer who observes certain boundaries. This is also described in Newton's "Abstinence as a role requirement of psychotherapy" describing the limits in social-psychological terms. (13) The emotional intensity ranges from (less intense) issues of the past, (except PTSD experiences), to (more intense) current life space, to (most intense) issues in the fantasy relationship in the here and now.

Level three: the individual interacts with the re-programmer, who responds with emotional responses and "authentic" personal disclosure. The client and re-programmer are in a *transactional relationship*. (Some consider this a breakdown of Level 2 boundaries.) Contemporary PSA, i.e. Langs, envisions a more mutual interaction. (16) Searles wrote several papers on the intense counter-transferences he experienced. (17) This change may occur when the patient is "acting in" behavior in the session. A presentation of Level three is found in Whitaker and Malone, ***The Roots Of Psychotherapy*** where it is called "experiential psychotherapy" because *the therapist and client are both engaged in the experience of the therapy*. They describe "therapist vectors", and "patient vectors" in both seeking to help and receive help from the other, often outside their awareness. (18) The therapist *can receive re-programming from the patient*, illustrated in the one act play ***EMERGENCY***, by Hellmuth Kaiser:

> **CLINICAL EXAMPLE EMERGENCY** *In this one act play, the wife of a psychiatrist asks another psychiatrist to pose as a patient, and seek therapy with her husband. The psychiatrist-husband is depressed and suicidal, but refuses to get treatment for himself or stop his practice. The psychiatrist-posing-as-patient engages the suicidal-psychiatrist to influence his emotional state. How often something like this happens in real therapy situations is unknown, because this topic has never been researched and rarely discussed. Both participants are always acting strategically towards each other for an outcome, which may be different from what each consciously understands. (19)*

The re-programmer's role differs between Levels Two and Three, but the boundary issue of gratification for the therapist does not change. When the process maintains integrity, the re-programmer engages more of his/her person, but still avoids exploiting the patient for *self-gratification*. If this fails, the relationship degrades into abuse or exploitation of the client, as when the therapist engages in sexual activity with the client. The asymmetrical relationship (usually) does not provide emotional support for the re-programmer. (13,15) The therapist derives only financial support, and perhaps some recognition of skill. There is general agreement that sexual relationships are not acceptable, but boundary "blurring" may occur, i.e. the giving of "gifts", or special favors, which may not be recognized by the psycho-therapist, i.e. the *real relationship* cannot be entirely eliminated. Changes in the structure and frequency of sessions are sometimes appropriate and sometimes indicate a problem in boundaries. Experiential interaction makes the therapist more vulnerable. The paradox is that "real" human relationships in everyday settings often have the most powerful impact on a person, for good or ill, and the more the re-programming approaches the real, the more the benefit, and risk.

> **SIDEBAR Countertransference and fee.** The payment of the therapist is a key element of the **therapeutic alliance** that grounds the fantasy relationship in reality: the therapist is not a "friend" but a "professional" being paid for services. When insurance payments, or clinic funding supports the treatment this can be confused as "the therapist cares so much about me that he does not charge". Similar problems arise if the therapist modifies the fee, or agrees to waive it, creating a "special" patient, often a counter transference. If the therapist makes the therapy relationship emotionally significant it is no longer the patient's fantasy! The therapist may see many people every week, so a significant emotional involvement with even a fraction of them creates emotional involvement that will eventually wear the therapist down (perhaps a reason why some discontinue doing therapy). Therapists who marry clients after terminating the treatment are another example of the danger of emotional involvement.

The most difficult challenge for the therapist is non-attachment to outcome. The patient apparently wishes to make life changes, and the therapist's self esteem is sometimes linked to the skill of producing change in clients. If being a "good therapist" depends on a positive outcome for validation, the client can manipulate progress to maintain attachment to the therapist. The professional must accept that no changes depend on his/her skill. This is more difficult when the funding source or employer pays for and expects the client to improve.

CLINICAL EXAMPLE *The angry woman with the lousy therapist.* A young woman was referred to a trainee. In the first session, she informed him that she had seen four previous trainees, and none of them knew anything or could help her, and that this would be no better. The trainee offered to try. The patient lived with her mother, had no job, and complained about her lack of social life. In each session, she complained bitterly about the therapist's lack of skill, and rejected any efforts at exploring her life. Comments or questions were met with derision and verbal attacks. The trainee stopped attempting to make "therapeutic comments" and simply acknowledged her disappointment. He discussed this in supervision without receiving any clarification. The sessions continued for the assigned six month cycle during which the client continued to complain angrily about her life, and the inadequacy of the therapist. After two months, the woman began a job for the first time in years. Toward the fifth month, between angry comments, she informed the therapist that she had decided to move out from living with her mother and had found an apartment she could afford. In the last month, the trainee reminded her that he would no longer be seeing her in several weeks. She responded that it was fine, because she didn't get any benefit anyway, and didn't think she would bother to enroll for another session of therapy, as she no longer thought she needed it. COMMENT The process of therapy is mysterious. Throughout the sessions the trainee wondered why the woman returned each week, but she was absolutely consistent. She had the opportunity to vent her anger and assert herself. Was this helpful or did she decide that therapy was worthless? There is no way to know whether the progress in her life had anything to do with her therapy experience.

Reprogramming may include others, using group therapy or family therapy. Group therapy, working with several clients at once in the same space and time, requires the ability to engage simultaneously with group members. Groups have their own dynamic evolution and can get sidelined with group process issues distracting from the primary task of therapeutic interventions. Special skills for managing group process are needed to utilize this technique. A separate literature and special training are available to learn the skills, including a famous text by Yalom, which explores the potential advantages. (21)

> **SIDEBAR Family therapy.** The family is the "original group" in which the individual is socialized (see chapter two). The family group already exists, and the therapist must join as an outsider, and therapists vary widely in their ability to do so. The ability to see the family as a system of interactive individuals, and also engage with the family, in the moment, is a special skill set, "participant observation". The decision to include the family in the therapy process is an important decision in assessment, as defined in the therapeutic alliance, and should respond to the realities of the situation. (22) The family therapy process may identify an **identified patient** whose symptoms are created in family interaction to stabilize family dysfunction. This concept is anomalous outside of the family therapy community, because most assessment assumes that the dysfunction resides entirely within the individual. (23) Neural pathways are organized by social interaction, often in the family, and may be dysfunctional for the individual, yet congruent to the family group. Working with families permits direct intervention with the interpersonal processes that influence pathways of the members, but requires special abilities to overcome habitual family patterns of interaction. Skilled practitioners are very effective using this technique, but special training, personal skills, and the ability to decode nonverbal communication are important skills to be effective. Specialized training is needed to be effective in family therapy involving a special skill set. This and the reluctance of insurers to pay for family therapy, especially using two therapists, makes the use of this powerful method infrequent. To effectively join an ongoing family group some Level 3 engagement is necessary.

Psychotherapy/Re-programming is interactive communication. The interpersonal relationship is the fundamental component and each experience is a different one, created by the therapist and client. The process, the organization and structure of these interactions, is specified in the therapeutic alliance; the messages transmitted are the content, determined by the client and therapist. Children may bring content to the session by way of play activities fantasy roles. Process and content jointly influence the re-programming, and careful attention to the content and its mode of expression is essential.

What information is transferred over which sensory modalities? The information exchanged includes cognitive and emotional messages, delivered by verbal or nonverbal channels of communication. Verbal communication is so typical that it is not usually emphasized except in its absence: dealing with the "silent patient". (24) Psychotherapy "expects" the client to communicate verbally. Some approaches emphasize the verbal content as *the* significant feature (ie Lacan (24)). Verbal communication includes non-verbal modulators that add information to the message, i.e. phrasing, tone of voice, changes in breathing, etc. Additional information is transmitted non-verbally between the participants using facial expression, and posture/gesture. Ekman and Friesen, working in facial expression, examined its role in the therapy process. (25) The therapist must be able to "tune in" to the combination of verbal and non-verbal messages being transmitted by the patient in order to sense the emotional communication. Reik's classic *Listening With The Third Ear* emphasized the nonverbal context of verbal communication, and suggestions for learning to recognize broader messages. (26) The *level of awareness* is described in the Johari window and may be at the verbal and/or nonverbal level for each quadrant:(27) Many events in the body and brain are not brought to awareness at every moment.

The Johari matrix:	KNOWN TO OTHER	UNKNOWN TO OTHER
KNOWN TO SELF	PUBLIC	PRIVATE
UNKNOWN TO SELF	BLIND SPOT	MYSTERY

Several researchers have attempted to study the patterns of nonverbal interaction during verbal psychotherapy, and socially effective adults acquire skills in observing subtle indicators of emotion in others, and use these skills, as when performing the therapist role. (28) Verbal encoding, "intellectualization", can improve emotional control. (29)

Physical behaviors performed by the patient during the therapy session ("acting in"), or before or after in the world outside of the therapy room ("acting out"), may be used to express emotion and/or cognitive reactions. The terms emphasize actions that result in negative consequences, the patient's loss of control. When working with children, young teenagers, and adults who show periods of developmental immaturity, these motor behaviors are part of the communication to the therapist and should be acknowledged. Whether the actions are supported or the client encouraged to substitute verbal for somatic motor behavior is an issue for the therapy. (31)

SIDEBAR Special physiological indicators. The polygraph was developed to assess somatic emotional response, but despite extensive use in Psychology, it has not been utilized by psychotherapists. (30) The pupillary response to emotion can be observed and used for detecting emotion.(A device for observing the pupillary response was featured in the science fiction movie, BLADE RUNNER.) L. Ron Hubbard advocated using a simple GSR device, he called an "e-meter", as part of the process called "clearing" in Scientology, (now a competitor for delivering mental health services as a religion).

Somatic empathy: some therapists have the ability to be aware of physical responses of emotion empathically. This can confirmed by asking the person in therapy "are you feeling xxxx in yyyy?" (for example, "tightness in your stomach"). A "yes" is confirming, a "no" may indicate denial, unawareness, or refusal to share. Luborsky's "symptom context method" involves a similar process (30). Most psychotherapists assume that their ability to assess nonverbal signals is either adequate, or not essential. Without some ability to be aware of the emotional response associated with verbal behavior, the re-programmer is limited to interventions that address cognitive behavior. Assessment of this skill is not directly included in training, but can often be observed by supervisors from the flow of "process tapes" and the trainee's response.

CLINICAL EXAMPLE Learning skills to express anger. The expression of anger/ aggression is learned developmentally. The earliest expressions of anger-assertion are non-specific responses and crying. The autonomic arousal and behavioral response of two year old "temper tantrums" demonstrate coordinated motor and emotional behavior attempting to impose the child's internal demands on the social environment. More coordinated patterns of anger-assertive behavior are learned like other emotional behaviors from observing parent or other caregiver responses, modeled at the child's level of cognitive-motor development. The adult response to the child's anger "shapes" the child's behavior to adaptive-acceptable patterns, or not. Child rearing practices which include physical expressions of anger toward the child's anger, both suppress the child's expression and model aggressive patterns of anger management, and families with spousal domestic violence model similar patterns. The child's anger may be suppressed by the caregiver, or encouraged to express appropriate anger for personal assertiveness. The

> *expression of anger progresses from diffuse behavior and emotion, to focused less destructive motor and emotional expression, to use of expletive verbal behavior, and finally to verbal behavior instrumental in achieving social goals. Many adults do not accomplish this sequence. This sequence, also discussed in chapter eight, is an essential element in anger and aggressive behavior.*

Therapy using art, dance, or music as the primary channel of communication between therapist and client offers options for **non-verbal** communication. Adolescent clients may bring selected songs reflecting mood to the therapist for consideration, and the response to this can be important to building (or blocking) the therapy relationship. Therapists working with children utilize non-verbal techniques to facilitate the child's expression of emotion in play therapy, sandboxes, or other "symbolic" techniques. (32) Several contemporary approaches to working with clients using nonverbal channels are available, massage therapy, different "body" therapies including Psychodrama, Alexander Technique, Rubenfeld synergy, Pesso-Boyden System, Bioenergetic analysis, etc. (32) *These are rarely reviewed, researched, or incorporated with other treatment methods.* Wilhelm Reich, a student of Freud explored nonverbal emotional communication of posture in the book **Character Armor: body postures and relationship to personality types**. Changes in posture, acquired in experience, may be permanent or transient. (The relationship between posture and personality is examined in chapter six.) Alexander Lowen, his student, developed a therapy, "bioenergetics" based on working with the body to release emotions stored in muscle tension. A range of therapeutic techniques might be developed based on the assumption that emotions are stored as patterns of muscle tension. (33)

These methods challenge the touch boundary of relationships and must be managed appropriately. Using touch to communicate via somatic channels between therapist and patient, or receiving touch from patients, is a consistent prohibition in modern psychotherapy. Contemporary therapists fear mis-interpretation of touch by patients as sexual, a violation of professional ethics. There is frequent confusion of messages in this channel, though how much confusion comes from which person is unclear. The prohibition of touch in general public interaction, usually interpreted as sexual, has led to a yearning for touch, (ref NYT opinion (2019)). Touch is an important channel of communication, emphasized by Harlow's work with primates (chapter seven). Massage therapists touch their clients and sometimes encounter sexual boundary issues, but most are able to maintain a professional boundary. (34) They report that massage sometimes opens up powerful emotional abreactions of traumatic childhood events, as in ***The Body Keeps The Score*** (33).

*CLINICAL EXAMPLE **Touch confused as an eating disorder.** A preteen girl was referred to a hospital for difficulty eating and losing weight. She was the second child of a rural family, and starting in childhood would refuse to eat various foods despite parental demands. She was also socially isolated, had few peers, but attended school with average performance. The parents had used various physical punishments to force her to eat without benefit, which bordered on abuse. In the hospital, the child was allowed to self-select foods, and a pattern was observed. An experiential therapist built rapport with the child and carried out a series of test responses to foods varying taste, consistency, origin, and other features. It became clear that the patient could not tolerate any food that was firm enough to cause oral pressure, and was sensitive to certain tastes, but readily ate bland soft foods and maintained weight without any pressure. COMMENT Her behavior suggested a mild autism syndrome, and the patients also sometimes have touch issues, including oral sensitivity. The parents were instructed about the situation and had no problem providing a tolerated diet.*

Any sensory channel can be used to communicate emotional content and it is rare that a therapist is skilled in attending to all of these channels, but may be able to access some. In addition to auditory-verbal, and visual-body language, other channels include auditory non-verbal, other visual, somatic empathy, olfactory signals, and taste (the powerful memory effect of a crepe madeleine in the famous example of Proust, and many persons/patients have strong emotional associations, positive and negative, to certain foods.) A problem in emotional learning, that occurred at an earlier developmental stage, may be easier to reorganize at the cognitive level at which it occurred. When therapy views verbal expression as the highest, most useful strategy, it excludes many non-verbal clients. "Talk therapists" are not trained to do massage or other body therapies, so coordinating treatment sessions between practitioners might be an alternative with appropriate patients.

> **SIDEBAR** *Combined therapy with other providers presents several challenges: Coordination of any two therapists requires mutual trust regarding professionalism and boundaries. There must be a common understanding of the patient's problems and treatment goals, which depends on working together regularly. One provider must not dominate the goals of both treatment processes or undermine the other provider. Shared liability for the combined therapy is rarely defined in any malpractice coverage. The cost of the double treatment is only supported by self payment. It is difficult to show effectiveness in many verbal therapy techniques, and virtually no evidence exists for nonverbal methods. Concerns about boundary violations must be handled effectively. Avoid referring for another therapist's services because the treatment process is stalling, which makes the referral is unacknowledged consultation, rather than a request for joint treatment. All these obstacles make coordination difficult. If coordination is impossible: Decide which channels the re-programmer is comfortable using. Learn to translate the nonverbal experience into verbal terms. (35)*

Do the interventions address cognitive patterns, emotional patterns, or both?

To manage emotional states effectively, the procedure must link cognitive and emotional states. "Cognitive therapies" examine emotion in objective verbal form to develop cognitive coping skills. Beck's Cognitive Therapy for Depression guides the client in a structured procedure to be aware of negative emotional self messages. Ellis developed Rational Emotive Therapy to guide "assumptions" about emotional experience. (Children, some teens, and adults with mental disabilities may be unable to abstract easily enough to use these methods.) The early writers of common features identified cognitive elements: Franks suggested developing a rationale, a conceptual scheme or myth to provide a plausible explanation for the patient's symptoms. (36)

Therapies that emphasize **emotional focus** facilitate the client's emotional experience to improve coping skills. Early PSA emphasized **abreaction,** an intense emotional experience of suppressed past emotion, modified by insight to help the patient cope with the emotion. Current approaches emphasize *improved management of emotional states*, not simple re-experiencing. Relaxation techniques are used to decondition anxiety arousing situations, or use "exposure deconditioning". (37) These methods presume that prefrontal cortical activity can directly regulate emotional response. (*Attitude theory* is a useful concept for combining cognitive, emotion, and behavior in a unified element. (38) For example, a **delusion** is an attitude in which the emotional element is so strong that it overwhelms the cognitive/sensory data which is unable to manage the impact on behavior.)

Personality, the cognitive behavior patterns of social interaction (chapter six) includes coping processes used to manage emotional communication. These represent the internal coordination of cognitive control of emotional expression. They are called "defenses" in PSA, relaxation techniques, focusing techniques, etc., in other methods, which are used as alternatives to psychopharmacology for managing emotional arousal (or combined with them). Anna Freud's ***Ego and The Mechanisms of Defense*** described these operations. Empirical validation of the continuity of coping method's is found in Vailliant's ***Adaptation to Life*** which identifies and classifies defense mechanisms, into neurotic, immature, or psychotic, and documents persistence of these coping styles over adult life. Marty Horowitz, described patients by their coping styles in response to PTSD events in ***Stress Response Syndromes***. He was able to classify *inhibitory* versus *switching* versus *denial* approaches to emotionally intense stressful situations. (39) **WRAP** is a structured approach for helping clients develop emotional containment by writing a specific personal plan for emotional management and utilizing it. *The lack of research on coping skills shows a lack of intellectual appreciation of their importance.* Difficulty in experiencing emotion, **alexithymia,** is also a challenge, sometimes seen with other patterns. The extreme of someone with extreme difficulty with emotional intimacy is described by Guntrip as the "schizoid compromise". (40)

CLINICAL EXAMPLE Love in the dance studio. *An unattached young adult male worked as a carpenter, and moved from one small town to the next as soon as the waitress in the local diner was familiar enough to know his name. After several years, he decided that he was too isolated, and started dancing lessons at a dance studio, became intensely attached to his instructor, and began stalking her. One night he got into a fight with another patron who was dancing with her, the police were called, and after evaluation, he was referred to treatment. He acknowledged that the attack was inappropriate, and that he had become too attached to the instructor, which was why he had avoided relationships in the past. After a few sessions, he left therapy and moved away.* **COMMENT** *He fits Guntrip's description of "schizoid", without any distortion of thought, only the profound fear of excessive attachment.*

CLINICAL EXAMPLE The Forgotten Appointment. *A therapist was treating a woman with ambivalent attachment who had never had a sustained relationship with another adult. She shared her everyday experiences in emotionally empty sessions. One day, the therapist was browsing a bookstore and had the thought, "I need to go back to my office." with no clear reason for the impulse, just feeling uneasy. Returning to the clinic, he saw this woman sitting in the waiting room, and the time for her session was three fourths over. In his office, the therapist apologized to her, and scheduled the next session, offering to talk about the error then. In the next session, and for many months, the woman discussed her profound terror about being abandoned, and the fear that something had happened to the therapist, and that she was going to lose the therapist. The event triggered feelings about abandonment and loss from childhood that controlled her life. After several months, the patient ended the therapy, and was participating in social activities and more emotionally engaged in her life.* **COMMENT** *A therapist cannot design an experience to be helpful to a patient. The authenticity of the process has a subconscious impact if correct, that enhances the therapy.*

A key feature of the interaction is not participating in the therapy in a way that has caused difficulties for the client in previous situations, by *"avoiding the disturbance perpetuating maneuver"*. The therapist must be aware of his/her interaction with patient and not respond to the patient's dysfunctional expectations. Hobbs: "the client has a sustained experience of intimacy with another human being without getting hurt." (20) Recent studies on coping strategies emphasize the particular ones used by students or other subjects. A more complex understanding of the pathways involved, and factors that limit choice for different individuals is not understood.(40)

***CLINICAL EXAMPLE** Masochism in psychotherapy.* Coping skills manage uncertainty and anxiety. Identifying problem coping skills in therapy is usually associated with the experience of anxiety, the discontinuation of old methods before new methods are acquired. The awareness of dysfunctional interaction causes a breakdown in the effectiveness of the defensive coping, and anxiety is experienced. This is not unique to the PSA method, but occurs whenever a problem coping skill is disrupted. The result is usually mild to moderate social anxiety and other defensive strategies. **In masochism, a pleasurable sensation is also generated from the discomfort, the process becomes rewarding, and reinforces the masochistic pattern of interaction.** The therapy is not effective because the interaction continues the masochistic pattern of pleasure at being hurt. The therapist is not *"avoiding the disturbance perpetuating maneuver".* This situation is difficult to recognize, because the patient participates freely in sessions, and acknowledges the dysfunctional coping behavior. This can continue for many sessions, and eventually the therapist will be aware that no change is occurring, and a close examination of the process reveals the patient's affirmative response has translated the anxiety or discomfort into a masochistic reward! COMMENT To address this issue, the therapist must get alignment with the client about the problem, subjective awareness, and the client must acknowledge the pleasurable discomfort each time, which will eventually rob it of reward value. This is not in the control of the therapist, and requires the **agency** of the patient. The same process can be used by the patient **silently** in other life situations to recognize masochistic interactions.

Is the patient/client actively involved? Does the therapist do something to change the client? Or is the client doing something to produce the change? A significant feature of interventions is **agency.** The individual must be able to make adaptive choices, and most symptoms of "mental illness" *include the loss of this ability.* Schwartz described a method for helping individuals with OCD symptoms learn to modify the symptoms by *self-directed intervention.* His book also includes other examples in animal and human research of reprogramming techniques that reorganize brain activity, not all of which were directed by the subject. (41) When designing re-programming experiences to modify a pathway, if the client is actively engaged, the intervention may be more effective. *The balance between active participation and passive response differs in different techniques, and is not always clearly defined in the Therapeutic Alliance.* Experiential learning is a situation in which the person does something to learn new patterns. The individual may be assigned a **specific task**, as in exposure therapy, and the experience occurs as the client performs the task. (42) How to use specific challenges to re-program pathways is not always clear, but every re-programming experience must include the possibility of learning new responses. The re-programmer may need to *not do* something, to allow the client to *learn by the experience*. (43) The expression of ***agency*** has a complex relationship with intention and consciousness of participation in the re-programming process. As PSA has evolved from emphasis on intra-personal to interpersonal dynamics, the interpersonal view puts more emphasis on active involvement and interpersonal awareness in the process, evident in procedures that emphasize focusing (see later). (44)

Matching the re-programmer and client includes: What level of interpersonal interaction is each participant comfortable experiencing? What channels of communication are preferred for each participant, verbal, non-verbal, or a combination? What balance of emotional and cognitive information is the person more comfortable expressing? What control over the process does each participant need? Personal and cultural features of the participants also play a role in matching or justifying the inability to engage. Gender, gender identity, racial-cultural background, and socio-economic status have all been identified as possibly important in forming the relationship. Intuitively, these features are important in the reprogramming process, so each participant's preferences must be considered in matching them, or creating complementary pairing. This is different from defining "effective modes of psychotherapy" but is probably related, since both participants must be comfortable with the process. (45) *A method for doing this matching does not exist.*

What specific procedures are used for reprogramming? The features of interpersonal communication are important in re-programming, but certain processes recur in re-programming methods. *Focusing attention* is a powerful tool. The attention process (described in chapter five) coordinates pathways, has an "operating system" function, and is directed by many different brain activities, including subjective awareness that can intentionally direct the focus. Using this system effectively requires skill and training, and much needs to be learned about utilizing this evolutionary gift, which is the basis of meditation, hypnosis, neurofeedback, EMDR, and other techniques. (46)

Meditation enhances awareness by training focus on a specific mental or sensory feature. Epstein wrote a preliminary attempt to blend Buddhist and PSA concepts. Kabat Zinn and colleagues have carried out studies training mindfulness meditation for relief of pain, improving general function, and other applications. (47) In experienced meditators, improved capacity for managing emotion may develop. *"Focusing"* is a method of using attention to become more self aware of emotional states and improve emotional regulation. The therapist instructs the individual in how to maintain awareness of the emotional state. (48) This has been incorporated into therapy for emotional reactivity, and attachment anxiety. Fonagy's group uses the term *mentalizing:* "cultivating awareness of mental states such as thoughts and feelings in self and others". The participant is trained to develop mentalization/awareness across four domains: Automatic/Controlled; Self/Other; Inner/Outer; Cognitive/Affective, and learns to balance the focus across all four. (49) Studies identify changes observed in the training. (50) Using controlled awareness is at an early stage in Western healing traditions compared to Eastern and Tibetan practices, with more advanced capabilities.

The Western method most resembling meditation is hypnosis, an *interpersonal process* which brings the subject into an altered "trance state" with potential therapeutic uses. Hypnosis has been utilized in mental health since (at least) Charcot and Janet in the 19th century, and influenced Freud. (51) The hypnotist directs a split in attention, utilizing the *dissociation process*, to facilitate changes in motivation and behavior. *Dissociation* is an observable, measurable cognitive defense, measured in ordinary people (often college students), which allows subjects to experience a "trance" state. The neural mechanisms involve control of the attention mechanisms, discussed in chapters five and six. (52) The hypnotic technique may provide access to information and facilitate awareness of inaccessible memories. (53) This is controversial because of the risk of suggesting false material incorporated into "memory" by the client. (54) It may allow the client to learn to focus attention on key skills through the facilitation of a skilled other, the hypnotist.

SIDEBAR Hypnosis And Milton Erickson. Milton Erickson, a psychiatrist practicing in the 1970s, was famous for his use of hypnotic techniques. Several books are available by Erickson and his students describing his methods. He was known for his ability to induce the trance state by subtle induction techniques. (55) He has discussed his understanding of the trance state and how these procedures work. Haley points out that Erickson uses hypnosis to address challenges of human development, identifying the key challenge at a life stage, and assigning an active response to overcome the challenge using hypnotic techniques. His phrase "my voice will go with you", often used at the end of the induction, extended the motivation beyond the session. **He was highly creative in devising exercises to address conflicts, requiring active behavior by the patient, outside of the hypnotherapy session, with a clear definition of task completion. He did not focus on diagnostic categories or symptoms, only life tasks and solutions.** *His method provides a model for reprogramming which contrasts to current methods emphasizing symptoms and diagnoses. Much of his technique can be accomplished without hypnotic induction, but studies documenting this have never been done.* The use of hypnosis in contemporary Western psychotherapy is limited because it depends on personal variables of the therapist and client, and entails learning special skills. (55)

Direct training of the attention process can be accomplished using *neurofeedback*. The client is linked to recording electrodes that detect EEG signals from scalp electrodes, fed to a computer and processed digitally. This is presented in real time on a computer screen in a visual format allowing the client to adjust the signal by altering his mental state. The client can learn to modify the distribution of brain wave frequencies, a personal variable otherwise inaccessible. It has been applied to improving focus in ADHD, and some studies explore use on amygdala response, but the broader implications of enhancing mental focus on reprogramming tasks have not been explored. (56) Neurofeedback is on the border of biological and information intervention, and adjusting overall EEG of a brain region (and related pathway) is not information specific but procedures could be designed to enhance pathway modifications using this technique.

SIDEBAR Techniques that combine neurofeedback and fMRI are in development. The relationship of EEG activity frequencies has been correlated to changing fMRI. Watanabe notes that external rewards help focus neurofeedback learning, and that multivariate techniques allows more sensitive neurofeedback control, and changes of connectivity in a targeted brain network. fMRI neurofeedback techniques include **decoded neurofeedback** (DecNef) applied to specific brain regions, and **functional connectivity-based neurofeedback** (FCNef), applied to connectivity strength between different brain regions. Learning to augment brain region activity while performing information tasks might facilitate altering neural pathways, but so far studies do not correlate with pathway abnormalities because they focus on diagnoses. Neurofeedback occurs on a different time scale than the measurements of fMRI, so the subject must maintain change of focus while the fMRI study is obtained. (57) More sophisticated research protocols will require normalizing values of different techniques clinically. Other sensory modes can also be used as input to regulate neural activity. *Whenever brain activity can be brought into subjective awareness, self modification is possible.* (58)

Several clinical syndromes are associated with changes in the attention process. Dissociation, a coping technique used early in development, is usually replaced by more cognitive methods, but continues to be used by persons with Borderline Syndrome, Dissociative Identity Disorder, and PTSD. Dissociation can be treated by focusing techniques redirecting attention pathways. In PTSD, the treatment often begins with the breakdown of blocked attention, discussed in chapter eight. The treatment requires three phases: i) methods for coping with the emerging anxiety and control of it in daily life so the person does not experience overwhelming anxiety. ii) Controlled re-experience of traumatic memories restored in different modes. iii) The person's life, especially the social interactions, must be revised and new patterns learned to replace those created by the trauma. (59) EMDR, a technique to modulate attention, is one of several techniques for treatment of PTSD with dissociation which directly modify the attention process. (60) *Borderline personality syndrome* involves a pathway disturbance of the attachment process, and does not respond to medication. (Details in chapter seven.) (61) Linehan developed an effective therapy, Dialectical Borderline Therapy (DBT) which helps the client develop emotional stabilization. (62) Fonagy's approach uses "mentalization". Both emphasize focus on affect using meditative techniques to develop emotional control. (63)

The human experience of grief has a specific technique for resolution. Lindemann's classic on working with grief describes the tasks the therapist and patient must accomplish, the same ones a mourner or family member uses to help the bereaved. *The reorganization of grieving, for any loss, is redirecting the interaction experiences (and rewards) away from the deceased, now gone, to memories and to new interactions with others.* (64) Kubler Ross describes "stages" of the process: denial, anger, bargaining, depression, acceptance and finding meaning. (65)

SIDEBAR: Stages of Grieving. *In the first stage of Denial, the person does not acknowledge a loss has occurred, the extreme of hallucinating the deceased. In the Anger-bargaining stage, the change is acknowledged and the person struggles to find ways to undo the loss or control it. A common childhood pattern is blaming the self for changes in family that are out of the child's control, because being out of control is more terrifying than feeling blame and responsibility, and gives the illusion of control. The acknowledgement of the loss is the awareness that the reward from the other is no longer possible. This sudden awareness of the loss of the rewards is often associated with depressed mood, showing the important role of reward in maintaining mood. Acceptance (and Finding Meaning) requires a reorganization of reward, by transferring the reward experiences to memory, substituting new rewards, or finding ways to self reward to replace the loss. These may include addiction, commitment to religion, a new social group, etc. These cognitive-emotional transitions are not always seen in this progression with every person. Being "stalled" at a "stage" may indicate the person is having problems transitioning. Depressed mood, including withdrawal and lack of motivation, may result from loss, the melancholia described by Freud. Grieving in a social setting brings others to facilitate the transitions, and alternative sources of reward. Goffman wrote "Cooling Out The Mark" to describe grieving in the person who loses money in a "confidence scam", which shows the grieving process is fundamental for adaptation to all loss. (66)*

CLINICAL EXAMPLE The Woman Who Grieved For A Father She Never Saw. *A single woman in her mid thirties was evaluated for depression. It began when her engagement was ended by her fiancée. She had been depressed on and off for many years, and unable to sustain a relationship with a male, and in previous counseling became aware that she was responsible for the breakups. She was conceived during father's leave from active duty, born during the war, but the father was captured and died a prisoner of war without ever seeing her. The mother remarried and had other children, and the patient's relationship to her stepfather was distant. She completed high school and college, had a responsible job, and a few social friends, but experienced depressions, and frustrated about not finding a partner. The therapist discovered that the patient had no knowledge of her biological father. Her mother rarely mentioned him while the patient was growing up. The patient sometimes fantasized "saving him" as a POW during childhood. And thought about him at special occasions like graduation, that he would have attended. The therapist encouraged her to ask her mother for whatever information about her father was available, and discovered that her mother had a collection of memorabilia which she had put away when she remarried, and had never shown them to the daughter to "avoid upsetting her". The patient proceeded to review and ruminate over this information, forming a clearer sense of the person she had lost. She had the insight that she was avoiding marriage because "he could not give me away". Over time her depressive episodes improved and she ended therapy.* COMMENT *Grieving is the replacement of real experiences with memories. The fewer the positive memory experiences the survivor has, the more difficult it is to grieve. This woman was an extreme circumstance.*

Psychosis is a specific pathway syndrome with multiple etiologies. (see chapter five) During a psychosis episode the *continuity of the self is interrupted*, and requires reintegration. Encouraging the patient to return to the previous life and ignore the interruption does not deal with the event, or the life situation that precipitated the episode. If no corrective intervention occurs, discontinuation of medication predicts return of psychosis in many patients. In order to repair the consequences of a psychotic state, the person must grieve for the loss of self in the previous life, recognize its ineffectiveness, and develop new patterns. C. G. Jung went through a period of psychosis, which he managed by intense self regulation, without medication, and described in a memoir. (see chapter five) (67) Recovery from *psychosis* includes both dealing with the event itself and addressing issues that lead to the loss of adaptive function. Psychotherapy after psychosis was available to affluent persons in specialized facilities before the extensive use of psychopharmacology. A literature of case reports and articles of treatment of psychosis and related conditions, in the 1950s to 60s, includes writings of Semrad, Harry Stack Sullivan, Frieda Fromm-Reichmann, and Searles, at Austen Riggs, Chestnut Lodge, and Institute of PA Hosp, and other institutions. The contemporary practice of brief hospitalization with high dose medication, and discharge to inconsistent followup does not include this. Preventing relapse of psychosis, without remedial therapy, leads to the contemporary strategy of chronic use of anti-psychotic medications to prevent future psychosis after the patient is no longer psychotic.(see chapter eleven) Learning to balance the use of medications and re-programming interventions requires training and experience. (68) *It is difficult to find a provider experienced in balancing the risk of psychotic deterioration with the ability to facilitate learning new skills, managing the interaction of psychopharmacology and psychotherapy.* (69) In psychosis associated with mania, a plan for addressing potential future episodes must be included, with discussion of use of various medications for prevention. In a patient with a schizophrenic disturbance, there will usually be antecedent cognitive difficulties, and problems with social and executive function. After stabilization, a plan for gradual improvement of cognitive skills is needed to prevent future episodes. Some newer CBT models have been developed to provide these skills (69).

Discontinuity in sense of self, experienced in psychosis, has been studied by R.J. Lifton with survivors coping with catastrophes, including the survivors of Hiroshima. Recovering from trauma requires formulating a continuation of narrative about the self, so the event does not interrupt the *continuity of self*. Lifton's approach uses scripting a "self narrative", usually done in groups, to help people verbalize traumatic experiences and visualize their future. He has also worked with American prisoners of war in Korea, Vietnam veterans, and others. The paradigm fits with *self as an experiential construction* (in insula pathways), and connects with Erikson's views of a formative "self", an organizing process for representing the integrated actions of the person, based on stored experiences. (70) Damasio has localized this in insula the place where convergence of pathways for this data occurs. (see chapter two) The Left brain is the "storyteller" because the formulation of this task is verbal, but children sometimes draw to create visual narratives with desirable outcomes, as in **dreams**.

The ability to "imagine the future", A unique human capacity, is the basis for Lifton's self narratives. The memory process is constructive, and memories of previous experience are "reassembled" in recall, or to produce a "fantasy vision" of the future. Gottschall reviews this narrative process in *The Storytelling Animal*. (71) Storytelling begins developmentally by the 3rd year in children and is universal. It contributes to the separate sense of self, and helps the small child deal with the fears experienced. Heroes overcoming fears are important themes, ages two to four, when attempts at assertion of autonomy ("no"), are opposed by "godlike" parental figures. Differences of male and female stories in roleplaying reveal the beginnings of gender identity. Fairy tales and bedtime stories provide hidden narratives about behavior and emotional control. Narratives can be used to re-program, as in rehearsing the experience of escaping danger to deal with anxiety.

Several therapeutic techniques have developed around the storytelling process using narrative, storytelling, and dreams for re-programming. These include the methods of the contemporary Jungians, Hillman et al, (72), and Pinkola Estes' **Women Who Run With The Wolves,** and other "teaching myths", which evoke and organize emotional responses. Berg's scaling therapy helps visualize positive outcomes. (72) Three separate skills are involved: Creating an heroic vision of self, which the individual can use to *formulate life goals*. Guided fantasy imagery using *visualization*, as in cancer treatment, to mobilize internal body defenses, or imagine internal *and external "rehearsal"* of actions. (73) Dream formation and interpretation has played a role in mental health from ancient times. Asklepios was the Greek healer/god and dreams were an integral part of the healing ritual.

> **SIDEBAR The Significance of Dreams.** *Dream interpretation is a feature of Freudian PSA, where it provides information on "unconscious conflict", and in Jungian therapy, where the dream enacts the narrative of the archetype. Other cultures use dreams to teach narrative lessons about social behavior and manage emotion. (74) The Psychoanalytic view that dreams are generated by desires of the dreamer is not consistent with the neurophysiology that REM states recur in 90 minute cycles by a coordinated neurophysiological mechanism for maintenance of sleep activity and stage 4 recuperative sleep. The structure of sleep cycles appears to be somewhat independent of psychological life. The recall of dreams is not closely related to their occurrence. REM states are characterized by low response to external stimuli, and therefore represent brain activity triggered by internal states. (Specific pontine signals appear to be the triggering mechanism.) Dream states are internal brain activity, free of structure by sensory input from external sources, which reflect internal memory and current emotional concerns. Patients in psychotherapy can learn to attend to dream states and wake to record them for later discussion. Given the different ways patients report dreams to therapists, it appears that the structuring of dreams is modified by the therapy context. Garfield reports use of dream states in other cultures that encourage the dreamer to take an active role in modifying the dream process, using changes in the state to reprogram at least some internal experience. (76) The Jungian method is more enactive and resembles traditional cultures in viewing the dreamer as an active participant in an alternate dream world. The dream state is mental activity that can be used to "reprogram" internal cognitive-emotional configurations. Special skills are needed to understand and use the information effectively, so most contemporary providers ignore this mental activity. "Dream time", the existence of a world parallel to waking reality, permits the dream world to feel more real and extend the everyday. Bosnak, a prominent Jungian dream specialist, studied Australian aboriginal culture and observed their dream process. (77) Aborigines experience "dream time" as an extension of waking activity, another level of reality, not engaging with the external sensory world, as in the Western view. The aboriginal view shows more balance between external and internal reality. The survival of the aborigines in a desolate environment suggests that this organization of the mind is adaptive.*

Narrative and dramatic expression have been part of the programming of mental health throughout human history. Greek theater characters form the names of contemporary emotional configurations ("Oedipus complex"), printed books expanded the distribution of narrative themes, the early films were described as dream equivalents, and new digital media allow anyone to create audio-visual

SIDEBAR NEW MEDIA. The evolution of narrative media in the 20th and 21st centuries provides a range of new opportunities for reprogramming. The evolution from oral sagas and Greek theater to mass publishing of written narratives provided "moral lessons", radio in the early 20th century expanded mass experience to sound and music, and movies created (eventually) full audio visual narratives. Films play a complex role in defining and guiding images of the self, body, and behavior. But limited access to production centralized the creative process in corporate hands until the development of compact, easy to use, digital recording and distribution media. This has expanded opportunities for expression not yet appreciated by the re-programming community. Teens and young adults share a range of (positive and negative) communications that transmit their personal concerns. *Lonely Girl,* and the current *Tiktok* site are examples of self generated resources. *There are opportunities for using these media productively both as records of difficult moments, and also to create coping programs for personal use.* Of less value are sites providing advice about mental health, training in coping skills, practicing techniques, and guided imagery, because self selection does not always lead to choosing effective resources. (79)

The use of digital devices to deliver formatted therapies has also expanded. EST manualized therapy techniques have been delivered via computer, (with studies that evaluate their effectiveness). (80) Social media have rarely been utilized for sharing mental health issues due to concerns about privacy and security, but new sites are being developed to respond to mental health crises and offer "secure" access to therapists online. (81)

The popularity of role playing games is focused on male teens and young adults as a venue for socialized aggression. A much broader range of opportunities is possible in these digital interaction media if designed for reprogramming goals, as a medium for development of experiences specifically tailored to individual issues, and suitable for children and teens. Several papers recognize the possibility, but developing effective tools for this purpose and implementing them successfully is not yet a reality.(82) Virtual reality simulation has been utilized to provide extinction trial experience for PTSD survivors. Combining life scripting and role playing simulation would allow the individual to script the identity of his/her character and experience simulated life consequences as fantasy learning experiences. (83) The opportunities these media provide are offset by the problems in regulation and selection for appropriate use.

narratives transferable to anyone else (for better or worse). The unknown factor is the effect of using interaction with digital representations as the alternative to live human experiences. This is likely to be tested in psychotherapy in the near future. New approaches may be able to combine different methods into complex reprogramming experiences. One approach is Joiner's FLEX system. (78)

The use of digital media for reprogramming raises concerns about expanding digital media experiences in place of direct human contact, which may not enhance social development. Children, teens, and young adults now spend more time in digital media than direct human interaction. The total time of "quasi-social interaction" including digital interaction has also increased. No studies of this aggregate have been done, though the various services certainly have part of the data. There is a need to assess the impact of this change in social communication, teach users to be aware of the different consequences, and potential dangers. Making this an issue of "protecting children" is short sighted, certain to be opposed by users, and creates an "enemy" out of a developing mode of communication, but it addresses the changing nature of the society and the need to manage it in human terms.

Combining psychopharmacology and reprogramming may provide new opportunities for pathway modification. The combination of the two interventions has used sedatives, antidepressants, and stimulants informally administered along with psychotherapy, but simply adding a second method, when the first is not effective, does not always improve the outcome. (84) Entrenched attitudes and licensing issues make it difficult to coordinate services. Stahl, a neuro-pharmacologist views psychotherapies as "drug-like effects" on specific brain vulnerabilities. (85) Adelman, a psychotherapist, describes medication treatment with borderline patients as "transitional objects", emphasizing the "placebo effect". Several recent papers explore other theories. (86)

Specific interactions can be described:

The pharmacological agent is used **to augment** *the reprogramming or vice versa.*

Many studies combine antidepressant SSRIs, and psychotherapy. Some are designed to compare which is better, but others look for augmentation effects in each modality. Typically, the STAR*D added CBT to treatment on a self selected basis without specific criteria for use, or benefit. Combination studies suffer from the same defect as the individual modality studies: failure to identify which groups are most likely to benefit. (87) One strategy uses medications to alter the motivation system component, while psychotherapy impacts the cortical/cognitive component. This concept has never been validated.

The pharmacological agent is used **to prepare/stabilize** *the client for reprogramming.*
The use of anti-psychotic medications to bring the patient out of psychosis, followed by return "home" and re-programming interventions is discussed in a previous section. This approach was occasionally used until most psychiatrists discontinued doing psychotherapy. The post psychotic patient is not an easy psychotherapy candidate. (88)

The pharmacological agent is used **to disrupt** *the patient for reprogramming,*
The use of psychopharmacology to enhance psychotherapy *by disrupting* has a strange history. "Psychedelic" chemicals and plants have been utilized for eons. Traditional cultures have extensive rituals intended to return a dysfunctional member to participation in the community, sometimes in conjunction with ingestion of hallucinogenic substances or other induction of **altered state**. Navaho rituals, described in anthropology, induce an "altered state" by chants, drumming, physical distress of sleeplessness, hunger and thirst. In the "vision quest", the emerging adult member of the tribe goes into the wilderness for an extended period to find new understanding to bring back to the tribe. The creation and discovery of LSD and related agents ushered in an era of confused exploration and negative reactions in American society (LSD was used for CIA interrogations!). An effort to reopen consideration of these chemicals and explore their possible potential has begun. (89) The chemicals produce states of disorganization at a variety of synaptic locations, which may also be disrupting pathway activity. Disrupting the pathway does not

guarantee developing a more adaptive one, and much of the failure of the 1960s-70s was the inability to organize more adaptive life strategies. If psycho-chemicals are to be used in treatment settings, a better strategy of conjoint interventions is needed. This method also runs the risk of disrupting functional pathways. The effect may be similar to ketamine in depression, or ECT. The major problem encountered in this as in other efforts to combine methods is the failure to make the re-programming component essential. Similar techniques are used in the military for training, and for interrogation. There is an assumption that after the patterns are broken down successful new patterns will be formed, but additional interventions are not always provided to ensure that new patterns are developed. (90)

*The two methods are combined in a **strategic plan**.*
An overall strategic plan for combining psychopharmacology and re-programming does not exist. The plan would have several components, none of which have current research data: What pathways are being modulated by each method? Is the combination complementary or augmenting? How to adjust dosage and timing to maximize the interaction? How to combine the administration of chemicals and other interpersonal interaction into *one relationship process*. The administration of chemicals, and personal interaction are different relationship modes, and the therapist and client must build a common relationship framework that incorporates both.

***CLINICAL EXAMPLE** Structuring the Session. A patient was evaluated for ongoing anxiety, at home and at work, and was taking anti-anxiety medication. He expressed concern about taking too much, but at each session would describe anxiety attacks, and ask if he was taking enough. This interfered with exploring the sources of anxiety in psychotherapy. The provider noted that the roles of therapist and medication provider were interfering with each other, and contracted with the patient to focus the session entirely on psychological and interpersonal issues until the last ten minutes, at which point, anxiety symptoms would be reviewed and a mutual decision made about medications. This was agreed, and became the structure of the sessions with beneficial results. COMMENT Two roles are involved in mixed treatment, which may interact constructively or interfere. The treatment alliance must be adjusted if necessary.*

How is the brain reorganized in "reprogramming"? The initial excitement of a study in 2000 documenting brain changes in re-programming has evolved into confusion and frustration about inconsistent results. Changes in fMRI occur after both medication treatments and psychotherapy, indicating that pathway changes are *correlated* with the treatments (see appendix chapter one). But efforts to "explain" how therapy works based on fMRI studies have limited data. Pre-frontal regions have a role in modulating the motivation/emotion regions of amygdala and hypothalamus (chapters three, five and six). Viamontes and Breitman proposed a three part model linking dorsolateral frontal cortex, orbito-frontal cortex, and cingulate & n. accumbens: i)sensory data (memory (hippocampal) data) enter DLPFC, ii) motivation data from subcortex enter pre-frontal cortex through OFC, iii) pre-frontal cortex performs the computation to determine behavior, iv) this is balanced by DMN, an expression of the attention process. (91) Their proposal is a variation on the decision making process described in chapter six. A meta-analysis by Messina et al of data from fMRI studies attempted to confirm this model by sampling for changes after treatment for anxiety and depression. It showed no changes in DLPFC, the region in which they expected to see most change, according to Viamontes' model, and no findings in amygdala regions (which were poorly visualized). Most changes were noted in temporal regions, esp left. They decided that the results were not consistent with the Viamontes proposal. It is probably more accurate to say that the meta-analysis data was too noisy to produce any clear conclusions. Also the assumption that DLPFC changes would reflect ongoing effects was very unlikely. The ability to measure pathway changes requires more specific criteria (see Appendix chapter one).

The growing body of fMRI data does not converge toward defining changes correlated with treatments, which may be due to several factors:

a) The relationship between pathway activity and fMRI (BOLD) connectivity is unknown.

SIDEBAR Other meta-reviews of fMRI of psychotherapy. Similar findings were noted in a more conventional meta-analysis of OCD treatment. (92) No consistent pattern of changes was noted in other studies and meta-reviews. A review of studies of fMRI in CBT treatment of various conditions, found results "interpreted as" **frontal suppression of emotional activity**. The authors decided that this supported the frontal control hypothesis of CBT but acknowledged that the exact mechanisms seem to be different in different modalities and patients! A meta-review by Porto et al is significant: CBT was compared with medication control for different anxiety diagnoses. Changes were noted between patients and controls across most CBT treatments in some brain regions, but the regions varied for different types of anxiety. The number of studies and total patients was small, and the review illustrates the value of more specific definitions of groups, and also the resulting problem with insufficient numbers. A truly heroic meta-analysis by Kalsiet. al. compared psychopharmacology and psychotherapy studies done with neural connectivity measurements. They reported overlap of a few specific regions across the studies, but no correlation of most. Why would they expect any correlations? (93)

b) Technical issues in fMRI measurement (discussed in appendix to chapter one) interfere with data accuracy. *(fMRI (BOLD)* techniques cannot separate *subcortical regions* consistently, so their role in pathways is missing.) The need for across laboratory standardization of procedures so that "normal" values are comparable across studies (without which "meta-analyses" are burdened with statistical noise). This standardization is also needed for any future clinical use.

c) The presumption that similar treatments create similar changes in different patients is unproven and likely to be incorrect, with variability, perhaps dramatic variability, because no one knows how reprogramming methods alter specific pathways.

d) The issue of "fidelity" is relevant in the studies; the "fidelity" of the same treatment intervention in different patients by different providers may not have the same effect.

Beauregard summarizes the confusion in an excellent review: *"Several potentially biasing factors may lead to contrasting results and render problematic a direct comparison between these studies....*" "*methodological factors that vary between neuroimaging studies of psychotherapy include the phenomena measured (eg, "metabolic activity" vs "hemodynamic activity"), the sensitivity and spatial/temporal resolutions of the neuroimaging techniques used, and the methods for examining regional brain activity (eg, voxel-based techniques, region-of-interest-based approaches). The sample size, the type of control participants (eg, healthy, waitlist), and the point of the second scan within the treatment course, may also lead to divergent results. .*"(94)

Linden's meta review concludes that the only way to standardize "connectivity relationships" is by correlation to external clinical validity. (95)

Finding brain changes "proves that psychotherapy is a biological process" but provides no other useful information so far. Brain measures by themselves do not document the effectiveness of techniques for improving social functioning, which requires an independent assessment of adaptation. This is the same issue when pathways are altered by psychopharmacology. Pathways changes are difficult to measure, and only validated for effectiveness by measuring improved adaptation. *(96)*

Evaluating re-programming interventions. The basis for evaluation of all mental health treatment is improved adaptation, not changes in symptoms. Although fMRI studies may indicate something has happened in some patients, the current state of biological measurement does not support using them to validate re-programming techniques. Research in the effectiveness of treatment has been performed for more than half a century, but rarely documents improved adaptation. (97) Validation of social improvement, or its absence, is too expensive for research budgets. (No one seems to have considered the strategy of using social media and patient cooperation to evaluate long term changes by self-report by secondary documentation.) It is unlikely that there are "universal" re-programming methods, any more than universal medication treatments. ***The task of fitting the treatment intervention to the***

person seeking help is rarely considered. The use of vague general diagnoses for medication treatment obscures individual differences in response, and creates a blurry "evidence based" standard of treatment. A similar problem has emerged in EST methods that claim to treat broad diagnostic categories. Studies show that EST treatments are not consistently successful, and comparison to general psychotherapy does not show dramatic differences. As in psychopharmacology, documentation of *functional improvement* is lacking. (98) *The mental health system is currently structured for the abilities and preferences of providers and available funding, not for the needs of the client.* The failure to identify common properties in patient groups that respond to treatment interventions, and other individual characteristics of the patients, has interfered with outcome evaluation in both psychopharmacology and re-programming. *People are different, and when they have problems, the problems have some features in common, and some not.* The differences sometimes respond to different treatments. (see comments in appendix to chapter one) Measurement techniques and research studies summarize the general results, but miss many details. (94) Designing research to compare different methods, with different therapists, and different patient groups (treatment and controls) soon balloons into so many separate groups with different treatments, that the numbers are too large for any realistic study. A different approach is needed: Differentiate patient groups and providers-interventions by statistical features, and evaluate them as statistical entities for outcome and other results. This amounts to a factor analysis approach seeking factors associated with treatment outcomes.

OR

Let provider and patient pairs self select treatment options and perform a treatment intervention. Evaluate the outcomes blind by pairings, allowing data to accumulate over time. Observe convergence for successful pairings, with clear preferred outcomes, (or, as in CATIE none occurs!). This proposal is similar to one by Castelnuovo, allowing patients with similar DSM diagnoses to pursue treatment choice, their outcomes are measured afterwards. He proposed a "sliding scale" self assessed scale of outcome, but this must also include adaptive social effect! (3)

THE SOCIAL CONTEXT OF MENTAL HEALTH

Just as the relationship between the individual and the social environment programs brain pathways for mental health, as described in chapter two, the system that delivers mental health services is embedded in and influenced by the surrounding social system. The many activities involved in mental health services, the providers licensed by the society, the clients, patients, and other recipients, and the organizations for delivering services are all influenced by this system. Different groups are responsible for the boundary between mental health services and the larger community, with each group advocating for its goals.

The social system of the United States is currently experiencing major dysfunction. There is conflict over the role of minorities and women in the society. There is a dramatically increasing wealth inequality with a growing class of economically excluded persons. Social media communications have altered the connections in the society. The integrity of the family as the basic structure of caring for and raising children, and managing elders has been undermined. Attempts to replace family services with paid services will bankrupt the system. Over 50% of children are born to one-parent families, and travel and relocation make inter-generational care difficult to arrange. Ordinary services like childcare for pregnancy, and balancing the work demands of two working parents are not addressed by the society. Children and teens are trained more for consuming than for productive work, and exposed to addictive substances at an early age for future use. The entire society is saturated with addictive behavior. Addictive use has killed off over 5% of youth in the population in the last two decades without serious efforts to prevent it. Any society that values income over developing children as future members is destined for major problems. Most citizens are aware of these problems, but only political action, not the efforts of individuals, can effect change. They all impact the mental health of the community

CHAPTER ONE REFERENCES

1) **CLINICAL EXAMPLE** These are *based on* clinical situations altered to maintain confidentiality. They are not "case reports".
2) Siegel,Dan J., *The Developing Mind.*
3) Shannon and weaver https://en.wikipedia.org/wiki/A_Mathematical_Theory_of_Communication
4) Pinker, S. (2009). How the Mind Works (1997/2009) (2009th ed.) . New York, NY: W. W. Norton & Company. p24
5) **Presti, David E. *Foundational Concepts in Neuroscience: A Brain-mind Odyssey.***
Ghaemi *"The fallacies of Psychiatry"* http://www.medscape.com/viewarticle/811956
6) Gérard Battail, Biology Needs Information Theory, April 2013,Biosemiotics 6(1)DOI: 10.1007/s12304-012-9152-6https://www.researchgate.net/publication/257780024_Biology_Needs_Information_Theory
Battail, G. (2008). Applying Semiotics and Information Theory to Biology: A Critical Comparison. Biosemiotics, 1-18.
Kendler K. S. (2014). The structure of psychiatric science. *The American journal of psychiatry, 171*(9), 931–938. **https://doi.org/10.1176/appi.ajp.2014.13111539** https://ajp.psychiatryonline.org/doi/full/10.1176/appi.ajp.2008.07071061
7) Lerner, T. N., Ye, L., & Deisseroth, K. (2016). Communication in Neural Circuits: Tools, Opportunities, and Challenges. *Cell, 164*(6), 1136–1150. https://doi.org/10.1016/j.cell.2016.02.027
8) **SIDEBARS** expand a particular subject in more detail and can be omitted without losing the theme of the chapter.
Hixon Symposium is available on download at http://calteches.library.caltech.edu/923/9) Norbert Weiner, ***CYBERNETICS*** Second Edition: Or the Control and Communication in the Animal and the Machine ISBN-10: 1614275025 ISBN-13: 978-1614275022
https://www.amazon.com/Cybernetics-Second-Control-Communication-Machine/dp/026273009X
10) Is the Brain a Digital Computer? - John Searle *https://philosophy.as.uky.edu › sites › default › files* PDF
John R. Searle Source: Proceedings and Addresses of the American Philosophical Association, Vol. 64, No. 3(Nov., 1990), pp. 21-37 http://www.jstor.org/stable/3130074 "The Mind as the Software of the Brain" by Ned Block New York
http://users.ecs.soton.ac.uk/harnad/Papers/Py104/searle.comp.html
Gerald M. Edelman, Naturalizing consciousness: A theoretical framework, Proceedings of the National Academy of Sciences Apr 2003, 100 (9) 5520-5524;

References

DOI: 10.1073/pnas.0931349100 https://www.pnas.org/content/100/9/5520
11) https://en.wikipedia.org/wiki/Turing_machine
McLaren, Niall. *Humanizing Psychiatry: The Biocognitive Model.* Ann Arbor, MI: Future Psychiatry, 2010. Print.
https://www.amazon.com/Humanizing-Psychiatry-Biocognitive-Model-Avail/dp/1615990119
12) https://en.wikipedia.org/wiki/Fuzzy_logic
Emil M. Petriu has written an overview: "Soft Computing: Neural Networks and Fuzzy Logic (PDF)" This paper clarifies the different properties of fuzzy logic networks including the brain neurons.
http://www.site.uottawa.ca/~petriu
http://www.site.uottawa.ca/~petriu/ELG5196-SoftComputing-NN_FL.pdf
13) Abbott, L. F., Regehr, Wade G., Synaptic computation, Nature, 2004/10/01, 796-803 (2004) https://doi.org/10.1038/nature03010
Turner et al , "Communication in Neural Circuits: Tools, Opportunities, and Challenges"Cell. 2016 Mar 10; 164(6): 1136–1150. doi: 10.1016/j.cell.2016.02.027
Zucker, R. S., & Regehr, W. G. (2002). Short-term synaptic plasticity. *Annual review of physiology*, *64*, 355–405. https://doi.org/10.1146/annurev.physiol.64.092501.114547
14) HEBB cell assembly pathways. For a recent overview:
Miguel A.L Nicolelis et al, "Hebb's Dream: The Resurgence of Cell Assemblies" NEURON Volume 19, ISSUE 2, P219-221, August 01, 1997 http://www.cell.com/neuron/fulltext/S0896-6273%2800%2980932-0
https://doi.org/10.1016/S0896-6273(00)80932-0
Hebb's original summary: D. O. Hebb **The ORGANIZATION OF BEHAVIOR**
15) https://en.wikipedia.org/wiki/Central_processing_unit
16) Kandel, A New Intellectual Framework for Psychiatry, *Am J Psychiatry 1998;155:457-469.*
http://ajp.psychiatryonline.org/doi/full/10.1176/ajp.155.4.457 Kandel's research on sea slugs is summarized in:
http://www.genomenewsnetwork.org/articles/2004/01/09/memories.php
17) Benjamín Callejas Bedregala,☐, Santiago Figueirab *On the computing power of fuzzy Turing machines | Request PDF*. Available from: https://www.researchgate.net/publication/222429253_On_the_computing_power_of_fuzzy_Turing_machines
18) MOORES LAW http://www.intel.com/content/www/us/en/electronic-innovations/moores-law-technology.html
19) http://whatis.techtarget.com/definition/operating-system-OS
Leonard, A. W. (2006, August 17). Your Brain Boots Up Like a Computer. https://www.livescience.com/980-brain-boots-computer.html
20) Torsten Wiesel "The Neural Basis of Visual Perception"
http://centennial.rucares.org/index.php?page=Neural_Basis_Visual_Perception

Martinez and Alonso, "COMPLEX RECEPTIVE FIELDS IN PRIMARY VISUAL CORTEX"
Neuroscientist. 2003 Oct; 9(5): 317–331. doi: 10.1177/1073858403252732
https://www.ncbi.nlm.nih.gov/pmc/articles/PMC2556291/
Yeo, B. T., Krienen, F. M., Sepulcre, J., Sabuncu, M. R., Lashkari, D., Hollinshead, M., Roffman, J. L., Smoller, J. W., Zöllei, L., Polimeni, J. R., Fischl, B., Liu, H., & Buckner, R. L. (2011). The organization of the human cerebral cortex estimated by intrinsic functional connectivity. *Journal of neurophysiology*, *106*(3), 1125–1165. https://doi.org/10.1152/jn.00338.2011
https://www.ncbi.nlm.nih.gov/pmc/articles/PMC3174820/
Casanova, M. F., & Casanova, E. L. (2019). The modular organization of the cerebral cortex: Evolutionary significance and possible links to neurodevelopmental conditions. *The Journal of comparative neurology*, *527*(10), 1720–1730. https://doi.org/10.1002/cne.24554
21) DeLong, M., & Wichmann, T. (2010). Changing views of basal ganglia circuits and circuit disorders. *Clinical EEG and neuroscience*, *41*(2), 61–67. https://doi.org/10.1177/155005941004100204
22) Posner M. I. (2016). Orienting of attention: Then and now. *Quarterly journal of experimental psychology (2006)*, *69*(10), 1864–1875. https://doi.org/10.1080/17470218.2014.937446
Vossel S, Geng JJ, Fink GR. Dorsal and Ventral Attention Systems: Distinct Neural Circuits but Collaborative Roles. *The Neuroscientist*. 2014;20(2):150-159. doi:10.1177/1073858413494269
https://journals.sagepub.com/doi/full/10.1177/1073858413494269
23) Adolph, A.R. Bulletin of Mathematical Biophysics (1959) 21: 195. https://appliedgo.net/perceptron/
24) http://www.humanconnectomeproject.org/
Connectome Workbench http://www.humanconnectome.org/software/connectome-workbench.html
Van Essen, D. C., Ugurbil, K., Auerbach, E., Barch, D., Behrens, T. E. J., Bucholz, R., ... Yacoub, E. (2012). The Human Connectome Project: A data acquisition perspective. *NeuroImage*, *62*(4), 2222–2231. https://doi.org/10.1016/j.neuroimage.2012.02.018   https://www.ncbi.nlm.nih.gov/pmc/articles/PMC3606888/
25) Stitt, I., Hollensteiner, K.J., Galindo-Leon, E. *et al.* Dynamic reconfiguration of cortical functional connectivity across brain states. *Sci Rep* **7**, 8797 (2017). https://doi.org/10.1038/s41598-017-08050-6https://www.nature.com/articles/s41598-017-08050-6
26) The Neuroscientist Who Wants To Upload Humanity To A Computer Randal Koene is recruiting top neuroscientists to help him make humans live forever. https://www.popsci.com/article/science/neuroscientist-who-wants-upload-humanity-computer/
https://www.fhi.ox.ac.uk/brain-emulation-roadmap-report.pdfAnd there is a site

to subscribe for future use https://carboncopies.org/
The Prospects of Whole Brain Emulation within the next Half-CenturyJournal of Artificial General Intelligence 4(3) 130-152, 2013DOI: 10.2478/jagi-2013-0008
Sandberg, A. & Bostrom, N. (2008): Whole Brain Emulation: A Roadmap, Technical Report #2008-3, Future ofHumanity Institute, Oxford University www.fhi.ox.ac.uk/reports/2008-3.pdf

27) Gerstner, W., Kreiter, A. K., Markram, H., & Herz, A. V. M. (1997). Neural codes: Firing rates and beyond. *Proceedings of the National Academy of Sciences*, *94*(24), 12740–12741. https://doi.org/10.1073/pnas.94.24.12740 https://www.pnas.org/content/94/24/12740   For detail and papers of Gerstein's work in spike trains see the bibliography at https://neurotree.org/beta/publications.php?pid=1365

Sengupta Abhronil, Ye Yuting, Wang Robert, Liu Chiao, Roy Kaushik, Going Deeper in Spiking Neural Networks: VGG and Residual Architectures, Frontiers in Neuroscience, 13, 2019 95 DOI=10.3389/fnins.2019.00095 https://www.frontiersin.org/articles/10.3389/fnins.2019.00095/full

Yao, Z., Hu, B., Xie, Y., Moore, P., & Zheng, J. (2015). A review of structural and functional brain networks: small world and atlas. Brain informatics, 2(1), 45–52. https://doi.org/10.1007/s40708-015-0009-z https://www.ncbi.nlm.nih.gov/pmc/articles/PMC4883160/

28) NEURO RESOURCES ONLINE multiple sites via
https://neuroscientificallychallenged.com/
https://www.teachthought.com/pedagogy/brain-based-learning-resources/
https://www.mcgill.ca/bic/neuroinformatics
https://thebrain.mcgill.ca/

29) https://www.yalescientific.org/2010/09/evolution-of-the-cerebral-cortex-makes-us-human/

Rakic P. (2009). Evolution of the neocortex: a perspective from developmental biology. *Nature reviews. Neuroscience*, *10*(10), 724–735. https://doi.org/10.1038/nrn2719   https://www.ncbi.nlm.nih.gov/pmc/articles/PMC2913577/

Hofman M. A. (2014). Evolution of the human brain: when bigger is better. *Frontiers in neuroanatomy*, *8*, 15. https://doi.org/10.3389/fnana.2014.00015 **https://www.ncbi.nlm.nih.gov/pmc/articles/PMC3973910/**

Pine, D. S., Wise, S. P., & Murray, E. A. (2021). Evolution, Emotion, and Episodic Engagement. *The American journal of psychiatry*, *178*(8), 701–714. https://doi.org/10.1176/appi.ajp.2020.20081187   https://www.ncbi.nlm.nih.gov/pmc/articles/PMC8378585/

Defelipe J. (2011). The evolution of the brain, the human nature of cortical circuits, and intellectual creativity. *Frontiers in neuroanatomy*, *5*, 29. https://doi.org/10.3389/fnana.2011.00029   **https://www.ncbi.nlm.nih.gov/pmc/articles/PMC3098448/**

Reilly, S. K., Yin, J., Ayoub, A. E., Emera, D., Leng, J., Cotney, J., Sarro, R.,

Rakic, P., & Noonan, J. P. (2015). Evolutionary genomics. Evolutionary changes in promoter and enhancer activity during human corticogenesis. *Science (New York, N.Y.)*, *347*(6226), 1155–1159. https://doi.org/10.1126/science.1260943 https://www.ncbi.nlm.nih.gov/pmc/articles/PMC4426903/
Sherwood, C. C., Subiaul, F., & Zawidzki, T. W. (2008). A natural history of the human mind: tracing evolutionary changes in brain and cognition. *Journal of anatomy*, *212*(4), 426–454. https://doi.org/10.1111/j.1469-7580.2008.00868.x https://www.ncbi.nlm.nih.gov/pmc/articles/PMC2409100/
https://www.livescience.com/48122-cerebellum-makes-humans-special.html
Fig 1.2: Brodmann's regions: OpenStax - https://cnx.org/contents/FPtK1zmh@8.25:fEI3C8Ot@10/Preface
Version 8.25 from the Textbook OpenStax Anatomy and Physiology Published May 18, 201
30) *The mapping is a complex mathematical process studied by several groups.*
David C Van Essen, James W Lewis, Heather A Drury, Nouchine Hadjikhani, Roger B.H Tootell, Muge Bakircioglu, Michael I Miller,Mapping visual cortex in monkeys and humans using surface-based atlases,Vision Research,Volume 41, Issues 10–11,2001,
Pages 1359-1378,ISSN 0042-6989,https://doi.org/10.1016/S0042-6989(01)00045-1.
https://www.sciencedirect.com/science/article/pii/S0042698901000451
Visualizing Flat Maps of the Human Brain   https://www.math.fsu.edu/~mhurdal/research/visualizemaps.html
Cerebral Cortex: A Cartographic Approach | Fewer Lacunae   https://kevinbinz.com/2015/10/29/cerebral-cortex/
31) For an estimate of number of cell columns, see Gazzaniga ref.
Cain N, Iyer R, Koch C, Mihalas S (2016) The Computational Properties of a Simplified Cortical Column Model. PLoS Comput Biol 12(9): e1005045. https://doi.org/10.1371/journal.pcbi.1005045   https://www.ncbi.nlm.nih.gov/pmc/articles/PMC5019422/
https://journals.plos.org/ploscompbiol/article?id=10.1371/journal.pcbi.1005045
Cortical Neurons and Circuits : A Tutorial Introduction Richard B. Wells Published 2005 a review of the structure, composition, and statistical modeling of the organization of the neocortex. http://www.mrc.uidaho.edu/~rwells/techdocs/reu06/Cortical Neurons and Circuits.pdf
White's rules are as follows. Rule 1. Every neuron within the target area of a projection receives input from the projection. Corollary to Rule 1. Axon terminals from any extrinsic or intrinsic source synapse onto every morphological or physiological neuron type within their terminal projection field. In practice this means that a pathway will form synapses with every element in their target region capable of forming the type of synapse normally made by the pathway (i.e., asymmetrical or symmetrical). Rule 2. Different dendrites of a single neuron form similar synaptic patterns; that is, the numbers, types proportions, and

spatial distribution of synapses is similar, provided the dendrites are exposed to similar synaptic inputs. Corollary to Rule 2. Axonal pathways form similar synaptic patterns onto all the dendrites of a single neuron, provided the dendrites occur within the target region of the axonal pathway. Rule 3. Neuronal types receive characteristic patterns of synaptic connections; the actual numbers, proportions, and spatial distribution of the synapses formed by each neuronal type occur within a range of values. Corollary to Rule 3. Different extrinsic and intrinsic synaptic pathways form specific proportions of their synapses with different postsynaptic elements (spines vs. dendritic shafts, one cell type vs. another). Rule 4. The receptive field properties of every cortical neuron are shaped by the spatial and temporal integration of inputs from a variety of excitatory and inhibitory sources. Inputs from a single source cannot be the sole determinant of the receptive field properties of cortical neurons. Rule 5. Only a fraction of the synaptic inputs to a cortical neuron are activated at one time. Therefore, despite the great variety of neuron types that occur in the nervous system, all neurons can be subsumed under a standard signal processing schema involving four elements: input element, integrative element, conductile element, and output element.

32) Markram, H., Muller, E., Ramaswamy, S., Reimann, M. W., Abdellah, M., Sanchez, C. A., Ailamaki, A., Alonso-Nanclares, L., Antille, N., Arsever, S., Kahou, G. A., Berger, T. K., Bilgili, A., Buncic, N., Chalimourda, A., Chindemi, G., Courcol, J. D., Delalondre, F., Delattre, V., Druckmann, S., … Schürmann, F. (2015). Reconstruction and Simulation of Neocortical Microcircuitry. *Cell*, *163*(2), 456–492. https://doi.org/10.1016/j.cell.2015.09.029 https://www.cell.com/abstract/S0092-8674%2815%2901191-5

33) Bloom, J. S., & Hynd, G. W. (2005). The role of the corpus callosum in interhemispheric transfer of information: excitation or inhibition?. *Neuropsychology review*, *15*(2), 59–71. https://doi.org/10.1007/s11065-005-6252-y

Eric Mooshagian, Anatomy of the Corpus Callosum Reveals Its Function, Journal of Neuroscience 13 February 2008, 28 (7) 1535-1536; DOI: 10.1523/JNEUROSCI.5426-07.2008 https://www.jneurosci.org/content/28/7/1535

Seymour, S. E., Reuter-Lorenz, P. A., & Gazzaniga, M. S. (1994). The disconnection syndrome. Basic findings reaffirmed. *Brain : a journal of neurology*, *117 (Pt 1)*, 105–115. https://doi.org/10.1093/brain/117.1.105

Human Motor Corpus Callosum: Topography, Somatotopy, and Link between Microstructure and Function, Mathias Wahl, Birgit Lauterbach-Soon, Elke Hattingen, Patrick Jung, Oliver Singer, Steffen Volz, Johannes C. Klein, Helmuth Steinmetz, Ulf Ziemann, Journal of Neuroscience 7 November 2007, 27 (45) 12132-12138; https://www.jneurosci.org/content/27/45/12132

34) S. Knecht, B. Dräger, M. Deppe, L. Bobe, H. Lohmann, A. Flöel, E.-B. Ringelstein, H. Henningsen, Handedness and hemispheric language dominance in healthy humans, *Brain*, Volume 123, Issue 12, December 2000, Pages

2512–2518, https://doi.org/10.1093/brain/123.12.2512
The language side is generally associated with handedness, though whether cortex determines handedness or vice versa is not entirely clear. The fact that children with brain injuries before the age of (roughly) 13 can transfer language processing to the contralateral cortex, but not readily after that, shows both the potential for use of the other side, and the loss as areas become more organized for specific functions.

Gerstenecker, A., & Lazar, R. M. (2019). Language recovery following stroke. *The Clinical neuropsychologist*, *33*(5), 928–947. https://doi.org/10.1080/13854046.2018.1562093

Paul, L., Brown, W., Adolphs, R. *et al.* Agenesis of the corpus callosum: genetic, developmental and functional aspects of connectivity. *Nat Rev Neurosci* **8**, 287–299 (2007). https://doi.org/10.1038/nrn2107

The mix of genetic and experiential factors is still debated in linguistics:
https://www.amazon.com/Language-Instinct-How-Mind-Creates/dp/1491514981
https://www.quora.com/What-do-neuroscientists-say-about-Noam-Chomskys-universal-grammar-theory

35) Roger Brown's "original word game"
https://www.oxfordhandbooks.com/view/10.1093/oxfordhb/9780199641604.001.0001/oxfordhb-9780199641604-e-024#oxfordhb-9780199641604-e-024-div1-16

Revisiting Roger Brown's "Original Word Game":An Experimental Approach to the Pseudo-Semantic Basis of
Language-Specific Speech Perception in Late Infancy, Reese M. Heitner
https://www.aaai.org/Library/MAICS/1999/maics99-010.php
https://www.semanticscholar.org/paper/Revisiting-Roger-Brown%27s-%22Original-Word-Game%22%3A-An-Heitner/f16be85aeb78e4b8e76773b6550259d7f79065e7

Broca and Wernicke and reading areas. https://carta.anthropogeny.org/moca/topics/brocas-and-wernickes-areas

Dehaene in **Reading In The Brain** argues that the more recent reading skill *(compared to speech) uses brain capacities linking multiple cortical regions.*
TABLE OF SPEECH ABNORMALITIES   https://www.ncbi.nlm.nih.gov/books/NBK356270/
TABLE OF READING ABNORMALITIES   https://www.nichd.nih.gov/health/topics/reading/conditioninfo/disorders

36) Corballis M. C. (2014). Left brain, right brain: facts and fantasies. *PLoS biology*, *12*(1), e1001767. https://doi.org/10.1371/journal.pbio.1001767
Detailed review of elements of lateralization.
https://constanttherapyhealth.com/brainwire/right-brain-injury-vs-left-brain-injury-understanding-impact-brain-injury-daily-life/
https://en.wikipedia.org/wiki/Myers%E2%80%93Briggs_Type_Indicator

37) Brodmann areas https://radiopaedia.org/articles/brodmann-areas?lang=us

Glasser, M., Coalson, T., Robinson, E. *et al.* A multi-modal parcellation of human cerebral cortex. *Nature* **536**, 171–178 (2016).
http://www.nature.com/nature/journal/v536/n7615/full/nature18933.html
https://www.ncbi.nlm.nih.gov/pmc/articles/PMC4990127/
38) The pattern recognition theory of mind is described by Kurzweil,
https://www.amazon.com/How-Create-Mind-Thought-Revealed/dp/0143124048
Bruner's work summarized in
https://www.amazon.com/Thinking-Goodnow-Austin-Science-Editons/dp/B007KL3O1E
Neisser https://archive.org/stream/CognitivePsychologyClassicEdition/Cognitive_Psychology_(Classic_Edition)_djvu.txt
39) Hawkins, J., Ahmad, S., & Cui, Y. (2017). A Theory of How Columns in the Neocortex Enable Learning the Structure of World. *Frontiers in neural circuits*, *11*, 81. https://doi.org/10.3389/fncir.2017.00081 https://www.ncbi.nlm.nih.gov/pmc/articles/PMC5661005/
40) https://en.wikipedia.org/wiki/Piaget's_theory_of_cognitive_development
Deviations from Piaget's concept of cognitive development:
https://w4dey.wordpress.com/2010/03/21/deviations-from-piaget%E2%80%99s-concept-of-cognitive-development/
Supekar K, Musen M, Menon V (2009) Development of Large-Scale Functional Brain Networks in Children. PLoS Biol 7(7): e1000157. https://doi.org/10.1371/journal.pbio.1000157
41) S.M. Maricich, P. Azizi, J.Y. Jones, M.C. Morriss, J.V. Hunter, E.O. Smith, G. Miller, Myelination as Assessed by Conventional MR Imaging is Normal in Young Children with Idiopathic Developmental Delay,
American Journal of Neuroradiology Sep 2007, 28 (8) 1602-1605; DOI: 10.3174/ajnr.A0602
http://www.ajnr.org/content/28/8/1602.full
Meyer, H. C., & Lee, F. S. (2019). Translating Developmental Neuroscience to Understand Risk for Psychiatric Disorders. *The American journal of psychiatry*, *176*(3), 179–185. https://doi.org/10.1176/appi.ajp.2019.19010091
Daniel J. Miller, Tetyana Duka, Cheryl D. Stimpson, Steven J. Schapiro, Wallace B. Baze, Mark J. McArthur, Archibald J. Fobbs, André M. M. Sousa, Nenad Šestan, Derek E. Wildman, Leonard Lipovich, Christopher W. Kuzawa, Patrick R. Hof, Chet C. Sherwood, Proceedings of the National Academy of Sciences Oct 2012, 109 (41) 16480-16485; DOI: 10.1073/pnas.1117943109
http://www.pnas.org/content/109/41/16480.full
Casey, B. J., Tottenham, N., Liston, C., & Durston, S. (2005). Imaging the developing brain: what have we learned about cognitive development?. *Trends in cognitive sciences*, *9*(3), 104–110. https://doi.org/10.1016/j.tics.2005.01.01
https://www.researchgate.net/publication/7995747_
Casey, B. J., Getz, S., & Galvan, A. (2008). The adolescent brain. *Developmental review : DR*, *28*(1), 62–77. https://doi.org/10.1016/j.

dr.2007.08.003   https://www.ncbi.nlm.nih.gov/pmc/articles/PMC2500212/
Naama Barnea-Goraly, Vinod Menon, Mark Eckert, Leanne Tamm, Roland Bammer, Asya Karchemskiy, Christopher C. Dant, Allan L. Reiss, White Matter Development During Childhood and Adolescence: A Cross-sectional Diffusion Tensor Imaging Study, *Cerebral Cortex*, Volume 15, Issue 12, December 2005, Pages 1848–1854, https://doi.org/10.1093/cercor/bhi062https://academic.oup.com/cercor/article/15/12/1848/339689
Chevalier, N., Kurth, S., Doucette, M. R., Wiseheart, M., Deoni, S. C., Dean, D. C., 3rd, O'Muircheartaigh, J., Blackwell, K. A., Munakata, Y., & LeBourgeois, M. K. (2015). Myelination Is Associated with Processing Speed in Early Childhood: Preliminary Insights. *PloS one*, *10*(10), e0139897. https://doi.org/10.1371/journal.pone.0139897   https://www.ncbi.nlm.nih.gov/pmc/articles/PMC4595421/
Sean C.L. Deoni, Douglas C. Dean, Justin Remer, Holly Dirks, Jonathan O'Muircheartaigh,Cortical maturation and myelination in healthy toddlers and young children,NeuroImage,Volume 115,2015,Pages 147-161,ISSN 1053-8119, https://doi.org/10.1016/j.neuroimage.2015.04.058. https://www.sciencedirect.com/science/article/pii/S1053811915003584
Tierney, A. L., & Nelson, C. A., 3rd (2009). Brain Development and the Role of Experience in the Early Years. *Zero to three*, *30*(2), 9–13. https://www.ncbi.nlm.nih.gov/pmc/articles/PMC3722610/
42) https://www.frontiersin.org/articles/10.3389/fnana.2012.00022/full
Defelipe Javier, Markram Henry, Rockland Kathleen, The Neocortical Column Frontiers in Neuroanatomy 6 2012, p22 DOI=10.3389/fnana.2012.00022 https://www.frontiersin.org/article/10.3389/fnana.2012.00022
43) Paul C. Lebby, BRAIN IMAGING: A Guide for Clinicians. ISBN-13: 978-0190239060
ISBN-10: 0190239069 https://en.wikipedia.org/wiki/Karl_Lashley
https://en.wikipedia.org/wiki/Halstead-Reitan_Neuropsychological_Battery
44) Forster, B. B., MacKay, A. L., Whittall, K. P., Kiehl, K. A., Smith, A. M., Hare, R. D., & Liddle, P. F. (1998). Functional magnetic resonance imaging: the basics of blood-oxygen-level dependent (BOLD) imaging. *Canadian Association of Radiologists journal = Journal l'Association canadienne des radiologistes*, *49*(5), 320–329. https://www.ncbi.nlm.nih.gov/pmc/articles/PMC3811098/
45) Glover G. H. (2011). Overview of functional magnetic resonance imaging. *Neurosurgery clinics of North America*, *22*(2), 133–vii. https://doi.org/10.1016/j.nec.2010.11.001
Turner R. (2016). Uses, misuses, new uses and fundamental limitations of magnetic resonance imaging in cognitive science. *Philosophical transactions of the Royal Society of London. Series B, Biological sciences*, *371*(1705), 20150349. https://doi.org/10.1098/rstb.2015.0349
46) https://en.wikipedia.org/wiki/Neurometrics

References

European Delirium Association, & American Delirium Society (2014). The DSM-5 criteria, level of arousal and delirium diagnosis: inclusiveness is safer. *BMC medicine*, *12*, 141. https://doi.org/10.1186/s12916-014-0141-2
https://www.ncbi.nlm.nih.gov/pmc/articles/PMC4177077/ https://jhupbooks.press.jhu.edu/content/traumatized-brain
https://www.atrainceu.com/content/2-causes-delirium-0
Development and Validation of a Dementia Risk Prediction Model in the General Population: An Analysis of Three Longitudinal StudiesPublished Online:11 Dec 2018 https://ajp.psychiatryonline.org/doi/10.1176/appi.ajp.2020.19101099

47) F. Lucy Raymond, Patrick Tarpey, The genetics of mental retardation, *Human Molecular Genetics*, Volume 15, Issue suppl_2, 15 October 2006, Pages R110–R116, https://doi.org/10.1093/hmg/ddl189

48) https://www.nia.nih.gov/health/what-is-dementia

Gardner, H., **Frames of Mind: The Theory of Multiple Intelligences, 3rd Ed**
ISBN-13: 978-0465024339 ISBN-10: 0465024335

49) Another approach has been presented by Williams using more recent circuit data including: DEFAULT MODE (rumination), SALIENCE(anxious avoidance), NEGATIVE AFFECT(negative threat bias), POSITIVE AFFECT(anhedonia), ATTENTION(inattention), and COGNITIVE CONTROL(dyscontrol). These overlap with some features of *Neuromind,* but issues discussed in the appendix to this chapter challenge the validity of circuit definitions.

Williams, Leanne M. "Precision Psychiatry: A Neural Circuit Taxonomy for Depression and Anxiety." *The Lancet Psychiatry*, vol. 3, no. 5, May 2016, pp. 472–480, www.ncbi.nlm.nih.gov/pmc/articles/PMC4922884 doi: 10.1016/S2215-0366(15)00579-9

Buckholz and Meyer-Lindenberg proposed this idea as a "transdiagnostic basis for risk of mental illness" Buckholtz, J. W., & Meyer-Lindenberg, A. (2012). Psychopathology and the Human Connectome: Toward a Transdiagnostic Model of Risk For Mental Illness. *Neuron*, *74*(6), 990–1004. https://doi.org/10.1016/j.neuron.2012.06.002
https://www.cell.com/neuron/fulltext/S0896-6273(12)00514-4

Insel, T. R. (2014). The NIMH Research Domain Criteria (RDoC) Project: Precision Medicine for Psychiatry. *American Journal of Psychiatry*, *171*(4), 395–397. https://doi.org/10.1176/appi.ajp.2014.14020138
https://ajp.psychiatryonline.org/doi/full/10.1176/appi.ajp.2014.14020138
The interview in Psychiatric annals 42.9 sept 2012 p350 is about defining brain operations for better diagnosis.

Gillihan, S. J., & Parens, E. (2011). Should We Expect "Neural Signatures" forDSMDiagnoses? *The Journal of Clinical Psychiatry*, *72*(10), 1383–1389**.
https://doi.org/10.4088/jcp.10r06332gre**

APPENDIX REFS
50) The various techniques are documented in Wikipedia for easy reference: For example https://en.wikipedia.org/wiki/CT_scan
Adey, W. R. (1967). Hippocampal states and functional relations with cortico-subcortical systems in attention and learning. *Progress in brain research*, *27*, 228-245.
51) Hurley, R. A. (2015). A Practical Update on Neuroimaging for Psychiatric Disorders. *Psychiatric Times*. https://doi.org/https://www.psychiatrictimes.com/node/734537 http://www.psychiatrictimes.com/cme/practical-update-neuroimaging-psychiatric-disorders
Peter, F., Andrea, S., & Nancy, A. (2018). Forty years of structural brain imaging in mental disorders: is it clinically useful or not? *Dialogues in Clinical Neuroscience*, *20*(3), 179–186. https://www.ncbi.nlm.nih.gov/pmc/articles/PMC6296397/
52) Sharma, P., Savy, L., Britton, J., Taylor, R., Howick, A., & Patton, M. (1996). Huntington's disease: a molecular genetic and CT comparison. *Journal of Neurology, Neurosurgery & Psychiatry*, *60*(2), 208. https://www.ncbi.nlm.nih.gov/pmc/articles/PMC1073808/
53) https://en.wikipedia.org/wiki/Magnetic_resonance_imaging
Ioannidis, J. P. A. (2011). Excess Significance Bias in the Literature on Brain Volume Abnormalities. *Archives of General Psychiatry*, *68*(8), 773. https://doi.org/10.1001/archgenpsychiatry.2011.28https://jamanetwork.com/journals/jamapsychiatry/fullarticle/1107236
54) https://en.wikipedia.org/wiki/Single-photon_emission_computed_tomography
55) https://en.wikipedia.org/wiki/Functional_magnetic_resonance_imaging
Mohamed, F. B. (2010). BOLD FMRI: A Guide to Functional Imaging for Neuroscientists. Netherlands: Springer New York.
Kalin N. H. (2021). Understanding the Value and Limitations of MRI Neuroimaging in Psychiatry. *The American journal of psychiatry*, *178*(8), 673–676. https://doi.org/10.1176/appi.ajp.2021.21060616
56) Wager, T. D., Lindquist, M., & Kaplan, L. (2007). Meta-analysis of functional neuroimaging data: current and future directions. *Social Cognitive and Affective Neuroscience*, *2*(2), 150–158. https://doi.org/10.1093/scan/nsm015 https://www.ncbi.nlm.nih.gov/pmc/articles/PMC2555451/
Alústiza, I., Radua, J., Albajes-Eizagirre, A., Domínguez, M., Aubá, E., & Ortuño, F. (2016). Meta-Analysis of
MacQueen, G. (2010). Will there be a role for neuroimaging in clinical psychiatry? *Journal of Psychiatry and Neuroscience*, *35*(5), 291–293. https://doi.org/10.1503/jpn.100129 https://www.ncbi.nlm.nih.gov/pmc/articles/PMC2928281/
Acar, F., Seurinck, R., Eickhoff, S. B., & Moerkerke, B. (2018). Assessing robustness against potential publication bias in Activation Likelihood Estimation

(ALE) meta-analyses for fMRI. *PloS one, 13*(11), e0208177. https://doi.org/10.1371/journal.pone.0208177
https://www.ncbi.nlm.nih.gov/pmc/articles/PMC6267999/
Samartsidis, P., Montagna, S., Nichols, T. E., & Johnson, T. D. (2017). The coordinate-based meta-analysis of neuroimaging data. *Statistical science : a review journal of the Institute of Mathematical Statistics, 32*(4), 580–599. https://doi.org/10.1214/17-STS624
C.R. Tench, Radu Tanasescu, C.S. Constantinescu, W.J. Cottam, D.P. Auer,Coordinate based meta-analysis of networks in neuroimaging studies,NeuroImage,Volume 205,2020,116259,ISSN 1053-8119, https://doi.org/10.1016/j.neuroimage.2019.116259.
(https://www.sciencedirect.com/science/article/pii/S105381191930850X)
Hutchison, R. M., Womelsdorf, T., Allen, E. A., Bandettini, P. A., Calhoun, V. D., Corbetta, M., Della Penna, S., Duyn, J. H., Glover, G. H., Gonzalez-Castillo, J., Handwerker, D. A., Keilholz, S., Kiviniemi, V., Leopold, D. A., de Pasquale, F., Sporns, O., Walter, M., & Chang, C. (2013). Dynamic functional connectivity: promise, issues, and interpretations. *NeuroImage, 80,* 360–378. https://doi.org/10.1016/j.neuroimage.2013.05.079 https://www.ncbi.nlm.nih.gov/pmc/articles/PMC3807588/
Brown, E. N., & Behrmann, M. (2017). Controversy in statistical analysis of functional magnetic resonance imaging data. *Proceedings of the National Academy of Sciences, 114*(17), E3368–E3369. https://doi.org/10.1073/pnas.1705513114
https://www.ncbi.nlm.nih.gov/pmc/articles/PMC5410776/
Can we trust statistics in fMRI studies? | PLOS Neuroscience Community. (2018, January 8). https://blogs.plos.org/neuro/2018/01/08/can-we-trust-statistics-in-fmri-studies/
57) Sporns O. (2013). Structure and function of complex brain networks. *Dialogues in clinical neuroscience, 15*(3), 247–262. https://doi.org/10.31887/DCNS.2013.15.3/osporns
58) DEFAULT MODE (rumination), SALIENCE(anxious avoidance), and COGNITIVE CONTROL(dyscontrol).
An alternate set of pathways has also been described by Williams et al.(49)
59) A number of mathematical techniques have been utilized to define "central nodes" identified via "centrality metrics", *with degree, betweenness, and eigenvector centrality being three of the most popular measures*. Degree identifies the most connected nodes, whereas *betweenness centrality* identifies those located on the most traveled paths. Eigenvector centrality considers *nodes connected to other high degree nodes* as highly central. a new centrality metric called **leverage centrality** considers the extent of connectivity of a node relative to the connectivity of its neighbors.
Joyce, K. E., Laurienti, P. J., Burdette, J. H., & Hayasaka, S. (2010). A New Measure of Centrality for Brain Networks. *PLoS ONE, 5*(8), e12200. https://doi.

org/10.1371/journal.pone.0012200
https://journals.plos.org/plosone/article?id=10.1371/journal.pone.0012200
Wang, J. (2010). Graph-based network analysis of resting-state functional MRI. *Frontiers in Systems Neuroscience.* https://doi.org/10.3389/fnsys.2010.00016
https://www.ncbi.nlm.nih.gov/pmc/articles/PMC2893007/
Wang, J.-H., Zuo, X.-N., Gohel, S., Milham, M. P., Biswal, B. B., & He, Y. (2011). Graph Theoretical Analysis of Functional Brain Networks: Test-Retest Evaluation on Short- and Long-Term Resting-State Functional MRI Data. *PLoS ONE, 6*(7), e21976. https://doi.org/10.1371/journal.pone.0021976 http://journals.plos.org/plosone/article?id=10.1371/journal.pone.0021976
Bullmore, E. T., & Bassett, D. S. (2011). Brain Graphs: Graphical Models of the Human Brain Connectome. *Annual Review of Clinical Psychology, 7*(1), 113–140. https://doi.org/10.1146/annurev-clinpsy-040510-143934
http://www.annualreviews.org/doi/abs/10.1146/annurev-clinpsy-040510-143934?journalCode=clinpsy&
Bundell, S. (2016). The ultimate brain map. *Nature.* https://doi.org/10.1038/d41586-019-00058-4
https://www.nature.com/articles/d41586-019-00058-4
60) Silbersweig D, Loscalzo J. Precision Psychiatry Meets Network Medicine: Network Psychiatry. *JAMA Psychiatry.* 2017;74(7):665–666. doi:10.1001/jamapsychiatry.2017.0580
Stanley, M. L., Moussa, M. N., Paolini, B. M., Lyday, R. G., Burdette, J. H., & Laurienti, P. J. (2013). Defining nodes in complex brain networks. *Frontiers in Computational Neuroscience, 7.* https://doi.org/10.3389/fncom.2013.00169
61) https://en.wikipedia.org/wiki/Diffusion_MRI
Roberts, R. E., Anderson, E. J., & Husain, M. (2013). White matter microstructure and cognitive function. *The Neuroscientist : a review journal bringing neurobiology, neurology and psychiatry, 19*(1), 8–15. https://doi.org/10.1177/1073858411421218
https://www.frontiersin.org/articles/10.3389/fnint.2018.00043/full
https://www.ncbi.nlm.nih.gov/pmc/articles/PMC3757996/
Wu, W., & Miller, K. L. (2017). Image formation in diffusion MRI: A review of recent technical developments. *Journal of Magnetic Resonance Imaging, 46*(3), 646–662
https://doi.org/10.1002/jmri.25664
https://www.ncbi.nlm.nih.gov/pmc/articles/PMC5574024/
Li, X., Weissman, M., Talati, A., Svob, C., Wickramaratne, P., Posner, J., & Xu, D. (2019). A diffusion tensor imaging study of brain microstructural changes related to religion and spirituality in families at high risk for depression. *Brain and Behavior, 9*(2), e01209. https://doi.org/10.1002/brb3.1209 https://www.ncbi.nlm.nih.gov/pmc/articles/PMC6379589/
Barysheva, M., Jahanshad, N., Foland-Ross, L., Altshuler, L. L., & Thompson, P. M. (2013). White matter microstructural abnormalities in bipolar disorder: A

whole brain diffusion tensor imaging study. *NeuroImage: Clinical*, *2*, 558–568. https://doi.org/10.1016/j.nicl.2013.03.016 https://www.ncbi.nlm.nih.gov/pmc/articles/PMC3777761/

KUBICKI, M., MCCARLEY, R., WESTIN, C., PARK, H., MAIER, S., KIKINIS, R., … SHENTON, M. (2007). A review of diffusion tensor imaging studies in schizophrenia. *Journal of Psychiatric Research*, *41*(1–2), 15–30. https://doi.org/10.1016/j.jpsychires.2005.05.005 https://www.ncbi.nlm.nih.gov/pmc/articles/PMC2768134/

Li, X., Lim, C., Li, K., Guo, L., & Liu, T. (2013). Detecting brain state changes via fiber-centered functional connectivity analysis. *Neuroinformatics*, *11*(2), 193–210. https://doi.org/10.1007/s12021-012-9157-y https://www.ncbi.nlm.nih.gov/pmc/articles/PMC3908655/

62) https://en.wikipedia.org/wiki/Electroencephalography
https://en.wikipedia.org/wiki/Quantitative_electroencephalography
Nuwer, M. (1997). Assessment of digital EEG, quantitative EEG, and EEG brain mapping: Report of the American Academy of Neurology and the American Clinical Neurophysiology Society. *Neurology*, *49*(1), 277–292. https://doi.org/10.1212/wnl.49.1.277
http://www.neurology.org/content/49/1/277.full.html

63) Snyder, S. M., & Hall, J. R. (2006). A Meta-analysis of Quantitative EEG Power Associated With Attention-Deficit Hyperactivity Disorder. *Journal of Clinical Neurophysiology*, *23*(5), 441–456. https://doi.org/10.1097/01.wnp.0000221363.12503.7
https://journals.lww.com/clinicalneurophys/Abstract/2006/10000/A_Meta_analysis_of_Quantitative_EEG_Power.9.aspx

64) Thatcher, R.W. and Lubar, J.F., HISTORY OF THE SCIENTIFIC STANDARDS OF QEEG NORMATIVE DATABASES, Introduction to QEEG and Neurofeedback: Advanced Theory and Applications" Thomas Budzinsky, H. Budzinski, J. Evans and A. Abarbanel editors, Academic Press, San Diego, CA, 2008. PDF

65) Grech, R., Cassar, T., Muscat, J., Camilleri, K. P., Fabri, S. G., Zervakis, M., … Vanrumste, B. (2008). Review on solving the inverse problem in EEG source analysis. *Journal of NeuroEngineering and Rehabilitation*, *5*(1), 25. https://doi.org/10.1186/1743-0003-5-25

Puskás, S. (2011). EEG source localization using LORETA (low resolution electromagnetic tomography). *Ideggyogyaszati Szemle*, *64*(3–4), 110–118. https://www.ncbi.nlm.nih.gov/pmc/articles/PMC2605581/
https://www.researchgate.net/publication/51100634_EEG_source_localization_using_LORETA_low_resolution_electromagnetic_tomography

66) Huster, R. J., Debener, S., Eichele, T., & Herrmann, C. S. (2012). Methods for Simultaneous EEG-fMRI: An Introductory Review. *Journal of Neuroscience*, *32*(18), 6053–6060. https://doi.org/10.1523/jneurosci.0447-12.2012
https://www.jneurosci.org/content/32/18/6053

Abreu, R., Leal, A., & Figueiredo, P. (2018). EEG-Informed fMRI: A Review of Data Analysis Methods. *Frontiers in Human Neuroscience, 12.* https://doi.org/10.3389/fnhum.2018.00029 https://www.frontiersin.org/articles/10.3389/fnhum.2018.00029/full
Mulert, C., Pogarell, O., & Hegerl, U. (2008). Simultaneous EEG-fMRI: Perspectives in Psychiatry. *Clinical EEG and Neuroscience, 39*(2), 61–64. https://doi.org/10.1177/155005940803900207 https://www.researchgate.net/publication/5402614_Simultaneous_EEG-fMRI_Perspectives_in_psychiatry
https://en.wikipedia.org/wiki/Magnetoencephalography
Marzetti, L., Basti, A., Chella, F., D'Andrea, A., Syrjälä, J., & Pizzella, V. (2019). Brain Functional Connectivity Through Phase Coupling of Neuronal Oscillations: A Perspective From Magnetoencephalography. *Frontiers in neuroscience, 13,* 964. https://doi.org/10.3389/fnins.2019.00964 https://www.frontiersin.org/articles/10.3389/fnins.2019.00964/full
Sharon, D., Hämäläinen, M. S., Tootell, R. B. H., Halgren, E., & Belliveau, J. W. (2007). The advantage of combining MEG and EEG: Comparison to fMRI in focally stimulated visual cortex. *NeuroImage, 36*(4), 1225–1235. https://doi.org/10.1016/j.neuroimage.2007.03.066 https://www.ncbi.nlm.nih.gov/pmc/articles/PMC2706118/
Liu, Z., Ding, L., & He, B. (2006). Integration of EEG/MEG with MRI and fMRI. *IEEE Engineering in Medicine and Biology Magazine : The Quarterly Magazine of the Engineering in Medicine & Biology Society, 25*(4), 46–53. https://doi.org/10.1109/memb.2006.1657787 https://www.ncbi.nlm.nih.gov/pmc/articles/PMC1815485/
Magnetoencephalography - Wikipedia
Lee, Adrian K.C., et al. "Mapping Cortical Dynamics Using Simultaneous MEG/EEG and Anatomically-Constrained Minimum-Norm Estimates: An Auditory Attention Example." *Journal of Visualized Experiments,* no. 68, 24 Oct. 2012, www.jove.com/video/4262/mapping-cortical-dynamics-using-simultaneous-megeeg-anatomically, 10.3791/4262. https://www.jove.com/video/4262/mapping-cortical-dynamics-using-simultaneous-megeeg-anatomically
Braeutigam S. (2013). Magnetoencephalography: fundamentals and established and emerging clinical applications in radiology. *ISRN radiology, 2013,* 529463. https://doi.org/10.5402/2013/529463 https://www.ncbi.nlm.nih.gov/pmc/articles/PMC4045536/
Uhlhaas, P. J., Liddle, P., Linden, D., Nobre, A. C., Singh, K. D., & Gross, J. (2017). Magnetoencephalography as a Tool in Psychiatric Research: Current Status and Perspective. *Biological psychiatry. Cognitive neuroscience and neuroimaging, 2*(3), 235–244. https://doi.org/10.1016/j.bpsc.2017.01.005 https://www.ncbi.nlm.nih.gov/pmc/articles/PMC5387180/
Hironaga, N., Takei, Y., Mitsudo, T., Kimura, T., & Hirano, Y. (2020).

References

Prospects for Future Methodological Development and Application of Magnetoencephalography Devices in Psychiatry. *Frontiers in psychiatry*, *11*, 863. https://doi.org/10.3389/fpsyt.2020.00863   https://www.ncbi.nlm.nih.gov/pmc/articles/PMC7472776/

67) Clinical Utility of Evoked Potentials: Overview, Visual Evoked Potential, Brainstem Auditory Evoked Potentials.
https://emedicine.medscape.com/article/1137451-overview

Walsh, P. (2005). The clinical role of evoked potentials. *Journal of Neurology, Neurosurgery & Psychiatry*, *76*(suppl_2), ii16–ii22. https://doi.org/10.1136/jnnp.2005.068130   https://www.ncbi.nlm.nih.gov/pmc/articles/PMC1765695/
https://www.sciencedirect.com/book/9780409950625/eeg-and-evoked-potentials-in-psychiatry-and-behavioral-neurology

68) Amit Etkin, A Reckoning and Research Agenda for Neuroimaging in Psychiatry,American Journal of Psychiatry 2019 176:7, 507

Etkin A. Addressing the Causality Gap in Human Psychiatric Neuroscience. *JAMA Psychiatry.* 2018;75(1):3–4. doi:10.1001/jamapsychiatry.2017.3610
https://jamanetwork.com/journals/jamapsychiatry/article-abstract/2664012

Dotson, N. M., Goodell, B., Salazar, R. F., Hoffman, S. J., & Gray, C. M. (2015). Methods, caveats and the future of large-scale microelectrode recordings in the non-human primate. *Frontiers in Systems Neuroscience*, *9*. https://doi.org/10.3389/fnsys.2015.00149
https://www.frontiersin.org/articles/10.3389/fnsys.2015.00149/full

Morita, T., Asada, M., & Naito, E. (2016). Contribution of Neuroimaging Studies to Understanding Development of Human Cognitive Brain Functions. *Frontiers in human neuroscience*, *10*, 464. https://doi.org/10.3389/fnhum.2016.00464

Supekar, K., Musen, M., & Menon, V. (2009). Development of Large-Scale Functional Brain Networks in Children. *PLoS Biology*, *7*(7), e1000157. https://doi.org/10.1371/journal.pbio.1000157

Deisseroth, K. (2010, October 20). Optogenetics: Controlling the Brain with Light https://www.scientificamerican.com/article/optogenetics-controlling/

Woodward, N. D., & Cascio, C. J. (2015). Resting-State Functional Connectivity in Psychiatric Disorders. *JAMA Psychiatry*, *72*(8), 743. https://doi.org/10.1001/jamapsychiatry.2015.0484
https://jamanetwork.com/journals/jamapsychiatry/fullarticle/2203837?resultClick=1
https://www.frontiersin.org/research-topics/5857/neuromodulation-of-circuits-in-brain-health-and-disease#articles
https://blogs.scientificamerican.com/cross-check/the-singularity-and-the-neural-code/

CHAPTER 2 REFERENCES

1) Same gene linked to bigger brains of dolphins and primates. Ed Yong Published September 11, 2012 https://www.nationalgeographic.com/science/article/dolphins-primates-gene-bigger-brains-aspm

2) Dunbar, R.I.M. "The Social Brain Hypothesis and Its Implications for Social Evolution." Annals of Human Biology, vol. 36, no. 5, Jan. 2009, pp. 562–572, 10.1080/03014460902960289. Accessed 26 Aug. 2019. https://anthropology.net/2008/04/23/the-social-brain-hypothesis-are-our-brains-hardwired-to-deal-with-social-hierarchies/
Dunbar, R. I. M., and S. Shultz. "Evolution in the Social Brain." Science, vol. 317, no. 5843, 7 Sept. 2007, pp. 1344–1347, 10.1126/science.1145463.

3) Bakker, Cornelis, et al. "The Social Brain: A Unifying Foundation for Psychiatry." Academic Psychiatry : The Journal of the American Association of Directors of Psychiatric Residency Training and the Association for Academic Psychiatry, vol. 26, no. 3, 2002,p219,https://www.researchgate.net/profile/Alan_Swann/publication/10693322_The_Social_Brain_A_Unifying_Foundation_for_Psychiatry/links/0912f50f349be6876b000000/The-Social-Brain-A-Unifying-Foundation-for-Psychiatry.pdf **https://ourgap.org/page-18120**

4) Academic Psychiatry 26:3, Fall 2002 Of Two Minds: An Anthropologist Looks at American Psychiatry: T.M. Luhrmann: 9780679744931: Amazon.com: Books. (2019). https://www.amazon.com/Two-Minds-Anthropologist-American-Psychiatry/dp/0679744932   Morton D. Sosland, The Social Brain and the Psychiatrist in Training, Psychiatric Annals, 35:10, pp 854-866, 2005. http://www.slackinc.com/reprints   https://www.giffordlectures.org/file/michael-gazzaniga-social-brain

5) See later section.

6) Frith, C. D. (2007). The social brain? Philosophical Transactions of the Royal Society B: Biological Sciences, 362(1480), 671–678. https://doi.org/10.1098/rstb.2006.2003   https://www.ncbi.nlm.nih.gov/pmc/articles/PMC1919402/

7) Van Overwalle, Frank. "Social Cognition and the Brain: A Meta-Analysis." Human Brain Mapping, vol. 30, no. 3, Mar. 2009, pp. 829–858, 10.1002/hbm.20547. Accessed 4 Sept. 2019.   https://www.ncbi.nlm.nih.gov/pubmed/18381770

8) Adolphs, R. (2009). The Social Brain: Neural Basis of Social Knowledge. Annual Review of Psychology, 60(1), 693–716. https://doi.org/10.1146/annurev.psych.60.110707.163514   https://www.ncbi.nlm.nih.gov/pmc/articles/PMC2588649/
Kennedy, D. P., & Adolphs, R. (2012). The social brain in psychiatric and neurological disorders. Trends in cognitive sciences, 16(11), 559–572. https://doi.org/10.1016/j.tics.2012.09.006

References

9) Hari, R., & Kujala, M. V. (2009). Brain Basis of Human Social Interaction: From Concepts to Brain Imaging. Physiological Reviews,89(2),453–479.https://doi.org/10.1152/physrev.00041.2007

10) Soto-Icaza, P., Aboitiz, F., & Billeke, P. (2015). Development of social skills in children: neural and behavioral evidence for the elaboration of cognitive models. Frontiers in neuroscience, 9, 333. https://doi.org/10.3389/fnins.2015.00333

11) Beier, J. S., & Spelke, E. S. (2012). Infants' Developing Understanding of Social Gaze. Child Development, 83(2), 486–496. https://doi.org/10.1111/j.1467-8624.2011.01702.x   Dev Sci. 2009 Sep; 12(5): 798–814. doi: 10.1111/j.1467-7687.2009.00833.x

Thorup, E., Nyström, P., Gredebäck, G., Bölte, S., Falck-Ytter, T., & EASE Team (2016). Altered gaze following during live interaction in infants at risk for autism: an eye tracking study. Molecular autism, 7, 12. *https://doi.org/10.1186/s13229-016-0069-9*

Angélina Vernetti, Nataşa Ganea, Leslie Tucker, Tony Charman, Mark H. Johnson, Atsushi Senju,Infant neural sensitivity to eye gaze depends on early experience of gaze communication,Developmental Cognitive Neuroscience,Volume 34,2018, Pages 1-6,ISSN 1878-9293, https://doi.org/10.1016/j.dcn.2018.05.007

12) Farroni, T., Menon, E., Rigato, S., & Johnson, M. H. (2007). The perception of facial expressions in newborns. The European Journal of Developmental Psychology, 4(1), 2–13.https://doi.org/10.1080/17405620601046832

Kaiser, J., Crespo-Llado, M. M., Turati, C., & Geangu, E. (2017). The development of spontaneous facial responses to others' emotions in infancy: An EMG study. Scientific Reports, 7(1). https://doi.org/10.1038/s41598-017-17556-y https://www.nature.com/articles/s41598-017-17556-y

Schultz, R. T. (2005). Developmental deficits in social perception in autism: the role of the amygdala and fusiform face area. International Journal of Developmental Neuroscience, 23(2–3), 125–141. https://doi.org/10.1016/j.ijdevneu.2004.12.012 https://www.sciencedirect.com/science/article/pii/S073657480400156X

Addabbo M, Longhi E, Marchis IC, Tagliabue P, Turati C (2018) Dynamic facial expressions of emotions are discriminated at birth. PLoS ONE 13(3): e0193868. https://doi.org/10.1371/journal.pone.0193868

12) Young, G. S., Merin, N., Rogers, S. J., & Ozonoff, S. (2009). Gaze behavior and affect at 6 months: predicting clinical outcomes and language development in typically developing infants and infants at risk for autism. Developmental science, 12(5), 798–814. https://doi.org/10.1111/j.1467-7687.2009.00833.x*Stein, A., Arteche, A., Lehtonen, A., Craske, M., Harvey, A., Counsell, N., & Murray, L. (2010). Interpretation of infant facial expression in the context of maternal postnatal depression. Infant Behavior and Development, 33(3),273–278. https://doi.org/10.1016/j.infbeh.2010.03.002*   https://www.sciencedirect.com/science/article/pii/S0163638310000287

Barry, R. A., Graf Estes, K., & Rivera, S. M. (2015). Domain general learning: Infants use social and non-social cues when learning object statistics. Frontiers in psychology, 6, 551. https://doi.org/10.3389/fpsyg.2015.00551

13) *Unmasking the Face: A Guide to Recognizing Emotions From Facial Expressions Paperback – December 2, 2003 ISBN = 1883536367* by Paul Ekman (Author), Wallace V. Friesen

14) Albonico, A., & Barton, J. (2019). Progress in perceptual research: the case of prosopagnosia. F1000Research, 8, F1000 Faculty Rev-765. https://doi.org/10.12688/f1000research.18492.1

15) Savic, I., Gulyas, B., Larsson, M., & Roland, P. (2000). Olfactory functions are mediated by parallel and hierarchical processing. Neuron, 26(3), 735–745. https://doi.org/10.1016/s0896-6273(00)81209-x

16) Hirstein, W., & Ramachandran, V. S. (1997). Capgras syndrome: a novel probe for understanding the neural representation of the identity and familiarity of persons. Proceedings. Biological sciences, 264(1380), 437–444. https://doi.org/10.1098/rspb.1997.0062

17) Kluver bucy syndrome Joe M Das; Waquar Siddiqui. https://www.ncbi.nlm.nih.gov/books/NBK544221/

18) Mathiak, K. A., Alawi, E. M., Koush, Y., Dyck, M., Cordes, J. S., Gaber, T. J., Zepf, F. D., Palomero-Gallagher, N., Sarkheil, P., Bergert, S., Zvyagintsev, M., & Mathiak, K. (2015). Social reward improves the voluntary control over localized brain activity in fMRI-based neurofeedback training. Frontiers in Behavioral Neuroscience, 9. https://doi.org/10.3389/fnbeh.2015.00136

McCormick, E. M., van Hoorn, J., Cohen, J. R., & Telzer, E. H. (2018). Functional connectivity in the social brain across childhood and adolescence. Social cognitive and affective neuroscience, 13(8), 819–830. https://doi.org/10.1093/scan/nsy064

Ivy F. Tso, Saige Rutherford, Yu Fang, Mike Angstadt, Stephan F. Taylor, The "social brain" is highly sensitive to the mere presence of social information: An automated meta-analysis and an independent study *https://doi.org/10.1371/journal.pone.0196503*
https://journals.plos.org/plosone/article?id=10.1371/journal.pone.0196503

Schilbach, L., Derntl, B., Aleman, A., Caspers, S., Clos, M., Diederen, K. M., Gruber, O., Kogler, L., Liemburg, E. J., Sommer, I. E., Müller, V. I., Cieslik, E. C., & Eickhoff, S. B. (2016). Differential Patterns of Dysconnectivity in Mirror Neuron and Mentalizing Networks in Schizophrenia. Schizophrenia bulletin, 42(5), 1135–1148. https://doi.org/10.1093/schbul/sbw015

19) Tzakis Nikolaos, Holahan Matthew R., Social Memory and the Role of the Hippocampal CA2 Region
Frontiers in Behavioral Neuroscience, 13, 2019, P233 https://www.frontiersin.org/articles/10.3389/fnbeh.2019.00233/full

20) Klinge, C., Röder, B., & Büchel, C. (2010). Increased amygdala activation to emotional auditory stimuli in the blind. Brain, 133(6), 1729–1736.

References

https://doi.org/10.1093/brain/awq102   https://academic.oup.com/brain/article/133/6/1729/355156

21) Music stimulates emotions through specific brain circuits. http://jonlieffmd.com/blog/music-stimulates-emotions-through-specific-brain-circuits

Nathalie Gosselin, Isabelle Peretz, Erica Johnsen, Ralph Adolphs,, Amygdala damage impairs emotion recognition from music, Neuropsychologia,Volume 45, Issue 2,2007,Pages 236-244,ISSN 0028-3932,https://doi.org/10.1016/j.neuropsychologia.2006.07.012. https://www.sciencedirect.com/science/article/pii/S0028393206003083

22) Kilner, J. M., & Lemon, R. N. (2013). What We Know Currently about Mirror Neurons. Current Biology, 23(23), R1057–R1062. https://doi.org/10.1016/j.cub.2013.10.051

Acharya, S., & Shukla, S. (2012). Mirror neurons: Enigma of the metaphysical modular brain. Journal of Natural Science, Biology and Medicine, 3(2), 118. https://doi.org/10.4103/0976-9668.101878

Cooper, R. P., Cook, R., Dickinson, A., & Heyes, C. M. (2013). Associative (not Hebbian) learning and the mirror neuron system. Neuroscience Letters, 540, 28–36. https://doi.org/10.1016/j.neulet.2012.10.002

Thomas, B. (n.d.). What's So Special about Mirror Neurons? Scientific American Blog Network. Retrieved February 13, 2020, from https://blogs.scientificamerican.com/guest-blog/whats-so-special-about-mirror-neurons/

Gallese, V. (2013). Mirror neurons, embodied simulation and a second-person approach to mindreading. Cortex, 49(10), 2954–2956. https://doi.org/10.1016/j.cortex.2013.09.008

Ferrari, P. F., & Rizzolatti, G. (2014). Mirror neuron research: the past and the future. Philosophical Transactions of the Royal Society B: Biological Sciences, 369(1644). https://doi.org/10.1098/rstb.2013.0169

Cattaneo, L., & Rizzolatti, G. (2009). The Mirror Neuron System. Archives of Neurology, 66(5). https://doi.org/10.1001/archneurol.2009.41   https://jamanetwork.com/journals/jamaneurology/fullarticle/796996

Perspectives on Imitation: Mechanisms of imitation and imitation in animals - Susan L. Hurley - Google Books

VS Ramachandran: The neurons that shaped civilization | Video on TED.com

Giacomo Rizzolatti and Laila Craighero

Annual Review of Neuroscience 2004 27:1, 169-192

https://www.annualreviews.org/doi/abs/10.1146/annurev.neuro.27.070203.144230?rfr_dat=cr_pub%3Dpubmed&url_ver=Z39.88-2003&rfr_id=ori%3Arid%3Acrossref.org&journalCode=neuro

23) Keysers, C., & Perrett, D. I. (2004). Demystifying social cognition: a Hebbian perspective. Trends in cognitive sciences, 8(11), 501–507. https://doi.org/10.1016/j.tics.2004.09.005

https://www.cell.com/trends/cognitive-sciences/fulltext/S1364-6613(04)00243-8?

M.A. Umiltà, E. Kohler, V. Gallese, L. Fogassi, L. Fadiga, C. Keysers, G. Rizzolatti,
I Know What You Are Doing: A Neurophysiological Study,Neuron,Volume 31, Issue 1,
2001,Pages 155-165,ISSN 0896-6273,https://doi.org/10.1016/S0896-6273(01)00337-3
https://www.sciencedirect.com/science/article/pii/S0896627301003373
Perry, A., Stiso, J., Chang, E. F., Lin, J. J., Parvizi, J., & Knight, R. T. (2018). Mirroring in the Human Brain: Deciphering the Spatial-Temporal Patterns of the Human Mirror Neuron System. Cerebral cortex (New York, N.Y. : 1991), 28(3), 1039–1048. https://doi.org/10.1093/cercor/bhx013
Jackson, P. L., Meltzoff, A. N., & Decety, J. (2006). Neural circuits involved in imitation and perspective-taking. NeuroImage, 31(1), 429–439. https://doi.org/10.1016/j.neuroimage.2005.11.026
Meltzoff, A. N., & Moore, M. K. (1997). Explaining Facial Imitation: A Theoretical Model. Early Development & Parenting, 6(3–4), 179–192. https://doi.org/10.1002/(SICI)1099-0917(199709/12)6:3/43.0.CO;2-R
Leslie, K. R., Johnson-Frey, S. H., & Grafton, S. T. (2004). Functional imaging of face and hand imitation: towards a motor theory of empathy. NeuroImage, 21(2), 601–607. https://doi.org/10.1016/j.neuroimage.2003.09.038
Buccino, G., Binkofski, F., & Riggio, L. (2004). The mirror neuron system and action recognition. Brain and Language, 89(2), 370–376. https://doi.org/10.1016/s0093-934x(03)00356-0
24) Mirror Neurons and the Evolution of Brain and Language - Google Books
25) Casile, A., Caggiano, V., & Ferrari, P. F. (2011). The mirror neuron system: a fresh view. The Neuroscientist : a review journal bringing neurobiology, neurology and psychiatry, 17(5), 524–538. https://doi.org/10.1177/1073858410392239
Sandrone S. (2013). Self through the Mirror (Neurons) and Default Mode Network: What Neuroscientists Found and What Can Still be Found There. Frontiers in human neuroscience, 7, 383. https://doi.org/10.3389/fnhum.2013.00383
Keromnes, G., Chokron, S., Celume, M. P., Berthoz, A., Botbol, M., Canitano, R., Du Boisgueheneuc, F., Jaafari, N., Lavenne-Collot, N., Martin, B., Motillon, T., Thirioux, B., Scandurra, V., Wehrmann, M., Ghanizadeh, A., & Tordjman, S. (2019). Exploring Self-Consciousness From Self- and Other-Image Recognition in the Mirror: Concepts and Evaluation. Frontiers in psychology, 10, 719. https://doi.org/10.3389/fpsyg.2019.00719
26) Stephani, C., Fernandez-Baca Vaca, G., Maciunas, R., Koubeissi, M., & Lüders, H. O. (2011). Functional neuroanatomy of the insular lobe. Brain structure & function, 216(2), 137–149.
27) Allman, J. M., Tetreault, N. A., Hakeem, A. Y., Manaye, K. F., Semendeferi, K., Erwin, J. M., Park, S., Goubert, V., & Hof, P. R. (2011). The von Economo neurons in fronto-insular and anterior cingulate cortex.

References

Annals of the New York Academy of Sciences, 1225, 59–71. https://doi.org/10.1111/j.1749-6632.2011.06011.x

Cauda, F., Geminiani, G. C., & Vercelli, A. (2014). Evolutionary appearance of von Economo's neurons in the mammalian cerebral cortex. Frontiers in Human Neuroscience, 8. https://doi.org/10.3389/fnhum.2014.00104 https://www.frontiersin.org/articles/10.3389/fnhum.2014.00104/full

28) Starr, C. J., Sawaki, L., Wittenberg, G. F., Burdette, J. H., Oshiro, Y., Quevedo, A. S., & Coghill, R. C. (2009). Roles of the Insular Cortex in the Modulation of Pain: Insights from Brain Lesions. Journal of Neuroscience, 29(9), 2684–2694. https://doi.org/10.1523/jneurosci.5173-08.2009

Droutman, V., Read, S. J., & Bechara, A. (2015). Revisiting the role of the insula in addiction. Trends in Cognitive Sciences, 19(7), 414–420. https://doi.org/10.1016/j.tics.2015.05.005

29) Nadine Gogolla,The insular cortex,Current Biology,Volume 27, Issue 12,2017,
Pages R580-R586,ISSN 0960-9822,
https://doi.org/10.1016/j.cub.2017.05.010   https://www.sciencedirect.com/science/article/pii/S0960982217305468

Persistence of Feelings and Sentience after Bilateral Damage of the Insula April2012Cerebral Cortex 23(4)DOI: 10.1093/cercor/bhs077
Damasio, Damasio and Tranel Cereb Cortex. 2013 Apr; 23(4): 833–846 doi: 10.1093/cercor/bhs077

Edmund T. Rolls,Functions of the anterior insula in taste, autonomic, and related functions,
Brain and Cognition,Volume 110,2016,Pages 4-19,ISSN 0278-2626,
https://doi.org/10.1016/j.bandc.2015.07.002. https://www.sciencedirect.com/science/article/pii/S027826261530004X

Andreja Varjačić, Dante Mantini, Jacob Levenstein, Elitsa D. Slavkova, Nele Demeyere, Céline R. Gillebert,The role of left insula in executive set-switching: Lesion evidence from an acute stroke cohort,Cortex,Volume 107,2018,Pages 92-101,ISSN 0010-9452,
https://doi.org/10.1016/j.cortex.2017.11.009. https://www.sciencedirect.com/science/article/pii/S0010945217303908

Emmerling F, Schuhmann T, Lobbestael J, Arntz A, Brugman S, Sack AT (2016) The Role of the Insular Cortex in Retaliation. PLoS ONE 11(4): e0152000. https://doi.org/10.1371/journal.pone.0152000

30) What does it mean to "represent" in the brain?
Genon, S., Reid, A., Langner, R., Amunts, K., & Eickhoff, S. B. (2018). How to Characterize the Function of a Brain Region. Trends in Cognitive Sciences, 22(4), 350–364. https://doi.org/10.1016/j.tics.2018.01.010
https://www.cell.com/trends/cognitive-sciences/fulltext/S1364-6613(18)30023-8

31) Menon, V., & Uddin, L. Q. (2010). Saliency, switching, attention and control: a network model of insula function. Brain Structure and Function,

214(5–6), 655–667. https://doi.org/10.1007/s00429-010-0262-0
Seeley, W. W., Menon, V., Schatzberg, A. F., Keller, J., Glover, G. H., Kenna, H., Reiss, A. L., & Greicius, M. D. (2007). Dissociable Intrinsic Connectivity Networks for Salience Processing and Executive Control. Journal of Neuroscience, 27(9), 2349–2356. https://doi.org/10.1523/jneurosci.5587-06.2007
Droutman, V., Bechara, A., & Read, S. J. (2015). Roles of the Different Sub-Regions of the Insular Cortex in Various Phases of the Decision-Making Process. Frontiers in Behavioral Neuroscience, 9. https://doi.org/10.3389/fnbeh.2015.00309
Sestito, M., Raballo, A., Stanghellini, G., & Gallese, V. (2017). Editorial: Embodying the Self: Neurophysiological Perspectives on the Psychopathology of Anomalous Bodily Experiences. Frontiers in human neuroscience, 11, 631. https://doi.org/10.3389/fnhum.2017.00631
Jacob and Jeannerod, 2005, The motor theory of social cognition: a critique. *Trends in cognitive sciences*, *9*(1), 21–25. https://doi.org/10.1016/j.tics.2004.11.003)
32) Giudice, M. D., Manera, V., & Keysers, C. (2009). Programmed to learn? The ontogeny of mirror neurons. Developmental Science, 12(2), 350–363. https://doi.org/10.1111/j.1467-7687.2008.00783.x
33) Catmur, C. (2013). Sensorimotor learning and the ontogeny of the mirror neuron system. Neuroscience Letters, 540, 21–27. https://doi.org/10.1016/j.neulet.2012.10.001
34) Byom, L. J., & Mutlu, B. (2013). Theory of mind: mechanisms, methods, and new directions. Frontiers in human neuroscience, 7, 413.https://www.frontiersin.org/articles/10.3389/fnhum.2013.00413   https://doi.org/10.3389/fnhum.2013.00413

Differentiation of "self" from "other" and separate storage of "self" and "other" is similar to animal behavior tests for "theory of mind" (= awareness of self). The test used by animal behaviorists to determine whether an animal species has "theory of mind" ie a sense of separate self identity is the mirror test. The animal is placed in front of a mirror observing its reflection. If the animal can recognize that the motions of the reflection are identical to its own motions, (in primates, dolphins, elephants) it has a sense of selfmind. If the species does not recognize itself, it will begin threat behaviors which are mirrored and escalate hostile behavior.

Gusnard, D. A., Akbudak, E., Shulman, G. L., & Raichle, M. E. (2001). Medial prefrontal cortex and self-referential mental activity: relation to a default mode of brain function. Proceedings of the National Academy of Sciences of the United States of America, 98(7), 4259–4264. https://doi.org/10.1073/pnas.071043098   https://www.ncbi.nlm.nih.gov/pmc/articles/PMC31213/
35) Medial prefrontal cortex and self-referential mental activity: Relation to a

References

default mode of brain function
The information on dorsomedial prefrontal cortex does not overlap easily with OFC and medial PFC. This region adjoins cingulate and DLPFC and has been associated with features of self representation and theory of mind. This aspect is reviewed in chapter 6. Roy, A., Perlovsky, L., Besold, T. R., Weng, J., & Edwards, J. (2018). Editorial: Representation in the Brain. Frontiers in psychology, 9, 1410. https://doi.org/10.3389/fpsyg.2018.01410 An entire issue devoted to this subject:
https://www.frontiersin.org/research-topics/4398/representation-in-the-brain
Martin A. (2007). The representation of object concepts in the brain. Annual review of psychology, 58, 25–45. https://doi.org/10.1146/annurev.psych.57.102904.190143
36) Wood, J. N., & Grafman, J. (2003). Human prefrontal cortex: processing and representational perspectives. Nature reviews. Neuroscience, 4(2), 139–147. https://doi.org/10.1038/nrn1033
Isoda Masaki, Noritake Atsushi,What makes the dorsomedial frontal cortex active during reading the mental states of others? Frontiers in Neuroscience 7 2013 P232 https://www.frontiersin.org/articles/10.3389/fnins.2013.00232/full
37) "scripts" are perceived patterns of social interaction, (as in GAMES PEOPLE PLAY, Berne.) The observer must compile multiple events to build a model of the expected behavior of the other.
Steinbeis N. (2016). The role of self-other distinction in understanding others' mental and emotional states: neurocognitive mechanisms in children and adults. Philosophical transactions of the Royal Society of London. Series B, Biological sciences, 371(1686), 20150074. https://doi.org/10.1098/rstb.2015.0074
Grossmann, T. (2013). The role of medial prefrontal cortex in early social cognition. Frontiers in Human Neuroscience, 7. https://doi.org/10.3389/fnhum.2013.00340   https://www.frontiersin.org/articles/10.3389/fnhum.2013.00340/full
Anderson, S., Bechara, A., Damasio, H. et al. Impairment of social and moral behavior related to early damage in human prefrontal cortex. Nat Neurosci **2**, 1032–1037 (1999). https://doi.org/10.1038/14833   https://www.nature.com/articles/nn1199_1032#citeas
Johnson, M. H., Grossmann, T., & Kadosh, K. C. (2009). Mapping functional brain development: Building a social brain through interactive specialization. *Developmental Psychology, 45*(1), 151–159. https://doi.org/10.1037/a0014548
Gilbert, C. D., & Sigman, M. (2007). Brain states: top-down influences in sensory processing. Neuron, 54(5), 677–696. https://doi.org/10.1016/j.neuron.2007.05.019
38) Hawco, C., Buchanan, R. W., Calarco, N., Mulsant, B. H., Viviano, J. D., Dickie, E. W., Argyelan, M., Gold, J. M., Iacoboni, M., DeRosse, P., Foussias, G., Malhotra, A. K., Voineskos, A. N., & SPINS Group (2019). Separable and Replicable Neural Strategies During Social Brain Function in People With and

Without Severe Mental Illness. The American journal of psychiatry, 176(7), 521–530. https://ajp.psychiatryonline.org/doi/10.1176/appi.ajp.2018.17091020
39) *Phineas Gage's Astonishing Brain Injury* By *Kendra Cherry* https://www.verywellmind.com/phineas-gage-2795244
40) Clinical and eeg investigation of prefrontal lobotomy patients, Harold Stevens And Abraham Mosovich American Journal of Psychiatry 1947 104:2, 73-80 https://ajp.psychiatryonline.org/doi/abs/10.1176/ajp.104.2.73
41) Damasio case https://www.scientificamerican.com/article/feeling-our-emotions/
42) Eight Problems for the Mirror Neuron Theory of Action Understanding in Monkeys and Humans Gregory Hickok J Cogn Neurosci. 2009 July; 21(7): 1229–1243. doi: 10.1162/jocn.2009.21189
43) *Recording multi-subjects' brain activities simultaneously, proposed by Montague et al. is called the "hyperscanning" technique, which refers to simultaneous recording of hemodynamic or neuro-electric activity of the brains from multiple subjects involved in social interactions. The "hyperscanning technique" has the potential to explore interpersonal brain mechanisms using modern techniques (e.g., EEG, fMRI, fNIRS). Which show correlation between interaction of two or more people in social interactions.*
Liu, D., Liu, S., Liu, X., Zhang, C., Li, A., Jin, C., Chen, Y., Wang, H., & Zhang, X. (2018). Interactive Brain Activity: Review and Progress on EEG-Based Hyperscanning in Social Interactions. Frontiers in psychology, 9, 1862. https://doi.org/10.3389/fpsyg.2018.01862
Montague, P. R., Berns, G. S., Cohen, J. D., McClure, S. M., Pagnoni, G., Dhamala, M., Wiest, M. C., Karpov, I., King, R. D., Apple, N., & Fisher, R. E. (2002). Hyperscanning: simultaneous fMRI during linked social interactions. NeuroImage, 16(4), 1159–1164. https://doi.org/10.1006/nimg.2002.1150
Michela Balconi & Erika Molteni (2016) Past and future of near-infrared spectroscopy in studies of emotion and social neuroscience, Journal of Cognitive Psychology, 28:2, 129-146, DOI: 10.1080/20445911.2015.1102919
Spiegelhalder, K., Ohlendorf, S., Regen, W., Feige, B., Tebartz van Elst, L., Weiller, C., Hennig, J., Berger, M., & Tüscher, O. (2014). Interindividual synchronization of brain activity during live verbal communication. Behavioural brain research, 258, 75–79. https://doi.org/10.1016/j.bbr.2013.10.015
Lindenberger, U., Li, S. C., Gruber, W., & Müller, V. (2009). Brains swinging in concert: cortical phase synchronization while playing guitar. BMC neuroscience, 10, 22. https://doi.org/10.1186/1471-2202-10-22
G. Dumas, F. Lachat, J. Martinerie, J. Nadel, N. George, From social behaviour to brain synchronization: Review and perspectives in hyperscanning,IRBM,Volume 32, Issue 1,2011,Pages 48-53,ISSN 1959-0318,https://doi.org/10.1016/j.irbm.2011.01.002.
Yun, K., Watanabe, K., & Shimojo, S. (2012). Interpersonal body and neural synchronization as a marker of implicit social interaction. Scientific reports, 2,

References

959. https://doi.org/10.1038/srep00959

Jahng, J., Kralik, J. D., Hwang, D. U., & Jeong, J. (2017). Neural dynamics of two players when using nonverbal cues to gauge intentions to cooperate during the Prisoner's Dilemma Game. NeuroImage, 157, 263–274. https://doi.org/10.1016/j.neuroimage.2017.06.024 https://pubmed.ncbi.nlm.nih.gov/28610901/

Hu, Y., Pan, Y., Shi, X., Cai, Q., Li, X., & Cheng, X. (2018). Inter-brain synchrony and cooperation context in interactive decision making. Biological psychology, 133, 54–62. https://doi.org/10.1016/j.biopsycho.2017.12.005

Goldstein, P., Weissman-Fogel, I., Dumas, G., & Shamay-Tsoory, S. G. (2018). Brain-to-brain coupling during handholding is associated with pain reduction. Proceedings of the National Academy of Sciences of the United States of America, 115(11), E2528–E2537. https://doi.org/10.1073/pnas.1703643115

44) Mathiak, K. A., Alawi, E. M., Koush, Y., Dyck, M., Cordes, J. S., Gaber, T. J., Zepf, F. D., Palomero-Gallagher, N., Sarkheil, P., Bergert, S., Zvyagintsev, M., & Mathiak, K. (2015). Social reward improves the voluntary control over localized brain activity in fMRI-based neurofeedback training. Frontiers in Behavioral Neuroscience, 9. https://doi.org/10.3389/fnbeh.2015.00136 https://www.ncbi.nlm.nih.gov/pmc/articles/PMC4452886/

Bhanji, J. P., & Delgado, M. R. (2014). The social brain and reward: social information processing in the human striatum. Wiley interdisciplinary reviews. Cognitive science, 5(1), 61–73. https://doi.org/10.1002/wcs.1266

Tanimizu, T., Kenney, J. W., Okano, E., Kadoma, K., Frankland, P. W., & Kida, S. (2017). Functional Connectivity of Multiple Brain Regions Required for the Consolidation of Social Recognition Memory. Journal of Neuroscience, 37(15), 4103–4116. https://doi.org/10.1523/JNEUROSCI.3451-16.2017 http://www.jneurosci.org/content/37/15/4103

45) John A. Richey Alison Rittenberg Lauren Hughes Cara R. Damiano Antoinette Sabatino Stephanie Miller Eleanor Hanna James W. Bodfish Gabriel S. Dichter, Common and distinct neural features of social and non-social reward processing in autism and social anxiety disorder. *Social Cognitive and Affective Neuroscience, Volume 9, Issue 3, 1 March 2014, Pages 367–377, https://doi.org/10.1093/scan/nss146*

46) https://www.scientificamerican.com/article/is-there-really-an-autism-epidemic/

Nevison, C., Blaxill, M., & Zahorodny, W. (2018). California Autism Prevalence Trends from 1931 to 2014 and Comparison to National ASD Data from IDEA and ADDM. Journal of autism and developmental disorders, 48(12), 4103–4117. https://doi.org/10.1007/s10803-018-3670-2

47) Current nomenclature of "autism spectrum" has replaced subcategories and "asperger's syndrome".

48) Agnes Moors, Agnes(2009) 'Theories of emotion causation: A review', Cognition & Emotion, 23: 4, 625 — 662,First published on: 31 March 2009

(iFirst) http://dx.doi.org/10.1080/02699930802645739 For example, Panksepp uses the term for any subjective awareness of motivation. Agnes Moors, Phoebe C. Ellsworth, Klaus R. Scherer, Appraisal Theories of Emotion: State of the Art and Future Development https://doi.org/10.1177/1754073912468165

49) Ekman, P., & Friesen, W. V. (1975). Unmasking the face: A guide to recognizing emotions from facial clues.
https://www.paulekman.com/facial-action-coding-system/

50) Schmidt, K. L., & Cohn, J. F. (2001). Human facial expressions as adaptations: Evolutionary questions in facial expression research. American journal of physical anthropology, Suppl 33, 3–24. https://doi.org/10.1002/ajpa.2001

51) Parkinson, B., Fischer, A.H., & Manstead, A.S.R. (2004). Emotion in Social Relations: Cultural, Group, and Interpersonal Processes (1st ed.). Psychology Press. https://doi.org/10.4324/9780203644966

52) Rom Harre: https://positioningtheory.wordpress.com/what-is-positioning-theory/

53) Gregory Johnson, Theories of Emotion,
https://www.researchgate.net/publication/242689923_Theories_of_Emotion

54) https://emotion.wisc.edu/wp-content/uploads/sites/1353/2020/11/Cannon_1927AmJPsych.pdf

55) This article was originally published with the title "Feeling Our Emotions" in SA Mind 16, 1, 14-15 (April 2005) doi:10.1038/scientificamericanmind0405-14

Antonio Damasio, **The Feeling of What Happens**
https://www.amazon.com/Feeling-What-Happens-Emotion-Consciousness/dp/0156010755

The **Schachter Singer approach** *suggest that external emotional input can influence the emotional state of the receiving person. The theory has two-steps. In the first step, stimulus input produces an undifferentiated state of physiological arousal. In the second step, the arousal is interpreted in light of the characteristics of that input. It is this cognitive process of attribution of arousal to the presumed cause of the arousal that produces a specific experience.*
https://replicationindex.com/2019/02/24/schachter-and-singer-1962-the-experiment-that-never-happened/

57) Lee, S. A., Kim, C. Y., & Lee, S. H. (2016). Non-Conscious Perception of Emotions in Psychiatric Disorders: The Unsolved Puzzle of Psychopathology. Psychiatry investigation, 13(2), 165–173. https://doi.org/10.4306/pi.2016.13.2.165

Rohr, M., & Wentura, D. (2021). Degree and Complexity of Non-conscious Emotional Information Processing - A Review of Masked Priming Studies. Frontiers in human neuroscience, 15, 689369. https://doi.org/10.3389/fnhum.2021.689369

58) Keltner, D., Sauter, D., Tracy, J., & Cowen, A. (2019). Emotional Expression: Advances in Basic Emotion Theory. Journal of nonverbal behavior, 43(2),

References

133–160. https://doi.org/10.1007/s10919-019-00293-3
Zakowski, S. G., Harris, C., Krueger, N., Laubmeier, K. K., Garrett, S., Flanigan, R., & Johnson, P. (2003). Social barriers to emotional expression and their relations to distress in male and female cancer patients. British journal of health psychology, 8(Pt 3), 271–286. https://doi.org/10.1348/135910703322370851
59) Ekman P. (2009). Darwin's contributions to our understanding of emotional expressions. Philosophical transactions of the Royal Society of London. Series B, Biological sciences, 364(1535), 3449–3451. https://doi.org/10.1098/rstb.2009.0189
60) https://library.psychology.edu/wp-files/uploads/2019/10/Instinct.100919.pdf
Kassam, K. S., Markey, A. R., Cherkassky, V. L., Loewenstein, G., & Just, M. A. (2013). Identifying Emotions on the Basis of Neural Activation. *PloS one*, *8*(6), e66032. https://doi.org/10.1371/journal.pone.0066032
61) Papez labeled his neural pathway for emotion, but it involves memory and significance, see chapter four.
62) https://psych-neuro.com/2019/05/04/acting-raw/
https://www.theatlantic.com/health/archive/2014/03/how-actors-create-emotions-a-problematic-psychology/284291/
https://en.wikipedia.org/wiki/Tourette_syndrome
Ahmed, A., & Simmons, Z. (2013). Pseudobulbar affect: prevalence and management. *Therapeutics and clinical risk management*, *9*, 483–489. https://doi.org/10.2147/TCRM.S5390
63) Szasz, Thomas S. The Myth of Mental Illness : Foundations of a Theory of Personal Conduct. New York, Harperperennial, 2010.
https://www.ncbi.nlm.nih.gov/pmc/articles/PMC5353517/
David, A., & Laing, R. D. (2010). The divided self : an existential study in sanity and madness. London: Penguin.
https://psychology.jrank.org/pages/367/Ronald-David-Laing.html https://www.researchgate.net/publication/226795096_Labeling_Theory
How Labeling Theory Can Help Us Understand Bias and Criminal Behavior.
https://www.thoughtco.com/labeling-theory-3026627
64) Scheff, T. J. (1975). Labeling madness. Englewood Cliffs, N.J.: Prentice-Hall, Inc.
Scheff, T. J. (1974). The Labelling Theory of Mental Illness. American Sociological Review, 39(3), 444. https://doi.org/10.2307/2094300 https://www.jstor.org/stable/2094300?seq=1
65) Rosenhan D. L. (1973). On being sane in insane places. Science (New York, N.Y.), 179(4070), 250–258. https://doi.org/10.1126/science.179.4070.250
https://en.wikipedia.org/wiki/Rosenhan_experiment
66) Emphasis of one etiology over another is a particular weakness in Psychiatry.
67) Seeman, M., & Goffman, E. (1964). Stigma: Notes on the Management of Spoiled Identity. American Sociological Review, 29(5), 770. https://doi.

org/10.2307/2091442 Goffman https://en.wikipedia.org/wiki/Asylums_(book)
68) Dawson, G., Carver, L., Meltzoff, A. N., Panagiotides, H., McPartland, J., & Webb, S. J. (2002). Neural correlates of face and object recognition in young children with autism spectrum disorder, developmental delay, and typical development. Child development, 73(3), 700–717. https://doi.org/10.1111/1467-8624.00433
69) Clements, C. C., Zoltowski, A. R., Yankowitz, L. D., Yerys, B. E., Schultz, R. T., & Herrington, J. D. (2018). Evaluation of the Social Motivation Hypothesis of Autism. JAMA Psychiatry, 75(8), 797. https://doi.org/10.1001/jamapsychiatry.2018.1100
Baron-Cohen, S., Bowen, D. C., Holt, R. J., Allison, C., Auyeung, B., Lombardo, M. V., Smith, P., & Lai, M. C. (2015). The "Reading the Mind in the Eyes" Test: Complete Absence of Typical Sex Difference in ~400 Men and Women with Autism. PloS one, 10(8), e0136521. https://doi.org/10.1371/journal.pone.0136521negative https://psycnet.apa.org/record/2016-54551-001
Self–Other Relations in Social Development and Autism: Multiple Roles for Mirror Neurons and Other Brain Bases Justin H.G. Williams Autism research 1 73-90 2008 https://onlinelibrary.wiley.com/doi/pdf/10.1002/aur.15
70)Rylaarsdam, L., & Guemez-Gamboa, A. (2019). Genetic Causes and Modifiers of Autism Spectrum Disorder. Frontiers in cellular neuroscience, 13, 385. https://doi.org/10.3389/fncel.2019.00385
https://embryo.asu.edu/pages/autistic-disturbances-affective-contact-1943-leo-kanner
Misra, V. (2014). The Social Brain Network and Autism. Annals of Neurosciences, 21(2). https://doi.org/10.5214/ans.0972.7531.210208
71) Lowe, J. K., Werling, D. M., Constantino, J. N., Cantor, R. M., & Geschwind, D. H. (2015). Social responsiveness, an autism endophenotype: genomewide significant linkage to two regions on chromosome 8. The American journal of psychiatry, 172(3), 266–275. https://doi.org/10.1176/appi.ajp.2014.14050576
Dawson, G., Carver, L., Meltzoff, A. N., Panagiotides, H., McPartland, J., & Webb, S. J. (2002). Neural correlates of face and object recognition in young children with autism spectrum disorder, developmental delay, and typical development. Child development, 73(3), 700–717. https://doi.org/10.1111/1467-8624.00433https://www.ncbi.nlm.nih.gov/pmc/articles/PMC3651041/
John A. Richey Alison Rittenberg Lauren Hughes Cara R. Damiano Antoinette Sabatino Stephanie Miller Eleanor Hanna James W. Bodfish Gabriel S. Dichter **Common and distinct neural features of social and non-social reward processing in autism and social anxiety disorder** Social Cognitive and Affective Neuroscience, Volume 9, Issue 3, 1 March 2014, Pages 367–377, https://doi.org/10.1093/scan/nss146
Abrams, D. A., Padmanabhan, A., Chen, T., Odriozola, P., Baker, A. E., Kochalka, J., Phillips, J. M., & Menon, V. (2019). Impaired voice processing in

References

reward and salience circuits predicts social communication in children with autism. eLife, 8, e39906. https://doi.org/10.7554/eLife.39906

72) Hoeft F, Walter E, Lightbody AA, et al. Neuroanatomical Differences in Toddler Boys With Fragile X Syndrome and Idiopathic Autism. *Arch Gen Psychiatry.* 2011;68(3):295–305. doi:10.1001/archgenpsychiatry.2010.153 https://jamanetwork.com/journals/jamapsychiatry/fullarticle/211180

Miles, J. Autism spectrum disorders—A genetics review. Genet Med **13**, 278–294 (2011). https://doi.org/10.1097/GIM.0b013e3181ff67ba https://www.nature.com/articles/gim9201151#citeas

Yoo H. (2015). Genetics of Autism Spectrum Disorder: Current Status and Possible Clinical Applications. Experimental neurobiology, 24(4), 257–272. https://doi.org/10.5607/en.2015.24.4.257

Davis, J. M., Heft, I., Scherer, S. W., & Sikela, J. M. (2019). A Third Linear Association Between Olduvai (DUF1220) Copy Number and Severity of the Classic Symptoms of Inherited Autism. The American journal of psychiatry, 176(8), 643–650. https://doi.org/10.1176/appi.ajp.2018.18080993

Manoli, D. S., & State, M. W. (2021). Autism Spectrum Disorder Genetics and the Search for Pathological Mechanisms. The American journal of psychiatry, 178(1), 30–38. https://doi.org/10.1176/appi.ajp.2020.20111608 https://ajp.psychiatryonline.org/doi/10.1176/appi.ajp.2020.20010015

Chawner, S., Doherty, J. L., Anney, R., Antshel, K. M., Bearden, C. E., Bernier, R., Chung, W. K., Clements, C. C., Curran, S. R., Cuturilo, G., Fiksinski, A. M., Gallagher, L., Goin-Kochel, R. P., Gur, R. E., Hanson, E., Jacquemont, S., Kates, W. R., Kushan, L., Maillard, A. M., McDonald-McGinn, D. M., ... van den Bree, M. (2021). A Genetics-First Approach to Dissecting the Heterogeneity of Autism: Phenotypic Comparison of Autism Risk Copy Number Variants. *The American journal of psychiatry*, *178*(1), 77–86. https://doi.org/10.1176/appi.ajp.2020.20010015

Hashem, S., Nisar, S., Bhat, A.A. et al. Genetics of structural and functional brain changes in autism spectrum disorder. Transl Psychiatry **10**, 229 (2020). https://doi.org/10.1038/s41398-020-00921-3 https://www.nature.com/articles/s41398-020-00921-3

Douard, E., Zeribi, A., Schramm, C., Tamer, P., Loum, M. A., Nowak, S., Saci, Z., Lord, M. P., Rodríguez-Herreros, B., Jean-Louis, M., Moreau, C., Loth, E., Schumann, G., Pausova, Z., Elsabbagh, M., Almasy, L., Glahn, D. C., Bourgeron, T., Labbe, A., Paus, T., ... Jacquemont, S. (2021). Effect Sizes of Deletions and Duplications on Autism Risk Across the Genome. The American journal of psychiatry, 178(1), 87–98. https://doi.org/10.1176/appi.ajp.2020.19080834

73) Brown, A. S., Cheslack-Postava, K., Rantakokko, P., Kiviranta, H., Hinkka-Yli-Salomäki, S., McKeague, I. W., Surcel, H. M., & Sourander, A. (2018). Association of Maternal Insecticide Levels With Autism in Offspring From a National Birth Cohort. The American journal of psychiatry, 175(11), 1094–1101.

https://doi.org/10.1176/appi.ajp.2018.17101129
Whitworth, M., Bricker, L., & Mullan, C. (2015). Ultrasound for fetal assessment in early pregnancy. The Cochrane database of systematic reviews, 2015(7), CD007058. https://doi.org/10.1002/14651858.CD007058.pub3
Rosman, N. P., Vassar, R., Doros, G., DeRosa, J., Froman, A., DiMauro, A., Santiago, S., & Abbott, J. (2018). Association of Prenatal Ultrasonography and Autism Spectrum Disorder. JAMA pediatrics, 172(4), 336–344. https://doi.org/10.1001/jamapediatrics.2017.5634
Newnham, J. P., Evans, S. F., Michael, C. A., Stanley, F. J., & Landau, L. I. (1993). Effects of frequent ultrasound during pregnancy: a randomised controlled trial. Lancet (London, England), 342(8876), 887–891. https://doi.org/10.1016/0140-6736(93)91944-h
Janecka, M., Kodesh, A., Levine, S. Z., Lusskin, S. I., Viktorin, A., Rahman, R., Buxbaum, J. D., Schlessinger, A., Sandin, S., & Reichenberg, A. (2018). Association of Autism Spectrum Disorder With Prenatal Exposure to Medication Affecting Neurotransmitter Systems. JAMA Psychiatry, 75(12), 1217–1224. https://doi.org/10.1001/jamapsychiatry.2018.2728
74) Daniel P. Kennedy, Ph.D., Neural Correlates of Autistic Traits in the General Population: Insights Into Autism
American Journal of Psychiatry 2009 166:8, 849-851 https://ajp.psychiatryonline.org/doi/full/10.1176/appi.ajp.2009.09060829
Gotts, S. J., Simmons, W. K., Milbury, L. A., Wallace, G. L., Cox, R. W., & Martin, A. (2012). Fractionation of social brain circuits in autism spectrum disorders. Brain : a journal of neurology, 135(Pt 9), 2711–2725. https://doi.org/10.1093/brain/aws160
Deuse, L., Rademacher, L. M., Winkler, L., Schultz, R. T., Gründer, G., & Lammertz, S. E. (2016). Neural correlates of naturalistic social cognition: brain-behavior relationships in healthy adults. Social cognitive and affective neuroscience, 11(11), 1741–1751. https://doi.org/10.1093/scan/nsw094
Byrge, L., Dubois, J., Tyszka, J. M., Adolphs, R., & Kennedy, D. P. (2015). Idiosyncratic brain activation patterns are associated with poor social comprehension in autism. The Journal of neuroscience : the official journal of the Society for Neuroscience, 35(14), 5837–5850. https://doi.org/10.1523/JNEUROSCI.5182-14.2015
75) Baribeau, D. A., Dupuis, A., Paton, T. A., Hammill, C., Scherer, S. W., Schachar, R. J., Arnold, P. D., Szatmari, P., Nicolson, R., Georgiades, S., Crosbie, J., Brian, J., Iaboni, A., Kushki, A., Lerch, J. P., & Anagnostou, E. (2019). Structural neuroimaging correlates of social deficits are similar in autism spectrum disorder and attention-deficit/hyperactivity disorder: analysis from the POND Network. Translational psychiatry, 9(1), 72. https://doi.org/10.1038/s41398-019-0382-0
Green, S. A., Hernandez, L., Lawrence, K. E., Liu, J., Tsang, T., Yeargin, J., Cummings, K., Laugeson, E., Dapretto, M., & Bookheimer, S. Y. (2019).

References

Distinct Patterns of Neural Habituation and Generalization in Children and Adolescents With Autism With Low and High Sensory Overresponsivity. The American journal of psychiatry, 176(12), 1010–1020. https://doi.org/10.1176/appi.ajp.2019.18121333

Solomon, M., Frank, M. J., Ragland, J. D., Smith, A. C., Niendam, T. A., Lesh, T. A., Grayson, D. S., Beck, J. S., Matter, J. C., & Carter, C. S. (2015). Feedback-driven trial-by-trial learning in autism spectrum disorders. The American journal of psychiatry, 172(2), 173–181. https://doi.org/10.1176/appi.ajp.2014.14010036

Dickstein, D. P., Pescosolido, M. F., Reidy, B. L., Galvan, T., Kim, K. L., Seymour, K. E., Laird, A. R., Di Martino, A., & Barrett, R. P. (2013). Developmental meta-analysis of the functional neural correlates of autism spectrum disorders. Journal of the American Academy of Child and Adolescent Psychiatry, 52(3), 279–289.e16. https://doi.org/10.1016/j.jaac.2012.12.012

Relationship Between Cingulo-Insular Functional Connectivity and Autistic Traits in Neurotypical Adults, Adriana Di Martino, M.D., Zarrar Shehzad, B.Sc., Clare Kelly, Ph.D., Amy Krain Roy, Ph.D., Dylan G. Gee, B.A., Lucina Q. Uddin, Ph.D., Kristin Gotimer, B.A., Donald F. Klein, M.D., D.Sc., F. Xavier Castellanos, M.D., and Michael P. Milham, M.D., Ph.D.

American Journal of Psychiatry 2009 166:8, 891-899 https://ajp.psychiatryonline.org/doi/abs/10.1176/appi.ajp.2009.08121894

LC Robertson, MR Lamb and RT Knight

Effects of lesions of temporal-parietal junction on perceptual and attentional processing in humans

Journal of Neuroscience 1 October 1988, 8 (10) 3757-3769; DOI: https://doi.org/10.1523/JNEUROSCI.08-10-03757.1988 http://www.jneurosci.org/content/8/10/3757.short

76) Chlebowski C, Green JA, Barton ML, Fein D. Using the childhood autism rating scale to diagnose autism spectrum disorders. *J Autism Dev Disord*. 2010;40(7):787-799. doi:10.1007/s10803-009-0926-x

77) Other adaptation scales are referenced in chapter ten.

78) Mark J. Hilsenroth, Ph.D. et al Reliability and Validity of DSM-IV Axis V (Am J Psychiatry 2000; 157:1858–1863) https://ajp.psychiatryonline.org/doi/pdf/10.1176/appi.ajp.157.11.1858 *The three axis V scales can be scored reliably. The Global Assessment of Relational Functioning Scale and the Social and Occupational Functioning Assessment Scale evaluate different constructs. These findings support the validity of the Global Assessment of Functioning Scale as a scale of global psychopathology, the Social and Occupational Functioning Assessment Scale as a measure of problems in social, occupational, and interpersonal functioning, and the Global Assessment of Relational Functioning Scale as an index of personality pathology.* The second problem discussed by Goldman et al is the exclusion of physical impairment from the Global Assessment of Functioning Scale. AmJ Psychiatry

157:11, November 2000 1859
79) Scott, J. G., Mihalopoulos, C., Erskine, H. E., Roberts, J., & Rahman, A. (2016). Childhood Mental and Developmental Disorders. Disease Control Priorities, Third Edition (Volume 4): Mental, Neurological, and Substance Use Disorders, 145–161.
https://doi.org/10.1596/978-1-4648-0426-7_ch8
Gardner, A. (2017). The purpose of adaptation. Interface Focus, 7(5), 20170005. https://doi.org/10.1098/rsfs.2017.0005
80) Lewis, J. M., Beavers, W. R., Gossett, J. T., & Phillips, V. A. (1976). *No single thread: Psychological health in family systems.* Brunner/Mazel. https://doi.org/10.1007/978-1-349-04049-0
81) Chess, S., & Thomas, A. (1996). Temperament: Theory and Practice. NY: Brunner/Mazel.
https://www.scientificamerican.com/article/does-birth-order-affect-personality/
82) Skuse, D., Gallagher, L. Genetic Influences on Social Cognition. Pediatr Res **69,** 85–91 (2011). https://doi.org/10.1203/PDR.0b013e318212f562
https://www.nature.com/articles/pr9201198#citeas
Domingue BW, Belsky DW (2017) The social genome: Current findings and implications for the study of human genetics. PLoS Genet 13(3): e1006615. https://doi.org/10.1371/journal.pgen.1006615
https://journals.plos.org/plosgenetics/article?id=10.1371/journal.pgen.1006615
Martin, A. K., Robinson, G., Dzafic, I., Reutens, D., & Mowry, B. (2014). Theory of mind and the social brain: implications for understanding the genetic basis of schizophrenia. Genes, brain, and behavior, 13(1), 104–117. https://doi.org/10.1111/gbb.12066
83) Parker G. (1982). Re-searching the schizophrenogenic mother. The Journal of nervous and mental disease, 170(8), 452–462. https://doi.org/10.1097/00005053-198208000-00003
84) https://exploringyourmind.com/salvador-minuchin-and-structural-family-therapy/
https://familybasedtraining.com/app/uploads/2021/02/SFT1982.pdf
85) Identified patient https://books.google.com/books?id=uUE7DwAAQBAJ&pg=PA75&lpg=PA75&dq=symptom+bearer+family+therapy&source=bl&ots=nLvNCFY2cg&sig=YkYtUYlGWaY94e32oB44FxX9w0E&hl=en&sa=X&ved=0ahUKEwiPrdaV5_jYAhVJ7GMKHXvDDQwQ6AEIYjAI#v=onepage&q=symptom%20bearer%20family%20therapy&f=false
86) https://www.pewresearch.org/social-trends/2015/12/17/1-the-american-family-today/
87) https://www.facebook.com/verywell. "Overview of Feral Child Genie Wiley." Verywell Mind,2019 https://www.verywellmind.com/genie-the-story-of-the-wild-child-2795241
Psychology Case Study: The Wild Boy of Aveyron | Study.com. (2020). Retrieved January 6, 2020, from Study.com website: https://study.com/academy/

References

lesson/psychology-case-study-the-wild-boy-of-aveyron.html
88) 10 Modern Cases of Feral Children - Listverse. https://listverse.com/2008/03/07/10-modern-cases-of-feral-children/
89) S. Vilska, L. Unkila-Kallio, R.-L. Punamäki, P. Poikkeus, L. Repokari, J. Sinkkonen, A. Tiitinen, M. Tulppala, Mental health of mothers and fathers of twins conceived via assisted reproduction treatment: a 1-year prospective study, *Human Reproduction*, Volume 24, Issue 2, February 2009, Pages 367–377, https://doi.org/10.1093/humrep/den427
90) De Bellis, M. D., & Zisk, A. (2014). The biological effects of childhood trauma. Child and adolescent psychiatric clinics of North America, 23(2), 185–vii. https://doi.org/10.1016/j.chc.2014.01.002 https://www.ncbi.nlm.nih.gov/pmc/articles/PMC3968319/
Humberto Nagera (1970) Children's Reactions to the Death of Important Objects, The Psychoanalytic Study of the Child, 25:1, 360-400, DOI: 10.1080/00797308.1970.11823287
91) Ünstündag-Budak, A. (2015). The replacement child syndrome following stillbirth: a reconsideration. Enfance, 3, 351-364. https://doi.org/10.3917/enf1.153.0351   https://www.cairn.info/journal-enfance2-2015-3-page-351.htm https://www.psychologytoday.com/us/blog/in-flux/201409/are-you-replacement-child
92) https://cdcr.ca.gov/Wellness/docs/Grief-Of-Parents-Lifetime-Journey.pdf
Ellis, J.B. Grieving for the loss of the perfect child: Parents of children with handicaps. Child Adolesc Soc Work J **6**, 259–270 (1989). https://doi.org/10.1007/BF00755220   https://link.springer.com/article/10.1007/BF00755220
Bruce, E.J., Schultz, C.L., Smyrnios, K.X. and Schultz, N.C. (1994), Grieving related to development: A preliminary comparison of three age cohorts of parents of children with intellectual disability. British Journal of Medical Psychology, 67: 37-52.
https://doi.org/10.1111/j.2044-8341.1994.tb01769.x
http://www.mindsparklearning.com/grieving-the-loss-of-the-ideal-child/
Bruce, E.J., Schultz, C.L., Smyrnios, K.X. and Schultz, N.C. (1994), Grieving related to development: A preliminary comparison of three age cohorts of parents of children with intellectual disability. British Journal of Medical Psychology, 67: 37-52. https://doi.org/10.1111/j.2044-8341.1994.tb01769.x
http://onlinelibrary.wiley.com/doi/10.1111/j.2044-8341.1994.tb01769.x/full
93) Obianuju O. Berry, M. D. (2020, February 20). Recognizing and Addressing Domestic Violence: Issues for Psychiatrists. Psychiatric Times. https://www.psychiatrictimes.com/cme/recognizing-and-addressing-domestic-violence-issues-psychiatrists
Stiles M. M. (2002). Witnessing domestic violence: the effect on children. American family physician, 66(11), .
https://www.aafp.org/afp/2002/1201/p2052.html

Stover C. S. (2005). Domestic violence research: what have we learned and where do we go from here?. Journal of interpersonal violence, 20(4), 448–454. https://doi.org/10.1177/0886260504267755

Levendosky, Alytia & Graham-Bermann, Sandra. (2001). Parenting in Battered Women: The Effects of Domestic Violence on Women and Their Children. J Fam Violence. 16. 10.1023/A:1011111003373. https://www.researchgate.net/publication/30845675_Parenting_in_Battered_Women_The_Effects_of_Domestic_Violence_on_Women_and_Their_Children

Claudia Garcia-Moreno, Henrica AFM Jansen, Mary Ellsberg, Lori Heise, Charlotte H Watts, Prevalence of intimate partner violence: findings from the WHO multi-country study on women's health and domestic violence, The Lancet,Volume 368, Issue 9543, 2006,Pages 1260-1269,ISSN 0140-6736,https://doi.org/10.1016/S0140-6736(06)69523-8, https://www.sciencedirect.com/science/article/pii/S0140673606695238 94

J Garbarino; J Eckenrode Understanding Abusive Families - An Ecological Approach to Theory and PracticeJossey-Bass Publishers Address989 Market Street, San Francisco, CA 94103-1741, United States https://www.ojp.gov/ncjrs/virtual-library/abstracts/understanding-abusive-families-ecological-approach-theory-and https://www.ncjrs.gov/App/Publications/abstract.aspx?ID=173432 94) K MacFarlane; J Waterman; S Conerly; L Damon; M Durfee; S Long Sexual Abuse of Young Children Guilford Publications, Inc. 72 Spring Street, New York, NY 10012, United States https://www.ncjrs.gov/App/abstractdb/AbstractDBDetails.aspx?id=115728

White, M. A., Grzankowski, J., Paavilainen, E., Astedt-Kurki, P., & Paunonen-Ilmonen, M. (2003). Family dynamics and child abuse and neglect in three Finnish communities. Issues in mental health nursing, 24(6-7), 707–722. https://doi.org/10.1080/01612840305329
https://www.ncbi.nlm.nih.gov/pubmed/12907385

Thompson, Ross A., "Understanding the Dynamics of Child Maltreatment: Child Harm, Family Healing, and Public Policy (Discussant's Commentary)" (2000). Faculty Publications. https://digitalcommons.unl.edu/psychfacpub/354
95) https://en.wikipedia.org/wiki/Mandatory_reporting_in_the_United_States
96) Frederick S. Cohen, Judianne Densen-Gerber,A study of the relationship between child abuse and drug addiction in 178 patients: Preliminary results,Child Abuse & Neglect,Volume 6, Issue 4,1982,Pages 383-387,ISSN 0145-2134, https://doi.org/10.1016/0145-2134(82)90081-3. https://www.sciencedirect.com/science/article/pii/0145213482900813
https://pdfs.semanticscholar.org/9570/7047840d2e41f16c181b24cd4154d68a06d4.pdf

Earley, L., & Cushway, D. (2002). The Parentified Child. Clinical Child Psychology and Psychiatry, 7(2), 163–178. https://doi.org/10.1177/13591045020

References

07002005The Development of a Scale for the Assessment of Parentification Mika, Patricia; Bergner, Raymond M; Baum, Michael C. **Family Therapy; Roslyn Heights, N.Y.** (Jan 1, 1987): 229.

97) Beutel, M. E., Tibubos, A. N., Klein, E. M., Schmutzer, G., Reiner, I., Kocalevent, R. D., & Brähler, E. (2017). Childhood adversities and distress - The role of resilience in a representative sample. PloS one, 12(3), e0173826. https://doi.org/10.1371/journal.pone.0173826

Cecil, C. A., Viding, E., Fearon, P., Glaser, D., & McCrory, E. J. (2017). Disentangling the mental health impact of childhood abuse and neglect. Child abuse & neglect, 63, 106–119. https://doi.org/10.1016/j.chiabu.2016.11.024 https://pubmed.ncbi.nlm.nih.gov/27914236/

98) Helen Link Egger, Jane E. Costello, Adrian Angold,School Refusal and Psychiatric Disorders: A Community Study,Journal of the American Academy of Child & Adolescent Psychiatry,Volume 42, Issue 7,2003,Pages 797-807,ISSN 0890-8567, https://doi.org/10.1097/01.CHI.0000046865.56865.79. (https://www.sciencedirect.com/science/article/pii/S0890856709609795)

Johnson, A. M., Falstein, E. I., Szurek, S. A., & Svendsen, M. (1941). School phobia. *American Journal of Orthopsychiatry, 11*(4), 702-711. http://dx.doi.org/10.1111/j.1939-0025.1941.tb05860.x

Kawsar MDS, Yilanli M, Marwaha R. School Refusal. (Updated 2022 Feb 7). In: StatPearls (Internet). Treasure Island (FL): StatPearls Publishing; 2022 Jan-. Available from: https://www.ncbi.nlm.nih.gov/books/NBK534195/

99) Ersilia Menesini & Christina Salmivalli (2017) Bullying in schools: the state of knowledge and effective interventions, Psychology, Health & Medicine, 22:sup1, 240-253, DOI: 10.1080/13548506.2017.1279740 https://www.tandfonline.com/doi/citedby/10.1080/13548506.2017.1279740

Kirk R. Williams, Nancy G. Guerra,Prevalence and Predictors of Internet Bullying, Journal of Adolescent Health,Volume 41, Issue 6, Supplement,2007,Pages S14-S21, ISSN 1054-139X,https://doi.org/10.1016/j.jadohealth.2007.08.018. https://www.sciencedirect.com/science/article/pii/S1054139X0700362X http://signewhitson.com/

100) Alavi, N., Reshetukha, T., Prost, E., Antoniak, K., Patel, C., Sajid, S., & Groll, D. (2017). Relationship between Bullying and Suicidal Behaviour in Youth presenting to the Emergency Department. Journal of the Canadian Academy of Child and Adolescent Psychiatry = Journal de l'Academie canadienne de psychiatrie de l'enfant et de l'adolescent, 26(2), 70–77.

Kim, Y. S., & Leventhal, B. (2008). Bullying and suicide. A review. International Journal of Adolescent Medicine and Health, 20(2). https://doi.org/10.1515/IJAMH.2008.20.2.133   https://www.academia.edu/7748522/Bullying_and_suicide_A_review

Leary, M.R., Kowalski, R.M., Smith, L., & Phillips, S. (2003). *Teasing, rejection, and violence: Case studies of the school shootings. Aggressive Behavior, 29, 202-214.*https://www.semanticscholar.org/paper/Teasing%2C-rejection%2C-and-violence%3A-Case-studies-of-Leary-Kowalski/73c85599bb2989e8749b2ee4be46e38b424168b5

101) Ragelienė T. (2016). Links of Adolescents Identity Development and Relationship with Peers: A Systematic Literature Review. Journal of the Canadian Academy of Child and Adolescent Psychiatry = Journal de l'Academie canadienne de psychiatrie de l'enfant et de l'adolescent, 25(2), 97

Akhtar S. (1984). The syndrome of identity diffusion. The American journal of psychiatry, 141(11), 1381–1385. https://pubmed.ncbi.nlm.nih.gov/6496782/

Goth, K., Foelsch, P., Schlüter-Müller, S., Birkhölzer, M., Jung, E., Pick, O., & Schmeck, K. (2012). Assessment of identity development and identity diffusion in adolescence - Theoretical basis and psychometric properties of the self-report questionnaire AIDA. Child and adolescent psychiatry and mental health, 6(1), 27. https://doi.org/10.1186/1753-2000-6-27

102) Singer M. Delinquency and Family Disciplinary Configurations: An Elaboration of the Superego Lacunae Concept. *Arch Gen Psychiatry.* 1974;31(6):795-798. doi:10.1001/archpsyc.1974.01760180035004 http://jamanetwork.com/journals/jamapsychiatry/article-abstract/491277

Senn, T. E., Carey, M. P., & Vanable, P. A. (2008). Childhood and adolescent sexual abuse and subsequent sexual risk behavior: evidence from controlled studies, methodological critique, and suggestions for research. Clinical psychology review, 28(5), 711–735. https://doi.org/10.1016/j.cpr.2007.10.002

103) Veru, F., Jordan, G., Joober, R., Malla, A., & Iyer, S. (2016). Adolescent vs. adult onset of a first episode psychosis: Impact on remission of positive and negative symptoms. Schizophrenia research, 174(1-3), 183–188. https://doi.org/10.1016/j.schres.2016.03.035 https://pubmed.ncbi.nlm.nih.gov/27102425/

Trotman, H. D., Holtzman, C. W., Ryan, A. T., Shapiro, D. I., MacDonald, A. N., Goulding, S. M., Brasfield, J. L., & Walker, E. F. (2013). The development of psychotic disorders in adolescence: a potential role for hormones. Hormones and behavior, 64(2), 411–419. https://doi.org/10.1016/j.yhbeh.2013.02.018

Goodyer, I. M., Herbert, J., Tamplin, A., & Altham, P. M. (2000). First-episode major depression in adolescents. Affective, cognitive and endocrine characteristics of risk status and predictors of onset. The British journal of psychiatry : the journal of mental science, 176, 142–149. https://doi.org/10.1192/bjp.176.2.142

Cook, M. N., Peterson, J., & Sheldon, C. (2009). Adolescent depression: an update and guide to clinical decision making. Psychiatry (Edgmont (Pa. : Township)), 6(9), 17–31.https://www.ncbi.nlm.nih.gov/pmc/articles/PMC2766285/

104) Karakos H. (2014). Positive Peer Support or Negative Peer Influence? The Role of Peers among Adolescents in Recovery High Schools. PJE. Peabody journal of education, 89(2), 214–228. https://doi.org/10.1080/016195

References

6X.2014.897094
Dishion, T. J., McCord, J., & Poulin, F. (1999). When interventions harm. Peer groups and problem behavior. The American psychologist, 54(9), 755–764. https://doi.org/10.1037//0003-066x.54.9.755
https://pubmed.ncbi.nlm.nih.gov/10510665/
105) Erikson, Erik, & J.M. Erikson, **Life Cycle Completed,** W. W. Norton & Company; Extended Version edition (June 17, 1998),
Levinson, D.J., **Season's of A Man's Life,** Ballantine Books; Reissue edition (May 12, 1986)
Levinson, D.J **The Season's of a Woman's Life,** Ballantine Books; 1st edition (February 11, 1997)
Gail Sheehy, **Passages, Predictable Crises of Adult Life,** January 2006
106) Southwick, S. M., Bonanno, G. A., Masten, A. S., Panter-Brick, C., & Yehuda, R. (2014). Resilience definitions, theory, and challenges: interdisciplinary perspectives. European journal of psychotraumatology, 5, 10.3402/ejpt.v5.25338. https://doi.org/10.3402/ejpt.v5.25338   https://www.ncbi.nlm.nih.gov/pmc/articles/PMC4185134/
Fleming, J., & Ledogar, R. J. (2008). Resilience, an Evolving Concept: A Review of Literature Relevant to Aboriginal Research. *Pimatisiwin, 6*(2), 7–23.
Haley, Jay, **Uncommon Therapy,** W. W. Norton & Company; ISBN-13: 978-0393310313
107)Holmes, T. H., & Rahe, R. H. (1967). The Social Readjustment Rating Scale. Journal of psychosomatic research, 11(2), 213–218. https://doi.org/10.1016/0022-3999(67)90010-4   https://pubmed.ncbi.nlm.nih.gov/6059863/
https://www.stress.org/holmes-rahe-stress-inventory
108) Hollingshead, A. B., & Redlich, F. C. (2007). Social class and mental illness: a community study. 1958. American journal of public health, 97(10), 1756–1757. https://doi.org/10.2105/ajph.97.10.1756
Pols H. (2007). August Hollingshead and Frederick Redlich: poverty, socioeconomic status, and mental illness. American journal of public health, 97(10), 1755. https://doi.org/10.2105/AJPH.2007.117606
109) Patrick, M. E., Wightman, P., Schoeni, R. F., & Schulenberg, J. E. (2012). Socioeconomic status and substance use among young adults: a comparison across constructs and drugs. Journal of studies on alcohol and drugs, 73(5), 772–782. https://doi.org/10.15288/jsad.2012.73.772   https://www.sciencedirect.com/topics/social-sciences/culture-of-poverty
J.D. Vance, **Hillbilly Elegy**
110) https://www.cdc.gov/nceh/lead/prevention/populations.htm
Reiss F. (2013). Socioeconomic inequalities and mental health problems in children and adolescents: a systematic review. Social science & medicine (1982), 90, 24–31. https://doi.org/10.1016/j.socscimed.2013.04.026
https://graphics.latimes.com/exide-battery-plant/

Masten, S. J., Davies, S. H., & Mcelmurry, S. P. (2016). Flint Water Crisis: What Happened and Why?. Journal - American Water Works Association, 108(12), 22–34. https://doi.org/10.5942/jawwa.2016.108.0195
111) https://listverse.com/2016/08/05/10-tragic-cases-of-suicide-by-pilot/
112) Cacioppo, J. T., Hawkley, L. C., Norman, G. J., & Berntson, G. G. (2011). Social isolation. Annals of the New York Academy of Sciences, 1231(1), 17–22. https://doi.org/10.1111/j.1749-6632.2011.06028.x
https://publichealth.tulane.edu/blog/effects-of-social-isolation-on-mental-health/
https://www.hrsa.gov/enews/past-issues/2019/january-17/loneliness-epidemic
http://bowlingalone.com/ **Bowling Alone** *is a review book of data showing the increasing social isolation in US.*
113) Jurblum, M., Ng, C. H., & Castle, D. J. (2020). Psychological consequences of social isolation and quarantine: Issues related to COVID-19 restrictions. Australian journal of general practice, 49(12), 778–783. https://doi.org/10.31128/AJGP-06-20-5481
https://pubmed.ncbi.nlm.nih.gov/33254205/
Brown, V., Morgan, T., & Fralick, A. (2021). Isolation and mental health: thinking outside the box. General psychiatry, 34(3), e100461. https://doi.org/10.1136/gpsych-2020-100461
114) Umberson, D., & Montez, J. K. (2010). Social relationships and health: a flashpoint for health policy. Journal of health and social behavior, 51 Suppl(Suppl), S54–S66. https://doi.org/10.1177/0022146510383501
Cuijpers, P., Geraedts, A. S., van Oppen, P., Andersson, G., Markowitz, J. C., & van Straten, A. (2011). Interpersonal psychotherapy for depression: a meta-analysis. *The American journal of psychiatry*, *168*(6), 581–592. https://doi.org/10.1176/appi.ajp.2010.10101411
115) de C Williams, A. C., & van der Merwe, J. (2013). The psychological impact of torture. British journal of pain, 7(2), 101–106. https://doi.org/10.1177/2049463713483596
Psychological And Physical Torture Have Similar Mental Effects. ScienceDaily. https://www.sciencedaily.com/releases/2007/03/070305202811.htm
https://www.law.berkeley.edu/files/EffectsofPsychologicalTorturepaper(Final)11June10.pdf
Okello, J., Nakimuli-Mpungu, E., Musisi, S., Broekaert, E., & Derluyn, I. (2014). The Association between Attachment and Mental Health Symptoms among School-Going Adolescents in Northern Uganda: The Moderating Role of War-Related Trauma. PLoS ONE, 9(3), e88494. https://doi.org/10.1371/journal.pone.0088494
116) Danneskiold-Samsøe, B., Bartels, E. M., & Genefke, I. (2007). Treatment of torture victims—a longitudinal clinical study. Torture : quarterly journal on rehabilitation of torture victims and prevention of torture, 17(1), 11–17.
Hensel-Dittmann, D., Schauer, M., Ruf, M., Catani, C., Odenwald, M., Elbert, T., & Neuner, F. (2011). Treatment of traumatized victims of war and torture: a

References

randomized controlled comparison of narrative exposure therapy and stress inoculation training. Psychotherapy and psychosomatics, 80(6), 345–352. https://doi.org/10.1159/000327253 https://pubmed.ncbi.nlm.nih.gov/21829046/
117) R.J. Lifton interview https://www.youtube.com/watch?v=1cvNvtJxxSE
118) https://kenud.com/2021/11/08/what-is-stockholm-syndrome/
https://www.rollingstone.com/culture/culture-features/scientology-children-second-generation-846732/
https://www.culteducation.com/
https://www.newyorker.com/magazine/2019/05/06/my-childhood-in-a-cult
119) Tart, Charles *Waking UP Overcoming the Obstacles to Human Potential* ISBN-13 : 978-0595196647
120) https://www.sciencedirect.com/topics/social-sciences/cultural-variation
https://www.greatamericancountry.com/places/local-life/living-in-a-multicultural-neighborhood
https://scholarsarchive.byu.edu/cgi/viewcontent.cgi?article=1278&context=facpub
https://en.wikipedia.org/wiki/The_Spirit_Catches_You_and_You_Fall_Down
Coyote Medicine: Lessons from Native American Healing (Paperback) (Jan 01, 1997) Mehl-Madrona, Lewis
121) Alarcón R. D. (2009). Culture, cultural factors and psychiatric diagnosis: review and projections. World psychiatry : official journal of the World Psychiatric Association (WPA), 8(3), 131–139. https://doi.org/10.1002/j.2051-5545.2009.tb00233.x
Culture-Specific Psychiatric Syndromes: A Review - Medscape - Aug 24, 2018. https://www.medscape.com/viewarticle/901027#vp_2 https://www.medscape.com/viewarticle/899520
122) Toppelberg, C. O., & Collins, B. A. (2010). Language, culture, and adaptation in immigrant children. Child and adolescent psychiatric clinics of North America, 19(4), 697–717. https://doi.org/10.1016/j.chc.2010.07.003 https://www.ncbi.nlm.nih.gov/pmc/articles/PMC3526379/ https://www.thoughtco.com/first-generation-immigrant-defined-1951570
123) https://allianceforclas.org/wpcontent/uploads/2013/05/CulturalCompetenceEvidenceBasedPractice.pdf
124) Tsutsumi, A., Izutsu, T., & Matsumoto, T. (2012). Risky sexual behaviors, mental health, and history of childhood abuse among adolescents. Asian Journal of Psychiatry, 5(1), 48–52. https://doi.org/10.1016/j.ajp.2011.12.004 https://www.ncbi.nlm.nih.gov/pubmed/26878947
Power, Robert A., et al. "Fecundity of Patients With Schizophrenia, Autism, Bipolar Disorder, Depression, Anorexia Nervosa, or Substance Abuse vs Their Unaffected Siblings." JAMA Psychiatry, vol. 70, no. 1, 1 Jan. 2013, p. 22, jamanetwork.com/journals/jamapsychiatry/fullarticle/1390257, 10.1001/jamapsychiatry.2013.268. Accessed 6 Jan. 2020. https://jamanetwork.com/journals/jamapsychiatry/fullarticle/1390257

Escott-Price, V., Pardiñas, A. F., Santiago, E., Walters, J., Kirov, G., Owen, M. J., & O'Donovan, M. C. (2019). The Relationship Between Common Variant Schizophrenia Liability and Number of Offspring in the UK Biobank. The American journal of psychiatry, 176(8), 661–666. https://doi.org/10.1176/appi.ajp.2018.18020140

125) GARDNER, A., and A. GRAFEN. "Capturing the Superorganism: A Formal Theory of Group Adaptation." Journal of Evolutionary Biology, vol. 22, no. 4, Apr. 2009, pp. 659–671, 10.1111/j.1420-9101.2008.01681.x. Accessed 6 Jan. 2020.
https://onlinelibrary.wiley.com/doi/full/10.1111/j.1420-9101.2008.01681.x

126) The Price of Altruism: George Price and the Search for the Origins of Kindness: Oren Harman: 9780393339994: Amazon.com: Books. (2019). Retrieved January 6, 2020, from Amazon.com website: https://www.amazon.com/Price-Altruism-George-Origins-Kindness/dp/0393339998

For readers wishing to brush up on mathematical genetics:
https://en.wikipedia.org/wiki/Fisher%27s_fundamental_theorem_of_natural_selection "The rate of increase in fitness of any organism at any time is equal to its genetic variance in fitness at that time."…"The rate of increase in the mean fitness of any organism at any time ascribable to natural selection acting through changes in gene frequencies is exactly equal to its genetic variance in fitness at that time".
http://equation-of-the-month.blogspot.com/2011/01/fishers-fundamental-theorem-on-natural.html *Largely as a result of Fisher's feud with the American geneticist Sewall Wright about adaptive landscapes, the theorem was widely misunderstood to mean that the average fitness of a population would always increase, even though models showed this not to be the case.* https://en.wikipedia.org/wiki/Price_equation https://en.wikipedia.org/wiki/Group_selection

Fisher, R. (2020). Why altruism paid off for our ancestors. Retrieved January 6, 2020, from New Scientist website: https://www.newscientist.com/article/dn10750-why-altruism-paid-off-for-our-ancestors/

Luo J. (2018). The Neural Basis of and a Common Neural Circuitry in Different Types of Pro-social Behavior. *Frontiers in psychology*, *9*, 859. https://doi.org/10.3389/fpsyg.2018.00859
https://www.ncbi.nlm.nih.gov/pmc/articles/PMC5996127/

127) Sapolsky, R. (2018). **Behave : the biology of humans at our best and worst**. London: Vintage.

Skinner, Michael. "Unified Theory of Evolution." Aeon, Aeon, 9 Nov. 2016, aeon.co/essays/on-epigenetics-we-need-both-darwin-s-and-lamarck-s-theories.

128) Pinker, S. (2010). The cognitive niche: Coevolution of intelligence, sociality, and language. Proceedings of the National Academy of Sciences , 107, 8893-8999.National Academy of Sciences (US, Avise, J. C., & Ayala, F. J. (2010).
https://www.ncbi.nlm.nih.gov/books/NBK210002/

James, B. (2018, June 10). Did Toolmaking Pave the Road for Human

Language? The Atlantic; The Atlantic. https://www.theatlantic.com/science/archive/2018/06/toolmaking-language-brain/562385/

Keller, L. (2009). Adaptation and the genetics of social behaviour. Philosophical Transactions of the Royal Society B: Biological Sciences, 364(1533), 3209–3216. https://doi.org/10.1098/rstb.2009.0108 https://royalsocietypublishing.org/doi/full/10.1098/rstb.2009.0108

129) Dual inheritance https://en.wikipedia.org/wiki/Dual_inheritance_theory#cite_note-48

"Three core principles are involved: 1) the basis for the storage and transmission of cultural information comes from genetic mechanisms, including social learning 2) cultural traits are transmitted through different mechanisms involving social learning, but also impact population survival, 3) "Cultural traits alter the social and physical environments under which genetic selection operates.

130) Lumsden and E.O. Wilson's **Genes, Mind and Culture**. This book outlined a series of mathematical models of how genetic evolution might favor the selection of cultural traits and how cultural traits might affect the speed of genetic evolution. Controversy surrounding Wilson's sociobiological theories may also have decreased the lasting effect of this book.

Clinton Richard Dawkins (2016). **The selfish gene**. Oxford: Oxford University Press.

Feldman, M.; Cavalli-Sforna, L. (1976). "Cultural and biological evolutionary processes, selection for a trait under complex transmission". Theoretical Population Biology. **9**: 238–59. doi:10.1016/0040-5809(76)90047-2. PMID 1273802.

Cavalli-Sforza and Feldman, **Cultural Transmission and Evolution: A Quantitative Approach.** Borrowing heavily from population genetics and epidemiology, this book built a mathematical theory concerning the spread of cultural traits.

The next significant DIT publication was Robert Boyd and Peter Richerson's (1985) **Culture and the Evolutionary Process**.

Orr, H. A. (2005). The genetic theory of adaptation: a brief history. Nature Reviews Genetics, 6(2), 119–127. https://doi.org/10.1038/nrg1523https://www.nature.com/articles/nrg1523

Drown, D. M., & Wade, M. J. (2014). Runaway Coevolution: Adaptation To Heritable And Nonheritable Environments. Evolution, 68(10), 3039–3046. https://doi.org/10.1111/evo.12470

CHAPTER THREE REFERENCES

1) Cooper, J. O., Heron, T. E., & Heward, W. L. (2007). *Applied behavior analysis*. Upper Saddle River, N.J.: Pearson/Merrill-Prentice Hall. Burrhus Frederic Skinner, *About behaviorism*. New York Random House.

2) Glickman, S. E., & Schiff, B. B. (1967). A biological theory of reinforcement. *Psychological review*, *74*(2), 81–109. https://doi.org/10.1037/h0024290
https://www.researchgate.net/publication/17827524_Glickman_SE_Schiff_BB_A_biological_theory_of_reinforcement_Psychol_Rev_74_81-109
3) E. S. *Valenstein*, 1966. The *anatomical locus of reinforcement*, Progr. Physiol. Psychol., Vol. 1, pp. 149-190. 35
Valenstein, E. S. (1969). Behavior Elicited by Hypothalamic Stimulation. *Brain, Behavior and Evolution*, *2*(4), 295–316. https://doi.org/10.1159/000125869
http://www.karger.com/Article/Abstract/125869
4) Lüscher, C. (2018). Dark past of deep-brain stimulation. *Nature*, *555*(7696), 306–307. https://doi.org/10.1038/d41586-018-02963-6 Original studies on patients in a New Orleans hospital have apparently disappeared.
5) B.F. Skinner's definition of "reinforcement" was the response of the animal to stimulus. Positive = repeated behavior. Negative = suppressed behavior, but ignores the procedures needed to motivate the animals to respond, and other details of the process.
6) Stellar, J. (2014). *Neurobiology of motivation and reward* .Springer.p154
7) https://en.wikipedia.org/wiki/Reward
https://en.wikipedia.org/wiki/Nucleus_accumbens
Neurosci. "Neuroscientifically Challenged." *Neuroscientifically Challenged*, 14 June 2014, www.neuroscientificallychallenged.com/blog/2014/6/11/know-your-brain-nucleus-accumbens.
Salgado, Sanjay, and Michael G. Kaplitt. "The Nucleus Accumbens: A Comprehensive Review." *Stereotactic and Functional Neurosurgery*, vol. 93, no. 2, 18 Feb. 2015, pp. 75–93, #ref251, 10.1159/000368279. www.karger.com/Article/FullText/368279
Shirayama, Y., & Chaki, S. (2006). Neurochemistry of the nucleus accumbens and its relevance to depression and antidepressant action in rodents. *Current neuropharmacology*, *4*(4), 277–291. https://doi.org/10.2174/157015906778520773
https://www.ncbi.nlm.nih.gov/pmc/articles/PMC2475798/
8) https://en.wikipedia.org/wiki/Mesolimbic_pathway
Rolls, Edmund T. "Limbic Systems for Emotion and for Memory, but No Single Limbic System." *Cortex*, vol. 62, Jan. 2015, pp. 119–157, 10.1016/j.cortex.2013.12.005.
9) Isaacson, R. L. (1982). *The limbic system*. New York: Plenum Press.
10) Valenstein, E. S., & Valenstein, T. (1964). Interaction of Positive and Negative Reinforcing Neural Systems. *Science*, *145*(3639) https://doi.org/10.1126/science.145.3639.1456
Hirose, S., Osada, T., Ogawa, A., Tanaka, M., Wada, H., Yoshizawa, Y., ... Konishi, S. (2016). Lateral–Medial Dissociation in Orbitofrontal Cortex–Hypothalamus Connectivity. *Frontiers in Human Neuroscience*, *10*. https://doi.org/10.3389/fnhum.2016.00244

References

Hahn JD, Fink G, Kruk MR and Stanley BG (2019) Editorial: Current Views of Hypothalamic Contributions to the Control of Motivated Behaviors. Front. Syst. Neurosci. 13:32. doi: 10.3389/fnsys.2019.00032\
11) Purves, D., Augustine, G. J., Fitzpatrick, D., Katz, L. C., Anthony-Samuel LaMantia, McNamara, J. O., & S Mark Williams. (2019). The Biogenic Amines. https://www.ncbi.nlm.nih.gov/books/NBK11035/
Wagner, H., Burns, H., Dannals, R., Wong, D., Langstrom, B., Duelfer, T., Frost, J., Ravert, H., Links, J., Rosenbloom, S., Lukas, S., Kramer, A., & Kuhar, M. (1983). Imaging dopamine receptors in the human brain by positron tomography. *Science*, *221*(4617), 1264–1266. https://doi.org/10.1126/science.6604315
Sasaki-Adams, D. (2001). Serotonin-Dopamine Interactions in the Control of Conditioned Reinforcement and Motor Behavior. *Neuropsychopharmacology*, *25*(3), 440–452. https://doi.org/10.1016/s0893-133x(01)00240-8
Charnay, Y., & Léger, L. (2010). Brain serotonergic circuitries. *Dialogues in Clinical Neuroscience*, *12*(4), 471–487. https://www.ncbi.nlm.nih.gov/pmc/articles/PMC3181988/
Berridge, C. W., & Waterhouse, B. D. (2003). The locus coeruleus–noradrenergic system: modulation of behavioral state and state-dependent cognitive processes. *Brain Research Reviews*, *42*(1), 33–84. https://doi.org/10.1016/s0165-0173(03)00143-7
Neuroanatomy and Physiology of Brain Reward II. (2020). http://ibg.colorado.edu/cadd1/a_drug/essays/essay4.htm
12) Hoffman, B. J., Hansson, S. R., Mezey, E., & Palkovits, M. (1998). Localization and dynamic regulation of biogenic amine transporters in the mammalian central nervous system. *Frontiers in Neuroendocrinology*, *19*(3), 187–231. https://doi.org/10.1006/frne.1998.0168
Charnay, Y., & Léger, L. (2010). Brain serotonergic circuitries. *Dialogues in Clinical Neuroscience*, *12*(4), 471–487. Retrieved from https://www.ncbi.nlm.nih.gov/pmc/articles/PMC3181988/
Purves, D., Augustine, G. J., Fitzpatrick, D., Katz, L. C., Anthony-Samuel LaMantia, McNamara, J. O., & S Mark Williams. (2012). Peptide Neurotransmitters. Retrieved January 14, 2020, from Nih.gov website: https://www.ncbi.nlm.nih.gov/books/NBK10873/
Ebrahim, I. O., Howard, R. S., Kopelman, M. D., Sharief, M. K., & Williams, A. J. (2002). The hypocretin/orexin system. *JRSM*, https://doi.org/10.1258/jrsm.95.5.227
Dyan Sellayah, Devanjan Sikder, Food for Thought: Understanding the Multifaceted Nature of Orexins, *Endocrinology*, Volume 154, Issue 11, 1 November 2013, Pages 3990–3999, https://doi.org/10.1210/en.2013-1488 https://academic.oup.com/endo/article/154/11/3990/2422573
13) Sternson, S. M., & Roth, B. L. (2014). Chemogenetic Tools to Interrogate Brain Functions. *Annual Review of Neuroscience*, *37*(1), 387–407. https://doi.org/10.1146/annurev-neuro-071013-014048

Guru, A., Post, R. J., Ho, Y.-Y., & Warden, M. R. (2015). Making Sense of Optogenetics. *International Journal of Neuropsychopharmacology*, *18*(11), pyv079. https://doi.org/10.1093/ijnp/pyv079

14) Meier, J. D. (2011). fMRI Studies of the Human Hypothalamus. *Princeton. Edu.* https://doi.org/http://arks.princeton.edu/ark:/88435/dsp01pv63g039r
This thesis shows the problems in visualizing hypothalamus, let alone comparison measures.

15) Oomura, Y., Ooyama, H., Yamamoto, T., & Naka, F. (1967). Reciprocal relationship of the lateral and ventromedial hypothalamus in the regulation of food intake. *Physiology & Behavior*, *2*(2), 97–115. https://doi.org/10.1016/0031-9384(67)90020-0
https://www.sciencedirect.com/science/article/abs/pii/0031938467900200

Behbehani, M., Park, M., & Clement, M. (1988). Interactions between the lateral hypothalamus and the periaqueductal gray. *The Journal of Neuroscience*, *8*(8), 2780–2787. https://doi.org/10.1523/jneurosci.08-08-02780.1988
http://www.jneurosci.org/content/8/8/2780.long

Karlsson, K. Æ., Windischberger, C., Gerstl, F., Mayr, W., Siegel, J. M., & Moser, E. (2010). Modulation of hypothalamus and amygdalar activation levels with stimulus valence. *NeuroImage*, *51*(1), 324–328. https://doi.org/10.1016/j.neuroimage.2010.02.029

Tamas L. Horvath, Sabrina Diano, Peter Sotonyi, Mark Heiman, Matthias Tschöp, Minireview: Ghrelin and the Regulation of Energy Balance—A Hypothalamic Perspective, *Endocrinology*, Volume 142, Issue 10, 1 October 2001, Pages 4163–4169, https://doi.org/10.1210/endo.142.10.8490

Ahima, R. S., & Antwi, D. A. (2008). Brain regulation of appetite and satiety. *Endocrinology and metabolism clinics of North America*, *37*(4), 811–823. https://doi.org/10.1016/j.ecl.2008.08.005

Ubuka, T., Haraguchi, S., Tobari, Y. et al. Hypothalamic inhibition of sociosexual behaviour by increasing neuroestrogen synthesis. *Nat Commun* **5,** 3061 (2014). https://doi.org/10.1038/ncomms4061 https://www.nature.com/articles/ncomms4061#citeas

Nieh, E. H., Vander Weele, C. M., Matthews, G. A., Presbrey, K. N., Wichmann, R., Leppla, C. A., Izadmehr, E. M., & Tye, K. M. (2016). Inhibitory Input from the Lateral Hypothalamus to the Ventral Tegmental Area Disinhibits Dopamine Neurons and Promotes Behavioral Activation. *Neuron*, *90*(6), 1286–1298. https://doi.org/10.1016/j.neuron.2016.04.035

Hahn Joel D., Fink George, Kruk Menno R., Stanley B. Glenn, Editorial: Current Views of Hypothalamic Contributions to the Control of Motivated Behaviors Frontiers in Systems Neuroscience https://www.frontiersin.org/article/10.3389/fnsys.2019.00032
https://www.frontiersin.org/articles/10.3389/fnbeh.2011.00026/full

16) Phelps, J. (2015). The Neural Basis of Bipolar Disorder. *Psychiatric Times*. http://www.psychiatrictimes.com/special-reports/neural-basis-bipolar-disorder/

References

page/0/2

17) Sternson, S. M. (2013). Hypothalamic Survival Circuits: Blueprints for Purposive Behaviors. *Neuron*, *77*(5), 810–824. https://doi.org/10.1016/j.neuron.2013.02.018   http://www.sciencedirect.com/science/article/pii/S0896627313001761

18) Tomás, J., Macário, M. C., Gaspar, E., & Santana, I. (2015). Severe post-influenza (H1N1) encephalitis involving pulvinar nuclei in an adult patient. *BMJ case reports*, *2015*, bcr2015212667. https://doi.org/10.1136/bcr-2015-212667

Panksepp, in *Affective Neuroscience,* defines these as "emotions" rather "motivations" emphasizing subjective awareness.

Panksepp, J. (1998). *Affective neuroscience: The foundations of human and animal emotions*. New York: Oxford University Press https://www.amazon.com/Affective-Neuroscience-Foundations-Emotions-Science/dp/019517805X

19) Hypothalamus: Structural Organization (Section 4, Chapter 1) Neuroscience Online: An Electronic Textbook for the Neurosciences | Department of Neurobiology and Anatomy - The University of Texas Medical School at Houston. (2020). Retrieved January 14, 2020, from Tmc.edu website: https://nba.uth.tmc.edu/neuroscience/m/s4/chapter01.html

20) Hopkins, M., Blundell, J., Halford, J., King, N., & Finlayson, G. (2016, March 30). The Regulation of Food Intake in Humans. Retrieved January 14, 2020, from Nih.gov website: https://www.ncbi.nlm.nih.gov/books/NBK278931/

Casper, R. C., Sullivan, E. L., & Tecott, L. (2008). Relevance of animal models to human eating disorders and obesity. *Psychopharmacology*, *199*(3), 313–329. https://doi.org/10.1007/s00213-008-1102-2

Ahima, R. S., & Lazar, M. A. (2008). Adipokines and the Peripheral and Neural Control of Energy Balance. *Molecular Endocrinology*, *22*(5), 1023–1031. https://doi.org/10.1210/me.2007-0529 https://academic.oup.com/mend/article/22/5/1023/2660958

Hurley, S. W., & Johnson, A. K. (2014). The role of the lateral hypothalamus and orexin in ingestive behavior: a model for the translation of past experience and sensed deficits into motivated behaviors. *Frontiers in Systems Neuroscience*, *8*. https://doi.org/10.3389/fnsys.2014.00216

Li, M. M., Madara, J. C., Steger, J. S., Krashes, M. J., Balthasar, N., Campbell, J. N., Resch, J. M., Conley, N. J., Garfield, A. S., & Lowell, B. B. (2019). The Paraventricular Hypothalamus Regulates Satiety and Prevents Obesity via Two Genetically Distinct Circuits. *Neuron*, *102*(3), 653–667.e6. https://doi.org/10.1016/j.neuron.2019.02.028

Teitelbaum P & Epstein A N. The lateral hypothalamic syndrome:recovery of feeding and drinking after lateral hypothalamic lesions.
Psychol. Rev. 69:74-90, 1962.

Liu, C. M., & Kanoski, S. E. (2018). Homeostatic and non-homeostatic controls of feeding behavior: Distinct vs. common neural systems. *Physiology & Behavior*, *193*, 223–231. https://doi.org/10.1016/j.physbeh.2018.02.011

Müller, M. (2010). Is there evidence for a set point that regulates human body weight? *F1000 Medicine Reports*, *2*. https://doi.org/10.3410/m2-59 https://www.ncbi.nlm.nih.gov/pmc/articles/PMC2990627/

Gautron, L., Elmquist, J. K., & Williams, K. W. (2015). Neural Control of Energy Balance: Translating Circuits to Therapies. *Cell*, *161*(1), 133–145. https://doi.org/10.1016/j.cell.2015.02.023 https://www.ncbi.nlm.nih.gov/pmc/articles/PMC4392840/

Donovan, M. H., & Tecott, L. H. (2013). Serotonin and the regulation of mammalian energy balance. *Frontiers in Neuroscience*, *7*. https://doi.org/10.3389/fnins.2013.00036 https://www.ncbi.nlm.nih.gov/pubmed/23543912

Williams, G., Harrold, J. A., & Cutler, D. J. (2000). The hypothalamus and the regulation of energy homeostasis: lifting the lid on a black box. *Proceedings of the Nutrition Society*, *59*(3), 385–396. https://doi.org/10.1017/s0029665100000434

Loeb, K. L., & le Grange, D. (2009). Family-Based Treatment for Adolescent Eating Disorders: Current Status, New Applications and Future Directions. *International Journal of Child and Adolescent Health*, *2*(2), 243–254. https://www.ncbi.nlm.nih.gov/pmc/articles/PMC2828763/

Salvador Minuchin, **Families and Family Therapy** ISBN-13: 978-0415664738

21) Mantilla, E. F., & Birgegård, A. (2015). The enemy within: the association between self-image and eating disorder symptoms in healthy, non help-seeking and clinical young women. *Journal of Eating Disorders*, *3*(1). https://doi.org/10.1186/s40337-015-0067-x

Lock, J., Garrett, A., Beenhakker, J., & Reiss, A. L. (2011). Aberrant Brain Activation During a Response Inhibition Task in Adolescent Eating Disorder Subtypes. *American Journal of Psychiatry*, *168*(1), 55–64.https://doi.org/10.1176/appi.ajp.2010.10010056

Boraska, V., Franklin, C. S., Floyd, J. A. B., Thornton, L. M., Huckins, L. M., Southam, L., ... Bulik, C. M. (2014). A genome-wide association study of anorexia nervosa. *Molecular Psychiatry*, *19*(10), 1085–1094. https://doi.org/10.1038/mp.2013.187

Paolacci, S., Kiani, A. K., Manara, E., Beccari, T., Ceccarini, M. R., Stuppia, L., Chiurazzi, P., Dalla Ragione, L., & Bertelli, M. (2020). Genetic contributions to the etiology of anorexia nervosa: New perspectives in molecular diagnosis and treatment. *Molecular genetics & genomic medicine*, *8*(7), e1244. https://doi.org/10.1002/mgg3.1244Though the conclusion seems encouraging, the findings are negative.

22) Fladung, A.-K., Grön, G., Grammer, K., Herrnberger, B., Schilly, E., Grasteit, S., ... von Wietersheim, J. (2010). A Neural Signature of Anorexia Nervosa in the Ventral Striatal Reward System. *American Journal of Psychiatry*, *167*(2), 206–212. https://doi.org/10.1176/appi.ajp.2009.09010071The images in the study show medial cingulate cortex close to tegmentum, not striate.

23) Watson, K. T., Simard, J. F., Henderson, V. W., Nutkiewicz, L., Lamers,

References

F., Nasca, C., Rasgon, N., & Penninx, B. (2021). Incident Major Depressive Disorder Predicted by Three Measures of Insulin Resistance: A Dutch Cohort Study. *The American journal of psychiatry*, *178*(10), 914–920. https://doi.org/10.1176/appi.ajp.2021.20101479

24) Kubik, J. F., Gill, R. S., Laffin, M., & Karmali, S. (2013). The Impact of Bariatric Surgery on Psychological Health. *Journal of Obesity*, *2013*, 1–5. https://doi.org/10.1155/2013/837989

Morgan DJR, Ho KM, Platell C. Incidence and Determinants of Mental Health Service Use After Bariatric Surgery. *JAMA Psychiatry.* 2020;77(1):60–67. doi:10.1001/jamapsychiatry.2019.2741 https://jamanetwork.com/journals/jamapsychiatry/fullarticle/2751532

25) Wright, H., Li, X., Fallon, N. B., Crookall, R., Giesbrecht, T., Thomas, A., … Stancak, A. (2016). Differential effects of hunger and satiety on insular cortex and hypothalamic functional connectivity. *European Journal of Neuroscience*, *43*(9), 1181–1189. https://doi.org/10.1111/ejn.13182

26) Liu, C., Lee, S., & Elmquist, J. K. (2014). Circuits Controlling Energy Balance and Mood: Inherently Intertwined or Just Complicated Intersections? *Cell Metabolism*, *19*(6), 902–909. https://doi.org/10.1016/j.cmet.2014.02.008

Timper, K., & Brüning, J. C. (2017). Hypothalamic circuits regulating appetite and energy homeostasis: pathways to obesity. *Disease models & mechanisms*, *10*(6), 679–689. https://doi.org/10.1242/dmm.026609

27) Teff, K. L., & Kim, S. F. (2011). Atypical antipsychotics and the neural regulation of food intake and peripheral metabolism. *Physiology & behavior*, *104*(4), 590–598. https://doi.org/10.1016/j.physbeh.2011.05.033

Riordan, H. J., Antonini, P., & Murphy, M. F. (2011). Atypical antipsychotics and metabolic syndrome in patients with schizophrenia: risk factors, monitoring, and healthcare implications. *American health & drug benefits*, *4*(5), 292–302.

28) Rao, U., Hammen, C. L., & Poland, R. E. (2009). Mechanisms Underlying the Comorbidity Between Depressive and Addictive Disorders in Adolescents: Interactions Between Stress and HPA Activity. *American Journal of Psychiatry*, *166*(3), 361–369. https://doi.org/10.1176/appi.ajp.2008.08030412

Marsh, R., Horga, G., Wang, Z., Wang, P., Klahr, K. W., Berner, L. A., … Peterson, B. S. (2011). An fMRI Study of Self-Regulatory Control and Conflict Resolution in Adolescents With Bulimia Nervosa. *American Journal of Psychiatry*, *168*(11), 1210–1220. https://doi.org/10.1176/appi.ajp.2011.11010094 http://ajp.psychiatryonline.org/doi/full/10.1176/appi.ajp.2011.11010094

Marsh, R., Steinglass, J. E., Gerber, A. J., Graziano O'Leary, K., Wang, Z., Murphy, D., … Peterson, B. S. (2009). Deficient Activity in the Neural Systems That Mediate Self-regulatory Control in Bulimia Nervosa. *Archives of General Psychiatry*, *66*(1), 51. https://doi.org/10.1001/archgenpsychiatry.2008.504 http://jamanetwork.com/journals/jamapsychiatry/fullarticle/482930

29) King B. M. (2006). The rise, fall, and resurrection of the ventromedial hypothalamus in the regulation of feeding behavior and body weight. *Physiology &*

behavior, 87(2), 221–244. https://doi.org/10.1016/j.physbeh.2005.10.007
Gautron, L. (2009). Neurobiology of inflammation-associated anorexia. *Frontiers in Neuroscience.* https://doi.org/10.3389/neuro.23.003.2009
Armangue, T., Petit-Pedrol, M., & Dalmau, J. (2012). Autoimmune Encephalitis in Children. *Journal of Child Neurology, 27*(11), 1460–1469. https://doi.org/10.1177/0883073812448838
30) https://en.wikipedia.org/wiki/Hypophyseal_portal_system   https://nba.uth.tmc.edu/neuroscience/m/s4/chapter02.html
Raisman, G. (1997). AN URGE TO EXPLAIN THE INCOMPREHENSIBLE: Geoffrey Harris and the Discovery of the Neural Control of the Pituitary Gland. *Annual Review of Neuroscience, 20*(1), 533–566. https://doi.org/10.1146/annurev.neuro.20.1.533
http://www.annualreviews.org/doi/abs/10.1146/annurev.neuro.20.1.533
31) Circadian Rhythms and the Brain | Department of Neurobiology. (2018). Retrieved January 15, 2020, from Harvard.edu website: https://neuro.hms.harvard.edu/harvard-mahoney-neuroscience-institute/brain-newsletter/and-brain-series/circadian-rhythms-and-brain
The Neurons That Tell Time | The New Yorker
Logan, R. W., & McClung, C. A. (2018). Rhythms of life: circadian disruption and brain disorders across the lifespan. *Nature Reviews Neuroscience, 20*(1), 49–65. https://doi.org/10.1038/s41583-018-0088-y
Borjigin, J., Samantha Zhang, L., & Calinescu, A.-A. (2012). Circadian regulation of pineal gland rhythmicity. *Molecular and Cellular Endocrinology, 349*(1), 13–19. https://doi.org/10.1016/j.mce.2011.07.009
32) Aslan, S., Ersoy, R., Kuruoglu, A. C., Karakoc, A., & Cakir, N. (2005). Psychiatric symptoms and diagnoses in thyroid disorders. *International Journal of Psychiatry in Clinical Practice, 9*(3), 187–192. https://doi.org/10.1080/13651500510029129
https://www.tandfonline.com/doi/abs/10.1080/13651500510029129?journalCode=ijpc20
Hage, M. P., & Azar, S. T. (2012). The Link between Thyroid Function and Depression. *Journal of Thyroid Research, 2012*, 1–8. https://doi.org/10.1155/2012/590648
Joffe, R. T. (2011). Hormone treatment of depression. *Dialogues in Clinical Neuroscience, 13*(1), 127–138.
33) Bargiota, S. I., Bonotis, K. S., Messinis, I. E., & Angelopoulos, N. V. (2013). The Effects of Antipsychotics on Prolactin Levels and Women's Menstruation. *Schizophrenia Research and Treatment, 2013*, 1–10. https://doi.org/10.1155/2013/502697
34) McEwen, B. S., & Milner, T. A. (2016). Understanding the broad influence of sex hormones and sex differences in the brain. *Journal of Neuroscience Research, 95*(1–2), 24–39. https://doi.org/10.1002/jnr.23809
Henderson, V. W., St. John, J. A., Hodis, H. N., McCleary, C. A., Stanczyk, F. Z.,

Karim, R., ... Mack, W. J. (2013). Cognition, mood, and physiological concentrations of sex hormones in the early and late postmenopause. *Proceedings of the National Academy of Sciences*, *110*(50), 20290–20295. https://doi.org/10.1073/pnas.1312353110

35) Nillni, Y. I., Toufexis, D. J., & Rohan, K. J. (2011). Anxiety sensitivity, the menstrual cycle, and panic disorder: A putative neuroendocrine and psychological interaction. *Clinical Psychology Review*, *31*(7), 1183–1191. https://doi.org/10.1016/j.cpr.2011.07.006

36) Azadzoi, K. M., & Siroky, M. B. (2010). Neurologic factors in female sexual function and dysfunction. *Korean journal of urology*, *51*(7), 443–449. https://doi.org/10.4111/kju.2010.51.7.443

37) A side effect of SSRI antidepressants is reducing sex drive.

38) Hantsoo, Liisa, and C. Neill Epperson. "Premenstrual Dysphoric Disorder: Epidemiology and Treatment." *Current Psychiatry Reports*, vol. 17, no. 11, 16 Sept. 2015, www.ncbi.nlm.nih.gov/pmc/articles/PMC4890701/

39) Baller, E. B., Wei, S.-M., Kohn, P. D., Rubinow, D. R., Alarcón, G., Schmidt, P. J., & Berman, K. F. (2013). Abnormalities of Dorsolateral Prefrontal Function in Women With Premenstrual Dysphoric Disorder: A Multimodal Neuroimaging Study. *American Journal of Psychiatry*, *170*(3), 305–314. https://doi.org/10.1176/appi.ajp.2012.12030385

40) Sacher, J., Wilson, A. A., Houle, S., Rusjan, P., Hassan, S., Bloomfield, P. M., ... Meyer, J. H. (2010). Elevated Brain Monoamine Oxidase A Binding in the Early Postpartum Period. *Archives of General Psychiatry*, *67*(5), 468. https://doi.org/10.1001/archgenpsychiatry.2010.32
https://jamanetwork.com/journals/jamapsychiatry/fullarticle/210763
Sacher, J., Rekkas, P. V., Wilson, A. A., Houle, S., Romano, L., Hamidi, J., ... Meyer, J. H. (2014). Relationship of Monoamine Oxidase-A Distribution Volume to Postpartum Depression and Postpartum Crying. *Neuropsychopharmacology*, *40*(2), 429–435.https://doi.org/10.1038/npp.2014.190

Sharma, V., & Pope, C. J. (2012). Pregnancy and Bipolar Disorder. *The Journal of Clinical Psychiatry*, *73*(11), 1447–1455. https://doi.org/10.4088/jcp.11r07499

41) Forman, D. R., O'hara, M. W., Stuart, S., Gorman, L. L., Larsen, K. E., & Coy, K. C. (2007). Effective treatment for postpartum depression is not sufficient to improve the developing mother–child relationship. *Development and Psychopathology*, *19*(02). https://doi.org/10.1017/s0954579407070289

Cutrona, C. E., & Troutman, B. R. (1986). Social Support, Infant Temperament, and Parenting Self-Efficacy: A Mediational Model of Postpartum Depression. *Child Development*, *57*(6), 1507. https://doi.org/10.2307/1130428
http://www.jstor.org/stable/1130428?seq=1#page_scan_tab_contents

42) Zarghami, M., Abdollahi, F., & Lye, M.-S. (2016). Perspective of postpartum depression theories: A narrative literature review. *North American Journal of Medical Sciences*,*8*(6), 232. https://doi.org/10.4103/1947-2714.185027

Yim, I. S., Tanner Stapleton, L. R., Guardino, C. M., Hahn-Holbrook, J., & Dunkel Schetter, C. (2015). Biological and Psychosocial Predictors of Postpartum Depression: Systematic Review and Call for Integration. *Annual Review of Clinical Psychology*, *11*(1), 99–137. https://doi.org/10.1146/annurev-clinpsy-101414-020426

Schmidt, P. J., Ben Dor, R., Martinez, P. E., Guerrieri, G. M., Harsh, V. L., Thompson, K., Koziol, D. E., Nieman, L. K., & Rubinow, D. R. (2015). Effects of Estradiol Withdrawal on Mood in Women With Past Perimenopausal Depression: A Randomized Clinical Trial. *JAMA psychiatry*, *72*(7), 714–726. https://doi.org/10.1001/jamapsychiatry.2015.0111

44) Terauchi, M., Hiramitsu, S., Akiyoshi, M., Owa, Y., Kato, K., Obayashi, S., ... Kubota, T. (2012). Associations between anxiety, depression and insomnia in peri- and post-menopausal women. *Maturitas*, *72*(1), 61–65. https://doi.org/10.1016/j.maturitas.2012.01.014   Dalal, P., & Agarwal, M. (2015). Postmenopausal syndrome. *Indian Journal of Psychiatry*, *57*(6), 222. https://doi.org/10.4103/0019-5545.161483

Walf, A. A., & Frye, C. A. (2006). A Review and Update of Mechanisms of Estrogen in the Hippocampus and Amygdala for Anxiety and Depression Behavior. *Neuropsychopharmacology*, *31*(6), 1097–1111. https://doi.org/10.1038/sj.npp.1301067

45) Rodgers, S., grosse Holtforth, M., Hengartner, M. P., Müller, M., Aleksandrowicz, A. A., Rössler, W., & Ajdacic-Gross, V. (2015). Serum Testosterone Levels and Symptom-Based Depression Subtypes in Men. *Frontiers in Psychiatry*, *6*. https://doi.org/10.3389/fpsyt.2015.00061   Walther, A., Breidenstein, J., & Miller, R. (2019). Association of Testosterone Treatment With Alleviation of Depressive Symptoms in Men: A Systematic Review and Meta-analysis. *JAMA psychiatry*, *76*(1), 31–40. https://doi.org/10.1001/jamapsychiatry.2018.2734

46) The Hypothalamic-Pituitary-Adrenal (HPA) Axis. (2012). https://www.mind-body-health.net/hpa-axis.shtml

Selye, H. (1950). Stress and the General Adaptation Syndrome. *BMJ*, *1*(4667), 1383–1392. https://doi.org/10.1136/bmj.1.4667.1383

Selye, H. (1976). Forty years of stress research: principal remaining problems and misconceptions. *Canadian Medical Association Journal*, *115*(1), 53–56.

Jackson, M. (2014, February). Evaluating the Role of Hans Selye in the Modern History of Stress: https://www.ncbi.nlm.nih.gov/books/NBK349158/

Janes, M., Kuster, S., Goldson, T. M., & Forjuoh, S. N. (2019). Steroid-induced psychosis. *Proceedings (Baylor University. Medical Center)*, *32*(4), 614–615. https://doi.org/10.1080/08998280.2019.1629223

48) Biological Psychology website: http://www.oxfordpresents.com/ms/lambert/the-neurobiology-of-voodoo-death/

Engel Ann Int Med 74: 771-782 1971

W Cannon AMER ANTHROPOL 44: 169-181 1942

References

49) Fountoulakis, K. N., Gonda, X., Rihmer, Z., Fokas, C., & Iacovides, A. (2008). Revisiting the Dexamethasone Suppression Test in unipolar major depression: an exploratory study. *Annals of General Psychiatry*, 7(1). https://doi.org/10.1186/1744-859x-7-22

50) The scale and references to work are found at https://en.wikipedia.org/wiki/Holmes_and_Rahe_stress_scale

Noone, P. A. (2017). The Holmes–Rahe Stress Inventory. *Occupational Medicine*, 67(7), 581–582. https://doi.org/10.1093/occmed/kqx099 https://academic.oup.com/occmed/article/67/7/581/4430935

The Holmes and Rahe Stress Scale. (2016). https://kresserinstitute.com/tools/holmes/

The Body Keeps The Score
Penguin Publishing Group; Reprint edition (September 8, 2015)
ISBN-10 : 0143127748 ISBN-13 : 978-0143127741

Epstein, F. H., & Reichlin, S. (1993). Neuroendocrine-Immune Interactions. *New England Journal of Medicine*, 329(17), 1246–1253. https://doi.org/10.1056/nejm199310213291708
http://www.nejm.org/doi/pdf/10.1056/NEJM199310213291708

Calogero, A. E., Gallucci, W. T., Chrousos, G. P., & Gold, P. W. (1988). Catecholamine effects upon rat hypothalamic corticotropin-releasing hormone secretion in vitro. *Journal of Clinical Investigation*, 82(3), 839–846. https://doi.org/10.1172/jci11368

Chung Thong Lim, & Khoo, B. (2017, October 24). *Normal Physiology of ACTH and GH Release in the Hypothalamus and Anterior Pituitary in Man.* Nih.Gov; MDText.com, Inc. https://www.ncbi.nlm.nih.gov/books/NBK279116/

Heim, C., Newport, D. J., Mletzko, T., Miller, A. H., & Nemeroff, C. B. (2008). The link between childhood trauma and depression: Insights from HPA axis studies in humans. *Psychoneuroendocrinology*, 33(6), 693–710. https://doi.org/10.1016/j.psyneuen.2008.03.008 https://www.researchgate.net/profile/Charles_Nemeroff/publication/5249983_The_link_between_childhood_trauma_and_depression_Insights_from_HPA_axis_studies_in_humans/links/0fcfd50903cef2e6b9000000.pdf

Morgan, C. A., Wang, S., Mason, J., Southwick, S. M., Fox, P., Hazlett, G., Charney, D. S., & Greenfield, G. (2000). Hormone profiles in humans experiencing military survival training. *Biological Psychiatry*, 47(10), 891–901. https://doi.org/10.1016/s0006-3223(99)00307-8

Varghese, F. P., & Brown, E. S. (2001). The Hypothalamic-Pituitary-Adrenal Axis in Major Depressive Disorder: A Brief Primer for Primary Care Physicians. *Primary Care Companion to the Journal of Clinical Psychiatry*, 3(4), 151–155. https://doi.org/10.4088/pcc.v03n0401

Heim, C., Newport, D. J., Heit, S., Graham, Y. P., Wilcox, M., Bonsall, R., Miller, A. H., & Nemeroff, C. B. (2000). Pituitary-adrenal and autonomic responses to stress in women after sexual and physical abuse in childhood. *JAMA,*

284(5), 592–597. https://doi.org/10.1001/jama.284.5.592

51) Psychoneuroimmunology - Wikipedia   Cousins Center for Psychoneuroimmunology

52) Tekampe J, van Middendorp H, Meeuwis S, H, van Leusden J, W, R, Pacheco-López G, Hermus A, R, M, M, Evers A, W, M: Conditioning Immune and Endocrine Parameters in Humans: A Systematic Review. Psychother Psychosom 2017;86:99-107. doi: 10.1159/000449470https://www.karger.com/Article/Fulltext/449470#

Gorczynski, R. M. (2001). Understanding classical conditioning of immune responses. *NeuroImmune Biology*, 237–254. https://doi.org/10.1016/s1567-7443(01)80021-1   https://www.sciencedirect.com/science/article/pii/S1567744301800211

53) Immunology and Psychiatry. (2015). Immunology and Psychiatry - From Basic Research to Therapeutic Interventions | Norbert Müller | Springer. https://www.springer.com/gp/book/9783319136011

Recent Advances in Psychiatry from Psycho-Neuro-Immunology Research: Autoimmunencephalitis, Autoimmune-Encephalopathy, Mild Encephalitis. (2016). https://www.frontiersin.org/research-topics/4931/recent-advances-in-psychiatry-from-psycho-neuro-immunology-research-autoimmunencephalitis-autoimmune

Haroon, E., Raison, C. L., & Miller, A. H. (2011). Psychoneuroimmunology Meets Neuropsychopharmacology: Translational Implications of the Impact of Inflammation on Behavior. *Neuropsychopharmacology*, *37*(1), 137–162. https://doi.org/10.1038/npp.2011.205

Miller, A. H., Haroon, E., & Felger, J. C. (2016). The Immunology of Behavior—Exploring the Role of the Immune System in Brain Health and Illness. *Neuropsychopharmacology*, *42*(1), 1–4. https://doi.org/10.1038/npp.2016.229

Felger J. C. (2018). Imaging the Role of Inflammation in Mood and Anxiety-related Disorders. *Current neuropharmacology*, *16*(5), 533–558. https://doi.org/10.2174/1570159X15666171123201142

Soria, V., Uribe, J., Salvat-Pujol, N., Palao, D., Menchón, J. M., & Labad, J. (2018). Psychoneuroimmunology of mental disorders. *Revista de Psiquiatría y Salud Mental (English Edition)*, *11*(2), 115–124. https://doi.org/10.1016/j.rpsmen.2017.07.002 https://www.elsevier.es/en-revista-revista-psiquiatria-salud-mental-486-articulo-psychoneuroimmunology-mental-disorders-S2173505018300177   https://www.sciencedirect.com/topics/neuroscience/psychoneuroimmunology

Graziella Orefici, Cardona, F., Cox, C. J., & Cunningham, M. W. (2016, February 10). Pediatric Autoimmune Neuropsychiatric Disorders Associated with Streptococcal Infections (PANDAS). Retrieved October 28, 2019, from Nih.gov website: https://www.ncbi.nlm.nih.gov/books/NBK333433/

Pace, T. W. W., & Heim, C. M. (2011). A short review on the

References

psychoneuroimmunology of posttraumatic stress disorder: From risk factors to medical comorbidities. *Brain, Behavior, and Immunity*, 25(1), 6–13. https://doi.org/10.1016/j.bbi.2010.10.003

Miller, A. H., & Raison, C. L. (2016). The role of inflammation in depression: from evolutionary imperative to modern treatment target. *Nature reviews. Immunology*, 16(1), 22–34. https://doi.org/10.1038/nri.2015.5

54) Dubé, B., Benton, T., Cruess, D. G., & Evans, D. L. (2005). Neuropsychiatric manifestations of HIV infection and AIDS. *Journal of Psychiatry & Neuroscience : JPN*, 30(4), 237–246.

Siris, S. (2005). Psychiatric Manifestations of HIV Infection and AIDS. *Psychiatric Times*. https://www.psychiatrictimes.com/neuropsychiatry/psychiatric-manifestations-hiv-infection-and-aids

Giunta, B., Hervey, W., Klippel, C., Obregon, D., Robben, D., Hartney, K., di Ciccone, B. L., & Fernandez, F. (2013). Psychiatric Complications of HIV Infection: An Overview. *Psychiatric Annals*, 43(5), 199–203. https://doi.org/10.3928/00485713-20130503-03

Goodkin, K., López, E., Hardy, D. J., & Hardy, W. D. (2013). Neurocognitive Decline in HIV Infection. *Psychiatric Annals*, 43(5), 204–211. https://doi.org/10.3928/00485713-20130503-04

Neurologic and psychiatric complications of antiretroviral agents. (2020) http://www.natap.org/2002/june/060702_2.htm

55) Susannah Cahalan, **Brain on Fire: My Month of Madness**, Simon & Schuster; ISBN-10: 1451621388

56) assau, J. H., Tien, K., & Fritz, G. K. (2007). Review of the Literature: Integrating Psychoneuroimmunology into Pediatric Chronic Illness Interventions. *Journal of Pediatric Psychology*, 33(2), 195–207. https://doi.org/10.1093/jpepsy/jsm076

Köhler, O., Benros, M. E., Nordentoft, M., Farkouh, M. E., Iyengar, R. L., Mors, O., & Krogh, J. (2014). Effect of Anti-inflammatory Treatment on Depression, Depressive Symptoms, and Adverse Effects. *JAMA Psychiatry*, 71(12), 1381. https://doi.org/10.1001/jamapsychiatry.2014.1611

Nitta, M., Kishimoto, T., Müller, N., Weiser, M., Davidson, M., Kane, J. M., & Correll, C. U. (2013). Adjunctive Use of Nonsteroidal Anti-inflammatory Drugs for Schizophrenia: A Meta-analytic Investigation of Randomized Controlled Trials. *Schizophrenia Bulletin*, 39(6), 1230–1241. https://doi.org/10.1093/schbul/sbt070 https://jamanetwork.com/journals/jamapsychiatry/fullarticle/1916904

O'Connor, M.-F., Irwin, M. R., & Wellisch, D. K. (2009). When grief heats up: Pro-inflammatory cytokines predict regional brain activation. *NeuroImage*, 47(3), 891–896. https://doi.org/10.1016/j.neuroimage.2009.05.049

Friedman, H. S. (2008). The multiple linkages of personality and disease. *Brain, Behavior, and Immunity*, 22(5), 668–675. https://doi.org/10.1016/j.bbi.2007.09.004

57) The microbiota–gut–brain axis. Nature. (2019, June 17).https://www.nature.com/articles/d42859-019-00021-3

Martin, C. R., Osadchiy, V., Kalani, A., & Mayer, E. A. (2018). The Brain-Gut-Microbiome Axis. *Cellular and Molecular Gastroenterology and Hepatology*, *6*(2), 133–148. https://doi.org/10.1016/j.jcmgh.2018.04.003

Liang, S., Wu, X., & Jin, F. (2018). Gut-Brain Psychology: Rethinking Psychology From the Microbiota–Gut–Brain Axis. *Frontiers in Integrative Neuroscience*, *12*. https://doi.org/10.3389/fnint.2018.00033

Deans, E. (2016). Microbiome and mental health in the modern environment. *Journal of Physiological Anthropology*, *36*(1). https://doi.org/10.1186/s40101-016-0101-y

58) Gould, Katherine. "The Vagus Nerve: Your Body's Communication Superhighway." *Livescience.Com*, Live Science, 12 Nov. 2019, www.livescience.com/vagus-nerve.html.

Vagus Nerve: Anatomy and Function, Diagram, Stimulation, Conditions. (2018). https://www.healthline.com/human-body-maps/vagus-nerve

Breit, S., Kupferberg, A., Rogler, G., & Hasler, G. (2018). Vagus Nerve as Modulator of the Brain–Gut Axis in Psychiatric and Inflammatory Disorders. *Frontiers in Psychiatry*, *9*. https://doi.org/10.3389/fpsyt.2018.00044

59) Muscatello, M. R. A., Bruno, A., Mento, C., Pandolfo, G., & Zoccali, R. A. (2016). Personality traits and emotional patterns in irritable bowel syndrome. *World Journal of Gastroenterology*, *22*(28), 6402. https://doi.org/10.3748/wjg.v22.i28.6402

Khayyam-Nekouei, Z., Neshatdoost, H., Yousefy, A., Sadeghi, M., & Manshaee, G. (2013). Psychological factors and coronary heart disease. *ARYA Atherosclerosis*, *9*(1), 102–111. Retrieved from

59) Ketterer, M. W., & Mahr, G. (2016). Evidence-Based Treatment of Emotional Distress in Patients with Ischemic Coronary Heart Disease. *Psychiatric Annals*, *46*(12), 677–682. https://doi.org/10.3928/00485713-20161026-02

Compare, A., Germani, E., Proietti, R., & Janeway, D. (2011). Clinical Psychology and Cardiovascular Disease: An Up-to-Date Clinical Practice Review for Assessment and Treatment of Anxiety and Depression. *Clinical practice and epidemiology in mental health : CP & EMH*, *7*, 148–156. https://doi.org/10.2174/1745017901107010148

60) The scales are copyrighted and cannot be reprinted but references show the range of symptoms:
https://www.ncbi.nlm.nih.gov/pmc/articles/PMC3195800/
https://www.mdcalc.com/hamilton-depression-rating-scale-ham-d
https://www.sciencedirect.com/topics/neuroscience/beck-depression-inventory
https://psycho-tests.com/test/becks-depression-inventory

61) Martinowich, K., Schloesser, R. J., & Manji, H. K. (2009). Bipolar disorder: from genes to behavior pathways. *Journal of Clinical Investigation*, *119*(4),

References

726–736. https://doi.org/10.1172/jci37703
https://www.jci.org/articles/view/37703 http://enigma.ini.usc.edu/ongoing/enigma-bipolar-working-group/
Fears, S. C., Service, S. K., Kremeyer, B., Araya, C., Araya, X., Bejarano, J., Ramirez, M., Castrillón, G., Gomez-Franco, J., Lopez, M. C., Montoya, G., Montoya, P., Aldana, I., Teshiba, T. M., Abaryan, Z., Al-Sharif, N. B., Ericson, M., Jalbrzikowski, M., Luykx, J. J., Navarro, L., … Bearden, C. E. (2014). Multisystem component phenotypes of bipolar disorder for genetic investigations of extended pedigrees. *JAMA psychiatry*, *71*(4), 375–387. https://doi.org/10.1001/jamapsychiatry.2013.4100
Croarkin, P. E., Luby, J. L., Cercy, K., Geske, J. R., Veldic, M., Simonson, M., Joshi, P. T., Wagner, K. D., Walkup, J. T., Nassan, M. M., Cuellar-Barboza, A. B., Casuto, L., McElroy, S. L., Jensen, P. S., Frye, M. A., & Biernacka, J. M. (2017). Genetic Risk Score Analysis in Early-Onset Bipolar Disorder. *The Journal of Clinical Psychiatry*, *78*(9), 1337–1343. https://doi.org/10.4088/jcp.15m10314
Bahrami, S., Steen, N. E., Shadrin, A., O'Connell, K., Frei, O., Bettella, F., Wirgenes, K. V., Krull, F., Fan, C. C., Dale, A. M., Smeland, O. B., Djurovic, S., & Andreassen, O. A. (2020). Shared Genetic Loci Between Body Mass Index and Major Psychiatric Disorders: A Genome-wide Association Study. *JAMA psychiatry*, *77*(5), 503–512. https://doi.org/10.1001/jamapsychiatry.2019.4188
McElroy, S. L., & Keck, P. E., Jr (2014). Metabolic syndrome in bipolar disorder: a review with a focus on bipolar depression. *The Journal of clinical psychiatry*, *75*(1), 46–61. https://doi.org/10.4088/JCP.13r08634
62) *9 Most Common Triggers for Bipolar Mood Episodes | Everyday Health*. (2017, October 18). EverydayHealth.Com. https://www.everydayhealth.com/bipolar-disorder-pictures/biggest-triggers-of-bipolar-mood-swings.aspx
Walz, R. (2008). Psychiatric disorders and traumatic brain injury. *Neuropsychiatric Disease and Treatment*, 797. https://doi.org/10.2147/ndt.s2653
Judd, L. L., Schettler, P. J., Brown, E. S., Wolkowitz, O. M., Sternberg, E. M., Bender, B. G., Bulloch, K., Cidlowski, J. A., de Kloet, E. R., Fardet, L., Joëls, M., Leung, D. Y., McEwen, B. S., Roozendaal, B., Van Rossum, E. F., Ahn, J., Brown, D. W., Plitt, A., & Singh, G. (2014). Adverse consequences of glucocorticoid medication: psychological, cognitive, and behavioral effects. *The American journal of psychiatry*, *171*(10), 1045–1051. https://doi.org/10.1176/appi.ajp.2014.13091264
Sharma, V., & Pope, C. J. (2012). Pregnancy and Bipolar Disorder. *The Journal of Clinical Psychiatry*, *73*(11), 1447–1455. https://doi.org/10.4088/jcp.11r07499
Pregnancy and bipolar disorder: a systematic review. – PubMed – NCBI
Altshuler, L. L., Kupka, R. W., Hellemann, G., Frye, M. A., Sugar, C. A., McElroy, S. L., … Suppes, T. (2010). Gender and Depressive Symptoms in 711 Patients With Bipolar Disorder Evaluated Prospectively in the Stanley Foundation Bipolar Treatment Outcome Network. *American Journal of*

Psychiatry, *167*(6), 708–715. https://doi.org/10.1176/appi.ajp.2009.09010105
https://ajp.psychiatryonline.org/doi/full/10.1176/appi.ajp.2009.09010105
Jorge, R. E., & Arciniegas, D. B. (2014). Mood Disorders After TBI.
Psychiatric Clinics of North America, *37*(1), 13–29. https://doi.org/10.1016/j.psc.2013.11.005
63) Oomura, Y., Ooyama, H., Yamamoto, T., & Naka, F. (1967). Reciprocal relationship of the lateral and ventromedial hypothalamus in the regulation of food intake. *Physiology & Behavior*, *2*(2), 97–115. https://doi.org/10.1016/0031-9384(67)90020-0https://www.sciencedirect.com/science/article/abs/pii/0031938467900200
Behbehani, M., Park, M., & Clement, M. (1988). Interactions between the lateral hypothalamus and the periaqueductal gray. *The Journal of Neuroscience*, *8*(8), 2780–2787. https://doi.org/10.1523/jneurosci.08-08-02780.1988
http://www.jneurosci.org/content/8/8/2780.long
Karlsson, K. Æ., Windischberger, C., Gerstl, F., Mayr, W., Siegel, J. M., & Moser, E. (2010). Modulation of hypothalamus and amygdalar activation levels with stimulus valence. *NeuroImage*, *51*(1), 324–328. https://doi.org/10.1016/j.neuroimage.2010.02.029
Hibar, D. P., Westlye, L. T., Doan, N. T., Jahanshad, N., Cheung, J. W., Ching, C. R. K., Versace, A., Bilderbeck, A. C., Uhlmann, A.,
Blond, B. N., Fredericks, C. A., & Blumberg, H. P. (2012). Functional neuroanatomy of bipolar disorder: structure, function, and connectivity in an amygdala-anterior paralimbic neural system. *Bipolar Disorders*, *14*(4), 340–355. https://doi.org/10.1111/j.1399-5618.2012.01015.x
64) Correlates of Treatment-Emergent Mania Associated With Antidepressant Treatment in Bipolar Depression, Mark A. Frye M.D.Gerhard Helleman Ph.D.Susan L. McElroy M.D.Lori L. Altshuler M.D.David O. Black Ph.D.Paul E. Keck Jr., M.D.Willem A. Nolen M.D., Ph.D.et alAmerican Journal of Psychiatry Volume 166, Issue 2THE AMERICAN JOURNAL OF PSYCHIATRY February 2009 Volume 166 Number 2
https://ajp.psychiatryonline.org/doi/abs/10.1176/appi.ajp.2008.08030322
Viktorin, A., Lichtenstein, P., Thase, M. E., Larsson, H., Lundholm, C., Magnusson, P. K., & Landén, M. (2014). The risk of switch to mania in patients with bipolar disorder during treatment with an antidepressant alone and in combination with a mood stabilizer. *The American journal of psychiatry*, *171*(10), 1067–1073. https://doi.org/10.1176/appi.ajp.2014.13111501
Frye, M. A., Helleman, G., McElroy, S. L., Altshuler, L. L., Black, D. O., Keck, P. E., ... Suppes, T. (2009). Correlates of Treatment-Emergent Mania Associated With Antidepressant Treatment in Bipolar Depression. *American Journal of Psychiatry*, *166*(2), 164–172. https://doi.org/10.1176/appi.ajp.2008.08030322
https://ajp.psychiatryonline.org/doi/abs/10.1176/appi.ajp.2008.08030322
El-Mallakh, R. S., Vöhringer, P. A., Ostacher, M. M., Baldassano, C. F., Holtzman, N. S., Whitham, E. A., Thommi, S. B., Goodwin, F. K., & Ghaemi,

References

S. N. (2015). Antidepressants worsen rapid-cycling course in bipolar depression: A STEP-BD randomized clinical trial. *Journal of affective disorders*, *184*, 318–321. https://doi.org/10.1016/j.jad.2015.04.054

Truman, C. J., Goldberg, J. F., Ghaemi, S. N., Baldassano, C. F., Wisniewski, S. R., Dennehy, E. B., Thase, M. E., & Sachs, G. S. (2007). Self-reported history of manic/hypomanic switch associated with antidepressant use: data from the Systematic Treatment Enhancement Program for Bipolar Disorder (STEP-BD). *The Journal of clinical psychiatry*, *68*(10), 1472–1479. https://doi.org/10.4088/jcp.v68n1002

65) Post R. M. (2007). Kindling and sensitization as models for affective episode recurrence, cyclicity, and tolerance phenomena. *Neuroscience and biobehavioral reviews*, *31*(6), 858–873. https://doi.org/10.1016/j.neubiorev.2007.04.003

Weiss, R. B., Stange, J. P., Boland, E. M., Black, S. K., LaBelle, D. R., Abramson, L. Y., & Alloy, L. B. (2015). Kindling of life stress in bipolar disorder: Comparison of sensitization and autonomy models. *Journal of Abnormal Psychology*, *124*(1), 4–16. https://doi.org/10.1037/abn0000014

Bender, R. E., & Alloy, L. B. (2011). Life stress and kindling in bipolar disorder: Review of the evidence and integration with emerging biopsychosocial theories. *Clinical Psychology Review*, *31*(3), 383–398. https://doi.org/10.1016/j.cpr.2011.01.004

66) Ghaemi, S. N., Boiman, E. E., & Goodwin, F. K. (1999). Kindling and second messengers: an approach to the neurobiology of recurrence in bipolar disorder. *Biological Psychiatry*, *45*(2), 137–144. https://doi.org/10.1016/s0006-3223(98)00256-x

67) Amann, B. L., Canales-Rodríguez, E. J., Madre, M., Radua, J., Monte, G., Alonso-Lana, S., Landin-Romero, R., Moreno-Alcázar, A., Bonnin, C. M., Sarró, S., Ortiz-Gil, J., Gomar, J. J., Moro, N., Fernandez-Corcuera, P., Goikolea, J. M., Blanch, J., Salvador, R., Vieta, E., McKenna, P. J., & Pomarol-Clotet, E. (2015). Brain structural changes in schizoaffective disorder compared to schizophrenia and bipolar disorder. *Acta Psychiatrica Scandinavica*, *133*(1), 23–33. https://doi.org/10.1111/acps.12440

Endres, D., Perlov, E., Feige, B., Fleck, M., Bartels, S., Altenmüller, D.-M., & Tebartz van Elst, L. (2016). Electroencephalographic findings in schizophreniform and affective disorders. *International Journal of Psychiatry in Clinical Practice*, *20*(3), 157–164. https://doi.org/10.1080/13651501.2016.1181184

Mathalon, D. (2009). Neurophysiological distinction between schizophrenia and schizoaffective disorder. *Frontiers in Human Neuroscience*. https://doi.org/10.3389/neuro.09.070.2009

Howells, F. M., Temmingh, H. S., Hsieh, J. H., van Dijen, A. V., Baldwin, D. S., & Stein, D. J. (2018). Electroencephalographic delta/alpha frequency activity differentiates psychotic disorders: a study of schizophrenia, bipolar disorder and methamphetamine-induced psychotic disorder. *Translational Psychiatry*, *8*(1). https://doi.org/10.1038/s41398-018-0105-y

https://www.nature.com/articles/s41398-018-0105-y
68) Beesdo, K., Lau, J. Y. F., Guyer, A. E., McClure-Tone, E. B., Monk, C. S., Nelson, E. E., Fromm, S. J., Goldwin, M. A., Wittchen, H.-U., Leibenluft, E., Ernst, M., & Pine, D. S. (2009). Common and Distinct Amygdala-Function Perturbations in Depressed vs Anxious Adolescents. *Archives of General Psychiatry*, *66*(3), 275. https://doi.org/10.1001/archgenpsychiatry.2008.545
Banks, Sarah J., et al. "Amygdala–Frontal Connectivity during Emotion Regulation." *Social Cognitive and Affective Neuroscience*, vol. 2, no. 4, 21 July 2007, pp. 303–312, 10.1093/scan/nsm029. Accessed 21 Mar. 2019.
Akirav, I., & Maroun, M. (2007). The Role of the Medial Prefrontal Cortex-Amygdala Circuit in Stress Effects on the Extinction of Fear. *Neural Plasticity*, *2007*, 1–11. https://doi.org/10.1155/2007/30873
69) Freed, P. J., Yanagihara, T. K., Hirsch, J., & Mann, J. J. (2009). Neural mechanisms of grief regulation. *Biological psychiatry*, *66*(1), 33–40. https://doi.org/10.1016/j.biopsych.2009.01.019
Sullivan, R. M. (2012). The Neurobiology of Attachment to Nurturing and Abusive Caregivers. *The Hastings Law Journal*, *63*(6), 1553–1570. https://www.ncbi.nlm.nih.gov/pmc/articles/PMC3774302/
Newman, L., Sivaratnam, C., & Komiti, A. (2015). Attachment and early brain development – neuroprotective interventions in infant–caregiver therapy. *Translational Developmental Psychiatry*, *3*(1), 28647. https://doi.org/10.3402/tdp.v3.28647
70) Baldwin, J. R., Reuben, A., Newbury, J. B., & Danese, A. (2019). Agreement Between Prospective and Retrospective Measures of Childhood Maltreatment: A Systematic Review and Meta-analysis. *JAMA psychiatry*, *76*(6), 584–593. https://doi.org/10.1001/jamapsychiatry.2019.0097
Williams, L. M., Debattista, C., Duchemin, A. M., Schatzberg, A. F., & Nemeroff, C. B. (2016). Childhood trauma predicts antidepressant response in adults with major depression: data from the randomized international study to predict optimized treatment for depression. *Translational psychiatry*, *6*(5), e799. https://doi.org/10.1038/tp.2016.61
Nanni, V., Uher, R., & Danese, A. (2012). Childhood maltreatment predicts unfavorable course of illness and treatment outcome in depression: a meta-analysis. *The American journal of psychiatry*, *169*(2), 141–151. https://doi.org/10.1176/appi.ajp.2011.11020335
Withers, A. C., Tarasoff, J. M., & Stewart, J. W. (2013). Is depression with atypical features associated with trauma history?. *The Journal of clinical psychiatry*, *74*(5), 500–506. https://doi.org/10.4088/JCP.12m07870
Pearson, R. M., Evans, J., Kounali, D., Lewis, G., Heron, J., Ramchandani, P. G., O'Connor, T. G., & Stein, A. (2013). Maternal depression during pregnancy and the postnatal period: risks and possible mechanisms for offspring depression at age 18 years. *JAMA psychiatry*, *70*(12), 1312–1319. https://doi.org/10.1001/jamapsychiatry.2013.2163

References

Tully, E. C., Iacono, W. G., & McGue, M. (2008). An adoption study of parental depression as an environmental liability for adolescent depression and childhood disruptive disorders. *The American journal of psychiatry*, *165*(9), 1148–1154. https://doi.org/10.1176/appi.ajp.2008.07091438

Plant, D. T., Pariante, C. M., Sharp, D., & Pawlby, S. (2015). Maternal depression during pregnancy and offspring depression in adulthood: role of child maltreatment. *The British journal of psychiatry : the journal of mental science*, *207*(3), 213–220. https://doi.org/10.1192/bjp.bp.114.156620

Björkenstam, E., Hjern, A., Björkenstam, C., & Kosidou, K. (2018). Association of Cumulative Childhood Adversity and Adolescent Violent Offending With Suicide in Early Adulthood. *JAMA psychiatry*, *75*(2), 185–193. https://doi.org/10.1001/jamapsychiatry.2017.3788

Jorge, R. E., Robinson, R. G., Moser, D., Tateno, A., Crespo-Facorro, B., & Arndt, S. (2004). Major depression following traumatic brain injury. *Archives of general psychiatry*, *61*(1), 42–50. https://doi.org/10.1001/archpsyc.61.1.42

Fann, J. R., Hart, T., & Schomer, K. G. (2009). Treatment for depression after traumatic brain injury: a systematic review. *Journal of neurotrauma*, *26*(12), 2383–2402. https://doi.org/10.1089/neu.2009.1091

Stein, M. B., Jain, S., Giacino, J. T., Levin, H., Dikmen, S., Nelson, L. D., Vassar, M. J., Okonkwo, D. O., Diaz-Arrastia, R., Robertson, C. S., Mukherjee, P., McCrea, M., Mac Donald, C. L., Yue, J. K., Yuh, E., Sun, X., Campbell-Sills, L., Temkin, N., Manley, G. T., TRACK-TBI Investigators, ... Zafonte, R. (2019). Risk of Posttraumatic Stress Disorder and Major Depression in Civilian Patients After Mild Traumatic Brain Injury: A TRACK-TBI Study. *JAMA psychiatry*, *76*(3), 249–258. https://doi.org/10.1001/jamapsychiatry.2018.4288

Leblanc, É., Dégeilh, F., Daneault, V., Beauchamp, M. H., & Bernier, A. (2017). Attachment Security in Infancy: A Preliminary Study of Prospective Links to Brain Morphometry in Late Childhood. *Frontiers in psychology*, *8*, 2141. https://doi.org/10.3389/fpsyg.2017.02141

73) Mayberg, H. S. (2003). Modulating dysfunctional limbic-cortical circuits in depression: towards development of brain-based algorithms for diagnosis and optimised treatment. *British Medical Bulletin*, *65*(1), 193–207. https://doi.org/10.1093/bmb/65.1.193
https://academic.oup.com/bmb/article/65/1/193/375334

Ramirez-Mahaluf, J. P., Roxin, A., Mayberg, H. S., & Compte, A. (2017). A Computational Model of Major Depression: the Role of Glutamate Dysfunction on Cingulo-Frontal Network Dynamics. *Cerebral cortex (New York, N.Y. : 1991)*, *27*(1), 660–679. https://doi.org/10.1093/cercor/bhv249

Stevens, F. L., Hurley, R. A., & Taber, K. H. (2011). Anterior Cingulate Cortex: Unique Role in Cognition and Emotion. *The Journal of Neuropsychiatry and Clinical Neurosciences*, *23*(2), 121–125. https://doi.org/10.1176/jnp.23.2.jnp121

Mayberg, H. S., Lozano, A. M., Voon, V., McNeely, H. E., Seminowicz, D., Hamani, C., Schwalb, J. M., & Kennedy, S. H. (2005). Deep Brain Stimulation for Treatment-Resistant Depression. *Neuron, 45*(5), 651–660. https://doi.org/10.1016/j.neuron.2005.02.014

Abend, R., Sar-el, R., Gonen, T., Jalon, I., Vaisvaser, S., Bar-Haim, Y., & Hendler, T.(2018). Modulating Emotional Experience Using Electrical Stimulation of the Medial Prefrontal Cortex: A Preliminary tDCS-fMRI Study. *Neuromodulation: Technology at the Neural Interface, 22*(8), 884–893. https://doi.org/10.1111/ner.12787 https://onlinelibrary.wiley.com/doi/abs/10.1111/ner.12787

74) Alves, P. N., Foulon, C., Karolis, V., Bzdok, D., Margulies, D. S., Volle, E., & Thiebaut de Schotten, M. (2019). An improved neuroanatomical model of the default-mode network reconciles previous neuroimaging and neuropathological findings. *Communications Biology, 2*(1). https://doi.org/10.1038/s42003-019-0611-3

https://www.neuroscientificallychallenged.com/blog/know-your-brain-default-mode-network

Beyond Feeling: Chronic Pain Hurts the Brain, Disrupting the Default-Mode Network Dynamics, Marwan N. Baliki, Paul Y. Geha, A. Vania Apkarian, Dante R. ChialvoJournal of Neuroscience 6 February 2008, 28 (6) 1398-1403; DOI: 10.1523/JNEUROSCI.4123-07.2008 https://www.jneurosci.org/content/28/6/1398

Anticevic, A., Cole, M. W., Murray, J. D., Corlett, P. R., Wang, X. J., & Krystal, J. H. (2012). The role of default network deactivation in cognition and disease. *Trends in cognitive sciences, 16*(12), 584–592. https://doi.org/10.1016/j.tics.2012.10.008

Hamilton, J. P., Chen, M. C., & Gotlib, I. H. (2013). Neural systems approaches to understanding major depressive disorder: an intrinsic functional organization perspective. *Neurobiology of disease, 52*, 4–11. https://doi.org/10.1016/j.nbd.2012.01.015

Kapogiannis, D., Reiter, D. A., Willette, A. A., & Mattson, M. P. (2013). Posteromedial cortex glutamate and GABA predict intrinsic functional connectivity of the default mode network. *NeuroImage, 64*, 112–119. https://doi.org/10.1016/j.neuroimage.2012.09.029

75) *Role of Default Mode Network in Depression | Psychiatry & Behavioral Health Learning Network.* (2012). Psychcongress.Com. https://www.psychcongress.com/blog/role-default-mode-network-depression

Hu, Y., Chen, X., Gu, H., & Yang, Y. (2013). Resting-state glutamate and GABA concentrations predict task-induced deactivation in the default mode network. *The Journal of neuroscience : the official journal of the Society for Neuroscience, 33*(47), 18566–18573. https://doi.org/10.1523/JNEUROSCI.1973-13.2013

Hamilton, J. P., Farmer, M., Fogelman, P., & Gotlib, I. H. (2015). Depressive Rumination, the Default-Mode Network, and the Dark Matter of Clinical Neuroscience. *Biological Psychiatry, 78*(4), 224–230. https://doi.org/10.1016/j.

biopsych.2015.02.020

Siegle, G. J., Thompson, W. K., Collier, A., Berman, S. R., Feldmiller, J., Thase, M. E., & Friedman, E. S. (2012). Toward clinically useful neuroimaging in depression treatment: prognostic utility of subgenual cingulate activity for determining depression outcome in cognitive therapy across studies, scanners, and patient characteristics. *Archives of general psychiatry*, *69*(9), 913–924. https://doi.org/10.1001/archgenpsychiatry.2012.65

Coutinho, J. F., Fernandesl, S. V., Soares, J. M., Maia, L., Gonçalves, Ó. F., & Sampaio, A. (2016). Default mode network dissociation in depressive and anxiety states. *Brain imaging and behavior*, *10*(1), 147–157. https://doi.org/10.1007/s11682-015-9375-7

Kaiser, R. H., Whitfield-Gabrieli, S., Dillon, D. G., Goer, F., Beltzer, M., Minkel, J., Smoski, M., Dichter, G., & Pizzagalli, D. A. (2015). Dynamic Resting-State Functional Connectivity in Major Depression. *Neuropsychopharmacology*, *41*(7), 1822–1830. https://doi.org/10.1038/npp.2015.352

Kaiser, R. H., Andrews-Hanna, J. R., Wager, T. D., & Pizzagalli, D. A. (2015). Large-Scale Network Dysfunction in Major Depressive Disorder. *JAMA Psychiatry*, *72*(6), 603. https://doi.org/10.1001/jamapsychiatry.2015.0071

Michael D. Greicius, Kaustubh Supekar, Vinod Menon, Robert F. Dougherty, Resting-State Functional Connectivity Reflects Structural Connectivity in the Default Mode Network, *Cerebral Cortex*, Volume 19, Issue 1, January 2009, Pages 72–78, https://doi.org/10.1093/cercor/bhn059

76) Gotlib, I. H., Hamilton, J. P., Cooney, R. E., Singh, M. K., Henry, M. L., & Joormann, J. (2010). Neural processing of reward and loss in girls at risk for major depression. *Archives of general psychiatry*, *67*(4), 380–387. https://doi.org/10.1001/archgenpsychiatry.2010.13

Ng, T.H., Alloy, L.B. & Smith, D.V. Meta-analysis of reward processing in major depressive disorder reveals distinct abnormalities within the reward circuit. *Transl Psychiatry* **9**, 293 (2019). https://doi.org/10.1038/s41398-019-0644-x https://www.nature.com/articles/s41398-019-0644-x#citeas

Admon, R., & Pizzagalli, D. A. (2015). Dysfunctional Reward Processing in Depression. *Current opinion in psychology*, *4*, 114–118. https://doi.org/10.1016/j.copsyc.2014.12.011

Naranjo, C. A., Tremblay, L. K., & Busto, U. E. (2001). The role of the brain reward system in depression. *Progress in neuro-psychopharmacology & biological psychiatry*, *25*(4), 781–823. https://doi.org/10.1016/s0278-5846(01)00156-7

Tremblay, L. K., Naranjo, C. A., Graham, S. J., Herrmann, N., Mayberg, H. S., Hevenor, S., & Busto, U. E. (2005). Functional neuroanatomical substrates of altered reward processing in major depressive disorder revealed by a dopaminergic probe. *Archives of general psychiatry*, *62*(11), 1228–1236. https://doi.org/10.1001/archpsyc.62.11.1228

Heller AS, Johnstone T, Peterson MJ, Kolden GG, Kalin NH, Davidson RJ. Increased Prefrontal Cortex Activity During Negative Emotion Regulation as a Predictor of Depression Symptom Severity Trajectory Over 6 Months. *JAMA Psychiatry*. 2013;70(11):1181–1189. doi:10.1001/jamapsychiatry.2013.2430 https://jamanetwork.com/journals/jamapsychiatry/fullarticle/1761298

77) Elliott R, Lythe K, Lee R, et al. Reduced Medial Prefrontal Responses to Social Interaction Images in Remitted Depression. *Arch Gen Psychiatry*. 2012;69(1):37–45. https://jamanetwork.com/journals/jamapsychiatry/fullarticle/1107383

Beck A. T. (2008). The evolution of the cognitive model of depression and its neurobiological correlates. *The American journal of psychiatry*, 165(8), 969–977. https://doi.org/10.1176/appi.ajp.2008.08050721

Lythe, K. E., Moll, J., Gethin, J. A., Workman, C. I., Green, S., Lambon Ralph, M. A., Deakin, J. F., & Zahn, R. (2015). Self-blame-Selective Hyperconnectivity Between Anterior Temporal and Subgenual Cortices and Prediction of Recurrent Depressive Episodes. *JAMA psychiatry*, 72(11), 1119–1126. https://doi.org/10.1001/jamapsychiatry.2015.1813

Howlett, J. R., & Paulus, M. P. (2013). Decision-Making Dysfunctions of Counterfactuals in Depression: Who Might I have Been?. *Frontiers in psychiatry*, 4, 143. https://doi.org/10.3389/fpsyt.2013.00143

Wilson, R. S., Nag, S., Boyle, P. A., Hizel, L. P., Yu, L., Buchman, A. S., Shah, R. C., Schneider, J. A., Arnold, S. E., & Bennett, D. A. (2013). Brainstem aminergic nuclei and late-life depressive symptoms. *JAMA psychiatry*, 70(12), 1320–1328. https://doi.org/10.1001/jamapsychiatry.2013.2224

Aizenstein, H. J., Andreescu, C., Edelman, K. L., Cochran, J. L., Price, J., Butters, M. A., Karp, J., Patel, M., & Reynolds, C. F., 3rd (2011). fMRI correlates of white matter hyperintensities in late-life depression. *The American journal of psychiatry*, 168(10), 1075–1082. https://doi.org/10.1176/appi.ajp.2011.10060853

Papakostas, G. I. (2013). Cognitive Symptoms in Patients With Major Depressive Disorder and Their Implications for Clinical Practice. *The Journal of Clinical Psychiatry*, 75(01), 8–14. https://doi.org/10.4088/jcp.13r08710

Zuckerman, H., Pan, Z., Park, C., Brietzke, E., Musial, N., Shariq, A. S., ... McIntyre, R. S. (2018). Recognition and Treatment of Cognitive Dysfunction in Major Depressive Disorder. *Frontiers in Psychiatry*, 9. https://doi.org/10.3389/fpsyt.2018.00655

Lam, R. W., Kennedy, S. H., McIntyre, R. S., & Khullar, A. (2014). Cognitive dysfunction in major depressive disorder: effects on psychosocial functioning and implications for treatment. *Canadian journal of psychiatry. Revue canadienne de psychiatrie*, 59(12), 649–654. https://doi.org/10.1177/070674371405901206

78) Seminowicz, D. ., Mayberg, H. ., McIntosh, A. ., Goldapple, K., Kennedy, S., Segal, Z., & Rafi-Tari, S. (2004). Limbic–frontal circuitry in major depression: a path modeling metanalysis. *NeuroImage*, 22(1), 409–418. https://doi.org/10.1016/j.neuroimage.2004.01.015

References

79) Drysdale, A. T., Grosenick, L., Downar, J., Dunlop, K., Mansouri, F., Meng, Y., Fetcho, R. N., Zebley, B., Oathes, D. J., Etkin, A., Schatzberg, A. F., Sudheimer, K., Keller, J., Mayberg, H. S., Gunning, F. M., Alexopoulos, G. S., Fox, M. D., Pascual-Leone, A., Voss, H. U., Casey, B. J., … Liston, C. (2017). Resting-state connectivity biomarkers define neurophysiological subtypes of depression. *Nature medicine*, *23*(1), 28–38. https://doi.org/10.1038/nm.4246

80) Xia, M., Si, T., Sun, X., Ma, Q., Liu, B., Wang, L., Meng, J., Chang, M., Huang, X., Chen, Z., Tang, Y., Xu, K., Gong, Q., Wang, F., Qiu, J., Xie, P., Li, L., He, Y., & DIDA-Major Depressive Disorder Working Group (2019). Reproducibility of functional brain alterations in major depressive disorder: Evidence from a multisite resting-state functional MRI study with 1,434 individuals. *NeuroImage*, *189*, 700–714. https://doi.org/10.1016/j.neuroimage.2019.01.074

Patel, M. J., Khalaf, A., & Aizenstein, H. J. (2015). Studying depression using imaging and machine learning methods. *NeuroImage. Clinical*, *10*, 115–123. https://doi.org/10.1016/j.nicl.2015.11.003

Yamashita A, Sakai Y, Yamada T, Yahata N, Kunimatsu A, Okada N, et al. (2020) Generalizable brain network markers of major depressive disorder across multiple imaging sites. PLoS Biol 18(12): e3000966. https://doi.org/10.1371/journal.pbio.3000966

Hahn, T., Marquand, A. F., Ehlis, A. C., Dresler, T., Kittel-Schneider, S., Jarczok, T. A., Lesch, K. P., Jakob, P. M., Mourao-Miranda, J., Brammer, M. J., & Fallgatter, A. J. (2011). Integrating neurobiological markers of depression. *Archives of general psychiatry*, *68*(4), 361–368. https://doi.org/10.1001/archgenpsychiatry.2010.178

81) A range of other etiologies include:

Moncrieff, J., Cooper, R.E., Stockmann, T. *et al.* The serotonin theory of depression: a systematic umbrella review of the evidence. *Mol Psychiatry* (2022). https://doi.org/10.1038/s41380-022-01661-0
https://www.nature.com/articles/s41380-022-01661-0

Association of Hormonal Contraception With Depression. *JAMA Psychiatry*, *73*(11), 1154. https://doi.org/10.1001/jamapsychiatry.2016.2387

Gestational Influenza and Bipolar Disorder in Adult Offspring. *JAMA Psychiatry.* 2013;70(7):677–685. doi:10.1001/jamapsychiatry.2013.896
http://jamanetwork.com/journals/jamapsychiatry/fullarticle/1686037?resultclick=1

The neurobiology of retinoic acid in affective disorders. *Progress in neuro-psychopharmacology & biological psychiatry*, *32*(2), 315–331. https://doi.org/10.1016/j.pnpbp.2007.07.001

Irritability and Its Clinical Utility in Major Depressive Disorder: Prediction of Individual-Level Acute-Phase Outcomes Using Early Changes in Irritability and Depression Severity. *American Journal of Psychiatry*, *176*(5), 358–366. https://doi.org/10.1176/appi.ajp.2018.18030355

Heterogeneity in Major Depressive Disorder: Lessons From Developmental Research on Irritability. *American Journal of Psychiatry*, *176*(5), 331–332. https://doi.org/10.1176/appi.ajp.2019.19020214
An approach to revealing clinically relevant subgroups across the mood spectrum. *Journal of affective disorders*, *203*, 265–274. https://doi.org/10.1016/j.jad.2016.06.019
Understanding the Clinical Heterogeneity of Major Depression Using Family Data. *Arch Gen Psychiatry.* 1986;43(5):430–434. doi:10.1001/archpsyc.1986.01800050028003 https://jamanetwork.com/journals/jamapsychiatry/article-abstract/493796

APPENDIX ON SUICIDE

82) Greg Eghigian, PhD A "Sickness of Our Time": How Suicide First Became a Research Question, Psychiatric Times, Vol 35 No 4, Volume 35, Issue 4 http://www.psychiatrictimes.com/cultural-psychiatry/sickness-our-time-how-suicide-first-became-research-question
83) *dolce et decorum est pro patria mori*
84) Zaorsky, N.G., Zhang, Y., Tuanquin, L. et al. Suicide among cancer patients. *Nat Commun* **10,** 207 (2019). https://doi.org/10.1038/s41467-018-08170-1
Chapple, A., Ziebland, S., McPherson, A., & Herxheimer, A. (2006). What people close to death say about euthanasia and assisted suicide: a qualitative study. *Journal of medical ethics*, *32*(12), 706–710. https://doi.org/10.1136/jme.2006.015883
Verkissen, M.N., Houttekier, D., Cohen, J. et al. End-of-life decision-making across cancer types: results from a nationwide retrospective survey among treating physicians. *Br J Cancer* **118,** 1369–1376 (2018). https://doi.org/10.1038/s41416-018-0070-5
85) https://www.newyorker.com/magazine/2015/06/22/the-death-treatment
http://gawker.com/in-belgium-doctors-will-help-you-kill-yourself-if-your-1711933134
86) Caine ED. Suicide and Attempted Suicide in the United States During the 21st Century. *JAMA Psychiatry.* 2017;74(11):1087–1088. doi:10.1001/jamapsychiatry.2017.2524 https://jamanetwork.com/journals/jamapsychiatry/article-abstract/2652964
87) Oquendo presentation to APA:The Neurobiology of Suicide Vulnerability distinct nb pathways to SB evolving concept 2020 05 11 v2.pdf https://www.nimh.nih.gov/health/statistics/suicide
Brent DA, Oquendo M, Birmaher B, et al. Familial Pathways to Early-Onset Suicide Attempt: Risk for Suicidal Behavior in Offspring of Mood-Disordered Suicide Attempters. *Arch Gen Psychiatry.* 2002;59(9):801–807. doi:10.1001/archpsyc.59.9.801
https://jamanetwork.com/journals/jamapsychiatry/fullarticle/206697
Eileen P. Ryan, D.O., and Maria A. Oquendo, M.D., Ph.D.

References

https://focus.psychiatryonline.org/doi/10.1176/appi.focus.20200011
88) Sisti DA, Joffe S. Implications of Zero Suicide for Suicide Prevention Research. *JAMA.* 2018;320(16):1633–1634. doi:10.1001/jama.2018.13083
Ursano RJ, Kessler RC, Naifeh JA, et al. Risk Factors Associated With Attempted Suicide Among US Army Soldiers Without a History of Mental Health Diagnosis. *JAMA Psychiatry.* 2018;75(10):1022–1032. doi:10.1001/jamapsychiatry.2018.2069
89) Bernanke, J. A., Stanley, B. H., & Oquendo, M. A. (2017). Toward fine-grained phenotyping of suicidal behavior: the role of suicidal subtypes. *Molecular psychiatry*, *22*(8), 1080–1081. https://doi.org/10.1038/mp.2017.123
Oquendo, M. A., Galfalvy, H., Russo, S., Ellis, S. P., Grunebaum, M. F., Burke, A., & Mann, J. J. (2004). Prospective study of clinical predictors of suicidal acts after a major depressive episode in patients with major depressive disorder or bipolar disorder. *The American journal of psychiatry*, *161*(8), 1433–1441. https://doi.org/10.1176/appi.ajp.161.8.1433
90) Klonsky E. D. (2009). The functions of self-injury in young adults who cut themselves: clarifying the evidence for affect-regulation. *Psychiatry research*, *166*(2-3), 260–268. https://doi.org/10.1016/j.psychres.2008.02.008
91) Alexis C. Edwards, Henrik Ohlsson, Eve Mościcki, Casey Crump, Jan Sundquist, Paul Lichtenstein, Kenneth S. Kendler, and Kristina Sundquist, On the Genetic and Environmental Relationship Between Suicide Attempt and Death by Suicide
American Journal of Psychiatry 2021 178:11, 1060-1069
Oquendo, M. A., & Bernanke, J. A. (2017). Suicide risk assessment: tools and challenges. *World psychiatry : official journal of the World Psychiatric Association (WPA)*, *16*(1), 28–29. https://doi.org/10.1002/wps.20396
DOI: 10.3928/00485713-20170801-01 how baseball explains risk assessment
Edwards, A. C., Ohlsson, H., Mościcki, E., Crump, C., Sundquist, J., Lichtenstein, P., Kendler, K. S., & Sundquist, K. (2021). On the Genetic and Environmental Relationship Between Suicide Attempt and Death by Suicide. *The American journal of psychiatry*, *178*(11), 1060–1069. https://doi.org/10.1176/appi.ajp.2020.20121705

The Collaborative Assessment and Management of Suicidality (CAMS) model is a prototype clinical framework organized around the cooperative completion of the quantitative and qualitative Suicide Status Form (SSF). This model, which encourages problem-solving to reduce the suicide "drivers" and boost coping, is designed to enhance the patient-clinician alliance, build motivation, and avoid inpatient hospitalization
When selecting a tool, consider whether it has been validated, has a quantitative component, can be repeated, is not diagnosis-specific, is available in a variety of formats, and is available in relevant languages. In our view, the Beck Scale for Suicide Ideation (SSI) and the Columbia-Suicide Severity Rating Scale (C-SSRS) are good options.

Hawes, M., Yaseen, Z., Briggs, J., & Galynker, I. (2017). The Modular Assessment of Risk for Imminent Suicide (MARIS): A proof of concept for a multi-informant tool for evaluation of short-term suicide risk. *Comprehensive psychiatry*, *72*, 88–96. https://doi.org/10.1016/j.comppsych.2016.10.00292)
Maciejewski, D. F., Creemers, H. E., Lynskey, M. T., Madden, P. A., Heath, A. C., Statham, D. J., Martin, N. G., & Verweij, K. J. (2014). Overlapping genetic and environmental influences on nonsuicidal self-injury and suicidal ideation: different outcomes, same etiology?. *JAMA psychiatry*, *71*(6), 699–705. https://doi.org/10.1001/jamapsychiatry.2014.89
93) Willour, V. L., Seifuddin, F., Mahon, P. B., Jancic, D., Pirooznia, M., Steele, J., Schweizer, B., Goes, F. S., Mondimore, F. M., Mackinnon, D. F., Bipolar Genome Study Consortium, Perlis, R. H., Lee, P. H., Huang, J., Kelsoe, J. R., Shilling, P. D., Rietschel, M., Nöthen, M., Cichon, S., Gurling, H., ... Potash, J. B. (2012). A genome-wide association study of attempted suicide. *Molecular psychiatry*, *17*(4), 433–444. https://doi.org/10.1038/mp.2011.4
94) Zhang, H., Chen, Z., Jia, Z., & Gong, Q. (2014). Dysfunction of neural circuitry in depressive patients with suicidal behaviors: a review of structural and functional neuroimaging studies. *Progress in neuro-psychopharmacology & biological psychiatry*, *53*, 61–66. https://doi.org/10.1016/j.pnpbp.2014.03.002
Ballard, E. D., Lally, N., Nugent, A. C., Furey, M. L., Luckenbaugh, D. A., & Zarate, C. A., Jr (2014). Neural correlates of suicidal ideation and its reduction in depression. *The international journal of neuropsychopharmacology*, *18*(1), pyu069. https://doi.org/10.1093/ijnp/pyu069
Sullivan, G. M., Oquendo, M. A., Milak, M., Miller, J. M., Burke, A., Ogden, R. T., Parsey, R. V., & Mann, J. J. (2015). Positron emission tomography quantification of serotonin(1A) receptor binding in suicide attempters with major depressive disorder. *JAMA psychiatry*, *72*(2), 169–178. https://doi.org/10.1001/jamapsychiatry.2014.2406
Hu, L., Xiao, M., Cao, J., Tan, Z., Wang, M., & Kuang, L. (2021). The Association Between Insular Subdivisions Functional Connectivity and Suicide Attempt in Adolescents and Young Adults with Major Depressive Disorder. *Brain topography*, *34*(3), 297–305. https://doi.org/10.1007/s10548-021-00830-8
Ballard, E. D., Gilbert, J. R., Fields, J. S., Nugent, A. C., & Zarate, C. A., Jr (2020). Network Changes in Insula and Amygdala Connectivity Accompany Implicit Suicidal Associations. *Frontiers in psychiatry*, *11*, 577628. https://doi.org/10.3389/fpsyt.2020.577628
95) Evolutionary psychiatrist and neuroscientist Martin Brüne of University Hospital Bochum and his colleagues detailed these findings online June 22 in *PLoS ONE*. https://www.scientificamerican.com/article/suicide-cells/
96) Bak, J., Shim, S. H., Kwon, Y. J., Lee, H. Y., Kim, J. S., Yoon, H., & Lee, Y. J. (2018). The Association between Suicide Attempts and *Toxoplasma gondii* Infection. *Clinical psychopharmacology and neuroscience : the official scientific journal of the Korean College of Neuropsychopharmacology*, *16*(1), 95–102.

References

https://doi.org/10.9758/cpn.2018.16.1.95
Zhang, Y., Träskman-Bendz, L., Janelidze, S., Langenberg, P., Saleh, A., Constantine, N., Okusaga, O., Bay-Richter, C., Brundin, L., & Postolache, T. T. (2012). Toxoplasma gondii immunoglobulin G antibodies and nonfatal suicidal self-directed violence. *The Journal of clinical psychiatry*, *73*(8), 1069–1076. https://doi.org/10.4088/JCP.11m07532

97) Glenn, C. R., & Nock, M. K. (2014). Improving the short-term prediction of suicidal behavior. *American journal of preventive medicine*, *47*(3 Suppl 2), S176–S180. https://doi.org/10.1016/j.amepre.2014.06.004
Nock, M. K., Park, J. M., Finn, C. T., Deliberto, T. L., Dour, H. J., & Banaji, M. R. (2010). Measuring the suicidal mind: implicit cognition predicts suicidal behavior. *Psychological science*, *21*(4), 511–517. https://doi.org/10.1177/0956797610364762
Keilp, J. G., Gorlyn, M., Russell, M., Oquendo, M. A., Burke, A. K., Harkavy-Friedman, J., & Mann, J. J. (2013). Neuropsychological function and suicidal behavior: attention control, memory and executive dysfunction in suicide attempt. *Psychological medicine*, *43*(3), 539–551. https://doi.org/10.1017/S0033291712001419
Mann, J. J., Currier, D., Stanley, B., Oquendo, M. A., Amsel, L. V., & Ellis, S. P. (2006). Can biological tests assist prediction of suicide in mood disorders?. *The international journal of neuropsychopharmacology*, *9*(4), 465–474. https://doi.org/10.1017/S1461145705005687

98) Posner, K., Brown, G. K., Stanley, B., Brent, D. A., Yershova, K. V., Oquendo, M. A., Currier, G. W., Melvin, G. A., Greenhill, L., Shen, S., & Mann, J. J. (2011). The Columbia-Suicide Severity Rating Scale: initial validity and internal consistency findings from three multisite studies with adolescents and adults. *The American journal of psychiatry*, *168*(12), 1266–1277. https://doi.org/10.1176/appi.ajp.2011.10111704

99) Mann, J. J., & Rizk, M. M. (2020). A Brain-Centric Model of Suicidal Behavior. *The American journal of psychiatry*, *177*(10), 902–916. https://doi.org/10.1176/appi.ajp.2020.20081224
Benedetti, F., Riccaboni, R., Locatelli, C., Poletti, S., Dallaspezia, S., & Colombo, C. (2014). Rapid treatment response of suicidal symptoms to lithium, sleep deprivation, and light therapy (chronotherapeutics) in drug-resistant bipolar depression. *The Journal of clinical psychiatry*, *75*(2), 133–140. https://doi.org/10.4088/JCP.13m08455
Oquendo, M. A., Galfalvy, H. C., Currier, D., Grunebaum, M. F., Sher, L., Sullivan, G. M., Burke, A. K., Harkavy-Friedman, J., Sublette, M. E., Parsey, R. V., & Mann, J. J. (2011). Treatment of suicide attempters with bipolar disorder: a randomized clinical trial comparing lithium and valproate in the prevention of suicidal behavior. *The American journal of psychiatry*, *168*(10), 1050–1056. https://doi.org/10.1176/appi.ajp.2011.11010163

100) The finding that antidepressants might "release" suicidal behavior in some

depressed patients, would be consistent with this notion that reducing depression makes the individual more able to act, but has been countered by pharmaceutically sponsored meta-analyses and pronouncements. (Gibbons and Mann, Psychiatric Times December 2016). Despite this, the FDA has not rescinded its warning on the risks of using SSRI in youth.

101) Grunebaum, M. F., Galfalvy, H. C., Choo, T. H., Keilp, J. G., Moitra, V. K., Parris, M. S., Marver, J. E., Burke, A. K., Milak, M. S., Sublette, M. E., Oquendo, M. A., & Mann, J. J. (2018). Ketamine for Rapid Reduction of Suicidal Thoughts in Major Depression: A Midazolam-Controlled Randomized Clinical Trial. *The American journal of psychiatry*, *175*(4), 327–335. https://doi.org/10.1176/appi.ajp.2017.17060647
https://ajp.psychiatryonline.org/doi/10.1176/appi.ajp.2017.17060647
Kellner, C. H., Fink, M., Knapp, R., Petrides, G., Husain, M., Rummans, T., Mueller, M., Bernstein, H., Rasmussen, K., O'connor, K., Smith, G., Rush, A. J., Biggs, M., McClintock, S., Bailine, S., & Malur, C. (2005). Relief of expressed suicidal intent by ECT: a consortium for research in ECT study. *The American journal of psychiatry*, *162*(5), 977–982. https://doi.org/10.1176/appi.ajp.162.5.977

102) Guille C, Zhao Z, Krystal J, Nichols B, Brady K, Sen S. Web-Based Cognitive Behavioral Therapy Intervention for the Prevention of Suicidal Ideation in Medical Interns: A Randomized Clinical Trial. *JAMA Psychiatry*. 2015;72(12):1192–1198. doi:10.1001/jamapsychiatry.2015.1880
Brown GK, Ten Have T, Henriques GR, Xie SX, Hollander JE, Beck AT. Cognitive Therapy for the Prevention of Suicide Attempts: A Randomized Controlled Trial. *JAMA*. 2005;294(5):563–570. doi:10.1001/jama.294.5.563

103) Serafini, G., Canepa, G., Adavastro, G., Nebbia, J., Belvederi Murri, M., Erbuto, D., Pocai, B., Fiorillo, A., Pompili, M., Flouri, E., & Amore, M. (2017). The Relationship between Childhood Maltreatment and Non-Suicidal Self-Injury: A Systematic Review. *Frontiers in psychiatry*, *8*, 149.
Björkenstam, E., Hjern, A., Björkenstam, C., & Kosidou, K. (2018). Association of Cumulative Childhood Adversity and Adolescent Violent Offending With Suicide in Early Adulthood. *JAMA psychiatry*, *75*(2), 185–193. https://doi.org/10.1001/jamapsychiatry.2017.3788
Liu, R. T., Scopelliti, K. M., Pittman, S. K., & Zamora, A. S. (2018). Childhood maltreatment and non-suicidal self-injury: a systematic review and meta-analysis. *The lancet. Psychiatry*, *5*(1), 51–64. https://doi.org/10.1016/S2215-0366(17)30469-8
Paul E. Bebbington, Ph.D., F.R.C.P., F.R.C.Psych., Claudia Cooper, Ph.D., M.R.C.Psych., Sarah Minot, M.Sc., M.R.C.Psych., Traolach S. Brugha, M.D., F.R.C.Psych., Rachel Jenkins, M.D., F.R.C.Psych., Howard Meltzer, Ph.D., and Michael Dennis, M.D., M.R.C.Psych., Suicide Attempts, Gender, and Sexual Abuse: Data From the 2000 British Psychiatric Morbidity Survey,American Journal of Psychiatry 2009 166:10, 1135-1140 https://ajp.psychiatryonline.org/

References

doi/full/10.1176/appi.ajp.2009.09030310
Guldin, M. B., Li, J., Pedersen, H. S., Obel, C., Agerbo, E., Gissler, M., Cnattingius, S., Olsen, J., & Vestergaard, M. (2015). Incidence of Suicide Among Persons Who Had a Parent Who Died During Their Childhood: A Population-Based Cohort Study. *JAMA psychiatry*, *72*(12), 1227–1234. https://doi.org/10.1001/jamapsychiatry.2015.2094
Qiu, H., Cao, B., Cao, J., Li, X., Chen, J., Wang, W., Lv, Z., Zhang, S., Fang, W., Ai, M., & Kuang, L. (2020). Resting-state functional connectivity of the anterior cingulate cortex in young adults depressed patients with and without suicidal behavior. *Behavioural brain research*, *384*, 112544. https://doi.org/10.1016/j.bbr.2020.112544
104) de Leon, J., Baca-García, E., & Blasco-Fontecilla, H. (2015). From the serotonin model of suicide to a mental pain model of suicide. *Psychotherapy and psychosomatics*, *84*(6), 323–329. https://doi.org/10.1159/000438510
105) Van Orden, K. A., Witte, T. K., Cukrowicz, K. C., Braithwaite, S. R., Selby, E. A., & Joiner, T. E., Jr (2010). The interpersonal theory of suicide. *Psychological review*, *117*(2), 575–600. https://doi.org/10.1037/a0018697
Heidi Hjelmeland & Birthe Loa Knizek (2020) The emperor's new clothes? A critical look at the interpersonal theory of suicide, Death Studies, 44:3, 168-178, DOI: 10.1080/07481187.2018.1527796
106) Malone J Affect Disord. 1995 Jun 8;34(3):173-85. Isometsa Can J Psychiatry. 2014 Mar; 59(3): 120–130. doi: 10.1177/070674371405900303

CHAPTER FOUR REFERENCES

1) Purves, D., Brannon, E. and Cabeza, R. (2013) Purves, D. (2013). *Principles of cognitive neuroscience*. Sinauer Associates.
2) The term "salience" is a proposed network, so "significance" was chosen. https://en.wikipedia.org/wiki/Salience_(neuroscience)
3) https://www.sfn.org/~/media/SfN/Documents/ClassicPapers/Emotion/papez.ashx
(RajMohan V, Mohandas E. The limbic system. Indian J Psychiatry (serial online) 2007 (cited 2017 Feb 6);49:132-9. http://www.indianjpsychiatry.org/text.asp?2007/49/2/132/33264
4) https://en.wikipedia.org/wiki/Kl%C3%BCver%E2%80%93Bucy_syndrome
5) Roy, A., Perlovsky, L., Besold, T. R., Weng, J., & Edwards, J. C. W. (2018). Editorial: Representation in the Brain. *Frontiers in Psychology*, *9*. https://doi.org/10.3389/fpsyg.2018.01410 https://www.frontiersin.org/articles/10.3389/fpsyg.2018.01410/full
6) Carroll, B. T., Goforth, H. W., & Raimonde, L. A. (2001). Partial Kluver-Bucy syndrome: two cases. *CNS Spectrums*, *6*(4), 329–332. https://doi.org/10.1017/s1092852900022033

Luef, G. J. (2008). Epilepsy and sexuality. *Seizure, 17*(2), 127–130. https://doi.org/10.1016/j.seizure.2007.11.009

Taylor, D. C. (1969). Sexual Behavior and epilepsy. *Archives of Neurology, 21*(5), 510–516. https://doi.org/10.1001/archneur.1969.00480170082008

7) Squire, L. R. (2009). The Legacy of Patient H.M. for Neuroscience. *Neuron, 61*(1), 6–9. https://doi.org/10.1016/j.neuron.2008.12.023

8) Kopelman, M. D., Thomson, A. D., Guerrini, I., & Marshall, E. J. (2009). The Korsakoff Syndrome: Clinical Aspects, Psychology and Treatment. *Alcohol and Alcoholism, 44*(2), 148–154. https://doi.org/10.1093/alcalc/agn118

Vann, S. D., & Nelson, A. J. D. (2015). The mammillary bodies and memory. *The Connected Hippocampus*, 163–185. https://doi.org/10.1016/bs.pbr.2015.03.006

9) Guenther K. (2016). Between Clinic and Experiment: Wilder Penfield's Stimulation Reports and the Search for Mind, 1929-55. https://doi.org/10.3138/cbmh.33.2.148-27012015

10) Cowan, N. (2008). *Attention and memory : an integrated framework*. Oxford University Press.

Eichenbaum, H. (2012). *The Cognitive neuroscience of memory : an introduction*. Oxford University Press, Cop.

Declarative Memory (Explicit Memory) and Procedural Memory (Implicit Memory) - Types of Memory - The Human Memory. (2018). Human-Memory.Net. http://www.human-memory.net/types_declarative.html

Norden, J. (n.d.). *Brain Areas involved in Different Types of Memory*. https://www.vanderbilt.edu/olli/classmaterials/Neuroscience_April4th.pdf

11) Amaral, D. G., Scharfman, H. E., & Lavenex, P. (2007). The dentate gyrus: fundamental neuroanatomical organization (dentate gyrus for dummies). *Progress in brain research, 163*, 3–22. https://doi.org/10.1016/S0079-6123(07)63001-5

Anderson, M. C., Bunce, J. G., & Barbas, H. (2016). Prefrontal-hippocampal pathways underlying inhibitory control over memory. *Neurobiology of learning and memory, 134 Pt A*(Pt A), 145–161. https://doi.org/10.1016/j.nlm.2015.11.008

Sauer, Jonas-Frederic and Bartos, Marlene. "The role of the dentate gyrus in mnemonic functions" *Neuroforum*, vol. 26, no. 4, 2020, pp. 247-254. https://doi.org/10.1515/nf-2020-0021

Bergmann, H. C., Daselaar, S. M., Fernández, G., & Kessels, R. P. (2016). Neural substrates of successful working memory and long-term memory formation in a relational spatial memory task. *Cognitive processing, 17*(4), 377–387. https://doi.org/10.1007/s10339-016-0772-7 Rugg, M. D., Vilberg, K. L., Mattson, J. T., Yu, S. S., Johnson, J. D., & Suzuki, M. (2012). Item memory, context memory and the hippocampus: fMRI evidence. *Neuropsychologia, 50*(13), https://doi.org/10.1016/j.neuropsychologia.2012.06.004

Woollett, K., & Maguire, E. A. (2011). Acquiring "the Knowledge" of London's

References

Layout Drives Structural Brain Changes. *Current Biology*, *21*(24), 2109–2114. https://doi.org/10.1016/j.cub.2011.11.018 https://www.ncbi.nlm.nih.gov/pmc/articles/PMC3268356
https://www.scientificamerican.com/article/london-taxi-memory/

Hartley, T., Lever, C., Burgess, N., & O'Keefe, J. (2013). Space in the brain: how the hippocampal formation supports spatial cognition. *Philosophical transactions of the Royal Society of London. Series B, Biological sciences*, *369*(1635), 20120510. https://doi.org/10.1098/rstb.2012.0510

Konkel, A., & Cohen, N. J. (2009). Relational memory and the hippocampus: representations and methods. *Frontiers in neuroscience*, *3*(2), 166–174. https://doi.org/10.3389/neuro.01.023.2009

O'Keefe, J., & Dostrovsky, J. (1971). The hippocampus as a spatial map. Preliminary evidence from unit activity in the freely-moving rat. *Brain Research*, *34*(1), 171–175. https://doi.org/10.1016/0006-8993(71)90358-1

Hafting, T., Fyhn, M., Molden, S., Moser, M.-B., & Moser, E. I. (2005). Microstructure of a spatial map in the entorhinal cortex. *Nature*, *436*(7052), 801–806. https://doi.org/10.1038/nature03721 https://www.nature.com/articles/nature03721

Shrager, Y., Bayley, P. J., Bontempi, B., Hopkins, R. O., & Squire, L. R. (2007). Spatial memory and the human hippocampus. *Proceedings of the National Academy of Sciences*, *104*(8), 2961–2966. https://doi.org/10.1073/pnas.0611233104

Caruso, C. (2017, March 9). *Don't Forget: You, Too, Can Acquire a Super Memory*. Scientific American. https://www.scientificamerican.com/article/dont-forget-you-too-can-acquire-a-super-memory/

Martin, A. (2007). The Representation of Object Concepts in the Brain. *Annual Review of Psychology*, *58*(1), 25–45. https://doi.org/10.1146/annurev.psych.57.102904.190143

James L. McGaugh, Larry Cahill, Benno Roozendaal, Involvement of the amygdala in memory storage: Interaction with other brain systems, Proceedings of the National Academy of Sciences Nov 1996, 93 (24) 13508-13514; DOI: 10.1073/pnas.93.24.13508 Martin, A., & Weisberg, J. (2003). Neural foundations for understanding social and mechanical concepts. *Cognitive neuropsychology*, *20*(3-6), 575–587. https://doi.org/10.1080/02643290342000005

12) Hitti, F. L., & Siegelbaum, S. A. (2014). The hippocampal CA2 region is essential for social memory. *Nature*, *508*(7494), 88–92. https://doi.org/10.1038/nature13028 https://www.ncbi.nlm.nih.gov/pmc/articles/PMC4000264/

Meira, T., Leroy, F., Buss, E. W., Oliva, A., Park, J., & Siegelbaum, S. A. (2018). A hippocampal circuit linking dorsal CA2 to ventral CA1 critical for social memory dynamics. *Nature Communications*, *9*(1). https://doi.org/10.1038/s41467-018-06501-w see ref #58

13) Albright, T. D. (2017). Why eyewitnesses fail. *Proceedings of the National Academy of Sciences*, *114*(30), 7758–7764. https://doi.org/10.1073/

pnas.1706891114 https://www.pnas.org/content/114/30/7758

14) Milner, B., Squire, L. R., & Kandel, E. R. (1998). Cognitive Neuroscience and the Study of Memory. *Neuron, 20*(3), 445–468. https://doi.org/10.1016/s0896-6273(00)80987-3 *http://www.cell.com/neuron/fulltext/S0896-6273(00)80987-3*

Davis, R. L., & Zhong, Y. (2017). The Biology of Forgetting-A Perspective. *Neuron, 95*(3), 490–503. https://doi.org/10.1016/j.neuron.2017.05.039 https://www.cell.com/neuron/fulltext/S0896-6273(17)30498-1

Liu, Y., Du, S., Lv, L., Lei, B., Shi, W., Tang, Y., Wang, L., & Zhong, Y. (2016). Hippocampal Activation of Rac1 Regulates the Forgetting of Object Recognition Memory. *Current biology : CB, 26*(17), 2351–2357. https://doi.org/10.1016/j.cub.2016.06.056

http://dx.doi.org/10.1016/j.cub.2016.06.056 https://www.quantamagazine.org/to-remember-the-brain-must-actively-forget-20180724/

Kumaran, D. (2008). Short-Term Memory and the Human Hippocampus. *Journal of Neuroscience, 28*(15), 3837–3838. https://doi.org/10.1523/jneurosci.0046-08.2008 http://www.jneurosci.org/content/28/15/3837

Robertson, H., & Pryor, R. (2006). Memory and cognitive effects of ECT: informing and assessing patients†. *Advances in Psychiatric Treatment, 12*(3), 228–237. https://doi.org/10.1192/apt.12.3.228 http://apt.rcpsych.org/content/12/3/228

Staba, R. J., & Worrell, G. A. (2014). What Is the Importance of Abnormal "Background" Activity in Seizure Generation? *Issues in Clinical Epileptology: A View from the Bench*, 43–54. https://doi.org/10.1007/978-94-017-8914-1_3 https://www.ncbi.nlm.nih.gov/pmc/articles/PMC4276130/

Andraus, M. E. C., & Alves-Leon, S. V. (2011). Non-epileptiform EEG abnormalities: an overview. *Arquivos de Neuro-Psiquiatria, 69*(5), 829–835. https://doi.org/10.1590/s0004-282x2011000600020

http://www.scielo.br/scielo.php?script=sci_arttext&pid=S0004-282X2011000600020 https://www.cdc.gov/epilepsy/about/types-of-seizures.htm

15) https://en.wikipedia.org/wiki/Temporal_lobe_epilepsy

Gupta, A. K., Jeavons, P. M., Hughes, R. C., & Covanis, A. (1983). Aura in temporal lobe epilepsy: clinical and electroencephalographic correlation. *Journal of Neurology, Neurosurgery & Psychiatry, 46*(12), 1079–1083. https://doi.org/10.1136/jnnp.46.12.1079

16) Slater, E., & Beard, A. W. (1963). The Schizophrenia-like Psychoses of Epilepsy. *British Journal of Psychiatry, 109*(458), 95–112. https://doi.org/10.1192/bjp.109.458.95 https://www.cambridge.org/core/journals/the-british-journal-of-psychiatry/article/schizophrenialike-psychoses-of-epilepsy/A9EA9E39A19F459BECFA993A4E49182E

17) MARGERISON, J. H., & CORSELLIS, J. A. N. (1966). EPILEPSY AND THE TEMPORAL LOBES. *Brain, 89*(3), 499–530. https://doi.org/10.1093/

brain/89.3.499 https://academic.oup.com/brain/article-abstract/89/3/499/313057?redirectedFrom=fulltext

de Lanerolle, N. C., Kim, J. H., Robbins, R. J., & Spencer, D. D. (1989). Hippocampal interneuron loss and plasticity in human temporal lobe epilepsy. *Brain Research*, *495*(2), 387–395. https://doi.org/10.1016/0006-8993(89)90234-5

18) FALCONER, M. A., SERAFETINIDES, E. A., & CORSELLIS, J. A. N. (1964). Etiology and Pathogenesis of Temporal Lobe Epilepsy. *Archives of Neurology*, *10*(3), 233–248. https://doi.org/10.1001/archneur.1964.00460150003001

Giannopoulou, I., Pagida, M.A., Briana, D.D. et al. Perinatal hypoxia as a risk factor for psychopathology later in life: the role of dopamine and neurotrophins. Hormones 17, 25–32 (2018). https://doi.org/10.1007/s42000-018-0007-7 https://link.springer.com/article/10.1007/s42000-018-0007-7#citeas

Haukvik, U. K., McNeil, T., Lange, E. H., Melle, I., Dale, A. M., Andreassen, O. A., & Agartz, I. (2014). Pre- and perinatal hypoxia associated with hippocampus/amygdala volume in bipolar disorder. *Psychological medicine*, *44*(5), 975–985. https://doi.org/10.1017/S0033291713001529

Dubovický M. (2010). Neurobehavioral manifestations of developmental impairment of the brain. *Interdisciplinary toxicology*, *3*(2), 59–67. https://doi.org/10.2478/v10102-010-0012-4

19) Taylor, D. C. (1975). Factors influencing the occurrence of schizophrenia-like psychosis in patients with temporal lobe epilepsy. *Psychological Medicine*, *5*(3), 249–254. https://doi.org/10.1017/s0033291700056609

Sano, K. (1953). Clinical Significance Of Sclerosis Of The Cornu Ammonis. *A.M.A. Archives of Neurology & Psychiatry*, *70*(1), 40. https://doi.org/10.1001/archneurpsyc.1953.02320310046003 https://jamanetwork.com/journals/archneurpsyc/article-abstract/651604

Malamud, N. (1967). Psychiatric Disorder With Intracranial Tumors of Limbic System. *Archives of Neurology*, *17*(2), 113–123. https://doi.org/10.1001/archneur.1967.00470260003001

20) Wall, M., Tuchman, M., & Mielke, D. (1985). Panic attacks and temporal lobe seizures associated with a right temporal lobe arteriovenous malformation: case report. *The Journal of Clinical Psychiatry*, *46*(4), 143–145. https://www.ncbi.nlm.nih.gov/pubmed/3980454

21) Blumer, D. (1967). Sexual Behavior in Temporal Lobe Epilepsy. *Archives of Neurology*, *16*(1), 37. https://doi.org/10.1001/archneur.1967.00470190041005 https://jamanetwork.com/journals/jamaneurology/article-abstract/567058

Dietrich Blumer MD McLean Hospital Journal June 1977 pp53-196 with a similar series of cases.

Blumer, D., Wakhlu, S., Davies, K. and Hermann, B. (1998), Psychiatric Outcome of Temporal Lobectomy for Epilepsy: Incidence and Treatment of Psychiatric Complications. Epilepsia, 39: 478-486. https://doi.org/10.1111/j.1528-1157.1998.tb01409.x

22) Waxman, S. G., & Geschwind, N. (1975). The interictal behavior syndrome of temporal lobe epilepsy. *Archives of General Psychiatry*, *32*(12), 1580–1586. https://doi.org/10.1001/archpsyc.1975.01760300118011

Devinsky, J., & Schachter, S. (2009). Norman Geschwind's contribution to the understanding of behavioral changes in temporal lobe epilepsy: The February 1974 lecture. Epilepsy & Behavior, 15(4), 417–424. https://doi.org/10.1016/j.yebeh.2009.06.006

23) Turetsky, B. I., & Moberg, P. J. (2009). An Odor-Specific Threshold Deficit Implicates Abnormal Intracellular Cyclic AMP Signaling in Schizophrenia. American Journal of Psychiatry, 166(2), 226–233. https://doi.org/10.1176/appi.ajp.2008.07071210

Allebone, J., Kanaan, R., & Wilson, S. J. (2017). Systematic review of structural and functional brain alterations in psychosis of epilepsy. *Journal of Neurology, Neurosurgery & Psychiatry*, *89*(6), 611–617. https://doi.org/10.1136/jnnp-2017-317102
http://jnnp.bmj.com/content/early/2017/12/23/jnnp-2017-317102.long

Jellinek, M. S., SZABO, C. P., & MAGNUS, C. (1999). Complex Partial Seizures in an Adolescent Psychiatric Inpatient Setting. Journal of the American Academy of Child & Adolescent Psychiatry, 38(4), 477–479. https://doi.org/10.1097/00004583-199904000-00022

Bernhardt, B. C., Hong, S., Bernasconi, A., & Bernasconi, N. (2013). Imaging structural and functional brain networks in temporal lobe epilepsy. *Frontiers in Human Neuroscience*, *7*. https://doi.org/10.3389/fnhum.2013.00624

van Diessen, E., Zweiphenning, W. J. E. M., Jansen, F. E., Stam, C. J., Braun, K. P. J., & Otte, W. M. (2014). Brain Network Organization in Focal Epilepsy: A Systematic Review and Meta-Analysis. *PLoS ONE*, *9*(12), e114606. https://doi.org/10.1371/journal.pone.0114606

Taylor, P. N., Han, C. E., Schoene-Bake, J.-C., Weber, B., & Kaiser, M. (2015). Structural connectivity changes in temporal lobe epilepsy: Spatial features contribute more than topological measures. *NeuroImage: Clinical*, *8*, 322–328. https://doi.org/10.1016/j.nicl.2015.02.004

Laufs, H., Hamandi, K., Salek-Haddadi, A., Kleinschmidt, A. K., Duncan, J. S., & Lemieux, L. (2006). Temporal lobe interictal epileptic discharges affect cerebral activity in "default mode" brain regions. *Human Brain Mapping*, *28*(10), 1023–1032. https://doi.org/10.1002/hbm.20323 https://onlinelibrary.wiley.com/doi/full/10.1002/hbm.20323

24) Van Buren, J. M. (1963). The abdominal aura. A study of abdominal sensations occurring in epilepsy and produced by depth stimulation. *Electroencephalography and Clinical Neurophysiology*, *15*, 1–19. https://doi.org/10.1016/0013-4694(63)90035-x

Henkel, A., Noachtar, S., Pfänder, M., & Lüders, H. O. (2002). The localizing value of the abdominal aura and its evolution. *Neurology*, *58*(2), 271–276. https://doi.org/10.1212/wnl.58.2.271 https://n.neurology.org/content/58/2/271.long

25) Lewis, D. O., Moy, E., Jackson, L. D., Aaronson, R., Restifo, N., Serra, S., & Simos, A. (1985). Biopsychosocial characteristics of children who later murder: *The American journal of psychiatry*, *142*(10), 1161–1167. https://doi.org/10.1176/ajp.142.10.1161

Schug, R. A., Yang, Y., Raine, A., Han, C., Liu, J., & Li, L. (2011). Resting EEG deficits in accused murderers with schizophrenia. *Psychiatry research*, *194*(1), 85–94. https://doi.org/10.1016/j.pscychresns.2010.12.017

Calzada-Reyes, A., Alvarez-Amador, A., Galán-García, L., & Valdés-Sosa, M. (2012). Electroencephalographic abnormalities in antisocial personality disorder. *Journal of forensic and legal medicine*, *19*(1), 29–34. https://doi.org/10.1016/j.jflm.2011.10.002

Pillmann, F., Rohde, A., Ullrich, S., Draba, S., Sannemüller, U., & Marneros, A. (1999). Violence, criminal behavior, and the EEG: significance of left hemispheric focal abnormalities. *The Journal of neuropsychiatry and clinical neurosciences*, *11*(4), 454–457. https://doi.org/10.1176/jnp.11.4.454 https://pubmed.ncbi.nlm.nih.gov/10570757/

26) *Dr. Amen's Love Affair with SPECT Scans*. (2020). Sciencebasedmedicine.Org. https://sciencebasedmedicine.org/dr-amens-love-affair-with-spect-scans/ https://www.amenclinics.com/

Santosh, P. J. (2000). Current topic: Neuroimaging in child and adolescent psychiatric disorders. *Archives of Disease in Childhood*, *82*(5), 412–419. https://doi.org/10.1136/adc.82.5.412

27) Rapp, P. E., Keyser, D. O., Albano, A., Hernandez, R., Gibson, D. B., Zambon, R. A., Hairston, W. D., Hughes, J. D., Krystal, A., & Nichols, A. S. (2015). Traumatic Brain Injury Detection Using Electrophysiological Methods. *Frontiers in Human Neuroscience*, *9*. https://doi.org/10.3389/fnhum.2015.00011

Ianof, J. N., & Anghinah, R. (2017). Traumatic brain injury: An EEG point of view. *Dementia & Neuropsychologia*, *11*(1), 3–5. https://doi.org/10.1590/1980-57642016dn11-010002 https://www.ncbi.nlm.nih.gov/pmc/articles/PMC5619208/

28) Max, J. E., Wilde, E. A., Bigler, E. D., MacLeod, M., Vasquez, A. C., Schmidt, A. T., Chapman, S. B., Hotz, G., Yang, T. T., & Levin, H. S. (2012). Psychiatric Disorders After Pediatric Traumatic Brain Injury: A Prospective, Longitudinal, Controlled Study. *The Journal of Neuropsychiatry and Clinical Neurosciences*, *24*(4), 427–436. https://doi.org/10.1176/appi.neuropsych.12060149

Max, J. E., Robin, D. A., Lindgren, S. D., Smith, W. L., Jr, Sato, Y., Mattheis, P. J., Stierwalt, J. A., & Castillo, C. S. (1997). Traumatic brain injury in children and adolescents: psychiatric disorders at two years. *Journal of the American Academy of Child and Adolescent Psychiatry*, *36*(9), 1278–1285. https://doi.

org/10.1097/00004583-199709000-00021
Rapp, P. E., Keyser, D. O., Albano, A., Hernandez, R., Gibson, D. B., Zambon, R. A., Hairston, W. D., Hughes, J. D., Krystal, A., & Nichols, A. S. (2015). Traumatic brain injury detection using electrophysiological methods. *Frontiers in human neuroscience*, *9*, 11. https://doi.org/10.3389/fnhum.2015.00011
Frederick K. Goodwin, MD S. Nassir Ghaemi, MD, The Conundrum of Schizoaffective Disorder: A Review of the Literature http://www.healio.com/psychiatry/journals/psycann/2010-3-40-3/%7B390ab01a-e542-4d4f-901c-5312f5fc42e7%7D/the-conundrum-of-schizoaffective-disorder-a-review-of-the-literature
29) Hirstein, W., & Ramachandran, V. S. (1997). Capgras syndrome: a novel probe for understanding the neural representation of the identity and familiarity of persons. *Proceedings. Biological sciences*, *264*(1380), 437–444. https://doi.org/10.1098/rspb.1997.0062
30) Cascella, N. G., Schretlen, D. J., & Sawa, A. (2009). Schizophrenia and epilepsy: Is there a shared susceptibility? Neuroscience Research, 63(4), 227–235. https://doi.org/10.1016/j.neures.2009.01.002
Gold, J. M., Hermann, B. P., Randolph, C., Wyler, A. R., Goldberg, T. E., & Weinberger, D. R. (1994). Schizophrenia and temporal lobe epilepsy. Archives of General Psychiatry, 51(4), 265–272. https://doi.org/10.1001/archpsyc.1994.03950040009001
Sachdev, P. (1998). Schizophrenia-Like Psychosis and Epilepsy: The Status of the Association. American Journal of Psychiatry, 155(3), 325–336. https://doi.org/10.1176/ajp.155.3.325
31) Barch, D. M. (2020). Schizophrenia spectrum disorders. In R. Biswas-Diener & E. Diener (Eds), *Noba textbook series: Psychology.* Champaign, IL: DEF publishers. Retrieved from http://noba.to/5d98nsy4
Jeffrey Alan Lieberman, M.D., Gabriella Dishy, M.A.Milestones in the History of Schizophrenia. A Comprehensive Chronology of Schizophrenia Research: What Do We Know and When Did We Know It https://doi.org/10.1176/appi.pn.2021.1.7
MacDonald, A. W., & Schulz, S. C. (2009). What We Know: Findings That Every Theory of Schizophrenia Should Explain. *Schizophrenia Bulletin*, *35*(3), 493–508. https://doi.org/10.1093/schbul/sbp017
McCarthy-Jones, S. (2017, August 24). *The concept of schizophrenia is coming to an end – here's why*. The Conversation. https://theconversation.com/the-concept-of-schizophrenia-is-coming-to-an-end-heres-why-82775
Allardyce, J., Gaebel, W., Zielasek, J., & van Os, J. (2007). Deconstructing Psychosis conference February 2006: the validity of schizophrenia and alternative approaches to the classification of psychosis. *Schizophrenia bulletin*, *33*(4), 863–867. https://doi.org/10.1093/schbul/sbm051
Kring, A. M., Gur, R. E., Blanchard, J. J., Horan, W. P., & Reise, S. P. (2013). The Clinical Assessment Interview for Negative Symptoms (CAINS): Final

References

Development and Validation. *American Journal of Psychiatry, 170*(2), 165–172. https://doi.org/10.1176/appi.ajp.2012.12010109

32) Arnedo, J., Svrakic, D. M., Del Val, C., Romero-Zaliz, R., Hernández-Cuervo, H., Molecular Genetics of Schizophrenia Consortium, Fanous, A. H., Pato, M. T., Pato, C. N., de Erausquin, G. A., Cloninger, C. R., & Zwir, I. (2015). Uncovering the hidden risk architecture of the schizophrenias: confirmation in three independent genome-wide association studies. *The American journal of psychiatry, 172*(2), 139–153. https://doi.org/10.1176/appi.ajp.2014.14040435

Avramopoulos D. (2018). Recent Advances in the Genetics of Schizophrenia. *Molecular neuropsychiatry, 4*(1), 35–51. https://doi.org/10.1159/000488679

Jablensky A. (2015). Schizophrenia or schizophrenias? The challenge of genetic parsing of a complex disorder. *The American journal of psychiatry, 172*(2), 105–107. https://doi.org/10.1176/appi.ajp.2014.14111452

Bassett, A. S., Lowther, C., Merico, D., Costain, G., Chow, E., van Amelsvoort, T., McDonald-McGinn, D., Gur, R. E., Swillen, A., Van den Bree, M., Murphy, K., Gothelf, D., Bearden, C. E., Eliez, S., Kates, W., Philip, N., Sashi, V., Campbell, L., Vorstman, J., Cubells, J., … International 22q11.2DS Brain and Behavior Consortium (2017). Rare Genome-Wide Copy Number Variation and Expression of Schizophrenia in 22q11.2 Deletion Syndrome. *The American journal of psychiatry, 174*(11), 1054–1063. https://doi.org/10.1176/appi.ajp.2017.16121417

Henriksen, M. G., Nordgaard, J., & Jansson, L. B. (2017). Genetics of Schizophrenia: Overview of Methods, Findings and Limitations. *Frontiers in human neuroscience, 11*, 322. https://doi.org/10.3389/fnhum.2017.00322 https://www.frontiersin.org/articles/10.3389/fnhum.2017.00322/full

Bergen, S. E., Ploner, A., Howrigan, D., CNV Analysis Group and the Schizophrenia Working Group of the Psychiatric Genomics Consortium, O'Donovan, M. C., Smoller, J. Zheutlin, A. B., Dennis, J., Karlsson Linnér, R., Moscati, A., Restrepo, N., Straub, P., Ruderfer, D., Castro, V. M., Chen, C. Y., Ge, T., Huckins, L. M., Charney, A., Kirchner, H. L., Stahl, E. A., Chabris, C. F., Davis, L. K., & Smoller, J. W. (2019). Penetrance and Pleiotropy of Polygenic Risk Scores for Schizophrenia in 106,160 Patients Across Four Health Care Systems. *The American journal of psychiatry, 176*(10), 846–855. https://doi.org/10.1176/appi.ajp.2019.18091085

In other words the predictive value was small and overlapped other disorders!

Weinberger D. R. (2019). Thinking About Schizophrenia in an Era of Genomic Medicine. *The American journal of psychiatry, 176*(1), 12–20. https://doi.org/10.1176/appi.ajp.2018.18111275

Bassett, A. S., Scherer, S. W., & Brzustowicz, L. M. (2010). Copy Number Variations in Schizophrenia: Critical Review and New Perspectives on Concepts of Genetics and Disease. *American Journal of Psychiatry, 167*(8), 899–914.

https://doi.org/10.1176/appi.ajp.2009.09071016
Fanous, A. H., Zhou, B., Aggen, S. H., Bergen, S. E., Amdur, R. L., Duan, J., Sanders, A. R., Shi, J., Mowry, B. J., Olincy, A., Amin, F., Cloninger, C. R., Silverman, J. M., Buccola, N. G., Byerley, W. F., Black, D. W., Freedman, R., Dudbridge, F., Holmans, P. A., ... Levinson, D. F. (2012). Genome-Wide Association Study of Clinical Dimensions of Schizophrenia: Polygenic Effect on Disorganized Symptoms. *American Journal of Psychiatry, 169*(12), 1309–1317. https://doi.org/10.1176/appi.ajp.2012.12020218
Greenwood, T. A., Lazzeroni, L. C., Murray, S. S., Cadenhead, K. S., Calkins, M. E., Dobie, D. J., Green, M. F., Gur, R. E., Gur, R. C., Hardiman, G., Kelsoe, J. R., Leonard, S., Light, G. A., Nuechterlein, K. H., Olincy, A., Radant, A. D., Schork, N. J., Seidman, L. J., Siever, L. J., ... Braff, D. L. (2011). Analysis of 94 Candidate Genes and 12 Endophenotypes for Schizophrenia From the Consortium on the Genetics of Schizophrenia. *American Journal of Psychiatry, 168*(9), 930–946. https://doi.org/10.1176/appi.ajp.2011.10050723
Agerbo, E., Sullivan, P. F., Vilhjálmsson, B. J., Pedersen, C. B., Mors, O., Børglum, A. D., Hougaard, D. M., Hollegaard, M. V., Meier, S., Mattheisen, M., Ripke, S., Wray, N. R., & Mortensen, P. B. (2015). Polygenic Risk Score, Parental Socioeconomic Status, Family History of Psychiatric Disorders, and the Risk for Schizophrenia: A Danish Population-Based Study and Meta-analysis. *JAMA psychiatry, 72*(7), 635–641. https://doi.org/10.1001/jamapsychiatry.2015.0346
33) Cardno, A. G., & Owen, M. J. (2014). Genetic Relationships Between Schizophrenia, Bipolar Disorder, and Schizoaffective Disorder. *Schizophrenia Bulletin, 40*(3), 504–515. https://doi.org/10.1093/schbul/sbu016
Allardyce, J., Leonenko, G., Hamshere, M., Pardiñas, A. F., Forty, L., Knott, S., Gordon-Smith, K., Porteous, D. J., Haywood, C., Di Florio, A., Jones, L., McIntosh, A. M., Owen, M. J., Holmans, P., Walters, J., Craddock, N., Jones, I., O'Donovan, M. C., & Escott-Price, V. (2018). Association Between Schizophrenia-Related Polygenic Liability and the Occurrence and Level of Mood-Incongruent Psychotic Symptoms in Bipolar Disorder. *JAMA psychiatry, 75*(1), 28–35. https://doi.org/10.1001/jamapsychiatry.2017.3485
Jonas, K.G., Lencz, T., Li, K. et al. Schizophrenia polygenic risk score and 20-year course of illness in psychotic disorders. *Transl Psychiatry* **9,** 300 (2019). https://doi.org/10.1038/s41398-019-0612-5
Moskvina, V., Craddock, N., Holmans, P. et al. Gene-wide analyses of genome-wide association data sets: evidence for multiple common risk alleles for schizophrenia and bipolar disorder and for overlap in genetic risk. *Mol Psychiatry* **14,** 252–260 (2009). https://doi.org/10.1038/mp.2008.133
Wolfers T, Doan NT, Kaufmann T, et al. Mapping the Heterogeneous Phenotype of Schizophrenia and Bipolar Disorder Using Normative Models. *JAMA Psychiatry.* 2018;75(11):1146–1155. doi: 10.1001/jamapsychiatry.2018.2467
Huang, J., Perlis, R. H., Lee, P. H., Rush, A. J., Fava, M., Sachs, G. S.,

References

Lieberman, J., Hamilton, S. P., Sullivan, P., Sklar, P., Purcell, S., & Smoller, J. W. (2010). Cross-disorder genomewide analysis of schizophrenia, bipolar disorder, and depression. *The American journal of psychiatry*, *167*(10), 1254–1263. https://doi.org/10.1176/appi.ajp.2010.09091335

34) ETIOLOGY the following are reported studies

Benros, M. E., Nielsen, P. R., Nordentoft, M., Eaton, W. W., Dalton, S. O., & Mortensen, P. B. (2011). Autoimmune Diseases and Severe Infections as Risk Factors for Schizophrenia: A 30-Year Population-Based Register Study. *American Journal of Psychiatry*, *168*(12), 1303–1310. https://doi.org/10.1176/appi.ajp.2011.11030516

Venables, P. H., & Raine, A. (2012). Poor Nutrition at Age 3 and Schizotypal Personality at Age 23: The Mediating Role of Age 11 Cognitive Functioning. *American Journal of Psychiatry*, *169*(8), 822–830. https://doi.org/10.1176/appi.ajp.2012.11081173

Brown, A. S., Vinogradov, S., Kremen, W. S., Poole, J. H., Deicken, R. F., Penner, J. D., McKeague, I. W., Kochetkova, A., Kern, D., & Schaefer, C. A. (2009). Prenatal Exposure to Maternal Infection and Executive Dysfunction in Adult Schizophrenia. *American Journal of Psychiatry*, *166*(6), 683–690. https://doi.org/10.1176/appi.ajp.2008.08010089

Brown, Alan S., and Elena J. Derkits. "Prenatal Infection and Schizophrenia: A Review of Epidemiologic and Translational Studies." *American Journal of Psychiatry*, vol. 167, no. 3, Mar. 2010, pp. 261–280, DOI: 10.1176/appi.ajp.2009.09030361

Khandaker, G. M., Dalman, C., Kappelmann, N., Stochl, J., Dal, H., Kosidou, K., Jones, P. B., & Karlsson, H. (2018). Association of Childhood Infection With IQ and Adult Nonaffective Psychosis in Swedish Men. JAMA Psychiatry, 75(4), 356. https://doi.org/10.1001/jamapsychiatry.2017.4491

Pedersen, M. G., Stevens, H., Pedersen, C. B., Nørgaard-Pedersen, B., & Mortensen, P. B. (2011). Toxoplasma Infection and Later Development of Schizophrenia in Mothers. *American Journal of Psychiatry*, *168*(8), 814–821. https://doi.org/10.1176/appi.ajp.2011.10091351

Prasad, K. M., Eack, S. M., Goradia, D., Pancholi, K. M., Keshavan, M. S., Yolken, R. H., & Nimgaonkar, V. L. (2011). Progressive Gray Matter Loss and Changes in Cognitive Functioning Associated With Exposure to Herpes Simplex Virus 1 in Schizophrenia: A Longitudinal Study. *American Journal of Psychiatry*, *168*(8), 822–830. https://doi.org/10.1176/appi.ajp.2011.10101423

Petersen, L., Mortensen, P. B., & Pedersen, C. B. (2011). Paternal Age at Birth of First Child and Risk of Schizophrenia. American Journal of Psychiatry, 168(1), 82–88. https://doi.org/10.1176/appi.ajp.2010.10020252

Jongsma, H. E., & Jones, P. B. (2018). Weaving Causal Explanations of Schizophrenia in Urban Areas. *JAMA Psychiatry*, *75*(9), 878. https://doi.org/10.1001/jamapsychiatry.2018.1795

Conroy, M. A., Finch, T., Levin, T. T., Merkler, A. E., Safdieh, J., Samuels, S.,

& Gordon Elliott, J. S. (2018). Chronic Schizophrenia Later Diagnosed with Anti-NMDA Receptor Encephalitis: Case Report and Review of the Literature. *Clinical Schizophrenia & Related Psychoses, 11*(4), 201–204. https://doi.org/10.3371/csrp.mctf.071317

Kendler, K. S., Ohlsson, H., Sundquist, J., & Sundquist, K. (2019). Prediction of Onset of Substance-Induced Psychotic Disorder and Its Progression to Schizophrenia in a Swedish National Sample. *The American journal of psychiatry, 176*(9), 711–719. https://doi.org/10.1176/appi.ajp.2019.18101217

Foti, D. J., Kotov, R., Guey, L. T., & Bromet, E. J. (2010). Cannabis Use and the Course of Schizophrenia: 10-Year Follow-Up After First Hospitalization. American Journal of Psychiatry, 167(8), 987–993. https://doi.org/10.1176/appi.ajp.2010.09020189

Rodrigo, C., & Rajapakse, S. (2009). Cannabis and schizophrenia spectrum disorders: A review of clinical studies. Indian Journal of Psychological Medicine, 31(2), 62. https://doi.org/10.4103/0253-7176.63575

Rathbone, J., Variend, H., & Mehta, H. (2008). Cannabis and schizophrenia. Cochrane Database of Systematic Reviews. https://doi.org/10.1002/14651858.cd004837.pub2

HALL, W., & DEGENHARDT, L. (2008). Cannabis use and the risk of developing a psychotic disorder. World Psychiatry, 7(2), 68–71. https://doi.org/10.1002/j.2051-5545.2008.tb00158.x

Bygrave, A. M., Masiulis, S., Kullmann, D. M., Bannerman, D. M., & Kätzel, D. (2019). Gene-Environment Interaction in a Conditional NMDAR-Knockout Model of Schizophrenia. *Frontiers in behavioral neuroscience, 12*, 332. https://doi.org/10.3389/fnbeh.2018.00332

Dickerson, F., Katsafanas, E., Origoni, A., Squire, A., Khushalani, S., Newman, T., Rowe, K., Stallings, C., Savage, C., Sweeney, K., Nguyen, T. T., Breier, A., Goff, D., Ford, G., Jones-Brando, L., & Yolken, R. (2021). Exposure to Epstein Barr virus and cognitive functioning in individuals with schizophrenia. *Schizophrenia research, 228*, 193–197. https://doi.org/10.1016/j.schres.2020.12.018

Colodro-Conde, L., Couvy-Duchesne, B., Whitfield, J. B., Streit, F., Gordon, S., Kemper, K. E., Yengo, L., Zheng, Z., Trzaskowski, M., de Zeeuw, E. L., Nivard, M. G., Das, M., Neale, R. E., MacGregor, S., Olsen, C. M., Whiteman, D. C., Boomsma, D. I., Yang, J., Rietschel, M., McGrath, J. J., ... Martin, N. G. (2018). Association Between Population Density and Genetic Risk for Schizophrenia. *JAMA psychiatry, 75*(9), 901–910. https://doi.org/10.1001/jamapsychiatry.2018.1581

Riglin, L., Hammerton, G., Heron, J., Collishaw, S., Arseneault, L., Thapar, A. K., Maughan, B., O'Donovan, M. C., & Thapar, A. (2019). Developmental Contributions of Schizophrenia Risk Alleles and Childhood Peer Victimization to Early-Onset Mental Health Trajectories. *The American journal of psychiatry, 176*(1), 36–43. https://doi.org/10.1176/appi.ajp.2018.18010075

References

Müller N. (2018). Inflammation in Schizophrenia: Pathogenetic Aspects and Therapeutic Considerations. *Schizophrenia bulletin*, *44*(5), 973–982. https://doi.org/10.1093/schbul/sby024

Clarke, M. C., Tanskanen, A., Huttunen, M., Leon, D. A., Murray, R. M., Jones, P. B., & Cannon, M. (2011). Increased Risk of Schizophrenia From Additive Interaction Between Infant Motor Developmental Delay and Obstetric Complications. *American Journal of Psychiatry*, *168*(12), 1295–1302. https://doi.org/10.1176/appi.ajp.2011.11010011

Periyasamy, S., John, S., Padmavati, R., Rajendren, P., Thirunavukkarasu, P., Gratten, J., Vinkhuyzen, A., McRae, A., Holliday, E. G., Nyholt, D. R., Nancarrow, D., Bakshi, A., Hemani, G., Nertney, D., Smith, H., Filippich, C., Patel, K., Fowdar, J., McLean, D., Tirupati, S., … Mowry, B. J. (2019). Association of Schizophrenia Risk With Disordered Niacin Metabolism in an Indian Genome-wide Association Study. *JAMA psychiatry*, *76*(10), 1026–1034. https://doi.org/10.1001/jamapsychiatry.2019.1335

Hakulinen C, Webb RT, Pedersen CB, Agerbo E, Mok PLH. Association Between Parental Income During Childhood and Risk of Schizophrenia Later in Life. *JAMA Psychiatry*. 2020;77(1):17–24. doi:10.1001/jamapsychiatry.2019.2299

35) Howes, O. D., & Kapur, S. (2009). The Dopamine Hypothesis of Schizophrenia: Version III—The Final Common Pathway. *Schizophrenia Bulletin*, *35*(3), 549–562. https://doi.org/10.1093/schbul/sbp006

Prata, D. P., Mechelli, A., Picchioni, M. M., Fu, C. H. Y., Toulopoulou, T., Bramon, E., Walshe, M., Murray, R. M., Collier, D. A., & McGuire, P. (2009). Altered Effect of Dopamine Transporter 3′UTR VNTR Genotype on Prefrontal and Striatal Function in Schizophrenia. *Archives of General Psychiatry*, *66*(11), 1162. https://doi.org/10.1001/archgenpsychiatry.2009.147

Howes, O. D., Kambeitz, J., Kim, E., Stahl, D., Slifstein, M., Abi-Dargham, A., & Kapur, S. (2012). The Nature of Dopamine Dysfunction in Schizophrenia and What This Means for Treatment. *Archives of General Psychiatry*, *69*(8). https://doi.org/10.1001/archgenpsychiatry.2012.169

Demjaha, A., Murray, R. M., McGuire, P. K., Kapur, S., & Howes, O. D. (2012). Dopamine Synthesis Capacity in Patients With Treatment-Resistant Schizophrenia. *American Journal of Psychiatry*, *169*(11), 1203–1210. https://doi.org/10.1176/appi.ajp.2012.12010144

Kegeles, L. S., Abi-Dargham, A., Frankle, W. G., Gil, R., Cooper, T. B., Slifstein, M., Hwang, D.-R., Huang, Y., Haber, S. N., & Laruelle, M. (2010). Increased synaptic dopamine function in associative regions of the striatum in schizophrenia. *Archives of General Psychiatry*, *67*(3), 231–239. https://doi.org/10.1001/archgenpsychiatry.2010.10

Öngür, D. (2017). Dopamine Dysfunction in Schizophrenia and Bipolar Disorder—Never the Twain Shall Meet? *JAMA Psychiatry*, *74*(12), 1187. https://

doi.org/10.1001/jamapsychiatry.2017.2330

36) Egerton, A., Modinos, G., Ferrera, D., & McGuire, P. (2017). Neuroimaging studies of GABA in schizophrenia: a systematic review with meta-analysis. *Translational psychiatry*, *7*(6), e1147. https://doi.org/10.1038/tp.2017.124

Frankle, W. G., Cho, R. Y., Prasad, K. M., Mason, N. S., Paris, J., Himes, M. L., Walker, C., Lewis, D. A., & Narendran, R. (2015). In vivo measurement of GABA transmission in healthy subjects and schizophrenia patients. *The American journal of psychiatry*, *172*(11), 1148–1159. https://doi.org/10.1176/appi.ajp.2015.14081031

Benes, F. (2001). GABAergic Interneurons Implications for Understanding Schizophrenia and Bipolar Disorder. *Neuropsychopharmacology*, *25*(1), 1–27. https://doi.org/10.1016/s0893-133x(01)00225-1

Inan, M., Petros, T. J., & Anderson, S. A. (2013). Losing your inhibition: Linking cortical GABAergic interneurons to schizophrenia. *Neurobiology of Disease*, *53*, 36–48. https://doi.org/10.1016/j.nbd.2012.11.013

Wang, X., Christian, K. M., Song, H., & Ming, G. (2018). Synaptic dysfunction in complex psychiatric disorders: from genetics to mechanisms. *Genome Medicine*, *10*(1). https://doi.org/10.1186/s13073-018-0518-5

37) Years of Research on Schizophrenia: The Ascendance of the Glutamatergic Synapse Joseph T. Coyle, M.D., W. Brad Ruzicka, M.D., Ph.D., Darrick T. Balu, Ph.D.Pages:1119–1128Published Online:1 December 2020 https://doi.org/10.1176/appi.ajp.2020.20101481

Volk, D. W., Eggan, S. M., & Lewis, D. A. (2010). Alterations in Metabotropic Glutamate Receptor 1α and Regulator of G Protein Signaling 4 in the Prefrontal Cortex in Schizophrenia. *American Journal of Psychiatry*, *167*(12), 1489–1498. https://doi.org/10.1176/appi.ajp.2010.10030318

38) Kahn, R. S., & Keefe, R. S. E. (2013). Schizophrenia Is a Cognitive Illness. *JAMA Psychiatry*, *70*(10), 1107. https://doi.org/10.1001/jamapsychiatry.2013.155

39) Halder, S and Mahato A K, Cognitive Impairment in Schizophrenia: An Overview of Assessment and Management, The International Journal of Indian Psychology ISSN 2348-5396 DOI: 10.25215/0204.047 http://oaji.net/articles/2015/1170-1438018804.pdf

Schulz, S. C., & Murray, A. (2016). Assessing Cognitive Impairment in Patients With Schizophrenia. The Journal of Clinical Psychiatry, 77(Suppl 2), 3–7. https://doi.org/10.4088/jcp.14074su1c.01

40) Kendler, K. S., Ohlsson, H., Sundquist, J., & Sundquist, K. (2015). IQ and schizophrenia in a Swedish national sample: their causal relationship and the interaction of IQ with genetic risk. *The American journal of psychiatry*, *172*(3), 259–265. https://doi.org/10.1176/appi.ajp.2014.14040516

41) Keefe R. S. (2014). The longitudinal course of cognitive impairment in schizophrenia: an examination of data from premorbid through posttreatment phases of illness. *The Journal of clinical psychiatry*, *75 Suppl 2*, 8–13. https://

References

doi.org/10.4088/JCP.13065su1.02

42) Leeson, V. C., Barnes, T. R., Hutton, S. B., Ron, M. A., & Joyce, E. M. (2009). IQ as a predictor of functional outcome in schizophrenia: a longitudinal, four-year study of first-episode psychosis. *Schizophrenia research*, *107*(1), 55–60. https://doi.org/10.1016/j.schres.2008.08.014

an index of general cognitive ability, IQ, may be a more sensitive and reliable predictor of outcome in first-episode schizophrenia..the most consistent finding was a relationship between IQ and the negative syndrome.

43) Kring, A. M., Gur, R. E., Blanchard, J. J., Horan, W. P., & Reise, S. P. (2013). The Clinical Assessment Interview for Negative Symptoms (CAINS): Final Development and Validation. American Journal of Psychiatry, 170(2), 165–172. https://doi.org/10.1176/appi.ajp.2012.12010109

Nordgaard, J., Arnfred, S. M., Handest, P., & Parnas, J. (2007). The Diagnostic Status of First-Rank Symptoms. *Schizophrenia Bulletin*, *34*(1), 137–154. https://doi.org/10.1093/schbul/sbm044

Kendler, K. S. (2018). The Development of Kraepelin's Mature Diagnostic Concepts of Paranoia (Die Verrücktheit) and Paranoid Dementia Praecox (Dementia Paranoides). *JAMA Psychiatry*, *75*(12), 1280. https://doi.org/10.1001/jamapsychiatry.2018.2377

44) Calkins, M. E. (2014). Cognitive Impairment in Schizophrenia: Characteristics, Assessment, and Treatment edited by HarveyPhilip D.. New York, Cambridge University Press, 2013, 328 pp., $95.00. *American Journal of Psychiatry*, *171*(6), 694–695. https://doi.org/10.1176/appi.ajp.2014.14010100

Green, M. F., & Harvey, P. D. (2014). Cognition in schizophrenia: Past, present, and future. *Schizophrenia Research: Cognition*, *1*(1), e1–e9. https://doi.org/10.1016/j.scog.2014.02.001

Smith, A. K., Edgar, J. C., Huang, M., Lu, B. Y., Thoma, R. J., Hanlon, F. M., McHaffie, G., Jones, A. P., Paz, R. D., Miller, G. A., & Cañive, J. M. (2010). Cognitive Abilities and 50- and 100-msec Paired-Click Processes in Schizophrenia. *American Journal of Psychiatry*, *167*(10), 1264–1275. https://doi.org/10.1176/appi.ajp.2010.09071059

Khandaker, G. M., Barnett, J. H., White, I. R., & Jones, P. B. (2011). A quantitative meta-analysis of population-based studies of premorbid intelligence and schizophrenia. *Schizophrenia Research*, *132*(2–3), 220–227. https://doi.org/10.1016/j.schres.2011.06.017

Reichenberg, A., Caspi, A., Harrington, H., Houts, R., Keefe, R. S. E., Murray, R. M., Poulton, R., & Moffitt, T. E. (2010). Static and Dynamic Cognitive Deficits in Childhood Preceding Adult Schizophrenia: A 30-Year Study. *American Journal of Psychiatry*, *167*(2), 160–169. https://doi.org/10.1176/appi.ajp.2009.09040574

Leitman, D. I., Sehatpour, P., Higgins, B. A., Foxe, J. J., Silipo, G., & Javitt, D. C. (2010). Sensory Deficits and Distributed Hierarchical Dysfunction in Schizophrenia. *American Journal of Psychiatry*, *167*(7), 818–827. https://doi.

org/10.1176/appi.ajp.2010.09030338

Knowles, E. E. M., David, A. S., & Reichenberg, A. (2010). Processing Speed Deficits in Schizophrenia: Reexamining the Evidence. *American Journal of Psychiatry*, *167*(7), 828–835. https://doi.org/10.1176/appi.ajp.2010.09070937

Schiffman, J., Sorensen, H. J., Maeda, J., Mortensen, E. L., Victoroff, J., Hayashi, K., Michelsen, N. M., Ekstrom, M., & Mednick, S. (2009). Childhood Motor Coordination and Adult Schizophrenia Spectrum Disorders. *American Journal of Psychiatry*, *166*(9), 1041–1047. https://doi.org/10.1176/appi.ajp.2009.08091400

Parnas, J., & Henriksen, M. G. (2014). Disordered self in the schizophrenia spectrum: a clinical and research perspective. *Harvard review of psychiatry*, *22*(5), 251–265. https://doi.org/10.1097/HRP.0000000000000040

Sehatpour, P., Dias, E. C., Butler, P. D., Revheim, N., Guilfoyle, D. N., Foxe, J. J., & Javitt, D. C. (2010). Impaired Visual Object Processing Across an Occipital-Frontal-Hippocampal Brain Network in Schizophrenia. *Archives of General Psychiatry*, *67*(8), 772. https://doi.org/10.1001/archgenpsychiatry.2010.85

Gold, R., Butler, P., Revheim, N., Leitman, D. I., Hansen, J. A., Gur, R. C., Kantrowitz, J. T., Laukka, P., Juslin, P. N., Silipo, G. S., & Javitt, D. C. (2012). Auditory Emotion Recognition Impairments in Schizophrenia: Relationship to Acoustic Features and Cognition. *American Journal of Psychiatry*, *169*(4), 424–432. https://doi.org/10.1176/appi.ajp.2011.11081230

Revheim, N., Corcoran, C. M., Dias, E., Hellmann, E., Martinez, A., Butler, P. D., Lehrfeld, J. M., DiCostanzo, J., Albert, J., & Javitt, D. C. (2014). Reading deficits in schizophrenia and individuals at high clinical risk: relationship to sensory function, course of illness, and psychosocial outcome. *The American journal of psychiatry*, *171*(9), 949–959. https://doi.org/10.1176/appi.ajp.2014.13091196

Patients with schizophrenia show severe deficits in reading ability that represent a potentially remediable cause of impaired socioeconomic function. Such deficits are not presently captured during routine clinical assessment.

Andreasen, N. C., Nopoulos, P., O'Leary, D. S., Miller, D. D., Wassink, T., & Flaum, M. (1999). Defining the phenotype of schizophrenia: cognitive dysmetria and its neural mechanisms. *Biological Psychiatry*, *46*(7), 908–920. https://doi.org/10.1016/s0006-3223(99)00152-3

Martínez, A., Gaspar, P. A., Hillyard, S. A., Andersen, S. K., Lopez-Calderon, J., Corcoran, C. M., & Javitt, D. C. (2018). Impaired Motion Processing in Schizophrenia and the Attenuated Psychosis Syndrome: Etiological and Clinical Implications. *The American journal of psychiatry*, *175*(12), 1243–1254. https://doi.org/10.1176/appi.ajp.2018.18010072

Fisher, M., McCoy, K., Poole, J. H., & Vinogradov, S. (2008). Self and Other in Schizophrenia: A Cognitive Neuroscience Perspective. American Journal of Psychiatry, 165(11), 1465–1472. https://doi.org/10.1176/appi.ajp.2008.07111806

References

Blakemore, S.-J., & Frith, C. (2003). Self-awareness and action. *Current Opinion in Neurobiology, 13*(2), 219–224. https://doi.org/10.1016/s0959-4388(03)00043-6

Sarah-Jayne Blakemore: "The Teenager's Sense of Social Self" | Edge.org. (2019). Edge.Org. https://www.edge.org/conversation/sarah_jayne_blakemore-sarah-jayne-blakemore-the-teenagers-sense-of-social-self

Blakemore, S.-J., & Decety, J. (2001). From the perception of action to the understanding of intention. *Nature Reviews Neuroscience, 2*(8), 561–567. https://doi.org/10.1038/35086023

Javitt, D. C., & Freedman, R. (2015). Sensory processing dysfunction in the personal experience and neuronal machinery of schizophrenia. *The American journal of psychiatry, 172*(1), 17–31. https://doi.org/10.1176/appi.ajp.2014.13121691

Anselmetti, S., Cavallaro, R., Bechi, M., Angelone, S. M., Ermoli, E., Cocchi, F., & Smeraldi, E. (2007). Psychopathological and neuropsychological correlates of source monitoring impairment in schizophrenia. *Psychiatry Research, 150*(1), 51–59. https://doi.org/10.1016/j.psychres.2005.12.004

Satterthwaite, T. D., Wolf, D. H., Loughead, J., Ruparel, K., Valdez, J. N., Siegel, S. J., Kohler, C. G., Gur, R. E., & Gur, R. C. (2010). Association of Enhanced Limbic Response to Threat With Decreased Cortical Facial Recognition Memory Response in Schizophrenia. American Journal of Psychiatry, 167(4), 418–426. https://doi.org/10.1176/appi.ajp.2009.09060808 http://ajp.psychiatryonline.org/doi/full/10.1176/appi.ajp.2009.09060808

Holt, D. J., Coombs, G., Zeidan, M. A., Goff, D. C., & Milad, M. R. (2012). Failure of Neural Responses to Safety Cues in Schizophrenia. *Archives of General Psychiatry, 69*(9), 893. https://doi.org/10.1001/archgenpsychiatry.2011.2310

Greenman, D., La, M., Shah, S., Chen, Q., Berman, K. F., Weinberger, D. R., & Tan, H. Y. (2020). Parietal-Prefrontal Feedforward Connectivity in Association With Schizophrenia Genetic Risk and Delusions. *The American journal of psychiatry, 177*(12), 1151–1158. https://doi.org/10.1176/appi.ajp.2020.19111176

Kuperberg, G. R. (2010). Language in Schizophrenia Part 1: An Introduction. *Language and Linguistics Compass, 4*(8), 576–589. https://doi.org/10.1111/j.1749-818x.2010.00216.x

Kuperberg, G. R. (2010). Language in Schizophrenia Part 2: What Can Psycholinguistics Bring to the Study of Schizophrenia…and Vice Versa? *Language and Linguistics Compass, 4*(8), 590–604. https://doi.org/10.1111/j.1749-818x.2010.00217.x

45) Lesh, T. A., Niendam, T. A., Minzenberg, M. J., & Carter, C. S. (2010). Cognitive Control Deficits in Schizophrenia: Mechanisms and Meaning. *Neuropsychopharmacology, 36*(1), 316–338. https://doi.org/10.1038/npp.2010.156

McGlashan TH, Fenton WS. The Positive-Negative Distinction in Schizophrenia: Review of Natural History Validators. *Arch Gen Psychiatry.* 1992;49(1):63–72. doi:10.1001/archpsyc.1992.01820010063008
https://jamanetwork.com/journals/jamapsychiatry/article-abstract/495627
Strauss, G. P., Nuñez, A., Ahmed, A. O., Barchard, K. A., Granholm, E., Kirkpatrick, B., Gold, J. M., & Allen, D. N. (2018). The Latent Structure of Negative Symptoms in Schizophrenia. *JAMA Psychiatry*, *75*(12), 1271. **https://doi.org/10.1001/jamapsychiatry.2018.2475**
Strauss, G. P., & Gold, J. M. (2012). A New Perspective on Anhedonia in Schizophrenia. *American Journal of Psychiatry*, *169*(4), 364–373. https://doi.org/10.1176/appi.ajp.2011.11030447
Buchanan R. W. (2007). Persistent negative symptoms in schizophrenia: an overview. *Schizophrenia bulletin*, *33*(4), 1013–1022. https://doi.org/10.1093/schbul/sbl057
Wheeler, A. L., Wessa, M., Szeszko, P. R., Foussias, G., Chakravarty, M. M., Lerch, J. P., DeRosse, P., Remington, G., Mulsant, B. H., Linke, J., Malhotra, A. K., & Voineskos, A. N. (2015). Further Neuroimaging Evidence for the Deficit Subtype of Schizophrenia. *JAMA Psychiatry*, *72*(5), 446. https://doi.org/10.1001/jamapsychiatry.2014.3020
45) Cook, J., Barbalat, G., & Blakemore, S.-J. (2012). Top-down modulation of the perception of other people in schizophrenia and autism. *Frontiers in Human Neuroscience*, *6*. https://doi.org/10.3389/fnhum.2012.00175
Kogler, L., Liemburg, E. J., Sommer, I. E., Müller, V. I., Cieslik, E. C., & Eickhoff, S. B. (2016). Differential Patterns of Dysconnectivity in Mirror Neuron and Mentalizing Networks in Schizophrenia. *Schizophrenia bulletin*, *42*(5), 1135–1148. https://doi.org/10.1093/schbul/sbw015
46) Frith *The Cognitive Neuropsychology of Schizophrenia - Christopher D. Frith -*
Cognitive Impairment in Schizophrenia - edited by Philip D. Harvey
Garrison, J. R., Bond, R., Gibbard, E., Johnson, M. K., & Simons, J. S. (2017). Monitoring what is real: The effects of modality and action on accuracy and type of reality monitoring error. *Cortex*, *87*, 108–117. https://doi.org/10.1016/j.cortex.2016.06.018
47) Brune, M. (2005). "Theory of Mind" in Schizophrenia: A Review of the Literature. *Schizophrenia Bulletin*, *31*(1), 21–42. https://doi.org/10.1093/schbul/sbi002 https://academic.oup.com/schizophreniabulletin/article/31/1/21/1884527
Bozikas, V. P., Giannakou, M., Kosmidis, M. H., Kargopoulos, P., Kioseoglou, G., Liolios, D., & Garyfallos, G. (2011). Insights into theory of mind in schizophrenia: The impact of cognitive impairment. *Schizophrenia Research*, *130*(1–3), 130–136. https://doi.org/10.1016/j.schres.2011.04.025
Scherzer, P., Leveillé, E., Achim, A., Boisseau, E., & Stip, E. (2012). A Study of Theory of Mind in Paranoid Schizophrenia: A Theory or Many Theories? *Frontiers in Psychology*, *3*. https://doi.org/10.3389/fpsyg.2012.00432

References

48) Penn, D. L., Sanna, L. J., & Roberts, D. L. (2007). Social Cognition in Schizophrenia: An Overview. *Schizophrenia Bulletin, 34*(3), 408–411. https://doi.org/10.1093/schbul/sbn014

Bowie, C. R., Reichenberg, A., Patterson, T. L., Heaton, R. K., & Harvey, P. D. (2006). Determinants of Real-World Functional Performance in Schizophrenia Subjects: Correlations With Cognition, Functional Capacity, and Symptoms. American Journal of Psychiatry, 163(3), 418–425. https://doi.org/10.1176/appi.ajp.163.3.418

Thakkar, K. N., Peterman, J. S., & Park, S. (2014). Altered Brain Activation During Action Imitation and Observation in Schizophrenia: A Translational Approach to Investigating Social Dysfunction in Schizophrenia. American Journal of Psychiatry, 171(5), 539–548. https://doi.org/10.1176/appi.ajp.2013.13040498

Li, P., Fan, TT., Zhao, RJ. *et al.* Altered Brain Network Connectivity as a Potential Endophenotype of Schizophrenia. *Sci Rep* 7, 5483 (2017). https://doi.org/10.1038/s41598-017-05774-3

50) **Psychosis is a separate clinical phenomenon that may be triggered by multiple etiologies, including emotional arousal associated with *the cognitive confusion of disturbed hippocampal messages*. (see chapter five.)**

Calabrese, J., & Yasir Al Khalili. (2019, October 27). *Psychosis*. Nih.Gov; StatPearls Publishing.
https://www.ncbi.nlm.nih.gov/books/NBK546579/

Ellison-Wright, I., Glahn, D. C., Laird, A. R., Thelen, S. M., & Bullmore, E. (2008). The Anatomy of First-Episode and Chronic Schizophrenia: An Anatomical Likelihood Estimation Meta-Analysis. *American Journal of Psychiatry*, 165(8), 1015–1023. https://doi.org/10.1176/appi.ajp.2008.07101562http://ajp.psychiatryonline.org/doi/full/10.1176/appi.ajp.2008.07101562

51) Tamminga, C. A., Stan, A. D., & Wagner, A. D. (2010). The Hippocampal Formation in Schizophrenia. *American Journal of Psychiatry*, 167(10), 1178–1193. https://doi.org/10.1176/appi.ajp.2010.09081187

Stark, C. E., & Squire, L. R. (2000). Functional magnetic resonance imaging (fMRI) activity in the hippocampal region during recognition memory. *The Journal of neuroscience : the official journal of the Society for Neuroscience*, 20(20), 7776–7781. https://doi.org/10.1523/JNEUROSCI.20-20-07776.2000

Greene, A. J., Gross, W. L., Elsinger, C. L., & Rao, S. M. (2006). An FMRI analysis of the human hippocampus: inference, context, and task awareness. *Journal of cognitive neuroscience*, 18(7), 1156–1173. https://doi.org/10.1162/jocn.2006.18.7.1156

Rasetti, R., Mattay, V. S., White, M. G., Sambataro, F., Podell, J. E., Zoltick, B., Chen, Q., Berman, K. F., Callicott, J. H., & Weinberger, D. R. (2014). Altered Hippocampal-Parahippocampal Function During Stimulus Encoding. JAMA Psychiatry, 71(3), 236. https://doi.org/10.1001/jamapsychiatry.2013.3911

Mattai, A., Hosanagar, A., Weisinger, B., Greenstein, D., Stidd, R., Clasen, L., Lalonde, F., Rapoport, J., & Gogtay, N. (2011). Hippocampal Volume Development in Healthy Siblings of Childhood-Onset Schizophrenia Patients. *American Journal of Psychiatry, 168*(4), 427–435. https://doi.org/10.1176/appi.ajp.2010.10050681

Achim, A. M., Bertrand, M.-C., Sutton, H., Montoya, A., Czechowska, Y., Malla, A. K., Joober, R., Pruessner, J. C., & Lepage, M. (2007). Selective Abnormal Modulation of Hippocampal Activity During Memory Formation in First-Episode Psychosis. *Archives of General Psychiatry, 64*(9), 999. https://doi.org/10.1001/archpsyc.64.9.999

Lepage, M., Hawco, C., & Bodnar, M. (2015). Relational Memory as a Possible Neurocognitive Marker of Schizophrenia. *JAMA psychiatry, 72*(9), 946–947. https://doi.org/10.1001/jamapsychiatry.2015.0488

Brown, P. L., Shepard, P. D., Elmer, G. I., Stockman, S., McFarland, R., Mayo, C. L., Cadet, J. L., Krasnova, I. N., Greenwald, M., Schoonover, C., & Vogel, M. W. (2012). Altered spatial learning, cortical plasticity and hippocampal anatomy in a neurodevelopmental model of schizophrenia-related endophenotypes. *The European journal of neuroscience, 36*(6), 2773–2781. https://doi.org/10.1111/j.1460-9568.2012.08204.x

Lieberman, J.A., Girgis, R.R., Brucato, G. et al. Hippocampal dysfunction in the pathophysiology of schizophrenia: a selective review and hypothesis for early detection and intervention. *Mol Psychiatry* **23,** 1764–1772 (2018). https://doi.org/10.1038/mp.2017.249

Rubin, R. D., Watson, P. D., Duff, M. C., & Cohen, N. J. (2014). The role of the hippocampus in flexible cognition and social behavior. *Frontiers in Human Neuroscience, 8.* https://doi.org/10.3389/fnhum.2014.00742

Tregellas, J. R., Smucny, J., Harris, J. G., Olincy, A., Maharajh, K., Kronberg, E., Eichman, L. C., Lyons, E., & Freedman, R. (2014). Intrinsic hippocampal activity as a biomarker for cognition and symptoms in schizophrenia. *The American journal of psychiatry, 171*(5), 549–556. https://doi.org/10.1176/appi.ajp.2013.13070981

Hippocampal abnormalities and memory deficits: New evidence of a strong pathophysiological link in schizophrenia. *Brain research reviews, 54*(1), 92–112. https://doi.org/10.1016/j.brainresrev.2006.12.008

Lisman, J. E., & Grace, A. A. (2005). The hippocampal-VTA loop: controlling the entry of information into long-term memory. *Neuron, 46*(5), 703–713. https://doi.org/10.1016/j.neuron.2005.05.002

52) Levitt, J. J., Nestor, P. G., Levin, L., Pelavin, P., Lin, P., Kubicki, M., McCarley, R. W., Shenton, M. E., & Rathi, Y. (2017). Reduced Structural Connectivity in Frontostriatal White Matter Tracts in the Associative Loop in Schizophrenia. *The American journal of psychiatry, 174*(11), 1102–1111. https://doi.org/10.1176/appi.ajp.2017.16091046

Greenman, D., La, M., Shah, S., Chen, Q., Berman, K. F., Weinberger, D. R., &

References

Tan, H. Y. (2020). Parietal-Prefrontal Feedforward Connectivity in Association With Schizophrenia Genetic Risk and Delusions. *The American journal of psychiatry*, *177*(12), 1151–1158. https://doi.org/10.1176/appi.ajp.2020.19111176

Dwivedi Y. (2020). Cell-Type-Specific Transcriptomic Analysis in the Dorsolateral Prefrontal Cortex Reveals Distinct Mitochondrial Abnormalities in Schizophrenia and Bipolar Disorder. *The American journal of psychiatry*, *177*(12), 1107–1109. https://doi.org/10.1176/appi.ajp.2020.20101455

53) Wheeler, A. L., & Voineskos, A. N. (2014). A review of structural neuroimaging in schizophrenia: from connectivity to connectomics. *Frontiers in Human Neuroscience*, *8*. https://doi.org/10.3389/fnhum.2014.00653

Nekovarova, T., Fajnerova, I., Horacek, J., & Spaniel, F. (2014). Bridging disparate symptoms of schizophrenia: a triple network dysfunction theory. *Frontiers in Behavioral Neuroscience*, *8*. https://doi.org/10.3389/fnbeh.2014.00171

Kambeitz, J., Kambeitz-Ilankovic, L., Cabral, C., Dwyer, D. B., Calhoun, V. D., van den Heuvel, M. P., Falkai, P., Koutsouleris, N., & Malchow, B. (2016). Aberrant Functional Whole-Brain Network Architecture in Patients With Schizophrenia: A Meta-analysis. Schizophrenia Bulletin, 42(suppl 1), S13–S21. https://doi.org/10.1093/schbul/sbv174

Lynall, M. E., Bassett, D. S., Kerwin, R., McKenna, P. J., Kitzbichler, M., Muller, U., & Bullmore, E. (2010). Functional connectivity and brain networks in schizophrenia. *The Journal of neuroscience : the official journal of the Society for Neuroscience*, *30*(28), 9477–9487. https://doi.org/10.1523/JNEUROSCI.0333-10.2010

Hadley, J., Kraguljac, N., White, D. *et al.* Change in brain network topology as a function of treatment response in schizophrenia: a longitudinal resting-state fMRI study using graph theory. *npj Schizophr* **2,** 16014 (2016). https://doi.org/10.1038/npjschz.2016.14

Ray, K. L., Lesh, T. A., Howell, A. M., Salo, T. P., Ragland, J. D., MacDonald, A. W., Gold, J. M., Silverstein, S. M., Barch, D. M., & Carter, C. S. (2017). Functional network changes and cognitive control in schizophrenia. NeuroImage. Clinical, 15, 161–170. https://doi.org/10.1016/j.nicl.2017.05.001

Wolf, D. H., Satterthwaite, T. D., Calkins, M. E., Ruparel, K., Elliott, M. A., Hopson, R. D., Jackson, C. T., Prabhakaran, K., Bilker, W. B., Hakonarson, H., Gur, R. C., & Gur, R. E. (2015). Functional Neuroimaging Abnormalities in Youth With Psychosis Spectrum Symptoms. *JAMA Psychiatry*, *72*(5), 456. https://doi.org/10.1001/jamapsychiatry.2014.3169

Gold, J. M. (2012). Negative Symptoms and the Failure to Represent the Expected Reward Value of Actions. *Archives of General Psychiatry*, *69*(2), 129. https://doi.org/10.1001/archgenpsychiatry.2011.1269

Wible, C. G. (2012). Hippocampal temporal-parietal junction interaction in the production of psychotic symptoms: a framework for understanding the schizophrenic syndrome. *Frontiers in Human Neuroscience*, *6*. https://doi.org/10.3389/fnhum.2012.00180

Wannan, C., Cropley, V. L., Chakravarty, M. M., Bousman, C., Ganella, E. P., Bruggemann, J. M., Weickert, T. W., Weickert, C. S., Everall, I., McGorry, P., Velakoulis, D., Wood, S. J., Bartholomeusz, C. F., Pantelis, C., & Zalesky, A. (2019). Evidence for Network-Based Cortical Thickness Reductions in Schizophrenia. *The American journal of psychiatry*, *176*(7), 552–563. https://doi.org/10.1176/appi.ajp.2019.18040380

Schilbach, L., Hoffstaedter, F., Müller, V., Cieslik, E. C., Goya-Maldonado, R., Trost, S., Sorg, C., Riedl, V., Jardri, R., Sommer, I., Kogler, L., Derntl, B., Gruber, O., & Eickhoff, S. B. (2015). Transdiagnostic commonalities and differences in resting state functional connectivity of the default mode network in schizophrenia and major depression. *NeuroImage. Clinical*, *10*, 326–335. https://doi.org/10.1016/j.nicl.2015.11.021

Liu, H., Kaneko, Y., Ouyang, X., Li, L., Hao, Y., Chen, E. Y., Jiang, T., Zhou, Y., & Liu, Z. (2012). Schizophrenic patients and their unaffected siblings share increased resting-state connectivity in the task-negative network but not its anticorrelated task-positive network. *Schizophrenia bulletin*, *38*(2), 285–294. https://doi.org/10.1093/schbul/sbq074

Nejad, A. B., Ebdrup, B. H., Glenthøj, B. Y., & Siebner, H. R. (2012). Brain connectivity studies in schizophrenia: unravelling the effects of antipsychotics. *Current neuropharmacology*, *10*(3), 219–230. https://doi.org/10.2174/157015912803217305

Javitt, D. C., & Freedman, R. (2015). Sensory processing dysfunction in the personal experience and neuronal machinery of schizophrenia. *The American journal of psychiatry*, *172*(1), 17–31. https://doi.org/10.1176/appi.ajp.2014.13121691

54) Barch, D. M., & Ceaser, A. (2012). Cognition in schizophrenia: core psychological and neural mechanisms. *Trends in Cognitive Sciences*, *16*(1), 27–34. https://doi.org/10.1016/j.tics.2011.11.015

Minzenberg, M. J., Laird, A. R., Thelen, S., Carter, C. S., & Glahn, D. C. (2009). Meta-analysis of 41 functional neuroimaging studies of executive function in schizophrenia. *Archives of general psychiatry*, *66*(8), 811–822. https://doi.org/10.1001/archgenpsychiatry.2009.91

Dauvermann, M. R., Whalley, H. C., Schmidt, A., Lee, G. L., Romaniuk, L., Roberts, N., Johnstone, E. C., Lawrie, S. M., & Moorhead, T. W. J. (2014). Computational Neuropsychiatry – Schizophrenia as a Cognitive Brain Network Disorder. *Frontiers in Psychiatry*, *5*. https://doi.org/10.3389/fpsyt.2014.00030

Green, M. F., Lee, J., Cohen, M. S., Engel, S. A., Korb, A. S., Nuechterlein, K. H., Wynn, J. K., & Glahn, D. C. (2009). Functional Neuroanatomy of Visual Masking Deficits in Schizophrenia. *Archives of General Psychiatry*, *66*(12), 1295. https://doi.org/10.1001/archgenpsychiatry.2009.132

Michael C. Anderson, Jamie G. Bunce, Helen Barbas, Prefrontal–hippocampal pathways underlying inhibitory control over

References

memory,Neurobiology of Learning and Memory, Volume 134, Part A,2016,Pages 145-161,ISSN 1074-7427,https://doi.org/10.1016/j.nlm.2015.11.008. (https://www.sciencedirect.com/science/article/pii/S1074742715002178)

Thierry, A. M., Gioanni, Y., Dégénétais, E., & Glowinski, J. (2000). Hippocampo-prefrontal cortex pathway: anatomical and electrophysiological characteristics. *Hippocampus, 10*(4), 411–419. https://doi.org/10.1002/1098-1063(2000)10:4<411::AID-HIPO7>3.0.CO;2-A

Bill P. Godsil, Janos P. Kiss, Michael Spedding, Thérèse M. Jay,The hippocampal–prefrontal pathway: The weak link in psychiatric disorders?,European Neuropsychopharmacology,Volume 23, Issue 10,2013,Pages 1165-1181, https://doi.org/10.1016/j.euroneuro.2012.10.018.

56) Lisman and Grace Lisman, J., Grace, A. A., & Duzel, E. (2011). A neo-Hebbian framework for episodic memory; role of dopamine-dependent late LTP. *Trends in Neurosciences, 34*(10), 536–547. https://doi.org/10.1016/j.tins.2011.07.006

Studies at many types of synapses indicate that the early phase of long-term potentiation (LTP) has Hebbian properties. However, it is now clear that the Hebb rule does not account for late LTP; this requires an additional signal that is nonlocal. For novel information and motivational events such as rewards this signal at hippocampal CA1 synapses is mediated by the neuromodulator, dopamine.

57) Leivada, E., & Boeckx, C. (2014). Schizophrenia and cortical blindness: protective effects and implications for language. *Frontiers in Human Neuroscience, 8.* https://doi.org/10.3389/fnhum.2014.00940

Morgan, V. A., Clark, M., Crewe, J., Valuri, G., Mackey, D. A., Badcock, J. C., & Jablensky, A. (2018). Congenital blindness is protective for schizophrenia and other psychotic illness. A whole-population study. *Schizophrenia Research, 202,* 414–416. https://doi.org/10.1016/j.schres.2018.06.061

Pollak, T. A., & Corlett, P. R. (2019). Blindness, Psychosis, and the Visual Construction of the World. *Schizophrenia Bulletin.* https://doi.org/10.1093/schbul/sbz098

Blindness and Schizophrenia: The Exception Proves the Rule. (2014). Psychology Today. https://www.psychologytoday.com/us/blog/the-imprinted-brain/201411/blindness-and-schizophrenia-the-exception-proves-the-rule

Alderson-Day, B., McCarthy-Jones, S., & Fernyhough, C. (2015). Hearing voices in the resting brain: A review of intrinsic functional connectivity research on auditory verbal hallucinations. *Neuroscience and biobehavioral reviews, 55,* 78–87. https://doi.org/10.1016/j.neubiorev.2015.04.016

Alderson-Day, B., Diederen, K., Fernyhough, C., Ford, J. M., Horga, G., Margulies, D. S., McCarthy-Jones, S., Northoff, G., Shine, J. M., Turner, J., van de Ven, V., van Lutterveld, R., Waters, F., & Jardri, R. (2016). Auditory Hallucinations and the Brain's Resting-State Networks: Findings and

Methodological Observations. *Schizophrenia bulletin*, *42*(5), 1110–1123. https://doi.org/10.1093/schbul/sbw078

Lee, J., Gosselin, F., Wynn, J. K., & Green, M. F. (2011). How Do Schizophrenia Patients Use Visual Information to Decode Facial Emotion? *Schizophrenia Bulletin*, *37*(5), 1001–1008. https://doi.org/10.1093/schbul/sbq006

Siemerkus, J., Irle, E., Schmidt-Samoa, C., Dechent, P., & Weniger, G. (2012). Egocentric spatial learning in schizophrenia investigated with functional magnetic resonance imaging. *NeuroImage : Clinical*, *1*(1), 153–163. https://doi.org/10.1016/j.nicl.2012.10.004

Anticevic, A., & Corlett, P. R. (2012). Cognition-Emotion Dysinteraction in Schizophrenia. *Frontiers in Psychology*, *3*. https://doi.org/10.3389/fpsyg.2012.00392

58) Hare, S. M., Law, A. S., Ford, J. M., Mathalon, D. H., Ahmadi, A., Damaraju, E., Bustillo, J., Belger, A., Lee, H. J., Mueller, B. A., Lim, K. O., Brown, G. G., Preda, A., van Erp, T., Potkin, S. G., Calhoun, V. D., & Turner, J. A. (2018). Disrupted network cross talk, hippocampal dysfunction and hallucinations in schizophrenia. *Schizophrenia research*, *199*, 226–234. https://doi.org/10.1016/j.schres.2018.03.004

Stephanie Hare, Judith Ford, Alicia Law, Aral Ahmadi, Eswar Damaraju, Aysenil Belger, Juan Bustillo, Hyo Jong Lee, Daniel Mathalon, Bryon Mueller, Adrian Preda, Theo Van Erp, Steven Potkin, Vince Calhoun, Jessica Turner, 75. Disrupted Network Cross Talk, Hippocampal Dysfunction, and Hallucinations in Schizophrenia, *Schizophrenia Bulletin*, Volume 43, Issue suppl_1, March 2017, Page S43, https://doi.org/10.1093/schbul/sbx021.114

Fernández-Ruiz, A., Oliva, A., Soula, M., Rocha-Almeida, F., Nagy, G.A., Martin-Vazquez, G., & Buzsáki, G. (2021). Gamma rhythm communication between entorhinal cortex and dentate gyrus neuronal assemblies. Science, 372.

Mueller, S., Wang, D., Pan, R., Holt, D. J., & Liu, H. (2015). Abnormalities in Hemispheric Specialization of Caudate Nucleus Connectivity in Schizophrenia. *JAMA Psychiatry*, *72*(6), 552. https://doi.org/10.1001/jamapsychiatry.2014.3176

McHugo, M., Talati, P., Armstrong, K., Vandekar, S. N., Blackford, J. U., Woodward, N. D., & Heckers, S. (2019). Hyperactivity and Reduced Activation of Anterior Hippocampus in Early Psychosis. *The American journal of psychiatry*, *176*(12), 1030–1038. https://doi.org/10.1176/appi.ajp.2019.19020151

Liu, L., Cui, L. B., Xi, Y. B., Wang, X. R., Liu, Y. C., Xu, Z. L., Wang, H. N., Yin, H., & Qin, W. (2019). Association Between Connectivity of Hippocampal Sub-Regions and Auditory Verbal Hallucinations in Schizophrenia. *Frontiers in neuroscience*, *13*, 424. https://doi.org/10.3389/fnins.2019.00424

Vicidomini, C., Guo, N., & Sahay, A. (2020). Communication, Cross Talk, and Signal Integration in the Adult Hippocampal Neurogenic Niche. *Neuron*, *105*(2), 220–235. https://doi.org/10.1016/j.neuron.2019.11.029

Ragland, J. D., Laird, A. R., Ranganath, C., Blumenfeld, R. S., Gonzales, S. M., & Glahn, D. C. (2009). Prefrontal Activation Deficits During Episodic Memory.

American Journal of Psychiatry, *166*(8), 863–874. https://doi.org/10.1176/appi.ajp.2009.08091307

Krystal, J. H., Murray, J. D., Chekroud, A. M., Corlett, P. R., Yang, G., Wang, X.-J., & Anticevic, A. (2017). Computational Psychiatry and the Challenge of Schizophrenia. *Schizophrenia Bulletin*, *43*(3), 473–475. https://doi.org/10.1093/schbul/sbx025

Alústiza, I., Radua, J., Albajes-Eizagirre, A., Domínguez, M., Aubá, E., & Ortuño, F. (2016). Meta-Analysis of Functional Neuroimaging and Cognitive Control Studies in Schizophrenia: Preliminary Elucidation of a Core Dysfunctional Timing Network. *Frontiers in psychology*, *7*, 192. https://doi.org/10.3389/fpsyg.2016.00192

Slifstein, M., van de Giessen, E., Van Snellenberg, J., Thompson, J. L., Narendran, R., Gil, R., Hackett, E., Girgis, R., Ojeil, N., Moore, H., D'Souza, D., Malison, R. T., Huang, Y., Lim, K., Nabulsi, N., Carson, R. E., Lieberman, J. A., & Abi-Dargham, A. (2015). Deficits in Prefrontal Cortical and Extrastriatal Dopamine Release in Schizophrenia. *JAMA Psychiatry*, *72*(4), 316. https://doi.org/10.1001/jamapsychiatry.2014.2414

Rocco, B. R., DeDionisio, A. M., Lewis, D. A., & Fish, K. N. (2017). Alterations in a Unique Class of Cortical Chandelier Cell Axon Cartridges in Schizophrenia. Biological Psychiatry, 82(1), 40–48. https://doi.org/10.1016/j.biopsych.2016.09.018

Martínez, A., Gaspar, P. A., Hillyard, S. A., Andersen, S. K., Lopez-Calderon, J., Corcoran, C. M., & Javitt, D. C. (2018). Impaired Motion Processing in Schizophrenia and the Attenuated Psychosis Syndrome: Etiological and Clinical Implications. *The American journal of psychiatry*, *175*(12), 1243–1254. https://doi.org/10.1176/appi.ajp.2018.18010072

Siemerkus, Jakob & Irle, Eva & Schmidt-Samoa, Carsten & Dechent, Peter & Weniger, Godehard. (2012). Egocentric spatial learning in schizophrenia investigated with functional magnetic resonance imaging. NeuroImage: Clinical. 1 DOI:10.1016/j.nicl.2012.10.004

Brady, R. O., Jr, Gonsalvez, I., Lee, I., Öngür, D., Seidman, L. J., Schmahmann, J. D., Eack, S. M., Keshavan, M. S., Pascual-Leone, A., & Halko, M. A. (2019). Cerebellar-Prefrontal Network Connectivity and Negative Symptoms in Schizophrenia. *The American journal of psychiatry*, *176*(7), 512–520. https://doi.org/10.1176/appi.ajp.2018.18040429

Hamilton, H. K., Williams, T. J., Ventura, J., Jasperse, L. J., Owens, E. M., Miller, G. A., Subotnik, K. L., Nuechterlein, K. H., & Yee, C. M. (2018). Clinical and Cognitive Significance of Auditory Sensory Processing Deficits in Schizophrenia. *The American journal of psychiatry*, *175*(3), 275–283. https://doi.org/10.1176/appi.ajp.2017.16111203

Ren, Z., Zhang, Y., He, H., Feng, Q., Bi, T., & Qiu, J. (2019). The Different Brain Mechanisms of Object and Spatial Working Memory: Voxel-Based Morphometry and Resting-State Functional Connectivity. *Frontiers in Human*

Neuroscience, 13. https://doi.org/10.3389/fnhum.2019.00248
Zhai, J., Zhang, Q., Cheng, L., Chen, M., Wang, K., Liu, Y., Deng, X., Chen, X., Shen, Q., Xu, Z., Ji, F., Liu, C., Dong, Q., Chen, C., & Li, J. (2011). Risk variants in the S100B gene, associated with elevated S100B levels, are also associated with visuospatial disability of schizophrenia. *Behavioural brain research, 217*(2), 363–368. https://doi.org/10.1016/j.bbr.2010.11.004
https://www.sciencedirect.com/science/article/abs/pii/S016643281000728X?via%3Dihub
Ursu, S., Kring, A. M., Gard, M. G., Minzenberg, M. J., Yoon, J. H., Ragland, J. D., Solomon, M., & Carter, C. S. (2011). Prefrontal Cortical Deficits and Impaired Cognition-Emotion Interactions in Schizophrenia. *American Journal of Psychiatry, 168*(3), 276–285.
https://doi.org/10.1176/appi.ajp.2010.09081215
Yoon, J. H., Minzenberg, M. J., Ursu, S., Walters, R., Wendelken, C., Ragland, J. D., & Carter, C. S. (2008). Association of Dorsolateral Prefrontal Cortex Dysfunction With Disrupted Coordinated Brain Activity in Schizophrenia: Relationship With Impaired Cognition, Behavioral Disorganization, and Global Function. *American Journal of Psychiatry, 165*(8), 1006–1014. https://doi.org/10.1176/appi.ajp.2008.07060945
Gold J. M. (2011). Imaging emotion in schizophrenia: not finding feelings in all the right places. *The American journal of psychiatry, 168*(3), 237–239. https://doi.org/10.1176/appi.ajp.2010.10111653
https://ajp.psychiatryonline.org/doi/full/10.1176/appi.ajp.2010.10111653
Kochunov, P., Coyle, T. R., Rowland, L. M., Jahanshad, N., Thompson, P. M., Kelly, S., Du, X., Sampath, H., Bruce, H., Chiappelli, J., Ryan, M., Fisseha, F., Savransky, A., Adhikari, B., Chen, S., Paciga, S. A., Whelan, C. D., Xie, Z., Hyde, C. L., ... Hong, L. E. (2017). Association of White Matter With Core Cognitive Deficits in Patients With Schizophrenia. JAMA Psychiatry, 74(9), 958. https://doi.org/10.1001/jamapsychiatry.2017.2228
Ferrarelli, F., Sarasso, S., Guller, Y., Riedner, B. A., Peterson, M. J., Bellesi, M., Massimini, M., Postle, B. R., & Tononi, G. (2012). Reduced Natural Oscillatory Frequency of Frontal Thalamocortical Circuits in Schizophrenia. *Archives of General Psychiatry, 69*(8). https://doi.org/10.1001/archgenpsychiatry.2012.147
Ferrarelli, F., Peterson, M. J., Sarasso, S., Riedner, B. A., Murphy, M. J., Benca, R. M., Bria, P., Kalin, N. H., & Tononi, G. (2010). Thalamic Dysfunction in Schizophrenia Suggested by Whole-Night Deficits in Slow and Fast Spindles. *American Journal of Psychiatry, 167*(11), 1339–1348. https://doi.org/10.1176/appi.ajp.2010.09121731
Anticevic, A., Haut, K., Murray, J. D., Repovs, G., Yang, G. J., Diehl, C., McEwen, S. C., Bearden, C. E., Addington, J., Goodyear, B., Cadenhead, K. S., Mirzakhanian, H., Cornblatt, B. A., Olvet, D., Mathalon, D. H., McGlashan, T. H., Perkins, D. O., Belger, A., Seidman, L. J., Tsuang, M. T., ... Cannon, T. D. (2015). Association of Thalamic Dysconnectivity and Conversion to Psychosis

in Youth and Young Adults at Elevated Clinical Risk. *JAMA psychiatry*, *72*(9), 882–891. https://doi.org/10.1001/jamapsychiatry.2015.0566

Keshavan, M. S., & Paus, T. (2015). Neurodevelopmental Trajectories, Disconnection, and Schizophrenia Risk. *JAMA psychiatry*, *72*(9), 943–945. https://doi.org/10.1001/jamapsychiatry.2015.1119

Woodward, N. D., & Cascio, C. J. (2015). Resting-State Functional Connectivity in Psychiatric Disorders. *JAMA psychiatry*, *72*(8), 743–744. https://doi.org/10.1001/jamapsychiatry.2015.0484

Kraguljac NV, McDonald WM, Widge AS, Rodriguez CI, Tohen M, Nemeroff CB. Neuroimaging Biomarkers in Schizophrenia. Am J Psychiatry. 2021 Jun;178(6):509-521. https://doi.org/10.1176/appi.ajp.2020.20030340

Arnsten, A., & Wang, M. (2020). The Evolutionary Expansion of mGluR3-NAAG-GCPII Signaling: Relevance to Human Intelligence and Cognitive Disorders. *The American journal of psychiatry*, *177*(12), 1103–1106. https://doi.org/10.1176/appi.ajp.2020.20101458

Klingberg, T., & McNab, F. (2009). Working Memory Remediation and the D1 Receptor. *American Journal of Psychiatry*, *166*(5), 515–515. https://doi.org/10.1176/appi.ajp.2009.09030343

Julayanont, P., Ruthirago, D., Alam, K., & Alderazi, Y. J. (2017). Behavioral Disconnection Syndrome Manifesting as Combined Mania and Visual-Auditory Hallucinations Secondary to Isolated Right Thalamic Hemorrhage. *The Journal of neuropsychiatry and clinical neurosciences*, *29*(4), 401–408. https://doi.org/10.1176/appi.neuropsych.16110308

Kang, D., Ding, M., Topchiy, I., Shifflett, L., & Kocsis, B. (2015). Theta-rhythmic drive between medial septum and hippocampus in slow-wave sleep and microarousal: a Granger causality analysis. *Journal of Neurophysiology*, *114*(5), 2797–2803. https://doi.org/10.1152/jn.00542.2015

Buzsáki, G. (2002). Theta Oscillations in the Hippocampus. *Neuron*, *33*(3), 325–340. https://doi.org/10.1016/s0896-6273(02)00586-x

Ferrarelli, F., Massimini, M., Peterson, M. J., Riedner, B. A., Lazar, M., Murphy, M. J., Huber, R., Rosanova, M., Alexander, A. L., Kalin, N., & Tononi, G. (2008). Reduced Evoked Gamma Oscillations in the Frontal Cortex in Schizophrenia Patients: A TMS/EEG Study. *American Journal of Psychiatry*, *165*(8), 996–1005. https://doi.org/10.1176/appi.ajp.2008.07111733

Woodward, N. D., Karbasforoushan, H., & Heckers, S. (2012). Thalamocortical Dysconnectivity in Schizophrenia. *American Journal of Psychiatry*, *169*(10), 1092–1099. https://doi.org/10.1176/appi.ajp.2012.12010056

Guller, Y., Ferrarelli, F., Shackman, A. J., Sarasso, S., Peterson, M. J., Langheim, F. J., Meyerand, M. E., Tononi, G., & Postle, B. R. (2012). Probing Thalamic Integrity in Schizophrenia Using Concurrent Transcranial Magnetic Stimulation and Functional Magnetic Resonance Imaging. *Archives of General Psychiatry*, *69*(7). https://doi.org/10.1001/archgenpsychiatry.2012.23

DANCKERT, J. (2004). Attention, motor control and motor imagery in schizophrenia: implications for the role of the parietal cortex. *Schizophrenia Research, 70*(2–3), 241–261. https://doi.org/10.1016/j.schres.2003.12.007

Bossong, M. G., Antoniades, M., Azis, M., Samson, C., Quinn, B., Bonoldi, I., Modinos, G., Perez, J., Howes, O. D., Stone, J. M., Allen, P., & McGuire, P. (2019). Association of Hippocampal Glutamate Levels With Adverse Outcomes in Individuals at Clinical High Risk for Psychosis. *JAMA psychiatry, 76*(2), 199–207. https://doi.org/10.1001/jamapsychiatry.2018.3252

Lisman, J. E., & Grace, A. A. (2005). The Hippocampal-VTA Loop: Controlling the Entry of Information into Long-Term Memory. *Neuron, 46*(5), 703–713. https://doi.org/10.1016/j.neuron.2005.05.002

Kupferschmidt, D. A., & Gordon, J. A. (2018). The dynamics of disordered dialogue: Prefrontal, hippocampal and thalamic miscommunication working memory deficits. *Brain and neuroscience advances*. https://doi.org/10.1177/2398212818771821

Funahashi S. (2013). Thalamic mediodorsal nucleus and its participation in spatial working memory processes: comparison with the prefrontal cortex. *Frontiers in systems neuroscience, 7*, 36. https://doi.org/10.3389/fnsys.2013.00036

Pu, W., Rolls, E. T., Guo, S., Liu, H., Yu, Y., Xue, Z., Feng, J., & Liu, Z. (2014). Altered functional connectivity links in neuroleptic-naïve and neuroleptic-treated patients with schizophrenia, and their relation to symptoms including volition. *NeuroImage. Clinical, 6*, 463–474. https://doi.org/10.1016/j.nicl.2014.10.004

Mazza, M., Catalucci, A., Pino, M. C., Giusti, L., Nigri, A., Pollice, R., Roncone, R., Casacchia, M., & Gallucci, M. (2013). Dysfunctional neural networks associated with impaired social interactions in early psychosis: an ICA analysis. *Brain imaging and behavior, 7*(3), 248–259. https://doi.org/10.1007/s11682-013-9223-6 resting state fMRI and cerebellum

Penner, J., Osuch, E. A., Schaefer, B., Théberge, J., Neufeld, R., Menon, R. S., Rajakumar, N., Bourne, J. A., & Williamson, P. C. (2018). Higher order thalamic nuclei resting network connectivity in early schizophrenia and major depressive disorder. *Psychiatry research. Neuroimaging, 272*, 7–16. https://doi.org/10.1016/j.pscychresns.2017.12.002

Palaniyappan, L., Simmonite, M., White, T. P., Liddle, E. B., & Liddle, P. F. (2013). Neural primacy of the salience processing system in schizophrenia. *Neuron, 79*(4), 814–828. https://doi.org/10.1016/j.neuron.2013.06.027

Anticevic, A., Gancsos, M., Murray, J. D., Repovs, G., Driesen, N. R., Ennis, D. J., Niciu, M. J., Morgan, P. T., Surti, T. S., Bloch, M. H., Ramani, R., Smith, M. A., Wang, X. J., Krystal, J. H., & Corlett, P. R. (2012). NMDA receptor function in large-scale anticorrelated neural systems with implications for cognition and schizophrenia. *Proceedings of the National Academy of Sciences of the United States of America, 109*(41), 16720–16725. https://doi.org/10.1073/pnas.1208494109

Pei-Chi Tu, Ying-Chiao Lee, Ying-Shiue Chen, Cheng-Ta Li,

References

Tung-Ping Su,Schizophrenia and the brain's control network: Aberrant within- and between-network connectivity of the frontoparietal network in schizophrenia,Schizophrenia Research,Volume 147, Issues 2–3,2013,Pages 339-347 https://doi.org/10.1016/j.schres.2013.04.011

Galindo, L., Bergé, D., Murray, G. K., Mané, A., Bulbena, A., Pérez, V., & Vilarroya, O. (2018). Default Mode Network Aberrant Connectivity Associated with Neurological Soft Signs in Schizophrenia Patients and Unaffected Relatives. *Frontiers in psychiatry*, *8*, 298. https://doi.org/10.3389/fpsyt.2017.00298

Waltz, J. A., Kasanova, Z., Ross, T. J., Salmeron, B. J., McMahon, R. P., Gold, J. M., & Stein, E. A. (2013). The roles of reward, default, and executive control networks in set-shifting impairments in schizophrenia. *PloS one*, *8*(2), e57257. https://doi.org/10.1371/journal.pone.0057257

60) Zanelli, J., Mollon, J., Sandin, S., Morgan, C., Dazzan, P., Pilecka, I., Reis Marques, T., David, A. S., Morgan, K., Fearon, P., Doody, G. A., Jones, P. B., Murray, R. M., & Reichenberg, A. (2019). Cognitive Change in Schizophrenia and Other Psychoses in the Decade Following the First Episode. *The American journal of psychiatry*, *176*(10), 811–819. https://doi.org/10.1176/appi.ajp.2019.18091088

Cai, L., & Huang, J. (2018). Schizophrenia and risk of dementia: a meta-analysis study. *Neuropsychiatric Disease and Treatment*, *Volume 14*, 2047–2055. https://doi.org/10.2147/ndt.s172933

Ribe, A. R., Laursen, T. M., Charles, M., Katon, W., Fenger-Grøn, M., Davydow, D., Chwastiak, L., Cerimele, J. M., & Vestergaard, M. (2015). Long-term Risk of Dementia in Persons With Schizophrenia. *JAMA Psychiatry*, *72*(11), 1095. https://doi.org/10.1001/jamapsychiatry.2015.1546

Lin, C.-E., Chung, C.-H., Chen, L.-F., & Chi, M.-J. (2018). Increased risk of dementia in patients with Schizophrenia: A population-based cohort study in Taiwan. *European Psychiatry*, *53*, 7–16. https://doi.org/10.1016/j.eurpsy.2018.05.005

Spreng, R. N., DuPre, E., Ji, J. L., Yang, G., Diehl, C., Murray, J. D., Pearlson, G. D., & Anticevic, A. (2019). Structural Covariance Reveals Alterations in Control and Salience Network Integrity in Chronic Schizophrenia. *Cerebral cortex (New York, N.Y. : 1991)*, *29*(12), 5269–5284. https://doi.org/10.1093/cercor/bhz064

Winkelbeiner, S., Leucht, S., Kane, J. M., & Homan, P. (2019). Evaluation of Differences in Individual Treatment: A Meta-analysis. *JAMA psychiatry*, *76*(10), 1063–1073. https://doi.org/10.1001/jamapsychiatry.2019.1530

61) Velligan, D., Carpenter, W., Waters, H. C., Gerlanc, N. M., Legacy, S. N., & Ruetsch, C. (2018). Relapse Risk Assessment for Schizophrenia Patients (RASP): A New Self-Report Screening Tool. *Clinical Schizophrenia & Related Psychoses*, *11*(4), 224–235. https://doi.org/10.3371/CSRP.DVWC.111717

Ortiz, B. B., Gadelha, A., Higuchi, C. H., Noto, C., Medeiros, D., Pitta, J., de Araújo Filho, G. M., Hallak, J., & Bressan, R. A. (2017). Disorganized Symptoms Predicted Worse Functioning Outcome in Schizophrenia Patients with Established Illness. *Clinical schizophrenia & related psychoses*, *11*(3), 151–155. https://doi.org/10.3371/CSRP.ORGA.022015

Kotov, R., Fochtmann, L., Li, K., Tanenberg-Karant, M., Constantino, E. A., Rubinstein, J., Perlman, G., Velthorst, E., Fett, A. J., Carlson, G., & Bromet, E. J. (2017). Declining Clinical Course of Psychotic Disorders Over the Two Decades Following First Hospitalization: Evidence From the Suffolk County Mental Health Project. *The American journal of psychiatry*, *174*(11), 1064–1074. https://doi.org/10.1176/appi.ajp.2017.16101191

62) Zipursky, R. B., Agid, O., & Remington, G. (2018). Improving outcomes in schizophrenia by preventing early relapses. *The lancet. Psychiatry*, *5*(5), 384–386. https://doi.org/10.1016/S2215-0366(18)30124-X

Zipursky, R. B., Reilly, T. J., & Murray, R. M. (2013). The myth of schizophrenia as a progressive brain disease. *Schizophrenia bulletin*, *39*(6), 1363–1372. https://doi.org/10.1093/schbul/sbs135

Galderisi, S., Rucci, P., Kirkpatrick, B., Mucci, A., Gibertoni, D., Rocca, P., Rossi, A., Bertolino, A., Strauss, G. P., Aguglia, E., Bellomo, A., Murri, M. B., Bucci, P., Carpiniello, B., Comparelli, A., Cuomo, A., De Berardis, D., Dell'Osso, L., Di Fabio, F., Gelao, B., ... Italian Network for Research on Psychoses (2018). Interplay Among Psychopathologic Variables, Personal Resources, Context-Related Factors, and Real-life Functioning in Individuals With Schizophrenia: A Network Analysis. *JAMA psychiatry*, *75*(4), 396–404. https://doi.org/10.1001/jamapsychiatry.2017.4607

Kirkpatrick, B., Miller, B., García-Rizo, C., & Fernandez-Egea, E. (2014). Schizophrenia. *Clinical Schizophrenia & Related Psychoses*, *8*(2), 73–79. https://doi.org/10.3371/csrp.kimi.031513

Olfson, M., Gerhard, T., Huang, C., Crystal, S., & Stroup, T. S. (2015). Premature Mortality Among Adults With Schizophrenia in the United States. *JAMA Psychiatry*, *72*(12), 1172. https://doi.org/10.1001/jamapsychiatry.2015.1737

Kulhara, P., & Gupta, S. (2010). What is schizophrenia: A neurodevelopmental or neurodegenerative disorder or a combination of both? A critical analysis. *Indian Journal of Psychiatry*, *52*(1), 21. https://doi.org/10.4103/0019-5545.58891

Relapse Risk Assessment for Schizophrenia Patients (RASP): A New Self-Report Screening Tool. - PubMed - NCBI

Harvey, P. D., Helldin, L., Bowie, C. R., Heaton, R. K., Olsson, A.-K., Hjärthag, F., Norlander, T., & Patterson, T. L. (2009). Performance-Based Measurement of Functional Disability in Schizophrenia: A Cross-National Study in the United States and Sweden. *American Journal of Psychiatry*, *166*(7), 821–827. https://doi.org/10.1176/appi.ajp.2009.09010106

Tiihonen J, Mittendorfer-Rutz E, Torniainen M, Alexanderson K, Tanskanen

References

A. Mortality and Cumulative Exposure to Antipsychotics, Antidepressants, and Benzodiazepines in Patients With Schizophrenia: An Observational Follow-Up Study. Am J Psychiatry. 2016 Jun 1;173(6):600-6. doi: 10.1176/appi. ajp.2015.15050618. Epub 2015 Dec 7. PMID:26651392https://ajp.psychiatryonline.org/doi/10.1176/appi.ajp.2015.15050618

Schnack, H. G., van Haren, N. E., Nieuwenhuis, M., Hulshoff Pol, H. E., Cahn, W., & Kahn, R. S. (2016). Accelerated Brain Aging in Schizophrenia: A Longitudinal Pattern Recognition Study. *The American journal of psychiatry*, *173*(6), 607–616. https://doi.org/10.1176/appi.ajp.2015.15070922

Green M. F. (2016). Impact of cognitive and social cognitive impairment on functional outcomes in patients with schizophrenia. *The Journal of clinical psychiatry*, *77 Suppl 2*, 8–11. https://doi.org/10.4088/JCP.14074su1c.02

Keefe RS,The longitudinal course of cognitive impairment in schizophrenia: an examination of data from premorbid through posttreatment phases of illness.The Journal of Clinical Psychiatry, 01 Jan 2014, 75 DOI: 10.4088/jcp.13065su1.02

Brian Kirkpatrick, Brian J. Miller, Inflammation and Schizophrenia, *Schizophrenia Bulletin*, Volume 39, Issue 6, November 2013, Pages 1174–1179, https://doi.org/10.1093/schbul/sbt141

Lieberman, J. A., Small, S. A., & Girgis, R. R. (2019). Early Detection and Preventive Intervention in Schizophrenia: From Fantasy to Reality. *The American journal of psychiatry*, *176*(10), 794–810. https://doi.org/10.1176/appi.ajp.2019.19080865

Zipursky RB. Why are the outcomes in patients with schizophrenia so poor? J Clin Psychiatry. 2014;75 doi: 10.4088/JCP.13065su1.05

Wyatt R. J. (1991). Neuroleptics and the natural course of schizophrenia. *Schizophrenia bulletin*, *17*(2), 325–351. https://doi.org/10.1093/schbul/17.2.325

Wyatt, R. J., & Henter, I. D. (1998). The effects of early and sustained intervention on the long-term morbidity of schizophrenia. *Journal of psychiatric research*, *32*(3-4), 169–177. https://doi.org/10.1016/s0022-3956(97)00014-9

Tiihonen, J., Lönnqvist, J., Wahlbeck, K., Klaukka, T., Niskanen, L., Tanskanen, A., & Haukka, J. (2009). 11-year follow-up of mortality in patients with schizophrenia: a population-based cohort study (FIN11 study). *Lancet (London, England)*, *374*(9690), 620–627. https://doi.org/10.1016/S0140-6736(09)60742-X

63) Reddy M. S. (2014). Attenuated psychosis syndrome. *Indian journal of psychological medicine*, *36*(1), 1–3. https://doi.org/10.4103/0253-7176.127239

Salazar de Pablo, G., Guinart, D., Cornblatt, B. A., Auther, A. M., Carrión, R. E., Carbon, M., Jiménez-Fernández, S., Vernal, D. L., Walitza, S., Gerstenberg, M., Saba, R., Lo Cascio, N., Brandizzi, M., Arango, C., Moreno, C., Van Meter, A., Fusar-Poli, P., & Correll, C. U. (2020). DSM-5 Attenuated Psychosis Syndrome in Adolescents Hospitalized With Non-psychotic Psychiatric Disorders. *Frontiers in psychiatry*, *11*, 568982. https://doi.org/10.3389/fpsyt.2020.568982

Salazar de Pablo, G., Catalan, A., & Fusar-Poli, P. (2020). Clinical Validity of DSM-5 Attenuated Psychosis Syndrome: Advances in Diagnosis, Prognosis, and Treatment. *JAMA psychiatry*, *77*(3), 311–320. https://doi.org/10.1001/jamapsychiatry.2019.3561

64) Buchanan, A., Sint, K., Swanson, J., & Rosenheck, R. (2019). Correlates of Future Violence in People Being Treated for Schizophrenia. *The American journal of psychiatry*, *176*(9), 694–701. https://doi.org/10.1176/appi.ajp.2019.18080909
https://doi.org/10.1176/appi.ajp.2019.18080909

Appelbaum P. S. (2019). In Search of a New Paradigm for Research on Violence and Schizophrenia. *The American journal of psychiatry*, *176*(9), 677–679. https://doi.org/10.1176/appi.ajp.2019.19070678
https://doi.org/10.1176/appi.ajp.2019.19070678

Pinkham, A. E., Liu, P., Lu, H., Kriegsman, M., Simpson, C., & Tamminga, C. (2015). Amygdala Hyperactivity at Rest in Paranoid Individuals With Schizophrenia. *The American journal of psychiatry*, *172*(8), 784–792. https://doi.org/10.1176/appi.ajp.2014.14081000

Grant, P. M., Huh, G. A., Perivoliotis, D., Stolar, N. M., & Beck, A. T. (2012). Randomized trial to evaluate the efficacy of cognitive therapy for low-functioning patients with schizophrenia. *Archives of General Psychiatry*, *69*(2), 121–127. https://doi.org/10.1001/archgenpsychiatry.2011.129

In an essay, Deborah Danner, who was killed in a police shooting, once described the challenges of living with mental illness, including interacting with law enforcement.Living-With-Schizophrenia-by-Deborah-Danner.pdf
https://www.nytimes.com/2016/09/22/well/live/living-with-schizophrenia-my-fathers-perfect-family.html

CHAPTER FIVE REFERENCES

1) Sujana Reddy, & Sandeep Sharma. (2018, October 27). *Physiology, Circadian Rhythm*. Nih.Gov; StatPearls Publishing.
https://www.ncbi.nlm.nih.gov/books/NBK519507/
https://www.livescience.com/8639-change-seasons-affects-animals-humans.html
Ebling F. J. (2015). Hypothalamic control of seasonal changes in food intake and body weight. *Frontiers in neuroendocrinology*, *37*, 97–107. https://doi.org/10.1016/j.yfrne.2014.10.003

Shinomiya, A., Shimmura, T., Nishiwaki-Ohkawa, T., & Yoshimura, T. (2014). Regulation of seasonal reproduction by hypothalamic activation of thyroid hormone. *Frontiers in endocrinology*, *5*, 12. https://doi.org/10.3389/fendo.2014.00012

2) Burton, S. A., Harsh, J. R., & Badia, P. (1988). Cognitive activity in sleep and responsiveness to external stimuli. *Sleep*, *11*(1), 61–68.

References

3) The different terms refer to the behavior of focusing on a stimulus, or the subjective awareness, or both. See later sections.
4) Ellenberger, Henri F. (1970). **The Discovery of the Unconscious: The History and Evolution of Dynamic Psychiatry**. New York: Basic Books. Ellenberger H. (1957). The unconscious before Freud. *Bulletin of the Menninger Clinic*, 21(1), 3–15.
5) Similar explorations were taking place in other fields of the social sciences surveyed *in*
Hughes, H. Stuart (1958). ***Consciousness and Society: The Reorientation of European Social Thought***, 1890-1930. Octagon Books.
Lindsay Grace W., Attention in Psychology, Neuroscience, and Machine Learning, Frontiers in Computational Neuroscience,14, 2020 https://www.frontiersin.org/article/10.3389/fncom.2020.00029
6) Petersen, S. E., & Posner, M. I. (2012). The attention system of the human brain: 20 years after. *Annual review of neuroscience*, 35, 73–89. https://doi.org/10.1146/annurev-neuro-062111-150525 *https://www.ncbi.nlm.nih.gov/pmc/articles/PMC3413263/*
https://www.semanticscholar.org/paper/The-attention-system-of-the-human-brain.-Posner-Petersen/94f1cbb8e88f524efe2a9034e25c1f83a6b2abf3?p2df
7) Posner, M. I., & Rothbart, M. K. (2007). Research on attention networks as a model for the integration of psychological science. *Annual review of psychology*, 58, 1–23. https://doi.org/10.1146/annurev.psych.58.110405.085516
8) Raz, A., & Buhle, J. (2006). Typologies of attentional networks. *Nature reviews. Neuroscience*, 7(5), 367–379. https://doi.org/10.1038/nrn1903 http://razlab.mcgill.ca/docs/attentionalnetworks.pdf
9) Yeo, S. S., Chang, P. H., & Jang, S. H. (2013). The Ascending Reticular Activating System from Pontine Reticular Formation to the Thalamus in the Human Brain. *Frontiers in Human Neuroscience*, 7. https://doi.org/10.3389/fnhum.2013.00416
10) Kinomura, S., Larsson, J., Gulyás, B., & Roland, P. E. (1996). Activation by Attention of the Human Reticular Formation and Thalamic Intralaminar Nuclei. *Science*, 271(5248), 512–515.https://doi.org/10.1126/science.271.5248.512
C. M. Portas, G. Rees, A. M. Howseman, O. Josephs, R. Turner and C. D. Frith, A Specific Role for the Thalamus in Mediating the Interaction of Attention and Arousal in Humans, Journal of Neuroscience 1 November 1998, 18 (21) 8979-8989; https://doi.org/10.1523/JNEUROSCI.18-21-08979.1998
Van der Werf, Y. D., Witter, M. P., & Groenewegen, H. J. (2002). The intralaminar and midline nuclei of the thalamus. Anatomical and functional evidence for participation in processes of arousal and awareness. *Brain research. Brain research reviews*, 39(2-3), 107–140. https://doi.org/10.1016/s0165-0173(02)00181-9 http://neuroscience.uth.tmc.edu/s3/chapter08.html
Liu, X., de Zwart, J.A., Schölvinck, M.L. *et al.* Subcortical evidence for a

contribution of arousal to fMRI studies of brain activity. *Nat Commun* **9**, 395 (2018). https://doi.org/10.1038/s41467-017-02815-3

11) Brown, E. N., Lydic, R., & Schiff, N. D. (2010). General anesthesia, sleep, and coma. *The New England journal of medicine*, *363*(27), 2638–2650. https://doi.org/10.1056/NEJMra0808281

12) Valdez P. (2019). Circadian Rhythms in Attention. *The Yale journal of biology and medicine*, *92*(1), 81–92.

13) Michael I. Posner and Steven E. Petersen, **The attention system of the human brain.**
Annual Review of Neuroscience Vol. 13:25-42 https://doi.org/10.1146/annurev.ne.13.030190.000325
Posner (1990) The attentional system of the human brain -bdb79ce-324a4e1c6f44353e5aaee0f164ad9.pdf
http://www.cogsci.ucsd.edu/~coulson/101b/VisualAttention.pdf

14) Schmid, S., Wilson, D. A., & Rankin, C. H. (2015). Habituation mechanisms and their importance for cognitive function. *Frontiers in integrative neuroscience*, *8*, 97. https://doi.org/10.3389/fnint.2014.00097

15) >>REF #30

16) Sokolov, E.N., Nezlina, N.I., Polyanskii, V.B. et al. The Orientating Reflex: The "Targeting Reaction" and "Searchlight of Attention". *Neurosci Behav Physiol* **32**, 347–362 (2002). https://doi.org/10.1023/A:1015820025297
Bradley M. M. (2009). Natural selective attention. *Psychophysiology*, *46*(1), 1–11. https://doi.org/10.1111/j.1469-8986.2008.00702.x
Nalivaiko, E., Bondarenko, E., Lidström, A., & Barry, R. J. (2012). Respiratory component of the orienting reflex: a novel sensitive index of sensory-induced arousal in rats. *Frontiers in physiology*, *2*, 114. https://doi.org/10.3389/fphys.2011.00114

17) Näätänen, R., & Michie, P. T. (1979). Early selective-attention effects on the evoked potential: a critical review and reinterpretation. *Biological psychology*, *8*(2), 81–136. https://doi.org/10.1016/0301-0511(79)90053-x
Walsh P, Kane N, Butler S, The clinical role of evoked potentials, Journal of Neurology, Neurosurgery & Psychiatry 2005;76:ii16-ii22. https://jnnp.bmj.com/content/76/suppl_2/ii16.full

18) Razran G. (1961). The observable unconscious and the inferable conscious in current Soviet psychophysiology: interoceptive conditioning, semantic conditioning, and the orienting reflex. *Psychological review*, *68*, 1–147. https://pubmed.ncbi.nlm.nih.gov/13740033/

19) *Norman, Donald A., Toward a theory of memory and attention. Psychological Review, Vol 75(6), Nov 1968, 522-536.* doi: 10.1037/h0026699
Kemp, I. R., & Kaada, B. R. (1975). The relation of hippocampal theta activity to arousal, attentive behaviour and somato-motor movements in unrestrained cats. *Brain research*, *95*(2-3), 323–342. https://doi.org/10.1016/0006-8993(75)90110-9

References

Bygrave, A.M., Jahans-Price, T., Wolff, A.R. et al. Hippocampal–prefrontal coherence mediates working memory and selective attention at distinct frequency bands and provides a causal link between schizophrenia and its risk gene *GRIA1*. *Transl Psychiatry* **9**, 142 (2019). https://doi.org/10.1038/s41398-019-0471-0

Alex Kafkas, Andrew R Mayes, Daniela Montaldi, Thalamic-Medial Temporal Lobe Connectivity Underpins Familiarity Memory, *Cerebral Cortex*, Volume 30, Issue 6, June 2020, Pages 3827–3837, https://doi.org/10.1093/cercor/bhz345

Barron, D. S., Tandon, N., Lancaster, J. L., & Fox, P. T. (2014). Thalamic structural connectivity in medial temporal lobe epilepsy. *Epilepsia*, *55*(6), e50–e55. https://doi.org/10.1111/epi.12637 https://www.ncbi.nlm.nih.gov/pmc/articles/PMC4791041/

20) Mennemeier, M. S., Chatterjee, A., Watson, R. T., Wertman, E., Carter, L. P., & Heilman, K. M. (1994). Contributions of the parietal and frontal lobes to sustained attention and habituation. *Neuropsychologia*, *32*(6), 703–716. https://doi.org/10.1016/0028-3932(94)90030-2 https://pubmed.ncbi.nlm.nih.gov/8084425/

Shuhei Yamaguchi, Laura A. Hale, Mark D'Esposito, Robert T. Knight, Rapid Prefrontal-Hippocampal Habituation to Novel Events
Journal of Neuroscience 9 June 2004, 24 (23) 5356-5363; DOI: https://doi.org/10.1523/JNEUROSCI.4587-03.2004

21) https://en.wikipedia.org/wiki/Sensory_deprivation

Brown, R., Milner, P. The legacy of Donald O. Hebb: more than the Hebb Synapse. *Nat Rev Neurosci* **4**, 1013–1019 (2003). https://doi.org/10.1038/nrn1257

Josef P. Rauschecker,Sensory Deprivation,Reference Module in Neuroscience and Biobehavioral Psychology,Elsevier,2018,
ISBN 9780128093245, https://doi.org/10.1016/B978-0-12-809324-5.03164-3

22) Fiske, Donald & Maddi, Salvatore. (1961). *The Functions of Varied Experience*. The American Journal of Psychology. 76. 10.2307/1419183.https://www.researchgate.net/publication/232418803_The_Functions_of_Varied_Experience

23) Mather E. (2013). Novelty, attention, and challenges for developmental psychology. *Frontiers in psychology*, *4*, 491. https://doi.org/10.3389/fpsyg.2013.00491

Khachiyants, N., Trinkle, D., Son, S. J., & Kim, K. Y. (2011). Sundown syndrome in persons with dementia: an update. *Psychiatry investigation*, *8*(4), 275–287. https://doi.org/10.4306/pi.2011.8.4.275

24) Calcott, R. D., & Berkman, E. T. (2014). Attentional flexibility during approach and avoidance motivational states: the role of context in shifts of attentional breadth. *Journal of experimental psychology. General*, *143*(3), 1393–1408. https://doi.org/10.1037/a0035060

25) Kluetsch, R. C., Schmahl, C., Niedtfeld, I., Densmore, M., Calhoun, V. D., Daniels, J., Kraus, A., Ludaescher, P., Bohus, M., & Lanius, R. A. (2012). Alterations in Default Mode Network Connectivity During Pain Processing in

Borderline Personality Disorder. *Archives of General Psychiatry, 69*(10), 993–1002. https://doi.org/10.1001/archgenpsychiatry.2012.476

26) Sawe, N., & Knutson, B. (2015). Neural valuation of environmental resources. *NeuroImage, 122*, 87–95. https://doi.org/10.1016/j.neuroimage.2015.08.010

27) Menon V., & Uddin, L. Q. (2010). Saliency, switching, attention and control: a network model of insula function. *Brain Structure and Function, 214*(5–6), 655–667. https://doi.org/10.1007/s00429-010-0262-0

William W. Seeley, The Salience Network: A Neural System for Perceiving and Responding to Homeostatic Demands,
Journal of Neuroscience 11 December 2019, 39 (50) 9878-9882; DOI: https://doi.org/10.1523/JNEUROSCI.1138-17.2019

28) Greicius, M. D., Supekar, K., Menon, V., & Dougherty, R. F. (2008). Resting-State Functional Connectivity Reflects Structural Connectivity in the Default Mode Network. *Cerebral Cortex, 19*(1), 72–78. https://doi.org/10.1093/cercor/bhn059

Nord, C. L., Lawson, R. P., & Dalgleish, T. (2021). Disrupted Dorsal Mid-Insula Activation During Interoception Across Psychiatric Disorders. *The American journal of psychiatry, 178*(8), 761–770. https://doi.org/10.1176/appi.ajp.2020.20091340

Paulus, M. P., & Khalsa, S. S. (2021). When You Don't Feel Right Inside: Homeostatic Dysregulation and the Mid-Insular Cortex in Psychiatric Disorders. *The American journal of psychiatry, 178*(8), 683–685. https://doi.org/10.1176/appi.ajp.2021.21060622

McTeague, L. M., Huemer, J., Carreon, D. M., Jiang, Y., Eickhoff, S. B., & Etkin, A. (2017). Identification of Common Neural Circuit Disruptions in Cognitive Control Across Psychiatric Disorders. *The American journal of psychiatry, 174*(7), 676–685. https://doi.org/10.1176/appi.ajp.2017.16040400

Jerath, R., & Crawford, M. W. (2015). Layers of human brain activity: a functional model based on the default mode network and slow oscillations. *Frontiers in Human Neuroscience, 9*. https://doi.org/10.3389/fnhum.2015.00248

Mars, R. B., Neubert, F.-X., Noonan, M. P., Sallet, J., Toni, I., & Rushworth, M. F. S. (2012). On the relationship between the "default mode network" and the "social brain." *Frontiers in Human Neuroscience, 6*. https://doi.org/10.3389/fnhum.2012.00189

For more details of DMN see chapter three.

29) Petersen, S. E., & Posner, M. I. (2012). The attention system of the human brain: 20 years after. *Annual review of neuroscience, 35*, 73–89. https://doi.org/10.1146/annurev-neuro-062111-150525

Orquin, J. L., & Mueller Loose, S. (2013). Attention and choice: a review on eye movements in decision making. *Acta psychologica, 144*(1), 190–206. https://doi.org/10.1016/j.actpsy.2013.06.003

Hayward, D. A., & Ristic, J. (2013). Measuring attention using the Posner cuing paradigm: the role of across and within trial target probabilities. *Frontiers in*

References

human neuroscience, 7, 205. https://doi.org/10.3389/fnhum.2013.00205
Scarpina, F., & Tagini, S. (2017). The Stroop Color Test. *Frontiers in psychology*, 8, 557. https://doi.org/10.3389/fpsyg.2017.00557
Amso, D., & Scerif, G. (2015). The attentive brain: insights from developmental cognitive neuroscience. *Nature reviews. Neuroscience*, 16(10), 606–619. https://doi.org/10.1038/nrn4025
30) Crick, F., & Koch, C. (1990). Towards a neurobiological theory of consciousness. *Seminars in the Neurosciences*, 2, 263–275.
https://authors.library.caltech.edu/40352/
http://authors.library.caltech.edu/40352/1/148.pdf
31) In electronic computer systems, the **"operating system** (software)" is a control program to manage input, output, display, and interface with humans via devices, or other computer systems via networks. The program (in various forms DOS, Windows, Linux, Mac OS, etc) has control points activated by external signals and internal program controls.
32) https://en.wikipedia.org/wiki/Global_workspace_theory
http://cogweb.ucla.edu/CogSci/GWorkspace.html Contrasting approaches to Baars at http://www.scholarpedia.org/article/Models_of_consciousness
A full statement of the theory at:*https://www.cs.helsinki.fi/u/ahyvarin/teaching/niseminar4/Baars2004.pdf*
This reference addresses a broader view of animal consciousness:
https://aeon.co/essays/the-study-of-the-mind-needs-a-copernican-shift-in-perspective
33) Gazzaniga, M. S. (2019). *The consciousness instinct : unraveling the mystery of how the brain makes the mind.* **Farrar, Straus And Giroux,**
Blackmore, S. J. (2017). *Consciousness : a very short introduction*. Oxford University Press.
https://www.newyorker.com/magazine/2017/03/27/daniel-dennetts-science-of-the-soul
34) Posner, M. I. (2012). Attention Networks &Consciousness. *Frontiers in Psychology*, 3. https://doi.org/10.3389/fpsyg.2012.00064
http://www.pnas.org/content/91/16/7398.full.pdf
http://authors.library.caltech.edu/40485/1/28.pdf
van Boxtel, J. J. A., Tsuchiya, N., & Koch, C. (2010). Consciousness and Attention: On Sufficiency and Necessity. *Frontiers in Psychology*, 1. https://doi.org/10.3389/fpsyg.2010.00217
Graziano, M. S., & Webb, T. W. (2015). The attention schema theory: a mechanistic account of subjective awareness. *Frontiers in psychology*, 6, 500. https://doi.org/10.3389/fpsyg.2015.00500
Michael S. A. Graziano *Consciousness and the Social Brain , Oxford University Press*
35) https://www.ninds.nih.gov/Disorders/All-Disorders/Coma-Information-Page
Heine, L., Soddu, A., Gómez, F., Vanhaudenhuyse, A., Tshibanda, L., Thonnard,

M., Charland-Verville, V., Kirsch, M., Laureys, S., & Demertzi, A. (2012). Resting state networks and consciousness: alterations of multiple resting state network connectivity in physiological, pharmacological, and pathological consciousness states. *Frontiers in psychology, 3*, 295. https://doi.org/10.3389/fpsyg.2012.00295 https://www.ncbi.nlm.nih.gov/pmc/articles/PMC3427917/
36) Christof Koch. (2004). *The quest for consciousness a neurobiological approach.* Englewood Roberts And Company Publishers.
http://calteches.library.caltech.edu/4112/1/Consciousness.pdf
Koch, C. (2009). A Theory of Consciousness. *Scientific American Mind, 20*(4), 16–19. https://doi.org/10.1038/scientificamericanmind0709-16
Tononi, G. (2008). Consciousness as Integrated Information: a Provisional Manifesto. *The Biological Bulletin, 215*(3), 216–242. https://doi.org/10.2307/25470707
Specifically: (i) the quantity of consciousness corresponds to the amount of integrated information generated by a complex of elements; (ii) the quality of experience is specified by the set of informational relationships generated within that complex. Integrated information (Φ) is defined as the amount of information generated by a complex of elements, above and beyond the information generated by its parts.
Tononi, G., & Koch, C. (2015). Consciousness: here, there and everywhere?. *Philosophical transactions of the Royal Society of London. Series B, Biological sciences, 370*(1668), 20140167. https://doi.org/10.1098/rstb.2014.0167
Cerullo M. A. (2015). The Problem with Phi: A Critique of Integrated Information Theory. *PLoS computational biology, 11*(9), e1004286. https://doi.org/10.1371/journal.pcbi.1004286
Ramachandran, V. S. (2004). **A brief tour of human consciousness: From impostor poodles to purple numbers.** New York, NY, US: Pi Press, an imprint of Pearson Technology Group.
37) **References on DTPS and Mediodorsal N. Thalamus:**
Mitchell, A. S., & Chakraborty, S. (2013). What does the mediodorsal thalamus do?. *Frontiers in systems neuroscience, 7*, 37. https://doi.org/10.3389/fnsys.2013.00037
Pergola, G., Danet, L., Pitel, A. L., Carlesimo, G. A., Segobin, S., Pariente, J., Suchan, B., Mitchell, A. S., & Barbeau, E. J. (2018). The Regulatory Role of the Human Mediodorsal Thalamus. *Trends in cognitive sciences, 22*(11), 1011–1025. https://doi.org/10.1016/j.tics.2018.08.006
Mitchell A. S. (2015). The mediodorsal thalamus as a higher order thalamic relay nucleus important for learning and decision-making. *Neuroscience and biobehavioral reviews, 54*, 76–88. https://doi.org/10.1016/j.neubiorev.2015.03.001
de Bourbon-Teles, J., Bentley, P., Koshino, S., Shah, K., Dutta, A., Malhotra, P., Egner, T., Husain, M., & Soto, D. (2014). Thalamic control of human attention. *Current biology : CB, 24*(9), 993–999. https://doi.org/10.1016/j.cub.2014.03.024

References

Bolkan, S. S., Stujenske, J. M., Parnaudeau, S., Spellman, T. J., Rauffenbart, C., Abbas, A. I., Harris, A. Z., Gordon, J. A., & Kellendonk, C. (2017). Thalamic projections sustain prefrontal activity during working memory maintenance. *Nature neuroscience, 20*(7), 987–996. https://doi.org/10.1038/nn.4568

Basilis Zikopoulos, Helen Barbas, Pathways for Emotions and Attention Converge on the Thalamic Reticular Nucleus in Primates, Journal of Neuroscience 11 April 2012, 32 (15) 5338-5350; DOI: https://doi.org/10.1523/JNEUROSCI.4793-11.2012

Shepherd, G., & Yamawaki, N. (2021). Untangling the cortico-thalamo-cortical loop: cellular pieces of a knotty circuit puzzle. *Nature reviews. Neuroscience, 22*(7), 389–406. https://doi.org/10.1038/s41583-021-00459-3 https://www.nature.com/articles/s41583-021-00459-3?proof=tNature

Golosio, B., De Luca, C., Capone, C., Pastorelli, E., Stegel, G., Tiddia, G., De Bonis, G., & Paolucci, P. S. (2021). Thalamo-cortical spiking model of incremental learning combining perception, context and NREM-sleep. *PLoS computational biology, 17*(6), e1009045. https://doi.org/10.1371/journal.pcbi.1009045

Metzger, C. D., van der Werf, Y. D., & Walter, M. (2013). Functional mapping of thalamic nuclei and their integration into cortico-striatal-thalamo-cortical loops via ultra-high resolution imaging-from animal anatomy to in vivo imaging in humans. *Frontiers in neuroscience, 7*, 24. https://doi.org/10.3389/fnins.2013.00024

Hwang, K., Bertolero, M. A., Liu, W. B., & D'Esposito, M. (2017). The Human Thalamus Is an Integrative Hub for Functional Brain Networks. *The Journal of neuroscience : the official journal of the Society for Neuroscience, 37*(23), 5594–5607. https://doi.org/10.1523/JNEUROSCI.0067-17.2017

Sterzer P. (2016). Moving forward in perceptual decision making. *Proceedings of the National Academy of Sciences of the United States of America, 113*(21), 5771–5773. https://doi.org/10.1073/pnas.1605619113

38) Decoding the neuroscience of consciousness, *Nature* **571**, S2-S5 (2019) doi: https://doi.org/10.1038/d41586-019-02207-1

Kotchoubey B. (2018). Human Consciousness: Where Is It From and What Is It for. *Frontiers in psychology, 9*, 567. https://doi.org/10.3389/fpsyg.2018.00567

Edelman, G. M., Gally, J. A., & Baars, B. J. (2011). Biology of Consciousness. *Frontiers in Psychology, 2*. https://doi.org/10.3389/fpsyg.2011.00004

Edelman, G. M. (2003). Naturalizing consciousness: A theoretical framework. *Proceedings of the National Academy of Sciences, 100*(9), 5520–5524. https://doi.org/10.1073/pnas.0931349100 http://www.pnas.org/content/100/9/5520.full

39) **Working memory references**:

Baddeley, A. (2012). Working Memory: Theories, Models, and Controversies. *Annual Review of Psychology, 63*(1), 1–29. https://doi.org/10.1146/annurev-psych-120710-100422

Cowan, N. (2008). ***Attention and memory : an integrated framework***. O U Press. DOI: 10.1093/acprof:oso/9780195119107.001.0001

Nelson Cowan, Dawei Li, Amanda Moffitt, Theresa M. Becker, Elizabeth

A. Martin, J. Scott Saults, Shawn E. Christ; A Neural Region of Abstract Working Memory. *J Cogn Neurosci* 2011; 23 (10): 2852–2863. doi: https://doi.org/10.1162/jocn.2011.21625

Persuh, M., LaRock, E., & Berger, J. (2018). Working Memory and Consciousness: The Current State of Play. *Frontiers in human neuroscience, 12*, 78. https://doi.org/10.3389/fnhum.2018.00078

Silvanto, J. and Jacobs, C. 2015. How is working memory content consciously experienced? The 'conscious copy' model of WM introspection. *Neuroscience & Biobehavioral Reviews.* 55, pp. 510-519. https://doi.org/10.1016/j.neubiorev.2015.06.003

Stein, T., Kaiser, D., & Hesselmann, G. (2016). Can working memory be non-conscious?. *Neuroscience of consciousness, 2016*(1), niv011. https://doi.org/10.1093/nc/niv011

Lara, A. H., & Wallis, J. D. (2015). The Role of Prefrontal Cortex in Working Memory: A Mini Review. *Frontiers in systems neuroscience, 9*, 173. https://doi.org/10.3389/fnsys.2015.00173 https://www.frontiersin.org/articles/10.3389/fnsys.2015.00173/full

Murray, J. D., Jaramillo, J., & Wang, X.-J. (2017). Working Memory and Decision-Making in a Frontoparietal Circuit Model. *Journal of Neuroscience, 37*(50), 12167–12186. https://doi.org/10.1523/JNEUROSCI.0343-17.2017

D'Esposito, M., & Postle, B. R. (2015). The Cognitive Neuroscience of Working Memory. *Annual Review of Psychology, 66*(1), 115–142. https://doi.org/10.1146/annurev-psych-010814-015031

Adams, E. J., Nguyen, A. T., & Cowan, N. (2018). Theories of Working Memory: Differences in Definition, Degree of Modularity, Role of Attention, and Purpose. *Language, speech, and hearing services in schools, 49*(3), 340–355. https://doi.org/10.1044/2018_LSHSS-17-0114

Classic papers: Goldman-Rakic, P. S. (1996). Regional and cellular fractionation of working memory. *Proceedings of the National Academy of Sciences of the United States of America, 93*(24), 13473–13480.

Goldman-Rakic, P. . (1995). Cellular basis of working memory. *Neuron, 14*(3), 477–485. https://doi.org/10.1016/0896-6273(95)90304-6

Arnsten, A. F. T. (2013). The Neurobiology of Thought: The Groundbreaking Discoveries of Patricia Goldman-Rakic 1937-2003. *Cerebral Cortex, 23*(10), 2269–2281. https://doi.org/10.1093/cercor/bht195

40) Baars, B. J., & Franklin, S. (2003). How conscious experience and working memory interact. *Trends in cognitive sciences, 7*(4), 166–172. https://doi.org/10.1016/s1364-6613(03)00056-1

Postle, B. R. (2006). Working Memory as an Emergent Property of the Mind and Brain. *Neuroscience, 139*(1), 23–38. https://doi.org/10.1016/j.neuroscience.2005.06.005

Motley S. E. (2018). Relationship Between Neuromodulation and Working Memory in the Prefrontal Cortex: It's Complicated. *Frontiers in neural circuits,*

References

12, 31. https://doi.org/10.3389/fncir.2018.00031
Barbey, Aron K., et al. "Dorsolateral Prefrontal Contributions to Human Working Memory." *Cortex*, vol. 49, no. 5, May 2013, pp. 1195–1205, 10.1016/j.cortex.2012.05.022. www.ncbi.nlm.nih.gov/pmc/articles/PMC3495093/
41) Akira Miyake. (2007). *Models of working memory : mechanisms of active maintenance and excutive control*. Cambridge Univ. Press. Chapter 3 An Embedded process Theory of Working Memory.
Velichkovsky, Boris B. "Consciousness and Working Memory: Current Trends and Research Perspectives." *Consciousness and Cognition*, vol. 55, Oct. 2017, pp. 35–45 DOI:10.1016/j.concog.2017.07.005
Mansouri, F. A., Rosa, M. G. P., & Atapour, N. (2015). Working Memory in the Service of Executive Control Functions. *Frontiers in Systems Neuroscience*, *9*. https://doi.org/10.3389/fnsys.2015.00166
Kriete, T., Noelle, D. C., Cohen, J. D., & O'Reilly, R. C. (2013). Indirection and symbol-like processing in the prefrontal cortex and basal ganglia. *Proceedings of the National Academy of Sciences*, *110*(41), 16390–16395. https://doi.org/10.1073/pnas.1303547110
Frank, M. J., Loughry, B., & O'reilly, R. C. (2001). Interactions between frontal cortex and basal ganglia in working memory: A computational model. *Cognitive, Affective, & Behavioral Neuroscience*, *1*(2), 137–160. https://doi.org/10.3758/cabn.1.2.137
42) **A pointer in a programming language stores a memory address. In working memory, the "address" is the current activated region of attention, this connection can be lost in certain circumstances.**
43) Soto, D., & Silvanto, J. (2014). Reappraising the relationship between working memory and conscious awareness. *Trends in cognitive sciences*, *18*(10), 520–525. https://doi.org/10.1016/j.tics.2014.06.005
David Soto, Juha Silvanto, Is conscious awareness needed for all working memory processes?, *Neuroscience of Consciousness*, Volume 2016, Issue 1, 2016, niw009, https://doi.org/10.1093/nc/niw009
https://www.amazon.com/Memory-Consciousness-Brain-Tallinn-Conference/dp/1841690155
44) The Feeling of what Happens: Body and Emotion in the Making of Consciousness - Antonio R. Damasio https://en.wikipedia.org/wiki/Damasio%27s_theory_of_consciousness
https://en.wikipedia.org/wiki/Neural_basis_of_self
45) Thompson, E., & Varela, F. J. (2001). Radical embodiment: neural dynamics and consciousness. *Trends in Cognitive Sciences*, *5*(10), 418–425. https://doi.org/10.1016/S1364-6613(00)01750-2
Varela, Francisco J, et al. *The Embodied Mind : Cognitive Science and Human Experience*. Cambridge, Massachusetts, The Mit Press, 2016 https://archive.org/details/FranciscoJ.VarelaEvanT.ThompsonEleanorRoschTheEmbodiedMindCognitiveScienceAndHum/page/

n15/mode/2up

46) There is no method of testing "meta awareness" except verbal report. *Verbal report varies across different subjects who give different verbal reports to the same environmental stimuli (giving rise to the term "qualia" for the unique qualities of individual subjective experience). Self report does not always correspond to outer world events, examples of incorrect observation, or incorrect reporting, occur, intentional or otherwise. Verbal report is not true or false in this sense, but observed behavior. See also chapter ten.* Without verbal report, determining whether animals (or computers) achieve "meta awareness" remains a mystery. *The "observer self" has the potential to experience both external sensory stimuli, and internal experiences generated from memory. Internal memory is also the source of the pathology of hallucinations, when the reference to self is confused or lost. This dilemma was described by Wittgenstein as the "beetle in the box": Everyone has something in their box, which they call a beetle, but no one knows how they compare.*
https://virtualphilosopher.com/2006/09/wittgenstein_an.html

47) https://en.wikipedia.org/wiki/Neuroscience_of_free_will

48) https://en.wikipedia.org/wiki/Benjamin_Libet
Neuroscience and Free Will: New study debunks Libet's interpretation « A Philosopher's TakeDilemma of determinism - Wikipedia, the free encyclopedia
https://blogs.scientificamerican.com/observations/how-a-flawed-experiment-proved-that-free-will-doesnt-exist/

49) Gazzaniga "Who's In Charge?: Free Will and the Science of the Brain." *The Gifford Lectures*, 30 Oct. 2014, www.giffordlectures.org/books/whos-charge-free-will-and-science-brain..

50 Bandura, A. (1989). Human agency in social cognitive theory. *American Psychologist*, 44(9), 1175–1184. https://doi.org/10.1037//0003-066x.44.9.1175
https://www.uky.edu/~eushe2/Bandura/Bandura1989AP.pdf

51) The Neuroscience of Mental Imagery as it Relates to Athlete Performance
https://kaylatilkes.medium.com/the-neuroscience-of-mental-imagery-as-it-relates-to-athlete-performance-a861bc4b3489

52) Chella, A., & Riccardo Manzotti. (2007). *Artificial consciousness*. Exeter: Imprint Academic.
https://www.amazon.com/Artificial-Consciousness-Antonio-Chella/dp/1845400704
Kurzweil, Ray. *The Age of Spiritual Machines : When Computers Exceed Human Intelligence*. New York, Penguin, 2000.

53) Di Perri, C., Thibaut, A., Heine, L., Soddu, A., Demertzi, A., & Laureys, S. (2014). Measuring consciousness in coma and related states. *World journal of radiology*, 6(8), 589–597. https://doi.org/10.4329/wjr.v6.i8.589
Henry, T. R., & Ezzeddine, M. A. (2012). Approach to the patient with transient alteration of consciousness. *Neurology: Clinical Practice*, 2(3), 179–186. https://doi.org/10.1212/cpj.0b013e31826af1be

References

https://www.nia.nih.gov/health/what-is-dementia

54) Gaebel, W., & Zielasek, J. (2015). Focus on psychosis. *Dialogues in Clinical Neuroscience*, *17*(1), 9–18.

Gur, R. E., Keshavan, M. S., & Lawrie, S. M. (2007). Deconstructing Psychosis With Human Brain Imaging. *Schizophrenia Bulletin*, *33*(4), 921–931. https://doi.org/10.1093/schbul/sbm045

Behavioral, Clinical, and Multimodal Imaging Phenotypes in Patients With Psychosis. *JAMA Psychiatry*, *75*(4), 386–395. https://doi.org/10.1001/jamapsychiatry.2017.4741

Thermenos, H. W., Juelich, R. J., DiChiara, S. R., Mesholam-Gately, R. I., Woodberry, K. A., Wojcik, J., Makris, N., Keshavan, M. S., Whitfield-Gabrieli, S., Woo, T. U., Petryshen, T. L., Goldstein, J. M., Shenton, M. E., McCarley, R. W., & Seidman, L. J. (2016). Hyperactivity of caudate, parahippocampal, and prefrontal regions during working memory in never-medicated persons at clinical high-risk for psychosis. *Schizophrenia research*, *173*(1-2), 1–12. https://doi.org/10.1016/j.schres.2016.02.023

Louis-David Lord, Paul Allen, Paul Expert, Oliver Howes, Matthew Broome, Renaud Lambiotte, Paolo Fusar-Poli, Isabel Valli, Philip McGuire, Federico E. Turkheimer, Functional brain networks before the onset of psychosis: A prospective fMRI study with graph theoretical analysis,NeuroImage: Clinical,Volume 1, Issue 1,2012,Pages 91-98,ISSN 2213-1582, https://doi.org/10.1016/j.nicl.2012.09.008 .

Gothelf, D., Hoeft, F., Ueno, T., Sugiura, L., Lee, A. D., Thompson, P., & Reiss, A. L. (2011). Developmental changes in multivariate neuroanatomical patterns that predict risk for psychosis in 22q11.2 deletion syndrome. *Journal of Psychiatric Research*, *45*(3), 322–331. https://doi.org/10.1016/j.jpsychires.2010.07.008

55) Kamath, V., Lasutschinkow, P., Ishizuka, K., & Sawa, A. (2018). Olfactory Functioning in First-Episode Psychosis. *Schizophrenia Bulletin*, *44*(3), 672–680. https://doi.org/10.1093/schbul/sbx107

Harvey, P. D. (2018). The Course of Cognition and Functioning in Patients at Ultrahigh Risk of Developing Psychosis. *JAMA Psychiatry*, *75*(9), 882. https://doi.org/10.1001/jamapsychiatry.2018.1618

Maureen, Pratik Talati, Kristan Armstrong, Simon N. Vandekar, Jennifer Urbano Blackford, Neil D. Woodward, and Stephan Heckers, Hyperactivity and Reduced Activation of Anterior Hippocampus in Early Psychosis,American Journal of Psychiatry 2019 176:12, 1030-1038 https://ajp.psychiatryonline.org/doi/10.1176/appi.ajp.2019.19020151

56) Cardno, A. G., & Owen, M. J. (2014). Genetic Relationships Between Schizophrenia, Bipolar Disorder, and Schizoaffective Disorder. *Schizophrenia Bulletin*, *40*(3), 504–515. https://doi.org/10.1093/schbul/sbu016

Bipolar Disorder and Schizophrenia Working Group of the Psychiatric Genomics Consortium. Electronic address: douglas.ruderfer@vanderbilt.

edu, & Bipolar Disorder and Schizophrenia Working Group of the Psychiatric Genomics Consortium (2018). Genomic Dissection of Bipolar Disorder and Schizophrenia, Including 28 Subphenotypes. *Cell*, *173*(7), 1705–1715.e16. https://doi.org/10.1016/j.cell.2018.05.046
Bigdeli, T. B., Fanous, A. H., Li, Y., Rajeevan, N., Sayward, F., Genovese, G., Gupta, R., Radhakrishnan, K., Malhotra, A. K., Sun, N., Lu, Q., Hu, Y., Li, B., Chen, Q., Mane, S., Miller, P., Cheung, K. H., Gur, R. E., Greenwood, T. A., Braff, D. L., … Harvey, P. D. (2021). Genome-Wide Association Studies of Schizophrenia and Bipolar Disorder in a Diverse Cohort of US Veterans. *Schizophrenia bulletin*, *47*(2), 517–529. https://doi.org/10.1093/schbul/sbaa133
Cross-Disorder Group of the Psychiatric Genomics Consortium (2013). Identification of risk loci with shared effects on five major psychiatric disorders: a genome-wide analysis. *Lancet (London, England)*, *381*(9875), 1371–1379. https://doi.org/10.1016/S0140-6736(12)62129-1
57) Kelleher, I., & Cannon, M. (2016). Putting Psychosis in Its Place. *The American journal of psychiatry*, *173*(10), 951–952. https://doi.org/10.1176/appi.ajp.2016.16070810
https://journals.sagepub.com/doi/abs/10.1177/0020764020922276?journalCode=ispa
58) Burgy, M. (2008). The Concept of Psychosis: Historical and Phenomenological Aspects. *Schizophrenia Bulletin*, *34*(6), 1200–1210. https://doi.org/10.1093/schbul/sbm136
59) Susanah Cahalan, **Brain On Fire**, *My month of Madness*. Simon & Schuster; ISBN-13 978-1451621389
Pojen Deng, M. D. (2020, January 29). *Autoimmune Encephalitis: What Psychiatrists Need to Know*. Psychiatric Times. https://www.psychiatrictimes.com/neuropsychiatry/autoimmune-encephalitis-what-psychiatrists-need-know
Association of Delirium Response and Safety of Pharmacological Interventions for the Management and Prevention of Delirium: A Network Meta-analysis. | Critical Care Medicine | JAMA Psychiatry | JAMA Network
https://jamanetwork.com/journals/jamapsychiatry/fullarticle/2726609?guestAccessKey=562bbbcb-7d1c-4fc3-80e4-308c28aedb86&utm_source=silverchair&utm_medium=email&utm_campaign=article_alert-jamapsychiatry&utm_content=olf&utm_term=022719
60) Arciniegas D. B. (2015). Psychosis. *Continuum (Minneapolis, Minn.)*, *21*(3 Behavioral Neurology and Neuropsychiatry), 715–736. https://doi.org/10.1212/01.CON.0000466662.89908.e7
61) Schmidt, A., Smieskova, R., Aston, J., Simon, A., Allen, P., Fusar-Poli, P., McGuire, P. K., Riecher-Rössler, A., Stephan, K. E., & Borgwardt, S. (2013). Brain Connectivity Abnormalities Predating the Onset of Psychosis: Correlation With the Effect of Medication. *JAMA Psychiatry*, *70*(9), 903–912. https://doi.org/10.1001/jamapsychiatry.2013.117
Deng, Y., Liu, K., Cheng, D., Zhang, J., Chen, H., Chen, B., Li, Y., Wang, W.,

References

Kong, Y., & Wen, G. (2019). Ventral and dorsal visual pathways exhibit abnormalities of static and dynamic connectivities, respectively, in patients with schizophrenia. *Schizophrenia research*, *206*, 103–110. https://doi.org/10.1016/j.schres.2018.12.005

Stepien, M., Manoliu, A., Kubli, R., Schneider, K., Tobler, P. N., Seifritz, E., Herdener, M., Kaiser, S., & Kirschner, M. (2018). Investigating the association of ventral and dorsal striatal dysfunction during reward anticipation with negative symptoms in patients with schizophrenia and healthy individuals. *PloS one*, *13*(6), e0198215. https://doi.org/10.1371/journal.pone.0198215

Vossel, S., Geng, J. J., & Fink, G. R. (2014). Dorsal and ventral attention systems: distinct neural circuits but collaborative roles. *The Neuroscientist : a review journal bringing neurobiology, neurology and psychiatry*, *20*(2), 150–159. doi: 10.1177/1073858413494269

Calhoun, V. D., Sui, J., Kiehl, K., Turner, J., Allen, E., & Pearlson, G. (2012). Exploring the psychosis functional connectome: aberrant intrinsic networks. *Frontiers in psychiatry*, *2*, 75. https://doi.org/10.3389/fpsyt.2011.00075

62) Stahl, S. (2018). Beyond the dopamine hypothesis of schizophrenia to three neural networks of psychosis: Dopamine, serotonin, and glutamate. *CNS Spectrums, 23*(3), 187-191. doi:10.1017/S1092852918001013

Farber, N. B. (2003). The Nmda Receptor Hypofunction Model Of Psychosis. *Annals of the New York Academy of Sciences*, *1003*(1), 119–130. https://doi.org/10.1196/annals.1300.008

Modinos, G., Şimşek, F., Azis, M. *et al.* Prefrontal GABA levels, hippocampal resting perfusion and the risk of psychosis. *Neuropsychopharmacol* **43,** 2652–2659 (2018). https://doi.org/10.1038/s41386-017-0004-6

Kim Geon Ha, Kang Ilhyang, Jeong Hyeonseok, Park Shinwon, Hong Haejin, Kim Jinsol, Kim Jung Yoon, Edden Richard A. E., Lyoo In Kyoon, Yoon Sujung, Low Prefrontal GABA Levels Are Associated With Poor Cognitive Functions in Professional Boxers, Frontiers in Human Neuroscience, 13 2019, 193 https://doi.org/10.3389/fnhum.2019.00193

David A. Parker, Rebekah L. Trotti, Jennifer E. McDowell, Sarah K. Keedy, S. Kristian Hill, Elliot S. Gershon, Elena I. Ivleva, Godfrey D. Pearlson, Matcheri S. Keshavan, Carol A. Tamminga, and Brett A. Clementz, Auditory Oddball Responses Across the Schizophrenia-Bipolar Spectrum and Their Relationship to Cognitive and Clinical Features, American Journal of Psychiatry 2021 178:10, 952-96

63) Kapur S. (2003). Psychosis as a state of aberrant salience: a framework linking biology, phenomenology, and pharmacology in schizophrenia. *The American journal of psychiatry*, *160*(1), 13–23. https://doi.org/10.1176/appi.ajp.160.1.13

Waters, F., Chiu, V., Atkinson, A., & Blom, J. D. (2018). Severe Sleep Deprivation Causes Hallucinations and a Gradual Progression Toward Psychosis With Increasing Time Awake. *Frontiers in psychiatry*, *9*, 303. https://doi.org/10.3389/fpsyt.2018.00303

65) ETIOLOGIES
Was C.T.E. Stealing His Mind? A Gunshot Provided the Answer - The New York Times
Khandaker, G. M., Dalman, C., Kappelmann, N., Stochl, J., Dal, H., Kosidou, K., Jones, P. B., & Karlsson, H. (2018). Association of Childhood Infection With IQ and Adult Nonaffective Psychosis in Swedish Men: A Population-Based Longitudinal Cohort and Co-relative Study. *JAMA psychiatry*, *75*(4), 356–362. https://doi.org/10.1001/jamapsychiatry.2017.4491
Kim Geon Ha, Kang Ilhyang, Jeong Hyeonseok, Park Shinwon, Hong Haejin, Kim Jinsol, Kim Jung Yoon, Edden Richard A. E., Lyoo In Kyoon, Yoon Sujung, Low Prefrontal GABA Levels Are Associated With Poor Cognitive Functions in Professional Boxers Frontiers in Human Neuroscience 13 2019 https://www.frontiersin.org/articles/10.3389/fnhum.2019.00193 DOI=10.3389/fnhum.2019.00193
Bourque, J., Afzali, M. H., & Conrod, P. J. (2018). Association of Cannabis Use With Adolescent Psychotic Symptoms. *JAMA psychiatry*, *75*(8), 864–866. https://doi.org/10.1001/jamapsychiatry.2018.1330
Large, M., Sharma, S., Compton, M. T., Slade, T., & Nielssen, O. (2011). Cannabis Use and Earlier Onset of Psychosis. *Archives of General Psychiatry*, *68*(6), 555. https://doi.org/10.1001/archgenpsychiatry.2011.5
Erritzoe, D., Frokjaer, V. G., Holst, K. K., Christoffersen, M., Johansen, S. S., Svarer, C., Madsen, J., Rasmussen, P. M., Ramsøy, T., Jernigan, T. L., & Knudsen, G. M. (2011). In Vivo Imaging of Cerebral Serotonin Transporter and Serotonin2A Receptor Binding in 3,4-Methylenedioxymethamphetamine (MDMA or "Ecstasy") and Hallucinogen Users. *Archives of General Psychiatry*, *68*(6), 562. https://doi.org/10.1001/archgenpsychiatry.2011.56
Walz, R. (2008). Psychiatric disorders and traumatic brain injury. *Neuropsychiatric Disease and Treatment*, 797. https://doi.org/10.2147/ndt.s2653
Morrow, E.M., Lafayette, J.M., Bromfield, E.B. et al. Postictal psychosis: pre-symptomatic risk factors and the need for further investigation of genetics and pharmacotherapy. *Ann Gen Psychiatry* **5**, 9 (2006). https://doi.org/10.1186/1744-859X-5-9
Croft, J., Heron, J., Teufel, C., Cannon, M., Wolke, D., Thompson, A., Houtepen, L., & Zammit, S. (2019). Association of Trauma Type, Age of Exposure, and Frequency in Childhood and Adolescence With Psychotic Experiences in Early Adulthood. *JAMA Psychiatry*, *76*(1), 79. https://doi.org/10.1001/jamapsychiatry.2018.3155
Brandt, L., Henssler, J., Müller, M., Wall, S., Gabel, D., & Heinz, A. (2019). Risk of Psychosis Among Refugees. *JAMA Psychiatry*, *76*(11), 1133. https://doi.org/10.1001/jamapsychiatry.2019.1937
Stangeland H, Orgeta V, Bell V, Poststroke psychosis: a systematic review Journal of Neurology, Neurosurgery & Psychiatry 2018;89:879-885. https://jnnp.bmj.com/content/89/8/879

References

Kelleher, I., Keeley, H., Corcoran, P., Ramsay, H., Wasserman, C., Carli, V., Sarchiapone, M., Hoven, C., Wasserman, D., & Cannon, M. (2013). Childhood Trauma and Psychosis in a Prospective Cohort Study: Cause, Effect, and Directionality. *American Journal of Psychiatry*, *170*(7), 734–741. https://doi.org/10.1176/appi.ajp.2012.12091169

Zavos, H. M. S., Freeman, D., Haworth, C. M. A., McGuire, P., Plomin, R., Cardno, A. G., & Ronald, A. (2014). Consistent Etiology of Severe, Frequent Psychotic Experiences and Milder, Less Frequent Manifestations. *JAMA Psychiatry*, *71*(9), 1049. https://doi.org/10.1001/jamapsychiatry.2014.994

66) Bowers, M. B. (1974). ***Retreat from sanity : the structure of emerging psychosis***. New York ISBN-13: 978-0877051343

67) DSMV category ATTENUATED PSYCHOSIS SYNDROME fails to address the issue, assuming that certain episodes, which do not produce sustained disability are different.

Werbeloff, N., Drukker, M., Dohrenwend, B. P., Levav, I., Yoffe, R., Os, J. van, Davidson, M., & Weiser, M. (2012). Self-reported Psychotic Symptoms as Forerunners of Severe Mental Disorders Later in Life. *Archives of General Psychiatry*, *69*(5), 467–475. https://doi.org/10.1001/archgenpsychiatry.2011.1580

Salazar de Pablo, G., Guinart, D., Cornblatt, B. A., Auther, A. M., Carrión, R. E., Carbon, M., Jiménez-Fernández, S., Vernal, D. L., Walitza, S., Gerstenberg, M., Saba, R., Lo Cascio, N., Brandizzi, M., Arango, C., Moreno, C., Van Meter, A., Fusar-Poli, P., & Correll, C. U. (2020). DSM-5 Attenuated Psychosis Syndrome in Adolescents Hospitalized With Non-psychotic Psychiatric Disorders. *Frontiers in psychiatry*, *11*, 568982. https://doi.org/10.3389/fpsyt.2020.568982

Salazar de Pablo G, Catalan A, Fusar-Poli P. Clinical Validity of *DSM-5* Attenuated Psychosis Syndrome: Advances in Diagnosis, Prognosis, and Treatment. *JAMA Psychiatry*. 2020;77(3):311–320. DOI: 10.1001/jamapsychiatry.2019.3561

68) Kim, WS., Shen, G., Liu, C. et al. Altered amygdala-based functional connectivity in individuals with attenuated psychosis syndrome and first-episode schizophrenia. *Sci Rep* **10,** 17711 (2020). https://doi.org/10.1038/s41598-020-74771-w

Prerona Mukherjee, Amri Sabharwal, Roman Kotov, Akos Szekely, Ramin Parsey, Deanna M. Barch, Aprajita Mohanty, Disconnection Between Amygdala and Medial Prefrontal Cortex in Psychotic Disorders, *Schizophrenia Bulletin*, Volume 42, Issue 4, July 2016, Pages 1056–1067, https://doi.org/10.1093/schbul/sbw012

70) Scheepers, F. E., de Mul, J., Boer, F., & Hoogendijk, W. J. (2018). Psychosis as an Evolutionary Adaptive Mechanism to Changing Environments. *Frontiers in psychiatry*, *9*, 237. https://doi.org/10.3389/fpsyt.2018.00237

71) R. D. Laing https://psychology.jrank.org/pages/367/Ronald-David-Laing.html

Mosher LR, Vallone R, Menn A. The Treatment of Acute Psychosis Without Neuroleptics: Six-Week Psychopathology Outcome Data From the Soteria Project. *International Journal of Social Psychiatry.* 1995;41(3):157-173. doi:10.1177/002076409504100301
https://www.researchgate.net/scientific-contributions/Loren-R-Mosher-77204065
72) Kirmayer L. J. (2013). The cultural diversity of healing: meaning, metaphor,and mechanism. *Heart views : the official journal of the Gulf Heart Association*, *14*(1), 39–40. https://doi.org/10.4103/1995-705x.107123   https://www.ncbi.nlm.nih.gov/pmc/articles/PMC3621226/
https://en.wikipedia.org/wiki/Ghost_Dance
https://www.newyorker.com/book/under-review/the-science-of-the-psychedelic-renaissance
73) Timothy Leary's Transformation From Scientist to Psychedelic Celebrity https://www.wired.com/2013/10/timothy-leary-archives/
74) Fuentes, J. J., Fonseca, F., Elices, M., Farré, M., & Torrens, M. (2020). Therapeutic Use of LSD in Psychiatry: A Systematic Review of Randomized-Controlled Clinical Trials. *Frontiers in psychiatry*, *10*, 943. https://doi.org/10.3389/fpsyt.2019.00943
Krebs, T. S., & Johansen, P. Ø. (2013). Psychedelics and mental health: a population study. *PloS one*, *8*(8), e63972. https://doi.org/10.1371/journal.pone.0063972
75) **MEMORIES DREAMS REFLECTIONS**, CG JUNG recorded and edited by Aniela Jaffe vintage ed 1961Random House, N Y
76) Gur, R. C., Calkins, M. E., Satterthwaite, T. D., Ruparel, K., Bilker, W. B., Moore, T. M., Savitt, A. P., Hakonarson, H., & Gur, R. E. (2014). Neurocognitive growth charting in psychosis spectrum youths. *JAMA psychiatry*, *71*(4), 366–374. https://doi.org/10.1001/jamapsychiatry.2013.4190
Fusar-Poli P, Bonoldi I, Yung AR, et al. Predicting Psychosis: Meta-analysis of Transition Outcomes in Individuals at High Clinical Risk. *Arch Gen Psychiatry.* 2012;69(3):220–229. doi: 10.1001/archgenpsychiatry.2011.1472
Fusar-Poli, P., Borgwardt, S., Bechdolf, A., Addington, J., Riecher-Rössler, A., Schultze-Lutter, F., Keshavan, M., Wood, S., Ruhrmann, S., Seidman, L. J., Valmaggia, L., Cannon, T., Velthorst, E., De Haan, L., Cornblatt, B., Bonoldi, I., Birchwood, M., McGlashan, T., Carpenter, W., McGorry, P., ... Yung, A. (2013). The psychosis high-risk state: a comprehensive state-of-the-art review. *JAMA psychiatry*, *70*(1), 107–120. https://doi.org/10.1001/jamapsychiatry.2013.269
D'Ardenne, K., Eshel, N., Luka, J., Lenartowicz, A., Nystrom, L. E., & Cohen, J. D. (2012). Role of prefrontal cortex and the midbrain dopamine system in working memory updating. *Proceedings of the National Academy of Sciences*, *109*(49), 19900–19909. https://doi.org/10.1073/pnas.1116727109   https://www.pnas.org/content/109/49/19900
77) Cannon, T. D., Yu, C., Addington, J., Bearden, C. E., Cadenhead, K. S., Cornblatt, B. A., Heinssen, R., Jeffries, C. D., Mathalon, D. H., McGlashan, T.

References

H., Perkins, D. O., Seidman, L. J., Tsuang, M. T., Walker, E. F., Woods, S. W., & Kattan, M. W. (2016). An Individualized Risk Calculator for Research in Prodromal Psychosis. *The American journal of psychiatry*, *173*(10), 980–988. https://doi.org/10.1176/appi.ajp.2016.15070890

Dana M. Allswede, Jean Addington, Carrie E. Bearden, Kristin S. Cadenhead, Barbara A. Cornblatt, Daniel H. Mathalon, Thomas McGlashan, Diana O. Perkins, Larry J. Seidman, Ming T. Tsuang, Elaine F. Walker, Scott W. Woods, and Tyrone D. Cannon,
Characterizing Covariant Trajectories of Individuals at Clinical High Risk for Psychosis Across Symptomatic and Functional Domains,American Journal of Psychiatry 2020 177:2, 164-171

Livny, A., Reichenberg, A., Fruchter, E., Yoffe, R., Goldberg, S., Fenchel, D., Burshtein, S., Bachar, E., Davidson, M., & Weiser, M. (2018). A Population-Based Longitudinal Study of Symptoms and Signs Before the Onset of Psychosis. *The American journal of psychiatry*, *175*(4), 351–358. https://doi.org/10.1176/appi.ajp.2017.16121384

78) Fusar-Poli, P., Rutigliano, G., Stahl, D., Davies, C., Bonoldi, I., Reilly, T., & McGuire, P. (2017). Development and Validation of a Clinically Based Risk Calculator for the Transdiagnostic Prediction of Psychosis. *JAMA Psychiatry*, *74*(5), 493. https://doi.org/10.1001/jamapsychiatry.2017.0284 https://jamanetwork.com/journals/jamapsychiatry/fullarticle/2612445

Carrión, R. E., Cornblatt, B. A., Burton, C. Z., Tso, I. F., Auther, A. M., Adelsheim, S., Calkins, R., Carter, C. S., Niendam, T., Sale, T. G., Taylor, S. F., & McFarlane, W. R. (2016). Personalized Prediction of Psychosis: External Validation of the NAPLS-2 Psychosis Risk Calculator. *The American journal of psychiatry*, *173*(10), 989–996 https://doi.org/10.1176/appi.ajp.2016.15121565

Koutsouleris, N., Kambeitz-Ilankovic, L., Ruhrmann, S., Rosen, M., Ruef, A., Dwyer, D. B., Paolini, M., Chisholm, K., Kambeitz, J., Haidl, T., Schmidt, A., Gillam, J., Schultze-Lutter, F., Falkai, P., Reiser, M., Riecher-Rössler, A., Upthegrove, R., Hietala, J., Salokangas, R. K. R., … Borgwardt, S. (2018). Prediction Models of Functional Outcomes for Individuals in the Clinical High-Risk State for Psychosis or With Recent-Onset Depression: A Multimodal, Multisite Machine Learning Analysis. *JAMA Psychiatry*, *75*(11), 1156–1172. https://doi.org/10.1001/jamapsychiatry.2018.2165

Carpenter W. T. (2016). Early Detection of Psychosis Vulnerability: Progress, Opportunity, and Caution. *The American journal of psychiatry*, *173*(10), 949–950. https://doi.org/10.1176/appi.ajp.2016.16060746

79) Disconnection syndrome references:
https://brainaacn.org/disconnection-syndromes/
https://en.wikipedia.org/wiki/Blindsight
Catani, M., & ffytche, D. H. (2005). The rises and falls of disconnection syndromes. *Brain : a journal of neurology*, *128*(Pt 10), 2224–2239. https://doi.org/10.1093/brain/awh622

80) M.-Marsel Mesulam, Fifty years of disconnexion syndromes and the Geschwind legacy, *Brain*, Volume 138, Issue 9, September 2015, Pages 2791–2799, https://doi.org/10.1093/brain/awv198

Schmahmann, J. D., & Pandya, D. N. (2008). Disconnection syndromes of basal ganglia, thalamus, and cerebrocerebellar systems. *Cortex 44*(8), 1037–1066. https://doi.org/10.1016/j.cortex.2008.04.004

Parton A, Malhotra P, Husain M, Hemispatial neglect, Journal of Neurology, Neurosurgery & Psychiatry 2004;75:13-21. https://jnnp.bmj.com/content/75/1/13

81) Gomes, D., Fonseca, M., Garrotes, M., Lima, M. R., Mendonça, M., Pereira, M., Lourenço, M., Oliveira, E., & Lavrador, J. P. (2017). Corpus Callosum and Neglect Syndrome: Clinical Findings After Meningioma Removal and Anatomical Review. *Journal of neurosciences in rural practice, 8*(1), 101–106. https://doi.org/10.4103/0976-3147.193549

Berthier, M., Starkstein, S. and Leiguarda, R. (1988), Asymbolia for pain: A sensory-limbic disconnection syndrome. Ann Neurol., 24: 41-49. https://doi.org/10.1002/ana.410240109 https://onlinelibrary.wiley.com/doi/abs/10.1002/ana.410240109 See #33 for Gazzaniga ref.

82) Ornstein, R. E. (2008). *Meditation and modern psychology*. Malor Books. Naranjo, C., & Ornstein, R. E. (1973). *On the psychology of meditation*. Viking Press.

83) https://historyofyesterday.com/the-monk-who-burned-himself-to-death-as-a-form-of-protest-35008d0ed8e2

84) Dusek, J. A., & Benson, H. (2009). Mind-Body Medicine. *Minnesota Medicine, 92*(5), 47–50.

Baars, B. J. (2013). A scientific approach to silent consciousness. *Frontiers in Psychology, 4*. https://doi.org/10.3389/fpsyg.2013.00678

Dr. Herbert Benson's Relaxation Response. (2013). Psychology Today. https://www.psychologytoday.com/us/blog/heart-and-soul-healing/201303/dr-herbert-benson-s-relaxation-response

85) Austin, J. H. (1999). *Zen and the brain : toward an understanding of meditation and consciousness*. Mit Press. http://www.zenandthebrain.com/

Austin, J. H. (2013). Zen and the brain: mutually illuminating topics. *Frontiers in Psychology, 4*. https://doi.org/10.3389/fpsyg.2013.00784

Austin, J. H. (2011). **Selfless insight : Zen and the meditative transformations of consciousness**. MIT Press.

Chiesa, A., Brambilla, P., & Serretti, A. (2010). Functional neural correlates of mindfulness meditations in comparison with psychotherapy, pharmacotherapy and placebo effect. Is there a link?. *Acta neuropsychiatrica, 22*(3), 104–117. https://doi.org/10.1111/j.1601-5215.2010.00460.x

86) *Mindfulness Meditation - Guided Mindfulness Meditation Practices with Jon Kabat-Zinn*. (n.d.). Www.Mindfulnesscds.Com. Retrieved February 24, 2020, from https://www.mindfulnesscds.com/

References

87) Voluntary Control of Breathing | CARTA   The Diving Reflex |
Breatheology
Diving reflex - Wikipedia   The Science of Breathing
88) https://hypnosisandsuggestion.org/theories-of-hypnosis.html
Trance and Treatment: The clinical uses of hypnosis, Spiegel and Spiegel, ISBN-13: 978-1585621903
Shore and Orne, *The Nature of Hypnosis*, ASIN‏ : ‎B00B93TB3Y Publisher‏ : ‎ Holt, Rinehart and Winston (January 1, 1965)
89) Jensen, M. P., Adachi, T., Tomé-Pires, C., Lee, J., Osman, Z. J., & Miró, J. (2015). Mechanisms of hypnosis: toward the development of a biopsychosocial model. *The International journal of clinical and experimental hypnosis*, *63*(1), 34–75. https://doi.org/10.1080/00207144.2014.961875
Jensen, M. P., Jamieson, G. A., Lutz, A., Mazzoni, G., McGeown, W. J., Santarcangelo, E. L., Demertzi, A., De Pascalis, V., Bányai, É. I., Rominger, C., Vuilleumier, P., Faymonville, M.-E., & Terhune, D. B. (2017). New directions in hypnosis research: strategies for advancing the cognitive and clinical neuroscience of hypnosis. *Neuroscience of Consciousness*, *2017*(1). https://doi.org/10.1093/nc/nix004
Hoeft, F., Gabrieli, J. D. E., Whitfield-Gabrieli, S., Haas, B. W., Bammer, R., Menon, V., & Spiegel, D. (2012). Functional Brain Basis of Hypnotizability. *Archives of General Psychiatry*, *69*(10), 1064. https://doi.org/10.1001/archgenpsychiatry.2011.2190
Jiang, H., White, M. P., Greicius, M. D., Waelde, L. C., & Spiegel, D. (2017). Brain Activity and Functional Connectivity Associated with Hypnosis. *Cerebral Cortex*, *27*(8), 4083–4093. https://doi.org/10.1093/cercor/bhw220
Zhang, Y., Wang, Y., Shen, C., Ye, Y., Shen, S., Zhang, B., Wang, J., Chen, W., & Wang, W. (2017). Relationship between hypnosis and personality trait in participants with high or low hypnotic susceptibility. *Neuropsychiatric Disease and Treatment*, *Volume 13*, 1007–1012. https://doi.org/10.2147/ndt.s134930
90) https://en.wikipedia.org/wiki/Biofeedback
Yu, B., Funk, M., Hu, J., Wang, Q., & Feijs, L. (2018). Biofeedback for Everyday Stress Management: A Systematic Review. *Frontiers in ICT*, *5*. https://doi.org/10.3389/fict.2018.00023
Enriquez-Geppert, S., Smit, D., Pimenta, M. G., & Arns, M. (2019). Neurofeedback as a Treatment Intervention in ADHD: Current Evidence and Practice. *Current Psychiatry Reports*, *21*(6). https://doi.org/10.1007/s11920-019-1021-4
91) Schwartz, J., & Roth, T. (2008). Neurophysiology of Sleep and Wakefulness: Basic Science and Clinical Implications. *Current Neuropharmacology*, *6*(4), 367–378. https://doi.org/10.2174/157015908787386050
Sleep - How Sleep Works - Neurological Mechanisms of Sleep
Fraigne, J. J., Torontali, Z. A., Snow, M. B., & Peever, J. H. (2015). REM Sleep at its Core - Circuits, Neurotransmitters, and Pathophysiology. *Frontiers in*

neurology, *6*, 123. https://doi.org/10.3389/fneur.2015.00123
https://www.frontiersin.org/articles/10.3389/fneur.2015.00123/full
Scammell, T. E., Arrigoni, E., & Lipton, J. O. (2017). Neural Circuitry of Wakefulness and Sleep. *Neuron*, *93*(4), 747–765. https://doi.org/10.1016/j.neuron.2017.01.014
92) Velluti, R. (1997). Interactions between sleep and sensory physiology. *Journal of Sleep Research*, *6*(2), 61–77. https://doi.org/10.1046/j.1365-2869.1997.00031.x
93) Borbély, A. A., Daan, S., Wirz-Justice, A., & Deboer, T. (2016). The two-process model of sleep regulation: a reappraisal. *Journal of sleep research*, *25*(2), 131–143. https://doi.org/10.1111/jsr.12371
Borbély, A. A., & Achermann, P. (1999). Sleep homeostasis and models of sleep regulation. *Journal of biological rhythms*, *14*(6), 557–568. https://doi.org/10.1177/074873099129000894
Ono, D., & Yamanaka, A. (2017). Hypothalamic regulation of the sleep/wake cycle. *Neuroscience research*, *118*, 74–81. https://doi.org/10.1016/j.neures.2017.03.013
Monti, J. M. (2013). The neurotransmitters of sleep and wake, a physiological reviews series. *Sleep Medicine Reviews*, *17*(4), 313–315. https://doi.org/10.1016/j.smrv.2013.02.004
Krystal, A. D., MD, MS, Benca, R. M., MD, PhD, Kilduff, T. S., & PhD. (2013). Understanding the Sleep-Wake Cycle: Sleep, Insomnia, and the Orexin System. *The Journal of Clinical Psychiatry*, *74*(suppl 1), 3–20. https://doi.org/10.4088/JCP.13011su1c
Oh, J., Petersen, C., Walsh, C. M., Bittencourt, J. C., Neylan, T. C., & Grinberg, L. T. (2019). The role of co-neurotransmitters in sleep and wake regulation. *Molecular Psychiatry*, *24*(9), 1284–1295. https://doi.org/10.1038/s41380-018-0291-2
de Lecea, L., & Huerta, R. (2014). Hypocretin (orexin) regulation of sleep-to-wake transitions. *Frontiers in pharmacology*, *5*, 16. https://doi.org/10.3389/fphar.2014.00016
94) Duffy, J. F., & Czeisler, C. A. (2009). Effect of Light on Human Circadian Physiology. *Sleep Medicine Clinics*, *4*(2), 165–177. https://doi.org/10.1016/j.jsmc.2009.01.004
Junfeng Chen, Kousuke Okimura, Takashi Yoshimura, Light and Hormones in Seasonal Regulation of Reproduction and Mood, *Endocrinology*, Volume 161, Issue 9, September 2020, bqaa130, https://doi.org/10.1210/endocr/bqaa130https://academic.oup.com/endo/article/161/9/bqaa130/5879749
Aulinas A. Physiology of the Pineal Gland and Melatonin. (Updated 2019 Dec 10). In: Feingold KR, Anawalt B, Boyce A, et al., editors. Endotext (Internet). South Dartmouth (MA): MDText.com, Inc.; 2000-.
95) Laposky, A. D., Bass, J., Kohsaka, A., & Turek, F. W. (2008). Sleep and circadian rhythms: key components in the regulation of energy metabolism. *FEBS*

References

letters, *582*(1), 142–151. https://doi.org/10.1016/j.febslet.2007.06.079
Morrissette, D. A. (2013). Twisting the night away: a review of the neurobiology, genetics, diagnosis, and treatment of shift work disorder. *CNS Spectrums*, *18*(s1), 42–54. https://doi.org/10.1017/s109285291300076x
https://www.cambridge.org/core/journals/cns-spectrums/article/twisting-the-night-away-a-review-of-the-neurobiology-genetics-diagnosis-and-treatment-of-shift-work-disorder/B37DA3A224B9F7BB597B96940774272C
Lockley, S. W., Arendt, J., & Skene, D. J. (2007). Visual impairment and circadian rhythm disorders. *Dialogues in Clinical Neuroscience*, *9*(3), 301–314.
Jehan, S., Zizi, F., Pandi-Perumal, S. R., Myers, A. K., Auguste, E., Jean-Louis, G., & McFarlane, S. I. (2017). Shift Work and Sleep: Medical Implications and Management. *Sleep medicine and disorders : international journal*, *1*(2), 00008.
Grivas, T. B., & Savvidou, O. D. (2007). Melatonin the "light of night" in human biology and adolescent idiopathic scoliosis. *Scoliosis*, *2*, 6. https://doi.org/10.1186/1748-7161-2-6
96) Akintomide, G. S., & Rickards, H. (2011). Narcolepsy: a review. *Neuropsychiatric disease and treatment*, *7*, 507–518. https://doi.org/10.2147/NDT.S23624
Wang, Y. G., Benmedjahed, K., Lambert, J., Evans, C. J., Hwang, S., Black, J., & Johns, M. W. (2017). Assessing narcolepsy with cataplexy in children and adolescents: development of a cataplexy diary and the ESS-CHAD. *Nature and Science of Sleep*, *9*, 201–211. https://doi.org/10.2147/NSS.S140143
97) Kales, J. D. (1980). Night Terrors. *Archives of General Psychiatry*, *37*(12), 1413. https://doi.org/10.1001/archpsyc.1980.01780250099012
Thorpy, M. J., & Plazzi, G. (2010). *The parasomnias and other sleep-related movement disorders*. Cambridge University Press.
Markov, D., Jaffe, F., & Doghramji, K. (2006). Update on Parasomnias. *Psychiatry (Edgmont)*, *3*(7), 69–76.
98) de Araújo Lima, T. F., da Silva Behrens, N. S., Lopes, E., Pereira, D., de Almeida Fonseca, H., Cavalcanti, P. O., Pradella-Hallinan, M., Castro, J., Tufik, S., & Coelho, F. M. (2014). Kleine-Levin Syndrome: A case report. *Sleep science (Sao Paulo, Brazil)*, *7*(2), 122–125. https://doi.org/10.1016/j.slsci.2014.09.001
Raju M. (1994). KLEINE - LEVIN SYNDROME (A Case Report). *Medical journal, Armed Forces India*, *50*(3), 229–231. https://doi.org/10.1016/S0377-1237(17)31071-7
A Mysterious Sleeping Disorder That Turns Life Into a Waking Dream. (2019, October 2). *The New York Times*. https://www.nytimes.com/2019/10/02/magazine/mysterious-sleeping-disorder-diagnosis.html
Kleine Levin syndrome | Genetic and Rare Diseases Information Center (GARD) – an NCATS Program. (n.d.). Rarediseases.Info.Nih.Gov. Retrieved February 20, 2020, from https://rarediseases.info.nih.gov/diseases/3117/

kleine-levin-syndrome
99) Chow, M., & Cao, M. (2016). The hypocretin/orexin system in sleep disorders: preclinical insights and clinical progress. *Nature and science of sleep*, 8, 81–86. https://doi.org/10.2147/NSS.S76711
Prinz, P. (2004). Sleep, Appetite, and Obesity—What Is the Link? *PLoS Medicine*, *1*(3), e61. https://doi.org/10.1371/journal.pmed.0010061
Beccuti, G., & Pannain, S. (2011). Sleep and obesity. *Current Opinion in Clinical Nutrition and Metabolic Care*, *14*(4), 402–412. https://doi.org/10.1097/MCO.0b013e3283479109
Plante D. T. (2021). The Evolving Nexus of Sleep and Depression. *The American journal of psychiatry*, *178*(10), 896–902. https://doi.org/10.1176/appi.ajp.2021.21080821
Ferrarelli F. (2021). Sleep Abnormalities in Schizophrenia: State of the Art and Next Steps. *The American journal of psychiatry*, *178*(10), 903–913. https://doi.org/10.1176/appi.ajp.2020.20070968
http://www.alaskasleep.com/blog/types-of-sleep-apnea-explained-obstructive-central-mixed
http://journals.sagepub.com/doi/abs/10.1177/019459989310800203
100) *What Causes Sleep Paralysis During REM Sleep?* (2019). Sleepfoundation.Org. https://www.sleepfoundation.org/articles/what-you-should-know-about-sleep-paralysis
Reiser, M. F. (2001). The Dream in Contemporary Psychiatry. *American Journal of Psychiatry*, *158*(3), 351–359. https://doi.org/10.1176/appi.ajp.158.3.351
http://ajp.psychiatryonline.org/doi/abs/10.1176/appi.ajp.158.3.351
101) https://www.sleepfoundation.org/dreams/lucid-dreamsn

CHAPTER SIX REFERENCES

1) Rosenbloom, M. H., Schmahmann, J. D., & Price, B. H. (2012). The Functional Neuroanatomy of Decision-Making. *The Journal of Neuropsychiatry and Clinical Neurosciences*, *24*(3), 266–277. https://doi.org/10.1176/appi.neuropsych.11060139
Rudebeck, P. H., Behrens, T. E., Kennerley, S. W., Baxter, M. G., Buckley, M. J., Walton, M. E., & Rushworth, M. F. S. (2008). Frontal Cortex Subregions Play Distinct Roles in Choices between Actions and Stimuli. *Journal of Neuroscience*, *28*(51), 13775–13785. https://doi.org/10.1523/jneurosci.3541-08.2008 https://www.jneurosci.org/content/28/51/13775.long
Diamond, A. (2013). Executive Functions. *Annual Review of Psychology*, *64*(1), 135–168.
https://doi.org/10.1146/annurev-psych-113011-143750
https://www.jneurosci.org/content/27/31 contents of issue with mult articles on executive fx

References

Ball, G., Stokes, P. R., Rhodes, R. A., Bose, S. K., Rezek, I., Wink, A.-M., Lord, L.-D., Mehta, M. A., Grasby, P. M., & Turkheimer, F. E. (2011). Executive Functions and Prefrontal Cortex: A Matter of Persistence? *Frontiers in Systems Neuroscience, 5*. https://doi.org/10.3389/fnsys.2011.00003

Carpenter, P. A., Just, M. A., & Reichle, E. D. (2000). Working memory and executive function: evidence from neuroimaging. *Current opinion in neurobiology, 10*(2), 195–199. https://doi.org/10.1016/s0959-4388(00)00074-x

Yuan, P., & Raz, N. (2014). Prefrontal cortex and executive functions in healthy adults: A meta-analysis of structural neuroimaging studies. *Neuroscience & Biobehavioral Reviews, 42*, 180–192. https://doi.org/10.1016/j.neubiorev.2014.02.005

2) *Control of peripheral somatic muscles depends on a subtle adjustment between motor neuron activation and the tension recorded by muscle spindles in muscle receptors, which provides smooth control of motion, modified by input from descending motor signals from basal ganglia (and pyramidal tracts)*
https://en.wikipedia.org/wiki/Motor_control

Merel, J., Botvinick, M. & Wayne, G. Hierarchical motor control in mammals and machines. *Nat Commun* **10**, 5489 (2019). https://doi.org/10.1038/s41467-019-13239-6

Abbas J. (2014) Neuromuscular Control Systems, Models of. In: Jaeger D., Jung R. (eds) Encyclopedia of Computational Neuroscience. Springer, New York, NY. https://doi.org/10.1007/978-1-4614-7320-6_711-1

3) Best, J. R., & Miller, P. H. (2010). A Developmental Perspective on Executive Function. *Child Development, 81*(6), 1641–1660. https://doi.org/10.1111/j.1467-8624.2010.01499.x

Moriguchi, Y. (2014). The early development of executive function and its relation to social interaction: a brief review. *Frontiers in Psychology, 5*. https://doi.org/10.3389/fpsyg.2014.00388

Brocki, K., Fan, J., & Fossella, J. (2008). Placing Neuroanatomical Models of Executive Function in a Developmental Context. *Annals of the New York Academy of Sciences, 1129*(1), 246–255. https://doi.org/10.1196/annals.1417.025

Sylvester, C. M., Smyser, C. D., Smyser, T., Kenley, J., Ackerman, J. J., Jr, Shimony, J. S., Petersen, S. E., & Rogers, C. E. (2018). Cortical Functional Connectivity Evident After Birth and Behavioral Inhibition at Age 2. *The American journal of psychiatry, 175*(2), 180–187. https://doi.org/10.1176/appi.ajp.2017.17010018

Konrad, K., Firk, C., & Uhlhaas, P. J. (2013). Brain development during adolescence: neuroscientific insights into this developmental period. *Deutsches Arzteblatt international, 110*(25), 425–431. https://doi.org/10.3238/arztebl.2013.0425

Blakemore, S. J., & Choudhury, S. (2006). Development of the adolescent brain: implications for executive function and social cognition. *Journal of child psychology and psychiatry, and allied disciplines, 47*(3-4), 296–312. https://doi.

org/10.1111/j.1469-7610.2006.01611.x
4) Isaacs, B. R., Forstmann, B. U., Temel, Y., & Keuken, M. C. (2018). The Connectivity Fingerprint of the Human Frontal Cortex, Subthalamic Nucleus, and Striatum. *Frontiers in Neuroanatomy, 12*. https://doi.org/10.3389/fnana.2018.00060
https://thebrain.mcgill.ca/flash/i/i_06/i_06_cr/i_06_cr_mou/i_06_cr_mou.html
5) Goldman Rakic projections (The resulting diagram is an approximation (see chapter 1 sidebar for discussion).)
6) Kopp, B. (2012). A simple hypothesis of executive function. *Frontiers in Human Neuroscience, 6*. https://doi.org/10.3389/fnhum.2012.00159
Davis, R. (2016, January 27). *Models of Frontal Lobe Functioning | BRAIN*. Brainaacn.Org.
https://brainaacn.org/models-of-frontal-lobe-functioning/
Rushworth, M. F., Noonan, M. P., Boorman, E. D., Walton, M. E., & Behrens, T. E. (2011). Frontal cortex and reward-guided learning and decision-making. *Neuron, 70*(6), 1054–1069. https://doi.org/10.1016/j.neuron.2011.05.014
Hoffmann M. (2013). The human frontal lobes and frontal network systems: an evolutionary, clinical, and treatment perspective. *ISRN neurology, 2013*, 892459. https://doi.org/10.1155/2013/892459
Balleine B. W. (2007). The Neural Basis of Choice and Decision Making. *The Journal of Neuroscience, 27*(31), 8159–8160.
DOI: https://doi.org/10.1523/JNEUROSCI.1939-07.2007
Corrado, G., & Doya, K. (2007). Understanding neural coding through the model-based analysis of decision making. *The Journal of neuroscience : the official journal of the Society for Neuroscience, 27*(31), 8178–8180.
DOI: https://doi.org/10.1523/JNEUROSCI.1939-07.2007
Fellows L. K. (2004). The cognitive neuroscience of human decision making: a review and conceptual framework. *Behavioral and cognitive neuroscience reviews, 3*(3), 159–172. https://doi.org/10.1177/1534582304273251
7) Rolls, E. T. (2004). The functions of the orbitofrontal cortex. *Brain and Cognition, 55*(1), 11–29. https://doi.org/10.1016/s0278-2626(03)00277-x
Rolls, E. T., & Grabenhorst, F. (2008). The orbitofrontal cortex and beyond: from affect to decision-making. *Progress in neurobiology, 86*(3), 216–244. https://doi.org/10.1016/j.pneurobio.2008.09.001
Duncan, J., & Owen, A. M. (2000). Common regions of the human frontal lobe recruited by diverse cognitive demands. *Trends in neurosciences, 23*(10), 475–483. https://doi.org/10.1016/s0166-2236(00)01633-7
Wheeler, E. Z., & Fellows, L. K. (2008). The human ventromedial frontal lobe is critical for learning from negative feedback. *Brain : a journal of neurology, 131*(Pt 5), 1323–1331. https://doi.org/10.1093/brain/awn041
THARP., B.R. (1972), Orbital Frontal Seizures. An Unique Electroencephalographic and Clinical Syndrome*. Epilepsia, 13: 627-642. https://doi.org/10.1111/j.1528-1157.1972.tb04398.x

References

8) Grossman, M., Eslinger, P. J., Troiani, V., Anderson, C., Avants, B., Gee, J. C., McMillan, C., Massimo, L., Khan, A., & Antani, S. (2010). The role of ventral medial prefrontal cortex in social decisions: converging evidence from fMRI and frontotemporal lobar degeneration. *Neuropsychologia, 48*(12), 3505–3512. https://doi.org/10.1016/j.neuropsychologia.2010.07.036

9) O'Driscoll, K., & Leach, J. P. (1998). "No longer gage": an iron bar through the head. Early observations of personality change after injury to the prefrontal cortex. *BMJ (Clinical Research Ed.), 317*(7174), 1673–1674. https://www.smithsonianmag.com/history/phineas-gage-neurosciences-most-famous-patient-11390067/

Miller A. (1967). The lobotomy patient—a decade later: a follow-up study of a research project started in 1948. *Canadian Medical Association journal, 96*(15), 1095–1103.
https://allthatsinteresting.com/rosemary-kennedy-lobotomy

10) Rudebeck, P. H., & Murray, E. A. (2014). The Orbitofrontal Oracle: Cortical Mechanisms for the Prediction and Evaluation of Specific Behavioral Outcomes. *Neuron, 84*(6), 1143–1156. https://doi.org/10.1016/j.neuron.2014.10.049
https://onlinelibrary.wiley.com/doi/abs/10.1111/j.1528-1157.1972.tb04398.x
https://en.wikipedia.org/wiki/Iowa_gambling_task

IOWA GAMBLING TASK AND REVERSAL LEARNING. *OFC is activated in studies of reversal learning in humans using the* **Iowa gambling task**. *Patients choose from four decks of cards: two 'bad' and two 'good'. Bad decks are associated with large gains on each trial, but also often led to large losses, whereas good decks led to relatively small gains on each trial, but had correspondingly small and less frequent losses. Although both normal and brain-damaged subjects began by choosing mostly from decks that yielded large rewards, normal subjects rapidly switched to choosing the small reward decks. This switching is associated with the development of elevated skin conductance, a proxy for arousal and anxiety, during impending choices of the bad deck. Patients with OFC damage, particularly in the ventromedial part, are impaired on* **the Iowa gambling task**. *Patients with ventromedial OFC damage fail to switch their choices, continuing to choose the bad decks long after controls had stopped, and also fail to manifest the skin conductance responses. ...* <u>*The results can also be interpreted as problems in using new environmental data about rewards to revise sensory-reward data.*</u> *The Iowa gambling task is seen as a reversal task for humans but actually* <u>*involves graduated assessment of reward values.*</u>

Bull, P. N., Tippett, L. J., & Addis, D. R. (2015). Decision making in healthy participants on the Iowa Gambling Task: new insights from an operant approach. *Frontiers in psychology, 6*, 391. https://doi.org/10.3389/fpsyg.2015.00391

O'DOHERTY, J. P. "Lights, Camembert, Action! The Role of Human Orbitofrontal Cortex in Encoding Stimuli, Rewards, and Choices." *Annals of the New York Academy of Sciences*, vol. 1121, no. 1, 10 Sept. 2007, pp. 254–272, 10.1196/annals.1401.036.

https://pdfs.semanticscholar.org/896f/d13e7e-591172004b3351e5982922b14b0f0e.pdf
D'Argembeau, A. (2013). On the Role of the Ventromedial Prefrontal Cortex in Self-Processing: The Valuation Hypothesis. *Frontiers in Human Neuroscience*, 7. https://doi.org/10.3389/fnhum.2013.00372
Hu, C., & Jiang, X. (2014). An emotion regulation role of ventromedial prefrontal cortex in moral judgment. *Frontiers in Human Neuroscience*, 8. https://doi.org/10.3389/fnhum.2014.00873
11) Potts, G. F., Martin, L. E., Burton, P., & Montague, P. R. (2006). When Things Are Better or Worse than Expected: The Medial Frontal Cortex and the Allocation of Processing Resources. *Journal of Cognitive Neuroscience*, *18*(7), 1112–1119. https://doi.org/10.1162/jocn.2006.18.7.1112
12) Stalnaker, T. A., Cooch, N. K., & Schoenbaum, G. (2015). What the orbitofrontal cortex does not do. *Nature Neuroscience*, *18*(5), 620–627. https://doi.org/10.1038/nn.3982
13) https://en.wikipedia.org/wiki/Dorsolateral_prefrontal_cortex
Levy, R., & Goldman-Rakic, P. S. (2000). Segregation of working memory functions within the dorsolateral prefrontal cortex. *Executive Control and the Frontal Lobe: Current Issues*, 23–32. https://doi.org/10.1007/978-3-642-59794-7_4
Dolan, R. J., Bench, C. J., Liddle, P. F., Friston, K. J., Frith, C. D., Grasby, P. M., & Frackowiak, R. S. (1993). Dorsolateral prefrontal cortex dysfunction in the major psychoses; symptom or disease specificity? *Journal of Neurology, Neurosurgery & Psychiatry*, *56*(12), 1290–1294. https://doi.org/10.1136/jnnp.56.12.1290
14) https://en.wikipedia.org/wiki/Wisconsin_Card_Sorting_Test
https://www.psytoolkit.org/experiment-library/wcst.html lets you try this online!
The WCST consists of two card packs having four stimulus cards and 64 response cards in each. Each card measures 7×7 cm, and there are various geometric shapes in different colors and numbers. The participants are expected to accurately sort every response card with one of four stimulus cards through the feedback (right or wrong) given to them based on a rule. The rule for matching may be changed, testing the ability to change response to changing reward.
Stuss, D. T., Levine, B., Alexander, M. P., Hong, J., Palumbo, C., Hamer, L., Murphy, K. J., & Izukawa, D. (2000). Wisconsin Card Sorting Test performance in patients with focal frontal and posterior brain damage: effects of lesion location and test structure on separable cognitive processes. *Neuropsychologia*, *38*(4), 388–402. https://doi.org/10.1016/s0028-3932(99)00093-7
15) Fujii, D., & Fujii, D. C. (2012). Psychotic disorder due to traumatic brain injury: analysis of case studies in the literature. *The Journal of neuropsychiatry and clinical neurosciences*, *24*(3), 278–289.https://doi.org/10.1176/appi.neuropsych.11070176
Snyder, H. R., Miyake, A., & Hankin, B. L. (2015). Advancing understanding

References

of executive function impairments and psychopathology: bridging the gap between clinical and cognitive approaches. *Frontiers in Psychology*, 6. https://doi.org/10.3389/fpsyg.2015.00328

Baetens, K. L. M. R., Ma, N., & Van Overwalle, F. (2017). The Dorsal Medial Prefrontal Cortex Is Recruited by High Construal of Non-social Stimuli. *Frontiers in Behavioral Neuroscience*, 11. https://doi.org/10.3389/fnbeh.2017.00044

Structural and Functional Alterations in Right Dorsomedial Prefrontal and Left Insular Cortex Co-Localize in Adolescents with Aggressive Behaviour: An ALE Meta-Analysis,Nora Maria Raschle , Willeke Martine Menks, Lynn Valérie Fehlbaum, Ebongo Tshomba, Christina StadlerPublished: September 4, 2015 https://doi.org/10.1371/journal.pone.0136553

Yoo, A. H., & Collins, A. (2022). How Working Memory and Reinforcement Learning Are Intertwined: A Cognitive, Neural, and Computational Perspective. *Journal of cognitive neuroscience*, *34*(4), 551–568. https://doi.org/10.1162/jocn_a_01808

16) Frank, M. J., Loughry, B., & O'Reilly, R. C. (2001). Interactions between frontal cortex and basal ganglia in working memory: a computational model. *Cognitive, affective & behavioral neuroscience*, *1*(2), 137–160. https://doi.org/10.3758/cabn.1.2.137

17) *The motor system was traditionally separated into the "pyramidal tracts", originating in pyramidal cells of the motor strip anterior to the central sulcus which provide direct input to spinal motor activity, and the system of "accessory motor areas", coordinating complex movements through a series of subcortical nuclei, "the basal ganglia" ("striate cortex"). Research in the 1990s clarified the interactions of the motor control process.* http://www.neuroanatomy.wisc.edu/coursebook/motor2.pdf
https://www.sciencedirect.com/science/article/pii/S0166411506800063

Alexander, G. E., DeLong, M. R., & Strick, P. L. (1986). Parallel Organization of Functionally Segregated Circuits Linking Basal Ganglia and Cortex. *Annual Review of Neuroscience*, *9*(1), 357–381. https://doi.org/10.1146/annurev.ne.09.030186.002041

Alexander, G. E., Crutcher, M. D., & DeLong, M. R. (1991). Chapter 6 Basal ganglia-thalamocortical circuits: Parallel substrates for motor, oculomotor, "prefrontal" and "limbic" functions. *Progress in Brain Research*, 119–146. https://doi.org/10.1016/s0079-6123(08)62678-3

DeLong, M., & Wichmann, T. (2009). Update on models of basal ganglia function and dysfunction. *Parkinsonism & related disorders*, *15 Suppl 3*(0 3), S237–S240. https://doi.org/10.1016/S1353-8020(09)70822-3

Schmahmann, J. D., & Pandya, D. N. (2008). Disconnection syndromes of basal ganglia, thalamus, and cerebrocerebellar systems. *Cortex;* *44*(8), 1037–1066. https://doi.org/10.1016/j.cortex.2008.04.004

DeLong, M., & Wichmann, T. (2010). Changing views of basal ganglia circuits and circuit disorders. *Clinical EEG and neuroscience*, *41*(2), 61–67. https://doi.org/10.1177/155005941004100204

Lanciego, J. L., Luquin, N., & Obeso, J. A. (2012). Functional Neuroanatomy of the Basal Ganglia. *Cold Spring Harbor Perspectives in Medicine*, *2*(12), a009621–a009621. https://doi.org/10.1101/cshperspect.a009621

Ring, H. A., & Serra-Mestres, J. (2002). Neuropsychiatry of the basal ganglia. *Journal of neurology, neurosurgery, and psychiatry*, *72*(1), 12–21. https://doi.org/10.1136/jnnp.72.1.12

Middleton, F. A., & Strick, P. L. (2000). Basal ganglia output and cognition: evidence from anatomical, behavioral, and clinical studies. *Brain and cognition*, *42*(2), 183–200. https://doi.org/10.1006/brcg.1999.1099

18) Ikemoto, S., Yang, C., & Tan, A. (2015). Basal ganglia circuit loops, dopamine and motivation: A review and enquiry. *Behavioural Brain Research*, *290*, 17–31. https://doi.org/10.1016/j.bbr.2015.04.018

Chau, B., Jarvis, H., Law, C. K., & Chong, T. T. (2018). Dopamine and reward: a view from the prefrontal cortex. *Behavioural pharmacology*, *29*(7), 569–583. https://doi.org/10.1097/FBP.0000000000000424

Haber, S. N., & Knutson, B. (2009). The Reward Circuit: Linking Primate Anatomy and Human Imaging. *Neuropsychopharmacology*, *35*(1), 4–26. https://doi.org/10.1038/npp.2009.129

Haber, S. N. (2011). *Neuroanatomy of Reward: A View from the Ventral Striatum*. Nih.Gov; CRC Press/Taylor https://www.ncbi.nlm.nih.gov/books/NBK92787/

Taylor, A. E., Saint-Cyr, J. A., & Lang, A. E. (1986). Frontal Lobe Dysfunction In Parkinson's Disease the Cortical Focus Of Neostriatal Outflow. *Brain*, *109*(5), 845–883. https://doi.org/10.1093/brain/109.5.845

Luo, S. X., & Huang, E. J. (2016). Dopaminergic Neurons and Brain Reward Pathways. *The American Journal of Pathology*, *186*(3), 478–488. https://doi.org/10.1016/j.ajpath.2015.09.023

19) Graybiel A. M. (1998). The basal ganglia and chunking of action repertoires. *Neurobiology of learning and memory*, *70*(1-2), 119–136. https://doi.org/10.1006/nlme.1998.3843

"Go" and... Dana Foundation; Dana Foundation. https://www.dana.org/article/go-and-nogo/

Bahuguna, J., Aertsen, A., & Kumar, A. (2015). Existence and Control of Go/No-Go Decision Transition Threshold in the Striatum. *PLOS Computational Biology*, *11*(4), e1004233. https://doi.org/10.1371/journal.pcbi.1004233

Maia, T. V., & Frank, M. J. (2011). From reinforcement learning models to psychiatric and neurological disorders. *Nature Neuroscience*, *14*(2), 154–162. https://doi.org/10.1038/nn.2723

https://studywolf.wordpress.com/2012/10/09/the-basal-ganglia-for-action-selection/

20) Houk J. C. (2005). Agents of the mind. *Biological cybernetics*, *92*(6),

References

427–437. https://doi.org/10.1007/s00422-005-0569-8

Houk, James. (2000). Neurophysiology of Frontal-Subcortical Loops. https://www.researchgate.net/publication/237321150_Neurophysiology_of_Frontal-Subcortical_Loops

Houk, J. C., & Wise, S. P. (1995). Feature Article: Distributed Modular Architectures Linking Basal Ganglia, Cerebellum, and Cerebral Cortex: Their Role in Planning and Controlling Action. *Cerebral Cortex*, *5*(2), 95–110. https://doi.org/10.1093/cercor/5.2.95

Schroll, H., & Hamker, F. H. (2013). Computational models of basal-ganglia pathway functions: focus on functional neuroanatomy. *Frontiers in Systems Neuroscience*, *7*. https://doi.org/10.3389/fnsys.2013.00122

21) Alexander, G. E., DeLong, M. R., & Crutcher, M. D. (2020). Do cortical and basal ganglionic motor areas use "motor programs" to control movement? *Behavioral and Brain Sciences*, *15*(4), 656–665. https://doi.org/10.1017/S0140525X00072575

Nakahara, H., Amari, S., & Hikosaka, O. (2002). Self-Organization in the Basal Ganglia with Modulation of Reinforcement Signals. *Neural Computation*, *14*(4), 819–844. https://doi.org/10.1162/089976602317318974

Jin, X., & Costa, R. M. (2015). Shaping action sequences in basal ganglia circuits. *Current opinion in neurobiology*, *33*, 188–196. https://doi.org/10.1016/j.conb.2015.06.011

Dhawale, A.K., Wolff, S.B.E., Ko, R. *et al.* The basal ganglia control the detailed kinematics of learned motor skills. *Nat Neurosci* **24**, 1256–1269 (2021). https://doi.org/10.1038/s41593-021-00889-3 https://www.biorxiv.org/content/10.1101/827261v1.full

Charlesworth, J. D., Warren, T. L., & Brainard, M. S. (2012). Covert skill learning in a cortical-basal ganglia circuit. *Nature*, *486*(7402), 251–255. https://doi.org/10.1038/nature11078

Ohbayashi Machiko, The Roles of the Cortical Motor Areas in Sequential Movements Frontiers in Behavioral Neuroscience, 15, 2021 https://www.frontiersin.org/article/10.3389/fnbeh.2021.640659

22) Beckmann, M., Johansen-Berg, H., & Rushworth, M. F. S. (2009). Connectivity-Based Parcellation of Human Cingulate Cortex. *Journal of Neuroscience*, *29*(4), 1175–1190. https://doi.org/10.1523/jneurosci.3328-08.2009

Kolling, N., Behrens, T., Wittmann, M., & Rushworth, M. (2016). Multiple signals in anterior cingulate cortex. *Current Opinion in Neurobiology*, *37*, 36–43. https://doi.org/10.1016/j.conb.2015.12.007

Stevens, F. L., Hurley, R. A., & Taber, K. H. (2011). Anterior Cingulate Cortex: Unique Role in Cognition and Emotion. *Journal of Neuropsychiatry*, *23*(2), 121–125. https://doi.org/10.1176/appi.neuropsych.23.2.121

García-Cabezas, M. Á., & Barbas, H. (2013). A direct anterior cingulate pathway to the primate primary olfactory cortex may control attention to olfaction. *Brain Structure and Function*, *219*(5), 1735–1754. https://doi.org/10.1007/

s00429-013-0598-3
Dedovic, K., Slavich, G. M., Muscatell, K. A., Irwin, M. R., & Eisenberger, N. I. (2016). Dorsal Anterior Cingulate Cortex Responses to Repeated Social Evaluative Feedback in Young Women with and without a History of Depression. *Frontiers in Behavioral Neuroscience, 10*. https://doi.org/10.3389/fnbeh.2016.00064

This is a typical programming branch point*: is desired result obtained?*
    Yes = return to 4) and repeat until motivational signal is extinguished
    No = return to 3) shift lookup to different behavior, continue to 4)

Plans and the structure of behavior. (2010) http://archive.org/stream/plansstructureof00mill#page/12/mode/2up

22) **Stroop task** When the name of a color (e.g., "blue", "green", or "red") is printed in a color which is not denoted by the name (i.e., the word "red" printed in blue ink instead of red ink), naming the color of the word takes longer and is more prone to errors than when the color of the ink matches the name of the color.

MacLeod, C.M. (1991). Half a century of research on the Stroop effect: An integrative review. *Psychological Bulletin, 109*, 163-203. http://psycnet.apa.org/doiLanding?doi=10.1037%2F0033-2909.109.2.163

Weissman, D. H. (2004). Dorsal Anterior Cingulate Cortex Resolves Conflict from Distracting Stimuli by Boosting Attention toward Relevant Events. *Cerebral Cortex, 15*(2), 229–237. https://doi.org/10.1093/cercor/bhh125

Kennerley, S. W., Walton, M. E., Behrens, T. E., Buckley, M. J., & Rushworth, M. F. (2006). Optimal decision making and the anterior cingulate cortex. *Nature neuroscience, 9*(7), 940–947. https://doi.org/10.1038/nn1724

23) https://en.wikipedia.org/wiki/Eriksen_flanker_task

ERIKSEN FLANKER TEST Targets were flanked by either a congruent or an incongruent set of letters. Using an image of a thumb (up, down, or neutral), participants received feedback on how much money they gained or lost. The researchers found greater rostral ACC activation when participants lost money during the trials. The participants reported being frustrated when making mistakes.

Gehring, W. J., Goss, B., Coles, M. G. H., Meyer, D. E., & Donchin, E. (1993). A Neural System for Error Detection and Compensation. *Psychological Science, 4*(6), 385–390. https://doi.org/10.1111/j.1467-9280.1993.tb00586.x

Taylor, S. F. (2006). Medial Frontal Cortex Activity and Loss-Related Responses to Errors. *Journal of Neuroscience, 26*(15), 4063–4070. https://doi.org/10.1523/jneurosci.4709-05.2006

24) Kolling, N., Behrens, T., Wittmann, M., & Rushworth, M. (2016). Multiple signals in anterior cingulate cortex. *Current Opinion in Neurobiology, 37*, 36–43. https://doi.org/10.1016/j.conb.2015.12.007

Apps, M. A. J., Rushworth, M. F. S., & Chang, S. W. C. (2016). The Anterior

References

Cingulate Gyrus and Social Cognition: Tracking the Motivation of Others. *Neuron, 90*(4), 692–707. https://doi.org/10.1016/j.neuron.2016.04.018

Rushworth, M. F. S., Behrens, T. E. J., Rudebeck, P. H., & Walton, M. E. (2007). Contrasting roles for cingulate and orbitofrontal cortex in decisions and social behaviour. *Trends in Cognitive Sciences, 11*(4), 168–176. https://doi.org/10.1016/j.tics.2007.01.004

25) Cecil, K. M., Brubaker, C. J., Adler, C. M., Dietrich, K. N., Altaye, M., Egelhoff, J. C., Wessel, S., Elangovan, I., Hornung, R., Jarvis, K., & Lanphear, B. P. (2008). Decreased brain volume in adults with childhood lead exposure. *PLoS medicine, 5*(5), e112. https://doi.org/10.1371/journal.pmed.0050112

26) Kolling, N., Wittmann, M., Behrens, T. et al. Value, search, persistence and model updating in anterior cingulate cortex. *Nat Neurosci* **19,** 1280–1285 (2016). https://doi.org/10.1038/nn.4382

Banks, S. J., Eddy, K. T., Angstadt, M., Nathan, P. J., & Phan, K. L. (2007). Amygdala–frontal connectivity during emotion regulation. *Social Cognitive and Affective Neuroscience, 2*(4), 303–312. https://doi.org/10.1093/scan/nsm029

Ramirez-Mahaluf, J. P., Perramon, J., Otal, B., Villoslada, P., & Compte, A. (2018). Subgenual anterior cingulate cortex controls sadness-induced modulations. *Scientific Reports, 8*(1). https://doi.org/10.1038/s41598-018-26317-4

Redgrave, P., Prescott, T. J., & Gurney, K. (1999). The basal ganglia: a vertebrate solution to the selection problem? *Neuroscience, 89*(4), 1009–1023. https://doi.org/10.1016/s0306-4522(98)00319-4

Prescott gives an evolutionary perspective on the development of these control systems based on simpler organisms that helps the understanding of the adaptive mechanisms of more complex brains.

http://users.sussex.ac.uk/~inmanh/adsys10/Readings/Prescott_-_Landmarks_in_the_evolution_of_action_selection_-_AB_2007.pdf

27) Critchley, H. D., Mathias, C. J., Josephs, O., O'Doherty, J., Zanini, S., Dewar, B. K., Cipolotti, L., Shallice, T., & Dolan, R. J. (2003). Human cingulate cortex and autonomic control: converging neuroimaging and clinical evidence. *Brain : a journal of neurology, 126*(Pt 10), 2139–2152. https://doi.org/10.1093/brain/awg216

Critchley, H. D., Tang, J., Glaser, D., Butterworth, B., & Dolan, R. J. (2005). Anterior cingulate activity during error and autonomic response. *NeuroImage, 27*(4), 885–895. https://doi.org/10.1016/j.neuroimage.2005.05.047

Matthews, S. (2004). Functional subdivisions within anterior cingulate cortex and their relationship to autonomic nervous system function. *NeuroImage.* https://doi.org/10.1016/s1053-8119(04)00149-1

Frysinger, R. ., & Harper, R. . (1986). Cardiac and respiratory relationships with neural discharge in the anterior cingulate cortex during sleep-waking states. *Experimental Neurology, 94*(2), 247–263.

Leech, R., & Sharp, D. J. (2014). The role of the posterior cingulate cortex in cognition and disease. *Brain : a journal of neurology, 137*(Pt 1), 12–32. https://

doi.org/10.1093/brain/awt162 https://doi.org/10.1093/brain/awt162
28) Critchley H. D. (2009). Psychophysiology of neural, cognitive and affective integration: fMRI and autonomic indicants. *International journal of psychophysiology : official journal of the International Organization of Psychophysiology*, 73(2), 88–94. https://doi.org/10.1016/j.ijpsycho.2009.01.012
29) Deen, B., Pitskel, N. B., & Pelphrey, K. A. (2010). Three Systems of Insular Functional Connectivity Identified with Cluster Analysis. *Cerebral Cortex*, 21(7), 1498–1506. https://doi.org/10.1093/cercor/bhq186
Ibañez, A., Gleichgerrcht, E., & Manes, F. (2010). Clinical effects of insular damage in humans. *Brain Structure and Function*, 214(5–6), 397–410. https://doi.org/10.1007/s00429-010-0256-y
Nord, Camilla & Lawson, Rebecca & Dalgleish, Tim. (2021). Disrupted Dorsal Mid-Insula Activation During Interoception Across Psychiatric Disorders. American Journal of Psychiatry. 178. appi.ajp.2020.2. 10.1176/appi.ajp.2020.20091340.
Lemieux, F., Lanthier, S., Chevrier, M.-C., Gioia, L., Rouleau, I., Cereda, C., & Nguyen, D. K. (2012). Insular Ischemic Stroke: Clinical Presentation and Outcome. *Cerebrovascular Diseases Extra*, 2(1), 80–87. https://doi.org/10.1159/000343177
Medford, N., & Critchley, H. D. (2010). Conjoint activity of anterior insular and anterior cingulate cortex: awareness and response. *Brain Structure and Function*, 214(5–6), 535–549. https://doi.org/10.1007/s00429-010-0265-x
Damasio A. R. (1996). The somatic marker hypothesis and the possible functions of the prefrontal cortex. *Philosophical transactions of the Royal Society of London. Series B, Biological sciences*, 351(1346), 1413–1420. https://doi.org/10.1098/rstb.1996.0125
Stephani, C., Fernandez-Baca Vaca, G., Maciunas, R., Koubeissi, M., & Lüders, H. O. (2010). Functional neuroanatomy of the insular lobe. *Brain Structure and Function*, 216(2), 137–149.https://doi.org/10.1007/s00429-010-0296-3
Starr, C. J., Sawaki, L., Wittenberg, G. F., Burdette, J. H., Oshiro, Y., Quevedo, A. S., & Coghill, R. C. (2009). Roles of the Insular Cortex in the Modulation of Pain: Insights from Brain Lesions. *Journal of Neuroscience*, 29(9), 2684–2694. https://doi.org/10.1523/jneurosci.5173-08.2009
Droutman, V., Read, S. J., & Bechara, A. (2015). Revisiting the role of the insula in addiction. *Trends in Cognitive Sciences*, 19(7), 414–420. https://doi.org/10.1016/j.tics.2015.05.005
Emmerling, F., Schuhmann, T., Lobbestael, J., Arntz, A., Brugman, S., & Sack, A. T. (2016). The Role of the Insular Cortex in Retaliation. *PLOS ONE*, 11(4), e0152000. https://doi.org/10.1371/journal.pone.0152000
Evrard, H. C., Forro, T., & Logothetis, N. K. (2012). Von Economo Neurons in the Anterior Insula of the Macaque Monkey. *Neuron*, 74(3), 482–489. https://doi.org/10.1016/j.neuron.2012.03.003
Bartra, O., McGuire, J. T., & Kable, J. W. (2013). The valuation system:

References

a coordinate-based meta-analysis of BOLD fMRI experiments examining neural correlates of subjective value. *NeuroImage, 76*, 412–427. https://doi.org/10.1016/j.neuroimage.2013.02.063

Cauda, F., Geminiani, G. C., & Vercelli, A. (2014). Evolutionary appearance of von Economo's neurons in the mammalian cerebral cortex. *Frontiers in human neuroscience, 8*, 104. https://doi.org/10.3389/fnhum.2014.00104 https://www.frontiersin.org/articles/10.3389/fnhum.2014.00104/full

30) Menon, V., & Uddin, L. Q. (2010). Saliency, switching, attention and control: a network model of insula function. *Brain structure & function, 214*(5-6), 655–667. https://doi.org/10.1007/s00429-010-0262-0

Seeley, W. W., Menon, V., Schatzberg, A. F., Keller, J., Glover, G. H., Kenna, H., Reiss, A. L., & Greicius, M. D. (2007). Dissociable Intrinsic Connectivity Networks for Salience Processing and Executive Control. *Journal of Neuroscience, 27*(9), 2349–2356. doi: 10.1523/JNEUROSCI.5587-06.2007

Seeley W. W. (2019). The Salience Network: A Neural System for Perceiving and Responding to Homeostatic Demands. *The Journal of neuroscience : the official journal of the Society for Neuroscience, 39*(50), 9878–9882. https://doi.org/10.1523/JNEUROSCI.1138-17.2019

Niendam, T. A., Laird, A. R., Ray, K. L., Dean, Y. M., Glahn, D. C., & Carter, C. S. (2012). Meta-analytic evidence for a superordinate cognitive control network subserving diverse executive functions. *Cognitive, Affective & Behavioral Neuroscience, 12*(2), 241–268. https://doi.org/10.3758/s13415-011-0083-5

Dosenbach, N. U., Fair, D. A., Cohen, A. L., Schlaggar, B. L., & Petersen, S. E. (2008). A dual-networks architecture of top-down control. *Trends in cognitive sciences, 12*(3), 99–105. https://doi.org/10.1016/j.tics.2008.01.001

31) King-Casas, B., Tomlin, D., Anen, C., Camerer, C. F., Quartz, S. R., & Montague, P. R. (2005). Getting to know you: reputation and trust in a two-person economic exchange. *Science (New York, N.Y.), 308*(5718), 78–83. https://doi.org/10.1126/science.1108062

https://en.wikipedia.org/wiki/Read_Montague

Xiang T, Ray D, Lohrenz T, Dayan P, Montague PR (2012) Computational Phenotyping of Two-Person Interactions Reveals Differential Neural Response to Depth-of-Thought. PLoS Comput Biol 8(12): e1002841. https://doi.org/10.1371/journal.pcbi.1002841

Other proposed models of the executive process sequence:
Miyake and Friedman's theory proposes three aspects: **updating, inhibition, and shifting**.[53] "Updating" is the continuous monitoring of contents within one's **working memory** in Step #2 of DLPFC. "Inhibition" **modifies responses** in step #5 through input of ACC. "Shifting" is flexibility to **switch between different tasks** or mental states. The shifting process is the effect of Step #5 correction and repeat iteration.

Miyake, A., Friedman, N. P., Emerson, M. J., Witzki, A. H., Howerter, A., &

Wager, T. D. (2000). The Unity and Diversity of Executive Functions and Their Contributions to Complex "Frontal Lobe" Tasks: A Latent Variable Analysis. *Cognitive Psychology, 41*(1), 49–100. https://doi.org/10.1006/cogp.1999.0734

Banich *defines a sequence based on studies using the Stroop Task 1)posterior DLPFC creates attentional set, or rules for the brain to accomplish the current goal. For the Stroop task, this involves activating the areas of the brain involved in color perception, and not those involved in word comprehension. It counteracts biases and irrelevant information, like the fact that the semantic perception of the word is more salient to most people than the color in which it is printed.2) Next, the mid-DLPFC selects the representation that will fulfill the goal. The task-relevant information must be separated from other sources of information in the task. In the example, this means focusing on the ink color and not the word. (STEP #2 and #6), 3)The posterior (ACC) is next in the cascade, and it is responsible for response selection. This is where the decision is made whether you will say green (the written word and the incorrect answer) or red (the font color and correct answer). 4)Following the response, the anterior dorsal ACC is involved in response evaluation, deciding whether you were correct or incorrect. Activity in this region increases when the probability of an error is higher. (Step #5)This model overlaps steps #2 #3 and #5 and ignores #1 and #4 because it focuses on a specific cognitive human task and was not concerned with motivation.*

Kopp B. (2012). A simple hypothesis of executive function. *Frontiers in human neuroscience, 6,* 159. https://doi.org/10.3389/fnhum.2012.00159

Miller, E. K., & Cohen, J. D. (2001). An integrative theory of prefrontal cortex function. *Annual review of neuroscience, 24,* 167–202. https://doi.org/10.1146/annurev.neuro.24.1.167

32) https://en.wikipedia.org/wiki/Benjamin_Libet
https://blogs.scientificamerican.com/observations/how-a-flawed-experiment-proved-that-free-will-doesnt-exist/

33) Gazzaniga, **Who's In Charge? Free Will And The Science Of The Brain.** *The Gifford Lectures*, 30 Oct. 2014, www.giffordlectures.org/books/whos-charge-free-will-and-science-brain.
https://drdansiegel.com

34) Bandura, A. (1989). Human agency in social cognitive theory. *American Psychologist, 44*(9), 1175–1184. https://doi.org/10.1037//0003-066x.44.9.1175
https://www.uky.edu/~eushe2/Bandura/Bandura1989AP.pdf

35) McLaren, N. (2009). ***Humanizing Psychiatry: The Biocognitive Model***. United States: Future Psychiatry Press. *a computational view and concludes that whatever the biocomputer computes, the organism is determined to do, and therefore there is no "free will"(not a very humanizing conclusion!).*

36) The Neuroscience of Mental Imagery as it Relates to Athlete Performance https://kaylatilkes.medium.com/the-neuroscience-of-mental-imagery-as-it-relates-to-athlete-performance-a861bc4b3489

37) This issue has been reevaluated by legal scholars in the light of new

information in neuroscience.
https://jgcrimlaw.com/blog/free-will-determinism-and-the-criminal-justice-system/

38) **Neuromind** *proposes a universal model of symptoms: changes in pathways that are maladaptive. This complicates assessment because certain behavior may be adaptive in one circumstance but not in another. This is the importance of adaptation as a criterion, see chapter ten.*

39) *Manzotti and Chella propose a self organizing computer system that demonstrates similar properties. This leads to the (uncomfortable) position, that if a system can demonstrate "free will" behaviors in humans, a similar one can be designed in electronic computer systems of sufficient power:*
Manzotti, R. (n.d.). *Intentional robots The design of a goal-seeking, environment-driven, agent.* Retrieved from http://www.consciousness.it/Docs/tesi.pdf Chella, A., & Manzotti, R. (n.d.). *Artificial Intelligence and Consciousness.* Retrieved February 24, 2020, from http://www.consciousness.it/CAI/online_papers/Chella%20Manzotti%20-%20Introductory%20Paper.pdf
https://www.amazon.com/Artificial-Consciousness-Antonio-Chella/dp/1845400704
(A similar view in Kurzweil, Ray. *The Age of Spiritual Machines : When Computers Exceed Human Intelligence.* New York, Penguin, 2000.)

40) Posture is learned in humans when children go from quadrapedal to bipedal locomation by observing this in adults.
Human Growth and development 2nd ED, Academic Press 2012 **Hardcover ISBN:** 9780123838827 **eBook ISBN:** 9780123846518
Erikson, *Eight Ages Of Man* focuses on the developmental stages as specific types of social interaction.
Kohlberg stages https://en.wikipedia.org/wiki/Lawrence_Kohlberg%27s_stages_of_moral_development
Fairchild, G., Passamonti, L., Hurford, G., Hagan, C. C., von dem Hagen, E. A., van Goozen, S. H., Goodyer, I. M., & Calder, A. J. (2011). Brain structure abnormalities in early-onset and adolescent-onset conduct disorder. *The American journal of psychiatry, 168*(6), 624–633. https://doi.org/10.1176/appi.ajp.2010.10081184
Guyer, A. E., Choate, V. R., Detloff, A., Benson, B., Nelson, E. E., Perez-Edgar, K., Fox, N. A., Pine, D. S., & Ernst, M. (2012). Striatal functional alteration during incentive anticipation in pediatric anxiety disorders. *The American journal of psychiatry, 169*(2), 205–212. https://doi.org/10.1176/appi.ajp.2011.11010006

41) Lange, K. W., Reichl, S., Lange, K. M., Tucha, L., & Tucha, O. (2010). The history of attention deficit hyperactivity disorder. *Attention deficit and hyperactivity disorders, 2*(4), 241–255. https://doi.org/10.1007/s12402-010-0045-8
https://www.psychologytoday.com/us/blog/saving-normal/201603/keith-connors-father-adhd-regrets-its-current-misuse
Ball, G., Malpas, C. B., Genc, S., Efron, D., Sciberras, E., Anderson, V.,

Nicholson, J. M., & Silk, T. J. (2019). Multimodal Structural Neuroimaging Markers of Brain Development and ADHD Symptoms. *The American journal of psychiatry*, *176*(1), 57–66. https://doi.org/10.1176/appi.ajp.2018.18010034

Stevens, M. C., Pearlson, G. D., Calhoun, V. D., & Bessette, K. L. (2018). Functional Neuroimaging Evidence for Distinct Neurobiological Pathways in Attention-Deficit/Hyperactivity Disorder. *Biological Psychiatry: Cognitive Neuroscience and Neuroimaging*, *3*(8), 675–685. https://doi.org/10.1016/j.bpsc.2017.09.005

Emond, V., Joyal, C., & Poissant, H. (2009). Structural and functional neuroanatomy of attention-deficit hyperactivity disorder (ADHD). *L'Encephale*, *35*(2), 107–114. https://doi.org/10.1016/j.encep.2008.01.005

Dickstein, S. G., Bannon, K., Xavier Castellanos, F., & Milham, M. P. (2006). The neural correlates of attention deficit hyperactivity disorder: an ALE meta-analysis. *Journal of Child Psychology and Psychiatry*, *47*(10), 1051–1062. https://doi.org/10.1111/j.1469-7610.2006.01671.x

Shim, S.-H., Yoon, H., Bak, J., Hahn, S.-W., & Kim, Y.-K. (2016). Clinical and neurobiological factors in the management of treatment refractory attention-deficit hyperactivity disorder. *Progress in Neuro-Psychopharmacology and Biological Psychiatry*, *70*, 237–244. https://doi.org/10.1016/j.pnpbp.2016.04.007

D'Onofrio, B. M., Class, Q. A., Rickert, M. E., Larsson, H., Långström, N., & Lichtenstein, P. (2013). Preterm birth and mortality and morbidity. *JAMA psychiatry*, *70*(11), 1231–1240. https://doi.org/10.1001/jamapsychiatry.2013.2107

Sujan AC, Rickert ME, Öberg AS, et al. Associations of Maternal Antidepressant Use During the First Trimester of Pregnancy With Preterm Birth, Small for Gestational Age, Autism Spectrum Disorder, and Attention-Deficit/Hyperactivity Disorder in Offspring. *JAMA*. 2017;317(15):1553–1562. doi:10.1001/jama.2017.3413 https://jamanetwork.com/journals/jama/fullarticle/2618619%20

42) Thapar A. (2018). Discoveries on the Genetics of ADHD in the 21st Century: New Findings and Their Implications. *The American journal of psychiatry*, *175*(10), 943–950. https://doi.org/10.1176/appi.ajp.2018.18040383

Poelmans, G., Pauls, D. L., Buitelaar, J. K., & Franke, B. (2011). Integrated Genome-Wide Association Study Findings: Identification of a Neurodevelopmental Network for Attention Deficit Hyperactivity Disorder. *American Journal of Psychiatry*, *168*(4), 365–377. https://doi.org/10.1176/appi.ajp.2010.10070948

Faraone, S. V., & Larsson, H. (2018). Genetics of attention deficit hyperactivity disorder. *Molecular Psychiatry*. https://doi.org/10.1038/s41380-018-0070-0 https://www.nature.com/articles/s41380-018-0070-0

Bornovalova, M. A., Hicks, B. M., Iacono, W. G., & McGue, M. (2010). Familial Transmission and Heritability of Childhood Disruptive Disorders. *American Journal of Psychiatry*, *167*(9), 1066–1074. https://doi.org/10.1176/appi.ajp.2010.09091272

Stergiakouli, E., Hamshere, M., Holmans, P., Langley, K., Zaharieva, I., Hawi,

References

Z., Kent, L., Gill, M., Williams, N., Owen, M. J., O'Donovan, M., & Thapar, A. (2012). Investigating the Contribution of Common Genetic Variants to the Risk and Pathogenesis of ADHD. *American Journal of Psychiatry, 169*(2), 186–194. https://doi.org/10.1176/appi.ajp.2011.11040551

Williams, N. M., Franke, B., Mick, E., Anney, R. J. L., Freitag, C. M., Gill, M., Thapar, A., O'Donovan, M. C., Owen, M. J., Holmans, P., Kent, L., Middleton, F., Zhang-James, Y., Liu, L., Meyer, J., Nguyen, T. T., Romanos, J., Romanos, M., Seitz, C., ... Faraone, S. V. (2012). Genome-Wide Analysis of Copy Number Variants in Attention Deficit Hyperactivity Disorder: The Role of Rare Variants and Duplications at 15q13.3. *American Journal of Psychiatry, 169*(2), 195–204. https://doi.org/10.1176/appi.ajp.2011.11060822

Xu, G., Strathearn, L., Liu, B., Yang, B., & Bao, W. (2018). Twenty-Year Trends in Diagnosed Attention-Deficit/Hyperactivity Disorder Among US Children and Adolescents, 1997-2016. *JAMA Network Open, 1*(4), e181471. https://doi.org/10.1001/jamanetworkopen.2018.1471

Nikolas, M., Friderici, K., Waldman, I., Jernigan, K., & Nigg, J. T. (2010). Gene x environment interactions for ADHD: synergistic effect of 5HTTLPR genotype and youth appraisals of inter-parental conflict. *Behavioral and brain functions : BBF, 6*, 23. https://doi.org/10.1186/1744-9081-6-23 https://www.ncbi.nlm.nih.gov/pmc/articles/PMC2865439/

van der Meer D, Hoekstra PJ, Zwiers M, et al.: Brain correlates of the interaction between 5-HTTLPR and psychosocial stress mediating attention deficit hyperactivity disorder severity. **Am J Psychiatry** 2015; 172:768–775 https://ajp.psychiatryonline.org/doi/10.1176/appi.ajp.2015.15050619

http://www.brainhealth.utdallas.edu/pdfs/Predictors_of_attention-deficit-hyperactivity_disorder_within_6_months_after_pediatric_traumatic_brain_injury.pdf

43) Rubia, K. "Neuro-Anatomic Evidence for the Maturational Delay Hypothesis of ADHD." *PNAS*, vol. 104, no. 50, 6 Dec. 2007, pp. 19663–19664, www.ncbi.nlm.nih.gov/pmc/articles/PMC2148352/ https://www.pnas.org/content/104/50/19663

Sripada, C. S., Kessler, D., & Angstadt, M. (2014). Lag in maturation of the brain's intrinsic functional architecture in attention-deficit/hyperactivity disorder. *Proceedings of the National Academy of Sciences of the United States of America, 111*(39), 14259–14264. https://doi.org/10.1073/pnas.1407787111

Miller, D. J., Duka, T., Stimpson, C. D., Schapiro, S. J., Baze, W. B., McArthur, M. J., Fobbs, A. J., Sousa, A. M. M., Sestan, N., Wildman, D. E., Lipovich, L., Kuzawa, C. W., Hof, P. R., & Sherwood, C. C. (2012). Prolonged myelination in human neocortical evolution. *Proceedings of the National Academy of Sciences of the United States of America, 109*(41), 16480–16485. https://doi.org/10.1073/pnas.1117943109 http://www.pnas.org/content/109/41/16480.full

Szekely, E., Sudre, G. P., Sharp, W., Leibenluft, E., & Shaw, P. (2017). Defining the Neural Substrate of the Adult Outcome of Childhood ADHD: A Multimodal Neuroimaging Study of Response Inhibition. *The American journal of*

psychiatry, *174*(9), 867–876. https://doi.org/10.1176/appi.ajp.2017.16111313
Shaw, P., Eckstrand, K., Sharp, W., Blumenthal, J., Lerch, J. P., Greenstein, D., Clasen, L., Evans, A., Giedd, J., & Rapoport, J. L. (2007). Attention-deficit/hyperactivity disorder is characterized by a delay in cortical maturation. *Proceedings of the National Academy of Sciences*, *104*(49), 19649–19654. https://doi.org/10.1073/pnas.0707741104
Shaw, P., Gilliam, M., Liverpool, M., Weddle, C., Malek, M., Sharp, W., Greenstein, D., Evans, A., Rapoport, J., & Giedd, J. (2011). Cortical development in typically developing children with symptoms of hyperactivity and impulsivity: support for a dimensional view of attention deficit hyperactivity disorder. *The American journal of psychiatry*, *168*(2), 143–151. https://doi.org/10.1176/appi.ajp.2010.10030385 http://ajp.psychiatryonline.org/doi/full/10.1176/appi.ajp.2010.10030385
Pingault, J. B., Tremblay, R. E., Vitaro, F., Carbonneau, R., Genolini, C., Falissard, B., & Côté, S. M. (2011). Childhood trajectories of inattention and hyperactivity and prediction of educational attainment in early adulthood: a 16-year longitudinal population-based study. *The American journal of psychiatry*, *168*(11), 1164–1170. https://doi.org/10.1176/appi.ajp.2011.10121732 http://ajp.psychiatryonline.org/doi/full/10.1176/appi.ajp.2011.10121732
Pingault, J.-B., Viding, E., Galéra, C., Greven, C. U., Zheng, Y., Plomin, R., & Rijsdijk, F. (2015). Genetic and Environmental Influences on the Developmental Course of Attention-Deficit/Hyperactivity Disorder Symptoms From Childhood to Adolescence. *JAMA Psychiatry*, *72*(7), 651. https://doi.org/10.1001/jamapsychiatry.2015.0469
44) Brent R. Collett, Ph.D., Jeneva L. Ohan, Ph.D., And Kathleen M. Myers, M.D., M.P.H.Ten-Year Review Of Rating Scales.V: Scales Assessing Attention-Deficit/Hyperactivity Disorder, J. AM. ACAD. CHILD ADOLESC. PSYCHIATRY, 42:9, SEPTEMBER
Swanson, J. M., Schuck, S., Porter, M. M., Carlson, C., Hartman, C. A., Sergeant, J. A., Clevenger, W., Wasdell, M., McCleary, R., Lakes, K., & Wigal, T. (2012). Categorical and Dimensional Definitions and Evaluations of Symptoms of ADHD: History of the SNAP and the SWAN Rating Scales. *The International journal of educational and psychological assessment*, *10*(1), 51–70.
Also popular is a computer based eye gaze system that tracks errors in response to rapid stimulus presentation. Though these do not correlate to other methods: Schatz, A. M., Ballantyne, A. O., & Trauner, D. A. (2001). Sensitivity and specificity of a computerized test of attention in the diagnosis of Attention-Deficit/Hyperactivity Disorder. *Assessment*, *8*(4), 357–365. https://doi.org/10.1177/107319110100800401
45) Castellanos, F. X., & Elmaghrabi, S. E. (2017). On the Road to Physiological Models of Brain Function in ADHD. *The American journal of psychiatry*, *174*(9), 825–826. https://doi.org/10.1176/appi.ajp.2017.17060667

References

46) Curatolo, P., D'Agati, E., & Moavero, R. (2010). The neurobiological basis of ADHD. *Italian Journal of Pediatrics*, *36*(1), 79. https://doi.org/10.1186/1824-7288-36-79

Sheridan, M. A., Hinshaw, S., & D'Esposito, M. (2010). Stimulant Medication and Prefrontal Functional Connectivity During Working Memory in ADHD. *Journal of Attention Disorders*, *14*(1), 69–78. https://doi.org/10.1177/1087054709347444

Dickstein, S. G., Bannon, K., Xavier Castellanos, F., & Milham, M. P. (2006). The neural correlates of attention deficit hyperactivity disorder: an ALE meta-analysis. *Journal of Child Psychology and Psychiatry*, *47*(10), 1051–1062. https://doi.org/10.1111/j.1469-7610.2006.01671.x https://onlinelibrary.wiley.com/doi/full/10.1111/j.1469-7610.2006.01671.x

47) Konrad, K., & Eickhoff, S. B. (2010). Is the ADHD brain wired differently? A review on structural and functional connectivity in attention deficit hyperactivity disorder. *Human brain mapping*, *31*(6), 904–916. https://doi.org/10.1002/hbm.21058

Cortese, S., Kelly, C., Chabernaud, C., Proal, E., Di Martino, A., Milham, M. P., & Castellanos, F. X. (2012). Toward Systems Neuroscience of ADHD: A Meta-Analysis of 55 fMRI Studies. *American Journal of Psychiatry*, *169*(10), 1038–1055. https://doi.org/10.1176/appi.ajp.2012.11101521

Wong, C. G., & Stevens, M. C. (2012). The effects of stimulant medication on working memory functional connectivity in attention-deficit/hyperactivity disorder. *Biological psychiatry*, *71*(5), 458–466. https://doi.org/10.1016/j.biopsych.2011.11.011

Hart, H., Radua, J., Nakao, T., Mataix-Cols, D., & Rubia, K. (2013). Meta-analysis of Functional Magnetic Resonance Imaging Studies of Inhibition and Attention in Attention-deficit/Hyperactivity Disorder. *JAMA Psychiatry*, *70*(2), 185. https://doi.org/10.1001/jamapsychiatry.2013.277 http://jamanetwork.com/journals/jamapsychiatry/fullarticle/1485446

Ivanov, I., Bansal, R., Hao, X., Zhu, H., Kellendonk, C., Miller, L., Sanchez-Pena, J., Miller, A. M., Chakravarty, M. M., Klahr, K., Durkin, K., Greenhill, L. L., & Peterson, B. S. (2010). Morphological abnormalities of the thalamus in youths with attention deficit hyperactivity disorder. *The American Journal of Psychiatry*, *167*(4), 397–408. https://doi.org/10.1176/appi.ajp.2009.09030398

Suskauer, S. J., Simmonds, D. J., Caffo, B. S., Denckla, M. B., Pekar, J. J., & Mostofsky, S. H. (2008). fMRI of Intrasubject Variability in ADHD: Anomalous Premotor Activity With Prefrontal Compensation. *Journal of the American Academy of Child & Adolescent Psychiatry*, *47*(10), 1141–1150. https://doi.org/10.1097/chi.0b013e3181825b1f

48) Teicher, M. H., Anderson, C. M., Polcari, A., Glod, C. A., Maas, L. C., & Renshaw, P. F. (2000). Functional deficits in basal ganglia of children with attention-deficit/hyperactivity disorder shown with functional magnetic resonance imaging relaxometry. *Nature Medicine*, *6*(4), 470–473. https://doi.

org/10.1038/74737 http://www.nature.com/nm/journal/v6/n4/abs/nm0400_470.html

Hoogman, M., Aarts, E., Zwiers, M., Slaats-Willemse, D., Naber, M., Onnink, M., Cools, R., Kan, C., Buitelaar, J., & Franke, B. (2011). Nitric Oxide Synthase Genotype Modulation of Impulsivity and Ventral Striatal Activity in Adult ADHD Patients and Healthy Comparison Subjects. *American Journal of Psychiatry, 168*(10), 1099–1106. https://doi.org/10.1176/appi.ajp.2011.10101446

Qiu, A., Crocetti, D., Adler, M., Mahone, E. M., Denckla, M. B., Miller, M. I., & Mostofsky, S. H. (2009). Basal Ganglia Volume and Shape in Children With Attention Deficit Hyperactivity Disorder. *American Journal of Psychiatry, 166*(1), 74–82. https://doi.org/10.1176/appi.ajp.2008.08030426 http://ajp.psychiatryonline.org/doi/full/10.1176/appi.ajp.2008.08030426

Hauser, T. U., Iannaccone, R., Ball, J., Mathys, C., Brandeis, D., Walitza, S., & Brem, S. (2014). Role of the Medial Prefrontal Cortex in Impaired Decision Making in Juvenile Attention-Deficit/Hyperactivity Disorder. *JAMA Psychiatry, 71*(10), 1165. https://doi.org/10.1001/jamapsychiatry.2014.1093 http://jamanetwork.com/journals/jamapsychiatry/fullarticle/1897301

Snyder, S. M., Rugino, T. A., Hornig, M., & Stein, M. A. (2015). Integration of an EEG biomarker with a clinician's ADHD evaluation. *Brain and Behavior, 5*(4), n/a-n/a. https://doi.org/10.1002/brb3.330

Surman, C. B., Biederman, J., Spencer, T., Yorks, D., Miller, C. A., Petty, C. R., & Faraone, S. V. (2011). Deficient emotional self-regulation and adult attention deficit hyperactivity disorder: a family risk analysis. *The American journal of psychiatry, 168*(6), 617–623. https://doi.org/10.1176/appi.ajp.2010.10081172 https://pubmed.ncbi.nlm.nih.gov/21498464/

Biederman, J., Petty, C. R., Monuteaux, M. C., Fried, R., Byrne, D., Mirto, T., Spencer, T., Wilens, T. E., & Faraone, S. V. (2010). Adult Psychiatric Outcomes of Girls With Attention Deficit Hyperactivity Disorder: 11-Year Follow-Up in a Longitudinal Case-Control Study. *American Journal of Psychiatry, 167*(4), 409–417. https://doi.org/10.1176/appi.ajp.2009.09050736

49) Makris, N., Biederman, J., Monuteaux, M. C., & Seidman, L. J. (2009). Towards conceptualizing a neural systems-based anatomy of attention-deficit/hyperactivity disorder. *Developmental neuroscience, 31*(1-2), 36–49. https://doi.org/10.1159/000207492

50) Baumgardner, D. J., Schreiber, A. L., Havlena, J. A., Bridgewater, F. D., Steber, D. L., & Lemke, M. A. (2010). Geographic analysis of diagnosis of Attention-Deficit/Hyperactivity Disorder in children: Eastern Wisconsin, USA. *International journal of psychiatry in medicine, 40*(4), 363–382. https://doi.org/10.2190/PM.40.4.a https://pubmed.ncbi.nlm.nih.gov/21391408/

Reyes, N., Baumgardner, D. J., Simmons, D. H., & Buckingham, W. (2013). The potential for sociocultural factors in the diagnosis of ADHD in children. *WMJ : official publication of the State Medical Society of Wisconsin, 112*(1), 13

Fairman KA, Peckham AM, Sclar DA. Diagnosis and Treatment of

References

ADHD in the United States: Update by Gender and Race. Journal of Attention Disorders. 2020;24(1):10-19. https://journals.sagepub.com/doi/full/10.1177/1087054716688534

Muñoz-Silva, A., Lago-Urbano, R., Sanchez-Garcia, M., & Carmona-Márquez, J. (2017). Child/Adolescent's ADHD and Parenting Stress: The Mediating Role of Family Impact and Conduct Problems. *Frontiers in psychology*, *8*, 2252. https://doi.org/10.3389/fpsyg.2017.02252

Sibley MH, Rohde LA, Swanson JM, et al.: Late-onset ADHD reconsidered with comprehensive repeated assessments between ages 10 and 25. **Am J Psychiatry** 2018; 175:140–149 https://ajp.psychiatryonline.org/doi/10.1176/appi.ajp.2017.17030298

51) Ptácek, R., Kuzelová, H., & Stefano, G. B. (2011). Dopamine D4 receptor gene DRD4 and its association with psychiatric disorders. *Medical science monitor : international medical journal of experimental and clinical research*, *17*(9), RA215–RA220. https://doi.org/10.12659/msm.881925

Volkow, N. D., Wang, G.-J., Newcorn, J. H., Kollins, S. H., Wigal, T. L., Telang, F., Fowler, J. S., Goldstein, R. Z., Klein, N., Logan, J., Wong, C., & Swanson, J. M. (2010). Motivation deficit in ADHD is associated with dysfunction of the dopamine reward pathway. *Molecular Psychiatry*, *16*(11), 1147–1154. https://doi.org/10.1038/mp.2010.97

Chau, B., Jarvis, H., Law, C. K., & Chong, T. T. (2018). Dopamine and reward: a view from the prefrontal cortex. *Behavioural pharmacology*, *29*(7), 569–583. https://doi.org/10.1097/FBP.0000000000000424

Luo, S. X., & Huang, E. J. (2016). Dopaminergic Neurons and Brain Reward Pathways. *The American Journal of Pathology*, *186*(3), 478–488. https://doi.org/10.1016/j.ajpath.2015.09.023

Ptácek, R., Kuzelová, H., & Stefano, G. B. (2011). Dopamine D4 receptor gene DRD4 and its association with psychiatric disorders. *Medical science monitor : international medical journal of experimental and clinical research*, *17*(9), RA215–RA220. https://doi.org/10.12659/msm.881925

Vanicek, T., Spies, M., Rami-Mark, C., Savli, M., Höflich, A., Kranz, G. S., Hahn, A., Kutzelnigg, A., Traub-Weidinger, T., Mitterhauser, M., Wadsak, W., Hacker, M., Volkow, N. D., Kasper, S., & Lanzenberger, R. (2014). The Norepinephrine Transporter in Attention-Deficit/Hyperactivity Disorder Investigated With Positron Emission Tomography. *JAMA Psychiatry*, *71*(12), 1340. https://doi.org/10.1001/jamapsychiatry.2014.1226 http://jamanetwork.com/journals/jamapsychiatry/fullarticle/1917887

Shaw P. (2018). Growing Up: Evolving Concepts of Adult Attention Deficit Hyperactivity Disorder. *The American journal of psychiatry*, *175*(2), 95–96. https://doi.org/10.1176/appi.ajp.2017.17111257

Rydén, E., Thase, M. E., Stråht, D., Aberg-Wistedt, A., Bejerot, S., & Landén, M. (2009). A history of childhood attention-deficit hyperactivity disorder

(ADHD) impacts clinical outcome in adult bipolar patients regardless of current ADHD. *Acta psychiatrica Scandinavica, 120*(3), 239–246. https://doi.org/10.1111/j.1600-0447.2009.01399.x

Jadidian, A., Hurley, R. A., & Taber, K. H. (2015). Neurobiology of Adult ADHD: Emerging Evidence for Network Dysfunctions. *The Journal of Neuropsychiatry and Clinical Neurosciences, 27*(3), 173–178. https://doi.org/10.1176/appi.neuropsych.15060142

52) Viding, E., & McCrory, E. (2020). Disruptive Behavior Disorders: The Challenge of Delineating Mechanisms in the Face of Heterogeneity. *The American journal of psychiatry, 177*(9), 811–817. https://doi.org/10.1176/appi.ajp.2020.20070998

Alegria, A. A., Radua, J., & Rubia, K. (2016). Meta-Analysis of fMRI Studies of Disruptive Behavior Disorders. *The American journal of psychiatry, 173*(11), 1119–1130. https://doi.org/10.1176/appi.ajp.2016.15081089

53) **Equifinality refers to the observation that in any open system a diversity of pathways may lead to the same outcome. Multifinality** means that any one component may function differently depending on the organization of the system in which it operates.

54) Shen, C., Luo, Q., Jia, T., Zhao, Q., Desrivières, S., Quinlan, E. B., Banaschewski, T., Millenet, S., Bokde, A., Büchel, C., Flor, H., Frouin, V., Garavan, H., Gowland, P., Heinz, A., Ittermann, B., Martinot, J. L., Artiges, E., Paillère-Martinot, M. L., Nees, F., ... IMAGEN consortium (2020). Neural Correlates of the Dual-Pathway Model for ADHD in Adolescents. *The American journal of psychiatry, 177*(9), 844–854. https://doi.org/10.1176/appi.ajp.2020.19020183

Disruptive Mood Dysregulation Disorder (DMDD). (2019). Aacap.Org. https://www.aacap.org/AACAP/Families_and_Youth/Facts_for_Families/FFF-Guide/Disruptive-Mood-Dysregulation-Disorder-_DMDD_-110.aspx

The OFC and mOFC are references 8) to 11) of this chapter.

Sparks, G. M., Axelson, D. A., Yu, H., Ha, W., Ballester, J., Diler, R. S., Goldstein, B., Goldstein, T., Hickey, M. B., Ladouceur, C. D., Monk, K., Sakolsky, D., & Birmaher, B. (2014). Disruptive mood dysregulation disorder and chronic irritability in youth at familial risk for bipolar disorder. *Journal of the American Academy of Child and Adolescent Psychiatry, 53*(4), 408–416. https://doi.org/10.1016/j.jaac.2013.12.026 https://www.ncbi.nlm.nih.gov/pmc/articles/PMC4049528/

Copeland, W. E., Shanahan, L., Egger, H., Angold, A., & Costello, E. J. (2014). Adult diagnostic and functional outcomes of DSM-5 disruptive mood dysregulation disorder. *The American journal of psychiatry, 171*(6), 668–674. https://doi.org/10.1176/appi.ajp.2014.13091213 https://www.ncbi.nlm.nih.gov/pmc/articles/PMC4106474/

Axelson, D., Findling, R. L., Fristad, M. A., Kowatch, R. A., Youngstrom, E. A., Horwitz, S. M., Arnold, L. E., Frazier, T. W., Ryan, N., Demeter, C., Gill, M. K.,

References

Hauser-Harrington, J. C., Depew, J., Kennedy, S. M., Gron, B. A., Rowles, B. M., & Birmaher, B. (2012). Examining the proposed disruptive mood dysregulation disorder diagnosis in children in the Longitudinal Assessment of Manic Symptoms study. *The Journal of clinical psychiatry*, *73*(10), 1342 https://doi.org/10.4088/JCP.12m07674

Buckholtz, J. W., Martin, J. W., Treadway, M. T., Jan, K., Zald, D. H., Jones, O., & Marois, R. (2015). From Blame to Punishment: Disrupting Prefrontal Cortex Activity Reveals Norm Enforcement Mechanisms. *Neuron*, *87*(6), 1369–1380. https://doi.org/10.1016/j.neuron.2015.08.023

Jennifer S. Lerner, Ye Li, Piercarlo Valdesolo, Karim S. Kassam, Emotion and Decision Making
Annual Review of Psychology 2015 66:1, 799-823 https://www.annualreviews.org/doi/10.1146/annurev-psych-010213-115043

55) Biederman, J., Faraone, S., Mick, E., Wozniak, J., Chen, L., Ouellette, C., Marrs, A., Moore, P., Garcia, J., Mennin, D., & Lelon, E. (1996). Attention deficit hyperactivity disorder and juvenile mania: an overlooked comorbidity?. *Journal of the American Academy of Child and Adolescent Psychiatry*, *35*(8), 997–1008. https://doi.org/10.1097/00004583-199608000-00010
(This work has been undermined by the discovery that he received significant unreported income from drug companies that benefited from this research: https://www.nytimes.com/2008/06/08/us/08conflict.html https://www.nature.com/articles/nn0908-983)

Birmaher B. (2013). Bipolar disorder in children and adolescents. *Child and adolescent mental health*, *18*(3), 140–148. https://doi.org/10.1111/camh.12021

Akiskal H. S. (1998). The childhood roots of bipolar disorder. *Journal of affective disorders*, *51*(2), 75–76. https://doi.org/10.1016/s0165-0327(98)00173-6

Fristad, M. A., Wolfson, H., Algorta, G. P., Youngstrom, E. A., Arnold, L. E., Birmaher, B., Horwitz, S., Axelson, D., Kowatch, R. A., & Findling, R. L. (2016). Disruptive Mood Dysregulation Disorder and Bipolar Disorder Not Otherwise Specified: Fraternal or Identical Twins? *Journal of Child and Adolescent Psychopharmacology*, *26*(2), 138–146. https://doi.org/10.1089/cap.2015.0062

Hosang, G. M., Lichtenstein, P., Ronald, A., Lundström, S., & Taylor, M. J. (2019). Association of Genetic and Environmental Risks for Attention-Deficit/Hyperactivity Disorder With Hypomanic Symptoms in Youths. *JAMA Psychiatry*, *76*(11), 1150. https://doi.org/10.1001/jamapsychiatry.2019.1949 https://jamanetwork.com/journals/jamapsychiatry/fullarticle/2747573

Moran, L. V., Guvenek-Cokol, P. E., & Perlis, R. H. (2019). Attention-Deficit/Hyperactivity Disorder, Hypomania, and Bipolar Disorder in Youth. *JAMA Psychiatry*, *76*(11), 1119. https://doi.org/10.1001/jamapsychiatry.2019.1926

Axelson, D., Findling, R. L., Fristad, M. A., Kowatch, R. A., Youngstrom, E. A., Horwitz, S. M., Arnold, L. E., Frazier, T. W., Ryan, N., Demeter, C., Gill, M. K., Hauser-Harrington, J. C., Depew, J., Kennedy, S. M., Gron, B. A., Rowles, B.

M., & Birmaher, B. (2012). Examining the proposed disruptive mood dysregulation disorder diagnosis in children in the Longitudinal Assessment of Manic Symptoms study. *The Journal of clinical psychiatry*, *73*(10), 1342–1350. https://doi.org/10.4088/JCP.12m07674

56) McLaughlin, K. A., Green, J. G., Hwang, I., Sampson, N. A., Zaslavsky, A. M., & Kessler, R. C. (2012). Intermittent Explosive Disorder in the National Comorbidity Survey Replication Adolescent Supplement. *Archives of General Psychiatry*, *69*(11). https://doi.org/10.1001/archgenpsychiatry.2012.592

Lee, R., Arfanakis, K., Evia, A. M., Fanning, J., Keedy, S., & Coccaro, E. F. (2016). White Matter Integrity Reductions in Intermittent Explosive Disorder. *Neuropsychopharmacology*, *41*(11), 2697–2703. https://doi.org/10.1038/npp.2016.74

Schreiber, L., Odlaug, B. L., & Grant, J. E. (2011). Impulse control disorders: updated review of clinical characteristics and pharmacological management. *Frontiers in psychiatry*, *2*, 1. https://doi.org/10.3389/fpsyt.2011.00001

Coccaro, E. F., Kavoussi, R. J., Berman, M. E., & Lish, J. D. (1998). Intermittent explosive disorder-revised: development, reliability, and validity of research criteria. *Comprehensive psychiatry*, *39*(6), 368–376. https://doi.org/10.1016/s0010-440x(98)90050-5

Montojo, C. A., Congdon, E., Hwang, L., Jalbrzikowski, M., Kushan, L., Vesagas, T. K., Jonas, R. K., Ventura, J., Bilder, R. M., & Bearden, C. E. (2015). Neural mechanisms of response inhibition and impulsivity in 22q11.2 deletion carriers and idiopathic attention deficit hyperactivity disorder. *NeuroImage. Clinical*, *9*, 310–321. https://doi.org/10.1016/j.nicl.2015.08.006

Kulendran, M., Wingfield, L. R., Sugden, C., Darzi, A., & Vlaev, I. (2016). Pharmacological manipulation of impulsivity: A randomized controlled trial. *Personality and Individual Differences*, *90*, 321–325. https://doi.org/10.1016/j.paid.2015.11.025

Kiehl K. A. (2006). A cognitive neuroscience perspective on psychopathy: evidence for paralimbic system dysfunction. *Psychiatry research*, *142*(2-3), 107–128. https://doi.org/10.1016/j.psychres.2005.09.013

57) Thériault, M. C., Lespérance, P., Achim, A., Tellier, G., Diab, S., Rouleau, G. A., Chouinard, S., & Richer, F. (2014). ODD irritability is associated with obsessive-compulsive behavior and not ADHD in chronic tic disorders. *Psychiatry research*, *220*(1-2), 447–452. https://doi.org/10.1016/j.psychres.2014.07.039

58) https://en.wikipedia.org/wiki/Lawrence_Kohlberg%27s_stages_of_moral_development

Parfitt, C. H., & Alleyne, E. (2020). Not the Sum of Its Parts: A Critical Review of the MacDonald Triad. *Trauma, violence & abuse*, *21*(2), 300–310. https://doi.org/10.1177/1524838018764164

Rubia, K., Smith, A. B., Halari, R., Matsukura, F., Mohammad, M., Taylor, E., & Brammer, M. J. (2009). Disorder-specific dissociation of orbitofrontal dysfunction in boys with pure conduct disorder during reward and ventrolateral prefrontal dysfunction in boys with pure ADHD during sustained attention. *The American journal of psychiatry*, *166*(1), 83–94. https://doi.org/10.1176/appi.ajp.2008.08020212 https://ajp.psychiatryonline.org/doi/full/10.1176/appi.ajp.2008.08020212

Samuel W. Hawes, Rebecca Waller, Amy L. Byrd, James M. Bjork, Anthony S. Dick, Matthew T. Sutherland, Michael C. Riedel, Michael J. Tobia, Nicholas Thomson, Angela R. Laird, and Raul Gonzalez

Reward Processing in Children With Disruptive Behavior Disorders and Callous-Unemotional Traits in the ABCD Study American Journal of Psychiatry 2021 178:4, 333-342 Published Online:31 Jul 2020https://doi.org/10.1176/appi.ajp.2020.191

https://www.encyclopedia.com/social-sciences/applied-and-social-sciences-magazines/rotters-internal-external-locus-control-scale

Johns, C. B., Lacadie, C., Vohr, B., Ment, L. R., & Scheinost, D. (2019). Amygdala functional connectivity is associated with social impairments in preterm born young adults. *NeuroImage. Clinical*, *21*, 101626. https://doi.org/10.1016/j.nicl.2018.101626

Adolphs R. (2010). What does the amygdala contribute to social cognition?. *Annals of the New York Academy of Sciences*, *1191*(1), 42–61. https://doi.org/10.1111/j.1749-6632.2010.05445.x

59) Maia, T. V., Cooney, R. E., & Peterson, B. S. (2008). The neural bases of obsessive–compulsive disorder in children and adults. *Development and Psychopathology*, *20*(4), 1251–1283. https://doi.org/10.1017/s0954579408000606

Saxena, S., Bota, R. G., & Brody, A. L. (2001). Brain-behavior relationships in obsessive-compulsive disorder. *Seminars in clinical neuropsychiatry*, *6*(2), 82–101. https://doi.org/10.1053/scnp.2001.21833

Yanagisawa N. (2018). Functions and dysfunctions of the basal ganglia in humans. *Proceedings of the Japan Academy. Series B, Physical and biological sciences*, *94*(7), 275–304. https://doi.org/10.2183/pjab.94.019

Boedhoe, P., Schmaal, L., Abe, Y., Alonso, P., Ameis, S. H., Anticevic, A., Arnold, P. D., Batistuzzo, M. C., Benedetti, F., Beucke, J. C., Bollettini, I., Bose, A., Brem, S., Calvo, A., Calvo, R., Cheng, Y., Cho, K., Ciullo, V., Dallaspezia, S., Denys, D., … ENIGMA OCD Working Group (2018). Cortical Abnormalities Associated With Pediatric and Adult Obsessive-Compulsive Disorder: Findings From the ENIGMA Obsessive-Compulsive Disorder Working Group. *The American journal of psychiatry*, *175*(5), 453–462. https://doi.org/10.1176/appi.ajp.2017.17050485

Norman LJ, Carlisi C, Lukito S, et al. Structural and Functional Brain Abnormalities in Attention-Deficit/Hyperactivity Disorder and Obsessive-Compulsive Disorder: A Comparative Meta-analysis . *JAMA Psychiatry*. 2016;73(8):815–825. http://jamanetwork.com/journals/jamapsychiatry/

article-abstract/2526239
Pauli P, Perriello C, Piacentini J, Piras F, Piras F, (Plus other authors ...) Subcortical Brain Volume, Regional Cortical Thickness, and Cortical Surface Area Across Disorders. Am J Psychiatry. 2020 Sep 1;177(9):834-843. https://doi.org/10.1176/appi.ajp.2020.19030331

Onnink, A. M. H., Zwiers, M. P., Hoogman, M., Mostert, J. C., Dammers, J., Kan, C. C., Vasquez, A. A., Schene, A.

de Wit, S. J., de Vries, F. E., van der Werf, Y. D., Cath, D. C., Heslenfeld, D. J., Veltman, E. M., van Balkom, A. J. L. M., Veltman, D. J., & van den Heuvel, O. A. (2012). Presupplementary Motor Area Hyperactivity During Response Inhibition: A Candidate Endophenotype of Obsessive-Compulsive Disorder. *American Journal of Psychiatry*, *169*(10), 1100–1108. https://doi.org/10.1176/appi.ajp.2012.12010073

60) Goodman, W. K., Price, L. H., Rasmussen, S. A., Mazure, C., Fleischmann, R. L., Hill, C. L., Heninger, G. R., & Charney, D. S. (1989). The Yale-Brown Obsessive Compulsive Scale. I. Development, use, and reliability. *Archives of general psychiatry*, *46*(11), 1006–1011. https://doi.org/10.1001/archpsyc.1989.01810110048007

YBOCD scale, a collection of symptoms reported by the subject to the interviewer or scored on a questionnaire was developed to measure the presence and severity of symptoms. Such scales improve observer reliability providing a standard set of questions, but the problem of defining the "cut off" needed to "qualify" for diagnosis is not externally validated. How many positives are needed to establish the diagnosis? The prevalence of OCD diagnosis in a population changes dramatically when the cutoff for a diagnosis is set lower or higher.

Murphy, D. L., Moya, P. R., Fox, M. A., Rubenstein, L. M., Wendland, J. R., & Timpano, K. R. (2013). Anxiety and affective disorder comorbidity related to serotonin and other neurotransmitter systems: obsessive-compulsive disorder as an example of overlapping clinical and genetic heterogeneity. *Philosophical transactions of the Royal Society of London. Series B, Biological sciences*, *368*(1615), 20120435. https://doi.org/10.1098/rstb.2012.0435

Ballard, I. C., Murty, V. P., Carter, R. M., MacInnes, J. J., Huettel, S. A., & Adcock, R. A. (2011). Dorsolateral Prefrontal Cortex Drives Mesolimbic Dopaminergic Regions to Initiate Motivated Behavior. *The Journal of Neuroscience*, *31*(28), 10340–10346. https://doi.org/10.1523/JNEUROSCI.0895-11.2011
https://www.ncbi.nlm.nih.gov/pmc/articles/PMC3182466/

Bradley, B., DeFife, J. A., Guarnaccia, C., Phifer, J., Fani, N., Ressler, K. J., & Westen, D. (2011). Emotion Dysregulation and Negative Affect: Association With Psychiatric Symptoms. *The Journal of Clinical Psychiatry*, *72*(5), 685–691. https://doi.org/10.4088/JCP.10m06409blu

Marsh, R., Maia, T. V., & Peterson, B. S. (2009). Functional disturbances within frontostriatal circuits across multiple childhood psychopathologies. *The*

References

American journal of psychiatry, 166(6), 664–674. https://doi.org/10.1176/appi.ajp.2009.08091354

Understanding the duality comes from the contrasting effects of dopamine and serotonin on the systems:
Graeme Fairchild, Ph.D., Shared or Distinct Alterations in Brain Structure in Disorders Across the Impulsivity-Compulsivity Spectrum: What Can We Learn From Cross-Disorder Comparisons of ADHD, ASD, and OCD?, American Journal of Psychiatry 2020 177:9, 799-801 https://doi.org/10.1176/appi.ajp.2020.20071031 https://ajp.psychiatryonline.org/doi/10.1176/appi.ajp.2020.20071031

den Ouden, H. E., Daw, N. D., Fernandez, G., Elshout, J. A., Rijpkema, M., Hoogman, M., Franke, B., & Cools, R. (2013). Dissociable effects of dopamine and serotonin on reversal learning. *Neuron, 80*(4), 1090–1100. https://doi.org/10.1016/j.neuron.2013.08.030

Caetano, M. S., Jin, L. E., Harenberg, L., Stachenfeld, K. L., Arnsten, A. F., & Laubach, M. (2013). Noradrenergic control of error perseveration in medial prefrontal cortex. *Frontiers in integrative neuroscience, 6*, 125. https://doi.org/10.3389/fnint.2012.00125

Clarke, H. F., Dalley, J. W., Crofts, H. S., Robbins, T. W., & Roberts, A. C. (2004). Cognitive inflexibility after prefrontal serotonin depletion. *Science (New York, N.Y.), 304*(5672), 878–880. https://doi.org/10.1126/science.1094987

Zhukovsky, P., Alsiö, J., Jupp, B., Xia, J., Giuliano, C., Jenner, L., Griffiths, J., Riley, E., Ali, S., Roberts, A. C., Robbins, T. W., & Dalley, J. W. (2017). Perseveration in a spatial-discrimination serial reversal learning task is differentially affected by MAO-A and MAO-B inhibition and associated with reduced anxiety and peripheral serotonin levels. *Psychopharmacology, 234*(9-10), 1557–1571. https://doi.org/10.1007/s00213-017-4569-x

Di Matteo, V., Pierucci, M., Esposito, E., Crescimanno, G., Benigno, A., & Di Giovanni, G. (2008). Serotonin modulation of the basal ganglia circuitry: therapeutic implication for Parkinson's disease and other motor disorders. *Progress in brain research, 172*, 423–463. https://doi.org/10.1016/S0079-6123(08)00921-7

Miguelez, C., Morera-Herreras, T., Torrecilla, M., Ruiz-Ortega, J. A., & Ugedo, L. (2014). Interaction between the 5-HT system and the basal ganglia: functional implication and therapeutic perspective in Parkinson's disease. *Frontiers in neural circuits, 8*, 21. https://doi.org/10.3389/fncir.2014.00021

Banks GP, Mikell CB, Youngerman BE, et al. Neuroanatomical Characteristics Associated With Response to Dorsal Anterior Cingulotomy for Obsessive-Compulsive Disorder. *JAMA Psychiatry.* 2015;72(2):127–135. doi:10.1001/jamapsychiatry.2014.2216

61) Pediatric-autoimmune-neuropsychiatric-disorders-associated-with-streptococcal-infections-Clinical-description-of-the-first-50-cases.pdf NIMH » PANDAS—Questions and Answers https://www.nimh.nih.gov/health/

publications/pandas/index.shtml
Chang, K., Frankovich, J., Cooperstock, M., Cunningham, M. W., Latimer, M. E., Murphy, T. K., Pasternack, M., Thienemann, M., Williams, K., Walter, J., Swedo, S. E., & PANS Collaborative Consortium (2015). Clinical evaluation of youth with pediatric acute-onset neuropsychiatric syndrome (PANS): recommendations from the 2013 PANS Consensus Conference. *Journal of child and adolescent psychopharmacology*, *25*(1), 3–13. https://doi.org/10.1089/cap.2014.0084

Frick, L. R., Rapanelli, M., Jindachomthong, K., Grant, P., Leckman, J. F., Swedo, S., Williams, K., & Pittenger, C. (2018). Differential binding of antibodies in PANDAS patients to cholinergic interneurons in the striatum. *Brain, behavior, and immunity*, *69*, 304–311. https://doi.org/10.1016/j.bbi.2017.12.004

Hyman S. E. (2021). PANDAS: Too Narrow a View of the Neuroimmune Landscape. *The American journal of psychiatry*, *178*(1), 5– https://doi.org/10.1176/appi.ajp.2020.20111598   http://pandasnetwork.org/wp-content/uploads/2012/01/PANDAS-OT-Article.pdf

Litwin, T., Dusek, P., Szafrański, T., Dzieżyc, K., Członkowska, A., & Rybakowski, J. K. (2018). Psychiatric manifestations in Wilson's disease: possibilities and difficulties for treatment. *Therapeutic advances in psychopharmacology*, *8*(7), 199–211. https://doi.org/10.1177/2045125318759461

62) Kennerley, S. W., & Walton, M. E. (2011). Decision making and reward in frontal cortex: complementary evidence from neurophysiological and neuropsychological studies. *Behavioral neuroscience*, *125*(3), 297–317. https://doi.org/10.1037/a0023575

Walton, M. E., Bannerman, D. M., Alterescu, K., & Rushworth, M. F. (2003). Functional specialization within medial frontal cortex of the anterior cingulate for evaluating effort-related decisions. *The Journal of neuroscience : the official journal of the Society for Neuroscience*, *23*(16), 6475–6479. https://doi.org/10.1523/JNEUROSCI.23-16-06475.2003

Euston, D. R., Gruber, A. J., & McNaughton, B. L. (2012). The role of medial prefrontal cortex in memory and decision making. *Neuron*, *76*(6), 1057–1070. https://doi.org/10.1016/j.neuron.2012.12.002

Haber, S. N., & Knutson, B. (2009). The Reward Circuit: Linking Primate Anatomy and Human Imaging. *Neuropsychopharmacology*, *35*(1), 4–26. https://doi.org/10.1038/npp.2009.129   https://www.nature.com/articles/npp2009129

Haber, S. N. (2011). *Neuroanatomy of Reward: A View from the Ventral Striatum*. Nih.Gov; CRC Press/Taylor & Francis. https://www.ncbi.nlm.nih.gov/books/NBK92777/

63) Phillips, K. A., Didie, E. R., Menard, W., Pagano, M. E., Fay, C., & Weisberg, R. B. (2006). Clinical features of body dysmorphic disorder in adolescents and adults. *Psychiatry research*, *141*(3), 305–314. https://doi.org/10.1016/j.psychres.2005.09.014

Phillips, K. A., Grant, J. E., Siniscalchi, J. M., Stout, R., & Price, L. H. (2005). A

References

retrospective follow-up study of body dysmorphic disorder. *Comprehensive psychiatry*, *46*(5), 315–321. https://doi.org/10.1016/j.comppsych.2004.12.001

Phillips K. A. (2004). Body dysmorphic disorder: recognizing and treating imagined ugliness. *World psychiatry : official journal of the World Psychiatric Association (WPA)*, *3*(1), 12–17. https://www.ncbi.nlm.nih.gov/pmc/articles/PMC1414653/

Hong, K., Nezgovorova, V., & Hollander, E. (2018). New perspectives in the treatment of body dysmorphic disorder. *F1000Research*, *7*, 361. https://doi.org/10.12688/f1000research.13700.1

MacNeill, L. P., Best, L. A., & Davis, L. L. (2017). The role of personality in body image dissatisfaction and disordered eating: discrepancies between men and women. *Journal of eating disorders*, *5*, 44. https://doi.org/10.1186/s40337-017-0177-8

Mufaddel, A., Osman, O. T., Almugaddam, F., & Jafferany, M. (2013). A review of body dysmorphic disorder and its presentation in different clinical settings. *The primary care companion for CNS disorders*. https://doi.org/10.4088/PCC.12r01464

Bjornsson, A. S., Didie, E. R., & Phillips, K. A. (2010). Body dysmorphic disorder. *Dialogues in clinical neuroscience*, *12*(2), 221–232. https://doi.org/10.31887/DCNS.2010.12.2/abjornsson https://www.ncbi.nlm.nih.gov/pmc/articles/PMC3181960/

Kamps, Cristi & Berman, Steven. (2011). Body image and identity formation: The role of identity distress. Revista Latinoamericana de Psicología. 43. 267-277. https://www.researchgate.net/publication/262444144_Body_image_and_identity_formation_The_role_of_identity_distress

Fernández-Aranda, F., Dahme, B., & Meermann, R. (1999). Body image in eating disorders and analysis of its relevance: a preliminary study. *Journal of psychosomatic research*, *47*(5), 419–428. https://doi.org/10.1016/s0022-3999(99)00027-6

https://www.frontiersin.org/articles/10.3389/fpsyg.2020.00030/full

Andrew W. Joseph, Lisa Ishii, Shannon S. Joseph, Jane I. Smith, Peiyi Su, Kristin Bater, Patrick Byrne, Kofi Boahene, Ira Papel, Theda Kontis, Raymond Douglas, Christine C. Nelson, and Masaru Ishii, JAMA Facial Plastic Surgery 2017 19:4, 269-274 https://www.liebertpub.com/full/doi/10.1001/jamafacial.2016.1535

Thomas, J. J., Weigel, T. J., Lawton, R. K., Levendusky, P. G., & Becker, A. E. (2012). Cognitive-behavioral treatment of body image disturbance in a congenitally blind patient with anorexia nervosa. *The American journal of psychiatry*, *169*(1), 16–20. https://doi.org/10.1176/appi.ajp.2010.10040555

Rajanala, S., Maymone, M., & Vashi, N. A. (2018). Selfies-Living in the Era of Filtered Photographs. *JAMA facial plastic surgery*, *20*(6), 443–444. https://doi.org/10.1001/jamafacial.2018.0486

64) Huey, E. D., Zahn, R., Krueger, F., Moll, J., Kapogiannis, D., Wassermann, E. M., & Grafman, J. (2008). A psychological and neuroanatomical model of obsessive-compulsive disorder. *The Journal of neuropsychiatry and clinical neurosciences*, *20*(4), 390–408. Huey, E. D., Zahn, R., Krueger, F., Moll, J., Kapogiannis, D., Wassermann, E. M., & Grafman, J. (2008). A psychological and neuroanatomical model of obsessive-compulsive disorder. *The Journal of neuropsychiatry and clinical neurosciences*, *20*(4), 390–408. https://doi.org/10.1176/jnp.2008.20.4.390

...the anxiety can form the basis of an obsession, and a compulsion can be an attempt to receive relief from the anxiety by repeating parts of, or an entire, SEC. The authors discuss empiric support for, and specific experimental predictions of, this model....

Dougherty, D. D., Brennan, B. P., Stewart, S. E., Wilhelm, S., Widge, A. S., & Rauch, S. L. (2018). Neuroscientifically Informed Formulation and Treatment Planning for Patients With Obsessive-Compulsive Disorder: A Review. *JAMA psychiatry*, *75*(10), 1081–1087. https://doi.org/10.1001/jamapsychiatry.2018.0930

The concept of abnormal fear extinction is central to OCD and to the underlying therapeutic mechanism of exposure and response prevention. A framework for understanding the neurochemistry of OCD focuses on both traditional monoaminergic systems and more recent evidence of glutamatergic and γ-aminobutyric

Brennan, B. P., Jacoby, R. J., & Widge, A. S. (2018). A Case of Severe Intractable Contamination-Based Obsessive-Compulsive Disorder. *JAMA psychiatry*, *75*(10), 1088–1089. https://doi.org/10.1001/jamapsychiatry.2018.0927

Goodwin G. M. (2015). The overlap between anxiety, depression, and obsessive-compulsive disorder. *Dialogues in clinical neuroscience*, *17*(3), 249–260. https://doi.org/10.31887/DCNS.2015.17.3/ggoodwin

Kong, X. Z., et. al. (2020). Mapping Cortical and Subcortical Asymmetry in Obsessive-Compulsive Disorder: Findings From the ENIGMA Consortium. *Biological psychiatry*, *87*(12), 1022–1034. https://doi.org/10.1016/j.biopsych.2019.04.022

Riesel, A., Endrass, T., Kaufmann, C., & Kathmann, N. (2011). Overactive error-related brain activity as a candidate endophenotype for obsessive-compulsive disorder: evidence from unaffected first-degree relatives. *The American journal of psychiatry*, *168*(3), 317–324. https://doi.org/10.1176/appi.ajp.2010.10030416

Del Casale, A., Kotzalidis, G. D., Rapinesi, C., Serata, D., Ambrosi, E., Simonetti, A., Pompili, M., Ferracuti, S., Tatarelli, R., & Girardi, P. (2011). Functional neuroimaging in obsessive-compulsive disorder. *Neuropsychobiology*, *64*(2), 61–85. https://doi.org/10.1159/000325223

Fan, Q., & Xiao, Z. (2013). Neuroimaging studies in patients with obsessive-compulsive disorder in China. *Shanghai archives of psychiatry*, *25*(2), 81–90. https://doi.org/10.3969/j.issn.1002-0829.2013.02.004

Moreira, P. S., Marques, P., Soriano-Mas, C., Magalhães, R., Sousa, N., Soares,

References

J. M., & Morgado, P. (2017). The neural correlates of obsessive-compulsive disorder: a multimodal perspective. *Translational Psychiatry*, *7*(8), e1224–e1224. https://doi.org/10.1038/tp.2017.189

Grover, S., Dua, D., Chakrabarti, S., & Avasthi, A. (2017). Obsessive Compulsive Symptoms/disorder in patients with schizophrenia: Prevalence, relationship with other symptom dimensions and impact on functioning. *Psychiatry research*, *250*, 277–284. https://doi.org/10.1016/j.psychres.2017.01.067

Harrison, B. J., Soriano-Mas, C., Pujol, J., Ortiz, H., López-Solà, M., Hernández-Ribas, R., Deus, J., Alonso, P., Yücel, M., Pantelis, C., Menchon, J. M., & Cardoner, N. (2009). Altered corticostriatal functional connectivity in obsessive-compulsive disorder. *Archives of general psychiatry*, *66*(11), 1189–1200. https://doi.org/10.1001/archgenpsychiatry.2009.152

Trevor W. Robbins, Matilde M. Vaghi, Paula Banca, Obsessive-Compulsive Disorder: Puzzles and Prospects, Neuron, Volume 102, Issue 1, 2019, Pages 27-47, ISSN 0896-6273, https://doi.org/10.1016/j.neuron.2019.01.046.

65) Grant, J. E., & Chamberlain, S. R. (2016). Trichotillomania. *The American journal of psychiatry*, *173*(9), 868–874. https://doi.org/10.1176/appi.ajp.2016.15111432 Grant, J. E., Odlaug, B. L., Chamberlain, S. R., Keuthen, N. J., Lochner, C., & Stein, D. J. (2012). Skin picking disorder. *The American journal of psychiatry*, *169*(11), https://doi.org/10.1176/appi.ajp.2012.12040508

FOdlaug, B. L., Hampshire, A., Chamberlain, S. R., & Grant, J. E. (2016). Abnormal brain activation in excoriation (skin-picking) disorder: evidence from an executive planning fMRI study. *The British journal of psychiatry : the journal of mental science*, *208*(2), 168–174. https://doi.org/10.1192/bjp.bp.114.155192

Tolin DF, Stevens MC, Villavicencio AL, et al. Neural Mechanisms of Decision Making in Hoarding Disorder. *Arch Gen Psychiatry*. 2012;69(8):832–841. http://jamanetwork.com/journals/jamapsychiatry/fullarticle/1307558?resultClick=1

64) Comings, D.E., Wu, S., Chiu, C., Ring, R.H., Gade, R., Ahn, C., MacMurray, J.P., Dietz, G. and Muhleman, D. (1996), Polygenic inheritance of Tourette syndrome, stuttering, attention deficit hyperactivity, conduct, and oppositional defiant disorder: The additive and subtractive effect of the three dopaminergic genes—DRD2, DβH, and DAT1. Am. J. Med. Genet., 67: 264-288. https://doi.org/10.1002/(SICI)1096-8628(19960531)67:3<264::AID-AJMG4>3.0.CO;2-N

Grados, M., Huselid, R., & Duque-Serrano, L. (2018). Transcranial Magnetic Stimulation in Tourette Syndrome: A Historical Perspective, Its Current Use and the Influence of Comorbidities in Treatment Response. *Brain sciences*, *8*(7), 129. https://doi.org/10.3390/brainsci8070129

65) Alexander, G. E., Crutcher, M. D., & DeLong, M. R. (1991). Chapter 6 Basal ganglia-thalamocortical circuits: Parallel substrates for motor, oculomotor, "prefrontal" and "limbic" functions. *Progress in Brain Research*, 119–146. https://doi.org/10.1016/s0079-6123(08)62678-3 https://www.sciencedirect.com/science/article/pii/S0079612308626783

Yu, D., Sul, J. H., Tsetsos, F., Nawaz, M. S., Huang, A. Y., Zelaya, I., Illmann, C., Osiecki, L., Darrow, S. M., Hirschtritt, M. E., Greenberg, E., Muller-Vahl, K. R., Stuhrmann, M., Dion, Y., Rouleau, G., Aschauer, H., Stamenkovic, M., Schlögelhofer, M., Sandor, P., Barr, C. L., ... Tourette Association of America International Consortium for Genetics, the Gilles de la Tourette GWAS Replication Initiative, the Tourette International Collaborative Genetics Study, and the Psychiatric Genomics Consortium Tourette Syndrome Working Group (2019). Interrogating the Genetic Determinants of Tourette's Syndrome and Other Tic Disorders Through Genome-Wide Association Studies. *The American journal of psychiatry*, *176*(3), https://doi.org/10.1176/appi.ajp.2018.18070857

Hirschtritt, M. E., Lee, P. C., Pauls, D. L., Dion, Y., Grados, M. A., Illmann, C., King, R. A., Sandor, P., McMahon, W. M., Lyon, G. J., Cath, D. C., Kurlan, R., Robertson, M. M., Osiecki, L., Scharf, J. M., & Mathews, C. A. (2015). Lifetime Prevalence, Age of Risk, and Genetic Relationships of Comorbid Psychiatric Disorders in Tourette Syndrome. *JAMA Psychiatry*, *72*(4), 325. https://doi.org/10.1001/jamapsychiatry.2014.2650

Yu, D., Mathews, C. A., Scharf, J. M., Neale, B. M., Davis, L. K., Gamazon, E. R., Derks, E. M., Evans, P., Edlund, C. K., Crane, J., Fagerness, J. A., Osiecki, L., Gallagher, P., Gerber, G., Haddad, S., Illmann, C., McGrath, L. M., Mayerfeld, C., Arepalli, S., Barlassina, C., ... Pauls, D. L. (2015). Cross-disorder genome-wide analyses suggest a complex genetic relationship between Tourette's syndrome and OCD. *The American journal of psychiatry*, *172*(1), 82–93. https://doi.org/10.1176/appi.ajp.2014.13101306

Albin, R. L., & Mink, J. W. (2006). Recent advances in Tourette syndrome research. *Trends in neurosciences*, *29*(3), 175–182. https://doi.org/10.1016/j.tins.2006.01.001

Wang, Z., Maia, T. V., Marsh, R., Colibazzi, T., Gerber, A., & Peterson, B. S. (2011). The neural circuits that generate tics in Tourette's syndrome. *The American journal of psychiatry*, *168*(12), 1326–1337. https://doi.org/10.1176/appi.ajp.2011.09111692
https://doi.org/10.1176/appi.ajp.2011.09111692

Mazzone, L., Yu, S., Blair, C., Gunter, B. C., Wang, Z., Marsh, R., & Peterson, B. S. (2010). An FMRI study of frontostriatal circuits during the inhibition of eye blinking in persons with Tourette syndrome. *The American journal of psychiatry*, *167*(3), 341–349. https://doi.org/10.1176/appi.ajp.2009.08121831

Caligiore, D., Mannella, F., Arbib, M. A., & Baldassarre, G. (2017). Dysfunctions of the basal ganglia-cerebellar-thalamo-cortical system produce motor tics in Tourette syndrome. *PLoS computational biology*, *13*(3), e1005395. https://doi.org/10.1371/journal.pcbi.1005395

Warsi, Q., Kirby, C., & Beg, M. (2017). Pediatric Tourette Syndrome: A Tic Disorder with a Tricky Presentation. *Case reports in gastroenterology*, *11*(1), 89–94. https://doi.org/10.1159/000456609

Morand-Beaulieu, S., Grot, S., Lavoie, J., Leclerc, J. B., Luck, D., & Lavoie, M.

References

E. (2017). The puzzling question of inhibitory control in Tourette syndrome: A meta-analysis. *Neuroscience and biobehavioral reviews*, *80*, 240–262. https://doi.org/10.1016/j.neubiorev.2017.05.006

Cannon, E., Silburn, P., Coyne, T., O'Maley, K., Crawford, J. D., & Sachdev, P. S. (2012). Deep brain stimulation of anteromedial globus pallidus interna for severe Tourette's syndrome. *The American journal of psychiatry*, *169*(8), 860–866. https://doi.org/10.1176/appi.ajp.2012.11101583

Lavoie, M.E.; O'Connor, K. Toward a Multifactorial Conception of the Gilles de la Tourette Syndrome and Persistent Chronic Tic Disorder. *Brain Sci.* **2017**, *7*, 61. https://doi.org/10.3390/brainsci7060061 http://www.mdpi.com/2076-3425/7/6/61/htm

Lipkin, P. H., Goldstein, I. J., & Adesman, A. R. (1994). Tics and dyskinesias associated with stimulant treatment in attention-deficit hyperactivity disorder. *Archives of pediatrics & adolescent medicine*, *148*(8), https://doi.org/10.1001/archpedi.1994.02170080089017

https://dig.pharmacy.uic.edu/faqs/2019-2/september-2019-faqs/do-psychostimulants-cause-tics/

Kurlan R. M. (2014). Treatment of Tourette syndrome. *Neurotherapeutics : the journal of the American Society for Experimental NeuroTherapeutics*, *11*(1), 161–165. https://doi.org/10.1007/s13311-013-0215-4

Waln, O., & Jankovic, J. (2013). An update on tardive dyskinesia: from phenomenology to treatment. *Tremor and other hyperkinetic movements (New York, N.Y.)*, *3*, tre-03-161-4138-1. https://doi.org/10.7916/D88P5Z71

66) Tamminga C.A., Thaker G.K., Chase T.N. (1985) GABA Dysfunction in the Pathophysiology of Tardive Dyskinesia. In: Casey D.E., Chase T.N., Christensen A.V., Gerlach J. (eds) Dyskinesia. Psychopharmacology Supplementum, vol 2. Springer, Berlin, Heidelberg. https://doi.org/10.1007/978-3-642-70140-5_16

Gerlach J. (1985). Pathophysiological mechanisms underlying tardive dyskinesia. *Psychopharmacology. Supplementum*, *2*, 98–103. https://doi.org/10.1007/978-3-642-70140-5_12

Tiwari, A. K., Deshpande, S. N., Rao, A. R., Bhatia, T., Mukit, S. R., Shriharsh, V., Lerer, B., Nimagaonkar, V. L., & Thelma, B. K. (2005). Genetic susceptibility to tardive dyskinesia in chronic schizophrenia subjects: I. Association of CYP1A2 gene polymorphism. *The pharmacogenomics journal*, *5*(1), 60–69. https://doi.org/10.1038/sj.tpj.6500282

67) Parkinsonism Relat Disord. 2009 Dec; 15(0 3): S237–S240. doi: 10.1016/S1353-8020(09)70822-3

Shin, H. W., & Chung, S. J. (2012). Drug-induced parkinsonism. *Journal of clinical neurology (Seoul, Korea)*, *8*(1), 15–21. https://doi.org/10.3988/jcn.2012.8.1.15 https://www.apdaparkinson.org/article/drug-induced-parkinsonism/

Boord, P., Madhyastha, T. M., Askren, M. K., & Grabowski, T. J. (2016). Executive attention networks show altered relationship with default mode network in PD. *NeuroImage. Clinical, 13*, 1–8. https://doi.org/10.1016/j.nicl.2016.11.004

68) Lewis K, O'Day CS. Dystonic Reactions. In: StatPearls (Internet). Treasure Island (FL): StatPearls Publishing; 2022 Jan-. Available from: https://www.ncbi.nlm.nih.gov/books/NBK531466/ dyston https://emedicine.medscape.com/article/814632-overview

69) Berman B. D. (2011). Neuroleptic malignant syndrome: a review for neurohospitalists. *The Neurohospitalist, 1*(1), 41–47. https://doi.org/10.1177/1941875210386491

Atypical Antipsychotics and Neuroleptic Malignant Syndrome, Stanley N Caroff, MD , Stephan C Mann, MD , and E Cabrina Campbell, MD May 01, 2000https://doi.org/10.3928/0048-5713-20000501-09Psychiatric AnnalsVol. 30, No. 5

https://www.healio.com/psychiatry/journals/psycann/2000-5-30-5/%7B5b89d89f-8c5e-4ee7-921a-2d408b991a1f%7D/atypical-antipsychotics-and-neuroleptic-malignant-syndrome
https://www.mhaus.org/nmsis/publications/published-articles-for-promising-new-investigators/neuroleptic-malignant-syndrome-answers-to-6-tough-questions/

70) Fricchione G, Bush G, Fozdar M, Francis A, Fink M. Recognition and Treatment of the Catatonic Syndrome. Journal of Intensive Care Medicine. 1997;12(3):135-147. doi:10.1177/088506669701200304
http://journals.sagepub.com/doi/abs/10.1177/088506669701200304

Rasmussen, S. A., Mazurek, M. F., & Rosebush, P. I. (2016). Catatonia: Our current understanding of its diagnosis, treatment and pathophysiology. *World journal of psychiatry, 6*(4), 391–398. https://doi.org/10.5498/wjp.v6.i4.391

George, R., & Langford, A. (2017). Intermittent catatonia and complex automatisms caused by frontal lobe epilepsy in dementia. *BMJ case reports, 2017*, bcr2017222444. https://doi.org/10.1136/bcr-2017-222444

Mythri, S. V., & Mathew, V. (2016). Catatonic Syndrome in Anti-NMDA Receptor Encephalitis. *Indian journal of psychological medicine, 38*(2), 152–154. https://doi.org/10.4103/0253-7176.178812

Wilcox, J. A., & Reid Duffy, P. (2015). The Syndrome of Catatonia. *Behavioral sciences (Basel, Switzerland), 5*(4), 576–588. https://doi.org/10.3390/bs5040576
https://www.ncbi.nlm.nih.gov/pmc/articles/PMC4695780/

71) Ellul, P., & Choucha, W. (2015). Neurobiological Approach of Catatonia and Treatment Perspectives. *Frontiers in psychiatry, 6*, 182. https://doi.org/10.3389/fpsyt.2015.00182   https://www.ncbi.nlm.nih.gov/pmc/articles/PMC4689858/

Castillo, E., Rubin, R. T., & Holsboer-Trachsler, E. (1989). Clinical differentiation between lethal catatonia and neuroleptic malignant syndrome. *The American journal of psychiatry, 146*(3), 324–328. https://doi.org/10.1176/ajp.146.3.324

Strawn, J. R., Keck, P. E., Jr, & Caroff, S. N. (2007). Neuroleptic malignant

References

syndrome. *The American journal of psychiatry*, *164*(6), 870–876. https://doi.org/10.1176/ajp.2007.164.6.870

72) Carroll B. T. (2000). The universal field hypothesis of catatonia and neuroleptic malignant syndrome. *CNS spectrums*, *5*(7), 26–33. https://doi.org/10.1017/s1092852900013365 *GABA agonists have been shown to alleviate catatonia and NMS; D2 antagonism increases likelihood of NMS and catatonia; 5-HT1A agonism combined with 5-HT2A antagonism are associated with catatonia and NMS; NMDA receptor antagonists, such as phencyclidine and ketamine, that reduce glutamate transmission increase the risk.*

73) Maurer, C. W., LaFaver, K., Ameli, R., Epstein, S. A., Hallett, M., & Horovitz, S. G. (2016). Impaired self-agency in functional movement disorders: A resting-state fMRI study. *Neurology*, *87*(6), 564–570. https://doi.org/10.1212/WNL.0000000000002940

Espay, A. J., Aybek, S., Carson, A., Edwards, M. J., Goldstein, L. H., Hallett, M., LaFaver, K., LaFrance, W. C., Jr, Lang, A. E., Nicholson, T., Nielsen, G., Reuber, M., Voon, V., Stone, J., & Morgante, F. (2018). Current Concepts in Diagnosis and Treatment of Functional Neurological Disorders. *JAMA neurology*, *75*(9), 1132–1141. https://doi.org/10.1001/jamaneurol.2018.1264

74) Personality Can Change Over A Lifetime, And Usually For The Better https://www.npr.org/sections/health-shots/2016/06/30/484053435/personality-can-change-over-a-lifetime-and-usually-for-the-better

You Can't See It, But You'll Be A Different Person In 10 Years https://www.npr.org/sections/health-shots/2013/01/03/168567019/you-cant-see-it-but-youll-be-a-different-person-in-10-years

Hopwood, C. J., Donnellan, M. B., Blonigen, D. M., Krueger, R. F., McGue, M., Iacono, W. G., & Burt, S. A. (2011). Genetic and environmental influences on personality trait stability and growth during the transition to adulthood: A three-wave longitudinal study. *Journal of Personality and Social Psychology*, *100*(3), 545–556. https://doi.org/10.1037/a0022409

Löckenhoff, C. E., Terracciano, A., Ferrucci, L., & Costa, P. T. (2012). Five-Factor Personality Traits and Age Trajectories of Self-Rated Health: The Role of Question Framing. *Journal of Personality*, *80*(2), 375–401. https://doi.org/10.1111/j.1467-6494.2011.00724.x

Bleidorn, W., Hill, P. L., Back, M. D., Denissen, J. J. A., Hennecke, M., Hopwood, C. J., Jokela, M., Kandler, C., Lucas, R. E., Luhmann, M., Orth, U., Wagner, J., Wrzus, C., Zimmermann, J., & Roberts, B. (2019). The policy relevance of personality traits. *American Psychologist, 74*(9), 1056–1067. https://doi.org/10.1037/amp0000503

Erikson, E. H. (2980). **Identity and the life cycle**. New York Norton.
Erikson, Erik H. **Childhood and Society**. London, Vintage Digital, 2014.
Levinson, D. J. (1978). **The seasons of a man's life** : With Charlotte N. Darrow a. o. Knopf.

75) Hallquist, M. N., & Lenzenweger, M. F. (2013). Identifying Latent

Trajectories of
Personality Disorder Symptom Change: Growth Mixture Modeling in the Longitudinal
Study of Personality Disorders. *Journal of Abnormal Psychology, 122*(1), 138–155.https://doi.org/10.1037/a0030060
76) Control of Human Voluntary Movement | J.C. Rothwell | Springer
77) Pierre Sachse, Ursula Beermann, Markus Martini, Thomas Maran, Markus Domeier, Marco R. Furtner,"The world is upside down" – The Innsbruck Goggle Experiments of Theodor Erismann (1883–1961) and Ivo Kohler (1915–1985),Cortex,Volume 92,2017,Pages 222-232,ISSN 0010-9452, https://doi.org/10.1016/j.cortex.2017.04.014.
(https://www.sciencedirect.com/science/article/pii/S0010945217301314)
Kohler reversed goggles and video: https://www.youtube.com/watch?v=JQJ5SFnytfo
78) Houk J. C. (2005). Agents of the mind. *Biological cybernetics, 92*(6), 427–437. https://doi.org/10.1007/s00422-005-0569-8
Bressler, S. L., & Tognoli, E. (2006). Operational principles of neurocognitive networks. *International journal of psychophysiology : official journal of the International Organization of Psychophysiology, 60*(2), 139–148. https://doi.org/10.1016/j.ijpsycho.2005.12.008
Earl K. Miller, Timothy J. Buschman, Rules through Recursion: How Interactions between the Frontal Cortex and Basal Ganglia May Build Abstract, Complex Rules from Concrete, Simple Ones 10.1093/acprof:oso/9780195314274.003.0022
In Bunge and Wallis, NEUROSCIENCE OF RULE GUIDED BEHAVIOR
79) Marmarosh C. L. (2012). Empirically supported perspectives on transference. *Psychotherapy (Chicago, Ill.), 49*(3), 364–369. https://doi.org/10.1037/a0028801
https://www.researchgate.net/publication/230827643_Empirically_Supported_Perspectives_on_Transference
Berne simplifies this model in **Games People Play,** *and* **Im OK, You're OK.** *With clever descriptions of typical patterns of social interaction. ID-EGO-SUPEREGO becomes CHILD-ADULT-PARENT and the triad has functions similar to PSA formulations. Whether these have any statistical validity or are projections we do onto each other is unclear.*
Johnson, J. G., Cohen, P., Brown, J., Smailes, E. M., & Bernstein, D. P. (1999). Childhood Maltreatment Increases Risk for Personality Disorders During Early Adulthood. *Archives of General Psychiatry, 56*(7), 600. https://doi.org/10.1001/archpsyc.56.7.600
Bierer, L. M., Yehuda, R., Schmeidler, J., Mitropoulou, V., New, A. S., Silverman, J. M., & Siever, L. J. (2003). Abuse and Neglect in Childhood: Relationship to Personality Disorder Diagnoses. *CNS Spectrums, 8*(10), https://doi.org/10.1017/s1092852900019118

References

Hovens, J. G. F. M., Giltay, E. J., Spinhoven, P., van Hemert, A. M., & Penninx, B. W. J. H. (2015). Impact of Childhood Life Events and Childhood Trauma on the Onset and Recurrence of Depressive and Anxiety Disorders. *The Journal of Clinical Psychiatry*, *76*(07), 931–938. https://doi.org/10.4088/jcp.14m09135

Levy, K. N., & Scala, J. W. (2012). Transference, transference interpretations, and transference-focused psychotherapies. *Psychotherapy (Chicago, Ill.)*, *49*(3), 391–403. https://doi.org/10.1037/a0029371 https://www.researchgate.net/publication/230827646_Transference_Transference_Interpretations_and_Transference-Focused_Psychotherapies

Fletcher, J. M., & Schurer, S. (2017). Origins of adulthood personality: The role of adverse childhood experiences. *The B.E. Journal of Economic Analysis & Policy*, *17*(2).

Hampson, S. E. (2008). Mechanisms by Which Childhood Personality Traits Influence Adult Well-Being. *Current Directions in Psychological Science*, *17*(4), 264–268. https://doi.org/10.1111/j.1467-8721.2008.00587.x

Goodman, M., Weiss, D. S., Koenigsberg, H., Kotlyarevsky, V., New, A. S., Mitropoulou, V., Silverman, J. M., O'Flynn, K., & Siever, L. J. (2003). The role of childhood trauma in differences in affective instability in those with personality disorders. *CNS spectrums*, *8*(10), 763–770. https://doi.org/10.1017/s1092852900019131

Essex, M. J., Klein, M. H., Slattery, M. J., Goldsmith, H. H., & Kalin, N. H. (2010). Early risk factors and developmental pathways to chronic high inhibition and social anxiety disorder in adolescence. *The American journal of psychiatry*, *167*(1), 40–46. https://doi.org/10.1176/appi.ajp.2009.07010051

Johnson JG, Cohen P, Brown J, Smailes EM, Bernstein DP. Childhood Maltreatment Increases Risk for Personality Disorders During Early Adulthood. *Arch Gen Psychiatry*. 1999;56(7):600–606. https://jamanetwork.com/journals/jamapsychiatry/fullarticle/205066

Agrawal, A., Nelson, E. C., Littlefield, A. K., Bucholz, K. K., Degenhardt, L., Henders, A. K., Madden, P. A. F., Martin, N. G., Montgomery, G. W., Pergadia, M. L., Sher, K. J., Heath, A. C., & Lynskey, M. T. (2012). Cannabinoid Receptor Genotype Moderation of the Effects of Childhood Physical Abuse on Anhedonia and Depression. *Archives of General Psychiatry*, *69*(7), 732–740. https://doi.org/10.1001/archgenpsychiatry.2011.2273

80) https://www.nytimes.com/1971/04/18/archives/wilhelm-reich-the-psychoanalyst-as-revolutionary-wilhelm-reich.html
https://www.lowenfoundation.org/about-alexander-lowen
https://www.rubenfeldsynergy.com/
https://pbsp.com/

Varela, F. J., Rosch, E., & Thompson, E. (2016). ***The embodied mind : cognitive science and human experience***. The Mit Press. https://archive.org/details/FranciscoJ.VarelaEvanT.ThompsonEleanorRoschTheEmbodiedMindCognitiveScienceAndHum/page/

n15/mode/2up
81) Sanchez-Roige, S., Gray, J. C., MacKillop, J., Chen, C.-H., & Palmer, A. A. (2017). The genetics of human personality. *Genes, Brain and Behavior, 17*(3), e12439. https://doi.org/10.1111/gbb.12439
Plomin, R., DeFries, J. C., Knopik, V. S., & Neiderhiser, J. M. (2016). Top 10 Replicated Findings from Behavioral Genetics. *Perspectives on Psychological Science : A Journal of the Association for Psychological Science, 11*(1), 3–23. https://doi.org/10.1177/1745691615617439
Genetics of personality Consortium, de Moor, M. H., van den Berg, S. M., Verweij, K. J., Krueger, R. F., Luciano, M., Arias Vasquez, A., Matteson, L. K., Derringer, J., Esko, T., Amin, N., Gordon, S. D., Hansell, N. K., Hart, A. B., Seppälä, I., Huffman, J. E., Konte, B., Lahti, J., Lee, M., Miller, M., ... Boomsma, D. I. (2015). Meta-analysis of Genome-wide Association Studies for Neuroticism, and the Polygenic Association With Major Depressive Disorder. *JAMA psychiatry, 72*(7), 642–650. https://doi.org/10.1001/jamapsychiatry.2015.0554
Milaneschi Y, Lamers F, Peyrot WJ, et al. Genetic Association of Major Depression With Atypical Features and Obesity-Related Immunometabolic Dysregulations. *JAMA Psychiatry.* 2017;74(12):1214–1225. doi:10.1001/jamapsychiatry.2017.3016
https://jamanetwork.com/journals/jamapsychiatry/fullarticle/2657483
Labonté, B., Suderman, M., Maussion, G., Navaro, L., Yerko, V., Mahar, I., Bureau, A., Mechawar, N., Szyf, M., Meaney, M. J., & Turecki, G. (2012). Genome-wide Epigenetic Regulation by Early-Life Trauma. *Archives of General Psychiatry, 69*(7). https://doi.org/10.1001/archgenpsychiatry.2011.2287
Plomin, R. (2019). ***Blueprint : how DNA makes us who we are.*** The Mit Press.
Briley, D. A., & Tucker-Drob, E. M. (2014). Genetic and environmental continuity in personality development: A meta-analysis. *Psychological Bulletin, 140*(5), 1303–1331. https://doi.org/10.1037/a0037091
12.3 Is Personality More Nature or More Nurture? Behavioural and Molecular Genetics – Introduction to Psychology – 1st Canadian Edition. (2014, October 17). Opentextbc.Ca. https://opentextbc.ca/introductiontopsychology/chapter/11-3-is-personality-more-nature-or-more-nurture-behavioral-and-molecular-genetics/
Chess, S., & Thomas, A. (1977). Temperamental Individuality from Childhood to Adolescence. *Journal of the American Academy of Child Psychiatry, 16*(2), 218–226. https://doi.org/10.1016/s0002-7138(09)60038-8
82) Namnyak, M., Tufton, N., Szekely, R., Toal, M., Worboys, S., & Sampson, E. L. (2008). 'Stockholm syndrome': psychiatric diagnosis or urban myth?. *Acta psychiatrica Scandinavica, 117*(1), 4–11. https://doi.org/10.1111/j.1600-0447.2007.01112.x
https://pubmed.ncbi.nlm.nih.gov/18028254/
de C Williams, A. C., & van der Merwe, J. (2013). The psychological

impact of torture. *British journal of pain*, *7*(2), 101–106. https://doi.org/10.1177/2049463713483596

Kienzler, H., & Sapkota, R. P. (2020). The Long-Term Mental Health Consequences of Torture, Loss, and Insecurity: A Qualitative Study Among Survivors of Armed Conflict in the Dang District of Nepal. *Frontiers in psychiatry*, *10*, 941. https://doi.org/10.3389/fpsyt.2019.00941

83) https://en.wikipedia.org/wiki/Genie_(feral_child)
Case Studies. (2018). Feral Children…. https://feralchildrenproject.weebly.com/case-studies.html
"Isabelle: The Story of a Child Kept in Extreme Isolation." *Edublox Online Tutor*, 31 Mar. 2018, www.edubloxtutor.com/isabelle-isolation/. *10 Modern Cases of Feral Children - Listverse*. (2017, April 21). Listverse. https://listverse.com/2008/03/07/10-modern-cases-of-feral-children/ feral child case study - Google Search. (n.d.). Www.Google.Com. Retrieved March 27, 2020, from https://www.google.com/search?client=firefox-b-1-d&q=feral+child+case+study&sa=X&ved=2ahUKEwjx77G3sKjiAhXZHjQIHXDXBjcQ1QIoBHoECAsQBQ&biw=858&bih=808

84) Germans, S., Van Heck, G. L., & Hodiamont, P. P. G. (2012). Results of the search for personality disorder screening tools: clinical implications. *The Journal of Clinical Psychiatry*, *73*(2), 165–173. https://doi.org/10.4088/JCP.11m07067

85) Minnesota Multiphasic Personality Inventory - an overview | ScienceDirect Topics. (n.d.). Www.Sciencedirect.Com. Retrieved March 27, 2020, from https://www.sciencedirect.com/topics/medicine-and-dentistry/minnesota-multiphasic-personality-inventory

Two classic personality tests: *MMPI and Rohrschach illustrate the problems and limitations of these methods: They differ on what is being evaluated: The MMPI was developed using hospitalized psychiatric patients who reported their symptoms and mental states. These were recreated as questions and sorted into scales (by statistical (factor) analysis) to use as a diagnostic instrument for major mental disorders. The test was re-standardized later using the scales as indications of milder "personality types", standardized against clinician diagnoses of personality features. The irony of the MMPI is that a tool for diagnosing major mental disorders was repurposed, without major changes in content, for self report of personality dysfunction. The high degree of statistical standardization for reliability is offset by questions about validity: what is it really measuring?*

A Swiss Psychiatrist, Hermann Rohrschach, created a method of evaluation by marking random ink blots on pages and folding the pages to create mirror image figures. The patient is asked to report what the images "look like" or "remind them of" and the responses recorded with the presumption that the subject will report objects or things, just as people sometimes see objects when viewing clouds. In the early years of use, the direct responses were reported and rated by the clinician, with attention to the content of the responses. This was found to be inconsistent and a literature developed identifying "common" and "uncommon and bizarre" responses to each figure as well as the perceptual quality of the response incorporating more or less of the image. (Exner scoring) This scoring system correlates with symptoms of mental disorganization. The responses are visual perceptions and therefore predominantly test the visual/emotional link. The Rohrschach was favored by many PSA for its supposed ability to elicit "unconscious preoccupations" in the ambiguous figures by projection. No external validation to personality categories exists and the test is was not used that way. Nor is there research that documents that it reveals emotional issues in the "Unconscious".

FORER B. R. (1949). The fallacy of personal validation; a classroom demonstration of gullibility. *Journal of abnormal psychology*, *44*(1), 118–123. https://doi.org/10.1037/h0059240 And this phenomenon and studies have been reviewed by Dickson and Kelly.

Dickson, D. H., & Kelly, I. W. (1985). The 'Barnum Effect' in Personality Assessment: A Review of the Literature. *Psychological Reports*, *57*(2), 367–382. https://doi.org/10.2466/pr0.1985.57.2.367

86) Trull, T. J., & Durrett, C. A. (2005). Categorical and Dimensional Models of Personality Disorder. *Annual Review of Clinical Psychology*, *1*(1), 355–380. https://doi.org/10.1146/annurev.clinpsy.1.102803.144009

Trull, T. J., & Widiger, T. A. (2013). Dimensional models of personality: the five-factor model and the DSM-5. *Dialogues in Clinical Neuroscience*, *15*(2), 135–146. https://www.ncbi.nlm.nih.gov/pmc/articles/PMC3811085/

Trull and Widiger are advocates for the **"five factor"** continuum model. The scale is formed from prior scales, not direct observation and categorization of behavior. A "factor analysis" of previous testing methods, a "scale of scales" not direct observations, whose validity is unclear. The FFM has "dimensions of personality" measured by separate scales: **extraversion (versus introversion)** a general measure of how attentive the person is to external interaction, **agreeableness (versus antagonism)**, an affiliation measure for degree of seeking interaction vs defensiveness **conscientiousness (or constraint)**, is difficult to interpret (OCD?) **emotional instability (or neuroticism)**, reflects rigid methods of dealing with anxiety vs inability to manage it, and **intellect (vs unconventionality or openness)**, reflects cognitive vs intuitive processing. (the acronym OCEAN). The separate factors correlate with traditional personality diagnoses, intended to show that the method would "identify" these clinical patterns, but clinicians were not convinced of its practicality and it has not been used.

Rottman, Benjamin M., et al. "Can Clinicians Recognize DSM-IV Personality Disorders from Five-Factor Model Descriptions of Patient Cases?" *The American Journal of Psychiatry*, vol. 166, no. 4, 1 Apr. 2009, pp. 427–433, 10.1176/appi.ajp.2008.08070972

Westen, D., & Shedler, J. (2007). Personality diagnosis with the Shedler-Westen Assessment Procedure (SWAP): Integrating clinical and statistical measurement and prediction. *Journal of Abnormal Psychology*, *116*(4), 810–822. https://doi.org/10.1037/0021-843x.116.4.810

Westen, D., Shedler, J., Bradley, B., & DeFife, J. A. (2012). An Empirically Derived Taxonomy for Personality Diagnosis: Bridging Science and Practice in Conceptualizing Personality. *American Journal of Psychiatry*, *169*(3), 273–284. https://doi.org/10.1176/appi.ajp.2011.11020274

Widiger, T. A., & Simonsen, E. (2005). Alternative Dimensional Models of Personality Disorder: Finding a Common Ground. *Journal of Personality Disorders*, *19*(2), 110–130. https://doi.org/10.1521/pedi.19.2.110.62628

Schmeck, K., Schlüter-Müller, S., Foelsch, P. A., & Doering, S. (2013). The role of identity in the DSM-5 classification of personality disorders. *Child and Adolescent Psychiatry and Mental Health*, *7*(1), 27. https://doi.org/10.1186/1753-2000-7-27

87) Bellak, Leopold, Marvin Hurvich, and Helen K. Gediman. *Ego Functions in Schizophrenics, Neurotics, and Normals: A Systematic Study of Conceptual, Diagnostic, and Therapeutic Aspects*. New York, NY: John Wiley, 1973.

Psychoanalisys - Defence mechanisms. (n.d.). Www.Freudfile.Org. Retrieved March 13, 2020, from http://www.freudfile.org/psychoanalysis/defence_mecanism.html

15 Common Defense Mechanisms. (2018, October 8). Psych Central. https://psychcentral.com/lib/15-common-defense-mechanisms/

Waude, A. (2016, May 16). *31 Psychological Defense Mechanisms Explained*. Psychologistworld.Com; Psychologist World. https://www.psychologistworld.com/freud/defence-mechanisms-list

Freud, Anna, **Ego And The Mechanisms Of Defense**.

Northoff, G., Bermpohl, F., Schoeneich, F., & Boeker, H. (2007). How Does Our Brain Constitute Defense Mechanisms? First-Person Neuroscience and Psychoanalysis. *Psychotherapy and Psychosomatics*, *76*(3), 141–153. https://doi.org/10.1159/000099841

Ochsner, K. N., & Gross, J. J. (2008). Cognitive Emotion Regulation: Insights from Social Cognitive and Affective Neuroscience. *Current directions in psychological science*, *17*(2), 153–158. https://doi.org/10.1111/j.1467-8721.2008.00566.x

88) Vaillant G. E. (1971). Theoretical hierarchy of adaptive ego mechanisms: a 30-year follow-up of 30 men selected for psychological health. *Archives of general psychiatry*, *24*(2), 107–118. https://doi.org/10.1001/archpsyc.1971.01750080011003

Malone, J. C., Cohen, S., Liu, S. R., Vaillant, G. E., & Waldinger, R. J. (2013). Adaptive midlife defense mechanisms and late-life health. *Personality and Individual Differences*, *55*(2), 85–89. https://doi.org/10.1016/j.paid.2013.01.025

89) Southwick, S. M., Bonanno, G. A., Masten, A. S., Panter-Brick, C., & Yehuda, R. (2014). Resilience definitions, theory, and challenges: interdisciplinary perspectives. *European journal of psychotraumatology*, *5*, 10.3402/ejpt.

v5.25338. https://doi.org/10.3402/ejpt.v5.25338 https://www.ncbi.nlm.nih.gov/pmc/articles/PMC4185134/

Born, M., Chevalier, V., & Humblet, I. (1997). Resilience, desistance and delinquent career of adolescent offenders. *Journal of adolescence*, *20*(6), 679–694. https://doi.org/10.1006/jado.1997.0119

Tugade, M. M., Fredrickson, B. L., & Barrett, L. F. (2004). Psychological resilience and positive emotional granularity: examining the benefits of positive emotions on coping and health. *Journal of personality*, *72*(6), 1161–1190. https://doi.org/10.1111/j.1467-6494.2004.00294.x

90) This understanding is also central to Buddhist psychology, which sees the "self" as experience of life events, and always changing. Kornfield, J. (n.d.). *No Self or True Self? — Identity and Selflessness in Buddhism.* Tricycle: The Buddhist Review. Retrieved March 27, 2020, from https://tricycle.org/magazine/no-self-or-true-self/

Damasio, A. R. (2012). **Self comes to mind : constructing the conscious brain**. Vintage.

extended self in a digital world - Google Search. (n.d.). Www.Google.Com. Retrieved March 11, 2020, from https://www.google.com/search?q=extended+self+in+a+digital+world&ie=utf-8&oe=utf-8

Hood, B. M. (2013). **The self illusion : how the social brain creates identity**. Oxford University Press.

Schmeck, K., Schlüter-Müller, S., Foelsch, P. A., & Doering, S. (2013). The role of identity in the DSM-5 classification of personality disorders. *Child and Adolescent Psychiatry and Mental Health*, *7*(1), 27. https://doi.org/10.1186/1753-2000-7-27

91) Gaetano, Phil, "David Reimer and John Money Gender Reassignment Controversy: The John/Joan Case". *Embryo Project Encyclopedia* (2017-11-15). ISSN: 1940-5030 http://embryo.asu.edu/handle/10776/13009. https://embryo.asu.edu/pages/david-reimer-and-john-money-gender-reassignment-controversy-johnjoan-case

92) References relative to table:
Gender ABACUS https://appadvice.com/app/the-gender-abacus/1211466227

93) Yatsenko, S. A., & Witchel, S. F. (2017). Genetic approach to ambiguous genitalia and disorders of sex development: What clinicians need to know. *Seminars in perinatology*, *41*(4), 232–243. https://doi.org/10.1053/j.semperi.2017.03.016

Miranda, A., & Sousa, N. (2018). Maternal hormonal milieu influence on fetal brain development. *Brain and Behavior*, *8*(2), e00920. https://doi.org/10.1002/brb3.920

Hines, M. (2011). Prenatal endocrine influences on sexual orientation and on sexually differentiated childhood behavior. *Frontiers in Neuroendocrinology*, *32*(2), 170–182. https://doi.org/10.1016/j.yfrne.2011.02.006

Bjørnerem, A., Straume, B., Øian, P., & Berntsen, G. K. R. (2006).

References

Seasonal Variation of Estradiol, Follicle Stimulating Hormone, and Dehydroepiandrosterone Sulfate in Women and Men. *The Journal of Clinical Endocrinology & Metabolism*, *91*(10), 3798–3802. https://doi.org/10.1210/jc.2006-0866

Martikainen, H., Ruokonen, A., Tomás, C., & Kauppila, A. (1996). Seasonal changes in pituitary function: amplification of midfollicular luteinizing hormone secretion during the dark season. *Fertility and Sterility*, *65*(4), 718–720. https://doi.org/10.1016/s0015-0282(16)58202-8

Ganna, A., Verweij, K., Nivard, M. G., Maier, R., Wedow, R., Busch, A. S., Abdellaoui, A., Guo, S., Sathirapongsasuti, J. F., 23andMe Research Team, Lichtenstein, P., Lundström, S., Långström, N., Auton, A., Harris, K. M., Beecham, G. W., Martin, E. R., Sanders, A. R., Perry, J., Neale, B. M., ... Zietsch, B. P. (2019). Large-scale GWAS reveals insights into the genetic architecture of same-sex sexual behavior. *Science (New York, N.Y.)*, *365*(6456), eaat7693. https://doi.org/10.1126/science.aat7693

Schecklmann, M., Engelhardt, K., Konzok, J., Rupprecht, R., Greenlee, M. W., Mokros, A., Langguth, B., & Poeppl, T. B. (2015). Sexual motivation is reflected by stimulus-dependent motor cortex excitability. *Social cognitive and affective neuroscience*, *10*(8), 1061–1065. https://doi.org/10.1093/scan/nsu157

P Fitzgibbons R. (2015). Transsexual attractions and sexual reassignment surgery: Risks and potential risks. *The Linacre quarterly*, *82*(4), 337–350. https://doi.org/10.1080/00243639.2015.1125574

Stoller RJ, Herdt GH. Theories of Origins of Male Homosexuality: A Cross-cultural Look. *Arch Gen Psychiatry*. 1985;42(4):399–404. doi:10.1001/archpsyc.1985.01790270089010

http://jamanetwork.com/journals/jamapsychiatry/article-abstract/493553

Discussion of recent studies claiming brain differentiation:
Richard Bränström and John E. Pachankis Reduction in Mental Health Treatment Utilization Among Transgender Individuals After Gender-Affirming Surgeries: A Total Population Study,American Journal of Psychiatry 2020 177:8, 727-734 https://ajp.psychiatryonline.org/doi/10.1176/appi.ajp.2019.19010080

BeckmanJan. 22, M., 2004, & Am, 12:00. (2004, January 22). *Once a Male, Always a Male*. Science | AAAS. https://www.sciencemag.org/news/2004/01/once-male-always-male

https://www.nytimes.com/2018/12/03/opinion/male-female-brains-mosaic.html

Wiik, A., Andersson, D. P., Brismar, T. B., Chanpen, S., Dhejne, C., Ekström, T. J., Flanagan, J. N., Holmberg, M., Kere, J., Lilja, M., Lindholm, M. E., Lundberg, T. R., Maret, E., Melin, M., Olsson, S. M., Rullman, E., Wåhlén, K., Arver, S., & Gustafsson, T. (2018). Metabolic and functional changes in transgender individuals following cross-sex hormone treatment: Design and methods of the GEnder Dysphoria Treatment in Sweden (GETS) study. *Contemporary Clinical Trials Communications*, *10*, 148–153. https://doi.org/10.1016/j.conctc.2018.04.005

Nguyen, H. B., Chavez, A. M., Lipner, E., Hantsoo, L., Kornfield, S. L., Davies, R. D., & Epperson, C. N. (2018). Gender-Affirming Hormone Use in Transgender Individuals: Impact on Behavioral Health and Cognition. *Current Psychiatry Reports, 20*(12). https://doi.org/10.1007/s11920-018-0973-0
T'Sjoen, G., Arcelus, J., Gooren, L., Klink, D. T., & Tangpricha, V. (2018). Endocrinology of Transgender Medicine. *Endocrine Reviews, 40*(1), 97–117. https://doi.org/10.1210/er.2018-00011
94) Manoli, D. S., & State, M. W. (2021). Autism Spectrum Disorder Genetics and the Search for Pathological Mechanisms. *The American journal of psychiatry, 178*(1), 30–38. https://doi.org/10.1176/appi.ajp.2020.20111608
95) Gillig P. M. (2009). Dissociative identity disorder: a controversial diagnosis. *Psychiatry (Edgmont (Pa. : Township)), 6*(3), 24–29. Dissociation is discussed in more detail in chapter nine, PTSD.

CHAPTER SEVEN REFERENCES

1) McLeod, S. A. (2018, Oct 31). Konrad Lorenz's imprinting theory. https://www.simplypsychology.org/Konrad-Lorenz.html
Critical periods in puppy development. (2019). Ucdavis.Edu. http://ice.ucdavis.edu/~robyn/Korina/BCIdeas/Criticalperiodsinpuppydevelopment.html
2) MacLean, P. D. (1985). Brain Evolution Relating to Family, Play, and the Separation Call. *Archives of General Psychiatry, 42*(4), 405–417. https://doi.org/10.1001/archpsyc.1985.01790270095011 https://jamanetwork.com/journals/jamapsychiatry/article-abstract/493555?redirect=true
3) Harlow, H. F., & Zimmermann, R. R. (1959). Affectional Response in the Infant Monkey: Orphaned baby monkeys develop a strong and persistent attachment to inanimate surrogate mothers. *Science, 130*(3373), 421–432. https://doi.org/10.1126/science.130.3373.421
Zhang, B. (2017). Consequences of early adverse rearing experience (EARE) on development: insights from non-human primate studies. *Zoological Research, 38*(1), 7–35. https://doi.org/10.13918/j.issn.2095-8137.2017.002
4) Spitz, R.A. (1945). Hospitalism—An Inquiry Into the Genesis of Psychiatric Conditions in Early Childhood. Psychoanalytic Study of the Child, 1, 53-74.
5) Bowlby The Nature Of The Child's Tie To His Mother, International Journal of Psycho-Analysis, 1958, 39, 350
http://www.psychology.sunysb.edu/attachment/online/nature%20of%20the%20childs%20tie%20bowlby.pdf
Bowlby went on to do research on depression in children after mother-child separation which was published in three books: Attachment, Separation, & Loss. Perhaps this was an important issue in London after world war II because of the separation of parents and children that occurred when children were sent away to avoid the bombings.

References

6) Schneider-Rosen, K. (2016). ***Social and emotional development : attachment relationships and the emerging self***. Macmillan.

7) Tell, D., Davidson, D., & Camras, L. A. (2014). Recognition of Emotion from Facial Expressions with Direct or Averted Eye Gaze and Varying Expression Intensities in Children with Autism Disorder and Typically Developing Children. *Autism Research and Treatment*, *2014*, 1–11. https://doi.org/10.1155/2014/816137

Awad, D., Emery, N. J., & Mareschal, I. (2019). The Role of Emotional Expression and Eccentricity on Gaze Perception. *Frontiers in Psychology*, *10*. https://doi.org/10.3389/fpsyg.2019.01129

8) Insel, T. R., & Young, L. J. (2001). The neurobiology of attachment. *Nature Reviews Neuroscience*, *2*(2), 129–136. https://doi.org/10.1038/35053579 A neurobiological basis of social attachment. (1997). *American Journal of Psychiatry*, *154*(6), 726–735. https://doi.org/10.1176/ajp.154.6.726

Insel, T. R. (2010). The Challenge of Translation in Social Neuroscience: A Review of Oxytocin, Vasopressin, and Affiliative Behavior. *Neuron*, *65*(6), 768–779. https://doi.org/10.1016/j.neuron.2010.03.005

Donaldson, Z. R., & Young, L. J. (2008). Oxytocin, vasopressin, and the neurogenetics of sociality. *Science (New York, N.Y.)*, *322*(5903), 900–904. https://doi.org/10.1126/science.1158668

9) Strathearn, L. (2011). Maternal Neglect: Oxytocin, Dopamine and the Neurobiology of Attachment. *Journal of Neuroendocrinology*, *23*(11), 1054–1065. https://doi.org/10.1111/j.1365-2826.2011.02228.x

10). Strathearn, L., Mamun, A. A., Najman, J. M., & O'Callaghan, M. J. (2009). Does Breastfeeding Protect Against Substantiated Child Abuse and Neglect? A 15-Year Cohort Study. *PEDIATRICS*, *123*(2), 483–493. https://doi.org/10.1542/peds.2007-3546

Georgescu, T., Swart, J. M., Grattan, D. R., & Brown, R. (2021). The Prolactin Family of Hormones as Regulators of Maternal Mood and Behavior. *Frontiers in global women's health*, *2*, 767467. https://doi.org/10.3389/fgwh.2021.767467

Carter, Carol. (2017). The Role of Oxytocin and Vasopressin in Attachment. Psychodynamic Psychiatry. 45. 499-517.https://www.researchgate.net/publication/321845637_The_Role_of_Oxytocin_and_Vasopressin_in_Attachment

Young, L. J., Lim, M. M., Gingrich, B., & Insel, T. R. (2001). Cellular Mechanisms of Social Attachment. *Hormones and Behavior*, *40*(2), 133–138. https://doi.org/10.1006/hbeh.2001.1691

Keverne, E. B., & Curley, J. P. (2004). Vasopressin, oxytocin and social behaviour. *Current opinion in neurobiology*, *14*(6), 777–783. https://doi.org/10.1016/j.conb.2004.10.006

Rees C. (2007). Childhood attachment. *The British journal of general practice : the journal of the Royal College of General Practitioners*, *57*(544), 920–922. https://doi.org/10.3399/096016407782317955

11) https://en.wikipedia.org/wiki/Stranger_anxiety

Brooker, R. J., Buss, K. A., Lemery-Chalfant, K., Aksan, N., Davidson, R. J., & Goldsmith, H. H. (2013). The development of stranger fear in infancy and toddlerhood: normative development, individual differences, antecedents, and outcomes. *Developmental Science*, n/a-n/a. https://doi.org/10.1111/desc.12058

12) Goleman, D. (1989, June 6). New Research Overturns A Milestone Of Infancy. *The New York Times*. https://www.nytimes.com/1989/06/06/science/new-research-overturns-a-milestone-of-infancy.html

13) Fraiberg, S. (1969). Libidinal Object Constancy and Mental Representation. *The Psychoanalytic Study of the Child*, 24(1), 9–47. https://doi.org/10.1080/00797308.1969.11822685

14) Denis, M. (n.d.). The psychic envelopes in psychoanalytic theories of infancy. *Frontiers in Psychology*. https://www.academia.edu/27596800/The_psychic_envelopes_in_psychoanalytic_theories_of_infancy

Zeanah, C. H., Berlin, L. J., & Boris, N. W. (2011). Practitioner Review: Clinical applications of attachment theory and research for infants and young children. *Journal of Child Psychology and Psychiatry*, 52(8), 819–833. https://doi.org/10.1111/j.1469-7610.2011.02399.x

15) Wan, M. W., Downey, D., Strachan, H., Elliott, R., Williams, S. R., & Abel, K. M. (2014). The Neural Basis of Maternal Bonding. *PLoS ONE*, 9(3). https://doi.org/10.1371/journal.pone.0088436

Kim, P. (2016). Human Maternal Brain Plasticity: Adaptation to Parenting. *New Directions for Child and Adolescent Development*, 2016(153), 47–58. https://doi.org/10.1002/cad.20168

How a mother's voice shapes her baby's developing brain – Kate Fehlhaber | Aeon Ideas. (n.d.). Aeon. Retrieved February 25, 2020, from https://aeon.co/ideas/how-a-mother-s-voice-shapes-her-baby-s-developing-brain

Noriuchi, M., Kikuchi, Y., Mori, K. et al. The orbitofrontal cortex modulates parenting stress in the maternal brain. *Sci Rep* **9,** 1658 (2019). https://doi.org/10.1038/s41598-018-38402-9   https://www.nature.com/articles/s41598-018-38402-9

Vrtička, P., & Vuilleumier, P. (2012). Neuroscience of human social interactions and adult attachment style. *Frontiers in Human Neuroscience*, 6. https://doi.org/10.3389/fnhum.2012.00212

Laurita, A. C., Hazan, C., & Spreng, R. N. (2019). An attachment theoretical perspective for the neural representation of close others. *Social cognitive and affective neuroscience*, 14(3), 237–251. https://doi.org/10.1093/scan/nsz010

Lenzi, D., Trentini, C., Pantano, P., Macaluso, E., Lenzi, G. L., & Ammaniti, M. (2013). Attachment models affect brain responses in areas related to emotions and empathy in nulliparous women. *Human brain mapping*, 34(6), 1399–1414. https://doi.org/10.1002/hbm.21520

Simpson, E. A., Murray, L., Paukner, A., & Ferrari, P. F. (2014). The mirror neuron system as revealed through neonatal imitation: presence from birth, predictive power and evidence of plasticity. *Philosophical transactions of the Royal*

Society of London. Series B, Biological sciences, *369*(1644), 20130289. https://doi.org/10.1098/rstb.2013.0289

Šešo-Šimić, Đ., Sedmak, G., Hof, P., & Šimić, G. (2010). Recent advances in the neurobiology of attachment behavior. Translational Neuroscience, 1(2). https://doi.org/10.2478/V10134-010-0020-0

Praszkier, Ryszard. (2014). Empathy, mirror neurons and SYNC. Mind & Society. 15.

Redlich, R., Grotegerd, D., Opel, N., Kaufmann, C., Zwitserlood, P., Kugel, H., Heindel, W., Donges, U. S., Suslow, T., Arolt, V., & Dannlowski, U. (2015). Are you gonna leave me? Separation anxiety is associated with increased amygdala responsiveness and volume. *Social cognitive and affective neuroscience*, *10*(2), 278–284. https://doi.org/10.1093/scan/nsu055

16) Winnicott in the paper "the Transitional Object and Transitional Phenomena." International Journal of Psycho-Analysis, Vol. 30+, Part 2 (1953): andin D. W Winnicott, Collected Papers: Through Pediatrics to Psycho-Analysis (1958a). London:Tavistock

Winnicott ch1. (2010). https://llk.media.mit.edu/courses/readings/Winnicott_ch1.pdf

MBernstein. (2009). *Winnicott D. Transitional Objects and Transitional Phenomena*. http://icpla.edu/wp-content/uploads/2013/02/Winnicott-D.-Transitional-Objects-and-Transitional-Phenomena.pdf

Fortuna, K., Baor, L., Israel, S., Abadi, A., & Knafo, A. (2014). Attachment to inanimate objects and early childcare: A twin study. *Frontiers in psychology*, *5*, 486. https://doi.org/10.3389/fpsyg.2014.00486

Ward, A., Ramsay, R., & Treasure, J. (2000). Attachment research in eating disorders. *The British journal of medical psychology*, *73 (Pt 1)*, 35–51. https://doi.org/10.1348/000711200160282

17) W describes this process as the child "hallucinating" the mother and attaching this onto the transitional object. In cognitive psychology terms, sensory memory-reward patterns are paired with objects in the external environment to become "transitional objects". This assignment of internal memory data to other external environmental cues is called "hallucinating" in adults.

Ratnapalan, S., & Batty, H. (2009). To be good enough. *Canadian family physician Medecin de famille canadien*, *55*(3), 239–242.

18) Benoit, D. (2004). Infant-parent attachment: Definition, types, antecedents, measurement and outcome. *Paediatrics & Child Health*, *9*(8), 541–545.

Moriceau, S., & Sullivan, R. M. (2005). Neurobiology of infant attachment. *Developmental Psychobiology*, *47*(3), 230–242. https://doi.org/10.1002/dev.20093

19) *Levy, K.N., Johnson, B.N., Clouthier, T.L., Scala, J.W., & Temes, C.M. (2015). An Attachment Theoretical Framework for Personality Disorders. Canadian Psychology, 56, 197-207.*

https://www.semanticscholar.org/paper/An-Attachment-Theoretical-Framework-for-Personality-Levy-Johnson/a262876e52069f44803b09d3cc271c131e363d77

Bartholomew, K., & Horowitz, L. M. (1991). Attachment styles among young adults: a test of a four-category model. *Journal of personality and social psychology*, *61*(2), 226–244. https://doi.org/10.1037//0022-3514.61.2.226

20) *A Brief Overview of Adult Attachment Theory and Research* | R. Chris Fraley. (2018). Illinois.Edu. http://labs.psychology.illinois.edu/~rcfraley/attachment.htm

21) Mahler M. S. (1974). Symbiosis and individuation. The psychological birth of the human infant. *The Psychoanalytic study of the child*, *29*, 89–106.

The devotion of the human dad separates us from other apes | Aeon Essays

'Touch Me Not' Review: Our Bodies Examined - The New York Times   a documentary about touch.

22) Fonagy **Attachment Theory And Psychoanalysis**

Fonagy, P. (2001). Attachment Theory and Psychoanalysis (1st ed.). Routledge. https://doi.org/10.4324/9780429472060

Fonagy, P., & Bateman, A. (2008). The development of borderline personality disorder—a mentalizing model. *Journal of personality disorders*, *22*(1), 4–21. https://doi.org/10.1521/pedi.2008.22.1.4

Salvia, E., Süß, M., Tivadar, R., Harkness, S., & Grosbras, M. H. (2016). Mirror Neurons System Engagement in Late Adolescents and Adults While Viewing Emotional Gestures. *Frontiers in psychology*, *7*, 1099. https://doi.org/10.3389/fpsyg.2016.01099

23) Stern, D. N. (2019). Motherhood Constellation : a unified view of parent-infant psychotherapy.

Stern D.N. *Non Interpretive Mechanisms in Psychoanalytic Therapy.* (n.d.). http://icpla.edu/wp-content/uploads/2012/10/Stern-D.N.-Non-Interpretive-Mechanisms-in-Psychoanalytic-Therapy.pdf

Mellier, D. (2014). The psychic envelopes in psychoanalytic theories of infancy. *Frontiers in Psychology*, *5*. https://doi.org/10.3389/fpsyg.2014.00734

24) https://en.wikipedia.org/wiki/Gay_A._Bradshaw

Bradshaw, G.A. (2009). Elephants on the edge: What animals teach us about humanity. New Haven: Yale University Press. http://yalepress.yale.edu/yupbooks/book.asp?isbn=9780300167832

25) Siegel, D.J. (2001). Toward An Interpersonal Neurobiology Of The Developing Mind: Attachment Relationships, "Mindsight," And Neural Integration. Tradition, 22, 67-94.

It is through the interactive process of two independently motivated individuals that social transaction occurs.

26) The Neurobiology of We - MOL 103 - IPNB and Relationships - The Neurobiology of We_0.pdf

The Developing Mind Quotes by Daniel J. Siegel

References

Cassidy, J., & Shaver, P. R. (2016). *Handbook of attachment : theory, research, and clinical applications*. The Guilford Press.

Coan, James. (2008). Toward a Neuroscience of Attachment (PDF) Toward a Neuroscience of Attachment

Šešo-Šimić, Đurđica & Sedmak, Goran & Hof, Patrick & Simic, Goran. (2010). Recent advances in the neurobiology of attachment behavior.Translational Neuroscience. 1. 148-159. 10.2478/v10134-010-0020-0.

27) Fricchione, Gregory. *Compassion and Healing in Medicine and Society: On the Nature and Use of Attachment Solutions to Separation Challenges* , 2011. Chap "13,14,15.". Print.

28) Cowan, P. A., & Cowan, C. P. (2007). Attachment Theory: Seven Unresolved Issues and Questions for Future Research. *Research in Human Development*, *4*(3–4), 181–201. https://doi.org/10.1080/15427600701663007

Waters, E., Merrick, S., Treboux, D., Crowell, J., & Albersheim, L. (2000). Attachment security in infancy and early adulthood: a twenty-year longitudinal study. *Child development*, *71*(3), 684–689. https://doi.org/10.1111/1467-8624.00176

Schore, J.R., & Schore, A.N. (2008). Modern Attachment Theory: The Central Role of Affect Regulation in Development and Treatment. Clinical Social Work Journal, 36, https://pdfs.semanticscholar.org/51c6/9755a627e34970db74b96d0f45755bcde3ef.pdf

Sullivan, Regina M. "The Neurobiology of Attachment to Nurturing and Abusive Caregivers." *The Hastings Law Journal*, vol. 63, no. 6, 2012, pp. 1553–1570, https://link.springer.com/article/10.1007/s10615-007-0111-7

29) Aviezer, O., Sagi, A., & van Ijzendoorn, M. (2002). Balancing the Family and the Collective in Raising Children: Why Communal Sleeping in Kibbutzim Was Predestined to End*. *Family Process*, *41*(3), 435–454. https://doi.org/10.1111/j.1545-5300.2002.41310.x

Levy-Shiff, R. (1983). Adaptation and Competence in Early Childhood: Communally Raised Kibbutz Children versus Family Raised Children in the City. *Child Development*, *54*(6), 1606. https://doi.org/10.2307/1129824

Scharf, M. (2001). A "Natural Experiment" in Childrearing Ecologies and Adolescents' Attachment and Separation Representations. *Child Development*, *72*(1), 236–251. https://doi.org/10.1111/1467-8624.00276

30) *Nonparental Daycare: What The Research Tells Us*. (2017). Psychology Today. https://www.psychologytoday.com/us/blog/insight-therapy/201710/nonparental-daycare-what-the-research-tells-us

Babes in Day Care. (n.d.). Www.Theatlantic.Com. Retrieved February 26, 2020, from https://www.theatlantic.com/past/docs/issues/88aug/babe.htm

What Really Matters When It Comes to Daycare | The Attached Family. (n.d.). Retrieved February 26, 2020, from http://theattachedfamily.com/membersonly/?article=what-really-matters-when-it-comes-to-daycare

31) https://www.britishpsychotherapyfoundation.org.uk/insights/blog/

joy-schaverien
https://www.joyschaverien.com/
32) M. King Adkins *Television Storyworlds as Virtual Space* (Lexington Books; Illustrated edition (September 15, 2018)
33) Gail Tittle, MSW, PhD, Non-organic Failure to Thrive Literature Review May, 2002
https://cfrc.illinois.edu/pubs/lr_20020501_Non-OrganicFailureToThrive.pdf
Rudolf, M. C. J. (2005). What is the long term outcome for children who fail to thrive? A systematic review. *Archives of Disease in Childhood*, *90*(9), 925–931. https://doi.org/10.1136/adc.2004.050179 http://adc.bmj.com/content/90/9/925.full
https://www.ncbi.nlm.nih.gov/pmc/articles/PMC1720590/pdf/v090p00925.pdf
Ward, M.J., Lee, S.S. and Lipper, E.G. (2000), Failure-to-thrive is associated with disorganized infant–mother attachment and unresolved maternal attachment. Infant Ment. Health J., 21: 428-442. https://doi.org/10.1002/1097-0355(200011/12)21:6<428::AID-IMHJ2>3.0.CO;2-B
34) Institute of Medicine (US) Committee for the Study of Health Consequences of the Stress of Bereavement, Osterweis, M., Solomon, F., & Green, M. (2013). *Bereavement During Childhood and Adolescence*. Nih.Gov; National Academies Press (US).
Coffino B. (2009). The role of childhood parent figure loss in the etiology of adult depression: findings from a prospective longitudinal study. *Attachment & human development*, *11*(5), 445–470. https://doi.org/10.1080/14616730903135993
Marks, N. F., Jun, H., & Song, J. (2007). Death of Parents and Adult Psychological and Physical Well-Being: A Prospective U.S. National Study. *Journal of Family Issues*, *28*(12), 1611–1638. https://doi.org/10.1177/0192513X07302728
Nagera, H. (1970). Children's Reactions to the Death of Important Objects. *The Psychoanalytic Study of the Child*, *25*(1), 360–400. https://doi.org/10.1080/00797308.1970.11823287
Heilbrunn, G. (1972). Children's Reactions to the Death of a Parent: A Review of the Psychoanalytic Literature. *American Journal of Psychotherapy*, *26*(2), 303–303. https://doi.org/10.1176/appi.psychotherapy.1972.26.2.303
Brent, D., Melhem, N., Donohoe, M. B., & Walker, M. (2009). The Incidence and Course of Depression in Bereaved Youth 21 Months After the Loss of a Parent to Suicide, Accident, or Sudden Natural Death. *The American Journal of Psychiatry*, *166*(7), 786–794. https://doi.org/10.1176/appi.ajp.2009.08081244
https://www.ncbi.nlm.nih.gov/pubmed/19411367
Ellis, J., Dowrick, C., & Lloyd-Williams, M. (2013). The long-term impact of early parental death: lessons from a narrative study. *Journal of the Royal Society of Medicine*, *106*(2), 57–67. https://doi.org/10.1177/0141076812472623
Baker, J. E. (2001). Mourning and the transformation of object relationships:

References

Evidence for the persistence of internal attachments. *Psychoanalytic Psychology, 18*(1), 55–73. https://doi.org/10.1037//0736-9735.18.1.55

Bowlby, J. (1960). *Grief and Mourning in Infancy and Early Childhood.* http://icpla.edu/wp-content/uploads/2012/10/Bowlby-J.-Grief-and-Mourning-in-Infancy-and-Early-Childhood-vol.15-p.9-52.pdf

Delvecchio, E., Di Riso, D., Salcuni, S., Lis, A., & George, C. (2014). Anorexia and attachment: dysregulated defense and pathological mourning. *Frontiers in psychology, 5*, 1218. https://doi.org/10.3389/fpsyg.2014.01218

Rice, K. G. (1990). Attachment in adolescence: A narrative and meta-analytic review. *Journal of Youth and Adolescence, 19*(5), 511–538. https://doi.org/10.1007/bf01537478 https://link.springer.com/article/10.1007/BF01537478

Moretti, M. M., & Peled, M. (2004). Adolescent-parent attachment: Bonds that support healthy development. *Paediatrics & Child Health, 9*(8), 551–555. https://doi.org/10.1093/pch/9.8.551

Dubois-Comtois K, Cyr C, Pascuzzo K, Lessard M (2013) Attachment Theory in Clinical Work with Adolescents. J Child Adolesc Behav 1:111. doi:10.4172/2375-4494.1000111

35) Opendak, M., Gould, E., & Sullivan, R. (2017). Early life adversity during the infant sensitive period for attachment: Programming of behavioral neurobiology of threat processing and social behavior. *Developmental Cognitive Neuroscience, 25*, 145–159. https://doi.org/10.1016/j.dcn.2017.02.002

Schore, J. R., & Schore, A. N. (2007). Modern Attachment Theory: The Central Role of Affect Regulation in Development and Treatment. *Clinical Social Work Journal, 36*(1), 9–20. https://doi.org/10.1007/s10615-007-0111-7

Mikulincer, M., & Shaver, P. R. (2012). An attachment perspective on psychopathology. *World Psychiatry : Official Journal of the World Psychiatric Association (WPA), 11*(1), 11–15.

Pascuzzo, K., Moss, E., & Cyr, C. (2015). Attachment and Emotion Regulation Strategies in Predicting Adult Psychopathology. *SAGE Open, 5*(3), 215824401560469. https://doi.org/10.1177/2158244015604695 https://www.researchgate.net/publication/281633318_Attachment_and_Emotion_Regulation_Strategies_in_Predicting_Adult_Psychopathology

36) Turner, G. (n.d.). *My Childhood in a Cult.* The New Yorker. Retrieved February 26, 2020, from https://www.newyorker.com/magazine/2019/05/06/my-childhood-in-a-cult

Ellis, E. E., & Abdolreza Saadabadi. (2019, January 13). *Reactive Attachment Disorder.* Nih.Gov; StatPearls Publishing. https://www.ncbi.nlm.nih.gov/books/NBK537155/

37) Vachon, D. D., Krueger, R. F., Rogosch, F. A., & Cicchetti, D. (2015). Different Forms of Child Maltreatment have Comparable Consequences Among Children from Low-Income Families. *JAMA Psychiatry, 72*(11), 1135–1142. https://doi.org/10.1001/jamapsychiatry.2015.1792

Bierer, L. M., Yehuda, R., Schmeidler, J., Mitropoulou, V., New, A. S., Silverman, J. M., & Siever, L. J. (2003). Abuse and Neglect in Childhood: Relationship to Personality Disorder Diagnoses. *CNS Spectrums, 8*(10), https://doi.org/10.1017/s1092852900019118

Kettler, S. (2019, July 30). *Inside Ted Bundy's Troubled and Disturbing Childhood.* Biography. https://www.biography.com/news/ted-bundy-childhood

Levy, K. N., Johnson, B. N., Clouthier, T. L., J. Wesley Scala, & Temes, C. M. (2015). An attachment theoretical framework for personality disorders. *Canadian Psychology/Psychologie Canadienne, 56*(2), 197–207. https://doi.org/10.1037/cap0000025

Johnson, A. M., Falstein, E. I., Szurek, S. A., & Svendsen, M. (1941). School phobia. *American Journal of Orthopsychiatry, 11*(4), 702-711. http://dx.doi.org/10.1111/j.1939-0025.1941.tb05860.x

38) Smyke, A. T., Zeanah, C. H., Gleason, M. M., Drury, S. S., Fox, N. A., Nelson, C. A., & Guthrie, D. (2012). A randomized controlled trial comparing foster care and institutional care for children with signs of reactive attachment disorder. *The American Journal of Psychiatry, 169*(5), 508–514. https://www.ncbi.nlm.nih.gov/pmc/articles/PMC4158103/
https://www.researchgate.net/profile/Charles_Zeanah/publication/228683818_Reactive_Attachment_Disorder_a_review_for_DSM-V/links/0deec51e86576d1e8c000000/Reactive-Attachment-Disorder-a-review-for-DSM-V.pdf

Zeanah, C. H., & Gleason, M. M. (2014). Annual Research Review: Attachment disorders in early childhood - clinical presentation, causes, correlates, and treatment. *Journal of Child Psychology and Psychiatry, 56*(3), 207–222. https://doi.org/10.1111/jcpp.12347

39) Zeanah, C. H., Egger, H. L., Smyke, A. T., Nelson, C. A., Fox, N. A., Marshall, P. J., & Guthrie, D. (2009). Institutional Rearing and Psychiatric Disorders in Romanian Preschool Children. *American Journal of Psychiatry, 166*(7), 777–785. https://doi.org/10.1176/appi.ajp.2009.08091438

40) Cassidy, J., Jones, J. D., & Shaver, P. R. (2013). Contributions of attachment theory and research: A framework for future research, translation, and policy. *Development and Psychopathology, 25*(4pt2), 1415–1434. https://doi.org/10.1017/s0954579413000692

41) Okello, J., Nakimuli-Mpungu, E., Musisi, S., Broekaert, E., & Derluyn, I. (2014). The Association between Attachment and Mental Health Symptoms among School-Going Adolescents in Northern Uganda: The Moderating Role of War-Related Trauma. *PLoS ONE, 9*(3), e88494. https://doi.org/10.1371/journal.pone.0088494

Stillman, S. (n.d.). *America's Other Family-Separation Crisis.* The New Yorker. Retrieved February 26, 2020, from https://www.newyorker.com/magazine/2018/11/05/americas-other-family-separation-crisis

Bresnahan, M., Hornig, M., Schultz, A. F., Gunnes, N., Hirtz, D., Lie, K. K.,

References

Magnus, P., Reichborn-Kjennerud, T., Roth, C., Schjølberg, S., Stoltenberg, C., Surén, P., Susser, E., & Lipkin, W. I. (2015). Association of Maternal Report of Infant and Toddler Gastrointestinal Symptoms With Autism. *JAMA Psychiatry*, *72*(5), 466–474. https://doi.org/10.1001/jamapsychiatry.2014.3034

42) Chaffin, M., Hanson, R., Saunders, B. E., Nichols, T., Barnett, D., Zeanah, C., Berliner, L., Egeland, B., Newman, E., Lyon, T., Letourneau, E., & Miller-Perrin, C. (2006). Report of the
APSAC Task Force on Attachment Therapy, Reactive Attachment Disorder, and Attachment Problems. *Child Maltreatment*, *11*(1), 76–89. https://doi.org/10.1177/1077559505283699

43) Amone-P'Olak, Kennedy. (2008). Attachment Disorder in Child Abductees in War Zones: the case of Children abducted in Northern Uganda. 20. 94 - 101. https://www.researchgate.net/publication/305221541_Attachment_Disorder_in_Child_Abductees_in_War_Zones_the_case_of_Children_abducted_in_Northern_Uganda

Dutton, D. G., & Painter, S. (1993). Emotional attachments in abusive relationships: a test of traumatic bonding theory. *Violence and victims*, *8*(2), 105–120.

44) Lahav, Y., Allende, S., Talmon, A., Ginzburg, K., & Spiegel, D. (2022). Identification With the Aggressor and Inward and Outward Aggression in Abuse Survivors. *Journal of interpersonal violence*, *37*(5-6), 2705–2728. https://doi.org/10.1177/0886260520938516

Howell E. F. (2014). Ferenczi's concept of identification with the aggressor: understanding dissociative structure with interacting victim and abuser self-states. *American journal of psychoanalysis*, *74*(1), 48–59. https://doi.org/10.1057/ajp.2013.40

Teague, S. J., Gray, K. M., Tonge, B. J., & Newman, L. K. (2017). Attachment in children with autism spectrum disorder:
A systematic review. *Research in Autism Spectrum Disorders*, *35*, 35–50.
Autism, Attachment and Parenting: A Comparison of Children with Autism Spectrum Disorder, Mental Retardation, Language Disorder, and Non-clinical Children. *Journal of Abnormal Child Psychology*, *35*(5). https://doi.org/10.1007/s10802-007-9139-y

45) *Treatment of Attachment and Trauma at Evergreen Psychotherapy Center.* (n.d.). Evergreen Psychotherapy Center. Retrieved February 26, 2020, from https://www.evergreenpsychotherapycenter.com/treatment/

Buckner, J. D., Lopez, C., Dunkel, S., & Joiner, T. E. (2008). Behavior Management Training for the Treatment of Reactive Attachment Disorder. *Child Maltreatment*, *13*(3), 289–297. https://doi.org/10.1177/1077559508318396

What is the Treatment for RAD? (2018, October 3). The Chaos and the Clutter. https://www.thechaosandtheclutter.com/archives/what-is-the-treatment-for-rad
https://www.mayoclinic.org/diseases-conditions/reactive-attachment-disorder/diagnosis-treatment/drc-20352945
https://www.quackwatch.org/01QuackeryRelatedTopics/at.html

Weinberg, H. A. (2010). Improved Functioning in Children Diagnosed with Reactive Attachment Disorder after SSRI Therapy. *Journal of the Canadian Academy of Child and Adolescent Psychiatry*, *19*(1), 48–50.

46) Parish-Plass N. (2008). Animal-assisted therapy with children suffering from insecure attachment due to abuse and neglect: a method to lower the risk of intergenerational transmission of abuse?. *Clinical child psychology and psychiatry*, *13*(1), 7–30. https://doi.org/10.1177/1359104507086338

Zilcha-Mano, S., Mikulincer, M., & Shaver, P. R. (2011). Pet in the therapy room: an attachment perspective on Animal-Assisted Therapy. *Attachment & human development*, *13*(6), 541–561. https://doi.org/10.1080/14616734.2011.608987

Julius, H., Beetz, A., Kotrschal, K., Turner, D., & Uvnäs-Moberg, K. (2012). **Attachment to Pets: An Integrative View of Human-Animal Relationships with Implications for Therapeutic Practice**. In *Google Books*. Hogrefe Publishing.

47) Boris, N. W., & Zeanah, C. H. (2005). Practice Parameter for the Assessment and Treatment of Children and Adolescents With Reactive Attachment Disorder of Infancy and Early Childhood. *Journal of the American Academy of Child & Adolescent Psychiatry*, *44*(11), 1206–1219. https://doi.org/10.1097/01.chi.0000177056.41655.ce

48) Rice, K. G. (1990). Attachment in adolescence: A narrative and meta-analytic review. *Journal of Youth and Adolescence*, *19*(5), 511–538. https://doi.org/10.1007/bf01537478
https://link.springer.com/article/10.1007%2FBF01537478?LI=true

49) Schafer, R. (1973). Concepts of Self and Identity and the Experience of Separation-Individuation in Adolescence. *The Psychoanalytic Quarterly*, *42*(1), 42–59. https://doi.org/10.1080/21674086.1973.11926619
https://www.tandfonline.com/doi/abs/10.1080/21674086.1973.11926619?journalCode=upaq20

This study describes a series of parent-teen evaluations:
Therriault, D.; Lemelin,J.-P.; Toupin, J.; Déry, M. Factors Associated with Parent–Adolescent Attachment Relationship Quality: A Longitudinal Study. Adolescents 2021,1, 159–174. https://doi.org/10.3390/adolescents1020013

50) *Health warning: social rejection doesn't only hurt – it kills – Elitsa Dermendzhiyska | Aeon Essays*. (n.d.). Aeon.
https://aeon.co/essays/health-warning-social-rejection-doesnt-only-hurt-it-kills

Stepp, S. D. (2011). Development of Borderline Personality Disorder in Adolescence and Young Adulthood: Introduction to the Special Section. *Journal of Abnormal Child Psychology*, *40*(1), 1–5.
https://doi.org/10.1007/s10802-011-9594-3

Miljkovitch, R., Deborde, A. S., Bernier, A., Corcos, M., Speranza, M., & Pham-Scottez, A. (2018). Borderline Personality Disorder in Adolescence as a Generalization of Disorganized Attachment. *Frontiers in psychology*, *9*, 1962. https://doi.org/10.3389/fpsyg.2018.01962

References

51) John G. Gunderson, M.D. Borderline Personality Disorder: Ontogeny of a Diagnosis,
American Journal of Psychiatry 2009 Volume 166, Issue 5, May, 2009, pp. 530-539
https://ajp.psychiatryonline.org/doi/full/10.1176/appi.ajp.2009.08121825
Gunderson JG, Stout RL, McGlashan TH, et al. Ten-Year Course of Borderline Personality Disorder: Psychopathology and Function From the Collaborative Longitudinal Personality Disorders Study. *Arch Gen Psychiatry.* 2011;68(8):827–837. https://jamanetwork.com/journals/jamapsychiatry/fullarticle/1107231
Gunderson J. G. (2010). Revising the borderline diagnosis for DSM-V: an alternative proposal. *Journal of personality disorders*, 24(6), 694–708. https://doi.org/10.1521/pedi.2010.24.6.694
Lieb, K., Zanarini, M. C., Schmahl, C., Linehan, M. M., & Bohus, M. (2004). Borderline personality disorder. *Lancet (London, England)*, 364(9432), 453-461. https://doi.org/10.1016/S0140-6736(04)16770-6
Leichsenring, F., Leibing, E., Kruse, J., New, A. S., & Leweke, F. (2011). Borderline personality disorder. *Lancet (London, England)*, 377(9759), 74–84. https://doi.org/10.1016/S0140-6736(10)61422-5
Reisch, T., Ebner-Priemer, U. W., Tschacher, W., Bohus, M., & Linehan, M. M. (2008). Sequences of emotions in patients with borderline personality disorder. *Acta psychiatrica Scandinavica*, 118(1), 42–48. https://doi.org/10.1111/j.1600-0447.2008.01222.x
John M. Oldham, M.D., M.S., Borderline Personality Disorder Comes of Age, American Journal of Psychiatry 2009 166:5, 509-511
https://doi.org/10.1176/appi.ajp.2009.09020262
52) Stanley, B., & Siever, L. J. (2010). The interpersonal dimension of borderline personality disorder: toward a neuropeptide model. *The American journal of psychiatry*, 167(1), 24–39. https://doi.org/10.1176/appi.ajp.2009.09050744
Dixon-Gordon, K. L., Peters, J. R., Fertuck, E. A., & Yen, S. (2017). Emotional processes in borderline personality disorder: An update for clinical practice. *Journal of Psychotherapy Integration*, 27(4), 425–438. https://doi.org/10.1037/int0000044
Borderline Personality Disorder, Otto F. Kernberg, M.D. and Robert Michels, M.D., American Journal of Psychiatry 2009 166:5, 505-508 https://doi.org/10.1176/appi.ajp.2009.09020263
53) Fonagy, P., Target, M., & Gergely, G. (2000). Attachment And Borderline Personality Disorder. *Psychiatric Clinics of North America*, 23(1), 103–122. https://doi.org/10.1016/s0193-953x(05)70146-5
Stepp, S. D. (2011). Development of Borderline Personality Disorder in Adolescence and Young Adulthood: Introduction to the Special Section. *Journal of Abnormal Child Psychology*, 40(1), 1–5. https://doi.org/10.1007/s10802-011-9594-3

Biskin, R. S. (2015). The Lifetime Course of Borderline Personality Disorder. *The Canadian Journal of Psychiatry*, *60*(7), 303–308. https://doi.org/10.1177/070674371506000702

Peter Fonagy Ph.D. and FBA, Mary Target Ph.D., George Gergely Ph.D., Jon G. Allen Ph.D. & Anthony W. Bateman M.A. and FRCPsych (2003) The Developmental Roots of Borderline Personality Disorder in Early Attachment Relationships: A Theory and Some Evidence, Psychoanalytic Inquiry, 23:3, 412-459, DOI: 10.1080/07351692309349042

Sansone, R. A., & Sansone, L. A. (2009). The families of borderline patients: the psychological environment revisited. *Psychiatry (Edgmont (Pa. : Township))*, *6*(2), 19–24. https://www.ncbi.nlm.nih.gov/pmc/articles/PMC2719448/

Gunderson, J. G., Zanarini, M. C., Choi-Kain, L. W., Mitchell, K. S., Jang, K. L., & Hudson, J. I. (2011). Family study of borderline personality disorder and its sectors of psychopathology. *Archives of general psychiatry*, *68*(7), 753–762. https://doi.org/10.1001/archgenpsychiatry.2011.65

Reichborn-Kjennerud, T., Ystrom, E., Neale, M. C., Aggen, S. H., Mazzeo, S. E., Knudsen, G. P., Tambs, K., Czajkowski, N. O., & Kendler, K. S. (2013). Structure of genetic and environmental risk factors for symptoms of DSM-IV borderline personality disorder. *JAMA psychiatry*, *70*(11), 1206–1214. https://doi.org/10.1001/jamapsychiatry.2013.1944
https://www.ncbi.nlm.nih.gov/pmc/articles/PMC3927987/

Fonagy, P., Luyten, P., Allison, E., & Campbell, C. (2017). What we have changed our minds about: Part 1. Borderline personality disorder as a limitation of resilience. *Borderline personality disorder and emotion dysregulation*, *4*, 11. https://doi.org/10.1186/s40479-017-0061-9   https://www.ncbi.nlm.nih.gov/pmc/articles/PMC5389119/

Fonagy, P., Luyten, P., Allison, E., & Campbell, C. (2017). What we have changed our minds about: Part 2. Borderline personality disorder, epistemic trust and the developmental significance of social communication. *Borderline personality disorder and emotion dysregulation*, *4*, 9. https://doi.org/10.1186/s40479-017-0062-8

Luyten, P., Campbell, C., & Fonagy, P. (2020). Borderline personality disorder, complex trauma, and problems with self and identity: A social-communicative approach. *Journal of personality*, *88*(1), 88–105. https://doi.org/10.1111/jopy.12483

54) Amad, A., Ramoz, N., Thomas, P., Jardri, R., & Gorwood, P. (2014). Genetics of borderline personality disorder: systematic review and proposal of an integrative model. *Neuroscience and biobehavioral reviews*, *40*, 6–19. https://doi.org/10.1016/j.neubiorev.2014.01.003

Nicolas Lorenzini and Peter Fonagy, Attachment and Personality Disorders: A Short Review, FOCUS 2013 11:2, 155-166
https://doi.org/10.1176/appi.focus.11.2.155

Agrawal, H. R., Gunderson, J., Holmes, B. M., & Lyons-Ruth, K. (2004).

Attachment Studies with Borderline Patients: A Review. *Harvard Review of Psychiatry, 12*(2), 94–104. https://doi.org/10.1080/10673220490447218

Martín-Blanco, A., Ferrer, M., Soler, J., Arranz, M. J., Vega, D., Calvo, N., Elices, M., Sanchez-Mora, C., García-Martinez, I., Salazar, J., Carmona, C., Bauzà, J., Prat, M., Pérez, V., & Pascual, J. C. (2016). The role of hypothalamus-pituitary-adrenal genes and childhood trauma in borderline personality disorder. *European archives of psychiatry and clinical neuroscience, 266*(4), 307–316. https://doi.org/10.1007/s00406-015-0612-2

Prossin, A. R., Love, T. M., Koeppe, R. A., Zubieta, J. K., & Silk, K. R. (2010). Dysregulation of regional endogenous opioid function in borderline personality disorder. *The American journal of psychiatry, 167*(8), https://doi.org/10.1176/appi.ajp.2010.09091348

New, A. S., & Stanley, B. (2010). An Opioid Deficit in Borderline Personality Disorder: Self-Cutting, Substance Abuse, and Social Dysfunction. *American Journal of Psychiatry, 167*(8), 882–885. https://doi.org/10.1176/appi.ajp.2010.10040634

Bertsch, K., Gamer, M., Schmidt, B., Schmidinger, I., Walther, S., Kästel, T., Schnell, K., Büchel, C., Domes, G., & Herpertz, S. C. (2013). Oxytocin and reduction of social threat hypersensitivity in women with borderline personality disorder. *The American journal of psychiatry, 170*(10), 1169–1177. https://doi.org/10.1176/appi.ajp.2013.13020263 https://pubmed.ncbi.nlm.nih.gov/23982273/

Bertsch, K., Gamer, M., Schmidt, B., Schmidinger, I., Walther, S., Kästel, T., Schnell, K., Büchel, C., Domes, G., & Herpertz, S. C. (2013). Oxytocin and reduction of social threat hypersensitivity in women with borderline personality disorder. *The American journal of psychiatry, 170*(10), 1169–1177. https://doi.org/10.1176/appi.ajp.2013.13020263

Bertsch, K., & Herpertz, S. C. (2018). Oxytocin and Borderline Personality Disorder. *Current topics in behavioral neurosciences, 35*, 499–514. https://doi.org/10.1007/7854_2017_26

Amad, A., Thomas, P., & Perez-Rodriguez, M. M. (2015). Borderline Personality Disorder and Oxytocin: Review of Clinical Trials and Future Directions. *Current pharmaceutical design, 21*(23), 3311–3316. https://doi.org/10.2174/1381612821666150619093019

Scott, L. N., Levy, K. N., & Pincus, A. L. (2009). Adult attachment, personality traits, and borderline personality disorder features in young adults. *Journal of personality disorders, 23*(3), 258–280. https://doi.org/10.1521/pedi.2009.23.3.258

Cackowski, S., Neubauer, T., & Kleindienst, N. (2016). The impact of post-traumatic stress disorder on borderline personality disorder. *Borderline personality disorder and emotion dysregulation, 3*, 7. https://doi.org/10.1186/s40479-016-0042-4

Perez-Rodriguez, M. M., Bulbena-Cabré, A., Bassir Nia, A., Zipursky,

G., Goodman, M., & New, A. S. (2018). The Neurobiology of Borderline Personality Disorder. *The Psychiatric clinics of North America, 41*(4), 633–650. https://doi.org/10.1016/j.psc.2018.07.012

Distel, M., Trull, T., Derom, C., Thiery, E., Grimmer, M., Martin, N., ... Boomsma, D. (2008). Heritability of borderline personality disorder features is similar across three countries. *Psychological Medicine, 38*(9), 1219-1229. doi:10.1017/S0033291707002024
https://www.cambridge.org/core/journals/psychological-medicine/article/abs/heritability-of-borderline-personality-disorder-features-is-similar-across-three-countries/00CADBAE31493D825F2EDBABFF58C5CD

Distel, M. A., Trull, T. J., Willemsen, G., Vink, J. M., Derom, C. A., Lynskey, M., Martin, N. G., & Boomsma, D. I. (2009). The five-factor model of personality and borderline personality disorder: a genetic analysis of comorbidity. *Biological psychiatry, 66*(12), 1131–1138. https://doi.org/10.1016/j.biopsych.2009.07.017

Martín-Blanco, A., Ferrer, M., Soler, J., Arranz, M. J., Vega, D., Calvo, N., Elices, M., Sanchez-Mora, C., García-Martinez, I., Salazar, J., Carmona, C., Bauzà, J., Prat, M., Pérez, V., & Pascual, J. C. (2016). The role of hypothalamus-pituitary-adrenal genes and childhood trauma in borderline personality disorder. *European archives of psychiatry and clinical neuroscience, 266*(4), 307–316. https://doi.org/10.1007/s00406-015-0612-2

Evardone, M., Alexander, G. M., & Morey, L. C. (2008). Hormones and Borderline Personality Features. *Personality and individual differences, 44*(1), 278–287. https://doi.org/10.1016/j.paid.2007.08.007

Rausch, J., Gäbel, A., Nagy, K., Kleindienst, N., Herpertz, S. C., & Bertsch, K. (2015). Increased testosterone levels and cortisol awakening responses in patients with borderline personality disorder: gender and trait aggressiveness matter. *Psychoneuroendocrinology, 55*, 116–127. https://doi.org/10.1016/j.psyneuen.2015.02.002

55) Ruocco, A. C., & Carcone, D. (2016). A Neurobiological Model of Borderline Personality Disorder: Systematic and Integrative Review. *Harvard review of psychiatry, 24*(5), 311–329. https://doi.org/10.1097/HRP.0000000000000123

Feldman, R. 2017). The Neurobiology of Human Attachments. *Trends in Cognitive Sciences, 21*(2), 80–99. https://doi.org/10.1016/j.tics.2016.11.007

R., Trisdorfer, R., Haznedar, M. M., Koenigsberg, H. W., Flory, J., & Siever, L. J. (2007). Amygdala–Prefrontal Disconnection in Borderline Personality Disorder. *Neuropsychopharmacology, 32*(7), 1629–1640. https://doi.org/10.1038/sj.npp.1301283
https://www.nature.com/articles/1301283

Salavert, J., Gasol, M., Vieta, E., Cervantes, A., Trampal, C., & Gispert, J. D. (2011). Fronto-limbic dysfunction in borderline personality disorder: a 18F-FDG positron emission tomography study. *Journal of affective disorders, 131*(1-3),

260–267. https://doi.org/10.1016/j.jad.2011.01.001

Herpertz, S. C., Dietrich, T. M., Wenning, B., Krings, T., Erberich, S. G., Willmes, K., Thron, A., & Sass, H. (2001). Evidence of abnormal amygdala functioning in borderline personality disorder: a functional MRI study. *Biological psychiatry*, *50*(4), 292–298. https://doi.org/10.1016/s0006-3223(01)01075-7

Krause-Utz, A., Winter, D., Niedtfeld, I., & Schmahl, C. (2014). The latest neuroimaging findings in borderline personality disorder. *Current psychiatry reports*, *16*(3), 438. https://doi.org/10.1007/s11920-014-0438-z

Denny, B. T., Fan, J., Fels, S., Galitzer, H., Schiller, D., & Koenigsberg, H. W. (2018). Sensitization of the Neural Salience Network to Repeated Emotional Stimuli Following Initial Habituation in Patients With Borderline Personality Disorder. *The American journal of psychiatry*, *175*(7), 657–664. https://doi.org/10.1176/appi.ajp.2018.17030367

Yang, X., Hu, L., Zeng, J. et al. Default mode network and frontolimbic gray matter abnormalities in patients with borderline personality disorder: A voxel-based meta-analysis. *Sci Rep* **6**, 34247 (2016). https://doi.org/10.1038/srep34247

Krause-Utz, A., Frost, R., Chatzaki, E., Winter, D., Schmahl, C., & Elzinga, B. M. (2021). Dissociation in Borderline Personality Disorder: Recent Experimental, Neurobiological Studies, and Implications for Future Research and Treatment. *Current psychiatry reports*, *23*(6), 37. https://doi.org/10.1007/s11920-021-01246-8

Pec, O., Bob, P., Simek, J., & Raboch, J. (2018). Dissociative states in borderline personality disorder and their relationships to psychotropic medication. *Neuropsychiatric Disease and Treatment*, *14*, 3253–3257. https://doi.org/10.2147/NDT.S179091

Eichelman B. (2010). Borderline personality disorder, PTSD, and suicide. *The American journal of psychiatry*, *167*(10), 1152–1154. https://doi.org/10.1176/appi.ajp.2010.10060870

Harned, M. S., Rizvi, S. L., & Linehan, M. M. (2010). Impact of co-occurring posttraumatic stress disorder on suicidal women with borderline personality disorder. *The American journal of psychiatry*, *167*(10), 1210–1217. https://doi.org/10.1176/appi.ajp.2010.09081213

van der Kolk, B. A., Perry, J. C., & Herman, J. L. (1991). Childhood origins of self-destructive behavior. *The American journal of psychiatry*, *148*(12), 1665–1671. https://doi.org/10.1176/ajp.148.12.1665
https://pubmed.ncbi.nlm.nih.gov/1957928/

56) Bateman, A., & Fonagy, P. (2010). Mentalization based treatment for borderline personality disorder. *World Psychiatry : Official Journal of the World Psychiatric Association (WPA)*, *9*(1), 11–15.

May, J. M., Richardi, T. M., & Barth, K. S. (2016). Dialectical behavior therapy as treatment for borderline personality disorder. *Mental Health Clinician*, *6*(2), 62–67. https://doi.org/10.9740/mhc.2016.03.62

57) McClellan, A. C., & Killeen, M. R. (2000). Attachment theory and violence toward women by male intimate partners. *Journal of nursing scholarship : an official publication of Sigma Theta Tau International Honor Society of Nursing*, *32*(4), 353–360. https://doi.org/10.1111/j.1547-5069.2000.00353.x

58) Velotti, P., Beomonte Zobel, S., Rogier, G., & Tambelli, R. (2018). Exploring Relationships: A Systematic Review on Intimate Partner Violence and Attachment. *Frontiers in psychology*, *9*, 1166. https://doi.org/10.3389/fpsyg.2018.01166

Sansone, R. A., & Sansone, L. A. (2010). Fatal attraction syndrome: stalking behavior and borderline personality. *Psychiatry (Edgmont (Pa. : Township))*, *7*(5), 42–46.

Sansone, R. A., & Sansone, L. A. (2011). Sexual behavior in borderline personality: a review. *Innovations in clinical neuroscience*, *8*(2), 14–18.

Corvo, Kenneth & Dutton, Donald & Chen, Wan-Yi. (2008). Toward Evidence-Based Practice with Domestic Violence Perpetrators. Journal of Aggression, Maltreatment & Trauma. DOI: 10.1080/10926770801921246

Jackson, M. A., Sippel, L. M., Mota, N., Whalen, D., & Schumacher, J. A. (2015). Borderline personality disorder and related constructs as risk factors for intimate partner violence perpetration. *Aggression and violent behavior*, *24*, 95–106. https://doi.org/10.1016/j.avb.2015.04.015

Mechanic, M. B., Weaver, T. L., & Resick, P. A. (2000). Intimate partner violence and stalking behavior: exploration of patterns and correlates in a sample of acutely battered women. *Violence and Victims*, *15*(1), 55–72.

Christina L. Patton, Matt R. Nobles, Kathleen A. Fox,Look who's stalking: Obsessive pursuit and attachment theory,Journal of Criminal Justice,Volume 38, Issue 3,2010,https://doi.org/10.1016/j.jcrimjus.2010.02.013.

Genest, Andrée-Anne, PhD(c) | Mathieu, Cynthia, PhD, Intimate Partner Violence: The Role of Attachment on Men's Anger
Partner AbuseVol 5Issue 4, DOI: 10.1891/1946-6560.5.4.375

Creamer CJ, Hand CJ. Intimate Partner Stalking/Pursuit: A Pathophysiology of Attachment Style. *International Journal of Offender Therapy and Comparative Criminology*. April 2021. doi:10.1177/0306624X211010289

Goldenson, J., Geffner, R., Foster, S. L., & Clipson, C. R. (2007). Female domestic violence offenders: their attachment security, trauma symptoms, and personality organization. *Violence and victims*, *22*(5), 532–545. https://doi.org/10.1891/088667007782312186

59) Paris J. (2012). The outcome of borderline personality disorder: good for most but not all patients. *The American journal of psychiatry*, *169*(5), 445–446. https://doi.org/10.1176/appi.ajp.2012.12010092

Zanarini, M. C., Frankenburg, F. R., Reich, D. B., & Fitzmaurice, G. (2012). Attainment and stability of sustained symptomatic remission and recovery among patients with borderline personality disorder and axis II comparison subjects: a 16-year prospective follow-up study. *The American journal of*

psychiatry, 169(5), 476–483. https://doi.org/10.1176/appi.ajp.2011.11101550
Zanarini, M. C., Frankenburg, F. R., Reich, D. B., Conkey, L. C., & Fitzmaurice, G. M. (2015). Treatment rates for patients with borderline personality disorder and other personality disorders: a 16-year study. *Psychiatric services (Washington, D.C.), 66*(1), 15–20. https://doi.org/10.1176/appi.ps.201400055
Identification and assessment of attachment difficulties. In *www.ncbi.nlm.nih.gov*. National Institute for Health and Care Excellence (UK). https://www.ncbi.nlm.nih.gov/books/NBK356191/
60) Estroff, S. E. (1989). Self, Identity, and Subjective Experiences of Schizophrenia: In Search of the Subject. *Schizophrenia Bulletin, 15*(2), 189–196. https://doi.org/10.1093/schbul/15.2.189
61) Brittany M. Mathes, Kiara R. Timpano, Amanda M. Raines, Norman B. Schmidt,Attachment theory and hoarding disorder: A review and theoretical integration,Behaviour Research and Therapy,Volume 125,2020,103549,ISSN 0005-7967,
https://doi.org/10.1016/j.brat.2019.103549 .
Frost, R. O., & Steketee, G. (Eds.). (2014). *The Oxford Handbook of Hoarding and Acquiring*. Oxford University Press. https://doi.org/10.1093/oxfordhb/9780199937783.001.0001
Phung, P. J., Moulding, R., Taylor, J. K., & Nedeljkovic, M. (2015). Emotional regulation, attachment to possessions and hoarding symptoms. *Scandinavian Journal of Psychology, 56*(5), 573–581. https://doi.org/10.1111/sjop.12239
Chen, D., Bienvenu, O. J., Krasnow, J., Wang, Y., Grados, M. A., Cullen, B., Goes, F. S., Maher, B., Greenberg, B. D., McLaughlin, N. C., Rasmussen, S. A., Fyer, A. J., Knowles, J. A., McCracken, J. T., Piacentini, J., Geller, D., Pauls, D. L., Stewart, S. E., Murphy, D. L., … Samuels, J. (2017). Parental bonding and hoarding in obsessive–compulsive disorder. *Comprehensive Psychiatry, 73*, 43–52. https://doi.org/10.1016/j.comppsych.2016.11.004
Dozier, M. E., & Ayers, C. R. (2017). The Etiology of Hoarding Disorder: A Review. *Psychopathology, 50*(5), 291–296. https://doi.org/10.1159/000479235 https://www.ncbi.nlm.nih.gov/pmc/articles/PMC7294599/
Yap, K., & Grisham, J. R. (2019). Unpacking the construct of emotional attachment to objects and its association with hoarding symptoms. *Journal of behavioral addictions, 8*(2), 249–258. https://doi.org/10.1556/2006.8.2019.15
62) Randy Frost, P. (2000, April 1). *People Who Hoard Animals*. Psychiatric Times. http://www.psychiatrictimes.com/obsessive-compulsive-disorder/people-who-hoard-animals
Reinisch, A. I. (2008). Understanding the human aspects of animal hoarding. *The Canadian Veterinary Journal, 49*(12), 1211–1214.
63) *McPartland J,Klin A (October 2006). "Asperger's syndrome". Adolescent Medicine Clinics. 17 (3): 771–88, abstract xiii. doi:10.1016/j.admecli.2006.06.010*

Effective Psychotherapy: The Contribution of Hellmuth Kaiser

Wisdom Moon Publishing (August 15, 2012) ISBN-13: 978-1938459108
64) Pini, S., Abelli, M., Mauri, M., Muti, M., Iazzetta, P., Banti, S., & Cassano, G. B. (2005). Clinical correlates and significance of separation anxiety in patients with bipolar disorder. *Bipolar Disorders*, *7*(4), 370–376. https://doi.org/10.1111/j.1399-5618.2005.00216.x   9 Most Common Triggers for Bipolar Mood Episodes | Everyday Health. (2017, October 18). EverydayHealth.Com. https://www.everydayhealth.com/bipolar-disorder-pictures/biggest-triggers-of-bipolar-mood-swings.aspx

65) Palmer, A. J., Harper, G., & Rivinus, T. M. (1983). The "adoption process" in the inpatient treatment of children and adolescents. *Journal of the American Academy of Child Psychiatry*, *22*(3), 286–293. https://doi.org/10.1016/s0002-7138(09)60379-4

Attachment Theory and the Psychotherapy Relationship | Society for the Advancement of Psychotherapy. (2019, January 3). Society for the Advancement of Psychotherapy. https://societyforpsychotherapy.org/attachment-theory-and-the-psychotherapy-relationship-summarizing-what-we-know/   Slade, A., & Holmes, J. (2019). Attachment and psychotherapy. *Current opinion in psychology*, *25*, 152–156. https://doi.org/10.1016/j.copsyc.2018.06.008

Bucci, S., Seymour-Hyde, A., Harris, A., & Berry, K. (2015). Client and Therapist Attachment Styles and Working Alliance. *Clinical Psychology & Psychotherapy*, *23*(2), 155–165. https://doi.org/10.1002/cpp.1944   Ruth Lanius, PhD. (2015, August 31). The Trauma Therapist Project. https://www.thetraumatherapistproject.com/podcast/ruth-lanius-phd/

66) Henderson, Exorcism, possession, and the Dracula cult: a synopsis of object-relations psychology.
Bull Menninger Clin. 1976 Nov;40(6):603-28.

67) John Money, Influence of Hormones on Sexual Behavior, Annual Review of Medicine (1965) 16:1, 67-82

Bancroft J. (1984). Hormones and human sexual behavior. *Journal of sex & marital therapy*, *10*(1), 3–21. https://doi.org/10.1080/00926238408405785

Pora, S., Pitukcheewanont, P., Kaufman, F. R., Nelson, J. C., & Gilsanz, V. (1999). Biochemical Markers of Bone Turnover and the Volume and the Density of Bone in Children at Different Stages of Sexual Development. *Journal of Bone and Mineral Research*, *14*(10), 1664–1671. https://doi.org/10.1359/jbmr.1999.14.10.1664   https://pubertycurriculum.com/ages-stages-of-healthy-childhood-sexual-development/   Kimberly J Jennings, Luis de Lecea, Neural and Hormonal Control of Sexual Behavior, *Endocrinology*, Volume 161, Issue 10, October 2020, bqaa150, https://doi.org/10.1210/endocr/bqaa150

Berenbaum, S. A., & Beltz, A. M. (2016). How early hormones shape gender development. *Current Opinion in Behavioral Sciences*, *7*, 53–60. https://doi.org/10.1016/j.cobeha.2015.11.011

Lee, J. Y., & Cho, K. S. (2013). Chemical castration for sexual offenders: physicians' views. *Journal of Korean medical science*, *28*(2), 171–172. https://doi.

References

org/10.3346/jkms.2013.28.2.171
MG.T. Marx,Technology and Social Control,
Editor(s): Neil J. Smelser, Paul B. Baltes,International Encyclopedia of the Social & Behavioral Sciences,Pergamon,2001,Pages 15506-15512,ISBN 9780080430768, https://doi.org/10.1016/B0-08-043076-7/00373-9.
68) Schecklmann, M., Engelhardt, K., Konzok, J., Rupprecht, R., Greenlee, M. W., Mokros, A., Langguth, B., & Poeppl, T. B. (2015). Sexual motivation is reflected by stimulus-dependent motor cortex excitability. *Social Cognitive and Affective Neuroscience*, *10*(8), 1061–1065. https://doi.org/10.1093/scan/nsu157
Carla Clark, PhD. (n.d.). *Brain Sex in Men and Women – From Arousal to Orgasm*. Www.Brainblogger.Com. https://www.brainblogger.com/2014/05/20/brain-sex-in-men-and-women-from-arousal-to-orgasm/
Baird, A. D., Wilson, S. J., Bladin, P. F., Saling, M. M., & Reutens, D. C. (2007). Neurological control of human sexual behaviour: insights from lesion studies. *Journal of Neurology, Neurosurgery & Psychiatry*, *78*(10), https://doi.org/10.1136/jnnp.2006.107193
Ortigue, S., & Bianchi-Demicheli, F. (2008). The chronoarchitecture of human sexual desire: A high-density electrical mapping study. *NeuroImage*, *43*(2), 337–345. https://doi.org/10.1016/j.neuroimage.2008.07.059
Aull-Watschinger, S., Pataraia, E., & Baumgartner, C. (2008). Sexual auras: predominance of epileptic activity within the mesial temporal lobe. *Epilepsy & Behavior: E&B*, *12*(1), 124–127. https://doi.org/10.1016/j.yebeh.2007.07.007
Chaukimath, S., & Patil, P. (2015). Orgasm Induced Seizures: A Rare Phenomenon. *Annals of Medical and Health Sciences Research*, *5*(6), 483–484. https://doi.org/10.4103/2141-9248.17799
What We Can Learn From Sexual Response Cycles. (2012). Retrieved November 25, 2019, from Psychology Today https://www.psychologytoday.com/us/blog/the-power-pleasure/201211/what-we-can-learn-sexual-response-cycles
Safron A. (2016). What is orgasm? A model of sexual trance and climax via rhythmic entrainment. *Socioaffective neuroscience & psychology*, *6*, 31763. https://doi.org/10.3402/snp.v6.31763
Krassioukov, A., & Elliott, S. (2017). Neural Control and Physiology of Sexual Function: Effect of Spinal Cord Injury. *Topics in spinal cord injury rehabilitation*, *23*(1), 1–10. https://doi.org/10.1310/sci2301-1
Sayin, Umit. (2011). Altered States of Consciousness Occurring During Expanded Sexual Response In The Human Female: Preliminary Definitions. NeuroQuantology. 9. 10.14704/nq.2011.9.4.486.
https://www.researchgate.net/publication/260385774_Altered_States_of_Consciousness_Occurring_During_Expanded_Sexual_Response_In_The_Human_Female_Preliminary_Definitions
69) **Masters and Johnson: Research, Study & Technique**. (n.d.). Study.Com. https://study.com/academy/lesson/masters-and-johnson-research-study-technique.html

70) Fisher, H. (2005). *Why we love : the nature and chemistry of romantic love.* New York: H. Holt. The Neurobiology of Romantic Love | SexInfo Online. (2011). Retrieved January 16, 2020, from Ucsb.edu website: https://sexinfo.soc.ucsb.edu/article/neurobiology-romantic-love
Fisher, H., Aron, A., & Brown, L. L. (2005). Romantic love: An fMRI study of a neural mechanism for mate choice. *The Journal of Comparative Neurology, 493*(1), 58–62. https://doi.org/10.1002/cne.20772
71) Stoller RJ, Herdt GH. Theories of Origins of Male Homosexuality: A Cross-cultural Look. *Arch Gen Psychiatry.* 1985;42(4):399–404. doi:10.1001/archpsyc.1985.01790270089010 https://www.ncsby.org/content/normative-sexual-behavior
https://www.ncbi.nlm.nih.gov/pmc/articles/PMC3030621/
Whyte, S., Brooks, R. C., Chan, H. F., & Torgler, B. (2021). Sex differences in sexual attraction for aesthetics, resources and personality across age. *PloS one, 16*(5), e0250151. https://doi.org/10.1371/journal.pone.0250151
72) Sex research at the Kinsey Institute. (n.d.). *Https://Www.Apa.Org.* Retrieved February 28, 2020, from https://www.apa.org/monitor/2015/10/research-kinsey
van de Bongardt, D., Verbeek, M. New Interview Method for Sketching the Dynamic Relational and Sexual History of Young Adults. *Sex Res Soc Policy* **18,** 1148–1164 (2021). https://doi.org/10.1007/s13178-020-00514-1
Aicken, C.R.H., Gray, M., Clifton, S. et al. Improving Questions on Sexual Partnerships: Lessons Learned from Cognitive Interviews for Britain's Third National Survey of Sexual Attitudes and Lifestyles ("Natsal-3"). *Arch Sex Behav* **42,** 173–185 (2013). https://doi.org/10.1007/s10508-012-9962-2
73) Louise M Howard, Anna M Ehrlich, Freya Gamlen, Sian Oram, Gender-neutral mental health research is sex and gender biased, Published:November 14, 2016DOI:https://doi.org/10.1016/S2215-0366(16)30209-7
https://www.ncsby.org/content/normative-sexual-behavior
74) Nargund G. (2009). Declining birth rate in Developed Countries: A radical policy re-think is required. *Facts, views & vision in ObGyn, 1*(3), 191–193.
75) Mullins, N., Ingason, A., Porter, H. et al. Reproductive fitness and genetic risk of psychiatric disorders in the general population. *Nat Commun* **8,** 15833 (2017). https://doi.org/10.1038/ncomms15833 https://www.nature.com/articles/ncomms15833#citeas
76) Robinson, M., Kleinman, A., Graff, M. et al. Genetic evidence of assortative mating in humans. *Nat Hum Behav* **1,** 0016 (2017). https://doi.org/10.1038/s41562-016-0016
77) https://my.clevelandclinic.org/health/diseases/14369-huntingtons-disease
78) Hoffman, MD, Freud's Theories about Sex as Relevant as Ever https://psychnews.psychiatryonline.org/doi/full/10.1176/pn.40.15.00400018
Lantz SE, Ray S. Freud Developmental Theory. In: StatPearls (Internet). Treasure Island (FL): StatPearls Publishing; 2021 Jan-. Available from: https://

References

www.ncbi.nlm.nih.gov/books/NBK557526/
https://www.psychologytoday.com/us/blog/psychoanalysis-unplugged/201805/7-things-about-sex-and-love-sigmund-freud-nailed
Stoléru S. (2014). Reading the Freudian theory of sexual drives from a functional neuroimaging perspective. *Frontiers in human neuroscience, 8,* 157. https://doi.org/10.3389/fnhum.2014.00157 https://www.ncbi.nlm.nih.gov/pmc/articles/PMC3957062/
79) https://www.psychologytoday.com/us/blog/insight-therapy/201412/laws-attraction-how-do-we-select-life-partner
Birnbaum, G. E. (2015). On the convergence of sexual urges and emotional bonds: The interplay of the sexual and attachment systems during relationship development. In J. A. Simpson & W. S. Rholes (Eds.), *Attachment theory and research: New directions and emerging themes* (pp. 170–194). The Guilford Press.
80) https://greekcitytimes.com/2020/02/14/the-8-ancient-greek-words-for-love/
81) Coria-Avila, G. A., Herrera-Covarrubias, D., Ismail, N., & Pfaus, J. G. (2016). The role of orgasm in the development and shaping of partner preferences. *Socioaffective neuroscience & psychology, 6,* 31815. https://doi.org/10.3402/snp.v6.31815
https://www.ncbi.nlm.nih.gov/pmc/articles/PMC5087697/
Reich, D. B., & Zanarini, M. C. (2008). Sexual orientation and relationship choice in borderline personality disorder over ten years of prospective follow-up. *Journal of personality disorders, 22*(6), 564–572. https://doi.org/10.1521/pedi.2008.22.6.564
https://www.ncbi.nlm.nih.gov/pmc/articles/PMC3203737/
Dickenson, J. A., Gleason, N., Coleman, E., & Miner, M. H. (2018). Prevalence of Distress Associated With Difficulty Controlling Sexual Urges, Feelings, and Behaviors in the United States. *JAMA network open, 1*(7), e184468. https://doi.org/10.1001/jamanetworkopen.2018.4468 https://www.ncbi.nlm.nih.gov/pmc/articles/PMC6324590/
82) *What Your Attachment Style May Reveal About Your Sex Life.* (n.d.). Psychology Today. Retrieved February 28, 2020, from https://www.psychologytoday.com/us/blog/intimately-connected/201902/what-your-attachment-style-may-reveal-about-your-sex-life
The Link Between Adult Attachment Styles and Sex and Love Addiction. (n.d.). https://www.psychologytoday.com/us/blog/sex-lies-trauma/201109/the-link-between-adult-attachment-styles-and-sex-and-love-addiction
Laschinger, B., Purnell, C., Schwartz, J., White, K., & Wingfield, R. (2004). Sexuality and attachment from a clinical point of view. *Attachment & human development, 6*(2), 151–164. https://doi.org/10.1080/14616730410001688194
Davis, D., Shaver, P. R., & Vernon, M. L. (2004). Attachment Style and Subjective Motivations for Sex. *Personality and Social Psychology Bulletin, 30*(8), 1076–1090. https://doi.org/10.1177/0146167204264794
Nia, A. S. N., Salari, P., Sharifi, N., & Nooghani, H. J. (2017). Effect of

Attachment Styles to Parents on Sexual Dysfunction Domains of Married Women. *Electronic Physician, 9*(1), 3605–3610. https://doi.org/10.19082/3605
Simpson, J. A., & Rholes, W. S. (2017). Adult attachment, stress, and romantic relationships. *Current Opinion in Psychology, 13*, 19–24. https://doi.org/10.1016/j.copsyc.2016.04.006
83) Bartholomew, K.J. (1990). Avoidance of Intimacy: An Attachment Perspective. *Journal of Social and Personal Relationships, 7,* 147 - 178.https://www.semanticscholar.org/paper/Avoidance-of-Intimacy%3A-An-Attachment-Perspective-Bartholomew/bbdf43e28662b4a06deb70960f475c7231bf18c9
84) Rakovec-Felser, Z. (2014). Domestic violence and abuse in intimate relationship from public health perspective. *Health Psychology Research, 2*(3). https://doi.org/10.4081/hpr.2014.1821 https://www.ncbi.nlm.nih.gov/pmc/articles/PMC4768593/
85) Middleton, W., Sachs, A., & Dorahy, M. J. (2017). The abused and the abuser: Victim–perpetrator dynamics. *Journal of Trauma & Dissociation, 18*(3), 249–258. https://doi.org/10.1080/15299732.2017.1295373
Sullivan, R., & Lasley, E. N. (2010). Fear in Love: Attachment, Abuse, and the Developing Brain. *Cerebrum: The Dana Forum on Brain Science, 2010.* https://www.ncbi.nlm.nih.gov/pmc/articles/PMC3574772/
Sullivan, R. M. (2012). The Neurobiology of Attachment to Nurturing and Abusive Caregivers. *The Hastings Law Journal, 63*(6), 1553–1570. https://www.ncbi.nlm.nih.gov/pmc/articles/PMC3774302/
Howell E. F. (2014). Ferenczi's concept of identification with the aggressor: understanding dissociative structure with interacting victim and abuser self-states. *American journal of psychoanalysis, 74*(1), 48–59. https://doi.org/10.1057/ajp.2013.40
https://en.wikipedia.org/wiki/Identification_with_the_Aggressor
86) Phyllis Greenacre (1969) The Fetish and the Transitional Object, The Psychoanalytic Study of the Child, 24:1, 144-164, DOI: 10.1080/00797308.1969.11822690 https://www.tandfonline.com/doi/abs/10.1080/00797308.1969.11822690?journalCode=upsc20
Phyllis Greenacre (1955) Further Considerations regarding Fetishism, The Psychoanalytic Study of the Child, 10:1, 187-194, DOI: 10.1080/00797308.1955.11822555 https://www.tandfonline.com/doi/abs/10.1080/00797308.1955.11822555?journalCode=upsc20
87) Duhn L. (2010). The importance of touch in the development of attachment. *Advances in neonatal care : official journal of the National Association of Neonatal Nurses, 10*(6), 294–300. https://doi.org/10.1097/ANC.0b013e3181fd2263
https://en.wikipedia.org/wiki/Haptic_communication
88) *Sexual Behaviors in Young Children: What's Normal, What's Not?* (2019). HealthyChildren.Org. https://www.healthychildren.org/English/ages-stages/

References

preschool/Pages/Sexual-Behaviors-Young-Children.aspx
N. D. Kellogg, Sexual Behaviors in Children, *Am Fam Physician*. 2010 Nov 15;82(10):1233-1238. https://www.aafp.org/afp/2010/1115/p1233.html
Kurtuncu, M., Akhan, L. U., Tanir, İ. M., & Yildiz, H. (2015). The Sexual Development and Education of Preschool Children: Knowledge and Opinions from Doctors and Nurses. *Sexuality and Disability*, *33*(2), 207–221. https://doi.org/10.1007/s11195-015-9393-9 Sandy K Wurtele Maureen C Kenny, Normative sexuality development in childhood: Implications for developmental guidance and prevention of childhood sexual abuse. December 2010. Journal of multicultural counseling and development 43(9):1-24
88) Spitoni, G.F., Zingaretti, P., Giovanardi, G. *et al.* Disorganized Attachment pattern affects the perception of Affective Touch. *Sci Rep* **10,** 9658 (2020). https://doi.org/10.1038/s41598-020-66606-5 https://www.sciencedirect.com/topics/psychology/sexual-touch
Carissa J. Cascio, David Moore, Francis McGlone, Social touch and human development,
Developmental Cognitive Neuroscience, Volume 35, 2019, Pages 5-11, ISSN 1878-9293,
https://doi.org/10.1016/j.dcn.2018.04.009 .
89) ***The Handbook of Touch: Neuroscience, Behavioral, and Health Perspectives***, Bonnie Bullough
Wagner SA, Mattson RE, Davila J, Johnson MD, Cameron NM. Touch me just enough: The intersection of adult attachment, intimate touch, and marital satisfaction. Journal of Social and Personal Relationships. 2020;37(6):1945-1967. doi:10.1177/0265407520910791
Davis, I., Rovers, M., & Petrella, C. (2017). Touch Deprivation and Counselling as Healing Touch. In M. Rovers, J. Malette, & M. Guirguis-Younger (Eds.), *Touch in the Helping Professions: Research, Practice and Ethics* (pp. 13–32). University of Ottawa Press. https://doi.org/10.2307/j.ctv5vdcvd.5
Hertenstein, M. J., & Keltner, D. (2011). Gender and the Communication of Emotion Via Touch. *Sex roles*, *64*(1-2), 70–80. https://doi.org/10.1007/s11199-010-9842-y
Jakubiak, B. K., & Feeney, B. C. (2017). Affectionate Touch to Promote Relational, Psychological, and Physical Well-Being in Adulthood: A Theoretical Model and Review of the Research. *Personality and social psychology review : an official journal of the Society for Personality and Social Psychology, Inc*, *21*(3), 228–252. https://doi.org/10.1177/1088868316650307
Hollender MH, Mercer AJ. Wish To Be Held and Wish To Hold in Men and Women. *Arch Gen Psychiatry*. 1976;33(1):49–51. https://jamanetwork.com/journals/jamapsychiatry/article-abstract/491476
Huang LT, Phares R, Hollender MH. The Wish To Be Held: A Transcultural Study. *Arch Gen Psychiatry*. 1976;33(1):41–43.

https://www.ncbi.nlm.nih.gov/pubmed/1247362
Johnson SM, Moser MB, Beckes L, Smith A, Dalgleish T, et al. (2014) Correction: Soothing the Threatened Brain: Leveraging Contact Comfort with Emotionally Focused Therapy. PLOS ONE 9(8): e105489. https://doi.org/10.1371/journal.pone.0105489
https://journals.plos.org/plosone/article?id=10.1371/journal.pone.0079314
90) *What Is Psoriasis? Symptoms, Causes, Diagnosis, Treatment, and Prevention | Everyday Health.* (n.d.). EverydayHealth.Com. Retrieved February 28, 2020, from https://www.everydayhealth.com/psoriasis/guide/
Armstrong, A. W., Cather, J. C., Paul, C. F., Edson-Heredia, E., Zhu, B., Hollister, K., Koo, J., Levin, E., & Bleakman, A. P. (2017). Association of Touch Avoidance with Disease Severity and Quality of Life in Psoriasis Patients. *Journal of Psoriasis and Psoriatic Arthritis*, 2(3), 57–63. https://doi.org/10.1177/247553031700200305
Gupta, M. A., Gupta, A. K., & Watteel, G. N. (1998). Deprivation Of Social Touch In Psoriasis And The Psychological Impact Of The Stigma Experience. *Psychosomatic Medicine*, 60(1), 131. https://doi.org/10.1097/00006842-199801000-00178
Patel, N., Nadkarni, A., Cardwell, L. A., Vera, N., Frey, C., Patel, N., & Feldman, S. R. (2017). Psoriasis, Depression, and Inflammatory Overlap: A Review. *American Journal of Clinical Dermatology*, 18(5), 613–620. https://doi.org/10.1007/s40257-017-0279-8 Patel, N., Nadkarni, A., Cardwell, L. A., Vera, N., Frey, C., Patel, N., & Feldman, S. R. (2017). Psoriasis, Depression, and Inflammatory Overlap: A Review. *American journal of clinical dermatology*, 18(5), 613–620. https://doi.org/10.1007/s40257-017-0279-8 Choi, J., & Koo, J. Y. M. (2003). Quality of life issues in psoriasis. *Journal of the American Academy of Dermatology*, 49(2, Supplement), 57–61. https://doi.org/10.1016/S0190-9622(03)01136-8 Kimball, A. B., Jacobson, C., Weiss, S., Vreeland, M. G., & Wu, Y. (2005). The Psychosocial Burden of Psoriasis. *American Journal of Clinical Dermatology*, 6(6), 383–392. https://doi.org/10.2165/00128071-200506060-00005

CHAPTER EIGHT REFERENCES

1) Adolph, K. E., Kretch, K. S., & LoBue, V. (2014). Fear of heights in infants?. *Current directions in psychological science*, 23(1), 60–66. https://doi.org/10.1177/0963721413498895
2) LeDoux, J. E. (1995). Emotion: Clues from the Brain. Annual Review of Psychology, 46(1), 209–235. https://doi.org/10.1146/annurev.ps.46.020195.001233
AbuHasan Q, Reddy V, Siddiqui W. Neuroanatomy, Amygdala. (Updated 2021 Jul 23). In: StatPearls (Internet). Treasure Island (FL): StatPearls Publishing;

References

2021 Jan-. https://www.ncbi.nlm.nih.gov/books/NBK537102/
anatomical diagrams:https://www.kenhub.com/en/library/anatomy/anatomy-of-amygdaloidal-complex
https://nba.uth.tmc.edu/neuroscience/s4/chapter06.html
3) LeDoux, J. E., & Pine, D. S. (2016). Using Neuroscience to Help Understand Fear and Anxiety: A Two-System Framework. American Journal of Psychiatry, 173(11), 1083–1093. https://doi.org/10.1176/appi.ajp.2016.16030353
LeDoux, J. E., & Brown, R. (2017). A higher-order theory of emotional consciousness. Proceedings of the National Academy of Sciences, 114(10), E2016–E2025. https://doi.org/10.1073/pnas.1619316114
Berridge K. C. (2018). Evolving Concepts of Emotion and Motivation. *Frontiers in psychology*, *9*, 1647. https://doi.org/10.3389/fpsyg.2018.01647
Dumont E. C. (2009). What is the bed nucleus of the stria terminalis?. *Progress in neuro-psychopharmacology & biological psychiatry*, *33*(8), 1289–1290. https://doi.org/10.1016/j.pnpbp.2009.07.006
Liberzon, I., Phan, K., Decker, L. *et al.* Extended Amygdala and Emotional Salience: A PET Activation Study of Positive and Negative Affect. *Neuropsychopharmacol* **28,** 726–733 (2003). https://doi.org/10.1038/sj.npp.1300113
Fudge, J. L., Kelly, E. A., Pal, R., Bedont, J. L., Park, L., & Ho, B. (2017). Beyond the Classic VTA: Extended Amygdala Projections to DA-Striatal Paths in the Primate. *Neuropsychopharmacology : official publication of the American College of Neuropsychopharmacology*, *42*(8), 1563–1576. https://doi.org/10.1038/npp.2017.38
Fox, A. S., & Shackman, A. J. (2019). The central extended amygdala in fear and anxiety: Closing the gap between mechanistic and neuroimaging research. *Neuroscience letters*, *693*, 58–67. https://doi.org/10.1016/j.neulet.2017.11.056
Alexander J. Shackman and Andrew S. Fox,Contributions of the Central Extended Amygdala to Fear and Anxiety, Journal of Neuroscience 3 August 2016, 36 (31) 8050-8063; DOI: https://doi.org/10.1523/JNEUROSCI.0982-16.2016
Kim, M. J., & Whalen, P. J. (2009). The Structural Integrity of an Amygdala-Prefrontal Pathway Predicts Trait Anxiety. Journal of Neuroscience, 29(37), 11614–11618. https://doi.org/10.1523/jneurosci.2335-09.2009
Sylvester, C. M., Yu, Q., Srivastava, A. B., Marek, S., Zheng, A., Alexopoulos, D., Smyser, C. D., Shimony, J. S., Ortega, M., Dierker, D. L., Patel, G. H., Nelson, S. M., Gilmore, A. W., McDermott, K. B., Berg, J. J., Drysdale, A. T., Perino, M. T., Snyder, A. Z., Raut, R. V., Laumann, T. O., … Dosenbach, N. (2020). Individual-specific functional connectivity of the amygdala: A substrate for precision psychiatry. *Proceedings of the National Academy of Sciences of the United States of America*, *117*(7), 3808–3818. https://doi.org/10.1073/pnas.1910842117
Yimeng Zeng, Fuxiang Tao, Zaixu Cui, Liyun Wu, Jiahua Xu, Wenshan

Dong, Chao Liu, Zhi Yang, Shaozheng Qin,Dynamic integration and segregation of amygdala subregional functional circuits linking to physiological arousal,NeuroImage,
Volume 238,2021,118224,ISSN 1053-8119,https://doi.org/10.1016/j.neuroimage.2021.118224.
Jimenez, J. C., Su, K., Goldberg, A. R., Luna, V. M., Biane, J. S., Ordek, G., Zhou, P., Ong, S. K., Wright, M. A., Zweifel, L., Paninski, L., Hen, R., & Kheirbek, M. A. (2018). Anxiety Cells in a Hippocampal-Hypothalamic Circuit. Neuron, 97(3), 670–683.e6. https://doi.org/10.1016/j.neuron.2018.01.016
4) Koski, J. E., Xie, H., & Olson, I. R. (2015). Understanding social hierarchies: The neural and psychological foundations of status perception. *Social neuroscience*, *10*(5), 527–550. https://doi.org/10.1080/17470919.2015.1013223
5) Martin, E. I., Ressler, K. J., Binder, E., & Nemeroff, C. B. (2009). The Neurobiology of Anxiety Disorders: Brain Imaging, Genetics, and Psychoneuroendocrinology. Psychiatric Clinics of North America, 32(3), 549–575. https://doi.org/10.1016/j.psc.2009.05.004
6) Craske, M. G., Rauch, S. L., Ursano, R., Prenoveau, J., Pine, D. S., & Zinbarg, R. E. (2009). What is an anxiety disorder?. Depression and anxiety, 26(12), 1066–1085. https://doi.org/10.1002/da.20633
Lenze, E. J., & Wetherell, J. L. (2011). A lifespan view of anxiety disorders. Dialogues in Clinical Neuroscience, 13(4), 381–399. https://www.ncbi.nlm.nih.gov/pmc/articles/PMC3263387/
Bocchio, M., McHugh, S. B., Bannerman, D. M., Sharp, T., & Capogna, M. (2016). Serotonin, Amygdala and Fear: Assembling the Puzzle. *Frontiers in neural circuits*, *10*, 24. https://doi.org/10.3389/fncir.2016.00024
Etkin, A., Prater, K. E., Schatzberg, A. F., Menon, V., & Greicius, M. D. (2009). Disrupted Amygdalar Subregion Functional Connectivity and Evidence of a Compensatory Network in Generalized Anxiety Disorder. Archives of General Psychiatry, 66(12), 1361–1372. https://doi.org/10.1001/archgenpsychiatry.2009.104
Jack B. Nitschke, Ph.D., Issidoros Sarinopoulos, Ph.D., Desmond J. Oathes, Ph.D., Tom Johnstone, Ph.D., Paul J. Whalen, Ph.D., Richard J. Davidson, Ph.D., and Ned H. Kalin, M.D., Anticipatory Activation in the Amygdala and Anterior Cingulate in Generalized Anxiety Disorder and Prediction of Treatment Response, AJP 2009 166:3, 302-310 https://doi.org/10.1176/appi.ajp.2008.07101682
Arnold, P.D., Zai, G. & Richter, M.A. Genetics of anxiety disorders. *Curr Psychiatry Rep* **6**, 243–254 (2004). https://doi.org/10.1007/s11920-004-0073-1
Gottschalk, M. G., & Domschke, K. (2017). Genetics of generalized anxiety disorder and related traits. *Dialogues in clinical neuroscience*, *19*(2), 159–168. https://doi.org/10.31887/DCNS.2017.19.2/kdomschke
7) Essex, M. J., Klein, M. H., Slattery, M. J., Goldsmith, H. H., & Kalin, N. H. (2010). Early risk factors and developmental pathways to chronic high inhibition

and social anxiety disorder in adolescence. *The American journal of psychiatry, 167*(1), 40–46. https://doi.org/10.1176/appi.ajp.2009.07010051

Blair, K. S., Geraci, M., Korelitz, K., Otero, M., Towbin, K., Ernst, M., Leibenluft, E., Blair, R. J., & Pine, D. S. (2011). The pathology of social phobia is independent of developmental changes in face processing. *The American journal of psychiatry, 168*(11), 1202–1209. https://doi.org/10.1176/appi.ajp.2011.10121740

Schneier, F. R. (2005). Neurobiological Mechanisms of Social Anxiety Disorder. CNS Spectrums, 10(10), 805h-805i. https://doi.org/10.1017/s1092852900010361

Mathew, S. J., Coplan, J. D., & Gorman, J. M. (2001). Neurobiological mechanisms of social anxiety disorder. *The American journal of psychiatry, 158*(10), 1558–1567. https://doi.org/10.1176/appi.ajp.158.10.1558

8) Roberson-Nay, R., & Kendler, K. (2011). Panic disorder and its subtypes: A comprehensive analysis of panic symptom heterogeneity using epidemiological and treatment seeking samples. *Psychological Medicine, 41*(11), 2411-2421. DOI: 10.1017/S0033291711000547

Redlich, R., Grotegerd, D., Opel, N., Kaufmann, C., Zwitserlood, P., Kugel, H., Heindel, W., Donges, U.-S., Suslow, T., Arolt, V., & Dannlowski, U. (2014). Are you gonna leave me? Separation anxiety is associated with increased amygdala responsiveness and volume. *Social Cognitive and Affective Neuroscience, 10*(2), 278–284. https://doi.org/10.1093/scan/nsu055

Gittelman, R., & Klein, D. F. (1984). Relationship between separation anxiety and panic and agoraphobic disorders. *Psychopathology, 17 Suppl 1*, 56–65. https://doi.org/10.1159/000284078

Davis, P., & Reijmers, L. G. (2018). The dynamic nature of fear engrams in the basolateral amygdala. *Brain research bulletin, 141*, 44–49. https://doi.org/10.1016/j.brainresbull.2017.12.004

Jo T. Van Winter, Gunnar B. Stickler,Panic attack syndrome,The Journal of Pediatrics,Volume 105, Issue 4,1984,Pages 661-665, https://doi.org/10.1016/S0022-3476(84)80444-8.

Weissman, M. M., Fyer, A. J., Haghighi, F., Heiman, G., Deng, Z., Hen, R., Hodge, S. E., & Knowles, J. A. (2000). Potential panic disorder syndrome: clinical and genetic linkage evidence. *American journal of medical genetics, 96*(1), 24–35. https://doi.org/10.1002/(sici)1096-8628(20000207)96:1<24::aid-ajmg7>3.0.co;2-e

Klein, Donald F.(1964), Delineation of two drug-responsive anxiety syndromes, Psychopharmacologia 397-408,VL 5,IS - 6, SN - 1432-2072 https://doi.org/10.1007/BF02193476

Pine, D. S., Klein, R. G., Coplan, J. D., Papp, L. A., Hoven, C. W., Martinez, J., Kovalenko, P., Mandell, D. J., Moreau, D., Klein, D. F., & Gorman, J. M. (2000). Differential carbon dioxide sensitivity in childhood anxiety disorders

and nonill comparison group. Archives of general psychiatry, 57(10), 960–967. https://doi.org/10.1001/archpsyc.57.10.960
Liebowitz, M. R., & Klein, D. F. (1981). Differential Diagnosis and Treatment of Panic Attacks and Phobic States. Annual Review of Medicine, 32(1), 583–599. https://doi.org/10.1146/annurev.me.32.020181.003055
Kim, J. E., Dager, S. R., & Lyoo, I. K. (2012). The role of the amygdala in the pathophysiology of panic disorder: evidence from neuroimaging studies. Biology of Mood & Anxiety Disorders, 2(1), 20. https://doi.org/10.1186/2045-5380-2-20
Buigues, J., & Vallejo, J. (1987). Therapeutic response to phenelzine in patients with panic disorder and agoraphobia with panic attacks. The Journal of Clinical Psychiatry, 48(2), 55–59.
Marchesi, C. (2008). Pharmacological management of panic disorder. Neuropsychiatric Disease and Treatment, 4(1), 93–106. Quitkin, F. M., Stewart, J. W., McGrath, P. J., Liebowitz, M. R., Harrison, W. M., Tricamo, E., Klein, D. F., Rabkin, J. G., Markowitz, J. S., & Wager, S. G. (1988). Phenelzine versus imipramine in the treatment of probable atypical depression: defining syndrome boundaries of selective MAOI responders. The American Journal of Psychiatry, 145(3), 306–311. https://doi.org/10.1176/ajp.145.3.306
Many providers have anxiety about using MAOI. http://www.shrinkrap.net/2008/03/why-this-shrink-doesnt-prescribe-maois.html
9) LaBar, K. S., Gatenby, J. C., Gore, J. C., LeDoux, J. E., & Phelps, E. A. (1998). Human Amygdala Activation during Conditioned Fear Acquisition and Extinction: a Mixed-Trial fMRI Study. Neuron, 20(5), 937–945. https://doi.org/10.1016/s0896-6273(00)80475-4
Graham, B. M., & Milad, M. R. (2011). The Study of Fear Extinction: Implications for Anxiety Disorders. American Journal of Psychiatry, 168(12), 1255–1265. https://doi.org/10.1176/appi.ajp.2011.11040557
10) LISTS OF PHOBIAS:
DSM-IV to DSM-5 Specific Phobia Comparison. Available from: https://www.ncbi.nlm.nih.gov/books/NBK519704/table/ch3.t11/
Lissek, S., Rabin, S., Heller, R. E., Lukenbaugh, D., Geraci, M., Pine, D. S., & Grillon, C. (2010). Overgeneralization of Conditioned Fear as a Pathogenic Marker of Panic Disorder. American Journal of Psychiatry, 167, https://doi.org/10.1176/appi.ajp.2009.09030410
11) Forster, S., Nunez Elizalde, A. O., Castle, E., & Bishop, S. J. (2015). Unraveling the Anxious Mind: Anxiety, Worry, and Frontal Engagement in Sustained Attention Versus Off-Task Processing. Cerebral Cortex (New York, NY), 25(3), 609–618. https://doi.org/10.1093/cercor/bht248
Etkin, A., Prater, K. E., Hoeft, F., Menon, V., & Schatzberg, A. F. (2010). Failure of anterior cingulate activation and connectivity with the amygdala during implicit regulation of emotional processing in generalized anxiety disorder. The American Journal of Psychiatry, 167(5), 545–554. https://doi.org/10.1176/appi.

References

ajp.2009.09070931
Robinson, O. J., Charney, D. R., Overstreet, C., Vytal, K., & Grillon, C. (2012). The adaptive threat bias in anxiety: amygdala- dorsomedial prefrontal cortex coupling and aversive amplification. Neuroimage, 60 https://doi.org/10.1016/j.neuroimage.2011.11.096

12) Beucke JC, Sepulcre J, Talukdar T, et al. Abnormally High Degree Connectivity of the Orbitofrontal Cortex in Obsessive-Compulsive Disorder. *JAMA Psychiatry.* 2013;70(6): https://jamanetwork.com/journals/jamapsychiatry/fullarticle/1679420

Milad MR, Furtak SC, Greenberg JL, et al. Deficits in Conditioned Fear Extinction in Obsessive-Compulsive Disorder and Neurobiological Changes in the Fear Circuit. *JAMA Psychiatry.* 2013;70(6):608–618. Doi:10.1001/jamapsychiatry.2013.914
https://jamanetwork.com/journals/jamapsychiatry/fullarticle/1679422

Hirschtritt, M. E., Bloch, M. H., & Mathews, C. A. (2017). Obsessive-Compulsive Disorder: Advances in Diagnosis and Treatment. *JAMA, 317*(13), 1358–1367. https://doi.org/10.1001/jama.2017.2200

Link to YBOCD scale: https://www.psychdb.com/_media/mood/yale-brown-ocd_full.pdf

13) Lack, Caleb & Huskey, Alisa & Weed, David & Highfill, Micah & Craig, Lauren. (2015). ***The etiology of Obsessive-Compulsive Disorder. In book: Obsessive-Compulsive Disorder: Etiology, Phenomenology, and Treatment,*** Edition: 1st, Publisher: Onus Books,

14) see ref #57) chapter seven.

15) Lokko, H. N., & Stern, T. A. (2015). Regression: Diagnosis, Evaluation, and Management. *The primary care companion for CNS disorders, 17*(3), 10.4088/PCC.14f01761. https://doi.org/10.4088/PCC.14f01761

Cox, D. J., Morris, J. B., Borowitz, S. M., & Sutphen, J. L. (2002). Psychological Differences Between Children With and Without Chronic Encopresis. Journal of Pediatric Psychology, 27(7), 585–591. https://doi.org/10.1093/jpepsy/27.7.585

Nelson, Theodora MD*; Chae, Heekyung MD*; Anbar, Ran D. MD†; Stein, Martin T. MD* Persistent Encopresis, Enuresis, and Anxiety in a 7-Year-Old Girl, Journal of Developmental & Behavioral Pediatrics: October 2017 - Volume 38 - Issue 8 - p 680-682 DOI: 10.1097/DBP.0000000000000504

16) Oyama, O., Paltoo, C., & Greengold, J. (2007). Somatoform disorders. *American family physician, 76*(9), 1333–1338. https://www.aafp.org/afp/2007/1101/p1333.html

Aybek, S., Nicholson, T. R., Zelaya, F., O'Daly, O. G., Craig, T. J., David, A. S., & Kanaan, R. A. (2014). Neural correlates of recall of life events in conversion disorder. *JAMA psychiatry, 71*(1), 52–60. Jan 01, 2014 | JAMA Psychiatry | JAMA Network

Unal, E. O., Unal, V., Gul, A., Celtek, M., Dıken, B., & Balcıoglu, İ. (2017). A

Serial Munchausen Syndrome by Proxy. *Indian journal of psychological medicine*, *39*(5), 671–674. https://doi.org/10.4103/0253-7176.217017
17) Bjornsson, A. S., Didie, E. R., & Phillips, K. A. (2010). Body dysmorphic disorder. *Dialogues in clinical neuroscience*, *12*(2), 221–232. https://doi.org/10.31887/DCNS.2010.12.2/abjornsson
Fernández-Aranda, F., Dahme, B., & Meermann, R. (1999). Body image in eating disorders and analysis of its relevance: a preliminary study. *Journal of psychosomatic research*, *47*(5), 419–428. https://doi.org/10.1016/s0022-3999(99)00027-6
Legenbauer Tanja, Radix Anne Kathrin, Naumann Eva, Blechert Jens, The Body Image Approach Test (BIAT): A Potential Measure of the Behavioral Components of Body Image Disturbance in Anorexia and Bulimia Nervosa? Frontiers in Psychology 11 2020, p30 https://www.frontiersin.org/article/10.3389/fpsyg.2020.00030 https://www.frontiersin.org/articles/10.3389/fpsyg.2020.00030/full
Hosseini SA, Padhy RK. ***Body Image Distortion***. Treasure Island https://www.ncbi.nlm.nih.gov/books/NBK546582/
18) Gauthier, I., & Nuss, P. (2015). Anxiety disorders and GABA neurotransmission: a disturbance of modulation. Neuropsychiatric Disease and Treatment, 165. https://doi.org/10.2147/ndt.s58841
Steimer, T. (2002). The biology of fear- and anxiety-related behaviors. Dialogues in Clinical Neuroscience, 4(3), 231–249.
Jie, F., Yin, G., Yang, W., Yang, M., Gao, S., Lv, J., & Li, B. (2018). Stress in Regulation of GABA Amygdala System and Relevance to Neuropsychiatric Diseases. Frontiers in Neuroscience, 12. https://doi.org/10.3389/fnins.2018.00562
19) Marksberry, K. (2011). Holmes- Rahe Stress Inventory - The American Institute of Stress. The American Institute of Stress. https://www.stress.org/holmes-rahe-stress-inventory
20) Selye, H. (1950). Stress and the General Adaptation Syndrome. BMJ, 1(4667), 1383–1392. https://doi.org/10.1136/bmj.1.4667.1383 the original paper is available online!
Jackson, M. (2014, February). Evaluating the Role of Hans Selye in the Modern History of Stress. Nih.Gov; University of Rochester Press. https://www.ncbi.nlm.nih.gov/books/NBK349158/
Martin, E. I., Ressler, K. J., Binder, E., & Nemeroff, C. B. (2009). The Neurobiology of Anxiety Disorders: Brain Imaging, Genetics, and Psychoneuroendocrinology. Psychiatric Clinics of North America, 32(3), 549–575. https://doi.org/10.1016/j.psc.2009.05.004
Rodrigues, S., Paiva, J., Dias, D., Aleixo, M., Filipe, R., & Cunha, J. (2018). Cognitive Impact and Psychophysiological Effects of Stress Using a Biomonitoring Platform. *International Journal of Environmental Research and Public Health*, *15*(6), 1080. https://doi.org/10.3390/ijerph15061080

References

Rong-Chang Jou, Chung-Wei Kuo, Mei-Ling Tang, A study of job stress and turnover tendency among air traffic controllers: The mediating effects of job satisfaction, Transportation Research Part E: Logistics and Transportation Review, Volume 57, 2013, Pages 95-104, ISSN 1366-5545, https://doi.org/10.1016/j.tre.2013.01.009

Leyro, T. M., Zvolensky, M. J., & Bernstein, A. (2010). Distress tolerance and psychopathological symptoms and disorders: a review of the empirical literature among adults. *Psychological bulletin*, *136*(4), 576–600. https://doi.org/10.1037/a0019712

Bartolomucci, A., Palanza, P., Sacerdote, P., Panerai, A. E., Sgoifo, A., Dantzer, R., & Parmigiani, S. (2005). Social factors and individual vulnerability to chronic stress exposure. *Neuroscience and biobehavioral reviews*, *29*(1), 67–81. https://doi.org/10.1016/j.neubiorev.2004.06.009

21) Learned Helplessness | Psychology Today. (2019). Psychology Today. https://www.psychologytoday.com/us/basics/learned-helplessness

Overmier, J. B., & Seligman, M. E. (1967). Effects of inescapable shock upon subsequent escape and avoidance responding. *Journal of Comparative and Physiological Psychology, 63*(1), 28–33. https://doi.org/10.1037/h0024166

22) Weber, Darren L. "Information Processing Bias in Post-Traumatic Stress Disorder." The Open Neuroimaging Journal, vol. 2, 10 June 2008, pp. 29–51. https://www.ncbi.nlm.nih.gov/pmc/articles/PMC2714576/

Nilsen, A. S., Blix, I., Leknes, S., Ekeberg, Ø., Skogstad, L., Endestad, T., Østberg, B. C., & Heir, T. (2016). Brain Activity in Response to Trauma-specific, Negative, and Neutral Stimuli. A fMRI Study of Recent Road Traffic Accident Survivors. Frontiers in Psychology, 7. https://doi.org/10.3389/fpsyg.2016.01173

Soares, J. M., Sampaio, A., Ferreira, L. M., Santos, N. C., Marques, P., Marques, F., Palha, J. A., Cerqueira, J. J., & Sousa, N. (2013). Stress Impact on Resting State Brain Networks. *PloS one*, *8*(6), e66500. https://doi.org/10.1371/journal.pone.0066500

Bramham, C. R., Alme, M. N., Bittins, M., Kuipers, S. D., Nair, R. R., Pai, B., Panja, D., Schubert, M., Soule, J., Tiron, A., & Wibrand, K. (2010). The Arc of synaptic memory. *Experimental brain research*, *200*(2), 125–140. https://doi.org/10.1007/s00221-009-1959-2

Germain, A. (2013). Sleep Disturbances as the Hallmark of PTSD: Where Are We Now? American Journal of Psychiatry, 170(4), 372–382. https://doi.org/10.1176/appi.ajp.2012.12040432

Jatzko, A., Rothenhöfer, S., Schmitt, A., Gaser, C., Demirakca, T., Weber-Fahr, W., Wessa, M., Magnotta, V., & Braus, D. F. (2006). Hippocampal volume in chronic posttraumatic stress disorder (PTSD): MRI study using two different evaluation methods. Journal of Affective Disorders, 94(1–3), 121–126. https://doi.org/10.1016/j.jad.2006.03.010

23) North, C. S., Suris, A. M., Davis, M., & Smith, R. P. (2009). Toward

validation of the diagnosis of posttraumatic stress disorder. The American Journal of Psychiatry, 166(1), 34–41. https://doi.org/10.1176/appi.ajp.2008.08050644

24) Nock, M. K., Stein, M. B., Heeringa, S. G., Ursano, R. J., Colpe, L. J., Fullerton, C. S., Hwang, I., Naifeh, J. A., Sampson, N. A., Schoenbaum, M., Zaslavsky, A. M., Kessler, R. C., & Army STARRS Collaborators (2014). Prevalence and correlates of suicidal behavior among soldiers: results from the Army Study to Assess Risk and Resilience in Servicemembers (Army STARRS). *JAMA psychiatry*, *71*(5), 514–522. https://doi.org/10.1001/jamapsychiatry.2014.30

McLaughlin K. A. (2016). Future Directions in Childhood Adversity and Youth Psychopathology. *Journal of clinical child and adolescent psychology : the official journal for the Society of Clinical Child and Adolescent Psychology, American Psychological Association, Division 53*, *45*(3), 361–382. https://doi.org/10.1080/15374416.2015.1110823

Kessler, R. C., Warner, C. H., Ivany, C., Petukhova, M. V., Rose, S., Bromet, E. J., Brown, M., 3rd, Cai, T., Colpe, L. J., Cox, K. L., Fullerton, C. S., Gilman, S. E., Gruber, M. J., Heeringa, S. G., Lewandowski-Romps, L., Li, J., Millikan-Bell, A. M., Naifeh, J. A., Nock, M. K., Rosellini, A. J., … Army STARRS Collaborators (2015). Predicting suicides after psychiatric hospitalization in US Army soldiers: the Army Study To Assess Risk and rEsilience in Servicemembers (Army STARRS). *JAMA psychiatry*, *72*(1), 49–57. https://doi.org/10.1001/jamapsychiatry.2014.1754

Kessler, R. C., Heeringa, S. G., Stein, M. B., Colpe, L. J., Fullerton, C. S., Hwang, I., Naifeh, J. A., Nock, M. K., Petukhova, M., Sampson, N. A., Schoenbaum, M., Zaslavsky, A. M., Ursano, R. J., & Army STARRS Collaborators (2014). Thirty-day prevalence of DSM-IV mental disorders among nondeployed soldiers in the US Army: results from the Army Study to Assess Risk and Resilience in Servicemembers (Army STARRS). *JAMA psychiatry*, *71*(5), 504–513. https://doi.org/10.1001/jamapsychiatry.2014.28

25) Acute Stress Disorder DSM 5. This diagnosis was proposed in DSM V to address the situation when a person has a traumatic experience of strong anxiety, and may enter the process that will eventually become PTSD. This cannot be diagnosed as PTSD without the associated symptoms.

26) Wolf, E. J., Miller, M. W., Reardon, A. F., Ryabchenko, K. A., Castillo, D., & Freund, R. (2012). A latent class analysis of dissociation and posttraumatic stress disorder: evidence for a dissociative subtype. Archives of general psychiatry, 69(7), 698–705. https://doi.org/10.1001/archgenpsychiatry.2011.1574

Nicholson, A. A., Rabellino, D., Densmore, M., Frewen, P. A., Paret, C., Kluetsch, R., Schmahl, C., Théberge, J., Ros, T., Neufeld, R., McKinnon, M. C., Reiss, J. P., Jetly, R., & Lanius, R. A. (2018). Intrinsic connectivity network dynamics in PTSD during amygdala downregulation using real-time fMRI neurofeedback: A preliminary analysis. *Human brain mapping*, *39*(11), 4258–4275.

References

https://doi.org/10.1002/hbm.24244

Nicholson, A. A., Rabellino, D., Densmore, M., Frewen, P. A., Paret, C., Kluetsch, R., Schmahl, C., Théberge, J., Neufeld, R. W., McKinnon, M. C., Reiss, J., Jetly, R., & Lanius, R. A. (2017). The neurobiology of emotion regulation in posttraumatic stress disorder: Amygdala downregulation via real-time fMRI neurofeedback. *Human brain mapping*, *38*(1), 541–560. https://doi.org/10.1002/hbm.23402

Lanius, R. A., Williamson, P. C., Densmore, M., Boksman, K., Neufeld, R. W., Gati, J. S., & Menon, R. S. (2004). The nature of traumatic memories: a 4-T FMRI functional connectivity analysis. The American Journal of Psychiatry, 161(1), 36–44. https://doi.org/10.1176/appi.ajp.161.1.36

Lanius, R. A., Vermetten, E., Loewenstein, R. J., Brand, B., Schmahl, C., Bremner, J. D., & Spiegel, D. (2010). Emotion modulation in PTSD: Clinical and neurobiological evidence for a dissociative subtype. The American journal of psychiatry, 167(6), 640–647. https://doi.org/10.1176/appi.ajp.2009.09081168

Frischholz, E. J., Braun, B. G., Sachs, R. G., Hopkins, L., et al. (1990). The Dissociative Experiences Scale: Further replication and validation. *Dissociation: Progress in the Dissociative Disorders*, *3*(3), 151–153.

https://www.columbiapsychiatry.org/research/research-areas/services-policy-and-law/structured-clinical-interview-dsm-disorders-scid

27) Alexander, J. E., Stimpson, K. H., Kittle, J., & Spiegel, D. (2021). The Hypnotic Induction Profile (HIP) in Clinical Practice and Research. The International journal of clinical and experimental hypnosis, 69(1), 72–82. https://doi.org/10.1080/00207144.2021.1836646

Amazon.com: Traumatic Dissociation: Neurobiology and Treatment (9781585621965): Eric Vermetten, Martin Dorahy, David Spiegel: Books

Heidi Jiang, Matthew P. White, Michael D. Greicius, Lynn C. Waelde, David Spiegel, Brain Activity and Functional Connectivity Associated with Hypnosis, *Cerebral Cortex*, Volume 27, Issue 8, August 2017, https://doi.org/10.1093/cercor/bhw220

Jensen, M. P., Jamieson, G. A., Lutz, A., Mazzoni, G., McGeown, W. J., Santarcangelo, E. L., Demertzi, A., De Pascalis, V., Bányai, É. I., Rominger, C., Vuilleumier, P., Faymonville, M. E., & Terhune, D. B. (2017). New directions in hypnosis research: strategies for advancing the cognitive and clinical neuroscience of hypnosis. Neuroscience of consciousness, 3(1), https://doi.org/10.1093/nc/nix004

Richard J. Davidson & Daniel J. Goleman (1977) The role of attention in meditation and hypnosis: A psychobiological perspective on transformations of consciousness, International Journal of Clinical and Experimental Hypnosis, 25:4, 291-308, DOI: 10.1080/00207147708415986

Iani, C., Ricci, F., Baroni, G., & Rubichi, S. (2009). Attention control and susceptibility to hypnosis. Consciousness and cognition, 18(4), 856–863. https://

doi.org/10.1016/j.concog.2009.07.002
Landry, M., Lifshitz, M., & Raz, A. (2017). Brain correlates of hypnosis: A systematic review and meta-analytic exploration. Neuroscience and biobehavioral reviews, 81(Pt A), 75–98. https://doi.org/10.1016/j.neubiorev.2017.02.020

28) Etkin, A., & Wager, T. D. (2007). Functional neuroimaging of anxiety: a meta-analysis of emotional processing in PTSD, social anxiety disorder, and specific phobia. The American Journal of Psychiatry, 164(10), 1476–1488. https://doi.org/10.1176/appi.ajp.2007.07030504

29) S., Fox, N. A., & Wald, I. (2010). Life-threatening danger and suppression of attention bias to threat. The American journal of psychiatry, 167(6), 694–698. https://doi.org/10.1176/appi.ajp.2009.09070956

Slopen, N., McLaughlin, K. A., Fox, N. A., Zeanah, C. H., & Nelson, C. A. (2012). Alterations in neural processing and psychopathology in children raised in institutions. Archives of general psychiatry, 69(10), 1022–1030. https://doi.org/10.1001/archgenpsychiatry.2012.444

Walsh, K. (2012). National Prevalence of Posttraumatic Stress Disorder Among Sexually Revictimized Adolescent, College, and Adult Household-Residing Women. Archives of General Psychiatry, 69(9), 935. https://doi.org/10.1001/archgenpsychiatry.2012.132

Copeland, W. E., Wolke, D., Angold, A., & Costello, E. J. (2013). Adult Psychiatric Outcomes of Bullying and Being Bullied by Peers in Childhood and Adolescence. JAMA Psychiatry, 70(4), 419. https://doi.org/10.1001/jamapsychiatry.2013.504

Taylor J. Keding, Sara A. Heyn, Justin D. Russell, Xiaojin Zhu, Josh Cisler, Katie A. McLaughlin, and Ryan J. Herringa, Differential Patterns of Delayed Emotion Circuit Maturation in Abused Girls With and Without Internalizing Psychopathology
American Journal of Psychiatry 2021 178:11, 1026-1036

30) Bryant, R. A., Creamer, M., O'Donnell, M., Forbes, D., McFarlane, A. C., Silove, D., & Hadzi-Pavlovic, D. (2017). Acute and Chronic Posttraumatic Stress Symptoms in the Emergence of Posttraumatic Stress Disorder: A Network Analysis. JAMA Psychiatry, 74(2), 135–142. https://doi.org/10.1001/jamapsychiatry.2016.3470

Ross, D. A., Arbuckle, M. R., Travis, M. J., Dwyer, J. B., van Schalkwyk, G. I., & Ressler, K. J. (2017). An Integrated Neuroscience Perspective on Formulation and Treatment Planning for Posttraumatic Stress Disorder An Educational Review. JAMA Psychiatry, 74(4), 407–415. https://doi.org/10.1001/jamapsychiatry.2016.3325

31) Arseneault, L., Cannon, M., Fisher, H. L., Polanczyk, G., Moffitt, T. E., & Caspi, A. (2011). Childhood trauma and children's emerging psychotic symptoms: A genetically sensitive longitudinal cohort study. The American journal of psychiatry, 168(1), 65–72. https://doi.org/10.1176/appi.ajp.2010.10040567

32) Tsai, J., Harpaz-Rotem, I., Pilver, C. E., Wolf, E. J., Hoff, R. A., Levy, K.

N., Sareen, J., & Pietrzak, R. H. (2014). Latent class analysis of personality disorders in adults with posttraumatic stress disorder: results from the National Epidemiologic Survey on Alcohol and Related Conditions. The Journal of clinical psychiatry, 75(3), 276–284. https://doi.org/10.4088/JCP.13m08466

Van Dam, N. T., Rando, K., Potenza, M. N., Tuit, K., & Sinha, R. (2014). Childhood maltreatment, altered limbic neurobiology, and substance use relapse severity via trauma-specific reductions in limbic gray matter volume. JAMA psychiatry, 71(8), 917–925. https://doi.org/10.1001/jamapsychiatry.2014.680

33) Lifton, R. J. *The Protean Self*, 「Basic Books (January 4, 1995) ISBN-13」:「978-0465064212

Stevens, J. S., Harnett, N. G., Lebois, L., van Rooij, S., Ely, T. D., Roeckner, A., Vincent, N., Beaudoin, F. L., An, X., Zeng, D., Neylan, T. C., Clifford, G. D., Linnstaedt, S. D., Germine, L. T., Rauch, S. L., Lewandowski, C., Storrow, A. B., Hendry, P. L., Sheikh, S., Musey, P. I., Jr, … Ressler, K. J. (2021). Brain-Based Biotypes of Psychiatric Vulnerability in the Acute Aftermath of Trauma. *The American journal of psychiatry*, 178(11), 1037–1049. https://doi.org/10.1176/appi.ajp.2021.20101526

34) Wisco, B. E., Marx, B. P., Miller, M. W., Wolf, E. J., Mota, N. P., Krystal, J. H., Southwick, S. M., & Pietrzak, R. H. (2016). Probable Posttraumatic Stress Disorder in the US Veteran Population According to DSM-5: Results From the National Health and Resilience in Veterans Study. The Journal of clinical psychiatry, 77(11), 1503–1510. https://doi.org/10.4088/JCP.15m10188

Yurgil, K. A., Barkauskas, D. A., Vasterling, J. J., Nievergelt, C. M., Larson, G. E., Schork, N. J., Litz, B. T., Nash, W. P., Baker, D. G., & Marine Resiliency Study Team (2014). Association between traumatic brain injury and risk of posttraumatic stress disorder in active-duty Marines. JAMA psychiatry, 71(2), 149–157. https://doi.org/10.1001/jamapsychiatry.2013.3080

van Zuiden, M., Heijnen, C. J., Maas, M., Amarouchi, K., Vermetten, E., Geuze, E., & Kavelaars, A. (2012). Glucocorticoid sensitivity of leukocytes predicts PTSD, depressive and fatigue symptoms after military deployment: A prospective study. Psychoneuroendocrinology, 37(11), 1822–1836. https://doi.org/10.1016/j.psyneuen.2012.03.018

van Zuiden, M., Geuze, E., Willemen, H. L., Vermetten, E., Maas, M., Heijnen, C. J., & Kavelaars, A. (2011). Pre-existing high glucocorticoid receptor number predicting development of posttraumatic stress symptoms after military deployment. The American journal of psychiatry, 168(1), 89–96. https://doi.org/10.1176/appi.ajp.2010.10050706

James, L. M., Engdahl, B. E., Leuthold, A. C., Lewis, S. M., Kampen, E. V., & Georgopoulos, A. P. (2013). Neural Network Modulation by Trauma as a Marker of Resilience: Differences Between Veterans With Posttraumatic Stress Disorder and Resilient Controls. JAMA Psychiatry, 70(4), 410–418. https://doi.org/10.1001/jamapsychiatry.2013.878

Shin, L. M., Bush, G., Milad, M. R., Lasko, N. B., Brohawn, K. H., Hughes,

K. C., Macklin, M. L., Gold, A. L., Karpf, R. D., Orr, S. P., Rauch, S. L., & Pitman, R. K. (2011). Exaggerated activation of dorsal anterior cingulate cortex during cognitive interference: a monozygotic twin study of posttraumatic stress disorder. The American Journal of Psychiatry, 168(9), 979–985. https://doi.org/10.1176/appi.ajp.2011.09121812

Delahanty D. L. (2011). Toward the predeployment detection of risk for PTSD. *The American journal of psychiatry, 168*(1), 9–11. https://doi.org/10.1176/appi.ajp.2010.10101519

Beevers, C. G., Lee, H. J., Wells, T. T., Ellis, A. J., & Telch, M. J. (2011). Association of predeployment gaze bias for emotion stimuli with later symptoms of PTSD and depression in soldiers deployed in Iraq. *The American journal of psychiatry, 168*(7), 735–741. https://doi.org/10.1176/appi.ajp.2011.10091309

Wiborg, J. F., Rademaker, A. R., Geuze, E., Twisk, J. W., Vermetten, E., & Knoop, H. (2016). Course and Predictors of Postdeployment Fatigue: A Prospective Cohort Study in the Dutch Armed Forces. The Journal of clinical psychiatry, 77(8), 1074–1079. https://doi.org/10.4088/JCP.15m09942

Victoria Tepe, PhD , Alison Cernich, PhD, ABPP-Cn , and James Kelly, MD, Polytraumatic TBI: Perspectives from Military Medicine, Published Online:July 03, 2013 DOI/ 10.3928:00485713-20130703-04

Stein, M. B., & McAllister, T. W. (2009). Exploring the Convergence of Posttraumatic Stress Disorder and Mild Traumatic Brain Injury. American Journal of Psychiatry, 166(7), 768–776. https://doi.org/10.1176/appi.ajp.2009.08101604

Peskind, E. R., Brody, D., Cernak, I., McKee, A., & Ruff, R. L. (2013). Military- and sports-related mild traumatic brain injury: clinical presentation, management, and long-term consequences. The Journal of clinical psychiatry, 74(2), 180–188. https://doi.org/10.4088/JCP.12011co1c

Mark D. Packer, MD , Tanisha Hammill, MPH , Jeremy T. Nelson, PhD , Jonathan S. Miller, PhD , Tonym D. Gover, PhD , and John M. Scherer, PhD, MT (ASCP), Integrated Care for Multisensory Injury Published Online:July 03, 2013 https://doi.org/10.3928/00485713-20130703-09

Morey, R. A., Gold, A. L., LaBar, K. S., Beall, S. K., Brown, V. M., Haswell, C. C., Nasser, J. D., Wagner, H. R., McCarthy, G., & Mid-Atlantic MIRECC Workgroup (2012). Amygdala volume changes in posttraumatic stress disorder in a large case-controlled veterans group. Archives of general psychiatry, 69(11), 1169–1178. https://doi.org/10.1001/archgenpsychiatry.2012.50

Drabant, E. M., Ramel, W., Edge, M. D., Hyde, L. W., Kuo, J. R., Goldin, P. R., Hariri, A. R., & Gross, J. J. (2012). Neural mechanisms underlying 5-HTTLPR-related sensitivity to acute stress. The American journal of psychiatry, 169(4), 397–405. https://doi.org/10.1176/appi.ajp.2011.10111699

35) Marjorie S. Campbell, Margaret Ryan, Daniel Wright, Maria D. Devore, and Charles W. Hoge,
Postdeployment PTSD and Addictive Combat Attachment Behaviors in U.S.

References

Military Service Members
American Journal of Psychiatry 2016 173:12, 1171-1176 https://doi.org/10.1176/appi.ajp.2015.15101297

36) Schon KR, Parker APJ, Woods CG. Congenital Insensitivity to Pain Overview.
In: Adam MP, Ardinger HH, Pagon RA, et al., editors. GeneReviews® (Internet). Seattle (WA): University of Washington, Seattle; https://www.ncbi.nlm.nih.gov/books/NBK481553/
https://www.sciencedirect.com/topics/neuroscience/congenital-insensitivity-to-pain

37) Blair R. (2012). Considering anger from a cognitive neuroscience perspective. Wiley interdisciplinary reviews. Cognitive science, 3(1), 65–74. https://doi.org/10.1002/wcs.154

38) Siever L. J. (2008). Neurobiology of aggression and violence. The American journal of psychiatry, 165(4), 429–442. https://doi.org/10.1176/appi.ajp.2008.07111774

Flavia Venetucci Gouveia, PhD, Clement Hamani, MD, PhD, Erich Talamoni Fonoff, MD, PhD, Helena Brentani, MD, PhD, Eduardo Joaquim Lopes Alho, MD, PhD, Rosa Magaly Campêlo Borba de Morais, MD, Aline Luz de Souza, MD, Sérgio Paulo Rigonatti, MD, PhD, Raquel C R Martinez, PhD, Amygdala and Hypothalamus: Historical Overview With Focus on Aggression, *Neurosurgery*, Volume 85, Issue 1, July 2019, Pages 11–30, https://doi.org/10.1093/neuros/nyy635

39) Modern society provides a wide range of active and identification experiences of aggressive training. Observing sports with significant aggressive elements, especially boxing, MMA, football, soccer, and ice hockey allow participants to channel aggressive patterns, derivatives of the Roman practices of gladiators. Role playing aggressive digital games encourage the participant to express anger and murderous aggression through symbolic patterns of interaction.

Williams, R. (2017). Anger as a Basic Emotion and Its Role in Personality Building and Pathological Growth: The Neuroscientific, Developmental and Clinical Perspectives. Frontiers in Psychology, 8, 1950. https://doi.org/10.3389/fpsyg.2017.01950

Recognize and Respond to the 6 Stages of Anger :: 1eighty Consulting. (n.d.). Retrieved March 6, 2020, from https://1eightyconsulting.com/recognize-and-respond-to-the-6-stages-of-anger/

12 Steps to Using Anger Constructively. (n.d.). Dummies. Retrieved March 6, 2020, from https://www.dummies.com/health/mental-health/12-steps-to-using-anger-constructively/

Cole, P. M., Tan, P. Z., Hall, S. E., Zhang, Y., Crnic, K. A., Blair, C. B., & Li, R. (2011). Developmental changes in anger expression and attention focus: Learning to wait. Developmental Psychology, 47(4), 1078–1089. https://doi.org/10.1037/a0023813

https://signewhitson.com/workshop-and-speaking/
how-to-be-angry-an-assertive-anger-expression-skills-workshop/

40) *A martian visitor viewing media production around the world would conclude that a major component of earthling mental activity is devising methods for self protection against a wide range of external aggressive threats. In many parts of the world, this is certainly true, and aggression is a necessary element of survival. It does not explain the popularity of these fantasies in persons in otherwise "safe" life circumstances.*

41) Matthies, S., Rüsch, N., Weber, M., Lieb, K., Philipsen, A., Tuescher, O., Ebert, D., Hennig, J., & van Elst, L. T. (2012). Small amygdala-high aggression? The role of the amygdala in modulating aggression in healthy subjects. The world journal of biological psychiatry : the official journal of the World Federation of Societies of Biological Psychiatry, 13(1), 75–81. https://doi.org/10.3109/15622975.2010.541282

The Size and Connectivity of the Amygdala Predicts Anxiety. (2013). Psychology Today. https://www.psychologytoday.com/us/blog/the-athletes-way/201311/the-size-and-connectivity-the-amygdala-predicts-anxiety

Pardini, D. A., Raine, A., Erickson, K., & Loeber, R. (2014). Lower amygdala volume in men is associated with childhood aggression, early psychopathic traits, and future violence. *Biological psychiatry*, *75*(1), 73–80. https://doi.org/10.1016/j.biopsych.2013.04.003

41) Fowles, D.C. (1980), The Three Arousal Model: Implications of Gray's Two-Factor Learning Theory for Heart Rate, Electrodermal Activity, and Psychopathy. Psychophysiology, 17: 87-104. https://doi.org/10.1111/j.1469-8986.1980.tb00117.x

Yamaguchi, T., Wei, D., Song, S.C. et al. Posterior amygdala regulates sexual and aggressive behaviors in male mice. *Nat Neurosci* **23**, 1111–1124 (2020). https://doi.org/10.1038/s41593-020-0675-x

Klasen, M., Wolf, D., Eisner, P. D., Eggermann, T., Zerres, K., Zepf, F. D., Weber, R., & Mathiak, K. (2019). Serotonergic Contributions to Human Brain Aggression Networks. *Frontiers in neuroscience*, *13*, 42. https://doi.org/10.3389/fnins.2019.00042

Bacq, A., Astori, S., Gebara, E. *et al.* Amygdala GluN2B-NMDAR dysfunction is critical in abnormal aggression of neurodevelopmental origin induced by St8sia2 deficiency. *Mol Psychiatry* **25**, (2020). https://doi.org/10.1038/s41380-018-0132-3

42) Psychophysiologic response in polygraph examination attempts to identify persons with low autonomic response, but the results are inconsistent enough to prevent their use in legal proceedings.
https://www.psychologytoday.com/us/blog/the-nature-deception/202001/do-lie-detector-tests-really-work
https://www.polygraph.org/polygraph-validity-research

References

Nora Maria Raschle, Willeke Martine Menks, Lynn Valérie Fehlbaum, Ebongo Tshomba, Christina Stadler, Structural and Functional Alterations in Right Dorsomedial Prefrontal and Left Insular Cortex Co-Localize in Adolescents with Aggressive Behaviour: An ALE Meta-Analysis, https://doi.org/10.1371/journal.pone.0136553 https://journals.plos.org/plosone/article?id=10.1371/journal.pone.0136553

Trimble, M. R., & Van Elst, L. T. (1999). On some clinical implications of the ventral striatum and the extended amygdala. Investigations of aggression. Annals of the New York Academy of Sciences, 877, 638–644. https://doi.org/10.1111/j.1749-6632.1999.tb09293.x

Coccaro E. F. (2012). Intermittent explosive disorder as a disorder of impulsive aggression for DSM-5. The American journal of psychiatry, 169(6), 577–588. https://doi.org/10.1176/appi.ajp.2012.11081259

43) Koenigs, M., Baskin-Sommers, A., Zeier, J., & Newman, J. P. (2010). Investigating the neural correlates of psychopathy: a critical review. Molecular Psychiatry, 16(8), 792–799. https://doi.org/10.1038/mp.2010.124

Blair, R. J. R. (2003). Neurobiological basis of psychopathy. British Journal of Psychiatry, 182(1), 5–7. https://doi.org/10.1192/bjp.182.1.5

R Blair R. J. (2013). Psychopathy: cognitive and neural dysfunction. Dialogues in clinical neuroscience, 15(2), 181–190. https://doi.org/10.31887/DCNS.2013.15.2/rblair https://www.ncbi.nlm.nih.gov/pmc/articles/PMC3811089/

Patrick, C.J. and Bernat, E.M. (2009). Neurobiology of Psychopathy. In Handbook of Neuroscience for the Behavioral Sciences (eds G.G. Berntson and J.T. Cacioppo). https://doi.org/10.1002/9780470478509.neubb002057

Siep, N., Tonnaer, F., van de Ven, V., Arntz, A., Raine, A., & Cima, M. (2019). Anger provocation increases limbic and decreases medial prefrontal cortex connectivity with the left amygdala in reactive aggressive violent offenders. *Brain imaging and behavior*, *13*(5), 1311–1323. https://doi.org/10.1007/s11682-018-9945-6

Seara-Cardoso, A., & Viding, E. (2014). Functional Neuroscience of Psychopathic Personality in Adults. Journal of Personality, 83(6), 723–737. https://doi.org/10.1111/jopy.12113

Hyde, L. W., Byrd, A. L., Votruba-Drzal, E., Hariri, A. R., & Manuck, S. B. (2014). Amygdala reactivity and negative emotionality: Divergent correlates of antisocial personality and psychopathy traits in a community sample. Journal of Abnormal Psychology, 123(1), 214–224. https://doi.org/10.1037/a0035467

Raine, A., & Yang, Y. (2006). Neural foundations to moral reasoning and antisocial behavior. Social Cognitive and Affective Neuroscience, 1(3), 203–213. https://doi.org/10.1093/scan/nsl033

Yang, Y., Glenn, A. L., & Raine, A. (2008). Brain abnormalities in antisocial individuals: implications for the law. Behavioral Sciences & the Law, 26(1), 65–83. https://doi.org/10.1002/bsl.788

Gao, Y., Glenn, A. L., Schug, R. A., Yang, Y., & Raine, A. (2009). The neurobiology of psychopathy: a neurodevelopmental perspective. Canadian journal of psychiatry. Revue canadienne de psychiatrie, 54(12), https://doi.org/10.1177/070674370905401204

Lozier, L. M., Cardinale, E. M., VanMeter, J. W., & Marsh, A. A. (2014). Mediation of the Relationship Between Callous-Unemotional Traits and Proactive Aggression by Amygdala Response to Fear Among Children With Conduct Problems. JAMA Psychiatry, 71(6), 627. https://doi.org/10.1001/jamapsychiatry.2013.4540

van Dongen J. (2020). The Empathic Brain of Psychopaths: From Social Science to Neuroscience in Empathy. Frontiers in psychology, 11, 695. https://doi.org/10.3389/fpsyg.2020.00695

Wang, P., Baker, L. A., Gao, Y., Raine, A., & Lozano, D. I. (2012). Psychopathic traits and physiological responses to aversive stimuli in children aged 9-11 years. Journal of abnormal child psychology, 40(5), 759–769 https://doi.org/10.1007/s10802-011-9606-3

Werner, K. B., Few, L. R., & Bucholz, K. K. (2015). Epidemiology, Comorbidity, and Behavioral Genetics of Antisocial Personality Disorder and Psychopathy. Psychiatric annals, 45(4), 195–199. https://doi.org/10.3928/00485713-20150401-08

Marsh, A. A., Finger, E. C., Mitchell, D. G. V., Reid, M. E., Sims, C., Kosson, D. S., Towbin, K. E., Leibenluft, E., Pine, D. S., & Blair, R. J. R. (2008). Reduced Amygdala Response to Fearful Expressions in Children and Adolescents With Callous-Unemotional Traits and Disruptive Behavior Disorders. American Journal of Psychiatry, 165(6), https://doi.org/10.1176/appi.ajp.2007.07071145

Silberg, J. L., Rutter, M., Tracy, K., Maes, H. H., & Eaves, L. (2007). Etiological heterogeneity in the development of antisocial behavior: the Virginia Twin Study of Adolescent Behavioral Development and the Young Adult Follow-Up. Psychological Medicine, 37(8), 1193–1202. https://doi.org/10.1017/S0033291707000293

Dolan, M. (2008). Neurobiological Disturbances in Callous-Unemotional Youths. American Journal of Psychiatry, 165(6), 668–670. https://doi.org/10.1176/appi.ajp.2008.08030393

White, S. F., Marsh, A. A., Fowler, K. A., Schechter, J. C., Adalio, C., Pope, K., Sinclair, S., Pine, D. S., & Blair, R. J. R. (2012). Reduced Amygdala Response in Youths With Disruptive Behavior Disorders and Psychopathic Traits: Decreased Emotional Response Versus Increased Top-Down Attention to Nonemotional Features. American Journal of Psychiatry, 169(7), 750–758. https://doi.org/10.1176/appi.ajp.2012.11081270

Hyde, L. W., Waller, R., Trentacosta, C. J., Shaw, D. S., Neiderhiser, J. M., Ganiban, J. M., Reiss, D., & Leve, L. D. (2016). Heritable and non-heritable pathways to early callous-unemotional behaviors. The American Journal of Psychiatry, 173(9), 903–910. https://doi.org/10.1176/appi.ajp.2016.15111381

Gao, Y., Raine, A., Venables, P. H., Dawson, M. E., & Mednick, S. A. (2010). Association of poor childhood fear conditioning and adult crime. The American journal of psychiatry, 167(1), 56–60. https://doi.org/10.1176/appi.ajp.2009.09040499

Barker, E. D., & Maughan, B. (2009). Differentiating early-onset persistent versus childhood-limited conduct problem youth. The American journal of psychiatry, 166(8), 900–908. https://doi.org/10.1176/appi.ajp.2009.08121770

44) "The Minority Report" Phil Dick.https://en.wikipedia.org/wiki/The_Minority_Report

Hofmann, S. G., Korte, K. J., & Suvak, M. K. (2009). The Upside of Being Socially Anxious: Psychopathic Attributes and Social Anxiety are Negatively Associated. *Journal of social and clinical psychology*, 28(6), 714–727. https://doi.org/10.1521/jscp.2009.28.6.714

Scott, S., Briskman, J., & O'Connor, T. G. (2014). Early prevention of antisocial personality: long-term follow-up of two randomized controlled trials comparing indicated and selective approaches. *The American journal of psychiatry, 171*(6), 649–657. https://doi.org/10.1176/appi.ajp.2014.13050697

CHAPTER NINE REFERENCES

1) DSM V criteria for addictive disorders. NIDA Research Monograph 54, 1984

2) Nestler, E. J. (1994). Molecular Neurobiology of Drug Addiction. *Neuropsychopharmacology*, 11(2), 77–87. https://doi.org/10.1038/npp.1994.37 https://www.nature.com/articles/npp199437.pdf?origin=ppub

Nestler, E. J. (2001). Molecular basis of long-term plasticity underlying addiction. *Nature Reviews Neuroscience*, 2(2), 119–128. https://doi.org/10.1038/35053570

3) Morse, R. M., & Flavin, D. K. (1992). The Definition of Alcoholism. *JAMA, 268*(8), 1012–1014. https://doi.org/10.1001/jama.1992.03490080086030 https://www.asam.org/quality-care/definition-of-addiction

4) https://en.wikipedia.org/wiki/Brain_stimulation_reward

The ability to use variable interval rewards extended out to create permanent response is documented but the evidence that animal subjects die as a result appears to be an "urban legend".

5) Volkow, N. D., & Boyle, M. (2018). Neuroscience of Addiction: Relevance to Prevention and Treatment. *The American journal of psychiatry, 175*(8), 729–740. https://doi.org/10.1176/appi.ajp.2018.17101174

Uhl, G. R., Koob, G. F., & Cable, J. (2019). The neurobiology of addiction. *Annals of the New York Academy of Sciences, 1451*(1), 5–28. https://doi.org/10.1111/nyas.13989

Hyman, S. E., Malenka, R. C., & Nestler, E. J. (2006). NEURAL MECHANISMS OF ADDICTION: The Role of Reward-Related Learning and Memory. *Annual Review of Neuroscience, 29*(1), 565–598. https://doi.org/10.1146/annurev.neuro.29.051605.113009

6) *Chapter 2—How Stimulants Affect the Brain and Behavior*. Nih.Gov; Substance Abuse and Mental Health Services Administration (US). https://www.ncbi.nlm.nih.gov/books/NBK64328/

Salgado, S., & Kaplitt, M. G. (2015). The Nucleus Accumbens: A Comprehensive Review. *Stereotactic and functional neurosurgery, 93*(2), 75–93. https://doi.org/10.1159/000368279

Shirayama, Y., & Chaki, S. (2006). Neurochemistry of the nucleus accumbens and its relevance to depression and antidepressant action in rodents. *Current neuropharmacology, 4*(4), 277–291. https://doi.org/10.2174/157015906778520773

Feltenstein, M. W., & See, R. E. (2008). The neurocircuitry of addiction: an overview. *British journal of pharmacology, 154*(2), 261–274. https://doi.org/10.1038/bjp.2008.51

Schippers, M. C., Bruinsma, B., Gaastra, M., Mesman, T. I., Denys, D., De Vries, T. J., & Pattij, T. (2017). Deep Brain Stimulation of the Nucleus Accumbens Core Affects Trait Impulsivity in a Baseline-Dependent Manner. *Frontiers in behavioral neuroscience, 11*, 52. https://doi.org/10.3389/fnbeh.2017.00052 https://www.ncbi.nlm.nih.gov/pmc/articles/PMC5362621/

Bardo, M. T. (1998). Neuropharmacological Mechanisms of Drug Reward: Beyond Dopamine in the Nucleus Accumbens. *Critical Reviews™ in Neurobiology, 12*(1–2), 37–68. https://doi.org/10.1615/critrevneurobiol.v12.i1-2.30

Smith-Roe, S. L., & Kelley, A. E. (2000). Coincident activation of NMDA and dopamine D1 receptors within the nucleus accumbens core is required for appetitive instrumental learning. The Journal of Neuroscience: The Official Journal of the Society for Neuroscience, 20(20), 7737–7742. https://www.ncbi.nlm.nih.gov/pubmed/11027236

7) Koob, G. F., & Volkow, N. D. (2009). Neurocircuitry of Addiction. *Neuropsychopharmacology, 35*(1), 217–238. https://doi.org/10.1038/npp.2009.110

Feltenstein, M. W., & See, R. E. (2009). The neurocircuitry of addiction: an overview. *British Journal of Pharmacology, 154*(2), 261–274. https://doi.org/10.1038/bjp.2008.51

8) *The Truth about Gateway Drugs and Addiction*. (2019). American Addiction Centers. https://americanaddictioncenters.org/the-addiction-cycle/gateway-drugs

Nkansah-Amankra, S., & Minelli, M. (2016). "Gateway hypothesis" and early drug use: Additional findings from tracking a population-based sample of adolescents to adulthood. *Preventive Medicine Reports, 4*, 134–141. https://doi.org/10.1016/j.pmedr.2016.05.003

9) Koob, G. F. (2009). Brain stress systems in the amygdala and addiction. *Brain Research, 1293*, 61–75. https://doi.org/10.1016/j.brainres.2009.03.038

References

Fox, A. S., & Shackman, A. J. (2019). The central extended amygdala in fear and anxiety: Closing the gap between mechanistic and neuroimaging research. *Neuroscience letters*, *693*, 58–67. https://doi.org/10.1016/j.neulet.2017.11.056

9) Wise, R. A., & Koob, G. F. (2013). The Development and Maintenance of Drug Addiction. *Neuropsychopharmacology*, *39*(2), 254–262. https://doi.org/10.1038/npp.2013.261

Koob GF, Arends MA, Le Moal M: Drugs, Addiction, and the Brain. San Diego, Academic Press, 2014.)

10) Piazza, P. V., & Deroche-Gamonet, V. (2013). A multistep general theory of transition to addiction. *Psychopharmacology*, *229*(3), 387–413. https://doi.org/10.1007/s00213-013-3224-4

Van Bockstaele E. J. (2012). The neurobiology of addiction-like behaviors. *ILAR journal*, *53*(1), 1–3. https://doi.org/10.1093/ilar.53.1.1a

Zubieta, J. K., & Stohler, C. S. (2009). Neurobiological mechanisms of placebo responses. *Annals of the New York Academy of Sciences*, *1156*, 198–210. https://doi.org/10.1111/j.1749-6632.2009.04424.x

11) Hyman, S. E., Malenka, R. C., & Nestler, E. J. (2006). NEURAL MECHANISMS OF ADDICTION: The Role of Reward-Related Learning and Memory. *Annual Review of Neuroscience*, *29*(1), 565–598. https://doi.org/10.1146/annurev.neuro.29.051605.113009

Beck SM, Locke HS, Savine AC, Jimura K, Braver TS (2010) Primary and Secondary Rewards Differentially Modulate Neural Activity Dynamics during Working Memory. PLoS ONE 5(2): e9251. https://doi.org/10.1371/journal.pone.0009251

Sescousse, G., Caldú, X., Segura, B., & Dreher, J.-C. (2013). Processing of primary and secondary rewards: A quantitative meta-analysis and review of human functional neuroimaging studies. *Neuroscience & Biobehavioral Reviews*, *37*(4), 681–696. https://doi.org/10.1016/j.neubiorev.2013.02.002

Wang, D., Liu, T., & Shi, J. (2017). Development of Monetary and Social Reward Processes. *Scientific Reports*, *7*(1), 1–10. https://doi.org/10.1038/s41598-017-11558-6

Lin, A., Adolphs, R., & Rangel, A. (2012). Social and monetary reward learning engage overlapping neural substrates. *Social Cognitive and Affective Neuroscience*, *7*(3), 274–281. https://doi.org/10.1093/scan/nsr006

Sescousse, G., Barbalat, G., Domenech, P., & Dreher, J. C. (2013). Imbalance in the sensitivity to different types of rewards in pathological gambling. *Brain : a journal of neurology*, *136*(Pt 8), 2527–2538. https://doi.org/10.1093/brain/awt126

Everitt, B. J., Belin, D., Economidou, D., Pelloux, Y., Dalley, J. W., & Robbins, T. W. (2008). Neural mechanisms underlying the vulnerability to develop compulsive drug-seeking habits and addiction. *Philosophical Transactions of the Royal Society B: Biological Sciences*, *363*(1507), 3125–3135. https://doi.org/10.1098/rstb.2008.0089

Everitt, B. J. (2014). Neural and psychological mechanisms underlying compulsive drug seeking habits and drug memories - indications for novel treatments of addiction. *European Journal of Neuroscience, 40*(1), 2163–2182. https://doi.org/10.1111/ejn.12644

Cooper, S., Robison, A. J., & Mazei-Robison, M. S. (2017). Reward Circuitry in Addiction. *Neurotherapeutics : the journal of the American Society for Experimental NeuroTherapeutics, 14*(3), 687–697. https://doi.org/10.1007/s13311-017-0525-z

Bernheim, B. D., & Rangel, A. (2002, November 1). *Addiction and Cue-Conditioned Cognitive Processes*. National Bureau of Economic Research. http://www.nber.org/papers/w9329

12) Nestler, E. J., Barrot, M., & Self, D. W. (2001). ΔFosB: A sustained molecular switch for addiction. *Proceedings of the National Academy of Sciences of the United States of America, 98*(20), 11042–11046. https://doi.org/10.1073/pnas.191352698

Vialou, V., Robison, A. J., Laplant, Q. C., Covington, H. E., 3rd, Dietz, D. M., Ohnishi, Y. N., Mouzon, E., Rush, A. J., 3rd, Watts, E. L., Wallace, D. L., Iñiguez, S. D., Ohnishi, Y. H., Steiner, M. A., Warren, B. L., Krishnan, V., Bolaños, C. A., Neve, R. L., Ghose, S., Berton, O., Tamminga, C. A., ... Nestler, E. J. (2010). DeltaFosB in brain reward circuits mediates resilience to stress and antidepressant responses. *Nature neuroscience, 13*(6), 745–752. https://doi.org/10.1038/nn.2551

Ruffle J. K. (2014). Molecular neurobiology of addiction: what's all the (Δ) FosB about?. *The American journal of drug and alcohol abuse, 40*(6), 428–437. https://doi.org/10.3109/00952990.2014.933840

Herman, M. A., & Roberto, M. (2015). The addicted brain: understanding the neurophysiological mechanisms of addictive disorders. *Frontiers in Integrative Neuroscience, 9.* https://doi.org/10.3389/fnint.2015.00018

Nora D. Volkow, Michael Michaelides, and Ruben Baler, The Neuroscience of Drug Reward and Addiction, Physiological Reviews 2019 99:4, 2115-2140 https://journals.physiology.org/action/showCitFormats?doi=10.1152%2Fphysrev.00014.2018

13) Schukit, M. A. (2014). A brief history of research on the genetics of alcohol and other drug use disorders. *Journal of Studies on Alcohol and Drugs. Supplement, 75 Suppl 17*(Suppl 17), 59–67.

Schuckit, M. A. (2009). An overview of genetic influences in alcoholism. *Journal of Substance Abuse Treatment, 36*(1), S5–14.

Edenberg, H. J., & Foroud, T. (2006). The genetics of alcoholism: identifying specific genes through family studies. *Addiction biology, 11*(3-4), 386–396. https://doi.org/10.1111/j.1369-1600.2006.00035.x

Radel, M., & Goldman, D. (2001). Pharmacogenetics of Alcohol Response and Alcoholism: The Interplay of Genes and Environmental Factors in Thresholds for Alcoholism. *Drug Metabolism and Disposition, 29*(4), 489–494. http://dmd.

References

aspetjournals.org/content/29/4/489.long

Koob G. F. (2015). Alcohol use disorders: tracts, twins, and trajectories. *The American journal of psychiatry*, *172*(6), 499–501. https://doi.org/10.1176/appi.ajp.2015.15020240 https://ajp.psychiatryonline.org/doi/10.1176/appi.ajp.2015.15020240

14) Ehlers, C. L., & Gizer, I. R. (2013). Evidence for a Genetic Component for Substance Dependence in Native Americans. *American Journal of Psychiatry*, *170*(2), 154–164. https://doi.org/10.1176/appi.ajp.2012.12010113

Walters RK, Polimanti R, Johnson EC, McClintick JN, **and multiple authors**. Transancestral GWAS of alcohol dependence reveals common genetic underpinnings with psychiatric disorders. Nat Neurosci. 2018 Dec;21(12) https://doi.org/10.1038/s41593-018-0275-1

Bevilacqua, L., & Goldman, D. (2009). Genes and addictions. *Clinical pharmacology and therapeutics*, *85*(4), 359–361. https://doi.org/10.1038/clpt.2009.6

Sanchez-Roige, S., Palmer, A. A., Fontanillas, P., Elson, S. L., 23andMe Research Team, the Substance Use Disorder Working Group of the Psychiatric Genomics Consortium, Adams, M. J., Howard, D. M., Edenberg, H. J., Davies, G., Crist, R. C., Deary, I. J., McIntosh, A. M., & Clarke, T. K. (2019). Genome-Wide Association Study Meta-Analysis of the Alcohol Use Disorders Identification Test (AUDIT) in Two Population-Based Cohorts. *The American journal of psychiatry*, *176*(2), 107–118. https://doi.org/10.1176/appi.ajp.2018.18040369

Pollock, J. D., & Lossie, A. C. (2019). Phenotype and Environment Matter: Discovering the Genetic and Epigenetic Architecture of Alcohol Use Disorders. *The American journal of psychiatry*, *176*(2), 92–95. https://doi.org/10.1176/appi.ajp.2018.18121364

McGue M. (1997). A behavioral-genetic perspective on children of alcoholics. *Alcohol health and research world*, *21*(3), 210–217.

Sigvardsson, S., Bohman, M., & Cloninger, C. R. (1996). Replication of the Stockholm Adoption Study of alcoholism. Confirmatory cross-fostering analysis. *Archives of general psychiatry*, *53*(8), 681–687. https://doi.org/10.1001/archpsyc.1996.01830080033007

Kendler, K. S., Sundquist, K., Ohlsson, H., Palmér, K., Maes, H., Winkleby, M. A., & Sundquist, J. (2012). Genetic and Familial Environmental Influences on the Risk for Drug Abuse. *Archives of General Psychiatry*, *69*(7). https://doi.org/10.1001/archgenpsychiatry.2011.2112

Kendler, K. S., & Myers, J. (2009). A developmental twin study of church attendance and alcohol and nicotine consumption: a model for analyzing the changing impact of genes and environment. *The American journal of psychiatry*, *166*(10), 1150–1155. https://doi.org/10.1176/appi.ajp.2009.09020182
https://en.wikipedia.org/wiki/Dionysian_Mysteries

15) Hancock, D. B., Markunas, C. A., Bierut, L. J., & Johnson, E. O. (2018). Human Genetics of Addiction: New Insights and Future Directions. *Current*

psychiatry reports, 20(2), 8. https://doi.org/10.1007/s11920-018-0873-3
Schellekens, A. F. A., Franke, B., Ellenbroek, B., Cools, A., Jong, C. A. J. de, Buitelaar, J. K., & Verkes, R.-J. (2012). Reduced Dopamine Receptor Sensitivity as an Intermediate Phenotype in Alcohol Dependence and the Role of the COMT Val158Met and DRD2 Taq1A Genotypes. *Archives of General Psychiatry, 69*(4), 339–348. https://doi.org/10.1001/archgenpsychiatry.2011.1335
16) Hah, J. M., Bateman, B. T., Ratliff, J., Curtin, C., & Sun, E. (2017). Chronic Opioid Use After Surgery: Implications for Perioperative Management in the Face of the Opioid Epidemic. *Anesthesia and analgesia, 125*(5), 1733–1740. https://doi.org/10.1213/ANE.0000000000002458
www.ncbi.nlm.nih.gov/pmc/articles/PMC6119469/pdf/nihms-1504139.pdf
Stanton, M. D. (1976). Drugs, Vietnam, and the Vietnam veteran: an overview. *The American Journal of Drug and Alcohol Abuse, 3*(4), 557–570. https://doi.org/10.3109/00952997609014295
Lee N. Robins, Darlene H. Davis, and David N. Nurco, 1974: How Permanent Was Vietnam Drug Addiction? American Journal of Public Health **64**, 38_43, https://doi.org/10.2105/AJPH.64.12_Suppl.38
Why Is Heroin So Addictive? (2018, February 13). Drug Rehab. https://www.drugrehab.com/addiction/drugs/heroin/why-is-heroin-so-addictive/
Hatsukami DK, Fischman MW. Crack Cocaine and Cocaine Hydrochloride: Are the Differences Myth or Reality? *JAMA.* 1996;276(19):1580–1588. doi:10.1001/jama.1996.03540190052029
https://jamanetwork.com/journals/jama/article-abstract/410806
17) Cheng, H., Liu, J. Alterations in Amygdala Connectivity in Internet Addiction Disorder. *Sci Rep* **10**, 2370 (2020). https://doi.org/10.1038/s41598-020-59195-w   https://www.nature.com/articles/s41598-020-59195-w#citeas
Goodman, J., & Packard, M. G. (2016). Memory Systems and the Addicted Brain. *Frontiers in psychiatry, 7*, 24. https://doi.org/10.3389/fpsyt.2016.00024
Oren Contreras-Rodriguez, Tracy Burrows, Kirrilly M. Pursey, Peter Stanwell, Linden Parkes, Carles Soriano-Mas, Antonio Verdejo-Garcia, Food addiction linked to changes in ventral striatum functional connectivity between fasting and satiety,Appetite,Volume 133,2019,Pages 18-23,ISSN 0195-6663, https://doi.org/10.1016/j.appet.2018.10.009
Morgenstern, J., Naqvi, N. H., Debellis, R., & Breiter, H. C. (2013). The contributions of cognitive neuroscience and neuroimaging to understanding mechanisms of behavior change in addiction. *Psychology of addictive behaviors : journal of the Society of Psychologists in Addictive Behaviors, 27*(2), 336–350. https://doi.org/10.1037/a0032435
Naqvi, N. H., & Morgenstern, J. (2015). Cognitive Neuroscience Approaches to Understanding Behavior Change in Alcohol Use Disorder Treatments. *Alcohol research : current reviews, 37*(1), 29–38.
Hu, Y., Salmeron, B. J., Gu, H., Stein, E. A., & Yang, Y. (2015). Impaired functional connectivity within and between frontostriatal circuits and its association

with compulsive drug use and trait impulsivity in cocaine addiction. *JAMA psychiatry*, *72*(6), 584–592. https://doi.org/10.1001/jamapsychiatry.2015.1

Yi-Yuan Tang, Michael I. Posner, Mary K. Rothbart, Nora D. Volkow, Circuitry of self-control and its role in reducing addiction, Trends in Cognitive Sciences Volume 19, ISSUE 8, P439-444, DOI:https://doi.org/10.1016/j.tics.2015.06.007

Seo, D., Lacadie, C. M., Tuit, K., Hong, K.-I., Constable, R. T., & Sinha, R. (2013). Disrupted Ventromedial Prefrontal Function, Alcohol Craving, and Subsequent Relapse Risk. *JAMA Psychiatry*, *70*(7), 727. https://doi.org/10.1001/jamapsychiatry.2013.762

Volkow, N. D., Tomasi, D., Wang, G.-J., Telang, F., Fowler, J. S., Logan, J., Maynard, L. J., & Wong, C. T. (2013). Predominance of D2 Receptors in Mediating Dopamine's Effects in Brain Metabolism: Effects of Alcoholism. *Journal of Neuroscience*, *33*(10), 4527–4535. https://doi.org/10.1523/jneurosci.5261-12.2013

18) Narendran, R., Tollefson, S., Himes, M. L., Paris, J., Lopresti, B., Ciccocioppo, R., & Mason, N. S. (2019). Nociceptin Receptors Upregulated in Cocaine Use Disorder: A Positron Emission Tomography Imaging Study Using (^{11}C)NOP-1A. *The American journal of psychiatry*, *176*(6), 468–476. https://doi.org/10.1176/appi.ajp.2019.18081007

Goldstein, R. Z., & Volkow, N. D. (2002). Drug addiction and its underlying neurobiological basis: neuroimaging evidence for the involvement of the frontal cortex. *The American journal of psychiatry*, *159*(10), 1642–1652. https://doi.org/10.1176/appi.ajp.159.10.1642

Hester, R., & Garavan, H. (2004). Executive dysfunction in cocaine addiction: evidence for discordant frontal, cingulate, and cerebellar activity. *The Journal of neuroscience : the official journal of the Society for Neuroscience*, *24*(49), 11017–11022. https://doi.org/10.1523/JNEUROSCI.3321-04.2004

Xun Liu, Jacqueline Hairston, Madeleine Schrier, Jin Fan,

Zhao, Y., Sallie, S. N., Cui, H., Zeng, N., Du, J., Yuan, T., Li, D., De Ridder, D., & Zhang, C. (2020). Anterior Cingulate Cortex in Addiction: New Insights for Neuromodulation. *Neuromodulation : journal of the International Neuromodulation Society*, 10.1111/ner.13291. Advance online publication. https://doi.org/10.1111/ner.13291

Volkow, N. D., Wang, G. J., Fowler, J. S., Tomasi, D., & Telang, F. (2011). Addiction: beyond dopamine reward circuitry. *Proceedings of the National Academy of Sciences of the United States of America*, *108*(37), 15037–15042. https://doi.org/10.1073/pnas.1010654108

Babor, T. F., Hofmann, M., DelBoca, F. K., Hesselbrock, V., Meyer, R. E., Dolinsky, Z. S., & Rounsaville, B. (1992). Types of alcoholics, I. Evidence for an empirically derived typology based on indicators of vulnerability and severity. *Archives of general psychiatry*, *49*(8), 599–608. https://doi.org/10.1001/archpsyc.1992.01820080007002

Schuckit, M. A., Tipp, J. E., Smith, T. L., Shapiro, E., Hesselbrock, V. M.,

Bucholz, K. K., Reich, T., & Nurnberger, J. I., Jr (1995). An evaluation of type A and B alcoholics. *Addiction (Abingdon, England)*, *90*(9), 1189–1203. https://doi.org/10.1046/j.1360-0443.1995.90911894.x

Litt MD, Babor TF, DelBoca FK, Kadden RM, Cooney NL. Types of Alcoholics, II: Application of an Empirically Derived Typology to Treatment Matching. *Arch Gen Psychiatry*. 1992;49(8):609–614. DOI: 10.1001/archpsyc.1992.01820080017003

Ducci, F., Roy, A., Shen, P. H., Yuan, Q., Yuan, N. P., Hodgkinson, C. A., Goldman, L. R., & Goldman, D. (2009). Association of substance use disorders with childhood trauma but not African genetic heritage in an African American cohort. *The American journal of psychiatry*, *166*(9), 1031–1040. https://doi.org/10.1176/appi.ajp.2009.08071068

19) Crews, F., He, J., & Hodge, C. (2007). Adolescent cortical development: a critical period of vulnerability for addiction. *Pharmacology, biochemistry, and behavior*, *86*(2), 189–199. https://doi.org/10.1016/j.pbb.2006.12.001

Chambers, R. A., Taylor, J. R., & Potenza, M. N. (2003). Developmental neurocircuitry of motivation in adolescence: a critical period of addiction vulnerability. *The American journal of psychiatry*, *160*(6), 1041–1052. https://doi.org/10.1176/appi.ajp.160.6.1041

Cousijn, J., Luijten, M., & Ewing, S. W. F. (2018). Adolescent resilience to addiction: a social plasticity hypothesis. *The Lancet. Child & Adolescent Health*, *2*(1), 69–78. https://doi.org/10.1016/S2352-4642(17)30148-7

20) Kendler, K. S., Ohlsson, H., Fagan, A. A., Lichtenstein, P., Sundquist, J., & Sundquist, K. (2018). Academic Achievement and Drug Abuse Risk Assessed Using Instrumental Variable Analysis and Co-relative Designs. *JAMA Psychiatry*, *75*(11), 1182–1188. https://doi.org/10.1001/jamapsychiatry.2018.2337

Morin, J. G., Afzali, M. H., Bourque, J., Stewart, S. H., Séguin, J. R., O'Leary-Barrett, M., & Conrod, P. J. (2019). A Population-Based Analysis of the Relationship Between Substance Use and Adolescent Cognitive Development. *The American journal of psychiatry*, *176*(2), 98–106. https://doi.org/10.1176/appi.ajp.2018.18020202

21) Keith McMahon, **The Fall of the God of Money: Opium Smoking in Nineteenth-Century China,** Rowan and Littlefield, 978-0-7425-1803-2 • Paperback • June 2002

Wartik, N. (2020, January 31). What Does It Mean to Have a Serious Drinking Problem? *The New York Times*. https://www.nytimes.com/2020/01/31/sunday-review/alcohol-drinking-problem.html

International Comparisons of Alcohol Consumption. (2015). Nih.Gov. https://pubs.niaaa.nih.gov/publications/arh27-1/95-109.htm

Marsh, S., Stefanou, E., & Guardian readers. (2018, March 4). *Which countries have the worst drinking cultures?* The Guardian; The Guardian. https://www.theguardian.com/society/2016/apr/15/

References

which-countries-worst-alcohol-binge-drinking-cultures

Dombrowski, K., Crawford, D., Khan, B., & Tyler, K. (2016). Current Rural Drug Use in the US Midwest. *Journal of Drug Abuse*, *2*(3), 22. https://www.ncbi.nlm.nih.gov/pmc/articles/PMC5119476/

Courtney, K. E., & Ray, L. A. (2014). Methamphetamine: an update on epidemiology, pharmacology, clinical phenomenology, and treatment literature. *Drug and alcohol dependence*, *143*, 11–21. https://doi.org/10.1016/j.drugalcdep.2014.08.003

Substance Use and Misuse in Rural Areas https://www.ruralhealthinfo.org/topics/substance-use

22) Luthar, S. S., & D'Avanzo, K. (1999). Contextual factors in substance use: a study of suburban and inner-city adolescents. *Development and psychopathology*, *11*(4), 845–867. https://doi.org/10.1017/s0954579499002357

Venkataramani, A. S., Bair, E. F., O'Brien, R. L., & Tsai, A. C. (2019). Association Between Automotive Assembly Plant Closures and Opioid Overdose Mortality in the United States. *JAMA Internal Medicine*. https://doi.org/10.1001/jamainternmed.2019.5686

Steven A. King, M. D. (2018, June 14). *The Opioid Epidemic: Who Is to Blame?* Psychiatric Times. https://www.psychiatrictimes.com/substance-use-disorder/opioid-epidemic-who-blamehttp://bowlingalone.com/

23) Whitesell, M., Bachand, A., Peel, J., & Brown, M. (2013). Familial, social, and individual factors contributing to risk for adolescent substance use. *Journal of addiction*, *2013*, 579310. https://doi.org/10.1155/2013/579310

Covington, J. (1997). The Social Construction Of the Minority Drug Problem. *Social Justice*, *24*(4 (70)), 117–147. https://www.jstor.org/stable/29767045?seq=1

https://www.nytimes.com/2018/04/21/opinion/an-opioid-crisis-foretold.html

24) Tay, N., Macare, C., Liu, Y., Ruggeri, B., Jia, T., Chu, C., Biondo, F., Ing, A., Luo, Q., Sarkysian, D., Banaschewski, T., Barker, G. J., Bokde, A., Bromberg, U., Büchel, C., Quinlan, E. B., Desrivières, S., Flor, H., Frouin, V., Garavan, H., … IMAGEN Consortium (2019). Allele-Specific Methylation of SPDEF: A Novel Moderator of Psychosocial Stress and Substance Abuse. *The American journal of psychiatry*, *176*(2), 146–155. https://doi.org/10.1176/appi.ajp.2018.17121360

Riehm, K. E., Feder, K. A., Tormohlen, K. N., Crum, R. M., Young, A. S., Green, K. M., … Mojtabai, R. (2019). Associations Between Time Spent Using Social Media and Internalizing and Externalizing Problems Among US Youth. *JAMA Psychiatry*, 1. https://doi.org/10.1001/jamapsychiatry.2019.2325

Bowling Alone: The Collapse And Revival Of American Community, by Robert D. Putnam

Wada, K. (2011). The history and current state of drug abuse in Japan. *Annals of the New York Academy of Sciences*, *1216*(1), 62–72. https://doi.org/10.1111/j.1749-6632.2010.05914.x

Japan, the place with the strangest drug debate in the world. (n.d.). OpenDemocracy. Retrieved March 8, 2020, from https://www.opendemocracy.net/en/japan-place-with-strangest-drug-debate-in-world/

Behrens, K. Y. (2004). A Multifaceted View of the Concept of Amae: Reconsidering the Indigenous Japanese Concept of Relatedness. *Human Development, 47*(1), https://www.jstor.org/stable/26763778

25) https://www.pewtrusts.org/en/research-and-analysis/issue-briefs/2018/03/more-imprisonment-does-not-reduce-state-drug-problems

https://www.hrw.org/news/2016/10/12/us-disastrous-toll-criminalizing-drug-use

Volkow, N.D. Addiction should be treated, not penalized. *Neuropsychopharmacol.* **46,** 2048–2050 (2021). https://doi.org/10.1038/s41386-021-01087-2

https://www.newyorker.com/news/annals-of-populism/is-there-a-case-for-legalizing-heroin?

A History of War in Six Drugs - The New York Times

26) Marks J. H. (2020). Lessons from Corporate Influence in the Opioid Epidemic: Toward a Norm of Separation. *Journal of bioethical inquiry, 17*(2), 173–189. https://doi.org/10.1007/s11673-020-09982-x

https://www.ncbi.nlm.nih.gov/pmc/articles/PMC7357445/

https://www.nytimes.com/2019/07/20/opinion/sunday/oxycontin-purdue-sacklers.html

https://www.nytimes.com/2019/07/19/health/opioids-trial-addiction-drugstores.html?searchResultPosition=1

https://www.nytimes.com/2019/05/13/books/review/bottle-of-lies-katherine-eban.html

https://www.newyorker.com/magazine/2017/10/30/the-family-that-built-an-empire-of-pain

https://www.nytimes.com/2021/04/23/us/fentanyl-overdoses-san-francisco.html

27) https://www.alliedmarketresearch.com/opioids-market

28) https://nida.nih.gov/publications/principles-drug-addiction-treatment-research-based-guide-third-edition/frequently-asked-questions/drug-addiction-treatment-worth-its-cost

https://www.fortunebusinessinsights.com/opioid-use-disorder-oud-market-102674

https://www.globenewswire.com/news-release/2020/02/20/1988216/0/en/Drug-Addiction-Treatment-Market-To-Reach-USD-31-17-Billion-By-2027-Reports-And-Data.html

29) Kirouac, M., & Witkiewitz, K. (2017). Identifying "Hitting Bottom" among Individuals with Alcohol Problems: Development and Evaluation of the Noteworthy Aspects of Drinking Important to Recovery (NADIR). *Substance Use & Misuse, 52*(12), 1602–1615. https://doi.org/10.1080/10826084.2017.1293104

https://www.streetdrugs.org/

References

https://www.drugabuse.gov/drugs-abuse/commonly-used-drugs-charts
30) Anton RF, Moak DH, Latham PK. The Obsessive Compulsive Drinking Scale: A New Method of Assessing Outcome in Alcoholism Treatment Studies. *Arch Gen Psychiatry.* 1996;53(3):225–231. doi:10.1001/archpsyc.1996.01830030047008 Obsessive Compulsive Drinking Scale (OCDS) - 45_OCDS.pdf
Babor TF, Hofmann M, DelBoca FK, et al. Types of Alcoholics, I: Evidence for an Empirically Derived Typology Based on Indicators of Vulnerability and Severity. *Arch Gen Psychiatry.* 1992;49(8):599–608. doi:10.1001/archpsyc.1992.01820080007002
31) Linda Carter Sobell, Mark B. Sobell,Using motivational interviewing techniques to talk with clients about their alcohol use,Cognitive and Behavioral Practice, Volume 10, Issue 3,2003,Pages 214-221,ISSN 1077-7229, https://doi.org/10.1016/S1077-7229(03)80033-0.
Miller, W. R., & Rose, G. S. (2009). Toward a theory of motivational interviewing. *The American psychologist*, 64(6), 527–537. https://doi.org/10.1037/a0016830
Parsons, J. T., Golub, S. A., Rosof, E., & Holder, C. (2007). Motivational interviewing and cognitive-behavioral intervention to improve HIV medication adherence among hazardous drinkers: a randomized controlled trial. *Journal of acquired immune deficiency syndromes (1999)*, 46(4), 443–450. https://doi.org/10.1097/qai.0b013e318158a461
32) Peele, A Different Path to Fighting Addiction - NYTimes.com http://www.nytimes.com/2014/07/06/nyregion/a-different-path-t S. A Moral Vision of Addiction: How People's Values Determine Whether They Become and Remain Addicts. Journal of Drug Issues. 1987;17(2):187-215. doi:10.1177/002204268701700205
33) http://silkworth.net/pages/aahistory/general/carljung_billw013061.php
34) https://centerforchange.com/discovering-your-purpose-an-essential-investment-on-the-recovery-path/
https://herrenwellness.com/discovering-your-why-addiction-recovery/
35) https://www.webmd.com/mental-health/addiction/addiction-detox-what-to-know
36) https://www.statnews.com/2017/10/29/opioid-epidemic-shares-chilling-similarities-with-past-drug-crises/
37) Mars S. (2003). Heroin Addiction Care and Control: the British System 1916 to 1984. *Journal of the Royal Society of Medicine*, 96(2), 99–100.https://transformdrugs.org/drug-policy/uk-drug-policy/heroin-assisted-treatment
38) Carroll, K. M., & Weiss, R. D. (2017). The Role of Behavioral Interventions in Buprenorphine Maintenance Treatment: A Review. *The American journal of psychiatry*, 174(8), 738–747. https://doi.org/10.1176/appi.ajp.2016.16070792
Volkow N. D. (2020). Personalizing the Treatment of Substance Use Disorders. *The American journal of psychiatry*, 177(2), 113–116. https://doi.org/10.1176/

appi.ajp.2019.19121284
https://ajp.psychiatryonline.org/doi/10.1176/appi.ajp.2019.19121284
Michael D. McGee , MD, The Optimal Management of Opioid Use Disorder: Leveraging Advances in Addiction Psychopharmacology to Enhance Treatment Outcomes https://doi.org/10.3928/00485713-20180417-01
Williams, A. R., Samples, H., Crystal, S., & Olfson, M. (2020). Acute Care, Prescription Opioid Use, and Overdose Following Discontinuation of Long-Term Buprenorphine Treatment for Opioid Use Disorder. *The American journal of psychiatry*, *177*(2), 117–124. https://doi.org/10.1176/appi.ajp.2019.19060612
Fiscella, K., Wakeman, S. E., & Beletsky, L. (2019). Buprenorphine Deregulation and Mainstreaming Treatment for Opioid Use Disorder: X the X Waiver. *JAMA psychiatry*, *76*(3), 229–230. https://doi.org/10.1001/jamapsychiatry.2018.3685
Fava, M., Memisoglu, A., Thase, M. E., Bodkin, J. A., Trivedi, M. H., de Somer, M., Du, Y., Leigh-Pemberton, R., DiPetrillo, L., Silverman, B., & Ehrich, E. (2016). Opioid Modulation With Buprenorphine/Samidorphan as Adjunctive Treatment for Inadequate Response to Antidepressants: A Randomized Double-Blind Placebo-Controlled Trial. *The American journal of psychiatry*, *173*(5), 499– https://doi.org/10.1176/appi.ajp.2015.15070921
Yovell, Y., Bar, G., Mashiah, M., Baruch, Y., Briskman, I., Asherov, J., Lotan, A., Rigbi, A., & Panksepp, J. (2016). Ultra-Low-Dose Buprenorphine as a Time-Limited Treatment for Severe Suicidal Ideation: A Randomized Controlled Trial. *The American journal of psychiatry*, *173*(5), 491–498. https://doi.org/10.1176/appi.ajp.2015.15040535https://doi.org/10.1176/appi.ajp.2015.15040535
voy KE, Hill LG, Groff L, Mazin L, Carlson CC, Reveles KR. Naloxone Accessibility Without a Prescriber Encounter Under Standing Orders at Community Pharmacy Chains in Texas. *JAMA.* 2018;320(18):1934–1937. doi:10.1001/jama.2018.15892
https://jamanetwork.com/journals/jama/fullarticle/2714520?guestAccessKey=f6f68ae6-7a39-495c-882c-f7fc720d8303
Puzantian, Talia, and James J Gasper. "Provision of Naloxone Without a Prescription by California Pharmacists 2 Years After Legislation Implementation." *JAMA* vol. 320,18 (2018): 1933-1934. https://www.ncbi.nlm.nih.gov/pmc/articles/PMC6248130/
https://www.nytimes.com/2019/01/14/us/opioids-car-crash-guns.html
The Prescription Drugs That Rich People Buy - The New York Times
The Worst Drug Crisis in American History - The New York Times
39) M., Gauthier, P., Hodgkins, C. C., King, J., Lindblad, R., Liu, D., Matthews, A. G., May, J., Peavy, K. M., Ross, S., Salazar, D., Schkolnik, P., Shmueli-Blumberg, D., ... Rotrosen, J. (2018). Comparative effectiveness of extended-release naltrexone versus buprenorphine-naloxone for opioid relapse prevention (X:BOT): a multicentre, open-label, randomised controlled trial. *Lancet (London, England)*, *391*(10118), 309–318. https://doi.org/10.1016/

References

S0140-6736(17)32812-X
Garcia-Portilla, M. P., Bobes-Bascaran, M. T., Bascaran, M. T., Saiz, P. A., & Bobes, J. (2014). Long term outcomes of pharmacological treatments for opioid dependence: does methadone still lead the pack?. *British journal of clinical pharmacology*, *77*(2), 272–284. https://doi.org/10.1111/bcp.12031
Sullivan, M. A., Bisaga, A., Pavlicova, M., Carpenter, K. M., Choi, C. J., Mishlen, K., Levin, F. R., Mariani, J. J., & Nunes, E. V. (2019). A Randomized Trial Comparing Extended-Release Injectable Suspension and Oral Naltrexone, Both Combined With Behavioral Therapy, for the Treatment of Opioid Use Disorder. *The American journal of psychiatry*, *176*(2), 129–137.
Long-term Effects of Buprenorphine & Methadone on Opioid Use. (n.d.). Recovery Research Institute.
https://www.recoveryanswers.org/research-post/long-term-effects-of-buprenorphine-methadone-on-opioid-use/
https://www.cochrane.org/CD002025/ADDICTN_buprenorphine-managing-opioid-withdrawal
Hurd, Y. L., & O'Brien, C. P. (2018). Molecular Genetics and New Medication Strategies for Opioid Addiction. *The American journal of psychiatry*, *175*(10), 935–942. https://doi.org/10.1176/appi.ajp.2018.18030352
Bart, G. (2012). Maintenance Medication for Opiate Addiction: The Foundation of Recovery. *Journal of Addictive Diseases*, *31*(3), 207–225. https://doi.org/10.1080/10550887.2012.694598
Nunes, E. V., Jr, Scodes, J. M., Pavlicova, M., Lee, J. D., Novo, P., Campbell, A., & Rotrosen, J. (2021). Sublingual Buprenorphine-Naloxone Compared With Injection Naltrexone for Opioid Use Disorder: Potential Utility of Patient Characteristics in Guiding Choice of Treatment. *The American journal of psychiatry*, *178*(7), 660–671. https://doi.org/10.1176/appi.ajp.2020.20060816
https://www.hhs.gov/about/news/2021/04/27/hhs-releases-new-buprenorphine-practice-guidelines-expanding-access-to-treatment-for-opioid-use-disorder.html
Sittambalam, C. D., Vij, R., & Ferguson, R. P. (2014). Buprenorphine Outpatient Outcomes Project: can Suboxone be a viable outpatient option for heroin addiction?. *Journal of community hospital internal medicine perspectives*, *4*(2). https://doi.org/10.3402/jchimp.v4.22902
Kattimani, S., Bharadwaj, B., & Arun, A. B. (2017). Benzodiazepine maintenance for alcohol dependence: A case series. *Journal of family medicine and primary care*, *6*(2), 431–433. https://doi.org/10.4103/2249-4863.220038
40) Weaver M. F. (2015). Prescription Sedative Misuse and Abuse. *The Yale journal of biology and medicine*, *88*(3), 247–256.
Post acute withdrawal is subjectively reported by persons in detox but not documented by any other measure. It has not been the subject of detailed research, for unknown reasons.
42) Gaval-Cruz, M., & Weinshenker, D. (2009). mechanism of disulfiram-induced cocaine abstinence: antabuse and cocaine relapse. *Molecular*

interventions, *9*(4), 175–187. https://doi.org/10.1124/mi.9.4.6

Anton, R. F., Latham, P., Voronin, K., Book, S., Hoffman, M., Prisciandaro, J., & Bristol, E. (2020). Efficacy of Gabapentin for the Treatment of Alcohol Use Disorder in Patients With Alcohol Withdrawal Symptoms: A Randomized Clinical Trial. *JAMA Internal Medicine*. https://doi.org/10.1001/jamainternmed.2020.0249

Johnson B. A. (2010). Medication treatment of different types of alcoholism. *The American journal of psychiatry*, *167*(6), 630–639. https://doi.org/10.1176/appi.ajp.2010.08101500 https://ajp.psychiatryonline.org/doi/full/10.1176/appi.ajp.2010.08101500

Kranzler, H. R., Covault, J., Feinn, R., Armeli, S., Tennen, H., Arias, A. J., Gelernter, J., Pond, T., Oncken, C., & Kampman, K. M. (2014). Topiramate treatment for heavy drinkers: moderation by a GRIK1 polymorphism. *The American journal of psychiatry*, *171*(4), 445–452. https://doi.org/10.1176/appi.ajp.2013.13081014   GABA receptor agonist - Wikipedia, the free encyclopedia

Laudet, A. B., Savage, R., & Mahmood, D. (2002). Pathways to long-term recovery: a preliminary investigation. *Journal of psychoactive drugs*, *34*(3), 305–311. https://doi.org/10.1080/02791072.2002.10399968

A Single Ketamine Infusion Combined With Motivational Enhancement Therapy for Alcohol Use Disorder: A Randomized Midazolam-Controlled Pilot Trial. *The American journal of psychiatry*, *177*(2), 125–133. https://doi.org/10.1176/appi.ajp.2019.19070684

Meryem Grabski, Amy McAndrew, Will Lawn, Beth Marsh, Laura Raymen, Tobias Stevens, Lorna Hardy, Fiona Warren, Michael Bloomfield, Anya Borissova, Emily Maschauer, Rupert Broomby, Robert Price, Rachel Coathup, David Gilhooly, Edward Palmer, Richard Gordon-Williams, Robert Hill, Jen Harris, O. Merve Mollaahmetoglu, H. Valerie Curran, Brigitta Brandner, Anne Lingford-Hughes, and Celia J.A. Morgan, Adjunctive Ketamine With Relapse Prevention–Based Psychological Therapy in the Treatment of Alcohol Use Disorder, American Journal of Psychiatry 2022 179:2, 152-162

Brown T. K. (2013). Ibogaine in the treatment of substance dependence. *Current drug abuse reviews*, *6*(1), 3–16. https://doi.org/10.2174/15672050113109990001 https://www.psychiatrictimes.com/view/psychedelics-and-the-future-of-psychiatry

Daryl Shorter (Assistant Professor), Coreen B Domingo (Assistant Professor) & Thomas R Kosten (Professor) (2015) Emerging drugs for the treatment of cocaine use disorder: a review of neurobiological targets and pharmacotherapy, Expert Opinion on Emerging Drugs, 20:1, 15-29, DOI: 10.1517/14728214.2015.985203

Allsop, D. J., Copeland, J., Lintzeris, N., Dunlop, A. J., Montebello, M., Sadler, C., Rivas, G. R., Holland, R. M., Muhleisen, P., Norberg, M. M., Booth, J., & McGregor, I. S. (2014). Nabiximols as an agonist replacement therapy during cannabis withdrawal: a randomized clinical trial. *JAMA psychiatry*, *71*(3),

References

281–291. https://doi.org/10.1001/jamapsychiatry.2013.3947
Bhardwaj, A. K., Allsop, D. J., Copeland, J., McGregor, I. S., Dunlop, A., Shanahan, M., Bruno, R., Phung, N., Montebello, M., Sadler, C., Gugusheff, J., Jackson, M., Luksza, J., Lintzeris, N., & Agonist Replacement for Cannabis Dependence (ARCD) study group (2018). Randomised Controlled Trial (RCT) of cannabinoid replacement therapy (Nabiximols) for the management of treatment-resistant cannabis dependent patients: a study protocol. *BMC psychiatry*, *18*(1), 140. https://doi.org/10.1186/s12888-018-1682-2

43) Vaillant, G. **Adaptation To Life, (1998) Harvard U Press**
Overcoming the Entitlement of 'King Baby Syndrome.' (2014, October 10). Drug Addiction Treatment. https://www.drugaddictiontreatment.com/addiction-in-the-news/addiction-news/overcoming-the-entitlement-of-king-baby-syndrome/

44) Melemis S. M. (2015). Relapse Prevention and the Five Rules of Recovery. *The Yale journal of biology and medicine*, *88*(3), 325–332. https://www.ncbi.nlm.nih.gov/pmc/articles/PMC4553654/

45) https://www.drugabuse.gov/publications/research-reports/common-comorbidities-substance-use-disorders/part-1-connection-between-substance-use-disorders-mental-illness

Farren, C. K., Hill, K. P., & Weiss, R. D. (2012). Bipolar disorder and alcohol use disorder: a review. *Current psychiatry reports*, *14*(6), 659–666. https://doi.org/10.1007/s11920-012-0320-9

Ostacher, M. J., Perlis, R. H., Nierenberg, A. A., Calabrese, J., Stange, J. P., Salloum, I., Weiss, R. D., Sachs, G. S., & STEP-BD Investigators (2010). Impact of substance use disorders on recovery from episodes of depression in bipolar disorder patients: prospective data from the Systematic Treatment Enhancement Program for Bipolar Disorder (STEP-BD). *The American journal of psychiatry*, *167*(3), 289–297. https://doi.org/10.1176/appi.ajp.2009.09020299

Pettorruso, M., De Risio, L., Di Nicola, M., Martinotti, G., Conte, G., & Janiri, L. (2014). Allostasis as a conceptual framework linking bipolar disorder and addiction. *Frontiers in psychiatry*, *5*, 173. https://doi.org/10.3389/fpsyt.2014.00173

Trull, T. J., Freeman, L. K., Vebares, T. J., Choate, A. M., Helle, A. C., & Wycoff, A. M. (2018). Borderline personality disorder and substance use disorders: an updated review. *Borderline personality disorder and emotion dysregulation*, *5*, 15. https://doi.org/10.1186/s40479-018-0093-9

Kienast, T., Stoffers, J., Bermpohl, F., & Lieb, K. (2014). Borderline Personality Disorder and Comorbid Addiction. *Deutsches Aerzteblatt Online*. https://doi.org/10.3238/arztebl.2014.0280

New, A. S., & Stanley, B. (2010). An opioid deficit in borderline personality disorder: self-cutting, substance abuse, and social dysfunction. *The American journal of psychiatry*, *167*(8), 882–885. https://doi.org/10.1176/appi.ajp.2010.10040634

Cope, L. M., Vincent, G. M., Jobelius, J. L., Nyalakanti, P. K., Calhoun, V. D., & Kiehl, K. A. (2014). Psychopathic traits modulate brain responses to drug cues in incarcerated offenders. *Frontiers in Human Neuroscience, 8*. https://doi.org/10.3389/fnhum.2014.00087

Berenz, E. C., & Coffey, S. F. (2012). Treatment of Co-occurring Posttraumatic Stress Disorder and Substance Use Disorders. *Current Psychiatry Reports, 14*(5), 469–477. https://doi.org/10.1007/s11920-012-0300-0

Alcohol, Tobacco, and Comorbid Psychiatric Disorders and Associations With Sexual Identity and Stress-Related Correlates
Rebecca J. Evans-Polce, Luisa Kcomt, Philip T. Veliz, Carol J. Boyd, and Sean Esteban McCabe
American Journal of Psychiatry 2020 177:11, 1073-1081 https://ajp.psychiatryonline.org/doi/abs/10.1176/appi.ajp.2020.20010005

Khantzian E. J. (1985). The self-medication hypothesis of addictive disorders: focus on heroin and cocaine dependence. *The American journal of psychiatry, 142*(11), 1259–1264. https://doi.org/10.1176/ajp.142.11.1259

Lembke A. (2012). Time to abandon the self-medication hypothesis in patients with psychiatric disorders. *The American journal of drug and alcohol abuse, 38*(6), 524–529. https://doi.org/10.3109/00952990.2012.694532

45) Awad AG, Voruganti LL. Revisiting the 'self-medication' hypothesis in light of the new data linking low striatal dopamine to comorbid addictive behavior. Therapeutic Advances in Psychopharmacology. 2015 Jun;5(3):172-178. https://europepmc.org/article/PMC/4502591

Koob, G. F., Powell, P., & White, A. (2020). Addiction as a Coping Response: Hyperkatifeia, Deaths of Despair, and COVID-19. *The American journal of psychiatry, 177*(11), 1031 https://doi.org/10.1176/appi.ajp.2020.20091375

46) https://www.scientificamerican.com/article/how-the-brain-gets-addicted-to-gambling/

Clark, L., Averbeck, B., Payer, D., Sescousse, G., Winstanley, C. A., & Xue, G. (2013). Pathological choice: the neuroscience of gambling and gambling addiction. *The Journal of neuroscience : the official journal of the Society for Neuroscience, 33*(45), 17617–17623. https://doi.org/10.1523/JNEUROSCI.3231-13.2013

Miedl, S. F., Peters, J., & Büchel, C. (2012). Altered neural reward representations in pathological gamblers revealed by delay and probability discounting. *Archives of general psychiatry, 69*(2), 177–186. https://doi.org/10.1001/archgenpsychiatry.2011.1552

Potenza, M. N., Fiellin, D. A., Heninger, G. R., Rounsaville, B. J., & Mazure, C. M. (2002). Gambling: an addictive behavior with health and primary care implications. *Journal of general internal medicine, 17*(9), 721–732. https://doi.org/10.1046/j.1525-1497.2002.10812.x

Internet Gaming Disorder Fact Sheet.pdf
Internet gaming addiction: current perspectives

References

Moore, T. J., Glenmullen, J., & Mattison, D. R. (2014). Reports of pathological gambling, hypersexuality, and compulsive shopping associated with dopamine receptor agonist drugs. *JAMA internal medicine*, *174*(12), 1930–1933. https://doi.org/10.1001/jamainternmed.2014.5262

47) Alcoholics Anonymous and other 12-step programs for alcohol use disorder https://www.cochranelibrary.com/cdsr/doi/10.1002/14651858.CD012880.pub2/full

48) Dutra, L., Stathopoulou, G., Basden, S. L., Leyro, T. M., Powers, M. B., & Otto, M. W. (2008). A meta-analytic review of psychosocial interventions for substance use disorders. *The American journal of psychiatry*, *165*(2), 179–187. https://doi.org/10.1176/appi.ajp.2007.06111851

Henwood, B. F., Padgett, D. K., & Tiderington, E. (2014). Provider views of harm reduction versus abstinence policies within homeless services for dually diagnosed adults. *The journal of behavioral health services & research*, *41*(1), 80–89. https://doi.org/10.1007/s11414-013-9318-2

In Rehab, 'Two Warring Factions': Abstinence vs. Medication - The New York Times

Humphreys KL, Eng T, Lee SS. Stimulant Medication and Substance Use Outcomes: A Meta-analysis. *JAMA Psychiatry*. 2013;70(7):740–749. doi:10.1001/jamapsychiatry.2013.1273

Falk, D. E., O'Malley, S. S., Witkiewitz, K., Anton, R. F., Litten, R. Z., Slater, M., Kranzler, H. R., Mann, K. F., Hasin, D. S., Johnson, B., Meulien, D., Ryan, M., Fertig, J., & Alcohol Clinical Trials Initiative (ACTIVE) Workgroup (2019). Evaluation of Drinking Risk Levels as Outcomes in Alcohol Pharmacotherapy Trials: A Secondary Analysis of 3 Randomized Clinical Trials. *JAMA psychiatry*, *76*(4), 374–381. https://doi.org/10.1001/jamapsychiatry.2018.3079

Sara K. Blaine, Stephanie Wemm, Nia Fogelman, Cheryl Lacadie, Dongju Seo, Dustin Scheinost, and Rajita Sinha, Association of Prefrontal-Striatal Functional Pathology With Alcohol Abstinence Days at Treatment Initiation and Heavy Drinking After Treatment Initiation American Journal of Psychiatry 2020 177:11, 1048-1059

Yip, S. W., Scheinost, D., Potenza, M. N., & Carroll, K. M. (2019). Connectome-Based Prediction of Cocaine Abstinence. *The American journal of psychiatry*, *176*(2), 156–164. https://doi.org/10.1176/appi.ajp.2018.17101147

49) Joshua B. Grubbs, K. Camille Hoagland, Brinna N. Lee, Jennifer T. Grant, Paul Davison, Rory C. Reid, Shane W. Kraus,Sexual addiction 25 years on: A systematic and methodological review of empirical literature and an agenda for future research,Clinical Psychology Review, Volume 82,2020,101925,ISSN 0272-7358,
https://doi.org/10.1016/j.cpr.2020.101925.https://www.sciencedirect.com/science/article/pii/S0272735820301136

Fong T. W. (2006). Understanding and managing compulsive sexual behaviors. *Psychiatry (Edgmont (Pa. : Township))*, *3*(11), 51–58.

Wired for Intimacy: How Pornography Hijacks the Male Brain: William M. Struthers: 9780830837007: Amazon.com: Books
Hilton, D. L., & Watts, C. (2011). Pornography addiction: A neuroscience perspective. *Surgical neurology international*, 2, 19. https://doi.org/10.4103/2152-7806.76977
Kühn, S., & Gallinat, J. (2014). Brain structure and functional connectivity associated with pornography consumption: the brain on porn. *JAMA psychiatry*, 71(7), 827–834. https://doi.org/10.1001/jamapsychiatry.2014.93
https://pubmed.ncbi.nlm.nih.gov/24871202/
Sex Addiction Is Not a Thing ByBeth Skwarecki
https://lifehacker.com/sex-addiction-is-not-a-thing-1846529088
50) Grosshans, M., Vollmert, C., Vollstädt-Klein, S., Tost, H., Leber, S., Bach, P., Bühler, M., von der Goltz, C., Mutschler, J., Loeber, S., Hermann, D., Wiedemann, K., Meyer-Lindenberg, A., & Kiefer, F. (2012). Association of leptin with food cue-induced activation in human reward pathways. *Archives of general psychiatry*, 69(5), 529–537. https://doi.org/10.1001/archgenpsychiatry.2011.1586
Carter, A., Hendrikse, J., Lee, N., Yücel, M., Verdejo-Garcia, A., Andrews, Z. B., & Hall, W. (2016). The Neurobiology of "Food Addiction" and Its Implications for Obesity Treatment and Policy. *Annual review of nutrition*, 36, 105–128. https://doi.org/10.1146/annurev-nutr-071715-050909
50) Hasin, D. S., Kerridge, B. T., Saha, T. D., Huang, B., Pickering, R., Smith, S. M., Jung, J., Zhang, H., & Grant, B. F. (2016). Prevalence and Correlates of DSM-5 Cannabis Use Disorder, 2012-2013: Findings from the National Epidemiologic Survey on Alcohol and Related Conditions-III. *The American journal of psychiatry*, 173(6), 588–599. https://doi.org/10.1176/appi.ajp.2015.15070907
https://medicalcannabis.com/cannabis-science/endocannabinoid-system/
Melvin, L. S., Milne, G. M., Johnson, M. R., Subramaniam, B., Wilken, G. H., & Howlett, A. C. (1993). Structure-activity relationships for cannabinoid receptor-binding and analgesic activity: studies of bicyclic cannabinoid analogs. *Molecular pharmacology*, 44(5), 1008–1015.
51) Hatsukami D; Bierut LJ;Department of Psychiatry, Washington University, St. Louis, MO, USA,Nicotine dependence and comorbid psychiatric disorders: Examination of specific genetic variants in the CHRNA5-A3-B4 nicotinic receptor genes
Drug Alcohol Depend. 2012; 123 Suppl 1:S42-51
Tiesler, C. M., & Heinrich, J. (2014). Prenatal nicotine exposure and child behavioural problems. *European child & adolescent psychiatry*, 23(10), 913–929. https://doi.org/10.1007/s00787-014-0615-y
Niemelä, S., Sourander, A., Surcel, H. M., Hinkka-Yli-Salomäki, S., McKeague, I. W., Cheslack-Postava, K., & Brown, A. S. (2016). Prenatal Nicotine Exposure and Risk of Schizophrenia Among Offspring in a National Birth Cohort. *The*

American journal of psychiatry, 173(8), 799–806. https://doi.org/10.1176/appi.ajp.2016.15060800

Grant, B. F., Shmulewitz, D., & Compton, W. M. (2020). Nicotine Use and DSM-IV Nicotine Dependence in the United States, 2001-2002 and 2012-2013. *The American journal of psychiatry, 177*(11), 1082–1090. https://doi.org/10.1176/appi.ajp.2020.19090900

52) https://www.nccih.nih.gov/health/cannabis-marijuana-and-cannabinoids-what-you-need-to-know

Volkow, N. D., Baler, R. D., Compton, W. M., & Weiss, S. R. (2014). Adverse health effects of marijuana use. *The New England journal of medicine, 370*(23), 2219–2227. https://doi.org/10.1056/NEJMra1402309

Bhattacharyya, S., Wilson, R., Appiah-Kusi, E., O'Neill, A., Brammer, M., Perez, J., Murray, R., Allen, P., Bossong, M. G., & McGuire, P. (2018). Effect of Cannabidiol on Medial Temporal, Midbrain, and Striatal Dysfunction in People at Clinical High Risk of Psychosis: A Randomized Clinical Trial. *JAMA psychiatry, 75*(11), 1107–1117. https://doi.org/10.1001/jamapsychiatry.2018.2309

52) Hurd, Y. L., Spriggs, S., Alishayev, J., Winkel, G., Gurgov, K., Kudrich, C., Oprescu, A. M., & Salsitz, E. (2019). Cannabidiol for the Reduction of Cue-Induced Craving and Anxiety in Drug-Abstinent Individuals With Heroin Use Disorder: A Double-Blind Randomized Placebo-Controlled Trial. *The American journal of psychiatry, 176*(11), 911–922. https://doi.org/10.1176/appi.ajp.2019.18101191

CHAPTER TEN REFERENCES

1) Goffman *Frame Analysis*: **An essay on the organization of experience**. ISBN-13 : 978-0930350918

2) Lazare, A., Eisenthal, S., & Wasserman, L. (1975). The customer approach to patienthood. Attending to patient requests in a walk-in clinic. *Archives of general psychiatry, 32*(5), 553–558. https://doi.org/10.1001/archpsyc.1975.01760230019001

3) In recent decades in the US, the shift to prison incarceration of mentally ill emphasizes the role of social deviance in intervention. A country, which once pioneered "humane" treatment for the mentally ill, is making them prisoners once again. Greenberg, G. A., & Rosenheck, R. A. (2008). Jail incarceration, homelessness, and mental health: a national study. *Psychiatric services (Washington, D.C.), 59*(2), 170–177. https://doi.org/10.1176/ps.2008.59.2.170

4) *Historical perspectives on the theories, diagnosis, and treatment of mental illness | British Columbia Medical Journal.* (2017). Bcmj.Org. https://www.bcmj.org/mds-be/historical-perspectives-theories-diagnosis-and-treatment-mental-illness

5) Harrington, A. (2019). A tale of two disorders: syphilis, hysteria and the

struggle to treat mental illness. *Nature*, *572*(7770), 436–437. https://doi.org/10.1038/d41586-019-02476-w

6) Lin, L.-R., Zhang, H.-L., Huang, S.-J., Zeng, Y.-L., Xi, Y., Guo, X.-J., Liu, G.-L., Tong, M.-L., Zheng, W.-H., Liu, L.-L., & Yang, T.-C. (2014). Psychiatric Manifestations as Primary Symptom of Neurosyphilis Among HIV-Negative Patients. *The Journal of Neuropsychiatry and Clinical Neurosciences*, *26*(3), 233–240. https://doi.org/10.1176/appi.neuropsych.13030064

7) Bar, K.-J., & Ebert, A. (2010). Emil Kraepelin: A pioneer of scientific understanding of psychiatry and psychopharmacology. *Indian Journal of Psychiatry*, *52*(2), 191. https://doi.org/10.4103/0019-5545.64591

Engstrom, E. J., & Kendler, K. S. (2015). Emil Kraepelin: Icon and Reality. *American Journal of Psychiatry*, *172*(12), 1190–1196. https://doi.org/10.1176/appi.ajp.2015.15050665

8) Crocq, M. A., & Crocq, L. (2000). From shell shock and war neurosis to post-traumatic stress disorder: a history of psychotraumatology. *Dialogues in clinical neuroscience*, *2*(1), 47–55. https://doi.org/10.31887/DCNS.2000.2.1/macrocq

9) Rosenhan, D. L. (1973). On Being Sane in Insane Places. *Science*, *179*(4070), 250–258. https://doi.org/10.1126/science.179.4070.250

Microsoft Word - On_Being_Sane_In_Insane_Places-1.doc - On_Being_Sane_In_Insane_Places-1.pdf

10) Carol Bernstein MD, in Psychiatric News mar 4 2011 46 #5

11) A "multi-axial approach" had separate axes for "medical" factors in etiology, and "social stress" to resolve the conflict between psychodynamic and biologically oriented practitioners, with different views of diagnosis and etiology, which is identified in Kendler's review. The review omits the impact of Rosenhan in 1973.

Kendler, K. S., Muñoz, R. A., & Murphy, G. (2010). The development of the Feighner criteria: a historical perspective. *The American journal of psychiatry*, *167*(2), https://doi.org/10.1176/appi.ajp.2009.09081155

12) Luria RE, McHugh PR. Reliability and Clinical Utility of the "Wing" Present State Examination. *Arch Gen Psychiatry*. 1974;30(6): https://jamanetwork.com/journals/jamapsychiatry/article-abstract/491160

13) Maj, M. (2005). 'Psychiatric comorbidity': an artefact of current diagnostic systems? *British Journal of Psychiatry*, *186*(3), 182–184. https://doi.org/10.1192/bjp.186.3.182

Rating scales and lists of symptoms aim to ensure that symptoms are reviewed with the client, to reduce the time demands of the clinician, and to improve "reliability" by consistency of questions asked. Diagnostic rating scales like the HAMD have arbitrarily defined cutoff points. The positive cut off point chosen will vary the estimate of mental illness prevalence and treatment response. There is no absolute cutoff.

Zimmerman, M., Martinez, J. H., Young, D., Chelminski, I., & Dalrymple, K. (2013). Severity classification on the Hamilton Depression Rating Scale.

References

Journal of affective disorders, *150*(2), 384–388. https://doi.org/10.1016/j.jad.2013.04.028

Zimmerman, M., Martinez, J. H., Friedman, M., Boerescu, D. A., Attiullah, N., & Toba, C. (2014). Speaking a more consistent language when discussing severe depression: a calibration study of 3 self-report measures of depressive symptoms. *The Journal of clinical psychiatry*, *75*(2), 141–146. https://doi.org/10.4088/JCP.13m08458 **Improved adaptation is not measured in the scales.** Zimmerman et al addresses this point. 353 depressed patients completed 3 different depression self rating scales with predetermined cutoffs. These were compared with the Hamilton evaluator rating scale and a cutoff of 25, higher than the usual 17. The correlation among scales and with the Hamilton was variable and the cutoff values varied across scales

Catherine Lord and Somer L. Bishop, Let's Be Clear That "Autism Spectrum Disorder Symptoms" Are Not Always Related to Autism Spectrum Disorder, American Journal of Psychiatry 2021 178:8, 680-682 https://ajp.psychiatryonline.org/doi/10.1176/appi.ajp.2021.21060578

14)The Conceptual Development of DSM-V https://www.psychotherapy.net/interview/allen-frances-interview https://www.psychologytoday.com/us/blog/dsm5-in-distress/201212/mislabeling-medical-illness-mental-disorder

15) Insel, T. R. (2014). The NIMH Research Domain Criteria (RDoC) Project: Precision Medicine for Psychiatry. *American Journal of Psychiatry*, *171*(4), 395–397. https://doi.org/10.1176/appi.ajp.2014.14020138 NIMH » Research Domain Criteria (RDoC)

Samet Kose & Mesut Cetin (2017) The Research Domain Criteria framework: transitioning from dimensional systems to integrating neuroscience and psychopathology, Psychiatry and Clinical Psychopharmacology, 27:1, 1-5, DOI: 10.1080/24750573.2017.1293255

There is overlap between Neuromind pathways and the domains of NIMH RDoC:

The **Negative Valence** system. This overlaps much of the function of aversive conditioning and fear discussed in Amygdala chapter 8 = Symptoms of danger signals. The range of functions identified corresponds to the notion of "extended amygdala".(see chapter 8)

Positive Valence system includes the reward and reinforcer paradigms of the chapter 3 system, but omits the wide range of other control variables involved in this system and also Symptoms related to interpretation of reward.

Cognitive systems This category overlaps Chapter #1 Cortical categorization, Chapter #4) and memory hippocampal symptoms. Chapter #5 the attention system.

The grouping of these elements probably reflects their co-association in cognitive psychology research and fails to differentiate their separate brain circuits.

Systems for social processes. This category emphasizes work on attachment. The role of emotional processes in social communication is not included, and the issues of mimicry and mirror neurons ignored. It corresponds to Chapter #2 and Chapter #7): Social brain and attachment processes.

Arousal/Regulatory systems corresponds to chapter 5, the core arousal system and its regulatory functions. The RDC does not recognize the "operating system" control function or the consciousness function of this component. (Chapters #5 and #6) and does not differentiate the attention and choice functions.

Yager, J., & Feinstein, R. E. (2017). Potential Applications of the National Institute of Mental Health's Research Domain Criteria (RDoC) to Clinical Psychiatric Practice: How RDoC Might Be Used in Assessment, Diagnostic Processes, Case Formulation, Treatment Planning, and Clinical Notes. *The Journal of clinical psychiatry*, *78*(4), 423–432. https://doi.org/10.4088/JCP.15nr10476

Weinberger DR, Glick ID, Klein DF. Whither Research Domain Criteria (RDoC)? The Good, the Bad, and the Ugly. *JAMA Psychiatry.* 2015;72(12):1161–1162. doi:10.1001/jamapsychiatry.2015.1743
https://jamanetwork.com/journals/jamapsychiatry/fullarticle/2469109

Kendler K. S. (2014). DSM issues: incorporation of biological tests, avoidance of reification, and an approach to the "box canyon problem". *The American journal of psychiatry*, *171*(12), 1248–1250. https://doi.org/10.1176/appi.ajp.2014.14081018

16) Heckers S. The Value of Psychiatric Diagnoses. *JAMA Psychiatry.* 2015;72(12):1165–1166.
https://jamanetwork.com/journals/jamapsychiatry/fullarticle/2469101

Pickersgill, M. D. (2013). Debating DSM-5: diagnosis and the sociology of critique. *Journal of Medical Ethics*, *40*(8), 521–525. https://doi.org/10.1136/medethics-2013-101762

Kotov, R., Ruggero, C. J., Krueger, R. F., Watson, D., Yuan, Q., & Zimmerman, M. (2011). New dimensions in the quantitative classification of mental illness. *Archives of general psychiatry*, *68*(10), 1003–1011. https://doi.org/10.1001/archgenpsychiatry.2011.107

Blanco, C., Krueger, R. F., Hasin, D. S., Liu, S. M., Wang, S., Kerridge, B. T., Saha, T., & Olfson, M. (2013). Mapping common psychiatric disorders: structure and predictive validity in the national epidemiologic survey on alcohol and related conditions. *JAMA psychiatry*, *70*(2), 199–208. https://doi.org/10.1001/jamapsychiatry.2013.281

Clarke, D. E., & Kuhl, E. A. (2014). DSM-5 cross-cutting symptom measures: a step towards the future of psychiatric care?. *World psychiatry : official journal of the World Psychiatric Association (WPA)*, *13*(3), 314–316. https://doi.org/10.1002/wps.20154

Gillihan, S. J., & Parens, E. (2011). Should We Expect "Neural Signatures" forDSMDiagnoses? *The Journal of Clinical Psychiatry*, *72*(10), 1383–1389. https://doi.org/10.4088/jcp.10r06332gre

References

17) Honnorat, N., Pfefferbaum, A., Sullivan, E. V., & Pohl, K. M. (2020). Deep Parametric Mixtures for Modeling the Functional Connectome. *PRedictive Intelligence in MEdicine. PRIME (Workshop)*, *12329*, 133–143. https://doi.org/10.1007/978-3-030-59354-4_13

Elliott, M. L., Romer, A., Knodt, A. R., & Hariri, A. R. (2018). A Connectome-wide Functional Signature of Transdiagnostic Risk for Mental Illness. *Biological psychiatry*, *84*(6), 452–459. https://doi.org/10.1016/j.biopsych.2018.03.012

McTeague, L. M., Rosenberg, B. M., Lopez, J. W., Carreon, D. M., Huemer, J., Jiang, Y., Chick, C. F., Eickhoff, S. B., & Etkin, A. (2020). Identification of Common Neural Circuit Disruptions in Emotional Processing Across Psychiatric Disorders. *The American journal of psychiatry*, *177*(5), 411–421. https://doi.org/10.1176/appi.ajp.2019.18111271

Goodkind, M., Eickhoff, S. B., Oathes, D. J., Jiang, Y., Chang, A., Jones-Hagata, L. B., Ortega, B. N., Zaiko, Y. V., Roach, E. L., Korgaonkar, M. S., Grieve, S. M., Galatzer-Levy, I., Fox, P. T., & Etkin, A. (2015). Identification of a common neurobiological substrate for mental illness. *JAMA psychiatry*, *72*(4), 305–315. https://doi.org/10.1001/jamapsychiatry.2014.2206

Sharma, A., Wolf, D. H., Ciric, R., Kable, J. W., Moore, T. M., Vandekar, S. N., Katchmar, N., Daldal, A., Ruparel, K., Davatzikos, C., Elliott, M. A., Calkins, M. E., Shinohara, R. T., Bassett, D. S., & Satterthwaite, T. D. (2017). Common Dimensional Reward Deficits Across Mood and Psychotic Disorders: A Connectome-Wide Association Study. *The American journal of psychiatry*, *174*(7), 657–666. https://doi.org/10.1176/appi.ajp.2016.16070774

18) Buckholtz, J. W., & Meyer-Lindenberg, A. (2012). Psychopathology and the human connectome: toward a transdiagnostic model of risk for mental illness. *Neuron*, *74*(6), 990–1004. https://doi.org/10.1016/j.neuron.2012.06.002

19) Kendler K. S. (2019). From Many to One to Many-the Search for Causes of Psychiatric Illness. *JAMA psychiatry*, *76*(10), 1085–1091. https://doi.org/10.1001/jamapsychiatry.2019.1200

Ritsner M.S., Gottesman I.I. (2009) Where Do We Stand in the Quest for Neuropsychiatric Biomarkers and Endophenotypes and What Next?. In: Ritsner M.S. (eds) The Handbook of Neuropsychiatric Biomarkers, Endophenotypes and Genes. Springer, Dordrecht. https://doi.org/10.1007/978-1-4020-9464-4_1

Moran, M. (2017). Imaging Advances Could Aid Prediction of Outcome in High-Risk Patients. *Psychiatric News*, *52*(10), 1–1. https://doi.org/10.1176/appi.pn.2017.5a2

20) Schulz P. (2019). Opportunities and challenges in psychopharmacology. *Dialogues in clinical neuroscience*, *21*(2), 119–130. https://doi.org/10.31887/DCNS.2019.21.2/pschulz

21) Engel G. L. (1980). The clinical application of the biopsychosocial model. *The American journal of psychiatry*, *137*(5), 535–544. https://doi.org/10.1176/ajp.137.5.535

Borrell-Carrió, F., Suchman, A. L., & Epstein, R. M. (2004). The biopsychosocial model 25 years later: principles, practice, and scientific inquiry. *Annals of family medicine*, *2*(6), 576–582. https://doi.org/10.1370/afm.245

Ghaemi S. N. (2009). The rise and fall of the biopsychosocial model. *The British journal of psychiatry : the journal of mental science*, *195*(1), 3–4. https://doi.org/10.1192/bjp.bp.109.063859

Benning T. B. (2015). Limitations of the biopsychosocial model in psychiatry. *Advances in medical education and practice*, *6*, 347–352. https://doi.org/10.2147/AMEP.S82937

22) https://www.ninds.nih.gov/Disorders/All-Disorders/Huntingtons-Disease-Information-Page

23) Lieff , This has never been published in a reviewed journal. https://jonlieffmd.com/blog/limitations-of-genetic-research-in-psychiatric-illness

Fundamental Neuroscience by Squire et al. (2003): *"The most compelling evidence is the 50% concordance rate for monozygotic twins relative to the 15% concordance for dizygotic twins" (Rapp and Bachevalier, 2003, p. 1193).*

Leo, J. (2003). *The Fallacy of the 50% Concordance Rate for Schizophrenia in Identical Twins. Human Nature Review* http://human-nature.com/nibbs/03/joseph.html

Copy number variants *multiple alleles at specific allele sites is an uncommon mode of genetic influence, and reliance on this model has hindered progress in research.*

Schizophrenia Working Group of the Psychiatric Genomics Consortium. Biological insights from 108 schizophrenia-associated genetic loci. *Nature* **511**, 421–427 (2014). https://doi.org/10.1038/nature13595

Gejman, P. V., Sanders, A. R., & Duan, J. (2010). The role of genetics in the etiology of schizophrenia. *The Psychiatric clinics of North America*, *33*(1), 35–66. https://doi.org/10.1016/j.psc.2009.12.003

Morris-Rosendahl D. J. (2002). Are there anxious genes?. *Dialogues in clinical neuroscience*, *4*(3), 251–260. https://doi.org/10.31887/DCNS.2002.4.3/dmrosendahl

Lawrence, R. E., & Appelbaum, P. S. (2011). Genetic testing in psychiatry: a review of attitudes and beliefs. *Psychiatry*, *74*(4), 315–331. https://doi.org/10.1521/psyc.2011.74.4.315

GWAS approach: *studying correlations of the entire genome of a large population of individuals correlated with diagnosis or other indicators, seeking statistical relationships of multiple loci.*

Collins, A., & Sullivan, P. (2013). Genome-wide association studies in psychiatry: What have we learned? *British Journal of Psychiatry, 202*(1), 1-4. http://bjp.rcpsych.org/content/202/1/1

Sullivan, P. F., Daly, M. J., & O'Donovan, M. (2012). Genetic architectures of psychiatric disorders: the emerging picture and its implications. *Nature reviews. Genetics*, *13*(8), https://doi.org/10.1038/nrg3240

Sullivan, P. F., & Geschwind, D. H. (2019). Defining the Genetic, Genomic,

References

Cellular, and Diagnostic Architectures of Psychiatric Disorders. *Cell, 177*(1), 162–183. https://doi.org/10.1016/j.cell.2019.01.015

Sullivan, P. F., Neale, M. C., & Kendler, K. S. (2000). Genetic epidemiology of major depression: review and meta-analysis. *The American journal of psychiatry, 157*(10), 1552–1562. https://doi.org/10.1176/appi.ajp.157.10.1552

Duncan, L. E., & Keller, M. C. (2011). A critical review of the first 10 years of candidate gene-by-environment interaction research in psychiatry. *The American journal of psychiatry, 168*(10), 1041–1049. https://doi.org/10.1176/appi.ajp.2011.11020191

Smoller J. W. (2019). Psychiatric Genetics Begins to Find Its Footing. *The American journal of psychiatry, 176*(8), 609–614. https://doi.org/10.1176/appi.ajp.2019.19060643

Border, R., Johnson, E. C., Evans, L. M., Smolen, A., Berley, N., Sullivan, P. F., & Keller, M. C. (2019). No Support for Historical Candidate Gene or Candidate Gene-by-Interaction Hypotheses for Major Depression Across Multiple Large Samples. *The American journal of psychiatry, 176*(5), 376–387. https://doi.org/10.1176/appi.ajp.2018.18070881

Sullivan, P. F., Agrawal, A., Bulik, C. M., Andreassen, O. A., Børglum, A. D., Breen, G., Cichon, S., Edenberg, H. J., Faraone, S. V., Gelernter, J., Mathews, C. A., Nievergelt, C. M., Smoller, J. W., O'Donovan, M. C., & Psychiatric Genomics Consortium (2018). Psychiatric Genomics: An Update and an Agenda. *The American journal of psychiatry, 175*(1), 15–27. https://doi.org/10.1176/appi.ajp.2017.17030283

24) *Medical genetics in other areas of medicine finds gene loci with specific genetic effects and related disorders. Some like "sickle cell" have adaptive value in some environments, but not others. Studies of the effect of radiation on genetic mutation encouraged the importance of point mutations in producing disease, a rare explanation for genetic variation.*

Murray, G. K., Lin, T., Austin, J., McGrath, J. J., Hickie, I. B., & Wray, N. R. (2021). Could Polygenic Risk Scores Be Useful in Psychiatry?: A Review. *JAMA psychiatry, 78*(2), 210–219. https://doi.org/10.1001/jamapsychiatry.2020.3042

Choi, S.W., Mak, T.SH. & O'Reilly, P.F. Tutorial: a guide to performing polygenic risk score analyses. *Nat Protoc* **15,** 2759–2772 (2020). https://doi.org/10.1038/s41596-020-0353-1

Bouwkamp, C. G., Kievit, A., Markx, S., Friedman, J. I., van Zutven, L., van Minkelen, R., Vrijenhoek, T., Xu, B., Sterrenburg-van de Nieuwegiessen, I., Veltman, J. A., Bonifati, V., & Kushner, S. A. (2017). Copy Number Variation in Syndromic Forms of Psychiatric Illness: The Emerging Value of Clinical Genetic Testing in Psychiatry. *The American journal of psychiatry, 174*(11), 1036–1050. https://doi.org/10.1176/appi.ajp.2017.16080946

Cross-Disorder Group of the Psychiatric Genomics Consortium (2013). Identification of risk loci with shared effects on five major psychiatric disorders: a genome-wide analysis. *Lancet (London, England), 381*(9875), 1371–1379.

https://doi.org/10.1016/S0140-6736(12)62129-1
Akbarian, S., Liu, C., Knowles, J. et al. The PsychENCODE project. *Nat Neurosci* **18,** 1707–1712 (2015). https://doi.org/10.1038/nn.4156 https://psychencode.synapse.org/
Gandal, M. J., Haney, J. R., Parikshak, N. N., Leppa, V., Ramaswami, G., Hartl, C., Schork, A. J., Appadurai, V., Buil, A., Werge, T. M., Liu, C., White, K. P., CommonMind Consortium, PsychENCODE Consortium, iPSYCH-BROAD Working Group, Horvath, S., & Geschwind, D. H. (2018). Shared molecular neuropathology across major psychiatric disorders parallels polygenic overlap. *Science (New York, N.Y.)*, *359*(6376), 693–697. https://doi.org/10.1126/science.aad6469
25) Lotan, A., Fenckova, M., Bralten, J., Alttoa, A., Dixson, L., Williams, R. W., & van der Voet, M. (2014). Neuroinformatic analyses of common and distinct genetic components associated with major neuropsychiatric disorders. *Frontiers in neuroscience*, *8*, 331. https://doi.org/10.3389/fnins.2014.00331
Hoehe, M. R., & Morris-Rosendahl, D. J. (2018). The role of genetics and genomics in clinical psychiatry. *Dialogues in clinical neuroscience*, *20*(3), 169–177. https://doi.org/10.31887/DCNS.2018.20.3/mhoehe
Fullerton, J. M., & Nurnberger, J. I. (2019). Polygenic risk scores in psychiatry: Will they be useful for clinicians?. *F1000Research*, *8*, F1000 Faculty Rev-1293. https://doi.org/10.12688/f1000research.18491.1
Gómez-Carrillo, A., Langlois-Thérien, T., & Kirmayer, L. J. (2018). Precision Psychiatry-Yes, but Precisely What?. *JAMA psychiatry*, *75*(12), 1302–1303. https://doi.org/10.1001/jamapsychiatry.2018.2651
International Schizophrenia Consortium, Purcell, S. M., Wray, N. R., Stone, J. L., Visscher, P. M., O'Donovan, M. C., Sullivan, P. F., & Sklar, P. (2009). Common polygenic variation contributes to risk of schizophrenia and bipolar disorder. *Nature*, *460*(7256), 748–752. https://doi.org/10.1038/nature08185
Doherty, J. L., & Owen, M. J. (2014). Genomic insights into the overlap between psychiatric disorders: implications for research and clinical practice. *Genome medicine*, *6*(4), 29. https://doi.org/10.1186/gm546
Cross-Disorder Group of the Psychiatric Genomics Consortium. Genetic relationship between five psychiatric disorders estimated from genome-wide SNPs. *Nat Genet* **45,** 984–994 (2013). https://doi.org/10.1038/ng.2711 https://www.nature.com/articles/ng.2711#citeas
http://www.wiringthebrain.com/2010/02/whats-in-name-genetic-overlap-between.html
26) Chess, S., Thomas, A., Rutter, M., & Birch, H. G. (1963). Interaction of temperament and environment in the production of behavioral disturbances in children. *The American journal of psychiatry*, *120*, 142–148. https://doi.org/10.1176/ajp.120.2.142
Chess, S., & Thomas, A. (2013). **Goodness of fit: Clinical applications, from infancy through adult life**. Routledge. McClowry, S. G., Rodriguez, E. T.,

References

& Koslowitz, R. (2008). Temperament-Based Intervention: Re-examining Goodness of Fit. *European journal of developmental science*, *2*(1-2), 120–135.

27) Koutsilieri, E., Scheller, C., Sopper, S., ter Meulen, V., & Riederer, P. (2002). Psychiatric complications in human immunodeficiency virus infection. *Journal of neurovirology*, *8 Suppl 2*, 129–133. https://doi.org/10.1080/13550280290167948

28) Chapman, M. R., & Vause, H. E. (2011). Anti-NMDA receptor encephalitis: diagnosis, psychiatric presentation, and treatment. *The American journal of psychiatry*, *168*(3), 245–251. https://doi.org/10.1176/appi.ajp.2010.10020181

Day, G. S., High, S. M., Cot, B., & Tang-Wai, D. F. (2011). Anti-NMDA-receptor encephalitis: case report and literature review of an under-recognized condition. *Journal of general internal medicine*, *26*(7), 811–816. https://doi.org/10.1007/s11606-011-1641-9

29) Madhusoodanan, S., Ting, M. B., Farah, T., & Ugur, U. (2015). Psychiatric aspects of brain tumors: A review. *World journal of psychiatry*, *5*(3), 273–285. https://doi.org/10.5498/wjp.v5.i3.273

Zhang, S., Xu, M., Liu, Z. J., Feng, J., & Ma, Y. (2020). Neuropsychiatric issues after stroke: Clinical significance and therapeutic implications. *World journal of psychiatry*, *10*(6), 125–138. https://doi.org/10.5498/wjp.v10.i6.125

30) http://dvbic.dcoe.mil/files/DVBIC_Research_Research-Review_TBI-Irritability-Agression_Feb2016_v1.0_2016-04-05.pdf

Gavett, B. E., Stern, R. A., & McKee, A. C. (2011). Chronic traumatic encephalopathy: a potential late effect of sport-related concussive and subconcussive head trauma. *Clinics in sports medicine*, *30*(1), 179–xi. https://doi.org/10.1016/j.csm.2010.09.007

Mez J, Daneshvar DH, Kiernan PT, et al. Clinicopathological Evaluation of Chronic Traumatic Encephalopathy in Players of American Football. *JAMA*. 2017;318(4):360–370. https://jamanetwork.com/journals/jama/fullarticle/2645104

Arciniegas, D. B., Frey, K. L., Newman, J., & Wortzel, H. S. (2010). Evaluation and Management of Posttraumatic Cognitive Impairments. *Psychiatric Annals*, *40*(11), 540–552. https://doi.org/10.3928/00485713-20101022-05

31) Breen, P. W., & Krishnan, V. (2020). Recent Preclinical Insights Into the Treatment of Chronic Traumatic Encephalopathy. *Frontiers in neuroscience*, *14*, 616. https://doi.org/10.3389/fnins.2020.00616

32) Victoria Tepe, PhD , Alison Cernich, PhD, ABPP-Cn , and James Kelly, MD, Polytraumatic TBI: Perspectives from Military Medicine, DOI/ 10.3928:00485713-20130703-04

Yurgil, K. A., Barkauskas, D. A., Vasterling, J. J., Nievergelt, C. M., Larson, G. E., Schork, N. J., Litz, B. T., Nash, W. P., Baker, D. G., & Marine Resiliency Study Team (2014). Association between traumatic brain injury and risk of posttraumatic stress disorder in active-duty Marines. *JAMA psychiatry*, *71*(2), 149–157. https://doi.org/10.1001/jamapsychiatry.2013.3080

33) Kendler K. S. (2020). A Prehistory of the Diathesis-Stress Model: Predisposing and Exciting Causes of Insanity in the 19th Century. *The American journal of psychiatry*, *177*(7), 576–588. https://doi.org/10.1176/appi.ajp.2020.19111213

Kendler, K. S., & Gardner, C. O. (2010). Dependent stressful life events and prior depressive episodes in the prediction of major depression: the problem of causal inference in psychiatric epidemiology. *Archives of general psychiatry*, *67*(11), 1120–1127. https://doi.org/10.1001/archgenpsychiatry.2010.136

Kendler KS, Prescott CA, Myers J, Neale MC. The Structure of Genetic and Environmental Risk Factors for Common Psychiatric and Substance Use Disorders in Men and Women. *Arch Gen Psychiatry*. 2003;60(9):929–937. http://jamanetwork.com/journals/jamapsychiatry/fullarticle/207813

Monzani B, Rijsdijk F, Harris J, Mataix-Cols D. The Structure of Genetic and Environmental Risk Factors for Dimensional Representations of *DSM-5* Obsessive-Compulsive Spectrum Disorders. *JAMA Psychiatry*. 2014;71(2):182–189. https://jamanetwork.com/journals/jamapsychiatry/fullarticle/1792141

Caspi, A., Hariri, A. R., Holmes, A., Uher, R., & Moffitt, T. E. (2010). Genetic sensitivity to the environment: the case of the serotonin transporter gene and its implications for studying complex diseases and traits. *The American journal of psychiatry*, *167*(5), https://doi.org/10.1176/appi.ajp.2010.09101452

Risch, N., Herrell, R., Lehner, T., Liang, K. Y., Eaves, L., Hoh, J., Griem, A., Kovacs, M., Ott, J., & Merikangas, K. R. (2009). Interaction between the serotonin transporter gene (5-HTTLPR), stressful life events, and risk of depression: a meta-analysis. *JAMA*, *301*(23), https://doi.org/10.1001/jama.2009.878

Karg, K., Burmeister, M., Shedden, K., & Sen, S. (2011). The serotonin transporter promoter variant (5-HTTLPR), stress, and depression meta-analysis revisited: evidence of genetic moderation. *Archives of general psychiatry*, *68*(5), 444–454. https://doi.org/10.1001/archgenpsychiatry.2010.189

Sen, S., Burmeister, M., & Ghosh, D. (2004). Meta-analysis of the association between a serotonin transporter promoter polymorphism (5-HTTLPR) and anxiety-related personality traits. *American journal of medical genetics. Part B, Neuropsychiatric genetics : the official publication of the International Society of Psychiatric Genetics*, *127B*(1), 85–89. https://doi.org/10.1002/ajmg.b.20158

Culverhouse, R. C., Saccone, N. L., Horton, A. C., Ma, Y., Anstey, K. J., Banaschewski, T., Burmeister, M., Cohen-Woods, S., Etain, B., Fisher, H. L., Goldman, N., Guillaume, S., Horwood, J., Juhasz, G., Lester, K. J., Mandelli, L., Middeldorp, C. M., Olié, E., Villafuerte, S., Air, T. M., … Bierut, L. J. (2018). Collaborative meta-analysis finds no evidence of a strong interaction between stress and 5-HTTLPR genotype contributing to the development of depression. *Molecular psychiatry*, *23*(1), 133–142. https://doi.org/10.1038/mp.2017.44

Dick D. M. (2011). Gene-environment interaction in psychological traits and disorders. *Annual review of clinical psychology*, *7*, 383–409. https://doi.org/10.1146/annurev-clinpsy-032210-104518

Duncan, L. E., & Keller, M. C. (2011). A critical review of the first 10 years of candidate gene-by-environment interaction research in psychiatry. *The American journal of psychiatry*, *168*(10), 1041–1049. https://doi.org/10.1176/appi.ajp.2011.11020191

34) Karcher, N. R., Barch, D. M., Demers, C. H., Baranger, D., Heath, A. C., Lynskey, M. T., & Agrawal, A. (2019). Genetic Predisposition vs Individual-Specific Processes in the Association Between Psychotic-like Experiences and Cannabis Use. *JAMA psychiatry*, *76*(1), 87–94 https://doi.org/10.1001/jamapsychiatry.2018.2546

35) Marmarosh C. L. (2012). Empirically supported perspectives on transference. *Psychotherapy (Chicago, Ill.)*, *49*(3), 364–369. https://doi.org/10.1037/a0028801

https://en.wikipedia.org/wiki/The_Four_Fundamental_Concepts_of_Psychoanalysis

Howard B. Levine M.D. (2014) Psychoanalysis and Trauma, Psychoanalytic Inquiry, 34:3, 214-224, DOI: 10.1080/07351690.2014.889475

Schaefer J. D. (2018). Use of Hierarchical Measures of Psychopathology to Capture the Long (and Wide) Shadow of Early Deprivation in the Bucharest Early Intervention Project Analysis. *JAMA psychiatry*, *75*(11), 1101–1102. https://doi.org/10.1001/jamapsychiatry.2018.2215

Weinberg, R. J., Dietz, L. J., Stoyak, S., Melhem, N. M., Porta, G., Payne, M. W., & Brent, D. A. (2013). A prospective study of parentally bereaved youth, caregiver depression, and body mass index. *The Journal of clinical psychiatry*, *74*(8), 834–840. https://doi.org/10.4088/JCP.12m08284

36) Dlin, B. M., & Fischer, H. K. (1979). The anniversary reaction: a meeting of Freud and Pavlov. *Psychosomatics*, *20*(11), 749–755. https://doi.org/10.1016/s0033-3182(79)73737-6

https://pubmed.ncbi.nlm.nih.gov/523592/

37) Rubin, R. T., Gunderson, E. K., & Arthur, R. J. (1972). Life stress and illness patterns in the US Navy. VI. Environmental, demographic, and prior life change variables in relation to illness onset in naval aviators during a combat cruise. *Psychosomatic medicine*, *34*(6), 533–547. https://doi.org/10.1097/00006842-197211000-00006

Holmes TH, Rahe RH (1967). "The Social Readjustment Rating Scale". J Psychosom Res. **11** *(2): 213–8. doi:10.1016/0022-3999(67)90010-4*

Weiner M. F. (1998). The Symptom-Context Method: Symptoms as Opportunities in Psychotherapy. *The Journal of Psychotherapy Practice and Research*, *7*(3), 259–260.

38) Aybek S, Nicholson TR, Zelaya F, et al. Neural Correlates of Recall of Life Events in Conversion Disorder. *JAMA Psychiatry.* 2014;71(1):52–60. doi:10.1001/jamapsychiatry.2013.2842

https://jamanetwork.com/journals/jamapsychiatry/fullarticle/1780023

39) Verduijn, J., Milaneschi, Y., van Hemert, A. M., Schoevers, R. A., Hickie, I.

B., Penninx, B. W., & Beekman, A. T. (2015). Clinical staging of major depressive disorder: an empirical exploration. *The Journal of clinical psychiatry, 76*(9), 1200–1208. https://doi.org/10.4088/JCP.14m09272

Forbes, D., Nickerson, A., Alkemade, N., Bryant, R. A., Creamer, M., Silove, D., McFarlane, A. C., Van Hooff, M., Fletcher, S. L., & O'Donnell, M. (2015). Longitudinal analysis of latent classes of psychopathology and patterns of class migration in survivors of severe injury. *The Journal of clinical psychiatry, 76*(9), 1193–1199. https://doi.org/10.4088/JCP.14m0907

Pugh WM, Erickson J, Rubin RT, Gunderson E, Rahe CRH. Cluster Analyses of Life Changes: II. Method and Replication in Navy Subpopulations. *Arch Gen Psychiatry.* 1971;25(4):333–339. doi:10.1001/archpsyc.1971.01750160045009

40) See chapter two for family issues. Loss of parent references in chapter eight. Early abuse references in chapter eight.

41) Lifton, R. J. **The Protean Self**, ʃBasic Books (January 4, 1995) ISBN-13ˀ : ʃ 978-0465064212

42) de C Williams, A. C., & van der Merwe, J. (2013). The psychological impact of torture. *British journal of pain, 7*(2), 101–106. https://doi.org/10.1177/2049463713483596

Holtz T. H. (1998). Refugee trauma versus torture trauma: a retrospective controlled cohort study of Tibetan refugees. *The Journal of nervous and mental disease, 186*(1), 24–34. https://doi.org/10.1097/00005053-199801000-00005

Singh, A. R., & Singh, A. N. (2010). The mental health consequences of being a child soldier - an international perspective. *International psychiatry : bulletin of the Board of International Affairs of the Royal College of Psychiatrists, 7*(3), 55–57.

43) Pols H. (2007). August Hollingshead and Frederick Redlich: poverty, socioeconomic status, and mental illness. *American journal of public health, 97*(10), 1755. https://doi.org/10.2105/AJPH.2007.117606

Shim, R., Koplan, C., Langheim, F. J. P., Manseau, M. W., Powers, R. A., & Compton, M. T. (2014). The social determinants of mental health: An overview and call to action. *Psychiatric Annals, 44*(1), 22–26. https://doi.org/10.3928/00485713-20140108-04

Schwartz, S., & Meyer, I. H. (2010). Mental health disparities research: the impact of within and between group analyses on tests of social stress hypotheses. *Social science & medicine (1982), 70*(8), 1111–1118. https://doi.org/10.1016/j.socscimed.2009.11.032

Meyer, I. H., Schwartz, S., & Frost, D. M. (2008). Social patterning of stress and coping: does disadvantaged social statuses confer more stress and fewer coping resources?. *Social science & medicine (1982), 67*(3), 368–379. https://doi.org/10.1016/j.socscimed.2008.03.012

M Rotter MTCompton The social determinants of mental health. New York State Office of Mental health. https://omh.ny.gov/omhweb/omh-institute/sdmh-white-paper.pdf

References

44) GOFFMAN, E., STIGMA Publisher: Touchstone (June 15, 1986) Length: 168 pages
ISBN13: 9780671622442
Crichton P. (2007). The Divided Self. *BMJ : British Medical Journal, 334*(7586), 211. https://doi.org/10.1136/bmj.39101.540347.BE
45) Walker, M.T. (2006). The Social Construction of Mental Illness and its Implications for the Recovery Model. **InternationalJournal of Psychosocial Rehabilitation. 10 (1), 71-87**
https://courses.lumenlearning.com/wmopen-introtosociology/chapter/reality-as-a-social-construct/
46) Alegría, M., NeMoyer, A., Falgàs Bagué, I., Wang, Y., & Alvarez, K. (2018). Social Determinants of Mental Health: Where We Are and Where We Need to Go. *Current psychiatry reports, 20*(11), 95. https://doi.org/10.1007/s11920-018-0969-9
47) Weissman M. M. (1975). The assessment of social adjustment. A review of techniques. *Archives of general psychiatry, 32*(3), 357–365. https://doi.org/10.1001/archpsyc.1975.01760210091006
Brief Psychiatric Rating Scale (BPRS)
https://priory.com/psych/bprs.htm HYPERLINK
Classification of Neurocognitive Disorders in DSM-5: A Work in Progress
http://jaapl.org/content/42/2/159/tab-article-info
Assessing levels of adaptive functioning: The Role Functioning Scale | SpringerLink 0c960514d5f56288cf000000.pdf
Los Reyes, A., Makol, B. A., Racz, S. J., Youngstrom, E. A., Lerner, M. D., & Keeley, L. M. (2019). The Work and Social Adjustment Scale for Youth: A Measure for Assessing Youth Psychosocial Impairment Regardless of Mental Health Status. *Journal of child and family studies, 28*(1), 1–16. https://doi.org/10.1007/s10826-018-1238-6
Gameroff, M. J., Wickramaratne, P., & Weissman, M. M. (2012). Testing the Short and Screener versions of the Social Adjustment Scale-Self-report (SAS-SR). *International journal of methods in psychiatric research, 21*(1), 52–65. https://doi.org/10.1002/mpr.358
48) Vaillant G. E. (2011). Involuntary coping mechanisms: a psychodynamic perspective. *Dialogues in clinical neuroscience, 13*(3), 366–370. https://doi.org/10.31887/DCNS.2011.13.2/gvaillant
Vaillant, G. E. (1992). ***Ego mechanisms of defense: A guide for clinicians and researchers***. American Psychiatric Association.
Martin-Joy, J. S., Malone, J. C., Cui, X. J., Johansen, P. Ø., Hill, K. P., Rahman, M. O., Waldinger, R. J., & Vaillant, G. E. (2017). Development of Adaptive Coping From Mid to Late Life: A 70-Year Longitudinal Study of Defense Maturity and Its Psychosocial Correlates. *The Journal of nervous and mental disease, 205*(9), 685–691. https://doi.org/10.1097/NMD.0000000000000711
Vaillant, G. E. (1977). ***Adaptation to Life***. Boston, MA: Little Brown and Co.

McCrae, Robert R. and John, Oliver P., "An Introduction to the Five-Factor Model and Its Applications" (1992). Public Health Resources. 556. https://digitalcommons.unl.edu/publichealthresources/556

Kernberg OF, Caligor E (2005) A psychoanalytic theory of personality disorders. In: Clarkin J F, Lenzenweger M F, *Major Theories of Personality Disorder*. Guilford, New York, USA, 114-156.

Gordon RM, Spektor V, Luu L (2019) Personality Organization Traits and Expected Countertransference and Treatment Interventions. Int J Psychol Psychoanal 5:039. https://www.clinmedjournals.org/articles/ijpp/international-journal-of-psychology-and-psychoanalysis-ijpp-5-039.php?jid=ijpp

DSM-5 Personality and Personality Disorders Work Group identified the following six:

1) *negative emotionality*, which includes "facets" of depression, anxiety, shame and guilt; 2) *introversion*, which includes withdrawal from social interaction;
3) *antagonism*, which includes an exaggerated sense of self-importance
4) *disinhibition*, which includes impulsivity;
5) *compulsivity*, which includes perfectionism and rigidity; and
6) *schizotypy*, which includes odd perceptions and beliefs.

49) Luthar, S. S., Cicchetti, D., & Becker, B. (2000). The construct of resilience: a critical evaluation and guidelines for future work. *Child development*, *71*(3), 543–562. https://doi.org/10.1111/1467-8624.00164

Hiebel Nina, Rabe Milena, Maus Katja, Peusquens Frank, Radbruch Lukas, Geiser Franziska, Resilience in Adult Health Science Revisited—A Narrative Review Synthesis of Process-Oriented Approaches, Frontiers in Psychology,12,2021 https://www.frontiersin.org/article/10.3389/fpsyg.2021.659395

Fleming, J., & Ledogar, R. J. (2008). Resilience, an Evolving Concept: A Review of Literature Relevant to Aboriginal Research. *Pimatisiwin*, *6*(2), 7–23.

50) *There are many reasons why the DSM AXIS V was not emphasized, but one is the impact of health insurance. Insurers required specific levels of disability to cover services, and discontinue coverage if the symptoms improve above this level. The chronic administration of medications is accepted as long term treatment, even when no improvement in social function occurs, but psycho-social interventions are no longer covered after specified sessions.*

51) Distinguishing insurable "medical" treatment that returns the individual to *adequate* social function, from intervention for "personal growth" which expands adaptive ability, and is a "learning" enhancement, and paid for in some other way.

52) https://www.sciencedirect.com/topics/social-sciences/professional-regulation
https://www.ama-assn.org/delivering-care/ethics/code-medical-ethics-professional-self-regulation

References

53) Alexander Brooks, Notes on Defining the "dangerousness" of the Mentally Ill.
Stanislaus A. (2013). Assessment of dangerousness in clinical practice. *Missouri medicine*, *110*(1), 61–64.
Sowislo, J., Gonet-Wirz, F., Borgwardt, S. *et al.* Perceived Dangerousness as Related to Psychiatric Symptoms and Psychiatric Service Use – a Vignette Based Representative Population Survey. *Sci Rep* **7**, 45716 (2017). https://doi.org/10.1038/srep45716
A variety of scales and etc have been developed to measure danger risk, none of which has any reliability.
54) Tarasoff: https://en.wikipedia.org/wiki/Tarasoff_v._Regents_of_the_University_of_California
https://www.apa.org/monitor/julaug05/jn
55) The situation in which a person is determined to be a danger to self, but not able to be sequestered safely for lack of placement is not unlikely in the current climate of reduced public health spending.
56) Snowden L. R. (2003). Bias in mental health assessment and intervention: theory and evidence. *American journal of public health*, *93*(2), 239–243. https://doi.org/10.2105/ajph.93.2.239
Jasmine R Marcelin, Dawd S Siraj, Robert Victor, Shaila Kotadia, Yvonne A Maldonado, The Impact of Unconscious Bias in Healthcare: How to Recognize and Mitigate It, *The Journal of Infectious Diseases*, Volume 220, Issue Supplement_2, 15 September 2019, Pages S62–S73, https://doi.org/10.1093/infdis/jiz214   https://academic.oup.com/jid/article/220/Supplement_2/S62/5552356
Measuring bias to health care in the military. https://www.rand.org/pubs/research_reports/RR1762.html
57) Theodor REIK, ***Listening With The Third Ear: The Inner Experience Of A Psychoanalyst***
58) (Fadiman, A. (2018). ***The spirit catches you and you fall down : a Hmong child, her American doctors, and the collision of two cultures***. Simon Fraser University Library.)
Lu, A.-P. (2004). **Theory of traditional Chinese medicine and therapeutic method of diseases.** *World Journal of Gastroenterology*, *10*(13), 1854. https://doi.org/10.3748/wjg.v10.i13.1854
59) Culture and psychiatric evaluation: operationalizing cultural formulation for DSM-5. - PubMed - NCBI
Stoller, R. J., & Herdt, G. H. (1985). Theories of origins of male homosexuality. A cross-cultural look. *Archives of general psychiatry*, *42*(4), 399–404. https://doi.org/10.1001/archpsyc.1985.01790270089010
60) Epstein, R. M., & Street, R. L., Jr (2011). The values and value of patient-centered care. *Annals of family medicine*, *9*(2), 100–103. https://doi.org/10.1370/afm.1239

*https://www.oneviewhealthcare.com/
the-eight-principles-of-patient-centered-care/*
61) Kendell, R., & Jablensky, A. (2003). Distinguishing between the validity and utility of psychiatric diagnoses. *The American journal of psychiatry, 160*(1), 4–12. https://doi.org/10.1176/appi.ajp.160.1.4
Voineskos A. N. (2018). Predicting Functional Outcomes in Early-Stage Mental Illness: Prognostic Precision Medicine Realized?. *JAMA psychiatry, 75*(11), 1105–1106. https://doi.org/10.1001/jamapsychiatry.2018.2410
Deif Reem, Salama Mohamed. Depression From a Precision Mental Health Perspective: Utilizing Personalized Conceptualizations to Guide Personalized Treatments, Frontiers in Psychiatry, 12, 2021, p662 https://www.frontiersin.org/article/10.3389/fpsyt.2021.650318
DeFife, J. A., Peart, J., Bradley, B., Ressler, K., Drill, R., & Westen, D. (2013). Validity of prototype diagnosis for mood and anxiety disorders. *JAMA psychiatry, 70*(2), 140–148. https://doi.org/10.1001/jamapsychiatry.2013.270
https://jamanetwork.com/journals/jamapsychiatry/fullarticle/1465613
62) Fusar-Poli, P., Hijazi, Z., Stahl, D., & Steyerberg, E. W. (2018). The Science of Prognosis in Psychiatry: A Review. *JAMA psychiatry, 75*(12), 1289–1297. https://doi.org/10.1001/jamapsychiatry.2018.2530
van Borkulo, C., Boschloo, L., Borsboom, D., Penninx, B. W., Waldorp, L. J., & Schoevers, R. A. (2015). Association of Symptom Network Structure With the Course of (corrected) Depression. *JAMA psychiatry, 72*(12), 1219–1226. https://doi.org/10.1001/jamapsychiatry.2015.2079
https://jamanetwork.com/journals/jamapsychiatry/fullarticle/2469105
A.I. Versus M.D. - The New Yorker
Mandl KD, Bourgeois FT. The Evolution of Patient Diagnosis: From Art to Digital Data-Driven Science. *JAMA*. 2017;318(19):1859–1860. doi:10.1001/jama.2017.15028
63) https://www.medpagetoday.com/opinion/kevinmd/97880
https://www.medicaleconomics.com/view/why-are-ehrs-still-so-terrible
The Algorithm Will See You Now. How Artificial Intelligence is Changing Medicine | Congress of Neurological Surgeons
Mandl KD, Bourgeois FT. The Evolution of Patient Diagnosis: From Art to Digital Data-Driven Science. *JAMA*. 2017;318(19):1859–1860. https://jamanetwork.com/journals/jama/article-abstract/2
Weissman, M. M., Pathak, J., & Talati, A. (2020). Personal Life Events-A Promising Dimension for Psychiatry in Electronic Health Records. *JAMA psychiatry, 77*(2), 115–116. https://doi.org/10.1001/jamapsychiatry.2019.321798

CHAPTER ELEVEN REFERENCES

1) Klemperer, F. (1992). No twisted thought without a twisted molecule. *Psychiatric Bulletin, 16*(3), 167-167. doi:10.1192/pb.16.3.167
https://www.psychiatrictimes.com/view/battle-soul-psychiatry-ronald-w-pies-md
https://qz.com/1162154/30-years-after-prozac-arrived-we-still-buy-the-lie-that-chemical-imbalances-cause-depression/
2) Rasmussen N. (2008). America's first amphetamine epidemic 1929-1971: a quantitative and qualitative retrospective with implications for the present. *American journal of public health, 98*(6), 974–985. https://doi.org/10.2105/AJPH.2007.110593
3) **Goldacre, Ben.** ***Bad Pharma: How Drug Companies Mislead Doctors and Harm Patients.*** **New York: Faber & Faber,, an Affiliate of Farrar, Straus and Giroux, 2014. Print.**
An Amazon book search of "big pharma" will produce a list of titles about this topic.
4) Nassir Ghaemi, S., Shirzadi, A. A., & Filkowski, M. (2008). Publication bias and the pharmaceutical industry: the case of lamotrigine in bipolar disorder. *Medscape journal of medicine, 10*(9), 211.
Turner, E. H., Matthews, A. M., Linardatos, E., Tell, R. A., & Rosenthal, R. (2008). Selective publication of antidepressant trials and its influence on apparent efficacy. *The New England journal of medicine, 358*(3), 252–260. https://doi.org/10.1056/NEJMsa065779
5) Citrome L. (2014). Quantifying clinical relevance. *Innovations in clinical neuroscience, 11*(5-6), 26–30.
"Evidence based" was introduced into medicine to identify treatments that have research documentation, compared to treatments based on clinicians' choices from practical experience. Patients and funding sources seek treatment with "scientific evidence" of effectiveness. "Evidence based" encourages a one-size-fits-all mentality about patient dosage, and clinicians need to adjust the "evidence" with clinical experience.
Kraemer, H. C., Wilson, G. T., Fairburn, C. G., & Agras, W. S. (2002). Mediators and moderators of treatment effects in randomized clinical trials. *Archives of general psychiatry, 59*(10), 877–883. https://doi.org/10.1001/archpsyc.59.10.877
Ho, G. J., Liew, S. M., Ng, C. J., Hisham Shunmugam, R., & Glasziou, P. (2016). Development of a Search Strategy for an Evidence Based Retrieval Service. *PloS one, 11*(12), e0167170. https://doi.org/10.1371/journal.pone.0167170
Patricia Benner; Ronda G. Hughes; Molly Sutphen, Chapter 6 Clinical Reasoning, Decisionmaking, and Action: Thinking Critically and Clinically https://www.ncbi.nlm.nih.gov/books/NBK2643/

Holyoak_Cheng_1995_PragmaticReasoning.pdf
7) Fleischhacker W. W. (2017). A Meta View on Meta-analyses. *JAMA psychiatry*, *74*(7), 684–685. https://doi.org/10.1001/jamapsychiatry.2017.1167https://pubmed.ncbi.nlm.nih.gov/28514464/
Mikolajewicz, N., & Komarova, S. V. (2019). Meta-Analytic Methodology for Basic Research: A Practical Guide. *Frontiers in physiology*, *10*, 203. https://doi.org/10.3389/fphys.2019.00203
8) https://thebrain.mcgill.ca/flash/capsules/pdf_articles/drugeffect_synapse.pdf
Lauffenburger, D. A., Linderman, J. (1993). **Receptors: Models for Binding, Trafficking, and Signaling**. United States: Oxford University Press.
Andrade, C., & Rao, N. S. (2010). How antidepressant drugs act: A primer on neuroplasticity as the eventual mediator of antidepressant efficacy. *Indian journal of psychiatry*, *52*(4), 378–386. https://doi.org/10.4103/0019-5545.74318
Chapter 6: Synaptic Transmission in the Central Nervous System John H. Byrne, Ph.D., https://nba.uth.tmc.edu/neuroscience/m/s1/chapter06.html
Kamel, F., & Hoppin, J. A. (2004). Association of pesticide exposure with neurologic dysfunction and disease. *Environmental health perspectives*, *112*(9), 950–958. https://doi.org/10.1289/ehp.7135
Purves D, Augustine GJ, Fitzpatrick D, et al., editors. Neuroscience. 2nd edition. Sunderland (MA): Sinauer Associates; 2001. Peptide Neurotransmitters. https://www.ncbi.nlm.nih.gov/books/NBK10873/
9) Wu, C., & Sun, D. (2015). GABA receptors in brain development, function, and injury. *Metabolic brain disease*, *30*(2), 367–379. https://doi.org/10.1007/s11011-014-9560-1
Decavel, C. and Van Den Pol, A.N. (1990), GABA: A dominant neurotransmitter in the hypothalamus. J. Comp. Neurol., 302: 1019-1037. https://doi.org/10.1002/cne.903020423
10) https://en.wikipedia.org/wiki/Monoamine_neurotransmitter
http://pittmedneuro.com/monoamines.html
Stephen R. Saklad; Graphic representation of pharmacology: Development of an alternative model. *Mental Health Clinician* 1 September 2017; 7 (5): 201–206. https://doi.org/10.9740/mhc.2017.09.201
https://meridian.allenpress.com/mhc/article/7/5/201/37224/Graphic-representation-of-pharmacology-Development
11) What is an inhibitory constant (Ki) and how does it relate to understanding drug interactions?
https://www.ebmconsult.com/articles/inhibitory-constant-ki-drug-interactions
Michaelis–Menten kinetics - Wikipedia
Anna Gaulton, Louisa J. Bellis, A. Patricia Bento, Jon Chambers, Mark Davies, Anne Hersey, Yvonne Light, Shaun McGlinchey, David Michalovich, Bissan Al-Lazikani, John P. Overington, ChEMBL: a large-scale bioactivity database for drug discovery, *Nucleic Acids Research*, Volume 40, Issue D1, 1 January 2012, Pages D1100–D1107, https://doi.org/10.1093/nar/gkr777

References

Keiser, M., Setola, V., Irwin, J. et al. Predicting new molecular targets for known drugs. *Nature* **462**, 175–181 (2009). https://doi.org/10.1038/nature08506 https://www.nature.com/articles/nature08506

12) Schwartz T. L. (2010). Psychopharmacology Today: Where are We and Where Do We Go From Here?. *Mens sana monographs*, *8*(1), 6–16. https://doi.org/10.4103/0973-1229.58816

Roden, D. M., Wilke, R. A., Kroemer, H. K., & Stein, C. M. (2011). Pharmacogenomics: the genetics of variable drug responses. *Circulation*, *123*(15), 1661–1670. https://doi.org/10.1161/CIRCULATIONAHA.109.914820

Greden, J. F., Parikh, S. V., Rothschild, A. J., Thase, M. E., Dunlop, B. W., DeBattista, C., ... Dechairo, B. (2019). Impact of pharmacogenomics on clinical outcomes in major depressive disorder in the GUIDED trial: A large, patient- and rater-blinded, randomized, controlled study. *Journal of Psychiatric Research*, *111*, 59–67. https://doi.org/10.1016/j.jpsychires.2019.01.003

Rosenblat, J. D., Lee, Y., & McIntyre, R. S. (2017). Does Pharmacogenomic Testing Improve Clinical Outcomes for Major Depressive Disorder? *The Journal of Clinical Psychiatry*, *78*(06), 720–729. https://doi.org/10.4088/jcp.15r10583

13) Mayberg, H. S., Silva, J. A., Brannan, S. K., Tekell, J. L., Mahurin, R. K., McGinnis, S., & Jerabek, P. A. (2002). The functional neuroanatomy of the placebo effect. *The American journal of psychiatry*, *159*(5), 728–737. https://doi.org/10.1176/appi.ajp.159.5.728

The Schachter-Singer experiment on emotion. Subjects given an injection of amphetamine experienced different social situations, and their report of emotional response reflected **both** *the arousal level and the social situation. There is a consistent failure to recognize the interaction of these two factors in medication administration, a collaborative interpersonal process in which both individuals must participate.* https://replicationindex.com/2019/02/24/schachter-and-singer-1962-the-experiment-that-never-happened/

Leon A. C. (2011). Two clinical trial designs to examine personalized treatments for psychiatric disorders. *The Journal of clinical psychiatry*, *72*(5), 593–597. https://doi.org/10.4088/JCP.09com05581whi

Balint E. (1969). The possibilities of patient-centered medicine. *The Journal of the Royal College of General Practitioners*, *17*(82), 269–276.

14) Mojtabai, R., & Olfson, M. (2014). National trends in long-term use of antidepressant medications: results from the U.S. National Health and Nutrition Examination Survey. *The Journal of clinical psychiatry*, *75*(2), 169–177. https://doi.org/10.4088/JCP.13m08443

Hillhouse, T. M., & Porter, J. H. (2015). A brief history of the development of antidepressant drugs: from monoamines to glutamate. *Experimental and clinical psychopharmacology*, *23*(1), 1–21. https://doi.org/10.1037/a0038550

Wang, H., Goehring, A., Wang, K. et al. Structural basis for action by diverse antidepressants on biogenic amine transporters. *Nature* **503**, 141–145 (2013). https://doi.org/10.1038/nature12648

Godlewska, B.R., Harmer, C.J. Cognitive neuropsychological theory of antidepressant action: a modern-day approach to depression and its treatment. *Psychopharmacology* **238**, 1265–1278 (2021). https://doi.org/10.1007/s00213-019-05448-0

De Vry J. (1995). 5-HT1A receptor agonists: recent developments and controversial issues. *Psychopharmacology*, *121*(1), 1–26. https://doi.org/10.1007/BF02245588

Mary L. Phillips, Henry W. Chase, Yvette I. Sheline, Amit Etkin, Jorge R.C. Almeida, Thilo Deckersbach, and Madhukar H. Trivedi, Identifying Predictors, Moderators, and Mediators of Antidepressant Response in Major Depressive Disorder: Neuroimaging Approaches, American Journal of Psychiatry 2015 172:2, 124-138 https://ajp.psychiatryonline.org/action/showCitFormats?doi=10.1176

Crane, N. A., Jenkins, L. M., Bhaumik, R., Dion, C., Gowins, J. R., Mickey, B. J., Zubieta, J. K., & Langenecker, S. A. (2017). Multidimensional prediction of treatment response to antidepressants with cognitive control and functional MRI. *Brain : a journal of neurology*, *140*(2), 472–486. https://doi.org/10.1093/brain/aww326

Malhi GS, Bell E, Morris G, Hamilton A. The delay in response to antidepressant therapy: A window of opportunity? Australian & New Zealand Journal of Psychiatry. 2020;54(2):127-129. https://journals.sagepub.com/doi/full/10.1177/0004867419900313

15) Maletic, V., Robinson, M., Oakes, T., Iyengar, S., Ball, S. G., & Russell, J. (2007). Neurobiology of depression: an integrated view of key findings. *International journal of clinical practice*, *61*(12), 2030–2040. https://doi.org/10.1111/j.1742-1241.2007.01602.x

Cowen, P. J., & Browning, M. (2015). What has serotonin to do with depression?. *World psychiatry : official journal of the World Psychiatric Association (WPA)*, *14*(2), https://doi.org/10.1002/wps.20229

16) Andrea Cipriani, Toshi A Furukawa, Georgia Salanti, Anna Chaimani, Lauren Z Atkinson, Yusuke Ogawa, Stefan Leucht, Henricus G Ruhe, Erick H Turner, Julian P T Higgins, Matthias Egger, Nozomi Takeshima, Yu Hayasaka, Hissei Imai, Kiyomi Shinohara, Aran Tajika, John P A Ioannidis, and John R Geddes, Comparative Efficacy and Acceptability of 21 Antidepressant Drugs for the Acute Treatment of Adults With Major Depressive Disorder: A Systematic Review and Network Meta-Analysis https://focus.psychiatryonline.org/doi/full/10.1176/appi.focus.16407

Pringle, A., & Harmer, C. J. (2015). The effects of drugs on human models of emotional processing: an account of antidepressant drug treatment. *Dialogues in clinical neuroscience*, *17*(4), 477–487. https://doi.org/10.31887/DCNS.2015.17.4/apringle

17) Rush A. J. (2007). STAR*D: what have we learned?. *The American journal of psychiatry*, *164*(2), 201–204. https://doi.org/10.1176/ajp.2007.164.2.201

References

18) *Peter D. Kramer* **Listening to Prozac** *Viking NY 1993*
Charles Barber **COMFORTABLY NUMB How Psychiatry is Medicating a Nation**
Pantheon Books NY 2008
19)) Kraemer, H. C., Wilson, G. T., Fairburn, C. G., & Agras, W. S. (2002). Mediators and moderators of treatment effects in randomized clinical trials. *Archives of general psychiatry*, *59*(10), 877–883. https://doi.org/10.1001/archpsyc.59.10.877
Kraemer, H. C., & Kupfer, D. J. (2006). Size of treatment effects and their importance to clinical research and practice. *Biological psychiatry*, *59*(11), 990–996. https://doi.org/10.1016/j.biopsych.2005.09.014
Walsh BT, Seidman SN, Sysko R, Gould M. Placebo Response in Studies of Major Depression: Variable, Substantial, and Growing. *JAMA*. 2002;287(14):1840–1847. doi:10.1001/jama.287.14.1840
https://jamanetwork.com/journals/jama/article-abstract/194819?redirect=true
Kirsch, I., Deacon, B. J., Huedo-Medina, T. B., Scoboria, A., Moore, T. J., & Johnson, B. T. (2008). Initial severity and antidepressant benefits: a meta-analysis of data submitted to the Food and Drug Administration. *PLoS medicine*, *5*(2), e45. https://doi.org/10.1371/journal.pmed.0050045
Enck, P., Klosterhalfen, S., Weimer, K., Horing, B., & Zipfel, S. (2011). The placebo response in clinical trials: more questions than answers. *Philosophical transactions of the Royal Society of London. Series B, Biological sciences*, *366*(1572), 1889–1895. https://doi.org/10.1098/rstb.2010.0384
20) Fried, E. I., & Nesse, R. M. (2015). Depression is not a consistent syndrome: An investigation of unique symptom patterns in the STAR*D study. *Journal of affective disorders*, *172*, 96–102. https://doi.org/10.1016/j.jad.2014.10.010
Mayberg, Utilizing the DSM-5 Anxious Distress Specifier to Develop Treatment Strategies for Patients With Major Depressive Disorder. (2017). *The Journal of Clinical Psychiatry*, *78*(9), 1351–1362. https://doi.org/10.4088/jcp.ot17015ah1
Schneck C. D. (2009). Mixed depression: the importance of rediscovering subtypes of mixed mood States. *The American journal of psychiatry*, *166*(2), 127–130. https://doi.org/10.1176/appi.ajp.2008.08111669
https://ajp.psychiatryonline.org/doi/full/10.1176/appi.ajp.2008.08111669
21) Noordam, R., Avery, C. L., Visser, L. E., & Stricker, B. H. (2016). Identifying genetic loci affecting antidepressant drug response in depression using drug-gene interaction models. *Pharmacogenomics*, *17*(9), 1029–1040. https://doi.org/10.2217/pgs-2016-0024
22) Barton DA, Esler MD, Dawood T, et al. Elevated Brain Serotonin Turnover in Patients With Depression: Effect of Genotype and Therapy. *Arch Gen Psychiatry*. 2008;65(1):38–46.
https://jamanetwork.com/journals/jamapsychiatry/fullarticle/482548
23) Crane, N. A., Jenkins, L. M., Bhaumik, R., Dion, C., Gowins, J. R., Mickey, B. J., Zubieta, J. K., & Langenecker, S. A. (2017). Multidimensional prediction

of treatment response to antidepressants with cognitive control and functional MRI. *Brain : a journal of neurology, 140*(2), 472–486. https://doi.org/10.1093/brain/aww326

Grzenda, A., & Widge, A. S. (2020). Electroencephalographic Biomarkers for Predicting Antidepressant Response. *JAMA Psychiatry.* https://doi.org/10.1001/jamapsychiatry.2019.3749

Widge, A. S., Bilge, M. T., Montana, R., Chang, W., Rodriguez, C. I., Deckersbach, T., Carpenter, L. L., Kalin, N. H., & Nemeroff, C. B. (2019). Electroencephalographic Biomarkers for Treatment Response Prediction in Major Depressive Illness: A Meta-Analysis. *The American journal of psychiatry, 176*(1), 44–56. https://doi.org/10.1176/appi.ajp.2018.17121358

Rolle, C. E., Fonzo, G. A., Wu, W., Toll, R., Jha, M. K., Cooper, C., … Etkin, A. (2020). Cortical Connectivity Moderators of Antidepressant vs Placebo Treatment Response in Major Depressive Disorder. *JAMA Psychiatry.* https://doi.org/10.1001/jamapsychiatry.2019.3867

Phillips, M. L., Chase, H. W., Sheline, Y. I., Etkin, A., Almeida, J. R., Deckersbach, T., & Trivedi, M. H. (2015). Identifying predictors, moderators, and mediators of antidepressant response in major depressive disorder: neuroimaging approaches. *The American journal of psychiatry, 172*(2), 124–138. https://doi.org/10.1176/appi.ajp.2014.14010076

O'Connell, C. P., Goldstein-Piekarski, A. N., Nemeroff, C. B., Schatzberg, A. F., Debattista, C., Carrillo-Roa, T., Binder, E. B., Dunlop, B. W., Craighead, W. E., Mayberg, H. S., & Williams, L. M. (2018). Antidepressant Outcomes Predicted by Genetic Variation in Corticotropin-Releasing Hormone Binding Protein. *The American journal of psychiatry, 175*(3), 251–261. https://doi.org/10.1176/appi.ajp.2017.17020172

Chin Fatt, C. R., Jha, M. K., Cooper, C. M., Fonzo, G., South, C., Grannemann, B., Carmody, T., Greer, T. L., Kurian, B., Fava, M., McGrath, P. J., Adams, P., McInnis, M., Parsey, R. V., Weissman, M., Phillips, M. L., Etkin, A., & Trivedi, M. H. (2020). Effect of Intrinsic Patterns of Functional Brain Connectivity in Moderating Antidepressant Treatment Response in Major Depression. *The American journal of psychiatry, 177*(2), 143–154. https://doi.org/10.1176/appi.ajp.2019.18070870

24) Rothschild A. J. (2016). Treatment for Major Depression With Psychotic Features (Psychotic Depression). *Focus (American Psychiatric Publishing), 14*(2), 207–209. https://doi.org/10.1176/appi.focus.20150045

25) Fried E. I. (2015). Problematic assumptions have slowed down depression research: why symptoms, not syndromes are the way forward. *Frontiers in psychology, 6*, 309. https://doi.org/10.3389/fpsyg.2015.00309

The most likely reason for failure to differentiate treatment is the lack of financial incentive for pharmas to do such studies. Specific syndrome studies with comparative medications would be expensive (needs a very large n), difficult to design, and would limit the value of medication to a smaller group of patients.

References

Robert M. Post, MD; Lori L. Altshuler, MD; Mark A. Frye, MD; Trisha Suppes, MD, PhD; Paul E. Keck Jr, MD; Susan L. McElroy, MD; Gabriele S. Leverich, LCSW; David A. Luckenbaugh, MA; Michael Rowe, PhD; Scott Pizzarello, BA; Ralph W. Kupka, MD, PhD; Heinz Grunze, MD, PhD; and Willem A. Nolen, MD, PhD, Complexity of Pharmacologic Treatment Required for Sustained Improvement in Outpatients With Bipolar Disorder, J Clin Psychiatry 2010;71(9):1176-1186 *The Journal of clinical psychiatry, 71*(9), 1176–1253. https://doi.org/10.4088/JCP.08m04811yel

Strawbridge, R., Young, A. H., & Cleare, A. J. (2017). Biomarkers for depression: recent insights, current challenges and future prospects. *Neuropsychiatric disease and treatment, 13*, 1245–1262. https://doi.org/10.2147/NDT.S114542

26) Rush, A. J., Trivedi, M. H., Wisniewski, S. R., Nierenberg, A. A., Stewart, J. W., Warden, D., Niederehe, G., Thase, M. E., Lavori, P. W., Lebowitz, B. D., McGrath, P. J., Rosenbaum, J. F., Sackeim, H. A., Kupfer, D. J., Luther, J., & Fava, M. (2006). Acute and longer-term outcomes in depressed outpatients requiring one or several treatment steps: a STAR*D report. *The American journal of psychiatry, 163*(11), 1905–1917. https://doi.org/10.1176/ajp.2006.163.11.1905

Pigott H. E. (2015). The STAR*D Trial: It Is Time to Reexamine the Clinical Beliefs That Guide the Treatment of Major Depression. *Canadian journal of psychiatry. Revue canadienne de psychiatrie, 60*(1), 9–13. https://doi.org/10.1177/070674371506000104

March, J., Silva, S., Vitiello, B., & TADS Team (2006). The Treatment for Adolescents with Depression Study (TADS): methods and message at 12 weeks. *Journal of the American Academy of Child and Adolescent Psychiatry, 45*(12), 1393–1403. https://doi.org/10.1097/01.chi.0000237709.35637.c0

Treatment for Adolescents With Depression Study (TADS) Team, March, J., Silva, S., Curry, J., Wells, K., Fairbank, J., Burns, B., Domino, M., Vitiello, B., Severe, J., Riedal, K., Goldman, M., Feeny, N., Findling, R., Stull, S., Baab, S., Weller, E. B., Robbins, M., Weller, R. A., Jessani, N., … Bartoi, M. (2009). The Treatment for Adolescents With Depression Study (TADS): outcomes over 1 year of naturalistic follow-up. *The American journal of psychiatry, 166*(10), 1141–1149. https://doi.org/10.1176/appi.ajp.2009.08111620

Kennard, B. D., Silva, S. G., Mayes, T. L., Rohde, P., Hughes, J. L., Vitiello, B., Kratochvil, C. J., Curry, J. F., Emslie, G. J., Reinecke, M. A., March, J. S., & TADS (2009). Assessment of safety and long-term outcomes of initial treatment with placebo in TADS. *The American journal of psychiatry, 166*(3), 337–344. https://doi.org/10.1176/appi.ajp.2008.08040487

Reinecke, M. A., Curry, J. F., & March, J. S. (2009). Findings from the Treatment for Adolescents with Depression Study (TADS): what have we learned? What do we need to know?. *Journal of clinical child and adolescent psychology : the official journal for the Society of Clinical Child and Adolescent Psychology, American Psychological Association, Division 53, 38*(6), 761–767. https://doi.org/10.1080/15374410903258991

Graham J. Emslie, Taryn Mayes, Giovanna Porta, Benedetto Vitiello, Greg Clarke, Karen Dineen Wagner, Joan Rosenbaum Asarnow, Anthony Spirito, Boris Birmaher, Neal Ryan, Betsy Kennard, Lynn DeBar, James McCracken, Michael Strober, Matthew Onorato, Jamie Zelazny, Marty Keller, Satish Iyengar, and David Brent,Treatment of Resistant Depression in Adolescents (TORDIA): Week 24 Outcomes, American Journal of Psychiatry 2010 167:7, https://ajp.psychiatryonline.org/doi/full/10.1176/appi.ajp.2010.09040552

27) El-Mallakh, R. S., Vöhringer, P. A., Ostacher, M. M., Baldassano, C. F., Holtzman, N. S., Whitham, E. A., Thommi, S. B., Goodwin, F. K., & Ghaemi, S. N. (2015). Antidepressants worsen rapid-cycling course in bipolar depression: A STEP-BD randomized clinical trial. *Journal of affective disorders*, *184*, 318–321. https://doi.org/10.1016/j.jad.2015.04.054

Gitlin, M.J. Antidepressants in bipolar depression: an enduring controversy. *Int J Bipolar Disord* **6**, 25 (2018). https://doi.org/10.1186/s40345-018-0133-9

28) *A list of various alternative treatments for depression.*
L-Tyrosine - Scientific Review on Usage, Dosage, Side Effects | Examine.com
Homocysteine, folate, methylation, and monoamine metabolism in depression | Journal of Neurology, Neurosurgery & Psychiatry
A double-blind, randomized controlled clinical trial comparing eicosapentaenoic acid versus docosahexaenoic acid for depression. - PubMed - NCBI

29) Conway, C. R., George, M. S., & Sackeim, H. A. (2017). Toward an Evidence-Based, Operational Definition of Treatment-Resistant Depression: When Enough Is Enough. *JAMA psychiatry*, *74*(1), 9–10. https://doi.org/10.1001/jamapsychiatry.2016.2586

30) Krystal, J. H., Abdallah, C. G., Sanacora, G., Charney, D. S., & Duman, R. S. (2019). Ketamine: A Paradigm Shift for Depression Research and Treatment. *Neuron*, *101*(5), 774–778. https://doi.org/10.1016/j.neuron.2019.02.005
Ketamine https://journals.healio.com/toc/psych/48/4

Singh, J. B., Fedgchin, M., Daly, E. J., De Boer, P., Cooper, K., Lim, P., Pinter, C., Murrough, J. W., Sanacora, G., Shelton, R. C., Kurian, B., Winokur, A., Fava, M., Manji, H., Drevets, W. C., & Van Nueten, L. (2016). A Double-Blind, Randomized, Placebo-Controlled, Dose-Frequency Study of Intravenous Ketamine in Patients With Treatment-Resistant Depression. *The American journal of psychiatry*, *173*(8), 816–826. https://doi.org/10.1176/appi.ajp.2016.16010037

Grunebaum, M. F., Galfalvy, H. C., Choo, T. H., Keilp, J. G., Moitra, V. K., Parris, M. S., Marver, J. E., Burke, A. K., Milak, M. S., Sublette, M. E., Oquendo, M. A., & Mann, J. J. (2018). Ketamine for Rapid Reduction of Suicidal Thoughts in Major Depression: A Midazolam-Controlled Randomized Clinical Trial. *The American journal of psychiatry*, *175*(4), 327–335. https://doi.org/10.1176/appi.ajp.2017.17060647

Phillips, J. L., Norris, S., Talbot, J., Birmingham, M., Hatchard, T., Ortiz, A., Owoeye, O., Batten, L. A., & Blier, P. (2019). Single, Repeated, and

References

Maintenance Ketamine Infusions for Treatment-Resistant Depression: A Randomized Controlled Trial. *The American journal of psychiatry*, *176*(5), 401–409. https://doi.org/10.1176/appi.ajp.2018.18070834
31) Popova, V., Daly, E. J., Trivedi, M., Cooper, K., Lane, R., Lim, P., Mazzucco, C., Hough, D., Thase, M. E., Shelton, R. C., Molero, P., Vieta, E., Bajbouj, M., Manji, H., Drevets, W. C., & Singh, J. B. (2019). Efficacy and Safety of Flexibly Dosed Esketamine Nasal Spray Combined With a Newly Initiated Oral Antidepressant in Treatment-Resistant Depression: A Randomized Double-Blind Active-Controlled Study. *The American journal of psychiatry*, *176*(6), 428–438. https://doi.org/10.1176/appi.ajp.2019.19020172
Daly EJ, Trivedi MH, Janik A, et al. Efficacy of Esketamine Nasal Spray Plus Oral Antidepressant Treatment for Relapse Prevention in Patients With Treatment-Resistant Depression: A Randomized Clinical Trial. *JAMA Psychiatry*. 2019;76(9):893–903. doi:10.1001/jamapsychiatry.2019.1189
https://jamanetwork.com/journals/jamapsychiatry/fullarticle/2735111
32) Can a Framework Be Established for the Safe Use of Ketamine?
https://ajp.psychiatryonline.org/doi/10.1176/appi.ajp.2018.18030290
Nichole Roxas, Chaarushi Ahuja, Jessica Isom, Samuel T. Wilkinson, and Noah Capurso, A Potential Case of Acute Ketamine Withdrawal: Clinical Implications for the Treatment of Refractory Depression, American Journal of Psychiatry 2021 178:7, 588-591
https://ajp.psychiatryonline.org/doi/10.1176/appi.ajp.2020.20101480
Roger S. McIntyre, Joshua D. Rosenblat, Charles B. Nemeroff, Gerard Sanacora, James W. Murrough, Michael Berk, Elisa Brietzke, Seetal Dodd, Philip Gorwood, Roger Ho, Dan V. Iosifescu, Carlos Lopez Jaramillo, Siegfried Kasper, Kevin Kratiuk, Jung Goo Lee, Yena Lee, Leanna M.W. Lui, Rodrigo B. Mansur, George I. Papakostas, Mehala Subramaniapillai, Michael Thase, Eduard Vieta, Allan H. Young, Carlos A. Zarate, Jr., and Stephen Stahl, Synthesizing the Evidence for Ketamine and Esketamine in Treatment-Resistant Depression: An International Expert Opinion on the Available Evidence and Implementation, American Journal of Psychiatry 2021 178:5, 383-399 https://doi.org/10.1176/appi.ajp.2020.20081251
Short, B., Fong, J., Galvez, V., Shelker, W., & Loo, C. K. (2018). Side-effects associated with ketamine use in depression: a systematic review. *The lancet. Psychiatry*, *5*(1), 65–78. https://doi.org/10.1016/S2215-0366(17)30272-9
Schatzberg A. F. (2019). A Word to the Wise About Intranasal Esketamine. *The American journal of psychiatry*, *176*(6), 422–424. https://doi.org/10.1176/appi.ajp.2019.19040423
Canuso, C. M., Singh, J. B., Fedgchin, M., Alphs, L., Lane, R., Lim, P., Pinter, C., Hough, D., Sanacora, G., Manji, H., & Drevets, W. C. (2018). Efficacy and Safety of Intranasal Esketamine for the Rapid Reduction of Symptoms of Depression and Suicidality in Patients at Imminent Risk for Suicide: Results of a Double-Blind, Randomized, Placebo-Controlled Study. *The American journal of*

psychiatry, 175(7), 620–630. https://doi.org/10.1176/appi.ajp.2018.17060720
33) Williams, N. R., Heifets, B. D., Blasey, C., Sudheimer, K., Pannu, J., Pankow, H., Hawkins, J., Birnbaum, J., Lyons, D. M., Rodriguez, C. I., & Schatzberg, A. F. (2018). Attenuation of Antidepressant Effects of Ketamine by Opioid Receptor Antagonism. *The American journal of psychiatry, 175*(12), 1205–1215. https://doi.org/10.1176/appi.ajp.2018.18020138
34) Keefe, R. S. E. (2007). Neurocognitive Effects of Antipsychotic Medications in Patients With Chronic Schizophrenia in the CATIE Trial. *Archives of General Psychiatry, 64*(6), 633. https://doi.org/10.1001/archpsyc.64.6.633
King D. J. (1998). Drug treatment of the negative symptoms of schizophrenia. *European neuropsychopharmacology : the journal of the European College of Neuropsychopharmacology, 8*(1), 33–42. https://doi.org/10.1016/s0924-977x(97)00041-2
Asenjo Lobos, C., Komossa, K., Rummel-Kluge, C., Hunger, H., Schmid, F., Schwarz, S., & Leucht, S. (2010). Clozapine versus other atypical antipsychotics for schizophrenia. *The Cochrane database of systematic reviews*, (11), CD006633. https://doi.org/10.1002/14651858.CD006633.pub2
Krause, M., Zhu, Y., Huhn, M. *et al.* Antipsychotic drugs for patients with schizophrenia and predominant or prominent negative symptoms: a systematic review and meta-analysis. *Eur Arch Psychiatry Clin Neurosci* **268,** 625–639 (2018). https://doi.org/10.1007/s00406-018-0869-3
35) Miranda Chakos, M.D., Jeffrey Lieberman, M.D., Elaine Hoffman, Ph.D., Daniel Bradford, M.D., and Brian Sheitman, M.D., Effectiveness of Second-Generation Antipsychotics in Patients With Treatment-Resistant Schizophrenia: A Review and Meta-Analysis of Randomized Trials
Published online: April 01, 2001 | https://doi.org/10.1176/appi.ajp.158.4.518
Myrto T. Samara, MD1; Markus Dold, MD2; Myrsini Gianatsi, MSc3; et al Adriani Nikolakopoulou, MSc3; Bartosz Helfer, MSc1; Georgia Salanti, PhD4,5,6; Stefan Leucht, MD1 Efficacy, Acceptability, and Tolerability of Antipsychotics in Treatment-Resistant SchizophreniaA Network Meta-analysis JAMA Psychiatry. 2016;73(3):199-210.
https://jamanetwork.com/journals/jamapsychiatry/fullarticle/2488040
The most surprising finding was that clozapine was not significantly better than most other drugs. Insufficient evidence exists on which antipsychotic is more efficacious for patients with treatment-resistant schizophrenia,
Essali, A., Al-Haj Haasan, N., Li, C., & Rathbone, J. (2009). Clozapine versus typical neuroleptic medication for schizophrenia. *The Cochrane database of systematic reviews, 2009*(1), CD000059. https://doi.org/10.1002/14651858.CD000059.pub2
Meltzer HY, Alphs L, Green AI, et al. Clozapine Treatment for Suicidality in Schizophrenia: International Suicide Prevention Trial (InterSePT). *Arch Gen Psychiatry.* 2003;60(1):82–91. Arch Gen Psychiatry. 2003;60(1):82-91. DOI: 10.1001/archpsyc.60.1.82

References

Joshi, Y. B., Thomas, M. L., Braff, D. L., Green, M. F., Gur, R. C., Gur, R. E., Nuechterlein, K. H., Stone, W. S., Greenwood, T. A., Lazzeroni, L. C., MacDonald, L. R., Molina, J. L., Nungaray, J. A., Radant, A. D., Silverman, J. M., Sprock, J., Sugar, C. A., Tsuang, D. W., Tsuang, M. T., Turetsky, B. I., … Light, G. A. (2021). Anticholinergic Medication Burden-Associated Cognitive Impairment in Schizophrenia. *The American journal of psychiatry*, *178*(9), 838–847. https://doi.org/10.1176/appi.ajp.2020.20081212

Shrestha, S., Agha, R. S., Khan, Z., Shah, K., & Jain, S. (2021). Considering Loxapine Instead of Clozapine: A Case Series and Literature Review. *Cureus*, *13*(1), https://doi.org/10.7759/cureus.12919

36) Squires, R. F., & Saederup, E. (1998). Clozapine and several other anti-psychotic/antidepressant drugs preferentially block the same 'core' fraction of GABA(A) receptors. *Neurochemical research*, *23*(10), 1283–1290. https://doi.org/10.1023/a:1020796200769

Benes, F., Berretta, S. GABAergic Interneurons: Implications for Understanding Schizophrenia and Bipolar Disorder. *Neuropsychopharmacol* **25**, 1–27 (2001). https://doi.org/10.1016/S0893-133X(01)00225-1

Pardiñas, A. F., Nalmpanti, M., Pocklington, A. J., Legge, S. E., Medway, C., King, A., Jansen, J., Helthuis, M., Zammit, S., MacCabe, J., Owen, M. J., O'Donovan, M. C., & Walters, J. (2019). Pharmacogenomic Variants and Drug Interactions Identified Through the Genetic Analysis of Clozapine Metabolism. *The American journal of psychiatry*, *176*(6), 477–486. https://doi.org/10.1176/appi.ajp.2019.18050589

Blackman, G., Oloyede, E., Horowitz, M., Harland, R., Taylor, D., MacCabe, J., & McGuire, P. (2022). Reducing the Risk of Withdrawal Symptoms and Relapse Following Clozapine Discontinuation-Is It Feasible to Develop Evidence-Based Guidelines?. *Schizophrenia bulletin*, *48*(1), 176–189. https://doi.org/10.1093/schbul/sbab103

37) Rajji, T. K., Mulsant, B. H., Davies, S., Kalache, S. M., Tsoutsoulas, C., Pollock, B. G., & Remington, G. (2015). Prediction of working memory performance in schizophrenia by plasma ratio of clozapine to N-desmethylclozapine. *The American journal of psychiatry*, *172*(6), 579–585. https://doi.org/10.1176/appi.ajp.2015.14050673

Takako Ohno-Shosaku, Yuto Sugawara, Chiho Muranishi, Keisuke Nagasawa, Kozue Kubono, Nami Aoki, Mitsuki Taguchi, Ryousuke Echigo, Naotoshi Sugimoto, Yui Kikuchi, Ryoko Watanabe, Mitsugu Yoneda, Effects of clozapine and N-desmethylclozapine on synaptic transmission at hippocampal inhibitory and excitatory synapses, Brain Research,Volume 1421,2011,Pages 66-77,ISSN 0006-8993, https://doi.org/10.1016/j.brainres.2011.08.073.

Michel, F. J., & Trudeau, L. E. (2000). Clozapine inhibits synaptic transmission at GABAergic synapses established by ventral tegmental area neurones in culture. *Neuropharmacology*, *39*(9), 1536–1543. https://doi.org/10.1016/s0028-3908(99)00239-7

Varma, S., Bishara, D., Besag, F. M., & Taylor, D. (2011). Clozapine-related EEG changes and seizures: dose and plasma-level relationships. *Therapeutic advances in psychopharmacology*, *1*(2), 47–66. https://doi.org/10.1177/2045125311405566

Tiihonen, J., Tanskanen, A., Bell, J. S., Dawson, J. L., Kataja, V., & Taipale, H. (2022). Long-term treatment with clozapine and other antipsychotic drugs and the risk of haematological malignancies in people with schizophrenia: a nationwide case-control and cohort study in Finland. *The lancet. Psychiatry*, *9*(5), 353–362. https://doi.org/10.1016/S2215-0366(22)00044-X

Toth, P., & Frankenburg, F. R. (1994). Clozapine and seizures: a review. *Canadian journal of psychiatry. Revue canadienne de psychiatrie*, *39*(4), 236–238. https://doi.org/10.1177/070674379403900409

Kikuchi, Y. S., Sato, W., Ataka, K., Yagisawa, K., Omori, Y., Kanbayashi, T., & Shimizu, T. (2014). Clozapine-induced seizures, electroencephalography abnormalities, and clinical responses in Japanese patients with schizophrenia. *Neuropsychiatric disease and treatment*, *10*, 1973–1978. https://doi.org/10.2147/NDT.S69784

Siafis, S., Tzachanis, D., Samara, M., & Papazisis, G. (2018). Antipsychotic Drugs: From Receptor-binding Profiles to Metabolic Side Effects. *Current neuropharmacology*, *16*(8), 1210–1223. https://doi.org/10.2174/1570159X15666170630163616 creative commons

38) *For unknown reasons, the antipsychotic medications are more likely to produce stroke or other lethal complications in elderly psychotic patients. This does not prohibit use, but puts the provider at increased liability. The treatment of agitation in elderly with dementia poses difficult challenges.*

Maust DT, Kim HM, Seyfried LS, et al. Antipsychotics, Other Psychotropics, and the Risk of Death in Patients With Dementia: Number Needed to Harm. *JAMA Psychiatry*. 2015;72(5):438–445. https://jamanetwork.com/journals/jamapsychiatry/fullarticle/2203833

Tampi, R. R., Tampi, D. J., Balachandran, S., & Srinivasan, S. (2016). Antipsychotic use in dementia: a systematic review of benefits and risks from meta-analyses. *Therapeutic advances in chronic disease*, *7*(5), 229–245. https://doi.org/10.1177/2040622316658463

Vigen, C. L. P., Mack, W. J., Keefe, R. S. E., Sano, M., Sultzer, D. L., Stroup, T. S., Dagerman, K. S., Hsiao, J. K., Lebowitz, B. D., Lyketsos, C. G., Tariot, P. N., Zheng, L., & Schneider, L. S. (2011). Cognitive Effects of Atypical Antipsychotic Medications in Patients With Alzheimer's Disease: Outcomes From CATIE-AD. *American Journal of Psychiatry*, *168*(8), 831–839. https://doi.org/10.1176/appi.ajp.2011.08121844

39) https://en.wikipedia.org/wiki/Tardive_dyskinesia

Cornett, E. M., Novitch, M., Kaye, A. D., Kata, V., & Kaye, A. M. (2017). Medication-Induced Tardive Dyskinesia: A Review and Update. *The Ochsner journal*, *17*(2), 162–174.

References

https://www.ncbi.nlm.nih.gov/pmc/articles/PMC5472076/
40) Ananth, J., Burgoyne, K. S., Gadasalli, R., & Aquino, S. (2001). How do the atypical antipsychotics work?. *Journal of psychiatry & neuroscience : JPN*, 26(5), 385–394.
https://www.ncbi.nlm.nih.gov/pmc/articles/PMC167197/
Atypical antipsychotics block serotonin 5-HT2 receptors. When the ratio of 5-HT2 to D2 receptor blocking is greater than 1, atypical antipsychotics have fewer EPS.
Kuroki, T., Nagao, N., & Nakahara, T. (2008). Neuropharmacology of second-generation antipsychotic drugs: a validity of the serotonin-dopamine hypothesis. *Progress in brain research*, 172, 199–212. https://doi.org/10.1016/S0079-6123(08)00910-2
Racz, R., Soldatos, T. G., Jackson, D., & Burkhart, K. (2018). Association Between Serotonin Syndrome and Second-Generation Antipsychotics via Pharmacological Target-Adverse Event Analysis. *Clinical and translational science*, 11(3), 322–329. https://doi.org/10.1111/cts.12543
41) Davis JM, Chen N, Glick ID. A Meta-analysis of the Efficacy of Second-Generation Antipsychotics. *Arch Gen Psychiatry*. 2003;60(6):553–564.
https://jamanetwork.com/journals/jamapsychiatry/fullarticle/207537
42) https://www.nimh.nih.gov/funding/clinical-research/practical/catie
43) Swartz, M. S., Stroup, T. S., McEvoy, J. P., Davis, S. M., Rosenheck, R. A., Keefe, R. S., Hsiao, J. K., & Lieberman, J. A. (2008). What CATIE found: results from the schizophrenia trial. *Psychiatric services (Washington, D.C.)*, 59(5), 500–506. https://doi.org/10.1176/ps.2008.59.5.500
https://www.ncbi.nlm.nih.gov/pmc/articles/PMC5033643/
Manschreck, T. C., & Boshes, R. A. (2007). The CATIE schizophrenia trial: results, impact, controversy. *Harvard review of psychiatry*, 15(5), 245–258. https://doi.org/10.1080/10673220701679838
Nasrallah H. A. (2007). The roles of efficacy, safety, and tolerability in antipsychotic effectiveness: practical implications of the CATIE schizophrenia trial. *The Journal of clinical psychiatry*, 68 Suppl 1, 5–11. https://pubmed.ncbi.nlm.nih.gov/17286522/
Weiden P. J. (2007). Discontinuing and switching antipsychotic medications: understanding the CATIE schizophrenia trial. *The Journal of clinical psychiatry*, 68 Suppl 1, 12–19.
https://pubmed.ncbi.nlm.nih.gov/17286523/
44) Leucht, S., Komossa, K., Rummel-Kluge, C., Corves, C., Hunger, H., Schmid, F., Asenjo Lobos, C., Schwarz, S., & Davis, J. M. (2009). A meta-analysis of head-to-head comparisons of second-generation antipsychotics in the treatment of schizophrenia. *The American journal of psychiatry*, 166(2), 152–163. https://doi.org/10.1176/appi.ajp.2008.08030368
45) Keks, N., Schwartz, D., & Hope, J. (2019). Stopping and switching antipsychotic drugs. *Australian prescriber*, 42(5), 152–157. https://doi.org/10.18773/

austprescr.2019.052
Hatta, K., Sugiyama, N., & Ito, H. (2018). Switching and augmentation strategies for antipsychotic medications in acute-phase schizophrenia: latest evidence and place in therapy. *Therapeutic advances in psychopharmacology*, *8*(6), 173–183. https://doi.org/10.1177/2045125318754472
Newcomer, J. W., Weiden, P. J., & Buchanan, R. W. (2013). Switching antipsychotic medications to reduce adverse event burden in schizophrenia: establishing evidence-based practice. *The Journal of clinical psychiatry*, *74*(11), 1108–1120. https://doi.org/10.4088/JCP.12028ah1
46) Stroup, T. S., & Gray, N. (2018). Management of common adverse effects of antipsychotic medications. *World psychiatry : official journal of the World Psychiatric Association (WPA)*, *17*(3), 341–356. https://doi.org/10.1002/wps.20567
Marketa Marvanova; Strategies for prevention and management of second generation antipsychotic-induced metabolic side effects. *Mental Health Clinician* 1 September 2013; 3 (3): 154–161. doi: https://doi.org/10.9740/mhc.n166832
Siegert, S., Factor, S., Liang, G., & Burke, J. (2018). Efficacy and safety of Valbenazine (NBI-98854) in subjects with tardive dyskinesia: Results of a long-term study (KINECT 3 extension). *Parkinsonism & Related Disorders*, *46*, e35. https://doi.org/10.1016/j.parkreldis.2017.11.113
Caroff, S. N., Aggarwal, S., & Yonan, C. (2018). Treatment of tardive dyskinesia with tetrabenazine or valbenazine: a systematic review. *Journal of comparative effectiveness research*, *7*(2), 135–148.
https://doi.org/10.2217/cer-2017-0065
Correll, C. U., Leucht, S., & Kane, J. M. (2004). Lower risk for tardive dyskinesia associated with second-generation antipsychotics: a systematic review of 1-year studies. *The American journal of psychiatry*, *161*(3), 414–425. https://doi.org/10.1176/appi.ajp.161.3.414
Hauser, R. A., Factor, S. A., Marder, S. R., Knesevich, M. A., Ramirez, P. M., Jimenez, R., Burke, J., Liang, G. S., & O'Brien, C. F. (2017). KINECT 3: A Phase 3 Randomized, Double-Blind, Placebo-Controlled Trial of Valbenazine for Tardive Dyskinesia. *The American journal of psychiatry*, *174*(5), 476–484. https://doi.org/10.1176/appi.ajp.2017.16091037 https://pubmed.ncbi.nlm.nih.gov/28320223/
Correll, C. U., Josiassen, R. C., Liang, G. S., Burke, J., & O'Brien, C. F. (2017). Efficacy of Valbenazine (NBI-98854) in Treating Subjects with Tardive Dyskinesia and Mood Disorder. *Psychopharmacology bulletin*, *47*(3), 53–60. https://www.ncbi.nlm.nih.gov/pmc/articles/PMC5546551/
47) Aronson J. K. (2004). In defence of polypharmacy. *British journal of clinical pharmacology*, *57*(2), 119–120. https://doi.org/10.1111/j.1365-2125.2004.02067.x
Christoph U. Correll, Christine Rummel-Kluge, Caroline Corves, John M. Kane, Stefan Leucht, Antipsychotic Combinations vs Monotherapy in Schizophrenia:

References

A Meta-analysis of Randomized Controlled Trials, *Schizophrenia Bulletin*, Volume 35, Issue 2, March 2009, Pages 443–457, https://doi.org/10.1093/schbul/sbn018https://academic.oup.com/schizophreniabulletin/article/35/2/443/1904239

Correll, C. U., & Gallego, J. A. (2012). Antipsychotic polypharmacy: a comprehensive evaluation of relevant correlates of a long-standing clinical practice. *The Psychiatric clinics of North America*, *35*(3), 661–681. https://doi.org/10.1016/j.psc.2012.06.007

Kukreja, S., Kalra, G., Shah, N., & Shrivastava, A. (2013). Polypharmacy in psychiatry: a review. *Mens sana monographs*, *11*(1), 82–99. https://doi.org/10.4103/0973-1229.104497

Correll CU, Rubio JM, Inczedy-Farkas G, Birnbaum ML, Kane JM, Leucht S. Efficacy of 42 Pharmacologic Cotreatment Strategies Added to Antipsychotic Monotherapy in Schizophrenia: Systematic Overview and Quality Appraisal of the Meta-analytic Evidence. *JAMA Psychiatry*. 2017;74(7):675–684. https://jamanetwork.com/journals/jamapsychiatry/article-abstract/2627699

Steven J. Kingsbury, Donna Yi, and George M. Simpson, Psychopharmacology: Rational and Irrational Polypharmacy, Psychiatric Services 2001 52:8, 1033-1036 https://ps.psychiatryonline.org/action/showCitFormats?doi=10.1176%2Fappi.ps.52.8.1033

48) Goff, D. C., & Dixon, L. (2011). Antipsychotic polypharmacy: are two ever better than one?. *The American journal of psychiatry*, *168*(7), 667–669. https://doi.org/10.1176/appi.ajp.2011.11020314

Tiihonen, J., Taipale, H., Mehtälä, J., Vattulainen, P., Correll, C. U., & Tanskanen, A. (2019). Association of Antipsychotic Polypharmacy vs Monotherapy With Psychiatric Rehospitalization Among Adults With Schizophrenia. *JAMA psychiatry*, *76*(5), 499–507. https://doi.org/10.1001/jamapsychiatry.2018.4320

Essock, S. M., Schooler, N. R., Stroup, T. S., McEvoy, J. P., Rojas, I., Jackson, C., Covell, N. H., & Schizophrenia Trials Network (2011). Effectiveness of switching from antipsychotic polypharmacy to monotherapy. *The American journal of psychiatry*, *168*(7), 702–708. https://doi.org/10.1176/appi.ajp.2011.10060908

Pandurangi, A. K., & Dalkilic, A. (2008). Polypharmacy with second-generation antipsychotics: a review of evidence. *Journal of psychiatric practice*, *14*(6), https://doi.org/10.1097/01.pra.0000341890.05383.45

David M. Gardner, Andrea L. Murphy, Heather O'Donnell, Franca Centorrino, and Ross J. Baldessarini
International Consensus Study of Antipsychotic Dosing, American Journal of Psychiatry 2010 167:6, 686-693 http://ajp.psychiatryonline.org/doi/full/10.1176/appi.ajp.2009.09060802

Clark, R. E., Bartels, S. J., Mellman, T. A., & Peacock, W. J. (2002). Recent trends in antipsychotic combination therapy of schizophrenia and schizoaffective disorder: implications for state mental health policy. *Schizophrenia bulletin*,

28(1), 75–84. https://doi.org/10.1093/oxfordjournals.schbul.a006928
49) Kondej, M., Stępnicki, P., & Kaczor, A. A. (2018). Multi-Target Approach for Drug Discovery against Schizophrenia. *International journal of molecular sciences, 19*(10), 3105. https://doi.org/10.3390/ijms19103105
Siafis, S., Tzachanis, D., Samara, M., & Papazisis, G. (2018). Antipsychotic Drugs: From Receptor-binding Profiles to Metabolic Side Effects. *Current neuropharmacology, 16*(8), 1210–1223. https://doi.org/10.2174/1570159X15666170630163616
50) Buchanan R. W. (2007). Persistent negative symptoms in schizophrenia: an overview. *Schizophrenia bulletin, 33*(4), 1013–1022. https://doi.org/10.1093/schbul/sbl057
Griswold, K. S., Del Regno, P. A., & Berger, R. C. (2015). Recognition and Differential Diagnosis of Psychosis in Primary Care. *American family physician, 91*(12), 856–863.
Wyatt, R. J., & Henter, I. D. (1998). The effects of early and sustained intervention on the long-term morbidity of schizophrenia. *Journal of psychiatric research, 32*(3-4), 169–177. https://doi.org/10.1016/s0022-3956(97)00014-9
Wyatt R. J. (1991). Neuroleptics and the natural course of schizophrenia. *Schizophrenia bulletin, 17*(2), 325–351. https://doi.org/10.1093/schbul/17.2.325
51) Goff, D. C., Falkai, P., Fleischhacker, W. W., Girgis, R. R., Kahn, R. M., Uchida, H., Zhao, J., & Lieberman, J. A. (2017). The Long-Term Effects of Antipsychotic Medication on Clinical Course in Schizophrenia. *The American journal of psychiatry, 174*(9), 840–849. https://doi.org/10.1176/appi.ajp.2017.16091016 https://pubmed.ncbi.nlm.nih.gov/28472900/
Yeisen, R.A.H., Bjornestad, J., Joa, I. *et al.* Experiences of antipsychotic use in patients with early psychosis: a two-year follow-up study. *BMC Psychiatry* **17,** 299 (2017). https://doi.org/10.1186/s12888-017-1425-9
Begemann, M., Thompson, I. A., Veling, W., Gangadin, S. S., Geraets, C., van 't Hag, E., Müller-Kuperus, S. J., Oomen, P. P., Voppel, A. E., van der Gaag, M., Kikkert, M. J., Van Os, J., Smit, H., Knegtering, R. H., Wiersma, S., Stouten, L. H., Gijsman, H. J., Wunderink, L., Staring, A., Veerman, S., … Sommer, I. (2020). To continue or not to continue? Antipsychotic medication maintenance versus dose-reduction/discontinuation in first episode psychosis: HAMLETT, a pragmatic multicenter single-blind randomized controlled trial. *Trials, 21*(1), 147. https://doi.org/10.1186/s13063-019-3822-5
Christine Merrild Posselt, Nikolai Albert, Merete Nordentoft, and Carsten Hjorthøj
The Danish OPUS Early Intervention Services for First-Episode Psychosis: A Phase 4 Prospective Cohort Study With Comparison of Randomized Trial and Real-World Data, American Journal of Psychiatry 2021 178:10, 941-951 https://doi.org/10.1176/appi.ajp.2021.20111596
Mayoral-van Son, J., de la Foz, V. O.-G., Martinez-Garcia, O., Moreno, T., Parrilla-Escobar, M., Valdizan, E. M., & Crespo-Facorro, B. (2015). Clinical

References

Outcome After Antipsychotic Treatment Discontinuation in Functionally Recovered First-Episode Nonaffective Psychosis Individuals. *The Journal of Clinical Psychiatry*, 77(04), 492–500. https://doi.org/10.4088/jcp.14m09540
52) Harrow, M., Jobe, T., & Tong, L. (2021). Twenty-year effects of antipsychotics in schizophrenia and affective psychotic disorders. *Psychological Medicine,* 1-11. doi:10.1017/S0033291720004778
https://www.cambridge.org/core/journals/psychological-medicine/article/abs/twentyyear-effects-of-antipsychotics-in-schizophrenia-and-affective-psychotic-disorders/24EF3F7E45EED8487F54A729C75EFF0A
53) *Historically, an amotivational state observed in CPZ treated schizophrenic patients (they were called "burnt out schizophrenic") was attributed to the disorder, while strongly denying the role of medication. Studies differentiating social withdrawal (a negative symptom) from drug impaired motivation have never been published.*
Whitaker, Robert, Anatomy of an epidemic, Ethical Human Psychology and Psychiatry, Vol 7, No 1, Spring 2005
An extensive historical review and critique can be found in Whitaker, *Anatomy Of An Epidemic*. *He makes the accusation that maintaining psychotic patients on high doses of dopamine blockers after remission of psychosis has resulted in "demotivated" individuals who have limited life adaptation and often are maintained on disability. This is disputed by the pharma industry, and complicated by financial circumstances in which the patient must qualify for disability to have payment for medication!*
54) Jeczmien, P., Levkovitz, Y., Weizman, A., & Carmel, Z. (2001). Post-psychotic depression in schizophrenia. *The Israel Medical Association journal : IMAJ*, 3(8), 589–592.
Sönmez, N., Romm, K.L., Andreasssen, O.A. et al. Depressive symptoms in first episode psychosis: a one-year follow-up study. *BMC Psychiatry* **13,** 106 (2013). https://doi.org/10.1186/1471-244X-13-106
Steffen Moritz, Stefanie J. Schmidt, Thies Lüdtke, Lea-Elena Braunschneider, Alisa Manske, Brooke C. Schneider, Ruth Veckstenstedt,Post-psychotic depression: Paranoia and the damage done,Schizophrenia Research,Volume 211,2019,Pages 79-85,
ISSN 0920-9964, https://doi.org/10.1016/j.schres.2019.06.022 .
Helfer, B., Samara, M. T., Huhn, M., Klupp, E., Leucht, C., Zhu, Y., Engel, R. R., & Leucht, S. (2016). Efficacy and Safety of Antidepressants Added to Antipsychotics for Schizophrenia: A Systematic Review and Meta-Analysis. *The American journal of psychiatry*, 173(9), 876–886. https://doi.org/10.1176/appi.ajp.2016.15081035
Woman who chose her symptoms:
https://www.nytimes.com/2022/05/17/magazine/antipsychotic-medications-mental-health.html
55) Ostuzzi, G., Bertolini, F., Del Giovane, C., Tedeschi, F., Bovo, C.,

Gastaldon, C., Nosé, M., Ogheri, F., Papola, D., Purgato, M., Turrini, G., Correll, C. U., & Barbui, C. (2021). Maintenance Treatment With Long-Acting Injectable Antipsychotics for People With Nonaffective Psychoses: A Network Meta-Analysis. *The American journal of psychiatry, 178*(5), https://doi.org/10.1176/appi.ajp.2020.20071120

Tiihonen, J., Haukka, J., Taylor, M., Haddad, P. M., Patel, M. X., & Korhonen, P. (2011). A nationwide cohort study of oral and depot antipsychotics after first hospitalization for schizophrenia. *The American journal of psychiatry, 168*(6), 603–609. https://doi.org/10.1176/appi.ajp.2011.10081224

The Use of Depot Medications in the Treatment of Schizophrenia John M. Davis American Journal of Psychiatry 2010 167:2, 125-126 Published online: February 01, 2010 | https://doi.org/10.1176/appi.ajp.2009.09111676

Weiden, P. J., Roma, R. S., Velligan, D. I., Alphs, L., DiChiara, M., & Davidson, B. (2015). The challenge of offering long-acting antipsychotic therapies: a preliminary discourse analysis of psychiatrist recommendations for injectable therapy to patients with schizophrenia. *The Journal of clinical psychiatry, 76*(6), 684–690. https://doi.org/10.4088/JCP.13m08946

56) El-Mallakh, R. S., & Briscoe, B. (2012). Studies of long-term use of antidepressants: how should the data from them be interpreted?. *CNS drugs, 26*(2), 97–109. https://doi.org/10.2165/11599450-000000000-00000

Lewis, G., Marston, L., Duffy, L., Freemantle, N., Gilbody, S., Hunter, R., Kendrick, T., Kessler, D., Mangin, D., King, M., Lanham, P., Moore, M., Nazareth, I., Wiles, N., Bacon, F., Bird, M., Brabyn, S., Burns, A., Clarke, C. S., Hunt, A., … Lewis, G. (2021). Maintenance or Discontinuation of Antidepressants in Primary Care. *The New England journal of medicine, 385*(14), 1257–1267. https://doi.org/10.1056/NEJMoa2106356

Maund, E., Stuart, B., Moore, M., Dowrick, C., Geraghty, A., Dawson, S., & Kendrick, T. (2019). Managing Antidepressant Discontinuation: A Systematic Review. *Annals of family medicine, 17*(1), 52–60. https://doi.org/10.1370/afm.2336

57) Zhang, TN., Gao, SY., Shen, ZQ. et al. Use of selective serotonin-reuptake inhibitors in the first trimester and risk of cardiovascular-related malformations: a meta-analysis of cohort studies. *Sci Rep* **7**, 43085 (2017). https://doi.org/10.1038/srep43085

Ross, E. J., Graham, D. L., Money, K. M., & Stanwood, G. D. (2015). Developmental consequences of fetal exposure to drugs: what we know and what we still must learn. *Neuropsychopharmacology : official publication of the American College of Neuropsychopharmacology, 40*(1), 61–87. https://doi.org/10.1038/npp.2014.147

Ross, L. E., Grigoriadis, S., Mamisashvili, L., Vonderporten, E. H., Roerecke, M., Rehm, J., Dennis, C. L., Koren, G., Steiner, M., Mousmanis, P., & Cheung, A. (2013). Selected pregnancy and delivery outcomes after exposure to antidepressant medication: a systematic review and meta-analysis. *JAMA psychiatry*,

References

70(4), 436–443. https://doi.org/10.1001/jamapsychiatry.2013.684

Lattimore, K., Donn, S., Kaciroti, N. et al. Selective Serotonin Reuptake Inhibitor (SSRI) Use during Pregnancy and Effects on the Fetus and Newborn: A Meta-Analysis. *J Perinatol* **25,** 595–604 (2005). https://doi.org/10.1038/sj.jp.7211352

Bar-Oz, B., Einarson, T., Einarson, A., Boskovic, R., O'Brien, L., Malm, H., Bérard, A., & Koren, G. (2007). Paroxetine and congenital malformations: meta-Analysis and consideration of potential confounding factors. *Clinical therapeutics*, *29*(5), 918–926. https://doi.org/10.1016/j.clinthera.2007.05.003

Einarson, A., Pistelli, A., DeSantis, M., Malm, H., Paulus, W. D., Panchaud, A., Kennedy, D., Einarson, T. R., & Koren, G. (2008). Evaluation of the risk of congenital cardiovascular defects associated with use of paroxetine during pregnancy. *The American journal of psychiatry*, *165*(6), 749–752. https://doi.org/10.1176/appi.ajp.2007.07060879

Bérard, A., Iessa, N., Chaabane, S., Muanda, F. T., Boukhris, T., & Zhao, J. P. (2016). The risk of major cardiac malformations associated with paroxetine use during the first trimester of pregnancy: a systematic review and meta-analysis. *British journal of clinical pharmacology*, *81*(4), 589–604. https://doi.org/10.1111/bcp.12849

Malm, H., Artama, M., Gissler, M., & Ritvanen, A. (2011). Selective serotonin reuptake inhibitors and risk for major congenital anomalies. *Obstetrics and gynecology*, *118*(1), 111–120. https://doi.org/10.1097/AOG.0b013e318220edcc

58) Ward, R. K., & Zamorski, M. A. (2002). Benefits and risks of psychiatric medications during pregnancy. *American family physician*, *66*(4), 629–636. https://www.aafp.org/afp/2002/0815/p629.html

Gail Erlick Robinson, Psychopharmacology in Pregnancy and Postpartum FOCUS 2012 10:1, 3-14
https://focus.psychiatryonline.org/doi/abs/10.1176/appi.focus.10.1.3

Yonkers, K. A., Vigod, S., & Ross, L. E. (2011). Diagnosis, pathophysiology, and management of mood disorders in pregnant and postpartum women. *Obstetrics and gynecology*, *117*(4), 961–977. https://doi.org/10.1097/AOG.0b013e31821187a7

59)https://www.researchgate.net/profile/Robert_Felix/publication/8156174_Postmarketing_surveillance_for_drug_safety_in_pregnancy_The_Organization_of_Teratology_Information_Services_Project/links/54db950f0cf28d3de65bbcdc.pdf

60) Trifu, S., Vladuti, A., & Popescu, A. (2019). The Neuroendocrinological Aspects Of Pregnancy And Postpartum Depression. *Acta endocrinologica (Bucharest, Romania : 2005)*, *15*(3), 410–415. https://doi.org/10.4183/aeb.2019.410

Edinoff, A. N., Odisho, A. S., Lewis, K., Kaskas, A., Hunt, G., Cornett, E. M., Kaye, A. D., Kaye, A., Morgan, J., Barrilleaux, P. S., Lewis, D., Viswanath, O., & Urits, I. (2021). Brexanolone, a GABA$_A$ Modulator, in the Treatment of

Postpartum Depression in Adults: A Comprehensive Review. *Frontiers in psychiatry*, *12*, 699740. https://doi.org/10.3389/fpsyt.2021.699740

61) Mayes, R., Bagwell, C., & Erkulwater, J. (2008). ADHD and the rise in stimulant use among children. *Harvard review of psychiatry*, *16*(3), 151–166. https://doi.org/10.1080/10673220802167782

Susan H. Busch, Medication Treatment For ADHD: Controversy Abounds Health Affairs 2009 28:5, 1549-1550 https://www.healthaffairs.org/doi/abs/10.1377/hlthaff.28.5.1549

Coghill D. (2004). Use of stimulants for attention deficit hyperactivity disorder: FOR. *BMJ (Clinical research ed.)*, *329*(7471), 907–908. https://doi.org/10.1136/bmj.329.7471.907

Clinical, and Sociodemographic Factors Associated With Stimulant Treatment Outcomes in ADHD. *The American journal of psychiatry*, *178*(9), 854–864. https://doi.org/10.1176/appi.ajp.2020.20121686

Castellanos F. X. (2021). A Biased Perspective on Brain Imaging of ADHD. *The American journal of psychiatry*, *178*(8), 694–700. https://doi.org/10.1176/appi.ajp.2021.21060609

Tung, Y. H., Lin, H. Y., Chen, C. L., Shang, C. Y., Yang, L. Y., Hsu, Y. C., Tseng, W. I., & Gau, S. S. (2021). Whole Brain White Matter Tract Deviation and Idiosyncrasy From Normative Development in Autism and ADHD and Unaffected Siblings Link With Dimensions of Psychopathology and Cognition. *The American journal of psychiatry*, *178*(8), 730–743. https://doi.org/10.1176/appi.ajp.2020.20070999

Luke J. Norman, Gustavo Sudre, Marine Bouyssi-Kobar, Wendy Sharp, and Philip Shaw,
A Longitudinal Study of Resting-State Connectivity and Response to Psychostimulant Treatment in ADHD
American Journal of Psychiatry 2021 178:8, 744-751
https://ajp.psychiatryonline.org/doi/abs/10.1176/appi.ajp.2021.20091342

62) Schertz, M., Adesman, A. R., Alfieri, N. E., & Bienkowski, R. S. (1996). Predictors of weight loss in children with attention deficit hyperactivity disorder treated with stimulant medication. *Pediatrics*, *98*(4 Pt 1), 763–769. https://pubmed.ncbi.nlm.nih.gov/8885958/

Mellström, E., Forsman, C., Engh, L., Hallerbäck, M. U., & Wikström, S. (2020). Methylphenidate and Reduced Overweight in Children With ADHD. *Journal of attention disorders*, *24*(2), 246–254. https://doi.org/10.1177/1087054718808045

63) https://amuedge.com/super-soldiers-performance-enhancing-drugs-and-the-military/
https://bartbernard.com/truck-accidents/the-3-most-common-drugs-truckers-use-behind-the-wheel/
https://smallwarsjournal.com/jrnl/art/swj-factsheet-pharmaceutical-soldier-performance-enhancing-drugs-battlefield-open-source

References

64) Cherkasova, M., Sulla, E. M., Dalena, K. L., Pondé, M. P., & Hechtman, L. (2013). Developmental course of attention deficit hyperactivity disorder and its predictors. *Journal of the Canadian Academy of Child and Adolescent Psychiatry = Journal de l'Academie canadienne de psychiatrie de l'enfant et de l'adolescent, 22*(1), 47–54. https://www.ncbi.nlm.nih.gov/pmc/articles/PMC3565715/

Agnew-Blais, J. C., Polanczyk, G. V., Danese, A., Wertz, J., Moffitt, T. E., & Arseneault, L. (2016). Evaluation of the Persistence, Remission, and Emergence of Attention-Deficit/Hyperactivity Disorder in Young Adulthood. *JAMA psychiatry, 73*(7), 713–720. https://doi.org/10.1001/jamapsychiatry.2016.0465

Sibley, M. H., Arnold, L. E., Swanson, J. M., Hechtman, L. T., Kennedy, T. M., Owens, E., Molina, B., Jensen, P. S., Hinshaw, S. P., Roy, A., Chronis-Tuscano, A., Newcorn, J. H., Rohde, L. A., & MTA Cooperative Group (2022). Variable Patterns of Remission From ADHD in the Multimodal Treatment Study of ADHD. *The American journal of psychiatry, 179*(2), 142–151. https://doi.org/10.1176/appi.ajp.2021.21010032

Volkow, N. D., & Swanson, J. M. (2008). Does childhood treatment of ADHD with stimulant medication affect substance abuse in adulthood?. *The American journal of psychiatry, 165*(5), 553–555. https://doi.org/10.1176/appi.ajp.2008.08020237

65) Stahl S. M. (2012). Psychotherapy as an epigenetic 'drug': psychiatric therapeutics target symptoms linked to malfunctioning brain circuits with psychotherapy as well as with drugs. *Journal of clinical pharmacy and therapeutics, 37*(3), 249–253. https://doi.org/10.1111/j.1365-2710.2011.01301.x

66) Adelman, S. A. (1985). Pills as Transitional Objects: A Dynamic Understanding of the Use of Medication in Psychotherapy. *Psychiatry, 48*(3), 246–253. https://doi.org/10.1080/00332747.1985.11024285

67) https://www.fda.gov/drugs/development-approval-process-drugs/drug-approvals-and-databases
https://www.fda.gov/patients/learn-about-expanded-access-and-other-treatment-options/understanding-unapproved-use-approved-drugs-label

68) Thomas Stephen Szasz, **Ceremonial Chemistry: The Ritual Persecution of Drugs, Addicts, and Pushers**

69) Lyon, E. R. (1999). A Review of the Effects of Nicotine on Schizophrenia and Antipsychotic Medications. *Psychiatric Services, 50*(10), 1346–1350. https://doi.org/10.1176/ps.50.10.1346

Manzella, F. (2015). Smoking in schizophrenic patients: A critique of the self-medication hypothesis. *World Journal of Psychiatry, 5*(1), 35. https://doi.org/10.5498/wjp.v5.i1.35

Nicotine is a significant drug activating acetylcholine receptors, used by humans for centuries before the current restrictions, with unknown addiction problems. It is marginally restricted to over 18 yrs old in US.

Potter, A. S., & Newhouse, P. A. (2008). Acute nicotine improves cognitive deficits in young adults with attention-deficit/hyperactivity disorder. *Pharmacology, biochemistry, and behavior*, 88(4), 407–417. https://doi.org/10.1016/j.pbb.2007.09.014

Potter, A. S., Dunbar, G., Mazzulla, E., Hosford, D., & Newhouse, P. A. (2014). AZD3480, a novel nicotinic receptor agonist, for the treatment of attention-deficit/hyperactivity disorder in adults. *Biological psychiatry*, 75(3), 207–214. https://doi.org/10.1016/j.biopsych.2013.06.002

William R. Martin, Glen R. Van Loon, Edgar T. Iwamoto, Layten David, ***Tobacco Smoking and Nicotine: A Neurobiological Approach,*** https://www.anunlikelystory.com/book/9781461290636

70) For discussion of factors in the current opiate crisis in the US, see chapter nine.

71) Rubin R. The Path to the First FDA-Approved Cannabis-Derived Treatment and What Comes Next. *JAMA.* 2018;320(12):1227–1229. https://jamanetwork.com/journals/jama/article-abstract/2702003

72) Sathyanarayana Rao, T. S., & Andrade, C. (2016). Classification of psychotropic drugs: Problems, solutions, and more problems. *Indian journal of psychiatry*, 58(2), 111–113. https://doi.org/10.4103/0019-5545.183771

Caraci, F., Enna, S. J., Zohar, J., Racagni, G., Zalsman, G., van den Brink, W., Kasper, S., Koob, G. F., Pariante, C. M., Piazza, P. V., Yamada, K., Spedding, M., & Drago, F. (2017). A new nomenclature for classifying psychotropic drugs. *British journal of clinical pharmacology*, 83(8), 1614–1616. https://doi.org/10.1111/bcp.13302

Ghaemi S. N. (2017). A new drug nomenclature for psychiatry - prospects and hazards. *British journal of clinical pharmacology*, 83(8), 1617–1618. https://doi.org/10.1111/bcp.13308

73) The European Neuropsychopharmacology work group proposed a revised multi-axial classification system for psychopharmacology:

Axis I primary pharmacological target (ie serotonin) and mechanism

Axis II family of agents, pharmacological-chemical group

Axis III neurobiological activities, transmitter site effects, phenotypes, brain circuits, gene expression, etc

Axis IV efficacy, including off label use, and major side effects

Axis V indications, ie FDA demonstrated or other validated applications

https://nbn2r.com/

https://www.slideshare.net/tulasiraman/structure-activity-relationships-antipsychotics

The system presented modifies the European proposal by emphasizing chemical and receptor properties, and combining neurobio-and clinical effects which are directly (not simply) related. Multiple receptor chemicals must be identified. The four properties are loosely related to each other: Different chemical structure may impact the same pharmacological site, and more than one site, so the relationship between A and B is usually complex. The relationship between B and C is the relationship between pharmacology research and clinical usage, the results of drug trials and "off label use".

APPENDIX

74) Kellner, C. H., Greenberg, R. M., Murrough, J. W., Bryson, E. O., Briggs, M. C., & Pasculli, R. M. (2012). ECT in treatment-resistant depression. *The American journal of psychiatry*, *169*(12), 1238–1244. https://doi.org/10.1176/appi.ajp.2012.12050648

75) Fosse, R., & Read, J. (2013). Electroconvulsive Treatment: Hypotheses about Mechanisms of Action. *Frontiers in psychiatry*, *4*, 94. https://doi.org/10.3389/fpsyt.2013.00094

76) Pfleiderer, B., Michael, N., Erfurth, A., Ohrmann, P., Hohmann, U., Wolgast, M., Fiebich, M., Arolt, V., & Heindel, W. (2003). Effective electroconvulsive therapy reverses glutamate/glutamine deficit in the left anterior cingulum of unipolar depressed patients. *Psychiatry research*, *122*(3), 185–192. https://doi.org/10.1016/s0925-4927(03)00003-9

77) Kho KH, van Vreeswijk MF, Simpson S, et al. A meta-analysis of electroconvulsive therapy efficacy in depression. 2003. In: Database of Abstracts of Reviews of Effects (DARE): Quality-assessed Reviews (Internet). York (UK): Centre for Reviews and Dissemination (UK); 1995-. Available from: https://www.ncbi.nlm.nih.gov/books/NBK69966/
https://www.ncbi.nlm.nih.gov/pubmedhealth/PMH0020583/

Haq, A. U., Sitzmann, A. F., Goldman, M. L., Maixner, D. F., & Mickey, B. J. (2015). Response of depression to electroconvulsive therapy: a meta-analysis of clinical predictors. *The Journal of clinical psychiatry*, *76*(10), 1374–1384. https://doi.org/10.4088/JCP.14r09528

Slade, E. P., Jahn, D. R., Regenold, W. T., & Case, B. G. (2017). Association of Electroconvulsive Therapy With Psychiatric Readmissions in US Hospitals. *JAMA psychiatry*, *74*(8), 798–804. https://doi.org/10.1001/jamapsychiatry.2017.1378

Sackeim HA. Modern Electroconvulsive Therapy: Vastly Improved yet Greatly Underused. *JAMA Psychiatry.* 2017;74(8):779–780. doi:10.1001/jamapsychiatry.2017.1670

Oremus C, Oremus M, McNeely H, et al
Effects of electroconvulsive therapy on cognitive functioning in patients with depression: protocol for a systematic review and meta-analysis BMJ Open 2015;5. http://bmjopen.bmj.com/content/5/3/e006966

UK ECT Review Group (2003). Efficacy and safety of electroconvulsive therapy in depressive disorders: a systematic review and meta-analysis. *Lancet (London, England)*, *361*(9360), 799–808. https://doi.org/10.1016/S0140-6736(03)12705-5

Medda, P., Toni, C., Mariani, M. G., De Simone, L., Mauri, M., & Perugi, G. (2015). Electroconvulsive therapy in 197 patients with a severe, drug-resistant bipolar mixed state: treatment outcome and predictors of response. *The Journal*

of clinical psychiatry, *76*(9), 1168–1173. https://doi.org/10.4088/JCP.14m09181
Medda, P., Toni, C., Mariani, M. G., De Simone, L., Mauri, M., & Perugi, G. (2015). Electroconvulsive therapy in 197 patients with a severe, drug-resistant bipolar mixed state: treatment outcome and predictors of response. *The Journal of clinical psychiatry*, *76*(9), 1168–1173. https://doi.org/10.4088/JCP.14m09181
78) Redlich R, Opel N, Grotegerd D, et al. Prediction of Individual Response to Electroconvulsive Therapy via Machine Learning on Structural Magnetic Resonance Imaging Data. *JAMA Psychiatry.* 2016;73(6):557–564. https://jamanetwork.com/journals/jamapsychiatry/fullarticle/2519363
Read, J., Harrop, C., Geekie, J., & Renton, J. (2018). An audit of ECT in England 2011-2015: Usage, demographics, and adherence to guidelines and legislation. *Psychology and psychotherapy*, *91*(3), 263–277. https://doi.org/10.1111/papt.12160
Read, J., Harrop, C., Geekie, J., Renton, J. and Cunliffe, S. (2021), A second independent audit of electroconvulsive therapy in England, 2019: Usage, demographics, consent, and adherence to guidelines and legislation. Psychol Psychother Theory Res Pract, 94: 603-619. https://doi.org/10.1111/papt.12335
McDonald, W. M., Weiner, R. D., Fochtmann, L. J., & McCall, W. V. (2016). The FDA and ECT. *The journal of ECT*, *32*(2), 75–77. https://doi.org/10.1097/YCT.0000000000000326
79) Argyelan, M., Lencz, T., Kang, S. et al. ECT-induced cognitive side effects are associated with hippocampal enlargement. *Transl Psychiatry* **11**, 516 (2021). https://doi.org/10.1038/s41398-021-01641-y
Heijnen, W. T., Birkenhäger, T. K., Wierdsma, A. I., & van den Broek, W. W. (2010). Antidepressant pharmacotherapy failure and response to subsequent electroconvulsive therapy: a meta-analysis. *Journal of clinical psychopharmacology*, *30*(5), 616–619. https://doi.org/10.1097/JCP.0b013e3181ee0f5f
Youssef, N. A., & McCall, W. V. (2014). Relapse prevention after index electroconvulsive therapy in treatment-resistant depression. *Annals of clinical psychiatry : official journal of the American Academy of Clinical Psychiatrists*, *26*(4), 288–296. ECT and continuation pharmacotherapy may be more effective than either alone for preventing relapse. However, more definitive randomized clinical trials are needed.
McClintock, S. M., Brandon, A. R., Husain, M. M., & Jarrett, R. B. (2011). A systematic review of the combined use of electroconvulsive therapy and psychotherapy for depression. *The journal of ECT*, *27*(3), 236–243. https://doi.org/10.1097/YCT.0b013e3181faaeca
Mukherjee, S., Sackeim, H. A., & Schnur, D. B. (1994). Electroconvulsive therapy of acute manic episodes: a review of 50 years' experience. *The American journal of psychiatry*, *151*(2), 169–176. https://doi.org/10.1176/ajp.151.2.169
Alby Elias, Naveen Thomas, and Harold A. Sackeim, Electroconvulsive Therapy in Mania: A Review of 80 Years of Clinical Experience, American Journal of Psychiatry 2021 178:3, 229-23

References

https://ajp.psychiatryonline.org/doi/abs/10.1176/appi.ajp.2020.20030238
Iodice, Aline J. MS, C.R.C.; McCall, W. Vaughn MD, MS ECT Resistance and Early Relapse, The Journal of ECT: December 2003 - Volume 19 - Issue 4 - p 238-241 https://journals.lww.com/ectjournal/Abstract/2003/12000/ECT_Resistance_and_Early_Relapse_Two_Cases_of.12.aspx

80) Aleman, A. (2013). Use of Repetitive Transcranial Magnetic Stimulation for Treatment in Psychiatry. *Clinical Psychopharmacology and Neuroscience*, *11*(2), 53–59. https://doi.org/10.9758/cpn.2013.11.2.53

81) Hallett M. (2007). Transcranial magnetic stimulation: a primer. *Neuron*, *55*(2), 187–199. https://doi.org/10.1016/j.neuron.2007.06.026

82) McClintock, S. M., Reti, I. M., Carpenter, L. L., McDonald, W. M., Dubin, M., Taylor, S. F., Cook, I. A., O'Reardon, J., Husain, M. M., Wall, C., Krystal, A. D., Sampson, S. M., Morales, O., Nelson, B. G., Latoussakis, V., George, M. S., & Lisanby, S. H. (2018). Consensus Recommendations for the Clinical Application of Repetitive Transcranial Magnetic Stimulation (rTMS) in the Treatment of Depression. *The Journal of Clinical Psychiatry*, *79*(1), 35–48. https://doi.org/10.4088/jcp.16cs10905

Bm, E., Fern, M., Fj, E., J, C. V., M, F., E, A., & I, T. (2019). Effects and Therapeutic Use of TMS in Psychiatric Disorders: An Evidence-Based Review. *Www.Jneuropsychiatry.Org*, *9*(1), 2140–2160. https://doi.org/10.4172/Neuropsychiatry.1000560

Health Quality Ontario (2016). Repetitive Transcranial Magnetic Stimulation for Treatment-Resistant Depression: A Systematic Review and Meta-Analysis of Randomized Controlled Trials. *Ontario health technology assessment series*, *16*(5), 1–66.

Gaynes, B. N., Lloyd, S. W., Lux, L., Gartlehner, G., Hansen, R. A., Brode, S., Jonas, D. E., Swinson Evans, T., Viswanathan, M., & Lohr, K. N. (2014). Repetitive transcranial magnetic stimulation for treatment-resistant depression: a systematic review and meta-analysis. *The Journal of clinical psychiatry*, *75*(5), 477–489. https://doi.org/10.4088/JCP.13r08815

Levkovitz, Y., Isserles, M., Padberg, F., Lisanby, S. H., Bystritsky, A., Xia, G., Tendler, A., Daskalakis, Z. J., Winston, J. L., Dannon, P., Hafez, H. M., Reti, I. M., Morales, O. G., Schlaepfer, T. E., Hollander, E., Berman, J. A., Husain, M. M., Sofer, U., Stein, A., Adler, S., ... Zangen, A. (2015). Efficacy and safety of deep transcranial magnetic stimulation for major depression: a prospective multicenter randomized controlled trial. *World psychiatry : official journal of the World Psychiatric Association (WPA)*, *14*(1), 64–73. https://doi.org/10.1002/wps.20199

Sampaio-Junior B, Tortella G, Borrione L, et al. Efficacy and Safety of Transcranial Direct Current Stimulation as an Add-on Treatment for Bipolar Depression: A Randomized Clinical Trial. *JAMA Psychiatry*. 2018;75(2):158–166. DOI: 10.1001/jamapsychiatry.2017.4040

83) Eleanor J. Cole, Katy H. Stimpson, Brandon S. Bentzley, Merve Gulser,

Kirsten Cherian, Claudia Tischler, Romina Nejad, Heather Pankow, Elizabeth Choi, Haley Aaron, Flint M. Espil, Jaspreet Pannu, Xiaoqian Xiao, Dalton Duvio, Hugh B. Solvason, Jessica Hawkins, Austin Guerra, Booil Jo, Kristin S. Raj, Angela L. Phillips, Fahim Barmak, James H. Bishop, John P. Coetzee, Charles DeBattista, Jennifer Keller, Alan F. Schatzberg, Keith D. Sudheimer, and Nolan R. Williams, Stanford Accelerated Intelligent Neuromodulation Therapy for Treatment-Resistant Depression, American Journal of Psychiatry 2020 177:8, 716-726 https://ajp.psychiatryonline.org/doi/abs/10.1176/appi.ajp.2019.19070720

Nauczyciel, C., Le Jeune, F., Naudet, F., Douabin, S., Esquevin, A., Vérin, M., Dondaine, T., Robert, G., Drapier, D., & Millet, B. (2014). Repetitive transcranial magnetic stimulation over the orbitofrontal cortex for obsessive-compulsive disorder: a double-blind, crossover study. *Translational psychiatry*, *4*(9), e436. https://doi.org/10.1038/tp.2014.62

Feffer, K., Fettes, P., Giacobbe, P., Daskalakis, Z. J., Blumberger, D. M., & Downar, J. (2018). 1Hz rTMS of the right orbitofrontal cortex for major depression: Safety, tolerability and clinical outcomes. *European neuropsychopharmacology : the journal of the European College of Neuropsychopharmacology*, *28*(1), 109–117. https://doi.org/10.1016/j.euroneuro.2017.11.011

Lan, M. J., Chhetry, B. T., Liston, C., Mann, J. J., & Dubin, M. (2016). Transcranial Magnetic Stimulation of Left Dorsolateral Prefrontal Cortex Induces Brain Morphological Changes in Regions Associated with a Treatment Resistant Major Depressive Episode: An Exploratory Analysis. *Brain stimulation*, *9*(4), 577–583. https://doi.org/10.1016/j.brs.2016.02.011

Laura Sagliano, Francesca D'Olimpio, Francesco Panico, Serena Gagliardi, Luigi Trojano, The role of the dorsolateral prefrontal cortex in early threat processing: a TMS study, *Social Cognitive and Affective Neuroscience*, Volume 11, Issue 12, December 2016, Pages 1992 https://doi.org/10.1093/scan/nsw105

84) Deuschl, G., Schade-Brittinger, C., Krack, P., Volkmann, J., Schäfer, H., Bötzel, K., Daniels, C., Deutschländer, A., Dillmann, U., Eisner, W., Gruber, D., Hamel, W., Herzog, J., Hilker, R., Klebe, S., Kloss, M., Koy, J., Krause, M., Kupsch, A., Lorenz, D., ... German Parkinson Study Group, Neurostimulation Section (2006). A randomized trial of deep-brain stimulation for Parkinson's disease. *The New England journal of medicine*, *355*(9), 896–908. https://doi.org/10.1056/NEJMoa060281

Follett, K. A., Weaver, F. M., Stern, M., Hur, K., Harris, C. L., Luo, P., Marks, W. J., Jr, Rothlind, J., Sagher, O., Moy, C., Pahwa, R., Burchiel, K., Hogarth, P., Lai, E. C., Duda, J. E., Holloway, K., Samii, A., Horn, S., Bronstein, J. M., Stoner, G., ... CSP 468 Study Group (2010). Pallidal versus subthalamic deep-brain stimulation for Parkinson's disease. *The New England journal of medicine*, *362*(22), 2077–2091. https://doi.org/10.1056/NEJMoa0907083

Bronstein JM, Tagliati M, Alterman RL, et al. Deep Brain Stimulation for Parkinson Disease: An Expert Consensus and Review of Key Issues. *Arch*

References

Neurol. 2011;68(2):165. doi:10.1001/archneurol.2010.260
https://jamanetwork.com/journals/jamaneurology/fullarticle/802237
85) Holtzheimer, P. E., 3rd, & Mayberg, H. S. (2010). Deep brain stimulation for treatment-resistant depression. *The American journal of psychiatry*, *167*(12), https://doi.org/10.1176/appi.ajp.2010.10010141
Chabardès, S., Polosan, M., Krack, P., Bastin, J., Krainik, A., David, O., Bougerol, T., & Benabid, A. L. (2013). Deep Brain Stimulation for Obsessive-Compulsive Disorder: Subthalamic Nucleus Target. *World Neurosurgery*, *80*(3), S31.e1–S31.e8. https://doi.org/10.1016/j.wneu.2012.03.010
Kennedy, S. H., Giacobbe, P., Rizvi, S. J., Placenza, F. M., Nishikawa, Y., Mayberg, H. S., & Lozano, A. M. (2011). Deep brain stimulation for treatment-resistant depression: follow-up after 3 to 6 years. *The American journal of psychiatry*, *168*(5), 502–510. https://doi.org/10.1176/appi.ajp.2010.10081187
Mayberg, H. S., Lozano, A. M., Voon, V., McNeely, H. E., Seminowicz, D., Hamani, C., Schwalb, J. M., & Kennedy, S. H. (2005). Deep brain stimulation for treatment-resistant depression. *Neuron*, *45*(5), 651–660. https://doi.org/10.1016/j.neuron.2005.02.014
http://www.cell.com/neuron/fulltext/S0896-6273(05)00156-X
Delaloye, S., & Holtzheimer, P. E. (2014). Deep brain stimulation in the treatment of depression. *Dialogues in clinical neuroscience*, *16*(1), 83–91. https://doi.org/10.31887/DCNS.2014.16.1/sdelaloye
Minichino, A., Enticott, P. G., Mazzarini, L., Khan, N., Antonacci, G., Raccah, R. N., Salviati, M., Delle Chiaie, R., Bersani, G., Fitzgerald, P. B., & Biondi, M. (2013). Deep transcranial magnetic stimulation as a treatment for psychiatric disorders: a comprehensive review. *European Psychiatry: The Journal of the Association of European Psychiatrists*, *28*(1), 30–39. https://doi.org/10.1016/j.eurpsy.2012.02.006
Nair, G., Evans, A., Bear, R. E., Velakoulis, D., & Bittar, R. G. (2014). The anteromedial GPi as a new target for deep brain stimulation in obsessive compulsive disorder. *Journal of Clinical Neuroscience*, *21*(5), 815–821. https://doi.org/10.1016/j.jocn.2013.10.003
McIntyre, C. C., Grill, W. M., Sherman, D. L., & Thakor, N. V. (2004). Cellular Effects of Deep Brain Stimulation: Model-Based Analysis of Activation and Inhibition. *Journal of Neurophysiology*, *91*(4), 1457–1469. https://doi.org/10.1152/jn.00989.2003
Bergfeld IO, Mantione M, Hoogendoorn MLC, et al. Deep Brain Stimulation of the Ventral Anterior Limb of the Internal Capsule for Treatment-Resistant Depression: A Randomized Clinical Trial. *JAMA Psychiatry.* 2016;73(5):456–464. doi:10.1001/jamapsychiatry.2016.0152
https://jamanetwork.com/journals/jamapsychiatry/fullarticle/2512238
https://www.omicsonline.org/open-access/deep-brain-stimulation-for-treatmentresistant-depression-review-of-the-literature-2168-975X-1000168.php?aid=55926

Youngerman, B. E., & Sheth, S. A. (2017). Deep brain stimulation for treatment-resistant depression: optimizing interventions while preserving valid trial design. *Annals of translational medicine*, *5*(Suppl 1), S1. https://doi.org/10.21037/atm.2017.03.40

Malone, D. A., Jr, Dougherty, D. D., Rezai, A. R., Carpenter, L. L., Friehs, G. M., Eskandar, E. N., Rauch, S. L., Rasmussen, S. A., Machado, A. G., Kubu, C. S., Tyrka, A. R., Price, L. H., Stypulkowski, P. H., Giftakis, J. E., Rise, M. T., Malloy, P. F., Salloway, S. P., & Greenberg, B. D. (2009). Deep brain stimulation of the ventral capsule/ventral striatum for treatment-resistant depression. *Biological psychiatry*, *65*(4), 267–275. https://doi.org/10.1016/j.biopsych.2008.08.029

Alonso, P., Cuadras, D., Gabriëls, L., Denys, D., Goodman, W., Greenberg, B. D., Jimenez-Ponce, F., Kuhn, J., Lenartz, D., Mallet, L., Nuttin, B., Real, E., Segalas, C., Schuurman, R., du Montcel, S. T., & Menchon, J. M. (2015). Deep Brain Stimulation for Obsessive-Compulsive Disorder: A Meta-Analysis of Treatment Outcome and Predictors of Response. *PloS one*, *10*(7), e0133591. https://doi.org/10.1371/journal.pone.0133591

Garnaat, S. L., Greenberg, B. D., Sibrava, N. J., Goodman, W. K., Mancebo, M. C., Eisen, J. L., & Rasmussen, S. A. (2014). Who qualifies for deep brain stimulation for OCD? Data from a naturalistic clinical sample. *The Journal of neuropsychiatry and clinical neurosciences*, *26*(1), 81–86. https://doi.org/10.1176/appi.neuropsych.12090226

86) O'Reardon, J. P., Cristancho, P., & Peshek, A. D. (2019). Vagus Nerve Stimulation (VNS) and Treatment of Depression: To the Brainstem and Beyond. *Psychiatry (Edgmont (Pa. : Township))*, *3*(5), 54–63.

Lv, H., Zhao, Y., Chen, J., Wang, D., & Chen, H. (2019). Vagus Nerve Stimulation for Depression: A Systematic Review. *Frontiers in Psychology*, *10*. https://doi.org/10.3389/fpsyg.2019.00064
https://www.frontiersin.org/articles/10.3389/fpsyg.2019.00064/full

Ronald G. Garcia, Justine E. Cohen, Arielle D. Stanford, Aileen Gabriel, Jessica Stowell, Harlyn Aizley, Riccardo Barbieri, David Gitlin, Vitaly Napadow, Jill M. Goldstein,Respiratory-gated auricular vagal afferent nerve stimulation (RAVANS) modulates brain response to stress in major depression, Journal of Psychiatric Research,Volume 142,2021,Pages 188-197,ISSN 0022-3956,
https://doi.org/10.1016/j.jpsychires.2021.07.048.

87) Staudt MD, Herring EZ, Gao K, Miller JP, Sweet JA. Evolution in the Treatment of Psychiatric Disorders: From Psychosurgery to Psychopharmacology to Neuromodulation. *Front Neurosci*. 2019;13:108. Published 2019 Feb 15. doi:10.3389/fnins.2019.00108

88) https://getpocket.com/explore/item/the-surgeon-who-wants-to-connect-you-to-the-internet-with-a-brain-implant

89) https://www.nih.gov/news-events/nih-research-matters/

device-allows-paralyzed-man-communicate-words
https://www.sciencedaily.com/releases/2017/02/170206084904.htm

CHAPTER TWELVE REFERENCES

1) For a general introduction to Freud see
"A general introduction to PSYCHOANALYSIS" presented at Clark University in 1924
Brenner, AN ELEMENTARY TEXTBOOK OF PSYCHOANALYSIS IUP NY 1955.
A comprehensive multivolume biography is 1953. Sigmund Freud: Life and Work. Vol 1: The Young Freud 1856–1900. London: Hogarth Press. 1955. Sigmund Freud: Life and Work. Vol 2: The Years of Maturity 1901–1919. London: Hogarth Press. 1957. Sigmund Freud: Life and Work. Vol 3: The Last Phase 1919–1939. London: Hogarth Press. 1961. *Sigmund Freud: Life and Work*. An abridgment of the preceding 3 volume work, by Lionel Trilling and Stephen Marcus, with Introduction by Lionel Trilling. New York: Basic Books.
Kenny, D.T. (2016). A brief history of psychoanalysis: From Freud to fantasy to folly. Psychotherapy and Counselling Journal of Australia. http://pacja.org.au/?p=29
https://www.researchgate.net/publication/307561841_A_brief_history_of_psychoanalysis_From_Freud_to_fantasy_to_folly
Ellman, Carolyn, Stanley Grand, Mark Silvan, and Steven Ellman *The Modern Freudians: Contemporary Psychoanalytic Technique* Publisher: Jason Aronson, 2000
Daniel Yankelovich and William Barrett, *EGO AND INSTINCT: The Psychoanalytic View Of Human Nature-Revised* Random House, 1970, ISBN-10 : 1199163082 https://www.amazon.com/Ego-instinct-psychoanalytic-human-nature-revised/dp/B0006C028M
Schalkwijk F (2018) A New Conceptualization of the Conscience. *Front. Psychol.* 9:1863. doi: 10.3389/fpsyg.2018.01863
https://www.frontiersin.org/articles/10.3389/fpsyg.2018.01863/full
Front. Psychol., 08 October 2018
Sec. Psychoanalysis and Neuropsychoanalysis
https://doi.org/10.3389/fpsyg.2018.01863
2) Jerome Frank, *Persuasion and Healing*, Shocken Books, New York, 1974
Common factors theory - Wikipedia
Strupp, H. H., & Hadley, S. W. (1979). Specific vs nonspecific factors in psychotherapy. A controlled study of outcome. *Archives of general psychiatry*, *36*(10), 1125–1136. https://doi.org/10.1001/archpsyc.1979.01780100095009 https://neurotree.org/beta/publications.php?pid=35328
"What Is Therapeutic Change?1" by Strupp, Hans H. PhD - Journal of Cognitive

Psychotherapy, Vol. 2, Issue 2, January 1, 1988 | Online Research Library: Questia
Stephen F Butler, and Hans H. Strupp. Specific and nonspecific factors in psychotherapy: A problematic paradigm for psychotherapy research, March 1986, Psychotherapy Theory Research Practice Training 23(1):30-40, DOI: 10.1037/h0085590
O'Malley, S. S., Suh, C. S., & Strupp, H. H. (1983). The Vanderbilt Psychotherapy Process Scale: A report on the scale development and a process-outcome study. *Journal of Consulting and Clinical Psychology, 51*(4), 581–586. https://doi.org/10.1037/0022-006X.51.4.581
Kernberg O. F. (2016). The four basic components of psychoanalytic technique and derived psychoanalytic psychotherapies. *World psychiatry : official journal of the World Psychiatric Association (WPA)*, *15*(3), 287–288. https://doi.org/10.1002/wps.20368 *Four aspects jointly determine the very essence of psychoanalytic technique: interpretation, transference analysis, technical neutrality, and countertransference analysis.*
Key factor research requires treatment & control groups with or without a certain factor, and therapists who consistently administer the factor (or omit it), and small effect sizes required large n for significance.
3) Wampold B. E. (2015). How important are the common factors in psychotherapy? An update. *World psychiatry : official journal of the World Psychiatric Association (WPA)*, *14*(3), 270–277. https://doi.org/10.1002/wps.20238
Castelnuovo G. (2010). Empirically supported treatments in psychotherapy: towards an evidence-based or evidence-biased psychology in clinical settings?. *Frontiers in psychology*, *1*, 27. https://doi.org/10.3389/fpsyg.2010.00027
Castelnuovo, G., Gaggioli, A., Mantovani, F., & Riva, G. (2003). From psychotherapy to e-therapy: the integration of traditional techniques and new communication tools in clinical settings. *Cyberpsychology & behavior : the impact of the Internet, multimedia and virtual reality on behavior and society*, *6*(4), 375–382. https://doi.org/10.1089/109493103322278754
Westen D, Bradley R. Empirically Supported Complexity: Rethinking Evidence-Based Practice in Psychotherapy. Current Directions in Psychological Science. 2005;14(5):266-271.
https://journals.sagepub.com/doi/10.1111/j.0963-7214.2005.00378.x
Evidence-Based Practice As Mental Health Policy: Three Controversies And A Caveat evidenced based practice in mental health - Google Scholar
Daniel Tadmon and Mark Olfson, Trends in Outpatient Psychotherapy Provision by U.S. Psychiatrists: 1996–2016 American Journal of Psychiatry 2022 179:2, https://doi.org/10.1176/appi.ajp.2021.21040338
A. John Rush, Making Therapy Widely Available: Clinical Research Triumph or Existential Catastrophe?
American Journal of Psychiatry 2022 179:2, 79-82 https://doi.org/10.1176/appi.ajp.2021.21121201

References

4) O'Donohue, W., Buchanan, J. A., & Fisher, J. E. (2000). Characteristics of empirically supported treatments. *The Journal of psychotherapy practice and research, 9*(2), 69–74.
SAMHSA: A Pocket Guide to Evidence-Based Practices (EBP) on the Web
SAMHSA: A Pocket Guide to Evidence-Based Practices (EBP) on the Web
NREPP | Home Evidence-Based Mental Health Treatment for Children and Adolescents
5) https://www.verywellmind.com/best-hypnosis-apps-4800547
6) https://www.portagepath.org/coping-skills-library/
Gladstone, T., Terrizzi, D., Stinson, A., Nidetz, J., Canel, J., Ching, E., Berry, A., Cantorna, J., Fogel, J., Eder, M., Bolotin, M., Thomann, L. O., Griffith, K., Ip, P., Aaby, D. A., Brown, C. H., Beardslee, W., Bell, C., Crawford, T. J., Fitzgibbon, M., … Van Voorhees, B. W. (2018). Effect of Internet-based Cognitive Behavioral Humanistic and Interpersonal Training vs. Internet-based General Health Education on Adolescent Depression in Primary Care: A Randomized Clinical Trial. *JAMA network open, 1*(7), e184278. https://doi.org/10.1001/jamanetworkopen.2018.4278
Culjak, G., Kowalenko, N., & Tennant, C. (2016). Awareness, Access and Use of Internet Self-Help Websites for Depression by University Students. *JMIR mental health, 3*(4), e48. https://doi.org/10.2196/mental.5311
7) https://www.bizjournals.com/philadelphia/news/2018/02/16/a-chance-encounter-could-be-a-life-changing-event.html
Bandura, A. (1982). The psychology of chance encounters and life paths. *American Psychologist, 37*(7), 747–755. https://doi.org/10.1037/0003-066X.37.7.747
LIST OF SELF HELP RESOURCES
https://mindremakeproject.org/2020/09/03/13-sites-for-self-help/
https://www.psywww.com/resource/selfhelp.htm
8) Greenson, R. R., & Wexler, M. (1969). The non-transference relationship in the psychoanalytic situation. *The International Journal of Psychoanalysis, 50*(1), 27–39.
Greensen, *A Technique in Practice of Psychoanalysis, vol.* 1, International University Press, New York, 1967
Ardito, R. B., & Rabellino, D. (2011). Therapeutic alliance and outcome of psychotherapy: historical excursus, measurements, and prospects for research. *Frontiers in psychology, 2*, 270. https://doi.org/10.3389/fpsyg.2011.00270
9) Szasz T. S. (1956). On the experiences of the analyst in the psychoanalytic situation; a contribution to the theory of psychoanalytic treatment. *Journal of the American Psychoanalytic Association, 4*(2), 197–223. https://doi.org/10.1177/000306515600400201
10) Gabbard G. O. (2020). The role of countertransference in contemporary psychiatric treatment. *World psychiatry : official journal of the World Psychiatric Association (WPA), 19*(2), 243–244. https://doi.org/10.1002/wps.20746

Evidence based Therapy Relationships, J C Norcross PhD ed, (2010)Chapter 12, Managing Countertransference. PDF A seminar of papers on EST
11) Richard M. Foxx,Applied Behavior Analysis Treatment of Autism: The State of the Art,Child and Adolescent Psychiatric Clinics of North America,Volume 17, Issue 4,2008,
Pages 821-834,ISSN 1056-4993, https://doi.org/10.1016/j.chc.2008.06.007 .
12) Carl Rogers, **On Becoming A Person**, Mariner Books; 2nd ed. edition (September 7, 1995)
Stern, D. N., Sander, L. W., Nahum, J. P., Harrison, A. M., Lyons-Ruth, K., Morgan, A. C., Bruschweiler-Stern, N., & Tronick, E. Z. (1998). Non-interpretive mechanisms in psychoanalytic therapy. The 'something more' than interpretation. The Process of Change Study Group. *The International journal of psycho-analysis, 79 (Pt 5)*, 903–921.
13) Peter M. Newton (1971) Abstinence as a Role Requirement in Psychotherapy, Psychiatry, 34:4, 391-400, DOI: 10.1080/00332747.1971.11023685
14) Oedipal Love in the Countertransference, Searles, Harold F. **The International Journal of Psycho-Analysis; London Vol. 40,** (Jan 1, 1959): 180.
Anna Maria Loiacono (2021) Countertransference and Oedipal love, International Forum of Psychoanalysis, DOI: 10.1080/0803706X.2021.1872799
15) Høglend, P., Bøgwald, K. P., Amlo, S., Marble, A., Ulberg, R., Sjaastad, M. C., Sørbye, O., Heyerdahl, O., & Johansson, P. (2008). Transference interpretations in dynamic psychotherapy: do they really yield sustained effects?. *The American journal of psychiatry, 165*(6), 763–771. https://doi.org/10.1176/appi.ajp.2008.07061028
Ralph Greenson, "Empathy and its Vicissitudes". https://www.proquest.com/openview/4c1877b2c04262c9343388cbff274f76/1?pq-origsite=gscholar&cbl=1818729
16) Langs, The Bipersonal field http://psychoanalyticmuse.blogspot.com/2011/12/robert-langs-bipersonal-field.html
Therapeutic interaction in the bipersonal field. Contributions of Robert Langs. http://www.regreynolds.ca/Articles/Psychotherapy/Contributions%20of%20Robert%20Langs%20to%20Clinical%20Psychoanalysis,%201973%20-%201979.pdf
Brie Turns, Paul R. Springer & D. Scott Sibley (2019) Removing the "mystery" in therapy: transparency as a continuous intervention in family psychotherapy, Journal of Family Psychotherapy, 30:1, 1-19, DOI: 10.1080/08975353.2018.1488127
Truax, C. B., & Carkhuff, R. R. (1965). Client and therapist transparency in the psychotherapeutic encounter. *Journal of Counseling Psychology, 12*(1), 3–9. https://doi.org/10.1037/h0021928

References

17) Searles, Harold, *Collected Papers on Schizophrenia and Related Subjects*, International University Press, New York, 1965.
Searles, H. F. (1979). *Countertransference and related subjects: Selected papers*. New York: International Universities Press. Searles, Hate in the countertransf
Szasz TS. On The Experiences of the Analyst in the Psychoanalytic Situation: A Contribution to the Theory of Psychoanalytic Treatment. *Journal of the American Psychoanalytic Association*. 1956;4(2):197-223. doi:10.1177/000306515600400201
https://www.psychiatrictimes.com/view/hateful-patient-revisited-transactional-view-difficult-physician-patient-relationships
18) CarlA. Whitaker MD and Thomas P. Malone Phd. MD *The Roots of Psychotherapy*   Brunner Mazel NY 1981https://www.amazon.com/Roots-Psychotherapy-Brunner-Classics-Psychoanalysis/dp/0876302657 (Chapter 13 and 14)
19) Louis Fierman,MD, "H Keiser and fusion fantasy" (unpublished)
Hellmuth Kaiser (1962) Emergency, Psychiatry, 25:2, 97-118, DOI: 10.1080/00332747.1962.11023302
20) *Hobbs, N. (1962). Sources of gain in psychotherapy. American Psychologist,17,741-7*
Glickauf-Hughes, C., & Wells, M. (1991). Current conceptualizations on masochism: genesis and object relations. *American journal of psychotherapy*, *45*(1), 53–68. https://doi.org/10.1176/appi.psychotherapy.1991.45.1.53
21) Yalom, *Theory and Practice of Group Psychotherapy*, Basic Books; 5th edition (March 3, 2008)
Janice L. DeLucia-Waack, Cynthia R. Kalodner , Maria Riva, *Handbook of Group Counseling and Psychotherapy 2nd Ed*
Fagan, J., & Shepherd, I. L. (1970). *Gestalt therapy now: Theory, techniques, applications*. Science & Behavior Books.. PsycINFO Database Record (c) 2016 APA,
A. K. Rice Institute for the Study of Social Systems
Group Relations Programme - The Tavistock Institute
22) William J. Doherty , Ralph LaRossa, Walter R. Schumm, Suzanne K. Steinmetz, *Sourcebook of Family Theories and Methods, A Contextual Approach*, ed Pauline Boss, Springer 1993
Jewell, T., Blessitt, E., Stewart, C., Simic, M., & Eisler, I. (2016). Family Therapy for Child and Adolescent Eating Disorders: A Critical Review. *Family process*, *55*(3) https://doi.org/10.1111/famp.12242
Heru A. M. (2018). Family Intervention in the Care of a Patient With Nonepileptic Seizures. *The American journal of psychiatry*, *175*(9), 824–830. https://doi.org/10.1176/appi.ajp.2018.18010021
Luby, J. L., Barch, D. M., Whalen, D., Tillman, R., & Freedland, K. E. (2018). A Randomized Controlled Trial of Parent-Child Psychotherapy Targeting Emotion

Development for Early Childhood Depression. *The American journal of psychiatry*, *175*(11), 1102–1110. https://doi.org/10.1176/appi.ajp.2018.18030321
23) https://archive.md/20130117102148/http://www.ayeconference.com/the-identified-patient-pattern/
24) Avery Weisman, Silence in Psychotherapy. Psychiatry 1955, vol 18, 241-260,
Ewbank, M. P., Cummins, R., Tablan, V., Bateup, S., Catarino, A., Martin, A. J., & Blackwell, A. D. (2020). Quantifying the Association Between Psychotherapy Content and Clinical Outcomes Using Deep Learning. *JAMA psychiatry*, *77*(1), 35–43. https://doi.org/10.1001/jamapsychiatry.2019.2664
Lacan created a unique branch of psychoanalysis that combines social, economic, and emotional elements in his idiosyncratic theory.
https://cla.purdue.edu/academic/english/theory/psychoanalysis/lacandevelop.html
https://lacan-psychoananalysisaspraxis.tumblr.com/post/150916856706/key-concepts-of-lacanian-psychoanalysis
Luepnitz, D.A. (2009), Thinking in the space between Winnicott and Lacan. The International Journal of Psychoanalysis, 90: 957-981. https://doi.org/10.1111/j.1745-8315.2009.00156.x
25) Ekman and Friesen, **FACIAL-Sign-Of-Emotional-Experience**.
Wolf K. (2015). Measuring facial expression of emotion. *Dialogues in clinical neuroscience*, *17*(4), 457–462. https://doi.org/10.31887/DCNS.2015.17.4/kwolf
Ernst Beier, **The Silent Language of Psychotherapy**, Aldean Publishing, Chicago, 1966
A review of the early work in non-verbal communication can be found in **Non-Verbal Communication**, edited by Shirley Weitz, Oxford University Press, New York, 1974.
Ray Birdwhistle, **Kinesics in Context**, U of Pennsylvania Press, Philadelphia 1970
Foley, G. N., & Gentile, J. P. (2010). Nonverbal communication in psychotherapy. *Psychiatry (Edgmont (Pa. : Township))*, *7*(6), 38–44. https://www.ncbi.nlm.nih.gov/pmc/articles/PMC2898840/
Sidney Jourard, **The Transparent Self**, Van Nostrom, New York 1971, revised edition.
26) Reik, T. (1948). *Listening with the third ear: The inner experience of a psychoanalyst*. New York: Farrar, Straus.
27) https://en.wikipedia.org/wiki/Johari_window
28) Schutte, N. S., Malouff, J. M., Hall, L. E., Haggerty, D. J., Cooper, J. T., Golden, C. J., & Dornheim, L. (1998). Development and validation of a measure of emotional intelligence. Personality and Individual Differences, 25(2), 167–177. https://doi.org/10.1016/S0191-8869(98)00001-4
Kaplowitz, M. J., Safran, J. D., & Muran, C. J. (2011). Impact of therapist emotional intelligence on psychotherapy. *The Journal of nervous and mental disease*,

References

199(2), 74–84. https://doi.org/10.1097/NMD.0b013e3182083efb

29) *Patients suitability for psychotherapy are sometimes given the informal acronym YAVIS, is Young, Attractive, Verbal, Intelligent and Successful. This group is less likely to need help than another group, people who are not comfortable in verbal social interaction.*

30) *The rejection of polygraph in psychotherapy seems to combine two issues, the polygraph is sometimes incorrect about responses, and "forcing someone to be truthful" does not fit well with a non-judgemental interpersonal relationship.*

Adrian Raine, Frances R. Chen, Rebecca Waller,The cognitive, affective and somatic empathy scales for adults,Personality and Individual Differences,Volume 185,2022, https://doi.org/10.1016/j.paid.2021.111238 .

Bradley, M. M., Miccoli, L., Escrig, M. A., & Lang, P. J. (2008). The pupil as a measure of emotional arousal and autonomic activation. *Psychophysiology*, *45*(4), 602–607. https://doi.org/10.1111/j.1469-8986.2008.00654.x

Paul Ekman and Wallace Friesen, **Non-Verbal Behavior in Psychothcrapy Research**, in Research and Psychotherapy, volume 3 1968. https://www.paulekman.com/wp-content/uploads/2013/07/Nonverbal-Behavior-In-Psychotherapy-Reseasrch.pdf

Some people have a sense of "somatic empathy" the intuition to experience in their body similar changes occurring in another. https://ericehrke.com/812-2/
https://www.scientology.org/what-is-scientology/the-practice-of-scientology/the-e-meter.html

Lester Luborsky and Arthur Auerbach, The Symptom Context Method, Journal of the American Psychoanalytic Association, Vol. 17, 1969, pg. 68-99.

Weiner M. F. (1998). The Symptom-Context Method: Symptoms as Opportunities in Psychotherapy. *The Journal of Psychotherapy Practice and Research*, *7*(3), 259–260. https://www.ncbi.nlm.nih.gov/pmc/articles/PMC3330505/

31) Some comments on acting out, and acting in: https://ebrary.net/54738/health/acting_outand_acting

Acting in: ACTING IN: "Sometimes therapy patients will engage in acting in, wherein they correlate their past experiences with others as being the same as what is occurring in the therapy settings, sometimes with their therapist." https://psychologydictionary.org/acting-in/

32) Landreth, G.L., **Play Therapy The Art of the relationship**

Ray, D et al (2001) The effectiveness of play therapy: Responding to the critics. Int J Play Therapy 10(1)85-108 https://doi.org/10.1037/h0089444

Pesso psychomotor training, http://books.wwnorton.com/books/detail-contents.aspx?ID=4294987187

Probst, Michel & Knapen, Jan & Poot, Greet & Vancampfort, Davy. (2010). Psychomotor Therapy and Psychiatry: What's in a Name?. Open Compl Med J. 2.

https://www.researchgate.net/

publication/228699942_Psychomotor_Therapy_and_Psychiatry_What%27s_in_a_Name https://www.rubenfeldsynergy.com/ https://alexandertechnique.com/
https://www.lowenfoundation.org/what-is-bioenergetics
33) Wilhelm Reich, **Character Armor**. **Language Of The Body, Betrayal Of The Body**,
http://www.bioenergetic-therapy.com/index.php/en/
van der Kolk, B. A. (2014). *The body keeps the score: Brain, mind, and body in the healing of trauma*. Viking.
https://www.amtamassage.org/publications/massage-therapy-journal/ethical-boundaries/
https://www.nytimes.com/2019/07/13/opinion/sunday/touch-intimacy.html
Touch boundaries of sex workers and sex surrogates. Sex workers are employed in many societies to perform sexual activities for money. This is morally rejected in some, disdained in some, and acceptable in others. No questions about the violations of boundaries occur in this setting, since the transfer of money focuses the reality that this is not a "real" relationship, just as in psychotherapy. (35) More confusing is a "sexual surrogate", a person whose task is to therapeutically enhance the sexual response of the client, not just provide an experience. Masters and Johnson carried out research and consultation with couples aiming to enhance their sexual experience, and faced strong criticism of their work in the medical community. This issue seems to reflect core cultural values (of the United States?). Sexual activities between two persons are categorically differentiated between experiences that have no relationship value, and experiences with relationship significance ("love" however that is interpreted). Everyday, individuals violate these norms on a consistent basis, yet it does not seem to change the norms of the broader society.
34) https://en.wikipedia.org/wiki/Sexual_surrogate
https://www.healthline.com/health/healthy-sex/sex-surrogate#what-it-is
https://www.surrogatetherapy.org/
35) https://www.ramonaclifton.com/blog/2014/6/25/can-i-have-two-therapists
36) Turner M. J. (2016). Rational Emotive Behavior Therapy (REBT), Irrational and Rational Beliefs, and the Mental Health of Athletes. *Frontiers in psychology*, 7, 1423. https://doi.org/10.3389/fpsyg.2016.01423
https://www.ncbi.nlm.nih.gov/pmc/articles/PMC5028385/
David, D., Cotet, C., Matu, S., Mogoase, C., & Stefan, S. (2018). 50 years of rational-emotive and cognitive-behavioral therapy: A systematic review and meta-analysis. *Journal of clinical psychology*, 74(3), 304–318. https://doi.org/10.1002/jclp.22514
https://beckinstitute.org/resources-for-professionals/research-corner/
https://beckinstitute.org/?s=derubeis
https://neurotree.org/beta/publications.php?pid=179737
Sloan DM, Marx BP, Lee DJ, Resick PA. A Brief Exposure-Based Treatment vs

References

Cognitive Processing Therapy for Posttraumatic Stress Disorder: A Randomized Noninferiority Clinical Trial. *JAMA Psychiatry.* 2018;75(3):233–239. doi:10.1001/jamapsychiatry.2017.4249
https://jamanetwork.com/journals/jamapsychiatry/fullarticle/2669771
37) Jackson S. W. (1994). Catharsis and abreaction in the history of psychological healing. *The Psychiatric clinics of North America, 17*(3), 471–491.
https://www.verywellmind.com/understanding-abreaction-1065382
38) Wendy Wood, Attitude Change: Persuasion and Social Influence, Annual Review of Psychology 2000 51:1, 539-570
Petty, R. E., Wheeler, S. C., & Tormala, Z. L. (2003). Persuasion and attitude change. In T. Millon & M. Lerner (Eds.), **Handbook of psychology: Personality and social psychology** (pp. 353-382). Hoboken, NJ: Wiley.
39) Anna Freud's **Ego and The Mechanisms of Defense** International University Press, New York,1946.
George Valliant, **Adaptation to Life**, Little Brown and Company, Boston, 1977.
Marty Horowitz, **Stress Response Syndromes**, Jason Arrinson, New York, 1976.
Marty J. Horowitz, **States of Mind** –Planom Medical Book Company, 1979, New York.
The Wellness Recovery Action Plan (WRAP) | Copeland Center for Wellness and Recovery https://copelandcenter.com/wellness-recovery-action-plan-wrap
40) Erskine, Richard. (2021). Relational Withdrawal, Attunement to Silence: Psychotherapy of the Schizoid Process. https://www.researchgate.net/publication/348339682_Relational_Withdrawal_Attunement_to_Silence_Psychotherapy_of_the_Schizoid_Process
Guntrip, H. The schizoid compromise and the therapeutic stalemate. https://bps-psychub.onlinelibrary.wiley.com/doi/10.1111/j.2044-8341.1962.tb00525.x
https://blogs.scientificamerican.com/mind-guest-blog/the-emotional-blindness-of-alexithymia/
Taylor, G. J., & Bagby, R. M. (2013). Psychoanalysis and empirical research: the example of alexithymia. *Journal of the American Psychoanalytic Association, 61*(1), https://doi.org/10.1177/0003065112474066
Goerlich K. S. (2018). The Multifaceted Nature of Alexithymia - A Neuroscientific Perspective. *Frontiers in psychology, 9*, 1614. https://doi.org/10.3389/fpsyg.2018.01614
Heffer, T., & Willoughby, T. (2017). A count of coping strategies: A longitudinal study investigating an alternative method to understanding coping and adjustment. *PloS one, 12*(10), e0186057. https://doi.org/10.1371/journal.pone.0186057
Wu, Y., Yu, W., Wu, X. et al. Psychological resilience and positive coping styles among Chinese undergraduate students: a cross-sectional study. *BMC Psychol* **8,** 79 (2020). https://doi.org/10.1186/s40359-020-00444-y
Babicka-Wirkus A, Wirkus L, Stasiak K, Kozłowski P (2021) University students' strategies of coping with stress during the coronavirus pandemic: Data

from Poland. PLoS ONE 16(7): e0255041. https://doi.org/10.1371/journal.pone.0255041

41) **The Mind and the Brain, Neuroplasticity and the Power of Mental Force**, Jeffrey M. Schwartz and Sharon Begley. Regin Books, Harper Collins 2002, New York, New York. *The book surveys techniques for working with brain injured patients and showing plasticity both in monkeys and in humans in using behavioral techniques for reprogramming: 1)Graybiel's study of TAN neurons.2)Taub experiments on monkey limbs.3) Merzenich and Kaas sensory relink mapping.4) Ramachandran phantom limb. 5)Hallett shows blind patients cross modal plasticity so that visual cortex responds to braile (touch).6) Tallal and Miller revising dyslexics.7) Leckman's work with tourettes. Etc.*

42) Greenberg, Leslie & Elliott, Robert & Lietaer, Germain. (2004). **Research on experiential psychotherapies.**
(2004). In M.J. Lambert (Ed.), Bergin & Garfield's **Handbook of psychotherapy and behavior change** (5th ed.) (pp. 493-539), New York: Wiley
Nature walks change the brain. https://www.rewireme.com/wellness/nature-walks-change-brain/
https://www.sensorimotorpsychotherapy.org/home/index.html
Use of drumming in therapy http://www.openculture.com/2015/08/the-neuroscience-of-drumming.html

43) Crits-Christoph, Paul & Cooper, Andrew & Luborsky, Lester. (1988). The accuracy of therapists' interpretations and the outcome of dynamic psychotherapy. J Consult Clin Psychol. 56. 490-5. https://doi.org/10.1037/0022-006X.56.4.490
Lomax, J. W., Kripal, J. J., & Pargament, K. I. (2011). Perspectives on "sacred moments" in psychotherapy. *The American journal of psychiatry*, *168*(1), 12–18. https://doi.org/10.1176/appi.ajp.2010.10050739

44) Cusumano EP and Raz A (2014) Harnessing psychoanalytical methods for a phenomenological neuroscience. *Front. Psychol.* **5**:334. doi: 10.3389/fpsyg.2014.00334
Unterrainer, H. F., Lewis, A. J., & Gruzelier, J. H. (2013). EEG-Neurofeedback in psychodynamic treatment of substance dependence. *Frontiers in psychology*, *4*, 692. https://doi.org/10.3389/fpsyg.2013.00692
Kato, T. A., & Kanba, S. (2013). Are microglia minding us? Digging up the unconscious mind-brain relationship from a neuropsychoanalytic approach. *Frontiers in human neuroscience*, *7*, 13. https://doi.org/10.3389/fnhum.2013.00013
Sharon Jane Calvert, Larry E. Beutler, and Marjorie Crago, Psychotherapy Outcome as a Function of Therapist-Patient Matching on Selected Variables Journal of Social and Clinical Psychology 1988 6:1, 104-117 https://guilfordjournals.com/doi/abs/10.1521/jscp.1988.6.1.104
O'Malley, S. S., Suh, C. S., & Strupp, H. H. (1983). The Vanderbilt Psychotherapy Process Scale: A report on the scale development and a

process-outcome study. *Journal of Consulting and Clinical Psychology, 51*(4), 581–586. https://doi.org/10.1037/0022-006X.51.4.581

Høglend P. (2014). Exploration of the patient-therapist relationship in psychotherapy. *The American journal of psychiatry, 171*(10), 1056–1066. https://doi.org/10.1176/appi.ajp.2014.14010121

Werbart, A., Hägertz, M., & Borg Ölander, N. (2018). Matching Patient and Therapist Anaclitic-Introjective Personality Configurations Matters for Psychotherapy Outcomes. *Journal of contemporary psychotherapy, 48*(4), 241–251.https://doi.org/10.1007/s10879-018-9389-8

Lingiardi, V., Muzi, L., Tanzilli, A., & Carone, N. (2018). Do therapists' subjective variables impact on psychodynamic psychotherapy outcomes? A systematic literature review. *Clinical psychology & psychotherapy, 25*(1), 85–101. https://doi.org/10.1002/cpp.2131

Marziliano, A., Applebaum, A., Moyer, A., Pessin, H., Rosenfeld, B., & Breitbart, W. (2021). The Impact of Matching to Psychotherapy Preference on Engagement in a Randomized Controlled Trial for Patients With Advanced Cancer. *Frontiers in psychology, 12*, 637519. https://doi.org/10.3389/fpsyg.2021.637519

45) MAES, J. L. (1968). The Role of Attention in Psychotherapy. *The Journal of Education, 150*(3), 82–91. http://www.jstor.org/stable/42772754

46) Mark Epstein, Md **Thoughts Without A Thinker**, Basic Books New York 1995

What_Do_We_Really_Know_About_Mindfulness20160310-26917-eqryx0-with-cover-page-v2.pdf

FOCUS The Hidden Driver of Excellence By Daniel Goleman 311 pp. Harper.

47) Niazi, A. K., & Niazi, S. K. (2011). Mindfulness-based stress reduction: a non-pharmacological approach for chronic illnesses. *North American journal of medical sciences, 3*(1), 20–23. https://doi.org/10.4297/najms.2011.320

Grossman P, Niemann L, Schmidt S, et al. Mindfulness-based stress reduction and health benefits: a meta-analysis. 2004. In: Database of Abstracts of Reviews of Effects (DARE): Quality-assessed Reviews (Internet). York (UK): Centre for Reviews and Dissemination (UK); 1995-. Available from: https://www.ncbi.nlm.nih.gov/books/NBK70854/

de Jong, M., Peeters, F., Gard, T., Ashih, H., Doorley, J., Walker, R., Rhoades, L., Kulich, R. J., Kueppenbender, K. D., Alpert, J. E., Hoge, E. A., Britton, W. B., Lazar, S. W., Fava, M., & Mischoulon, D. (2018). A Randomized Controlled Pilot Study on Mindfulness-Based Cognitive Therapy for Unipolar Depression in Patients With Chronic Pain. *The Journal of clinical psychiatry, 79*(1), 15m10160. https://doi.org/10.4088/JCP.15m10160

Hoge, E. A., Bui, E., Marques, L., Metcalf, C. A., Morris, L. K., Robinaugh, D. J., Worthington, J. J., Pollack, M. H., & Simon, N. M. (2013). Randomized controlled trial of mindfulness meditation for generalized anxiety disorder:

effects on anxiety and stress reactivity. *The Journal of clinical psychiatry*, *74*(8), 786–792. https://doi.org/10.4088/JCP.12m08083

Hoge, E. A., Bui, E., Palitz, S. A., Schwarz, N. R., Owens, M. E., Johnston, J. M., Pollack, M. H., & Simon, N. M. (2018). The effect of mindfulness meditation training on biological acute stress responses in generalized anxiety disorder. *Psychiatry research*, *262*, 328–332. https://doi.org/10.1016/j.psychres.2017.01.006

48) The Focusing Institute: Focusing is direct access to a bodily knowing. The following website lists available references. https://www.focusingtherapy.org/information-resources/articles/

Eugene T. Gendlin, FOCUSING ORIENTED PSYCHOTHERAPY (1996) Guilford
https://www.google.com/books/edition/Focusing_Oriented_Psychotherapy/

49) Fonagy, P., & Bateman, A. W. (2006). Mechanisms of change in mentalization-based treatment of BPD. *Journal of clinical psychology*, *62*(4), 411–430. https://doi.org/10.1002/jclp.20241

Bateman, A., & Fonagy, P. (2010). Mentalization based treatment for borderline personality disorder. *World psychiatry : official journal of the World Psychiatric Association (WPA)*, *9*(1), 11–15. https://doi.org/10.1002/j.2051-5545.2010.tb00255.x

James F. Masterson – **Psychotherapy of the Borderline Adult, A Developmental Approach**, Brunner Mazel, New York, 1976.

50) Bormann, J. E., Oman, D., Kemppainen, J. K., Becker, S., Gershwin, M., & Kelly, A. (2006). Mantram repetition for stress management in veterans and employees: a critical incident study. *Journal of advanced nursing*, *53*(5), 502–512. https://doi.org/10.1111/j.1365-2648.2006.03752.x

51) https://en.wikipedia.org/wiki/History_of_hypnosis

Martin T. Orne (1971) The simulation of hypnosis: Why, how, and what it means, International Journal of Clinical and Experimental Hypnosis, 19:4, 183-210, DOI: 10.1080/00207147108407167

52) Frankel F. H. (1990). Hypnotizability and dissociation. *The American journal of psychiatry*, *147*(7), 823–829. https://doi.org/10.1176/ajp.147.7.823

Herbert Spiegel, MD and David Spiegel MD, *Trance and Treatment: Clinical Uses of Hypnosis*, American Psychiatric Publications; 2nd edition (April 19, 2004)

Dissociative Experiences Scale

Mazzoni, G., Venneri, A., McGeown, W. J., & Kirsch, I. (2013). Neuroimaging resolution of the altered state hypothesis. *Cortex*, *49*(2), 400–410. https://doi.org/10.1016/j.cortex.2012.08.005

Jensen, M. P., Jamieson, G. A., Lutz, A., Mazzoni, G., McGeown, W. J., Santarcangelo, E. L., Demertzi, A., De Pascalis, V., Bányai, É. I., Rominger, C., Vuilleumier, P., Faymonville, M.-E., & Terhune, D. B. (2017). New directions in hypnosis research: strategies for advancing the cognitive and clinical neuroscience of hypnosis. *Neuroscience of Consciousness, 2017*(1). https://doi.org/10.1093/nc/nix004

53) Ruth A. Lanius, M. D. (2008, November 1). *Reexperiencing/Hyperaroused and Dissociative States in Posttraumatic Stress Disorder*. Psychiatric Times. https://www.psychiatrictimes.com/articles/reexperiencinghyperaroused-and-dissociative-states-posttraumatic-stress-disorder

54) FALSE MEMORY SYNDROME Memory storage of experience is not precise. Memory is recreation and therefore subject to distortion. Experiments in psychology reveal that memory storage process is inexact and highly influenced by external factors. Techniques that explore past history especially of dissociative events risk creating false recall. This can result in "false memory" suits against therapists who report child abuse from patient recall. Emotional experience is valid but the factual source may be different from recall.

Kaplan, R., & Manicavasagar, V. (2001). Is there a false memory syndrome? A review of three cases. *Comprehensive psychiatry*, *42*(4), 342 348. https://doi.org/10.1053/comp.2001.24588

https://news.isst-d.org/the-rise-and-fall-of-the-false-memory-syndrome-foundation/

55) John O. Beahrs M.D. (1971) The Hypnotic Psychotherapy of Milton H. Erickson, American Journal of Clinical Hypnosis, 14:2, 73-90, DOI: 10.1080/00029157.1971.10402155

Jay Haley **Uncommon Therapy: The Psychiatric Techniques Of Milton H Erikson Md** Norton NY1973

Milton H. Erickson, MD and Ernest Lawrence Rossi, Phd. **The February Man** Brunner Mazel New YORK 1989

56) Marzbani, H., Marateb, H. R., & Mansourian, M. (2016). Neurofeedback: A Comprehensive Review on System Design, Methodology and Clinical Applications. *Basic and clinical neuroscience*, *7*(2), 143–158. https://doi.org/10.15412/J.BCN.03070208

Neurofeedback, Biofeedback, QEEG Brain Maps, Mindfulness & Self-regulation Training. (408) 984-3333. Professional Neurofeedback, Biofeedback, QEEG, Brain Mapping, Mindfulness & Peak Performance Training.

Micoulaud-Franchi, J. A., Geoffroy, P. A., Fond, G., Lopez, R., Bioulac, S., & Philip, P. (2014). EEG neurofeedback treatments in children with ADHD: an updated meta-analysis of randomized controlled trials. *Frontiers in human neuroscience*, *8*, 906. https://doi.org/10.3389/fnhum.2014.00906

Young, K. D., Zotev, V., Phillips, R., Misaki, M., Drevets, W. C., & Bodurka, J. (2018). Amygdala real-time functional magnetic resonance imaging neurofeedback for major depressive disorder: A review. *Psychiatry and clinical neurosciences*, *72*(7), 466–481. https://doi.org/10.1111/pcn.12665

57) Watanabe, T., Sasaki, Y., Shibata, K., & Kawato, M. (2017). Advances in fMRI Real-Time Neurofeedback. *Trends in cognitive sciences*, *21*(12), 997–1010. https://doi.org/10.1016/j.tics.2017.09.010

58) *Other sensory pathways are available for exploring how they activate brain regions: Patterns of sound can create brain wave coherence, with secondary effects on sleep and focusing. Visual strobe effects impact brain pathways, and pose risks in those sensitive to seizure triggering, but are sought by youth in "raves" or other dance clubs, so finding ways to utilize this modality safely would be another option. Synthetic reality techniques have been incorporated into PTSD desensitization with variable results. The olfactory channel is documented in the herbal literature, and is now widely used in cosmetics, perfumes, and household products, with limited consideration for its emotional consequences, as in pheromones. A calming scent is used in felines. Somatic stimulation is also controllable using vibration tables. The calming effect of rocking chairs, and swings is a feature of human activity, and likely activates evolutionarily primitive vestibular signals. The range of sensory modalities offers a spectrum of access to brain activation, which can be observed indirectly in evoked potential and neurofeedback, and self regulated by the subject. Understanding how the processes alter pathways allows them to be used to design effective interactions. Studies exploring the use of these methods are rare.*

Visual strobe: Minamisawa, G., Funayama, K., Matsumoto, N., Matsuki, N., & Ikegaya, Y. (2017). Flashing Lights Induce Prolonged Distortions in Visual Cortical Responses and Visual Perception. *eNeuro, 4*(3), ENEURO.0304-16.2017. https://doi.org/10.1523/ENEURO.0304-16.2017

Virtual Reality glasses: https://ameliavirtualcare.com/home-professional/
Boeldt, D., McMahon, E., McFaul, M., & Greenleaf, W. (2019). Using Virtual Reality Exposure Therapy to Enhance Treatment of Anxiety Disorders: Identifying Areas of Clinical Adoption and Potential Obstacles. *Frontiers in psychiatry, 10*, 773. https://doi.org/10.3389/fpsyt.2019.00773

Babar Ali, Naser Ali Al-Wabel, Saiba Shams, Aftab Ahamad, Shah Alam Khan, Firoz Anwar,Essential oils used in aromatherapy: A systemic review,Asian Pacific Journal of Tropical Biomedicine,Volume 5, Issue 8,2015,Pages 601-611 https://doi.org/10.1016/j.apjtb.2015.05.007

Doty RL. Human Pheromones: Do They Exist? In: Mucignat-Caretta C, editor. Neurobiology of Chemical Communication. Boca Raton (FL): CRC Press/ Taylor & Francis; 2014. Chapter 19. Available from: https://www.ncbi.nlm.nih.gov/books/NBK200980/

Cross, R. L., White, J., Engelsher, J., & O'Connor, S. S. (2018). Implementation of Rocking Chair Therapy for Veterans in Residential Substance Use Disorder Treatment (Formula: see text). *Journal of the American Psychiatric Nurses Association, 24*(3), 190–198. https://doi.org/10.1177/1078390317746726

Rojiani, R., Zhang, X., Noah, A., & Hirsch, J. (2018). Communication of emotion via drumming: dual-brain imaging with functional near-infrared spectroscopy. *Social cognitive and affective neuroscience, 13*(10), 1047–1057. https://doi.org/10.1093/scan/nsy076

59) https://www.mayoclinic.org/diseases-conditions/dissociative-disorders/

References

symptoms-causes/syc-20355215
https://www.ptsd.va.gov/professional/treat/essentials/dissociative_subtype.asp
Krause-Utz, A., Frost, R., Chatzaki, E., Winter, D., Schmahl, C., & Elzinga, B. M. (2021). Dissociation in Borderline Personality Disorder: Recent Experimental, Neurobiological Studies, and Implications for Future Research and Treatment. *Current psychiatry reports*, *23*(6), 37. https://doi.org/10.1007/s11920-021-01246-8
Stein, D. J., Koenen, K. C., Friedman, M. J., Hill, E., McLaughlin, K. A., Petukhova, M., Ruscio, A. M., Shahly, V., Spiegel, D., Borges, G., Bunting, B., Caldas-de-Almeida, J. M., de Girolamo, G., Demyttenaere, K., Florescu, S., Haro, J. M., Karam, E. G., Kovess-Masfety, V., Lee, S., ... Kessler, R. C. (2013). Dissociation in Posttraumatic Stress Disorder: Evidence from the World Mental Health Surveys. *Biological Psychiatry*, *73*(4), 302–312. https://doi.org/10.1016/j.biopsych.2012.08.022
Vermetten, E., Dorahy, M., & Spiegel, D. (Eds.). (2007). *Traumatic dissociation: Neurobiology and treatment.* American Psychiatric Publishing, Inc..
In Lanius, U. F., In Paulsen, S., & In Corrigan, F. M. (2014). *Neurobiology and treatment of traumatic dissociation: Toward an embodied self.*
Lauren A.M. Lebois, Meiling Li, Justin T. Baker, Jonathan D. Wolff, Danhong Wang, Ashley M. Lambros, Elizabeth Grinspoon, Sherry Winternitz, Jianxun Ren, Atilla Gönenç, Staci A. Gruber, Kerry J. Ressler, Hesheng Liu, and Milissa L. Kaufman, Large-Scale Functional Brain Network Architecture Changes Associated With Trauma-Related Dissociation, American Journal of Psychiatry 2021 178:2, 165-173
https://ajp.psychiatryonline.org/doi/abs/10.1176/appi.ajp.2020.19060647
60) Merz J, Schwarzer G, Gerger H. Comparative Efficacy and Acceptability of Pharmacological, Psychotherapeutic, and Combination Treatments in Adults With Posttraumatic Stress Disorder: A Network Meta-analysis. *JAMA Psychiatry.* 2019;76(9):904–913. https://jamanetwork.com/journals/jamapsychiatry/fullarticle/2735127
Marmar CR, Schlenger W, Henn-Haase C, et al. Course of Posttraumatic Stress Disorder 40 Years After the Vietnam War: Findings From the National Vietnam Veterans Longitudinal Study. *JAMA Psychiatry.* 2015;72(9):875–881 https://jamanetwork.com/journals/jamapsychiatry/fullarticle/2398184
Hien, D. A., Jiang, H., Campbell, A. N., Hu, M. C., Miele, G. M., Cohen, L. R., Brigham, G. S., Capstick, C., Kulaga, A., Robinson, J., Suarez-Morales, L., & Nunes, E. V. (2010). Do treatment improvements in PTSD severity affect substance use outcomes? A secondary analysis from a randomized clinical trial in NIDA's Clinical Trials Network. *The American journal of psychiatry*, *167*(1), 95–101. https://doi.org/10.1176/appi.ajp.2009.09091261
The government recommendations also include EMDR
https://www.ptsd.va.gov/understand_tx/tx_basics.asp
Bradley, R., Greene, J., Russ, E., Dutra, L., & Westen, D. (2005). A

multidimensional meta-analysis of psychotherapy for PTSD. *The American journal of psychiatry*, *162*(2), 214–227. https://doi.org/10.1176/appi.ajp.162.2.214
61) Krause-Utz, A., Frost, R., Winter, D., & Elzinga, B. M. (2017). Dissociation and Alterations in Brain Function and Structure: Implications for Borderline Personality Disorder. *Current psychiatry reports*, *19*(1), 6.https://doi.org/10.1007/s11920-017-0757-y
Biskin R. S. (2015). The Lifetime Course of Borderline Personality Disorder. *Canadian journal of psychiatry. Revue canadienne de psychiatrie*, *60*(7), 303 https://doi.org/10.1177/070674371506000702
62)Allan Schore, MD **Affect Regulation and the Origin of the Self**, Norton 1994
Allan Schore, "Attachment Trauma and the Developing Right Brain: Origins of Pathological Dissociation", Ch 8 **Dissociation and the Dissociation Disorders**
https://psychcentral.com/lib/an-overview-of-dialectical-behavior-therapy
Harned, M. S., Korslund, K. E., Foa, E. B., & Linehan, M. M. (2012). Treating PTSD in suicidal and self-injuring women with borderline personality disorder: development and preliminary evaluation of a Dialectical Behavior Therapy Prolonged Exposure Protocol. *Behaviour research and therapy*, *50*(6), 381–386. https://doi.org/10.1016/j.brat.2012.02.011   https://www.ncbi.nlm.nih.gov/pmc/articles/PMC3348973/
McMain, S. F., Guimond, T., Streiner, D. L., Cardish, R. J., & Links, P. S. (2012). Dialectical behavior therapy compared with general psychiatric management for borderline personality disorder: clinical outcomes and functioning over a 2-year follow-up. *The American journal of psychiatry*, *169*(6), 650–661. https://doi.org/10.1176/appi.ajp.2012.11091416
Cristea, I. A., Gentili, C., Cotet, C. D., Palomba, D., Barbui, C., & Cuijpers, P. (2017). Efficacy of Psychotherapies for Borderline Personality Disorder: A Systematic Review and Meta-analysis. *JAMA psychiatry*, *74*(4), 319–328. https://doi.org/10.1001/jamapsychiatry.2016.4287
63) https://depthcounseling.org/blog/peter-fonagy-mentalization
https://www.google.com/books/edition/
The_Handbook_of_Mentalization_Based_Trea/
64) Lindemann E. (1994). Symptomatology and management of acute grief. 1944. *The American journal of psychiatry*, *151*(6 Suppl), 155–160. https://doi.org/10.1176/ajp.151.6.155
65) https://grief.com/the-five-stages-of-grief/
66) GOFFMAN E. (1952). On cooling the mark out; some aspects of adaptation to failure. *Psychiatry*, *15*(4), 451–463. https://doi.org/10.1080/00332747.1952.11022896
Crooked Psychics and Cooling the Mark Out | The New Yorker
67) *Memories Dreams Reflections CG Jung* recorded and edited by Aniela Jaffe vintage ed 1961random house new york
68) Garety P. A. (2003). The future of psychological therapies for psychosis.

References

World psychiatry : official journal of the World Psychiatric Association (WPA), 2(3), 147–152.https://www.ncbi.nlm.nih.gov/pmc/articles/PMC1525111/

David Fowler, Jo Hodgekins, Paul French, Max Marshall, Nick Freemantle, Paul McCrone, Linda Everard, Anna Lavis, Peter B Jones, Tim Amos, Swaran Singh, Vimal Sharma, Max Birchwood, Social recovery therapy in combination with early intervention services for enhancement of social recovery in patients with first-episode psychosis (SUPEREDEN3): a single-blind, randomised controlled trial,
The Lancet Psychiatry,Volume 5, Issue 1,2018,Pages 41-50,ISSN 2215-0366, https://doi.org/10.1016/S2215-0366(17)30476-5

Bjornestad, J., Veseth, M., Davidson, L., Joa, I., Johannessen, J. O., Larsen, T. K., Melle, I., & Hegelstad, W. (2018). Psychotherapy in Psychosis: Experiences of Fully Recovered Service Users. *Frontiers in psychology*, 9, 1675. https://doi.org/10.3389/fpsyg.2018.01675

Haram, A., Fosse, R., Jonsbu, E., & Holc, T. (2019). Impact of Psychotherapy in Psychosis: A Retrospective Case Control Study. *Frontiers in psychiatry*, 10, 204. https://doi.org/10.3389/fpsyt.2019.00204

Good M. I. (2009). Elvin V. Semrad (1909-1976): experiencing the heart and core of psychotherapy training. *American journal of psychotherapy*, 63(2), 183–205. https://doi.org/10.1176/appi.psychotherapy.2009.63.2.183

Best, M. W., Gale, D., Tran, T., Haque, M. K., & Bowie, C. R. (2019). Brief executive function training for individuals with severe mental illness: Effects on EEG synchronization and executive functioning. *Schizophrenia research*, 203, 32–40. https://doi.org/10.1016/j.schres.2017.08.052

69) Eells T. D. (2000). Psychotherapy of Schizophrenia. *The Journal of psychotherapy practice and research*, 9(4), 250–254.

Vita, A., Barlati, S., Ceraso, A., Nibbio, G., Ariu, C., Deste, G., & Wykes, T. (2021). Effectiveness, Core Elements, and Moderators of Response of Cognitive Remediation for Schizophrenia: A Systematic Review and Meta-analysis of Randomized Clinical Trials. *JAMA psychiatry*, 78(8), 848–858. https://doi.org/10.1001/jamapsychiatry.2021.0620

Barlati, S., Deste, G., De Peri, L., Ariu, C., & Vita, A. (2013). Cognitive remediation in schizophrenia: current status and future perspectives. *Schizophrenia research and treatment*, 2013, 156084. https://doi.org/10.1155/2013/156084

Hamm, J. A., Hasson-Ohayon, I., Kukla, M., & Lysaker, P. H. (2013). Individual psychotherapy for schizophrenia: trends and developments in the wake of the recovery movement. *Psychology research and behavior management*, 6, 45–54. https://doi.org/10.2147/PRBM.S47891

Nordgaard, J., Henriksen, M. G., Jansson, L., Handest, P., Møller, P., Rasmussen, A. R., Sandsten, K. E., Nilsson, L. S., Zandersen, M., Zahavi, D., & Parnas, J. (2021). Disordered Selfhood in Schizophrenia and the Examination of Anomalous Self-Experience: Accumulated Evidence and Experience. *Psychopathology*, 54(6), 275–281. https://doi.org/10.1159/000517672

Lysaker, P. H., Glynn, S. M., Wilkniss, S. M., & Silverstein, S. M. (2010). Psychotherapy and recovery from schizophrenia: A review of potential applications and need for future study. *Psychological services*, *7*(2), 75–91. https://doi.org/10.1037/a0019115

Til Wykes, Craig Steel, Brian Everitt, Nicholas Tarrier, Cognitive Behavior Therapy for Schizophrenia: Effect Sizes, Clinical Models, and Methodological Rigor, *Schizophrenia Bulletin*, Volume 34, Issue 3, May 2008, Pages 523–537, https://doi.org/10.1093/schbul/sbm114

Best, M. W., Milanovic, M., Iftene, F., & Bowie, C. R. (2019). A Randomized Controlled Trial of Executive Functioning Training Compared With Perceptual Training for Schizophrenia Spectrum Disorders: Effects on Neurophysiology, Neurocognition, and Functioning. *The American journal of psychiatry*, *176*(4), 297–306. https://doi.org/10.1176/appi.ajp.2018.18070849
https://ajp.psychiatryonline.org/doi/10.1176/appi.ajp.2018.18070849

70) Robert Jay Lifton - Wikipedia, the free encyclopedia
R. J. Lifton, *The Life Of The Self* simon and shuster ny 1976
Lifton, Robert Jay. "Chap. 3." *The Life of the Self: Toward a New Psychology*. New York: Basic, 1983. N. pag. Print.

71) Gottschall, Jonathan. *The Storytelling Animal*. 1st ed. Boston: Mariner Books, 2013.
Our Brains Tell Stories So We Can Live - Issue 75: Story - Nautilus

72) Re-Visioning Psychology: James Hillman: 9780060905637: Amazon.com: Books
Re-Visioning Psychology (James Hillman) on Amazon.com.
Pinkola Estes, **Women Who Run With The Wolves**
Insoo Kim Berg, **Solution Focused Therapy Interview**.

73) Singer, Jerome & Pope, Kenneth. (1978). **The Use of Imagery and Fantasy Techniques in Psychotherapy**. 10.1007/978-1-4613-3941-0_1.
https://www.researchgate.net/publication/289378162_The_Use_of_Imagery_and_Fantasy_Techniques_in_Psychotherapy

Singer JL. Towards the Scientific Study of Imagination. *Imagination, Cognition and Personality*. 1981;1(1):5-28. doi:10.2190/PVEB-NUD8-HK3U-0X8U

Klisch, Mary Lou R.N., M.S.N. The Simonton Method of Visualization, Cancer Nursing: August 1980 - Volume 3 - Issue 4 - p 295 https://simonton.eu/index.php/en/simontonmethod

74) https://www.ancient-origins.net/history-ancient-traditions/dream-incubation-ancient-greece-009287

Reiser, M. F. (2001). The Dream in Contemporary Psychiatry. *American Journal of Psychiatry*, *158*(3), 351–359. http://ajp.psychiatryonline.org/doi/abs/10.1176/appi.ajp.158.3.351
https://en.wikipedia.org/wiki/Psychoanalytic_dream_interpretation

Zhang, W., & Guo, B. (2018). Freud's Dream Interpretation: A Different Perspective Based on the Self-Organization Theory of Dreaming. *Frontiers in*

References

Psychology, 9. https://doi.org/10.3389/fpsyg.2018.01553
75) *Laberge, S. (2000). Lucid dreaming: Evidence and methodology. Behavioral and Brain Sciences, 23, 962 - 964.*
76) *Jung and Dreams | Society of Analytical Psychology.* (2015). Society of Analytical Psychology. https://www.thesap.org.uk/resources/articles-on-jungian-psychology-2/carl-gustav-jung/dreams/
Garfield, P. L. (1995). **Creative dreaming : plan and control your dreams to develop creativity, overcome fears, solve problems, and create a better self.** Simon & Schuster.https://en.wikipedia.org/wiki/Dreamtime
Anne Faraday, **Dream Power, The Dream Game,**
77) Bosnak is a well respected Jungian therapist with special interest in dreaming.
Robert Bosnak talk to CG Jung Society: "The Phenomenal Power of Asclepian Dream Incubation" - YouTube
Bosnak, **Tracks in the wilderness of Dreaming.**
78) Driscoll, Kimberly & Cukrowicz, K.C. & Reardon, Maureen & Joiner, T.E.. (2014). Simple treatments for complex problems: A flexible cognitive behavior analysis system approach to psychotherapy. Simple Treatments for Complex Problems: A Flexible Cognitive Behavior Analysis System Approach to Psychotherapy. https://en.wikipedia.org/wiki/Cognitive_behavioral_analysis_system_of_psychotherapy
Kimberly A. Driscoll, Kelly C. Cukrowicz, Maureen Lyons Reardon, Thomas E. Joiner Jr., **Simple Treatments for Complex Problems: A Flexible Cognitive Behavior Analysis System Approach To Psychotherapy 1st Edition**
79) https://www.nytimes.com/2012/04/29/fashion/jane-mcgonigal-designer-of-superbetter-moves-games-deeper-into-daily-life.html https://www.ted.com/speakers/jane_mcgonigal
https://janemcgonigal.com/meet-me/
Jane McGonigal, **Reality Is Broken**, Penguin, NY, 2011
Allison, S. E., von Wahlde, L., Shockley, T., & Gabbard, G. O. (2006). The development of the self in the era of the internet and role-playing fantasy games. *The American journal of psychiatry*, *163*(3), 381–385. https://doi.org/10.1176/appi.ajp.163.3.381
http://education.ucdavis.edu/faculty-profile/cynthia-carter-ching
Want to build a better you?
https://www.yahoo.com/entertainment/want-to-build-a-better-1351798905954358.html?guccounter=1
80) **computer assisted CBT**
Kiluk, B. D., Nich, C., Buck, M. B., Devore, K. A., Frankforter, T. L., LaPaglia, D. M., Muvvala, S. B., & Carroll, K. M. (2018). Randomized Clinical Trial of Computerized and Clinician-Delivered CBT in Comparison With Standard Outpatient Treatment for Substance Use Disorders: Primary Within-Treatment and Follow-Up Outcomes. *The American journal of psychiatry*, *175*(9),

853–863. https://doi.org/10.1176/appi.ajp.2018.17090978
Thase, M. E., Wright, J. H., Eells, T. D., Barrett, M. S., Wisniewski, S. R., Balasubramani, G. K., McCrone, P., & Brown, G. K. (2018). Improving the Efficiency of Psychotherapy for Depression: Computer-Assisted Versus Standard CBT. *The American journal of psychiatry*, *175*(3), 242–250. https://doi.org/10.1176/appi.ajp.2017.17010089
Craske, M. G., Rose, R. D., Lang, A., Welch, S. S., Campbell-Sills, L., Sullivan, G., Sherbourne, C., Bystritsky, A., Stein, M. B., & Roy-Byrne, P. P. (2009). Computer-assisted delivery of cognitive behavioral therapy for anxiety disorders in primary-care settings. *Depression and anxiety*, *26*(3), 235–242. https://doi.org/10.1002/da.20542
81) https://www.top10.com/online-therapy/comparison
82) Enfield, G. (2007). Becoming the hero: The use of role-playing games in psychotherapy. In L. C. Rubin (Ed.), *Using superheroes in counseling and play therapy* (pp. 227–241). Springer Publishing Co.
Mendoza, Jonathan, "Gaming Intentionally: A Literature Review of the Viability of Role-Playing Games as
Drama-Therapy-Informed Interventions" (2020). Expressive Therapies Capstone Theses. 322.
https://digitalcommons.lesley.edu/expressive_theses/322
83) Boeldt, D., McMahon, E., McFaul, M., & Greenleaf, W. (2019). Using Virtual Reality Exposure Therapy to Enhance Treatment of Anxiety Disorders: Identifying Areas of Clinical Adoption and Potential Obstacles. *Frontiers in psychiatry*, *10*, 773. https://doi.org/10.3389/fpsyt.2019.00773
https://www.thrivingcenterofpsych.com/contents/feat-services/virtual-reality-exposure-therapy
https://ameliavirtualcare.com/home-professional/
84) Dunlop, B. W., LoParo, D., Kinkead, B., Mletzko-Crowe, T., Cole, S. P., Nemeroff, C. B., Mayberg, H. S., & Craighead, W. E. (2019). Benefits of Sequentially Adding Cognitive-Behavioral Therapy or Antidepressant Medication for Adults With Nonremitting Depression. *The American journal of psychiatry*, *176*(4), 275–286. https://doi.org/10.1176/appi.ajp.2018.18091075
H., Kheirkhah, F., Mergl, R., Miranda, J., Mohr, D. C., Rush, A. J., Segal, Z. V., Siddique, J., ... Cuijpers, P. (2016). Divergent Outcomes in Cognitive-Behavioral Therapy and Pharmacotherapy for Adult Depression. *The American journal of psychiatry*, *173*(5), 481–490. https://doi.org/10.1176/appi.ajp.2015.15040492
Vittengl, J. R., Jarrett, R. B., Weitz, E., Hollon, S. D., Twisk, J., Cristea, I., David, D., DeRubeis, R. J., Dimidjian, S., Dunlop, B. W., Faramarzi, M., Hegerl, U., Kennedy, S. H., Kheirkhah, F., Mergl, R., Miranda, J., Mohr, D. C., Rush, A. J., Segal, Z. V., Siddique, J., ... Cuijpers, P. (2016). Divergent Outcomes in Cognitive-Behavioral Therapy and Pharmacotherapy for Adult Depression. *The American journal of psychiatry*, *173*(5), 481–490. https://doi.org/10.1176/appi.

ajp.2015.15040492

DeRubeis, R. J., Siegle, G. J., & Hollon, S. D. (2008). Cognitive therapy versus medication for depression: treatment outcomes and neural mechanisms. *Nature reviews. Neuroscience*, *9*(10), 788–796. https://doi.org/10.1038/nrn2345

85) Stahl S. M. (2012). Psychotherapy as an epigenetic 'drug': psychiatric therapeutics target symptoms linked to malfunctioning brain circuits with psychotherapy as well as with drugs. *Journal of clinical pharmacy and therapeutics*, *37*(3), 249–253. https://doi.org/10.1111/j.1365-2710.2011.01301.x

86) Adelman, S. A. (1985). Pills as Transitional Objects: A Dynamic Understanding of the Use of Medication in Psychotherapy. *Psychiatry*, *48*(3), 246 https://doi.org/10.1080/00332747.1985.11024285

Gorman, J. M. (2016). Combining Psychodynamic Psychotherapy and Pharmacotherapy. *Psychodynamic Psychiatry*, *44*(2), 183–209. https://doi.org/10.1521/pdps.2016.44.2.183

87) Nakagawa, A., Mitsuda, D., Sado, M., Abe, T., Fujisawa, D., Kikuchi, T., Iwashita, S., Mimura, M., & Ono, Y. (2017). Effectiveness of Supplementary Cognitive-Behavioral Therapy for Pharmacotherapy-Resistant Depression: A Randomized Controlled Trial. *The Journal of clinical psychiatry*, *78*(8), 1126–1135. https://doi.org/10.4088/JCP.15m10511

Rauch, S. A. M., Kim, H. M., Powell, C., Tuerk, P. W., Simon, N. M., Acierno, R., Allard, C. B., Norman, S. B., Venners, M. R., Rothbaum, B. O., Stein, M. B., Porter, K., Martis, B., King, A. P., Liberzon, I., Phan, K. L., & Hoge, C. W. (2019). Efficacy of Prolonged Exposure Therapy, Sertraline Hydrochloride, and Their Combination Among Combat Veterans With Posttraumatic Stress Disorder: A Randomized Clinical Trial. *JAMA Psychiatry*, *76*(2), 117–126. https://doi.org/10.1001/jamapsychiatry.2018.3412

Merz, J., Schwarzer, G., & Gerger, H. (2019). Comparative Efficacy and Acceptability of Pharmacological, Psychotherapeutic, and Combination Treatments in Adults With Posttraumatic Stress Disorder: A Network Meta-analysis. *JAMA psychiatry*, *76*(9), 904–913. https://doi.org/10.1001/jamapsychiatry.2019.0951

Zoellner, L. A., Roy-Byrne, P. P., Mavissakalian, M., & Feeny, N. C. (2019). Doubly Randomized Preference Trial of Prolonged Exposure Versus Sertraline for Treatment of PTSD. *The American journal of psychiatry*, *176*(4), 287–296. https://doi.org/10.1176/appi.ajp.2018.17090995
https://ajp.psychiatryonline.org/doi/10.1176/appi.ajp.2018.17090995

88) References for psychotherapy of psychosis/schizophrenia at #69. All included medication.

89) Dyck E. (2015). LSD: a new treatment emerging from the past. *CMAJ : Canadian Medical Association journal = journal de l'Association medicale canadienne*, *187*(14), 1079–1080. Advance online publication. https://doi.org/10.1503/cmaj.141358

Fuentes, J. J., Fonseca, F., Elices, M., Farré, M., & Torrens, M. (2020).

Therapeutic Use of LSD in Psychiatry: A Systematic Review of Randomized-Controlled Clinical Trials. *Frontiers in psychiatry*, *10*, 943. https://doi.org/10.3389/fpsyt.2019.00943

Effects of Psilocybin-Assisted Therapy on Major Depressive Disorder | Depressive Disorders | JN Learning | AMA Ed Hub FDA Permits Psilocybin to Be Tested for Refractory Depression

LSD, Reconsidered for Therapy - NYTimes.com http://www.nytimes.com/2014/03/04/health/lsd-reconsidered-for...

Harris J. C. (2021). Psychedelic-Assisted Psychotherapy and Carl Jung's Red Book. *JAMA psychiatry*, 10.1001/jamapsychiatry.2021.1207. https://doi.org/10.1001/jamapsychiatry.2021.1207

https://www.theatlantic.com/health/archive/2014/09/the-accidental-discovery-of-lsd/379564/

90) MAPS – MDMA-Assisted Psychotherapy
http://www.maps.org/research/mdma Founded in 1986, the Multidisciplinary Association for Psychedelic Studies (MAPS) is a 501(c)(3) non-profit research and educational organization that develops medical, legal, and cultural contexts for people to benefit from the careful uses of psychedelics and marijuana.

MDMA Therapy - https://thedea.org/mdma-ecstasy-molly-users-guide/mdma-therapy/

Carbonaro, T. M., Bradstreet, M. P., Barrett, F. S., MacLean, K. A., Jesse, R., Johnson, M. W., & Griffiths, R. R. (2016). Survey study of challenging experiences after ingesting psilocybin mushrooms: Acute and enduring positive and negative consequences. *Journal of psychopharmacology (Oxford, England)*, *30*(12), 1268–1278. https://doi.org/10.1177/0269881116662634

Furukawa, T. A., Efthimiou, O., Weitz, E. S., Cipriani, A., Keller, M. B., Kocsis, J. H., Klein, D. N., Michalak, J., Salanti, G., Cuijpers, P., & Schramm, E. (2018). Cognitive-Behavioral Analysis System of Psychotherapy, Drug, or Their Combination for Persistent Depressive Disorder: Personalizing the Treatment Choice Using Individual Participant Data Network Metaregression. *Psychotherapy and psychosomatics*, *87*(3), 140–153. https://doi.org/10.1159/000489227

91) Gabbard, G. (2000). A neurobiologically informed perspective on psychotherapy. *British Journal of Psychiatry, 177*(2), 117-122. doi:10.1192/bjp.177.2.117

Psychotherapeutic Change Part I: The Default Brain, George I. Viamontes, MD, PhD; Bernard D. Beitman, MD **Psychiatric Annals. 2006;36(4)**
https://www.yumpu.com/en/document/view/35438298/neural-substrates-of-psychotherapeutic-change-bernard-beitman-
http://www.healio.com/journals/psycann/2006-4-36-4/%7B40eb5880-85c8-4704-af68-3d0dc1257ef1%7D/neural-substrates-of-psychotherapeutic-change-part-i-the-default-brain

George I. Viamontes, MD, PhD; Bernard D. Beitman, MD , Neural Substrates of

References

Psychotherapeutic Change Part II: Beyond Default Mode, **Psychiatric Annals.** 2006;36(4)
http://www.healio.com/journals/psycann/2006-4-36-4/%7B81833356-0fea-4ea5-89d0-85dbe2c8a585%7D/neural-substrates-of-psychotherapeutic-change-part-ii-beyond-default-mode
https://www.researchgate.net/publication/299108485_Neural_substrates_of_psychotherapeutic_change_-_Part_II_Beyond_default_mode
Andrews-Hanna, J. R., Reidler, J. S., Sepulcre, J., Poulin, R., & Buckner, R. L. (2010). Functional-Anatomic Fractionation of the Brain's Default Network. *Neuron, 65*(4), 550–562. https://doi.org/10.1016/j.neuron.2010.02.005
Kounios, J., Fleck, J. I., Green, D. L., Payne, L., Stevenson, J. L., Bowden, E. M., & Jung-Beeman, M. (2008). The origins of insight in resting-state brain activity. *Neuropsychologia, 46*(1), 281–291. https://doi.org/10.1016/j.neuropsychologia.2007.07.013
92) Messina, I., Sambin, M., Palmieri, A., & Viviani, R. (2013). Neural correlates of psychotherapy in anxiety and depression: a meta-analysis. *PloS one, 8*(9), e74657. https://doi.org/10.1371/journal.pone.0074657
http://journals.plos.org/plosone/article?id=10.1371/journal.pone.0074657
Thorsen, A. L., van den Heuvel, O. A., Hansen, B., & Kvale, G. (2015). Neuroimaging of psychotherapy for obsessive-compulsive disorder: A systematic review. *Psychiatry research, 233*(3), 306–313. https://doi.org/10.1016/j.pscychresns.2015.05.004
Fonzo, G. A., Goodkind, M. S., Oathes, D. J., Zaiko, Y. V., Harvey, M., Peng, K. K., Weiss, M. E., Thompson, A. L., Zack, S. E., Mills-Finnerty, C. E., Rosenberg, B. M., Edelstein, R., Wright, R. N., Kole, C. A., Lindley, S. E., Arnow, B. A., Jo, B., Gross, J. J., Rothbaum, B. O., & Etkin, A. (2017). Selective Effects of Psychotherapy on Frontopolar Cortical Function in PTSD. *The American journal of psychiatry, 174*(12), 1175–1184. https://doi.org/10.1176/appi.ajp.2017.16091073
Porto, P. R., Oliveira, L., Mari, J., Volchan, E., Figueira, I., & Ventura, P. (2009). Does cognitive behavioral therapy change the brain? A systematic review of neuroimaging in anxiety disorders. *The Journal of neuropsychiatry and clinical neurosciences, 21*(2), 114–125. https://doi.org/10.1176/jnp.2009.21.2.114
93) Kalsi, N., Altavilla, D., Tambelli, R., Aceto, P., Trentini, C., Di Giorgio, C., & Lai, C. (2017). Neural Correlates of Outcome of the Psychotherapy Compared to Antidepressant Therapy in Anxiety and Depression Disorders: A Meta-Analysis. *Frontiers in psychology, 8*, 927. https://doi.org/10.3389/fpsyg.2017.00927
Lueken, U., Straube, B., Konrad, C., Wittchen, H. U., Ströhle, A., Wittmann, A., Pfleiderer, B., Uhlmann, C., Arolt, V., Jansen, A., & Kircher, T. (2013). Neural substrates of treatment response to cognitive-behavioral therapy in panic disorder with agoraphobia. *The American journal of psychiatry, 170*(11), 1345–1355. https://doi.org/10.1176/appi.ajp.2013.12111484

Hahn T, Kircher T, Straube B, et al. Predicting Treatment Response to Cognitive Behavioral Therapy in Panic Disorder With Agoraphobia by Integrating Local Neural Information. *JAMA Psychiatry.* 2015;72(1):
https://jamanetwork.com/journals/jamapsychiatry/fullarticle/1936093
94) Beauregard M. (2014). Functional neuroimaging studies of the effects of psychotherapy. *Dialogues in clinical neuroscience, 16*(1), 75–81. https://doi.org/10.31887/DCNS.2014.16.1/mbeauregard
95) Linden, D. How psychotherapy changes the brain – the contribution of functional neuroimaging. *Mol Psychiatry* **11,** 528–538 (2006). https://doi.org/10.1038/sj.mp.4001816
Skottnik, L., & Linden, D. (2019). Mental Imagery and Brain Regulation-New Links Between Psychotherapy and Neuroscience. *Frontiers in psychiatry, 10,* 779.https://doi.org/10.3389/fpsyt.2019.00779
Perez, D.L., Vago, D.R., Pan, H., Root, J., Tuescher, O., Fuchs, B.H., Leung, L., Epstein, J., Cain, N.M., Clarkin, J.F., Lenzenweger, M.F., Kernberg, O.F., Levy, K.N., Silbersweig, D.A. and Stern, E. (2016), Neural mechanisms of psychotherapy. Psychiatry Clin Neurosci, 70: 51-61. https://doi.org/10.1111/pcn.12357
http://onlinelibrary.wiley.com/doi/10.1111/pcn.12357/full
96) Kanda, P., Anghinah, R., Smidth, M. T., & Silva, J. M. (2009). The clinical use of quantitative EEG in cognitive disorders. *Dementia & neuropsychologia, 3*(3), 195–203.
https://doi.org/10.1590/S1980-57642009DN30300004
Neuner, I., Arrubla, J., Werner, C. J., Hitz, K., Boers, F., Kawohl, W., & Shah, N. J. (2014). The Default Mode Network and EEG Regional Spectral Power: A Simultaneous fMRI-EEG Study. *PLoS ONE, 9*(2). https://doi.org/10.1371/journal.pone.0088214
Grawe (Grawe, K. (2007). Neuropsychotherapy: How the neurosciences inform effective psychotherapy. New York, NY: Psychology Press.) The proposal amounts to using insights from understanding of the circuit models of neuro-phsiology to inform more effective techniques in psychotherapy. Very premature!
https://www.thescienceofpsychotherapy.com/
97) Sandell, R., Blomberg, J., Lazar, A., Carlsson, J., Broberg, J., & Schubert, J. (2000). Varieties of long-term outcome among patients in psychoanalysis and long-term psychotherapy. A review of findings in the Stockholm Outcome of Psychoanalysis and Psychotherapy Project (STOPP). *The International journal of psycho-analysis, 81 (Pt 5),* 921–942. https://doi.org/10.1516/0020757001600291
Even this PSA study was faulted for lack of data on long term adaptation.
98) Thoma, N. C., McKay, D., Gerber, A. J., Milrod, B. L., Edwards, A. R., & Kocsis, J. H. (2012). A quality-based review of randomized controlled trials of cognitive-behavioral therapy for depression: an assessment and metaregression. *The American journal of psychiatry, 169*(1), 22–30. https://doi.org/10.1176/appi.

References

ajp.2011.11030433

Westen, D., & Morrison, K. (2001). A multidimensional meta-analysis of treatments for depression, panic, and generalized anxiety disorder: an empirical examination of the status of empirically supported therapies. *Journal of consulting and clinical psychology*, *69*(6), 875–899.

Westen, D., Novotny, C. M., & Thompson-Brenner, H. (2004). The empirical status of empirically supported psychotherapies: assumptions, findings, and reporting in controlled clinical trials. *Psychological bulletin*, *130*(4), 631–663. https://doi.org/10.1037/0033-2909.130.4.631
http://citeseerx.ist.psu.edu/viewdoc/download?doi=10.1.1.536.6948&rep=rep1&type=pdf

Other studies of outcome

Lewandowski, K. E., Sperry, S. H., Cohen, B. M., Norris, L. A., Fitzmaurice, G. M., Ongur, D., & Keshavan, M. S. (2017). Treatment to Enhance Cognition in Bipolar Disorder (TREC-BD): Efficacy of a Randomized Controlled Trial of Cognitive Remediation Versus Active Control. *The Journal of clinical psychiatry*, *78*(9), e1242–e1249. https://doi.org/10.4088/JCP.17m11476

Elliott, R. (2011). Qualitative Methods for Studying Psychotherapy Change Processes. In Qualitative Research Methods in Mental Health and Psychotherapy (eds D. Harper and A.R. Thompson).
https://doi.org/10.1002/9781119973249.ch6

Elliott R. (2010). Psychotherapy change process research: realizing the promise. *Psychotherapy research : journal of the Society for Psychotherapy Research*, *20*(2), 123–135. https://doi.org/10.1080/10503300903470743

Swartz, H. A., & Fournier, J. (2019). Can Network Meta-analysis Substitute for Direct Comparisons in Psychotherapy Trials?. *JAMA psychiatry*, *76*(7), 678–679. https://doi.org/10.1001/jamapsychiatry.2019.0243

Leichsenring, F., Salzer, S., Beutel, M. E., Herpertz, S., Hiller, W., Hoyer, J., Huesing, J., Joraschky, P., Nolting, B., Poehlmann, K., Ritter, V., Stangier, U., Strauss, B., Tefikow, S., Teismann, T., Willutzki, U., Wiltink, J., & Leibing, E. (2014). Long-term outcome of psychodynamic therapy and cognitive-behavioral therapy in social anxiety disorder. *The American journal of psychiatry*, *171*(10), 1074–1082. https://doi.org/10.1176/appi.ajp.2014.13111514

Steinert, C., Munder, T., Rabung, S., Hoyer, J., & Leichsenring, F. (2017). Psychodynamic Therapy: As Efficacious as Other Empirically Supported Treatments? A Meta-Analysis Testing Equivalence of Outcomes. *The American journal of psychiatry*, *174*(10), 943–953. https://doi.org/10.1176/appi.ajp.2017.17010057

Cuijpers, P., Donker, T., Weissman, M. M., Ravitz, P., & Cristea, I. A. (2016). Interpersonal Psychotherapy for Mental Health Problems: A Comprehensive Meta-Analysis. *The American journal of psychiatry*, *173*(7), 680–687. https://doi.org/10.1176/appi.ajp.2015.15091141

Jennissen, S., Huber, J., Ehrenthal, J. C., Schauenburg, H., & Dinger, U. (2018).

Association Between Insight and Outcome of Psychotherapy: Systematic Review and Meta-Analysis. *The American journal of psychiatry*, *175*(10), 961–969. https://doi.org/10.1176/appi.ajp.2018.17080847

David, D., Cristea, I., & Hofmann, S. G. (2018). Why Cognitive Behavioral Therapy Is the Current Gold Standard of Psychotherapy. *Frontiers in psychiatry*, *9*, 4. https://doi.org/10.3389/fpsyt.2018.00004

Leichsenring F, Steinert C. Is Cognitive Behavioral Therapy the Gold Standard for Psychotherapy? The Need for Plurality in Treatment and Research. *JAMA*. 2017;318(14):1323–1324.

Schneider, R. A., Grasso, J. R., Chen, S. Y., Chen, C., Reilly, E. D., & Kocher, B. (2020). Beyond the Lab: Empirically Supported Treatments in the Real World. *Frontiers in psychology*, *11*, 1969. https://doi.org/10.3389/fpsyg.2020.01969

CPSIA information can be obtained
at www.ICGtesting.com
Printed in the USA
LVHW022225151122
732907LV00008B/239